The Covenant Renewal in Ezra-Nehemiah (Neh 7:72b–10:40)

SOCIETY OF BIBLICAL LITERATURE

SBL
DISSERTATION SERIES
Michael V. Fox, Old Testament Editor
Mark Allan Powell, New Testament Editor

Number 164
THE COVENANT RENEWAL IN EZRA-
NEHEMIAH (NEH 7:72B–10:40)
by
Michael W. Duggan

Michael W. Duggan

THE COVENANT RENEWAL IN EZRA-NEHEMIAH (NEH 7:72B–10:40)

An Exegetical, Literary, and Theological Study

Society of Biblical Literature
Atlanta

THE COVENANT RENEWAL IN EZRA-NEHEMIAH (NEH 7:72B–10:40)
An Exegetical, Literary, and Theological Study

by
Michael W. Duggan

Copyright © 2001 by the Society of Biblical Literature

All rights reserved. No part of this work may be reproduced or transmitted in any form or by any means, electronic or mechanical, including photocopying and recording, or by means of any information storage or retrieval system, except as may be expressly permitted by the 1976 Copyright Act or in writing from the publisher. Requests for permission should be addressed in writing to the Rights and Permissions Office, Society of Biblical Literature, 825 Houston Mill Road, Atlanta, GA 30329 USA.

Library of Congress Cataloging-in-Publication Data
Duggan, Michael.
    The covenant renewal in Ezra-Nehemiah : (Neh 7:72b–10:40) : an exegetical, literary and theological study/ by Michael W. Duggan.
        p. cm. — (Dissertation series / Society of Biblical Literature ; no. 164)
    A revision of the author's thesis (Ph.D.—Catholic University of America).
    Includes bibliographical references.
    ISBN 1-58983-014-8 (cloth : alk. paper)
        1-58983-169-1 (pbk. : alk. paper)
    1. Bible. O. T. Ezra—Criticism, interpretation, etc. 2. Bible. O.T. Nehemiah—Criticism, interpretation, etc. 3. Covenants—Biblical teaching. I. Title. II. Dissertation series (Society of Biblical Literature) ; no. 164.

BS1344.6.C6 D84 2001
222'.806—dc21
                                        98-011393

Printed in the United States of America
on acid-free paper

Contents

Acknowledgments vii
Abbreviations ix

1. The History of Research on Nehemiah 7:72b–10:40 1
   The Diachronic Approach 1
   The Synchronic Approach 38

2. The Context and Structure of the Covenant-Renewal Account (Nehemiah 7:72b–10:40) 59
   Outline of Ezra-Nehemiah 59
   The Delimitation of the Covenant-Renewal Account 68
   The Structure of the Covenant-Renewal Account
   (Nehemiah 7:72b–10:40) 73

3. The Reading of the Law and the Festival of Booths (Nehemiah 7:72b–8:18) 79
   The First Reading of the Law (Nehemiah 7:72b–8:12) 79
      Translation 79
      Textual Criticism 80
      Literary Analysis 81
      Lexical Examination 95
      Thematic Summary 120
   The Study of the Law and the Festival of Booths
   (Nehemiah 8:13–18) 122
      Translation 122
      Textual Criticism 123
      Literary Analysis 123
      Lexical Examination 129

Thematic Summary 136

4. The Penitential Rites (Nehemiah 9:1–5) **139**
Translation 139
Textual Criticism 140
Literary Analysis...140
Lexical Examination..149
Thematic Summary 155

5. The Levites' Prayer (Nehemiah 9:6–37)..........................**157**
Translation 157
Textual Criticism 161
Literary Analysis...161
The Language and Form of the Prayer 199
Thematic Summary 230

6. The Covenant Commitment (Nehemiah 10:1–40)...........**235**
Translation 235
Textual Criticism 237
Literary Analysis...238
Lexical Examination..255
Thematic Summary 286

7. Conclusion...**291**
Literary Features..291
Dramatic Development of Content..295

Works Consulted...301
Primary Sources 301
Secondary Literature 302

Index of Primary Sources 331
Index of Modern Authors 362
Index of Subjects 365
Index of Select Hebrew Words 371

Acknowledgments

This examination of the covenant renewal in Ezra-Nehemiah is a Ph.D. dissertation that I submitted to the Catholic University of America in 1996. The work represents the state of research up to that date. I have not made revisions in light of subsequent monographs and articles. The fine studies that have emerged recently testify to the vitality of Ezra-Nehemiah research.

The covenant-renewal account (Neh 7:72b–10:40) underlines the necessity of interpreting the written text within a community setting. I acknowledge my debt to instructors, colleges, friends, and family members who comprise the community within which I have studied this text. I express gratitude to the Department of Biblical Studies at the Catholic University of America. The dissertation took shape under the direction of Professor Christopher T. Begg. His remarkable acquaintance with the research and his exceptional insight guided the development of the study. I am indebted to Professor Alexander A. Di Lella, a mentor who sharpened my accuracy in reading the text and communicated his infectious enthusiasm for refined scholarship. I thank Professor Joseph Jensen for his conscientious assessment of the dissertation. In addition, I express appreciation to Bob Buller for his meticulous care in typesetting the text, composing the indices, and attending to critical editorial details.

Moreover, I extend thanks to friends and family. Throughout the time of research and writing, Jeremy Corley offered the type of friendship that was the topic of his dissertation in Ben Sira. During the past year, Dr. Terrence Downey, President of St. Mary's College, along with administrators and faculty, persistently encouraged the publication of this study. My sister, Mary Nora Lorieau, my brother-in-law Maurice, and my nephew Michael sustained me through their love and kindness. I am particularly grateful to my father, Bill, who has been a constant advocate of my doing this work. I dedicate this book to my family and to the memory of my mother.

Abbreviations

AASOR	Annual of the American Schools of Oriental Research
AB	Anchor Bible
ABD	*Anchor Bible Dictionary*, ed. D. N. Freedman. 6 vols. New York: Doubleday, 1992.
AJSL	*American Journal of Semitic Languages and Literature*
AnBib	Analecta biblica
Ant.	Josephus, *Jewish Antiquities*
AOAT	Alter Orient und Altes Testament
CAP	Cowley, A. E, *Aramaic Papyri of the Fifth Century B.C.* Oxford: Clarendon, 1923.
ATD	Das Alte Testament Deutsch
AUNVAO	Avhandlinger utgitt av Det Norske Videnskaps-Akademi i Oslo. 2. Hist.-Filos. Klasse 1952.
AUSS	*Andrews University Seminary Studies*
b.	Babylonian Talmud
B. Bat.	*Baba Batra*
BA	*Biblical Archaeologist*
BASOR	*Bulletin of the American Schools of Oriental Research*
BBB	Bonner biblische Beiträge
BDB	Brown, F., S. R. Driver, and C. A. Briggs, *A Hebrew and English Lexicon of the Old Testament.* Oxford: Oxford University Press, 1907.
BeO	*Bibbia e oriente*
BEvT	Beiträge zur evangelischen Theologie
BHK	*Biblia Hebraica.* Edited by R. Kittel. Stuttgart: Deutsche Bibelgesellschaft, 1951.
BHS	*Biblia Hebraica Stuttgartensia.* Edited by K. Elliger and W. Rudolph. Stuttgart: Deutsche Bibelgesellschaft, 1983.
BHT	Beiträge zur historischen Theologie
Bib	*Biblica*
Bijdr	*Bijdragen: Tijdschrift voor filosofie en theologie*
BJRL	*Bulletin of the John Rylands University Library of Manchester*
BN	*Biblische Notizen*
BRev	*Bible Review*
BSac	*Bibliotheca sacra*

BT	*The Bible Translator*
BTB	*Biblical Theology Bulletin*
BWANT	Beiträge zur Wissenschaft vom Alten und Neuen Testament
BZ	*Biblische Zeitschrift*
BZAW	Beihefte zur Zeitschrift für die alttestamentliche Wissenchaft
CBC	Cambridge Bible Commentary
CBQ	*Catholic Biblical Quarterly*
CC	Continental Commentaries
CTM	*Concordia Theological Monthly*
CurBS	*Currents in Research: Biblical Studies*
DBSup	*Dictionnaire de la Bible: Supplément.* Edited by L. Pirot and A. Robert. Paris: Letouzey et Ane, 1928–.
EM	Ezra Memoir
ErIsr	*Eretz-Israel*
EstBib	*Estudios bíblicos*
EvQ	*Evangelical Quarterly*
ExpTim	*Expository Times*
FRLANT	Forschungen zur Religion und Literatur des Alten und Neuen Testaments
GBH	Joüon, P., and T. Muraoka. *A Grammar of Biblical Hebrew.* 2 vols. Subsidia Biblica 14.1, 2. Rome: Biblical Institute, 1991.
GKC	*Gesenius' Hebrew Grammar.* Edited by E. Kautzsch. Translated by A. E. Cowley. 2d ed. Oxford: Oxford University Press, 1910.
GTA	Göttinger theologischer Arbeiten
HAL	Koehler, L., W. Baumgartner, and J. J. Stamm. *Hebräisches und aramäisches Lexikon zum Alten Testament.* 5 vols. Leiden: Brill, 1967–1995.
HAT	Handbuch zum Alten Testament
Hist. eccl.	Eusebius, *Historia ecclesiastica*
HSM	Harvard Semitic Monographs
HTR	*Harvard Theological Review*
HUCA	*Hebrew Union College Annual*
HvTSt	*Hervormde teologiese studies*
IBC	Interpretation: A Bible Commentary for Teaching and Preaching
ICC	International Critical Commentary
IDB	*The Interpreter's Dictionary of the Bible,* ed. G. A. Buttrick. 12 vols. Nashville: Abingdon, 1952–1957.

IDBSup	*Interpreter's Dictionary of the Bible: Supplementary Volume*, ed. K. Crim. Nashville: Abingdon, 1976.
IEJ	*Israel Exploration Journal*
Int	*Interpretation*
ITC	International Theological Commentary
JAOS	*Journal of the American Oriental Society*
JBL	*Journal of Biblical Literature*
JBLMS	Journal of Biblical Literature Monograph Series
JCS	*Journal of Cuneiform Studies*
JJS	*Journal of Jewish Studies*
JNES	*Journal of Near Eastern Studies*
JNSL	*Journal of Northwest Semitic Languages*
JPSV	The Jewish Publication Society Version
JQR	*Jewish Quarterly Review*
JR	*Journal of Religion*
JSJ	*Journal for the Study of Judaism in the Persian, Hellenistic, and Roman Periods*
JSOT	*Journal for the Study of the Old Testament*
JSOTSup	Journal for the Study of the Old Testament: Supplement Series
JSP	*Journal for the Study of the Pseudepigrapha*
JSS	*Journal of Semitic Studies*
JTS	*Journal of Theological Studies*
KAT	Kommentar zum Alten Testament
Laur	*Laurentianum*
LXX	Septuagint
MT	Masoretic Text
NAB	New American Bible
NCB	New Century Bible
NICOT	New International Commentary on the Old Testament
NJB	New Jerusalem Bible
NM	Nehemiah Memoir
NRSV	New Revised Standard Version
NTS	*New Testament Studies*
OBO	Orbis biblicus et orientalis
OLA	Orientalia lovaniensia analecta
OTE	*Old Testament Essays*
OTG	Old Testament Guides
OTL	Old Testament Library
OTM	Old Testament Message
OTS	Old Testament Studies
OtSt	*Oudtestamentische Studiën*
RB	*Revue biblique*

REB	Revised English Bible
ResQ	*Restoration Quarterly*
RevQ	*Revue de Qumran*
RSV	Revised Standard Version
RSO	*Revista degli studi orientali*
RTL	*Revue théologique de Louvain*
RTR	*Reformed Theological Review*
Salm	*Salmanticensis*
SBLDS	Society of Biblical Literature Dissertation Series
SBLMS	Society of Biblical Literature Monograph Series
SBLSCS	Society of Biblical Literature Septuagint and Cognate Studies
SBT	Studies in Biblical Theology
SC	Sources chrétiennes
ScrHier	Scripta hierosolymitana
SemeiaSt	Semeia Studies
SP	Samaritan Papyrus
SSN	Studia semitica neerlandica
ST	*Studia theologica*
SUNVAO	Skrifter utigitt av Det Norske Videnskaps-Akademi i Oslo. 2. Hist.-Filos. Klasse. Ny Serie.
Syr	Syriac
TB	Theologische Bücherei: Neudrucke und Berichte aus dem 20. Jahrhundert
TBT	*The Bible Today*
TD	*Theology Digest*
TDOT	*Theological Dictionary of the Old Testament*, ed. G. J. Botterweck and H. Ringgren, trans. J. T. Willis et al. 10 vols. Grand Rapids: Eerdmans, 1974–.
TMs	Typewritten manuscript
TOTC	Tyndale Old Testament Commentaries
Transeu	*Transeuphratène*
TRE	*Theologische Realenzyklopädie*. Edited by G. Krause and G. Müller. Berlin: Walter de Gruyter, 1977–
USQR	*Union Seminary Quarterly Review*
Vg	Vulgate
VT	*Vetus Testamentum*
VTSup	Supplements to Vetus Testamentum
WBC	Word Biblical Commentary
WMANT	Wissenschaftliche Monographien zum Alten und Neuen Testament
WTJ	*Westminster Theological Journal*
ZAW	*Zeitschrift für die alttestamentliche Wissenschaft*

1

The History of Research on Nehemiah 7:72b–10:40

The narrative of the covenant-renewal ceremony initiated by Ezra (Neh 7:72b–10:40)[1] constitutes the climax of the book of Ezra-Nehemiah. Various factors identify this section as the crux of interpretation for the whole work: (1) the description of Ezra's activity (Neh 7:72b–8:18) occurs in the midst of the account of Nehemiah's mission (Neh 1:1–7:5; 12:27–13:31) and interlocks the missions of the two protagonists; (2) the reading of the law (Neh 7:72b–8:18) represents an essential ingredient of Ezra's reform (Ezra 7:1–10:44); (3) the prayerful recounting of Israel's history (Neh 9:6–37) constitutes the only psalm in the whole work; and (4) the temple-related stipulations in the written oath (Neh 10:29–40) anticipate the activities that conclude Nehemiah's mission (Neh 13:4–31).

Factors such as these have prompted various studies on the covenant-renewal ceremony (Neh 7:72b–10:40), including its role within the entire Ezra-Nehemiah complex. This chapter reviews previous research on Neh 7:72b–10:40. From the first half of the nineteenth century until the last decade, commentators approached the text almost exclusively from a diachronic perspective. Therefore, this survey gives an overview of the issues and results of diachronic analyses that historical-critical studies typify. Against this background, a detailed summary of recent studies from a synchronic perspective emphasizes the promise contained in this new development in the history of research on Ezra-Nehemiah. Ultimately, my survey of research suggests the timeliness of a detailed synchronic study of the covenant-renewal ceremony for the advancement of Ezra-Nehemiah research.

THE DIACHRONIC APPROACH

Ezra's covenant-renewal ceremony has been the subject of extensive study in the fields of both historical and literary criticism. The primary historical questions concern the dating and duration of Ezra's mission to Jerusalem. Literary concerns span a broad spectrum of issues, including

---

[1] All citations follow the numbering in *BHS*.

the sources of the Ezra material, the contents of Ezra's law book, and the design of the covenant-renewal ceremony, as well as more generally the relationship between Ezra-Nehemiah and Chronicles and the unity of Ezra-Nehemiah.

HISTORICAL QUESTIONS

In the realm of historical criticism, the narrative of covenant renewal raises two related questions: (1) How should one date the missions of Ezra and Nehemiah in view of the overlap implied in the simultaneous references to these leaders (Neh 8:9; 10:2; cf. 12:26; 12:36, 38)? (2) Did Ezra's mission actually have a thirteen-year duration—as the text implies—from the time of his arrival in Jerusalem to his reading of the law at the Water Gate (see Ezra 7:7-9; Neh 1:1; 8:1)?

On the question of the relative chronology of the missions of Ezra and Nehemiah, the date of Nehemiah's arrival in Jerusalem is securely fixed in the twentieth year of Artaxerxes I, 445 B.C.E. (Neh 1:1; 2:1).[2] Twelve years

---

[2] Three Persian kings bore the name Artaxerxes: Artaxerxes I (Longimanus) (465–425 B.C.E.), Artaxerxes II (Mnemon) (404–358 B.C.E.), and Artaxerxes III (Ochus) (359–338 B.C.E.). Mention of the "thirty-second year of King Artaxerxes" (Neh 13:6) eliminates the possibility of reference to Artaxerxes III, since he reigned for only twenty-one years. An Aramaic papyrus from Elephantine dated to 407 B.C.E. ("the seventeenth year of Darius II," CAP 30:30) mentions both "Johanan the high priest ... in Jerusalem" (CAP 30:18) and "Delaiah and Shelemiah, the sons of Sanballat governor [פחת] of Judah" (CAP 30:29) as recipients of two different official letters from the Jewish community in Elephantine (A. Cowley, *Aramaic Papyri of the Fifth Century B.C.* [Oxford: Clarendon, 1923], 108–19). Johanan would have been the grandson of Eliashib, the high priest during Nehemiah's mission (Neh 12:10–11, 22). Furthermore, Sanballat would have been the nemesis of Nehemiah (Neh 2:10, 19; 3:33–34; 4:1; 6:1, 2, 5, 12, 14; 13:28). Thus, Nehemiah's contemporaries, namely Eliashib the high priest and Sanballat the Samaritan official, were in office at least one generation prior to the reign of Artaxerxes II. Their respective tenures—and therefore Nehemiah's missions—must be dated in the reign of Artaxerxes I. See H. H. Rowley, "Nehemiah's Mission and its Background," *BJRL* 37 (1954–155): 528–61, esp. 552–53; R. W. Klein, "Ezra and Nehemiah in Recent Studies," in *Magnalia Dei: The Mighty Acts of God. Essays on the Bible and Archaeology in Memory of G. Ernest Wright* (ed. F. M. Cross, W. E. Lemke, and P. D. Miller; Garden City, N.Y.: Doubleday, 1976), 370; idem, "Ezra-Nehemiah, Books of," *ABD* 2:735–37.

Two unrelated theories propose to date Nehemiah's arrival in Jerusalem to a year other than 445 B.C.E. First, R. J. Saley argues that the king under whom Nehemiah served could have been equally either Artaxerxes II or Artaxerxes I ("The Date of Nehemiah Reconsidered," in *Biblical and Near Eastern Studies: Essays in Honor of William Sanford LaSor* [ed. G. A. Tuttle; Grand Rapids: Eerdmans, 1978], 151–65). Therefore, the date of Nehemiah's arrival in Jerusalem (Neh 1:1; 2:1) could have been 384 B.C.E. (instead of 445 B.C.E.), and his return there after his sojourn in

later (in 433 B.C.E.), Nehemiah departed Jerusalem for a sojourn of unspecified length to meet with Artaxerxes before returning to further his work in Jerusalem (Neh 13:6–7a; cf. 5:14).

The date of Ezra's arrival in Jerusalem is the controversial issue. Attempts to explain various aspects of the relevant biblical data cluster around three proposals: (1) Ezra preceded Nehemiah to Jerusalem before the middle of the fifth century B.C.E.; (2) Ezra and Nehemiah carried out their respective missions in Jerusalem—at least in part—as contemporaries in the second half of the fifth century B.C.E.; or (3) Nehemiah preceded Ezra, who reached Jerusalem only at the beginning of the fourth century B.C.E.[3] The most probable of these proposals is the first, which maintains

---

Babylon (Neh 13:6–7a) could have been after 372 B.C.E. (instead of after 433 B.C.E.). Saley proposes this hypothesis by reading the list of priests in Neh 12:10–11, 22–23 in view of material in Josephus (*Ant.* 11.297–328). At the same time, Saley questions the validity of CAP 30 as evidence because the Elephantine papyrus does not mention Nehemiah while Josephus does. A. R. W. Green reviews the evidence and concludes that the fifth-century date is preferable from a plain reading of the evidence in Neh 12:1–26 and in CAP 30 ("The Date of Nehemiah: A Reexamination," *AUSS* 28 [1990]: 195–209). Green notes that only the material from Josephus suggests the possibility of a fourth-century date for Nehemiah. Saley's correlating the material in Josephus with the biblical account in order to arrive at a fourth-century date for Nehemiah rests on at least two implausible conjectures: (1) identifying Bagoas (*Ant.* 11.297–301) with a cohort of Artaxerxes III, not with the governor of Judah in the late fifth century (CAP 30); and (2) postulating a Sanballat III—who is unknown in any extant records—as the Sanballat to whom Josephus refers (*Ant.* 11.309–311).

Second, L. McFall attempts to date Nehemiah's first mission to Jerusalem in the twelve-year period from 465 to 454 B.C.E. and his second visit to a period of less than a year beginning in 445 B.C.E. ("Was Nehemiah Contemporary with Ezra in 458 BC?" *WTJ* 53 [1991]: 263–93). According to this proposal, Ezra and Nehemiah would have been contemporaries for at least one year, in 458 B.C.E. However, McFall's thesis demands a most dubious reading of the evidence that, on the one hand, would calculate the dates in Neh 5:14 and 13:6 according to a dynastic reckoning featuring Xerxes I (486–465 B.C.E.) and not Artaxerxes (in flagrant contradiction to the obvious sense of Neh 5:14 and 13:6!) and, on the other hand, would date Neh 2:1 according to the reign of Artaxerxes I. McFall's attempts to override the obvious sense of Neh 5:14 and 13:6 as well as the conjectural nature of his proposal of two systems of dating in the Nehemiah material render his thesis untenable.

[3] For summaries of the issues involved and the arguments used, see G. Widengren, "The Persian Period," in *Israelite and Judaean History* (ed. J. H. Hayes and J. M. Miller; Philadelphia: Westminster, 1977), 503–9 (who favors the fourth-century date); J. Bright, *A History of Israel* (3d ed.; Philadelphia: Westminster, 1981), 391–402 (who advocates a date in the last half of the fifth century); and H. G. M. Williamson, *Ezra, Nehemiah* (WBC 16; Waco, Tex.: Word, 1985), xxxix–xliv (who espouses a mid-fifth-century date).

the conventional dating of Ezra's arrival in Jerusalem to 458 B.C.E. The evidence that substantiates this date is the plain sense of "the seventh year of King Artaxerxes" (Ezra 7:7), understood as a reference to the reign of Artaxerxes I Longimanus (465–425 B.C.E.).[4] The second proposal, which dates Ezra's arrival to 428 B.C.E., strives at all costs to account for the simultaneity of the missions of Ezra and Nehemiah in accordance with the indications in Neh 8:9; 12:26, 36 (cf. 12:38).[5] However, this proposal requires a textual emendation that is unsubstantiated by any manuscript evidence (reading the "thirty-seventh" instead of the "seventh" year of Artaxerxes I [Ezra 7:7]).[6] The third proposal, that Ezra arrived in 398 B.C.E., derives from viewing Ezra 7:7 as a reference to the reign of Artaxerxes II.[7] This is a more likely alternative to the first proposal, but it does not explain why the narrative recounts the mission of Ezra before that of Nehemiah. It also does not discuss the fact that the narrative does not indicate that Ezra served under a different Artaxerxes than did Nehemiah.

The description of the renewal ceremony also raises the problem of the duration of Ezra's mission. The most obvious reading of the text dates

---

[4] For further evidence in favor of dating Ezra's arrival to 458 B.C.E., see, e.g., R. de Vaux, "Israel (Histoire d')," *DBSup* 4 (1949): 763–69; and F. M. Cross, "A Reconstruction of the Judean Restoration," *JBL* 94 (1975): 4–18. For a groundbreaking treatment of the social and political background of the missions of Ezra and Nehemiah, see K. G. Hoglund, *Achaemenid Imperial Administration of Syria-Palestine and the Missions of Ezra and Nehemiah* (SBLDS 125; Atlanta: Scholars Press, 1992).

[5] V. Pavlovsky argues extensively in favor of dating Ezra's arrival to 428 B.C.E. ("Die Chronologie der Tätigkeit Esdras. Versuch einer neuen Lösung," *Bib* 38 [1957]: 278–305, 428–56). For a critique of this position, see J. A. Emerton, "Did Ezra Go to Jerusalem in 428 B.C.?" *JTS* 17 (1966): 1–19. W. Rudolph (*Esra und Nehemia* [HAT 20; Tübingen: Mohr, 1949], xxvi–xxvii, 65–71) maintains that Ezra carried out his mission in Jerusalem for one year in the gap between Nehemiah's original twelve-year term (445–433 B.C.E.; Neh 5:14; 13:6) and subsequent return to Jerusalem (Neh 13:7). According to this view, Ezra arrived in Jerusalem no earlier than 433 B.C.E. and departed Jerusalem by 430 B.C.E.

[6] The emendation presumes to correct an error of haplography arising from homoioarkton in the numbers שבע and שלשים. See Pavolvsky, "Die Chronologie," 443–45; and W. F. Albright, *The Biblical Period from Abraham to Ezra* (New York: Harper & Row, 1963), 93, 112–13 n. 193.

[7] For argumentation in support of dating Ezra's arrival in Jerusalem to 398 B.C.E., see A. van Hoonacker, "La Succession Chronologique. Néhémie-Esdras," *RB* 32 (1923): 481–94; 33 (1924): 33–64; H. Cazelles, "La Mission d'Esdras," *VT* 4 (1954): 113–40; H. H. Rowley, "The Chronological Order of Ezra and Nehemiah," in *The Servant of the Lord and Other Essays on the Old Testament* (2d ed.; Oxford: Blackwell, 1952), 137–68; and S. Mowinckel, *Studien zu dem Buche Ezra-Nehemia III: Die Ezrageschichte und das Gesetz Moses* (SUNVAO 7; Oslo: Universitetsforlaget, 1965), 99–106.

Ezra's departure from Babylon to the first day of the first month and his arrival in Jerusalem to the fifth month of the seventh year of Artaxerxes I (458 B.C.E., Ezra 7:7–9). Nehemiah departed from Susa and arrived in Jerusalem in the twentieth year (445 B.C.E., Neh 1:1; 2:1). By implication, the "seventh month" in which Ezra read the law (Neh 8:2) would have been in the twentieth year of Artaxerxes, some thirteen years after Ezra's arrival in Jerusalem (445 B.C.E.). How can one account for the gap of thirteen years between the time of Ezra's arrival with the law (Ezra 7:9) and his actual proclamation of the law to the people (Neh 8:2)?

Even F. C. Fensham,[8] a conservative scholar who strives to maintain the historical reliability of the text in its present order, implicitly admits that a thirteen-year gap is too long a time between Ezra's arrival with the mandate to implement the law (Ezra 8:12, 14, 24–25) and his actual proclamation of the law (Neh 8:1–18). He seeks refuge in the conjecture that, after initiating his reforms in Jerusalem (in 458 B.C.E., Ezra 7–10), Ezra would have gone to Susa (not Babylon), only to return to Jerusalem to advance his reforms (Neh 7:72b–10:40) after Nehemiah had established himself as governor in Jerusalem (beginning in 445 B.C.E., Neh 1–7). However, the text does not substantiate this scenario of Ezra's departing Jerusalem in between two purported missions to the city.

From the historical perspective, a more likely reconstruction begins with the thesis of the literary unity of Ezra 7–10 and Neh 8. Reading Neh 8 between Ezra 8 and 9 as a component of a preexisting Ezra source provides a perfectly reasonable chronological sequence for Ezra's mission: after departing Babylon on the first day of the first month (Ezra 7:9), he arrived in Jerusalem in the fifth month (Ezra 7:8), read the law on the first day of the seventh month (Neh 7:72b; 8:2), initiated his marriage reform in the ninth month (Ezra 10:9), took up work on the specific cases in the tenth month (10:16), and completed his marriage reform by the first day of the first month (Ezra 10:17), precisely one year after his departure from Babylon.[9] Therefore, in terms of actual history, all of Ezra's activities most likely took place within a time span of one year. Consequently, the impression of a thirteen-year gap between his arrival in Jerusalem and his reading of the law is due entirely to literary rather than historical factors, namely, the transposition of Neh 7:72b–8:18 from its original setting in the Ezra Memoir (in which the "seventh month" refers to the seventh year of Artaxerxes: Neh 7:72b; cf. Ezra 7:7–9) to its present location following the

---

[8] See F. C. Fensham, *The Books of Ezra and Nehemiah* (NICOT; Grand Rapids: Eerdmans, 1982), 6–7.

[9] On the one-year duration of Ezra's mission, see Rudolph, *Esra und Nehemia*, xxvi–xxvii; Williamson, *Ezra, Nehemiah*, xxxi–xxxii, 279–86; and J. Blenkinsopp, *Ezra-Nehemiah* (OTL; Philadelphia: Westminster, 1988), 44–46.

description of Nehemiah's work on the walls (in which the "seventh month" refers, by implication, to the twentieth year of Artaxerxes; Neh 7:72b; cf. Neh 2:1).

LITERARY QUESTIONS

The problem of the duration of Ezra's mission necessarily moves the discussion from historical concerns into matters of literary criticism. The literary issues that require consideration here include: (1) the original arrangement of the Ezra material; (2) the putative existence of an Ezra source; (3) the contents of Ezra's law book; (4) the covenant-renewal prototype for the ceremony in Neh 7:72b–10:40; (5) the relationship between Ezra-Nehemiah and Chronicles; and (6) the unity of Ezra-Nehemiah.

THE ORIGINAL ORDER OF THE EZRA MATERIAL

An alternative version of the Ezra story in Greek, 1 Esdras, provides evidence that, in the tradition, the arrangement of the Ezra material was not absolutely fixed. In 1 Esdras, Neh 7:72–8:13a follows directly after Ezra 10:44 and constitutes the conclusion to the Ezra narrative (see especially 1 Esd 8:1–9:55; cf. Ezra 7:1–10:44 and Neh 7:72b–8:12). Some scholars consider the sequence of 1 Esdras to be the original order of the Ezra narrative.[10]

Nevertheless, the arrangement of the material proposed above (Ezra 7–8; Neh 8; Ezra 9–10) as the original sequence appears preferable to the hypothesis that Neh 8 earlier followed Ezra 10. The value of 1 Esdras as a witness to the original order of the Ezra material is questionable insofar as 1 Esdras exhibits remarkable differences in content vis-à-vis Ezra-Nehemiah.[11] Reading Neh 8 between Ezra 7–8 and Ezra 9 makes more sense from a logical as well as a chronological perspective. Artaxerxes had commissioned Ezra with a double mandate pertaining, on the one hand, to the deposition of goods at the temple (Ezra 7:13–20, 21–24) and, on the

---

[10] Mowinckel supports this sequence by noting that Josephus (*Ant.* 11.120–158) relates the Ezra story according to the order in 1 Esdras (*Studien III*, 7–11). A. S. Kapelrud subscribes to this order advocated by his mentor, Mowinckel (*The Question of Authorship in the Ezra-Narrative: A Lexical Investigation* [SUNVAO 1; Oslo: Dybwad, 1944], 7).

[11] Briefly, 1 Esdras consists of: (1) 2 Chr 35:1–36:23 in paraphrase; (2) Ezra 1:1–10:44 (with the letters between Rehum and Artaxerxes [Ezra 4:7–24] following immediately after Ezra 1:1–11); (3) the story of the three young guards (1 Esd 3:1–5:6), which is inserted into the Ezra narrative after Ezra 4:7–24 and before Ezra 2:1–4:5; and (4) the account of Ezra's reading of the law (Neh 7:72–8:13a). See K.-F. Pohlmann, *Studien zum dritten Esra* (FRLANT 104; Göttingen: Vandenhoeck & Ruprecht, 1970), 14–15. Further consideration of 1 Esdras follows below within the discussion of the Ezra source.

other hand, to the implementation of the law in society (Ezra 7:14, 25–26).[12] Once he had fulfilled his responsibilities at the temple (Ezra 8:24–30, 32–34, 35–36), Ezra would have devoted his energies to the public proclamation of the law (Neh 8:1–18), likely within a couple of months of his arrival in Jerusalem (Neh 8:2; cf. Ezra 7:8). The crisis over marriages with foreigners would have developed as a consequence of the people hearing the stipulations of the law (Neh 8:9; cf. Ezra 9:1–4). The resolution of the particular cases of mixed marriage, especially among the leaders, would have followed in subsequent months (Ezra 10:1–15, especially 10:9, 16) and reached completion by the beginning of the new year (Ezra 10:17). According to this scenario, Ezra's proclamation of the law was the driving force propelling the marriage reforms. By contrast, the alternative presentation (in 1 Esdras) casts the reading of the law as the ceremonial ratification of the marriage reforms separated by a seven-month delay (Neh 8:2; cf. Ezra 10:17; 1 Esd 9:16–17; cf. 9:37).[13] The primacy of the law in Ezra's imperial mandate (Ezra 7:12–14, 25–26) points rather toward the greater likelihood of an official proclamation of the law sometime during the course of his reforms than at their conclusion.

THE EZRA SOURCE

Rearranging the text in the manner just proposed rests on the hypothesis of a preexistent Ezra source that contained the material of Ezra 7–10 and Neh 8. Scholars who reject the existence of such a source base their objection primarily on the similarity in style and vocabulary between these chapters and other parts of both Ezra-Nehemiah and Chronicles.[14]

---

[12] Ezra 7:14 unites the two concerns insofar as it describes Ezra's commission to examine the state of the whole populace but primarily with a view to supporting the temple.

[13] Mowinckel, who subscribes to the order of 1 Esdras (see n. 10), views the description of Ezra's reading the law to be "the crowning conclusion" of the work: "Das Fest der Bundeserneuerung war aber seit alters [sic] her das Neujahrs- und Laubhüttenfest. Damit ist auch gegeben, dass Neh 8 nicht von dem Anfang des ezranischen Reformwerkes handelt, sondern von dem krönenden Abschluss desselben erzählen will" (Studien III, 9–10).

[14] Those who reject the hypothesis of an Ezra source nevertheless acknowledge the cohesiveness of the Ezra material. They attribute this cohesiveness to the single author responsible for the entire Ezra-Nehemiah complex. As a result of his comparative analysis of terminology and stylistic features in Ezra 7–10 and Neh 8–10, C. C. Torrey concludes that these chapters are the composition of the Chronicler himself (*The Composition and Historical Value of Ezra-Nehemiah* [BZAW 2; Giessen: J. Ricker'sche Buchhandlung, 1896], 16–29). Torrey's study, along with the list of terminology common to Chronicles and Ezra-Nehemiah compiled by S. R. Driver (*An Introduction to the Literature of the Old Testament* [Edinburgh:

Nevertheless, a combination of four primary considerations suggests the likelihood of a distinct Ezra source: (1) the cohesiveness of the Ezra narrative (however one arranges Ezra 7–10 and Neh 8); (2) the testimony of 1 Esdras to a tradition that presented the Ezra material as a whole, independent of any reference to Nehemiah; (3) the possibility of rearranging the Ezra material according to a self-consistent chronology (see above); and (4) the material's specifications regarding geography (Ezra 8:15, 17, 21, 31), as well as time and season (Ezra 10:9, 13), which are quite irrelevant to the story in its present form.[15]

Discussion of the Ezra source raises a variety of issues, including the extent of its contents; the relationship of the rescript of Artaxerxes (Ezra 7:12–26) and other archival material (Ezra 8:1–14; 10:20–44) to the Ezra narrative; the specific nature of the Ezra source as either a "memoir" or a "narrative"; the status of the Ezra source as either genuine or counterfeit history; and the purpose and authorship of the Ezra source.

The parameters of the Ezra source

The Ezra source encompassed at least Ezra 7–10 and Neh 8 (however one arranges this material).[16] In comparison, significant evidence, both external and internal, suggests that the bulk of Neh 9 and 10 did not form part of the Ezra source. In terms of external evidence, 1 Esdras does not include the material in these chapters; furthermore, Josephus makes Neh 8 the definitive conclusion of the Ezra material by following this immediately

---

T&T Clark, 1898], 534–40), was utilized by M. Noth (*The Chronicler's History* [trans. H. G. M. Williamson; JSOTSup 50; Sheffield: JSOT Press, 1987], 62–66), who likewise identifies the Chronicler as the author of Ezra 7–10 and Neh 8–10. At the conclusion of his fresh study of terminology in Ezra 7–10 and Neh 8, Kapelrud offers a threefold nuance on the relationship between the Chronicler and the Ezra material: (1) "Chronicle circles," not the Chronicler, gave the Ezra material its present form; (2) this Ezra material originated in an earlier tradition; but (3) it is impossible to identify this "original Ezra" (*The Question of Authorship*, 95).

[15] Cf. Williamson, *Ezra, Nehemiah*, xxviii–xxxii, esp. xxxi. See also F. Ahlemann, "Zur Esra-Quelle," *ZAW* 59 (1942–1943): 77–98; Rudolph, *Esra und Nehemia*, 163–67; Mowinckel, *Studien III*, 11–17; K. Koch, "Ezra and the Origins of Judaism," *JSS* 19 (1974): 176–79.

[16] Evidence both external and internal indicates this combination. The external evidence is the witness of 1 Esdras that associates Neh 7:72–8:13a directly with Ezra 7:1–10:44 (1 Esd 8:1–9:55). The internal evidence involves several basic links between Ezra's reading of the law and previous descriptions of his work: setting (the square in Jerusalem: Ezra 10:9; Neh 7:72b–8:1), subject matter (the law: Ezra 7:6, 10, 11, 13–14, 25–26; cf. Neh 8:1, 7–8), and personalities (Ezra, the people from Jerusalem and surrounding areas, and the Levites: Neh 8:1–18; cf. Ezra 8:15–20; 10:1–5).

The History of Research on Nehemiah 7:72b–10:40

with the announcement of the priest-scribe's death (*Ant.* 11.154–158). The most noteworthy internal evidence, however, is that Ezra's name does not occur in either Neh 9 or 10.[17] Furthermore, the formulations of Nehemiah's extensive psalm (Neh 9:6–37) seem too generic to have arisen directly out of Ezra's work of marriage reform. Finally, the stipulations of the oath-taking (Neh 10:29–40) are not intimately related to the mandate governing Ezra's activities at the temple (Ezra 7:14–24; 8:24–34).

Only one verse in each of the two chapters provides an obvious linkage to Ezra's reform: the description of the adherents to the law separating themselves from foreigners in general (Neh 9:2) and their making a commitment not to permit their children to intermarry with "people of the land" (Neh 10:31). The declaration of separation from foreigners within a penitential setting on "the twenty-fourth day of this month" (Neh 9:1–2) would provide a consistent and fitting sequel to the decisions taken on "the twentieth day" of the "ninth month" (Ezra 10:9–15) prior to the discussions between Ezra and the leaders that began on "the first day of the tenth month" (Ezra 10:16).[18] Although the oath by parents pledging not to allow their children to intermarry with foreigners (Neh 10:31) does not fit a specific context within the Ezra narrative (cf. Ezra 9:1–2), it does relate to concerns that Nehemiah will express (Neh 13:23–25). In summary, the evidence indicates that, along with Neh 8, only a tiny portion (Neh 9:1–2) of the narrative introduction to the historical psalm belonged originally to the Ezra source.[19] It seems unlikely that either the remainder of Neh 9 or all of Neh 10 were part of the Ezra source.[20]

Archival documents in the Ezra source

The Aramaic of Artaxerxes' rescript (Ezra 7:12–26) constitutes an intrusion into the Hebrew narrative (Ezra 7:1–11; 7:27–10:44) at the beginning of the Ezra source. The fact that the text is cited in Aramaic substantiates the claim that it is "a copy" of an official document of the Achaemenid

---

[17] This assertion presumes a reading of Neh 9:6 according to the MT rather than an emendation based on the Greek text, which reads, "And Ezra said..." (LXX 2 Esd 19:6).

[18] This is the proposal of Williamson, *Ezra, Nehemiah*, 309–10.

[19] This is the thesis of Williamson, ibid.

[20] There are two major differing views on the extent of the Ezra material. The first view considers all of Neh 8–10 as belonging to an Ezra narrative that the Chronicler authored (see C. C. Torrey, *Ezra Studies* [1910; repr., New York: Ktav, 1970], 252–84). The second view accepts only Neh 8 and 9 as part of the Ezra source. See, e.g., H. H. Schaeder, *Esra der Schreiber* (BHT 5; Tübingen: Mohr [Siebeck], 1930), 8–9; and D. J. A. Clines, *Ezra, Nehemiah, Esther* (NCB; Grand Rapids: Eerdmans, 1992), 6–8.

administration (Ezra 7:11) and, at the same time, relates this decree to the other items of official correspondence in Aramaic in the preceding chapters of Ezra (Ezra 4:11–16, 17–22; 5:7b–17; 6:3–12). The format of the rescript corresponds to the conventions of Aramaic letter-writing in the Persian era.[21]

However, its contents have provoked suspicion about the authenticity of the document on two fronts. First, in light of what is known of the imperial administration, some have questioned the likelihood either of the Persians' recognizing Ezra's title (Ezra 7:12, 21) or granting him authority both to make judicial appointments throughout the province Beyond the River and to impose the sanction of capital punishment (Ezra 7:25–26).[22] Second, with regard to the legal tradition of the decrees, some have noted the presence of non-Persian—indeed distinctively Jewish—elements in it.[23] In summary, the rescript of Artaxerxes betrays the work of a Jewish hand.

---

[21] J. A. Fitzmyer treats the letters in Ezra within the context of a study that examines some fifty letters written in Aramaic during the fifth and fourth centuries B.C.E. ("Aramaic Epistolography," in *A Wandering Aramean: Collected Aramaic Essays* [Missoula, Mont.: Scholars Press, 1979], 183–204). He identifies a five-part outline for such letters: (1) *praescriptio;* (2) salutation; (3) secondary greetings; (4) message; and (5) conclusion. Lastly, he states, "As for the biblical letters, those in Ezra supply the closest parallels to the extra biblical material" (p. 196). The letter in Ezra 7:12–26 exhibits elements 1, 2, and 4 of Fitzmyer's outline. Artaxerxes' rescript to Ezra (7:12–26) parallels the structure of his response to Rehum, Shimshai, and their companions ordering work on the city walls to cease (4:17–22), using the following elements: (1) *praescriptio* (4:17; cf. 7:12); (2) salutation (4:17; cf. 7:12); (3) particle indicating the beginning of the message (כענת: "and now," 4:17; 7:12); and (4) vocabulary of the message itself (e.g., שים טעם: מני "a decree was issued from me," 4:19, 21; 7:13; מדה בלו הלך: "tribute, custom, and toll," 4:20; 7:24; and a rhetorical question asking "Why [should harm come] to the king?" 4:22; 7:23b; cf. Williamson, *Ezra, Nehemiah,* 98). For a discussion of the Persian archival material in Ezra, see L. V. Hensley, "The Official Persian Documents in the Book of Ezra" (Ph.D. diss., University of Liverpool, 1977).

[22] Whereas Schaeder (*Esra der Schreiber,* 39–53) asserts that the rescript endowed Ezra with an official position as "minister of Jewish affairs," Kapelrud (*The Question of Authorship,* 27–42) rejects the authenticity of the rescript since he finds its contents implausible.

[23] Blenkinsopp (*Ezra-Nehemiah,* 147–51), notes the following Jewish elements: (1) Ezra's title in the *praescriptio* (7:12; cf. 7:21), which reflects the narrative introduction (7:6, 10, 11); (2) mention of "bulls, rams, and lambs" in the traditional MT order (Ezra 7:17; cf. 2 Chr 29:32), these being related to flour and drink offerings in accordance with the law (Ezra 7:17; cf. Num 15:1–16); (3) employment of the noun "wrath" (קצף, 7:23), a technical term that refers, in the MT tradition, exclusively to a reaction of God (Ezra 7:23; cf. Num 1:53; 2 Chr 19:10); and (4) the implementation of a judicial system throughout the countryside that approximates the one envisioned by the Deuteronomic tradition (Ezra 7:25; cf. Deut 1:16–17; 16:18; 17:8–13).

But in which stage in the development of the text did this hand intervene? One proposal considers the Jewish content as integral to the genesis of the document even to the point of attributing that content to Ezra himself on the supposition that he played an instrumental role in the original formulation of the decree by the Persian administration.[24] An alternative proposal ascribes the Jewish content rather to the final stage of redaction, attributing it to an editor who revised the Persian document when he inserted the Ezra source into the Ezra-Nehemiah complex.[25]

A close inspection of the rescript uncovers evidence that is essential for deciding its provenance. The king's communication to the treasurers in the province Beyond the River (7:21–24) is an independent document that has been inserted into the order that Artaxerxes addressed to Ezra (7:12–20, 25–26). The rescript commissioned Ezra to act in two spheres: first, in Jerusalem and more specifically at the temple, granting him permission to take priests and Levites from Babylon to Jerusalem, hand over the king's money to the temple, purchase sacrificial offerings, and deliver precious utensils (7:13–20); and, second, in the countryside throughout the province, authorizing him to appoint magistrates and judges to teach the laws (7:25–26; cf. 7:14). The Ezra source subsequently describes Ezra fulfilling his commission in the first sphere, pertaining to the priests, Levites, and temple in Jerusalem (8:15–23, 24–30, 32–34, 35).

Possibly the Ezra source also presented Ezra carrying out his commission in the second sphere, relating to the populace in the countryside (7:14, 25–26), though not precisely according to the king's prescription. Specifically, he would have fulfilled the commission to teach the laws (Ezra 7:25b) in his reading of the scroll with the assistance of the Levites, who interpreted the text for the people from the towns who had gathered at the square of the Water Gate (Neh 7:72b–8:8).[26] In the original order of the Ezra source, the description of this event (Neh 7:72b–8:18) would have followed the narrative about Ezra's summons of the Levites and handing over of wealth and utensils to the priests (Ezra 8:15–34; cf. 7:13–20).[27] In other

---

[24] Williamson, *Ezra, Nehemiah*, 98–99.

[25] Blenkinsopp attributes the revision to the Chronicler (*Ezra-Nehemiah*, 147–52).

[26] Noth asserts that the connection between Artaxerxes' rescript and Ezra's reading of the law is so strong that it provides the basis for relating Neh 8–10 to Ezra 7–10 (*The Chronicler's History*, 47). He states, "It is obvious that this account [Neh 8–10] represents the fulfillment of Ezra's mission according to Ezra 7.14, 25f. (cf. earlier 7.10) and that it therefore belongs very closely with the Ezra history in Ezra 7–10."

[27] One might add that the material that follows immediately (8:35–36) establishes a further correspondence between the rescript and the narrative: the offering of sacrifices at the temple (Ezra 8:35; cf. 7:16–17) and the Persian officials in the

words, the sequence of events in the Ezra source (Ezra 8–Neh 8) would have corresponded to the order of the prescriptions in the final version of Artaxerxes' rescript (Ezra 7:14–26). This correspondence makes it possible that the decree's present wording may be from Ezra in his role as imperial delegate, either in advance of his mission, as the appointee whose expertise influenced the original wording of the king's decree, or, subsequent to his mission, as the author of an official report outlining how his activities in Jerusalem and Judah complied with the commission he had received.

Besides the rescript of Artaxerxes (Ezra 7:12–26), the Ezra source contains two other archival documents, namely, the list of family heads who went up from Babylon to Jerusalem with Ezra (Ezra 8:1–14) and the list of those who had divorced their foreign wives in response to Ezra's marriage reform (Ezra 10:18–44). The fact that, in each case, a narrative seam (8:1; 10:18) introduces the list suggests that both lists represent preexisting archival materials that were incorporated into the Ezra narrative. The list of those who journeyed with Ezra interrupts the first-person narrative, which breaks off in Ezra 7:28 and resumes in 8:15 (with a linkage supplied by the verb ואקבצה ["and I gathered"] in each of these verses).[28] Furthermore, the vocabulary of the list's title (8:1) reiterates earlier material (ראשים: "heads," עלה: "to go up," 8:1 and 7:28; "King Artaxerxes," 8:1 and 7:1, 11, 21). The list of those who divorced their foreign wives (Ezra 10:18–44) appears to be an appendix inasmuch as it follows a summary statement concerning the date of the conclusion of the marriage reform (Ezra 10:17). At the same time, however, this list fits well into the present context both insofar as the actual names testify to the reality of the marriage reform and the vocabulary of marriage and divorce in the list is consistent with that of the narrative (ישב נשים נכריות [*hip'il*]: "to marry foreign women," 10:18; cf. 10:2, 10, 14, 17; יצא נשים [*hip'il*]: "to send away wives," 10:19; cf. 10:3).[29] In summary, both the introductory seams (8:1; 10:17–18) and their distinctive content identify these lists as insertions, while the links in terminology between the lists and the narrative (8:1; cf. 7:28 and 8:15; 10:18, 19; cf. 10:2–3) indicate that the author of the Ezra source is responsible for incorporating them into their present contexts.

---

province accepting the king's decree (Ezra 8:36; cf. 7:21–24). However, the third-person narrative form distinguishes this brief unit from the first-person autobiographical style of the surrounding context (Ezra 8:15–34; 9:1–15) and indicates that Ezra 8:35–36 is an editorial insertion. Rudolph (*Esra und Nehemia*, 84–85) and, more tentatively, Williamson (*Ezra, Nehemiah*, 116, 122) ascribe these verses to the editor who moved Neh 8:1–18 to its present location.

[28] Compare Noth, *The Chronicler's History*, 44.

[29] Williamson, *Ezra, Nehemiah*, 148–49.

The Ezra source: "narrative" or "memoir"?

Consideration of the respective settings in which the above two lists occur raises questions about the original form of the Ezra source. The list of those who went up from Babylon to Jerusalem with Ezra (8:1–14) is incorporated into a narrative in the first person (Ezra 7:27–9:15), while the list of those who divorced their foreign wives (Ezra 10:18–44) is an extension of a narrative in the third person (Ezra 10:1–17). Was the Ezra source, then, a third-person narrative or a first-person memoir?

Responding to this question requires investigating the relationship between the passages in the third person (Ezra 7:1–10; 10:1–44; Neh 8:1–18)[30] and those in the first person (Ezra 7:12–9:15).[31] Do the two narrative types represent two distinct sources? The first-person account manifests continuity, if not completeness (Ezra 7:12–9:15). The first part of the king's commission (7:12–20) seems to have inspired the initial part of the narrative, which describes the deposition of the vessels at the temple (8:24–34). But the correspondence between Ezra's mandated application of the laws of God and of the king (7:26) and his actual work of marriage reform (9:1–4) is, at best, oblique.[32] Nevertheless, the first-person account exhibits a certain artistry: Ezra's concluding prayer (9:6–15) provides an inclusion with his opening acclamation of praise (7:27–28), wherein prayers frame the autobiographical narrative (8:1–9:5). However, his final prayer does not offer an adequate conclusion for the autobiographical section, which, by itself, lacks a resolution to the crisis of mixed marriages.

The third-person narrative (Ezra 10:1–44; Neh 8:1–18) picks up the story in mid-course and lacks the requisite introduction for its description of the marriage crisis.[33] This narrative does not recount the early stages of

---

[30] Ezra 7:11 and 8:35–36 are editorial compositions in the third person. On Ezra 7:11, see n. 31 below, and on Ezra 8:35–36, see n. 27 above.

[31] The rescript of Artaxerxes (Ezra 7:12–26) could be read either as a continuation of the third-person narrative (see 7:11) or as the beginning of the first-person account. The latter alternative is preferable since Artaxerxes' rescript takes the form of a personal order that employs the "I-you" style of discourse. Ezra 7:11 is an editorial seam that provides the transition from the introduction (7:1–10) to the rescript (7:12–26).

[32] I have noted above (pp. 11–12) that Neh 8 probably constitutes the narrative fulfillment of Ezra 7:14, 25–26. If Neh 8 originally stood between Ezra 8 and 9, it would have been composed in the first person as well. The relocation of Ezra's reading of the law would have necessitated the transposition of its first-person account into the third-person narrative in order to distinguish the activities of Ezra from those of Nehemiah (which are narrated in the first person in Neh 1:1–7:5). See Williamson, *Ezra, Nehemiah*, xxxi, 147, 283–86.

[33] Most of Ezra 7:1–10 is an editorial composition. H. W. M. van Grol identifies a narrative thread in 7:1a, 6a, 8a: "In the reign of King Artaxerxes of Persia, Ezra

Ezra's mission, including the story of his journey to Jerusalem and his activities in relation to the temple (cf. Ezra 8:24-34); nevertheless, it does mention all the significant dates in Ezra's mission.[34] In summary, whereas the autobiographical section lacks an adequate conclusion, the narrative section lacks a sufficient introduction.

There is overlap in the two segments' descriptions of how the marriage crisis came to light (Ezra 9:1-5; cf. 10:1-5). The first-person account and the third-person narrative share the following details: leader(s) bringing the matter to Ezra's attention (9:1; cf. 10:2); mention of "those who tremble" at the words (commandments) of God (9:4; cf. 10:3); and Ezra's response of fasting (9:4-5; cf. 10:6). Nevertheless, the issue at stake in each account, while similar, is not identical. The autobiographical account mainly deals with parents allowing their children to marry foreigners (Ezra 9:2; cf. 9:12), whereas the third-person narrative deals more exclusively with men who have married foreigners (10:2-3). This evidence can be interpreted in one of two ways: either the elements that are common to the two accounts suggest that the same event is being recounted on the basis of two different sources (one in the first person and the other in the third person), both of which the editor preserved; or the difference in the precise issue indicates that two distinct episodes are being described similarly. The latter interpretation is preferable since it suggests a refined literary touch that is also apparent in these episodes being united in time (9:4, 5, "the evening sacrifice") and space (10:1, 6a, "before the house of God") and bound by subsequent temporal (10:6, "night") and spatial (10:6, "the chamber of Jehohanan") transitions.

Neither the memoir nor the narrative account constitutes a complete story in itself. Only the combination of the two provides a narrative whole. The problem of marriage with foreigners that first arises in the autobiographical section (9:1-4) is resolved in the narrative section (10:9-44).

So remarkable is the manner in which the two narratives complement each other that S. Mowinckel defends the integrity of the story as it stands. In search of precedents, he points to examples in Mesopotamian and

---

went up from Babylon and came to Jerusalem in the fifth month of the seventh year of the king" ("Ezra 7, 1-10: Een Literair-Stilistische Analyse," *Bijdr* 51 [1990]: 21-37). I would ascribe the dates in 7:9 to the original narrative. Even in its present expanded form, Ezra 7:1-10 does not provide a sufficient introduction to the matters recounted in Ezra 10:1-44 and Neh 8:1-18. Williamson (*Ezra, Nehemiah*, 90) thinks Ezra 7:1-10 is the work of the editor who assembled the Ezra-Nehemiah complex. In so doing, this editor rewrote an earlier introduction which was originally composed in the first person.

[34] The dates that can be rearranged into a complete one-year time span for Ezra's mission are all found in sections narrated in the third person (Ezra 7:7-9; Neh 8:2; Ezra 10:9, 16, 17).

Egyptian literature in which first-person autobiography follows third-person narrative.[35] However, the comparatively late texts of Tobit and Daniel are the only two Jewish texts to which he can appeal as exhibiting a narrative mixture of the first and third persons.[36]

Because neither account is sufficient by itself, recourse to separate sources cannot explain the composition of the present text. In principle, insertion into the present literary context could have demanded an alteration in the original form of a source. In fact, all of the contexts in which the narrative portions of the Ezra material appear require the third-person form. The third-person introduction to the Ezra material (Ezra 7:1–10) provides the required stylistic transition from the first part of the book (Ezra 1:1–6:22), which, except for some of the archival material (Ezra 1:2–4; 4:11–16; 4:17–22; 5:7–17; 6:3–12), takes the form of third-person narrative. The third-person account of the completion of the marriage reforms (Ezra 10:1–44) serves a double function by concluding the Ezra block in the same form as it began (7:1–10) and by providing a stylistic distinction separating the Ezra material from the first-person Nehemiah Memoir (NM) that follows immediately (Neh 1:1–7:5).

Similarly, the third-person account of Ezra's reading of the law provides a stylistic marker that distinguishes the activity of Nehemiah (Neh 1:1–7:5, autobiography) from the activity of Ezra (Neh 8:1–18, narrative). In summary, their present contexts necessitated that these major portions of Ezra material be narrated in the third person. This situation opens the possibility that the whole Ezra source could have been written originally as a first-person memoir that the editor subsequently transposed into the third person and inserted into the present contexts.[37] This hypothesis supports the convention of designating this source as the Ezra Memoir (EM). Because the Ezra material, at least in part, appears to be a memoir, I shall employ the designation EM while, of course, acknowledging its conjectural nature.

---

[35] S. Mowinckel, "'Ich' und 'Er' in der Esrageschichte," in *Verbannung und Heimkehr: Beiträge zur Geschichte und Theologie Israels im 6. und 5. Jahrhundert v. Chr.* (ed. A. Kuschke; Tübingen: Mohr [Siebeck], 1961), 220–22.

[36] Mowinckel ("'Ich' und 'Er,'" 222) notes that, in Tobit, the genealogical introduction in the third person (1:1–2) leads into the first-person account (1:3–2:14). Tobit's prayer (3:1–6) provides the transition to the narrative in the third person that pervades the remainder of the book. In Daniel, the evidence is even sparser, with Dan 10:1 providing the third-person introduction to a vision that—like all the visions in Daniel—is recounted in the first person. The Ezra material might have provided a stylistic precedent for Tobit and Daniel, which are later texts. The evidence that Ezra was composed prior to Tobit and Daniel precludes the possibility that the latter could have influenced the former.

[37] Williamson, *Ezra, Nehemiah*, xxxi–xxxii, 147–49.

The Ezra Memoir: authentic or counterfeit history?

The term *memoir* is central to the debate about the authenticity of the Ezra material and its reliability as a preexistent "source." In addition to being conjectural, the application of the term *memoir* to the Ezra material is based on its contiguity with the Nehemiah material. A wider convention applies the designation *memoir* to the Nehemiah source[38] because the first-person form is consistently maintained throughout its account of Nehemiah building the wall around Jerusalem (Neh 1:1–6:19) and continues—at least in piecemeal fashion—in the remainder of the Nehemiah material (Neh 7:1–5; 12:31–32, 37–40, 43; 13:4–31). Basically, the NM consists of Neh 1:1–7:5a; 12:27–43; and 13:4–31.[39]

How might one account for the observations that the Ezra and Nehemiah materials share the literary form of "memoir" and that these are the only examples of such memoirs in biblical literature?[40] Proposals to resolve this question fall into four basic categories: (1) the EM is not a "source" but a literary imitation of the NM that the Chronicler composed either with or without a historical foundation; (2) the EM is a source that was composed as an edifying history to rival the NM; (3) the EM derives from an oral tradition that shared the same ethos as the NM;

---

[38] However, S. Mowinckel disputes the application of the term *memoir* to the Nehemiah material (*Studien zu dem Buche Ezra-Nehemia II: Die Nehemia-Denkschrift* [SUNVAO 5; Oslo: Universitetsforlaget, 1964], 50–92). He emphasizes that the form (*Gattung*) of the Nehemiah material is unique in the MT. The terms *memoir* and *autobiography* are anachronistic when applied to such material of the ancient Near East (cf. Mowinckel, *Studien III*, 96–97).

[39] The precise content of the NM is open to debate particularly in connection with the following passages: (1) the roster of workers on the walls (3:1–32); (2) the explicit prayers for divine remembrance (Neh 5:14–19; cf. 13:4–14, 15–22, 23–31); (3) the census list (Neh 7:6–72a; cf. Ezra 2:1–70); and (4) the third-person account of the repopulation of Jerusalem (Neh 11:1–2). A broader view of the NM would include the census list (7:5b–72a) and the account of repopulating Jerusalem (but in the first person [11:1–2]). By this estimation, the NM would consist of Neh 1:1–7:72a; 11:1–2; 12:27–43; and 13:4–31. Cf. Klein, "Ezra-Nehemiah," 733–34.

[40] Since 1900, many German scholars have spoken of Isa 6:1–8:18 (or 6:1–9:6) as the prophet's *Denkschrift*. However, this portion of Isaiah differs from the EM and NM insofar as it consists more of prophetic oracles than of narrative, and it lacks the narrative continuity evident in both the EM and the NM. Furthermore, there is greater scholarly consensus supporting the term *memoir* for the Ezra and Nehemiah material than for the Isaian material. See S. A. Irvine, "The Isaianic *Denkschrift*: Reconsidering an Old Hypothesis," *ZAW* 104 (1992): 216–31; cf. O. Eissfeldt, *The Old Testament: An Introduction* (trans. P. R. Ackroyd; Oxford: Blackwell, 1966), 310–11; J. Jensen, *Isaiah 1–39* (OTM 8; Wilmington, Del.: Glazier, 1984), 82–83; H. Wildberger, *Isaiah 1–12: A Commentary* (trans. T. H. Tropp; CC; Minneapolis: Fortress, 1991), esp. 252, 258–59, 379.

and (4) the EM is an authentic independent autobiographical source parallel to the NM. C. C. Torrey advocates the first proposal and interprets their common (and unique) literary form as evidence that the EM was composed in imitation of the NM and, as such, was not a "source" but a free prose composition of "the Chronicler."[41] In Torrey's estimation, the EM is counterfeit history, nothing more than an invention of the Chronicler to legitimate the status of Judah (over against the Samaritans) as the genuine religious heir of preexilic Israel, the custodian of the true temple, and—as the faithful remnant that returned from Babylon—the preserver of the divine law. He judges that Ezra the scribe is not a historical figure but rather a character whom the Chronicler created to serve as the guarantor of the Torah.[42]

Subsequent commentators adhere to Torrey's thesis of the EM as a composition of the Chronicler in imitation of the NM while rejecting Torrey's radical judgment against the existence of a historical Ezra. M. Noth, for example, grants the historicity of Ezra while denying the existence of an Ezra source or "memoir." He accepts the rescript of Artaxerxes (Ezra 7:12–26) as an authentic source, along with the list of returnees (Ezra 8:1–14) as well as the NM, which together provided the raw material for the Chronicler's composition of the EM.[43] U. Kellermann subscribes to a similar position insofar as he admits Ezra's historicity without subscribing to the theory of an Ezra source. He views the Ezra material as the Chronicler's "midrash" on comparatively meager source material, which he limits to Ezra 7:12–23, 26 (and possibly 8:26–27).[44]

A second proposal is that of Mowinckel, who describes the EM as an "edifying historical narrative" (*erbauliche Geschichtserzählung*) that was composed perhaps a quarter-century after Ezra's mission by an eyewitness who intended to illustrate the superiority of Ezra over Nehemiah in the unfolding of God's plan for the restoration of Jerusalem and the people.[45]

---

[41] Torrey, *Ezra Studies*, 243–46; idem, *The Composition and Historical Value*, 28–29. As a result of his comparative analysis of vocabulary, syntax, and style, Torrey asserts that Neh 1:1–6:19 (except Neh 3:1–32) is a genuine source that the Chronicler only retouched (*The Composition and Historical Value*, 35–42). By contrast, he maintains that the Ezra material is a prime example of the Chronicler's own handiwork (*Ezra Studies*, 241).

[42] Torrey, *The Composition and Historical Value*, 57–62; idem, *Ezra Studies*, 247–48.

[43] Noth, *The Chronicler's History*, 63–66.

[44] U. Kellermann, *Nehemia: Quellen, Überlieferung und Geschichte* (BZAW 102; Berlin: Töpelmann, 1967), 56–69. In light of the limited historical value he ascribes to the Ezra material, Kellermann dates Ezra's mission to just before 448 B.C.E. ("Erwägungen zum Problem der Esradatierung," *ZAW* 80 [1968]: 55–87).

[45] Mowinckel, *Studien III*, 96–112.

A. S. Kapelrud, for his part, defends the authenticity of the Ezra material by tracing it back to oral traditions circulating in various Chronistic circles that, in turn, eventually gave definitive shape to the Ezra narrative. By contrast, the distinctiveness of the NM is due to its having already assumed written form when these Chronistic circles took it over.[46]

The fourth proposal is the most conventional one, gaining its strongest impetus from the thesis of H. H. Schaeder, who identifies Ezra himself as the author of the memoir, which originally constituted his report as an official of the Persian administration to that administration, accounting for his activities in Jerusalem in accordance with his imperial mandate. The Chronicler edited this original memoir to give it definitive form.[47]

Torrey stands alone in his refusal to ascribe any historical credibility to Ezra and the material concerning him. All other commentators maintain that at least a kernel of the Ezra material is securely grounded in history.

The purpose and authorship of the Ezra source

All the above proposals concerning the formation of the Ezra material have in common the supposition that the author of the Ezra-Nehemiah complex gave the Ezra material its definitive shape. No one suggests that the text preserves the EM in its original form. Opinions on the identity of the original author of the Ezra material vary from Ezra himself (Schaeder, Rudolph, Williamson) to a second-generation admirer (Mowinckel) to a Chronistic circle (Kapelrud) to the Chronicler (Torrey, Noth, Kellermann). Similarly, proposed identifications of the source's literary form range from an official government report (Schaeder, Rudolph, Williamson) to a Chronistic synthesis of oral tradition (Kapelrud) to an edifying historical narrative (Mowinckel) to a midrashic elaboration of an imperial rescript (Kellermann) to a Chronistic novella that only mimics history (Torrey).

---

[46] Kapelrud, *The Question of Authorship*, 95–97.

[47] Schaeder describes Ezra's composition as an official report to his Persian superiors: "Aber um private Aufzeichnungen kann es sich nicht handeln. Esra schrieb für andere und zwar in erster Linie für solche, die nicht Augenzeugen seines Handelns gewesen waren. Das waren einerseits der König und seine Minister; denn als Beamter in außerordentlicher und heikler Mission war Esra gehalten, seinen Vorgesetzten Rechenschaft zu geben" (*Esra der Schreiber*, 36). Rudolph asserts that Ezra's records were the only source for the activity of Ezra available to the Chronicler (*Esra und Nehemia*, xxiv). Williamson similarly maintains that the source used was Ezra's firsthand report to the Persian authorities to account for his mission (*Ezra-Nehemiah*, xxxi–xxxii). Schaeder argues that the phrase ספר דתא די־אלה שמיא ("scribe of the law of the God of heaven," Ezra 7:12) is an official title designating Ezra as a commissioner for Judahite affairs in the Persian administration (*Esra der Schreiber*, 48–57).

A definitive resolution is beyond the reach of this discussion. However, the consensus would sustain these presuppositions regarding the EM: (1) the historicity of Ezra; (2) the authenticity of at least some documents embedded within the Ezra material; (3) the development of a tradition concerning the words and deeds of Ezra; and (4) the marked influence on the EM of a redactional enterprise that aligned the account of Ezra's mission with that of Nehemiah.

EZRA'S BOOK OF THE LAW

The authenticity of the Ezra material determines the very possibility of identifying the contents of Ezra's book of the law. If the narrative is based on a firsthand EM, it can provide reliable indicators of the scope of Ezra's law book. If, on the contrary, the story is predominantly a work of tradition and redaction, it will reflect the law as known to the tradents and editors.

Historical evidence confirms the possibility that the Persian administration would have encouraged Ezra to articulate and implement a law code for the population of Yehud. Ezra's mandate as priest and scribe to the Judahites under Artaxerxes I exhibits similarities to that of Udjahorresnet the Egyptian to his own people under Darius I.[48] Moreover, Ezra's commission in service of the law is reminiscent of an order of Darius that Egyptian priests and scribes draw up a code of their laws.[49] Finally,

---

[48] J. Blenkinsopp highlights these features of Udjahorresnet, the Egyptian commissioned by the Persian king around 518 B.C.E.: (1) his title as "scribe" and the probability of his being of priestly stock; and (2) his mandate to reform the temple cult (at Neith) by banishing foreigners, purifying the sanctuary, reinstating legitimate cultic officials, and reimplementing the proper calendar of festivals ("The Mission of Udjahorresnet and Those of Ezra and Nehemiah," *JBL* 106 [1987]: 409–21).

[49] See W. Spiegelberg, *Die sogennante demotische Chronik des Pap. 215 der Bibliothèque Nationale zu Paris nebst den auf der Rückseite des Papyrus stehenden Texten* (Demotische Studien 7; Leipzig: Hinrichs, 1914). This papyrus dates from the Ptolemaic era, apparently sometime in the third century B.C.E. The recto of the papyrus contains the so-called "Demotic Chronicle," a coherent oracular text representative of an Egyptian temple ambiance. The verso (ibid., 30–32), however, consists of five different texts, one of which recounts the fact that, in 519–518 B.C.E., Darius directed the satraps in Egypt to gather "warriors, scribes, and priests," who would make a collection of the laws that had been in force up to 526 B.C.E. The text recounts that the delegation finished its task in 495 B.C.E. A copy of the resultant document (which is no longer extant) was written on a single roll of papyrus in two types of script: the official Aramaic and the less formal demotic. For an elaboration of the possible implications of the so-called "Demotic Chronicle" for understanding Ezra's commission, see N. J. Reich, "The Codification of the Egyptian Laws by Darius and the Origin of the 'Demotic Chronicle'," *Mizraim* 1 (1933), 178–85; A. T. Olmstead,

implementation of Judahite law to stabilize the province of Yehud would have furthered Persian interests especially in 458 B.C.E., following upon the Egyptian revolt against the Persians (460 B.C.E.) and the Greek conquest of Memphis (459 B.C.E.).[50]

The history of research has generated five categories of proposals regarding the content of Ezra's "book of the law" (Neh 8:3; cf. 8:1, 8, 14, 18; 9:3; 13:1): (1) identifying Ezra's book with the Pentateuch (the classical thesis) understands "the book of the law of Moses" (Neh 8:1) in the broadest terms as designating the entire Pentateuch;[51] (2) limiting the book to the Priestly Code is based on the allegedly exclusive references to P legislation in Neh 8:13–18 and Neh 10:29–40;[52] (3) identifying the law book with Deuteronomy appeals to the Deuteronomic coloring of Artaxerxes' rescript (Ezra 7:12–26);[53] (4) the lack of consistency in the evidence of the Ezra material suggests to some scholars that the law book comprised a compilation of material drawn from the various law codes of the Pentateuch;[54] and (5) divergences between the Ezra material and the pentateuchal laws stimulate the suggestion that Ezra's law book was an independent work that was not preserved.[55]

Extensive research on the topic has practically exhausted the options and suggests that the sketchy nature of the evidence makes it impossible to determine the precise content of Ezra's law book. A more fruitful avenue of investigation might consider Ezra's reforms as witness to an exegetical reinterpretation of traditional legislation made necessary by unprecedented situations.[56]

"Darius as Lawgiver," *AJSL* 51 (1934–1935): 247–49; and R. de Vaux, "Les Décrets de Cyrus et de Darius sur la Reconstruction du Temple," *RB* 46 (1937): 37–40.

[50] See O. Margalith, "The Political Role of Ezra As Persian Governor," *ZAW* 98 (1986): 110–12; and Hoglund, *Achaemenid Administration*, 86–91, 226–36.

[51] M. Kegel, *Die Kultusreformation des Esra: Außagen moderner Kritik über Neh. 8–10 kritisch beleuchtet* (Gütersloh: Bertelsmann, 1921), 214; Cazelles, "La Mission," 113–40; and Mowinckel, *Studien III*, 124–41.

[52] See Kellermann, "Erwägungen," 376–77, for commentators advocating this view.

[53] Ibid., 373–85.

[54] See, e.g., G. von Rad, *Das Geschichtsbild des Chronistischen Werkes* (BWANT 3; Stuttgart: Kohlhammer, 1930), 38–41; cf. idem, *Old Testament Theology* (trans. D. M. G. Stalker; 2 vols.; Edinburgh: Oliver & Boyd, 1962), 1:88–89; M. Noth, *The History of Israel* (trans. P. R. Ackroyd; 2d ed.; New York: Harper & Row, 1960), 335–36.

[55] B. D. Eerdmans, "Ezra and the Priestly Code," *The Expositor*, 7th ser., 10 (1910): 306–26; C. Houtman, "Ezra and the Law. Observations on the Supposed Relation between Ezra and the Pentateuch," *OtSt* 21 (1981): 91–115.

[56] See D. J. A. Clines, "Nehemiah 10 As an Example of Early Jewish Biblical Exegesis," *JSOT* 21 (1981): 111–17; M. Fishbane, *Biblical Interpretation in Ancient Israel* (Oxford: Clarendon, 1985), 107–34.

THE COVENANT-RENEWAL PROTOTYPE OF THE CEREMONY IN NEHEMIAH 7:72B–10:40

The book of the law takes center stage in the ceremonial gathering in the square before the Water Gate (Neh 7:72b–10:40). The form-critical studies of K. Baltzer and D. J. McCarthy have identified the event described as a covenant-renewal ceremony.[57] Baltzer examines Neh 9–10 in light of the covenants ratified under Moses (Exod 19–24; 34) and Joshua (Josh 24). His analysis of Neh 9–10 highlights the aspect of covenant renewal implicit in these chapters' references to the breaking of the Sinai pact (Neh 9:13–14; 10:30; cf. 9:32) and the consequent need for repentance (9:26, 31).[58] He notes the following characteristic components of a covenant formula: (1) a historical review of YHWH's acts of salvation (9:6–37); (2) identification of the signatories' document as a "firm covenant" (אמנה) as a synonym for ברית in 10:1);[59] (3) a listing of stipulations (10:31–40); (4) sanctions implied in the taking of an oath and curse (10:30); and (5) the sealing of the document (10:1).[60]

McCarthy discusses Neh 8–10 against the background of covenant and law in Chronicles. He directs attention to the three kings who—in Chronicles as in the Deuteronomistic History—initiate covenant renewals: Asa (2 Chr 15:1–18), Hezekiah (2 Chr 29:3–31:21), and Josiah (2 Chr 34:3–35:18). He likewise refers to three covenant renewals in Ezra-Nehemiah: Ezra's assembly to deal with marriages to foreigners (Ezra

---

[57] K. Baltzer, *The Covenant Formulary in Old Testament, Jewish and Early Christian Writings* (Philadelphia: Fortress, 1971); D. J. McCarthy, "Covenant and Law in Chronicles-Nehemiah," *CBQ* 44 (1982): 25–44.

[58] Baltzer, *Covenant Formulary*, 43–47. Baltzer (pp. 47–48) also describes Ezra 9–10 as a covenant renewal in light of the following elements: (1) historical review (within a confession of past sins, Ezra 9:6–15); (2) acknowledgment of present sin (10:2); (3) stipulation (10:3, with explicit use of the term ברית); and (4) oath of commitment first by the leaders (10:5), and then by the whole people (10:9–44). Basing himself upon Baltzer's study, Kellermann asserts that the Chronicler provided Neh 8–10; Ezra 9–10; 2 Chr 15:1–18; 29:1–31:21; and 34:29–35:19 with the same basic structure of the covenant-renewal ceremony, which consists of reading of the law, prayer of repentance, and a new oath-taking (*Nehemia*, 90–92).

[59] P. Kalluveettil suggests the possibility that כרת אמנה in Neh 10:1 is a synonym for the technical term כרת ברית (*Declaration and Covenant: A Comprehensive Review of Covenant Formulae from the Old Testament and the Ancient Near East* [AnBib 88; Rome: Biblical Institute Press, 1982], 50–61).

[60] From Baltzer's comments (*Covenant Formulary*, 44–47), one notes three features that are unique to Neh 9–10 as a covenant renewal: (1) the temple replaces YHWH as the one whom the people will not forsake (10:40; cf. Josh 24:16); (2) the review of YHWH's deeds takes the form of a confession of sins (Neh 9:6–37); and (3) the people formulate the stipulations to which they pledge themselves in the first person rather than in the second or third person (10:31–40; cf. Exod 34:17–26).

9–10), Nehemiah's initiatives against usury and debt-slavery (Neh 5:8–13), and Ezra's reading of the law (Neh 8–10).

McCarthy detects a structure common to all these covenant renewals in the Chronistic History: "(1) parenesis...; (2) covenant-making; (3) purification of land and people; (4) renewed cult."[61] He asserts that, while this structure does not reflect that of other biblical covenants, it does follow the model of Assyrian loyalty oaths.[62] He notes as well five features that distinguish Neh 8–10 (as well as Ezra 9–10 and Neh 5:8–13) from the covenant renewals in Chronicles: (1) the introductory parenesis places greater accent on the penitential aspect but without the distinctly prophetic overtones evident in Chronicles; (2) the written law has a higher profile and a more pervasive role than in the comparable events of Chronicles; (3) the community is a more active participant in the covenant event; (4) the stipulations are elaborated in a detail unprecedented in the Chronicler's History; and (5) the joy of the celebration is somewhat muted and tinged with sadness as compared with the undiluted jubilation evident in Chronicles.[63]

THE RELATIONSHIP BETWEEN EZRA-NEHEMIAH AND CHRONICLES

McCarthy's discernment of the different emphases in the covenant renewals in Ezra-Nehemiah compared to those in Chronicles prompts him to conclude his study with profound skepticism about the possibility of their common authorship.[64] His view reflects a more pervasive questioning that has developed over the past quarter-century regarding the relationship between Chronicles and Ezra-Nehemiah and the likelihood of their coming from the same author.

Beginning in the first half of the nineteenth century and extending throughout the subsequent 135 years, a scholarly consensus basically subscribed to the thesis of L. Zunz,[65] who asserted that Ezra-Nehemiah is the

---

[61] McCarthy, "Covenant and Law," 36.

[62] Indeed, the Assyrian term for such an oath (*adû*) seems to be reflected in the expression "stipulate covenant-stipulations" (העיד עדות; cf. Neh 9:34; ibid., 38).

[63] Ibid., 43–44.

[64] McCarthy evaluates the variations between the covenant-renewal format in Chronicles and Ezra-Nehemiah thusly: "The unity [of covenant-renewal type] is there, but it is stretched very thin by variation in structure, ideas, and especially in language where it is unnecessary. Does this point to different origins? Different authors? At best, a school? It would be a school which dealt so differently with climactic points as to stretch the concept of a single school so thin that it seems to lose any real meaning" (ibid., 44).

[65] L. Zunz, "Dibre-Hayamin oder die Bücher der Chronik," in *Die gottesdienstliche Vorträge der Juden historisch entwickelt. Ein Beitrag zur Alterthumskunde*

work of the same author as Chronicles. While scholars acknowledged variations between the two books in vocabulary, style, and content, they explained such variance by understanding "the Chronicler" alternatively as one person both using sources and composing freely (Torrey, Noth) or as a school or circle (Kapelrud) or as the originator of a literary tradition (Freedman).[66]

In 1968, such consensus definitively broke down under the weight of S. Japhet's discussion of linguistic traits that distinguish Ezra-Nehemiah from Chronicles.[67] Japhet's investigation attempted to demonstrate that "the books could not have been written or compiled by the same author."[68] Williamson's dissertation supported Japhet's conclusion with further evidence, namely, his examination of the relationship between the end of Chronicles and the beginning of Ezra, the relevance of 1 Esdras, the distinctive theological emphases in Chronicles compared to Ezra-Nehemiah, plus additional linguistic considerations.[69] The studies of Japhet and Williamson in particular have generated such strong support for the thesis of a distinct author for Ezra-Nehemiah over against Chronicles that this has become the dominant scholarly opinion.[70] The concept of a cohesive literary work embracing Chronicles and Ezra-Nehemiah and the idea of a common authorship for these books are now matters of extensive debate.

---

und biblischer Kritik zur Literatur- und Religionsgeschichte (1832; repr., Frankfurt: Kauffmann, 1892), 13–36.

[66] D. N. Freedman argues that the Chronicler wrote Ezra 1:1–4:5 (plus a conclusion to this section that 4:6–6:18 has replaced) as well as 1 and 2 Chronicles, whereas Ezra 7–Neh 13 constitutes a later addition ("The Chronicler's Purpose," *CBQ* 23 [1961]: 436–42). F. M. Cross developed Freedman's thesis and posited three editions of the work: Chr$_1$ comprised 1 Chr 10:1–29:30; 2 Chr 1:1–36:23 + Ezra 1:1–3:13 around 520 B.C.E.; Chr$_2$, from the years following 458 B.C.E., added the Ezra narrative according to the *Vorlage* of 1 Esdras (Ezra 7:1–10:44 + Neh 7:72b–8:12) and the Aramaic material in Ezra 5:1–6:19; Chr$_3$, from the early fourth century, introduced the genealogical material in 1 Chr 1:1–9:44 ("Reconstruction," 4–18).

[67] S. Japhet, "The Supposed Common Authorship of Chronicles and Ezra-Nehemia Investigated Anew," *VT* 18 (1968): 330–71.

[68] Ibid., 332–33.

[69] H. G. M. Williamson, *Israel in the Books of Chronicles* (Cambridge: Cambridge University Press, 1977), 5–86.

[70] More recently, I. Kalimi has argued that Chronicles is distinct from Ezra-Nehemiah both in authorship and in date of composition ("Die Abfassungszeit der Chronik—Forschungsstand und Perspektiven," *ZAW* 105 [1993]: 223–33; also, *Zur Geschichtsschreibung des Chronisten: Literarisch-historiographische Abweichungen der Chronik von ihren Paralleltexten in den Samuel- und Königsbüchern* [BZAW 226; Berlin: Walter de Gruyter, 1995], 8–9).

The discussion focuses on five issues: (1) the duplication of the edict of Cyrus at the end of Chronicles (2 Chr 36:22-23) and at the beginning of Ezra (Ezra 1:1-3a); (2) the extent of 1 Esdras that presents, as a literary unity, material from Chronicles (2 Chr 35-36), Ezra (Ezra 7-10), and Nehemiah (Neh 7:72b-8:12); (3) the language of Ezra-Nehemiah compared to that of Chronicles; (4) the respective ideological emphases in these works; and (5) the literary characteristics that distinguish them from one another.[71]

Those who argue on behalf of the unity of Chronicles and Ezra-Nehemiah attribute the repetition of Cyrus's edict at the end of Chronicles (2 Chr 36:22-23) and at the beginning of Ezra (Ezra 1:1-3a) to the secondary separation of these books, which originally constituted a continuous narrative. That separation is seen as the result of the canonical process on the presumption that their sequential order in the MT canon indicates that Ezra-Nehemiah was canonized prior to Chronicles. The repetition of Cyrus's edict is explained as either a scribal error (misjudging the break between Chronicles and Ezra in a unified exemplar)[72] or an editorial signal (indicating that the book of Ezra represents the continuation of Chronicles).[73]

Those who argue for the original independence of Ezra-Nehemiah from Chronicles base their view on the simple fact that, in both the MT and the LXX, these books appear separately. In addition, evidence is lacking that Ezra-Nehemiah was canonized prior to Chronicles. Furthermore, examination of form and function suggests the distinctiveness of 2 Chr 36:22-23 and Ezra 1:1-3a. The elongated spelling of Jeremiah's name (ירמיהו, 2 Chr 36:22; cf. ירמיה, Ezra 1:1) is characteristic of Chronicles vis-à-vis Ezra-Nehemiah.[74] Chronicles' quotation of Cyrus's edict in connection with a prophecy by Jeremiah (2 Chr 36:22-23; cf. Jer 51:11; Isa 45:13) links with its preceding allusion to the end of the exile using another word of the

---

[71] The discussion that follows in the text briefly summarizes the different viewpoints. For a more complete treatment of the issues, see: Williamson, *Israel in Chronicles*, 5-86; T. C. Eskenazi, *In an Age of Prose: A Literary Approach to Ezra-Nehemiah* (SBLMS 36; Atlanta: Scholars Press, 1988); and the works cited in the following footnotes.

[72] L. W. Batten, *The Books of Ezra and Nehemiah* (ICC; Edinburgh: T&T Clark, 1913), 1-2.

[73] E. L. Curtis and A. A. Madsen, *The Books of Chronicles* (ICC; Edinburgh: T&T Clark, 1910), 3. M. Haran accounts for the duplication with the presupposition that one scroll could contain all of Chronicles but not also Ezra-Nehemiah ("Explaining the Identical Lines at the End of Chronicles and the Beginning of Ezra," *BRev* 2 [Fall 1986]: 18-20). The reference to Cyrus's edict at the end of Chronicles would thus serve as a catch line indicating that the scroll of Ezra-Nehemiah continues the Chronistic narrative.

[74] See Japhet, "The Supposed Common Authorship," 338-41.

same prophet (2 Chr 36:20–21; cf. Jer 29:10–12). The declaration of the end of the exile (2 Chr 36:22–23) concludes the work with an optimism analogous to the editorial addition of a prophecy of hope for the future following a description of judgment (see, e.g., Amos 9:11–15).

Both Williamson and Eskenazi conclusively argue that 1 Esdras cannot be used as evidence for the original unity of Chronicles and Ezra-Nehemiah.[75] Those who view 1 Esdras as an original fragment of a united Chronicles-Ezra-Nehemiah work must account for the ideological distinctiveness of this work in comparison with Ezra-Nehemiah. The absence of any material pertaining to Nehemiah and the insertion of the contest between the bodyguards of King Darius (1 Esd 3:1–5:6) represent the most obvious distinguishing characteristics of 1 Esdras. The contest of the bodyguards serves to exalt Zerubbabel (1 Esd 3:1–5:6) to the stature of a temple reformer equal to Josiah (1 Esd 1:1–58) and Ezra (1 Esd 5:7–9:59), between whom he stands. Eskenazi argues that the ideology of 1 Esdras corresponds with that of Chronicles but is markedly distinct from that of Ezra-Nehemiah.[76] The evidence suggests, at least, that 1 Esdras is subsequent to Ezra-Nehemiah and, as such, cannot testify to an original relationship between Chronicles and Ezra-Nehemiah.

Japhet's close examination of the linguistic peculiarities of Chronicles compared to Ezra-Nehemiah provides the basis for her distinguishing their authors, thus shattering the previous consensus about their original unity.[77] However, subsequent challenges to her work demonstrate that linguistic evidence alone cannot conclusively resolve the question of authorship. Against Japhet, F. M. Cross points out that orthographic distinctions in different documents do not necessarily indicate a diversity of authorship.[78] Similarly, R. Polzin identifies fifteen linguistic features common to Chronicles and Ezra that, in his estimation, provide "an extremely strong case for similarity in authorship of Chr and Ezr."[79] He then extends this

---

[75] Williamson, *Israel in Chronicles*, 12–36; Eskenazi, *In an Age of Prose*, 34–35, 155–74.

[76] T. C. Eskenazi ("The Chronicler and the Composition of 1 Esdras," *CBQ* 48 [1986]: 39–61; *In an Age of Prose*, 155–74) takes the position that 1 Esdras is a separate work of the Chronicler based on material that he derived from Ezra-Nehemiah (a book by another hand).

[77] Japhet, "The Supposed Common Authorship," 334–71.

[78] Cross ("Reconstruction," 14 n. 58) states, "Some of [Japhet's] arguments are based on distinctions between different orthographic practice and the use of archaic or pseudo-archaic forms; these arguments do not hold, I believe, as can be seen by an examination of the two Isaiah scrolls of Qumran Cave 1, or a comparison of 4QSam^a and 4QSam^b, where common authorship is certain."

[79] R. Polzin, *Late Biblical Hebrew: Toward an Historical Typology of Biblical Hebrew Prose* (HSM 12; Missoula. Mont.: Scholars Press, 1976), 71.

observation by pointing out the linguistic affinity of Neh 7:6–12:26 with the material in Chronicles and Ezra.[80] According to Polzin, only the NM (Neh 1:1–7:5; 12:27–13:31) comes from a hand that is notably distinct from Chronicles and the remainder of Ezra-Nehemiah.

M. A. Throntveit applies Williamson's criteria for evidence of authorship to Polzin's data on the similarities, first, between Chronicles and Ezra and, second, between Chronicles-Ezra and Neh 7:6–12:26 (N^2).[81] Throntveit modifies Polzin's conclusion by asserting that this evidence testifies to a "similarity of language" in this material but not to a "similarity of authorship." More in consonance with Japhet, Throntveit maintains that one should work from the presupposition of separate authorship for Chronicles and Ezra-Nehemiah.[82]

D. Talshir calls into question the validity of such a presupposition in his twofold study consisting of, first, a reexamination of all the linguistic evidence that Japhet, Williamson, Polzin, and Throntveit adduced and, second, a comparative analysis of the linguistic affinity between Chronicles and each of four segments of Ezra-Nehemiah (the EM, the rest of Ezra, the NM, and the rest of Nehemiah).[83] The first part of his study indicates that the linguistic evidence proffered by previous scholarship is insufficient to determine whether or not Chronicles and Ezra-Nehemiah come from the same author.[84] As a result of the second part of his study, Talshir reaches a conclusion similar to Polzin's insofar as he notes the lexical distinctiveness of the NM vis-à-vis the lexical similarity of the remaining parts of Ezra-Nehemiah with Chronicles. In summary, Talshir proposes that all parts of Chronicles and Ezra-Nehemiah come from the same time period and that, with the exception

---

[80] Polzin states, "We hope that, by contrasting the late language of Esther and N^1 [Neh 1:1–7:5; 12:27–13:31] with that of Chr, Ezr and N^2 [Neh 7:6–12:26], the amazing linguistic similarity of the last three has been made clear" (Ibid., 75).

[81] M. A. Throntveit, "Linguistic Analysis and the Question of Authorship in Chronicles, Ezra and Nehemiah," *VT* 32 (1982): 201–16.

[82] Ibid., 215.

[83] D. Talshir, "A Reinvestigation of the Linguistic Relationship between Chronicles and Ezra-Nehemiah," *VT* 38 (1988): 165–93.

[84] Even before undertaking his analysis, Talshir states this principle: "affinity in language between two literary works is no proof of unity of authorship" (ibid., 167). Japhet, in a subsequent paper, favorably quotes this statement of Talshir and then adds, "The study of Late Biblical Hebrew is in many ways still at its beginning, but it has become abundantly clear that linguistic evidence can no longer be utilized as proof for common authorship" ("The Relationship between Chronicles and Ezra-Nehemiah," *Congress Volume Leuven, 1989* [VTSup 43; Leiden: Brill, 1991], 298–313, 304).

of the NM, the remainder of the compendium might come from the same circle.[85]

Because the linguistic evidence has proven inconclusive, a comparison of ideological emphases in Chronicles and Ezra-Nehemiah has become increasingly determinative in the debate over the common origin and authorship of these works. A brief survey will be sufficient to indicate the complex thematic relationship between the two books.[86] Both express a keen interest in the temple, its clergy, its sacred vessels, and the celebration of major feasts. More specifically, the accounts in Ezra of the erection of the altar (Ezra 3:1–13) and of the dedication of the Second Temple (Ezra 6:13–22) recall the preparations for (1 Chr 21:18–22:16; 25:1–31), construction of (2 Chr 2:15–16), and dedication of the First Temple (2 Chr 5:12–13). The Passover festival as described in Ezra 6:19–22 relates the dedication of the second temple to the reforms of Hezekiah (2 Chr 30:13–27) and Josiah (2 Chr 35:10–18).

However, the two books exhibit distinctive outlooks even on some themes that they share. Both speak of David appointing personnel and establishing standards for music and liturgy (1 Chr 23:1–25:31; cf. Ezra 3:10; Neh 12:45–46), but Chronicles portrays David as the head of a divinely ordained, everlasting dynasty (1 Chr 17:1–27), whereas Ezra-Nehemiah never mentions the Davidic line, even in connection with Zerubbabel (Ezra 3:2, 8; 4:3; 5:2).[87]

---

[85] Talshir states: "It would appear, then, that this examination supports the acceptance of the conventional assumption that the writer of the NM is someone other than the writer of Chr. and Ezra-Neh., and that the lexical affinity mentioned above reflects their similarity of provenance and age, but not identity of authorship. On the other hand, the similarity in both grammar and vocabulary of the three sections [the EM, the remainder of Ezra, and the remainder of Nehemiah outside of the NM] of Ezra-Neh. to Chr. is noteworthy, and if this does not absolutely prove a single author for both books, it certainly attests proximity of time and place, and perhaps even the same circle" ("A Reinvestigation," 192).

[86] For a more comprehensive treatment of the comparative ideologies in Chronicles and Ezra-Nehemiah, see J. D. Newsome, "Toward a New Understanding of the Chronicler and His Purposes," *JBL* 94 (1975): 201–17; Williamson, *Israel in Chronicles*, 60–70; H. Cazelles, review of *Israel in the Books of Chronicles*, by H. G. M. Williamson, *VT* 29 (1979): 375–80; R. L. Braun, "Chronicles, Ezra, and Nehemiah: Theology and Literary History," in *Studies in the Historical Books of the Old Testament* (VTSup 30; Leiden: Brill, 1979), 52–64; Blenkinsopp, *Ezra-Nehemiah*, 47–54; Japhet, "Relationship," 298–313; and S. Talmon, "Esra-Nehemia: Historiographie oder Theologie?" in *Ernten, was man sät. Festschrift für Klaus Koch zu seinem 65. Geburtstag* (ed. D. R. Daniels, U. Glessmer, and M. Rösel; Neukirchen-Vluyn: Neukirchener, 1991), 329–56.

[87] The genealogy in 1 Chr 3:19, as well as the prophecies of Haggai (Hag 2:1–9, 20–23) and Zechariah (Zech 4:6–10; 6:12–13), identifies Zerubbabel as a Davidic

Both works have a concern for "all Israel," but Chronicles explicitly incorporates the northern tribes under this designation (1 Chr 11:1; 2 Chr 15:9–15; 30:25), whereas Ezra-Nehemiah, while acknowledging the tradition of the twelve tribes (Ezra 6:17), apparently limits the authentic Israel to Judah and Benjamin along with Levi (Ezra 10:9). Hezekiah's invitation of the northerners to the Passover in Chronicles (2 Chr 30:1–12) contrasts with Zerubbabel's rejection of the northerners' offer to help rebuild the temple in Ezra (Ezra 4:1–3).

Both works stress the essential role of kingship in constructing and preserving the temple, but in Chronicles these kings are exclusively from the Davidic line in Judah, whereas in Ezra-Nehemiah Persian monarchs assume this role (1 Chr 28:1–21; 2 Chr 29:1–36; cf. Ezra 1:1–4; 7:12–26). Furthermore, each makes frequent reference to the Levites, but Chronicles provides a more universally positive portrait of them (1 Chr 15:1–2; 23:1–32) than does Ezra-Nehemiah (cf. Ezra 8:15–20).

Ezra-Nehemiah likewise diverges from Chronicles on some basic theological issues. The manner of God's action in history constitutes a fundamental difference: Chronicles describes God's immediate action in history by way of direct divine discourse (2 Chr 7:13–16) and miraculous interventions (2 Chr 20:22–23), especially in response to prayer; Ezra-Nehemiah does not narrate a single explicit intervention of God either in word or deed. Immediate divine retribution is practically a principle of history in Chronicles (1 Chr 28:9; 2 Chr 35:22–24), whereas in Ezra-Nehemiah the theme of retribution surfaces only in the penitential prayers, where it is mitigated by divine mercy (Ezra 9:6–15; Neh 9:6–37). The vision of history in Neh 9:6–37, with its concentration on the Mosaic covenant and the exodus and its failure to mention David in connection with the temple, contrasts greatly with Chronicles, which concentrates on the Davidic covenant in service of the temple with comparatively muted reference to the wilderness era (e.g., 2 Chr 6:5). Finally, Nehemiah's denunciation of Solomon for his marriages to foreigners is unparalleled in Chronicles, where Solomon appears as the perfect king (Neh 13:26; cf. 2 Chr 8:11; 1 Kgs 3:1; 11:1–8).

The distinctive literary features of Chronicles and Ezra-Nehemiah complement the foregoing linguistic and ideological evidence. Regardless of particular estimates of their provenance, the universal consensus is that these books constitute a compendium and should be read in light of one another.[88]

---

descendant. On the implications of this point for the relationship between Chronicles and Ezra-Nehemiah, see S. Japhet, "Sheshbazzar and Zerubbabel—Against the Background of the Historical and Religious Tendencies of Ezra-Nehemiah," *ZAW* 94 (1982): 66–98.

[88] On this point, see P. R. Ackroyd, "Chronicles-Ezra-Nehemiah: The Concept of Unity," *ZAW* 100 (1988): 189–201.

Their common literary features include: a concern for legitimation in the form of either genealogical records or census lists (e.g., 1 Chr 1:1–9:44; 24:1–27:34; cf. Ezra 2:1–70; Neh 10:1–28); the quotation of kingly decrees as divinely inspired mandates for the erection and preservation of the temple and its cult (2 Chr 30:6–9; cf. Ezra 1:2–4); and the incorporation of official documents and written sources into the text (extensive portions of Samuel and Kings as sources for Chronicles [e.g., 2 Sam 7:1–29 in 1 Chr 17:1–27]; cf. the archival documents in Ezra 4:7–22; 5:7–17; 6:3–12; 7:12–26).

However, three literary factors distinguish Chronicles from Ezra-Nehemiah: (1) the prophetic word that propels history in Chronicles (e.g., 2 Chr 15:1–7) has no counterpart in Ezra-Nehemiah (cf. Ezra 5:1–2; 6:14–15; Neh 9:26, 30, 32);[89] (2) the death of most of the kings of Judah is formally recorded in Chronicles (e.g., 2 Chr 12:12–16; 13:19–23),[90] whereas the final end of the leaders in Ezra-Nehemiah is unmentioned; and (3) the "Levitical sermon," an essential literary form in Chronicles (e.g., 2 Chr 13:4–12), is without parallel in Ezra-Nehemiah, whose own penitential prose prayers (Ezra 9:6–15; Neh 1:5–11; 9:6–37) have no equivalent in Chronicles.[91]

In summary, research indicates that Chronicles and Ezra-Nehemiah stand in a close but complex relationship to one another. The nature of this relationship cannot be elucidated by further speculation about the issue of authorship. However, a more precise insight into the relationship can be gained by a close comparative literary study of texts from these two works. For example, the narrative of Ezra's covenant renewal (Neh 7:72b–10:40) hints at an elusive but certain connection between these books: the editorial comment about the Festival of Booths at the time of Ezra's renewal (Neh 8:17: "from the days of Jeshua son of Nun to that day, the people had not done so") echoes analogous comments about the Festival of Passover during the reforms of Josiah (2 Chr 35:18: "No Passover like it had been kept in Israel since the days of the prophet Samuel") and Hezekiah (2 Chr 30:26: "since the time of Solomon son of King David of Israel there had been nothing like this

---

[89] In the NM, the narrative does not merely lack direct quotations of the prophets; it actually presents contemporary prophets as enemies of the protagonist (Neh 6:10–14; cf. 6:7).

[90] Chronicles mentions the death of every king from David to Josiah (1 Chr 29:28; 2 Chr 11:31; 12:16; 13:23; 16:14; 21:1, 19–20; 22:9; 24:25–26; 25:27–28; 26:23; 27:9; 28:27; 29:33; 33:20, 24; 35:24–25). However, such is not the case for any of the last four kings (Jehoahaz, Jehoiakim, Jehoiachin, and Zedekiah), who figure in the last chapter of Chronicles (2 Chr 36:1–13).

[91] These last two literary features are mentioned by Japhet, "Relationship," 306–8.

in Jerusalem").[92] Such evidence suggests the potential benefits of an intertextual examination of these texts.

THE UNITY OF EZRA-NEHEMIAH

More recently, the salutary challenge to the previously-held consensus regarding the unity of Chronicles and Ezra-Nehemiah has inspired J. C. VanderKam to question the practically unanimous opinion that Ezra and Nehemiah comprise one book.[93] While VanderKam attempts to distinguish the two books by contrasting their language and handling of archival material, D. Kraemer adds an ideological argument that the two books represent a study in contrasts.[94] I will summarize and evaluate their arguments, then cite evidence in favor of viewing Ezra-Nehemiah as one book.

The case for distinct books

Language. Within the texts that Williamson identifies as editorial in the two books,[95] VanderKam identifies four[96] distinguishing linguistic features: (1) the title "king of Persia" occurs in Ezra (1:1, 2, 8; 3:7; 4:3, 5, 7, 24; 6:14; 7:1; 9:9: מלך פרס) but not Nehemiah (cf. 12:22: מלכות דריוש הפרסי); (2) the

---

[92] Blenkinsopp, *Ezra-Nehemiah*, 54.

[93] J. C. VanderKam, "Ezra-Nehemiah or Ezra and Nehemiah?" in *Priests, Prophets and Scribes: Essays on the Formation and Heritage of Second Temple Judaism in Honour of Joseph Blenkinsopp* (ed. E. Ulrich, J. W. Wright, R. P. Carroll, and P. R. Davies; JSOTSup 149; Sheffield: JSOT Press, 1992), 55–75. All the major commentaries treat Ezra-Nehemiah as one book; see, e.g., Batten, *Ezra and Nehemiah*, 1–2; Rudolph, *Esra und Nehemia*, iii–iv, xxii–xxvii; Fensham, *Ezra and Nehemiah*, 1; J. M. Myers, *Ezra, Nehemiah* (AB 14; Garden City, N.Y.: Doubleday, 1983), xxxviii–xli; A. H. J. Gunneweg, *Esra* (KAT; Gütersloh: Gerd Mohn, 1985), 19–20, 28–31; Williamson, *Ezra, Nehemiah*, xxi–xxiii; Blenkinsopp, *Ezra-Nehemiah*, 38–39; Clines, *Ezra, Nehemiah, Esther*, 2–4.

[94] D. Kraemer, "On the Relationship of the Books of Ezra and Nehemiah," *JSOT* 59 (1993): 73–92.

[95] Williamson, *Ezra, Nehemiah*, xxiv–xxxiii. According to the reckoning of VanderKam ("Ezra and Nehemiah?" 63–64), the editorial verses in Ezra-Nehemiah total 67 (45 in Ezra + 22 in Nehemiah). VanderKam admits that the large percentage of source material and the comparatively meager amount of editorial comment in each book effectively undermines the linguistic argument.

[96] Two other items which VanderKam ("Ezra and Nehemiah?" 64–65) proposes as linguistic distinctions between Ezra and Nehemiah are inaccurate: (1) his contention that בית יהוה occurs only in Ezra, not in Nehemiah, fails to note Neh 10:36; and (2) his assertion that Ezra (6:22) identifies the Persian monarch typologically as "King of Assyria" whereas Nehemiah (9:32) employs that title rather for the actual Assyrian kings ignores the historical Esarhaddon "king of Assyria" in Ezra 4:2.

books diverge in the Hebrew phrasing of their parallel expressions regarding "the sound [or joy] heard from afar" (Ezra 3:13; cf. Neh 12:43);[97] (3) differences in terminology characterize the confessional psalm of the people (Neh 9:6–37) and Ezra's penitential prayer (Ezra 9:6–15);[98] and (4) the designation "the God of Israel" recurs throughout Ezra but is absent in Nehemiah.[99]

These observations necessitate a response. First, the title "king of Persia" does not so much distinguish Ezra from Nehemiah as attest to an emphasis in Ezra 1–6 that is not as important for Ezra 7–Neh 13.[100] Second, while VanderKam calls attention to the minor variations in the Hebrew phrases describing the sound of the people being heard from afar (Ezra 3:13; cf. Neh 12:43), he neglects to point out that the theme of "joy" (שמחה) in both texts is a significant unifying element in Ezra-Nehemiah.[101]

---

[97] Ezra 3:13 הקול נשמע עד למרחוק
Neh 12:43 ותשמע שמחת ירושלם מרחוק

[98] VanderKam, "Ezra and Nehemiah?" 65. Four words in Ezra 9:6–15 do not occur anywhere in Nehemiah: אשמה ("iniquity," Ezra 9:6, 7, 13, 15; cf. 10:10, 19); כלם nip'al ("to be disgraced," Ezra 9:6); בוש ("to be ashamed," Ezra 9:6); and יתד (a "stake," Ezra 9:8). Two words in Ezra's prayer (Ezra 9:6–15) do not occur in the people's confessional psalm (Neh 9:6–37) but are found elsewhere in Nehemiah: עון ("guilt," Ezra 9:6, 7, 13; cf. Neh 3:37; 9:2), and פליטה ("remnant," Ezra 9:8, 13, 14, 15; cf. Neh 1:2). On the other hand, two terminological items in Neh 9:6–37 do not occur anywhere in Ezra: מעלליהם ("evil deeds," Neh 9:35), and its designations for God, i.e., אלה (Neh 9:17) and אל (Neh 9:31, 32; cf. 1:5). Finally, the prayers' listings of the leaders who sinned differ: "we, our kings, our priests" (Ezra 9:7); cf. "our kings, our princes, our priests, our prophets, and our ancestors" (Neh 9:32) and "our kings, our princes, our priests, and our ancestors" (Neh 9:34).

[99] אלהי ישראל occurs thirteen times in Ezra, but never in Nehemiah: three times in Aramaic (אלה ישראל: Ezra 5:1; 6:14; 7:15); and ten times in Hebrew (six times in Ezra 1–6 [1:3; 3:2; 4:1, 3; 6:21, 22], and four times in Ezra 7–10 [7:6; 8:35; 9:4, 15].)

[100] Outside Ezra 1–6 (which mentions three different kings), the title "king of Persia" occurs only twice, once in reference to Artaxerxes (7:1, referring back to 6:14, thereby linking Ezra 7–10 with Ezra 1–6), and once in a general reference to "the kings of Persia" (9:9, perhaps another allusion to 6:14). Moreover, the alternative designation of the Persian kings as "king of Babylon" occurs in both books (Ezra 5:12 [Cyrus]; Neh 13:6 [Artaxerxes]).

[101] In eight of its nine occurrences, the noun "joy" (שמחה) is mentioned in connection with the four major festivals recounted in the two books: the laying of the temple foundations (Ezra 3:12–13); the Festival of Unleavened Bread (Ezra 6:22); Ezra's reading of the Torah (Neh 8:12, 17); and the dedication of the walls (Neh 12:27, 43). The one further occurrence of שמחה (Neh 12:44) echoes the preceding double employment of the noun that brings the dedication of the walls to a climax (12:43). The four occurrences of the verb שמח ("to rejoice") arise exclusively in the dedication of the temple (Ezra 6:16) and in the dedication of the city walls (12:43 [3x]). Note also the dedication of the temple "with joy" (Aramaic בחדוה [2x], Ezra 6:16; cf. Neh 8:10).

Third, the words of Ezra's prayer (Ezra 9:6–15) that VanderKam highlights have more to say about the prayer's cohesiveness with its immediate context of the EM (Ezra 7:27–10:44) than about either its relationship to the rest of Ezra or its distinctiveness vis-à-vis Nehemiah.[102]

Finally, the phrase "the God of Israel" (אלה ישראל/אלהי ישראל) occurs only in Ezra because the expression originated in the source material of Ezra (Ezra 7:15) and is intimately connected to both the construction of the temple and Ezra's treatment of mixed marriages.[103] By contrast, the term "the God of Israel" is absent from Nehemiah, since it did not occur in

---

[102] In particular, two terms connect the prayer to the surrounding narrative: בוש ("to be ashamed," Ezra 9:6; cf. 8:22), and אשמה ("guilt," Ezra 9:6, 7, 13, 15; cf. 10:10, 19). Two terms provide bridges to Nehemiah: עון ("iniquity," Ezra 9:6, 7, 13; cf. Neh 3:37; 9:2), and פליטה ("remnant," Ezra 9:8, 13, 14, 15; cf. Neh 1:2). Two of the prayer's terms are irrelevant to the discussion because they do not occur anywhere else in Ezra-Nehemiah: כלם nip'al ("to be disgraced," Ezra 9:6) and יתד ("a stake," Ezra 9:8). Two elements of the prose psalm (Neh 9:6–37) are not characteristic of the remainder of Nehemiah and therefore do not distinguish the two books from one another: the words for God (אל [9:17] and אלה [9:31, 32; cf. 1:5]) and the various categories of the people (9:31, 32).

[103] See C. Steuernagel, "Jahwe, der Gott Israels," in *Studien zur semitischen Philologie und Religionsgeschichte* (FS J. Wellhausen; BZAW 27; ed. K. Marti; Gieben: Töpelmann, 1914), 331–49, esp. 338–40. Steuernagel (339) asserts, "Der Jerusalemer יהוה heißt [יהוה אלהי ישראל] im Sinne des genuin israelitischen Jahwe und im Unterschied von dem auf den Höhen verehrten ethnisierten Jahwe." Since this title sets YHWH in Jerusalem apart from other gods, it also serves to separate the Israelites from pagan—which is precisely the common objective of the two projects described in the book of Ezra: the building of the temple and the breakup of marriages with foreign wives. Ten of the book's thirteen uses of the phrase "God of Israel" pertain directly to the temple (Ezra 1:3; 3:2; 4:1, 3; 5:1; 6:14, 21, 22; 7:15; 8:35). Seven of the eight occurrences in Ezra 1–6 draw on the traditional language of Solomon's blessing at the dedication of the original temple (Ezra 1:3; 3:2; 4:1, 3; 5:1; 6:14, 22; cf. 1 Kgs 8:15, 17, 20 = 2 Chr 6:4, 7, 10; 1 Chr 22:6), while the remaining instance describes the proselytes' separating themselves from the nations "to seek the Lord, the God of Israel" (Ezra 6:21; cf. 2 Chr 11:16; 30:1, 5). In the three instances in which the phrase "God of Israel" does not refer directly to the temple, the phrase bears upon Ezra's mission: (1) the introduction of Ezra as "a scribe skilled in the Torah of Moses that the Lord God of Israel had given" (Ezra 7:6) links Ezra 7–10 with Ezra 1–6, both by the repetition of the divine epithet (cf. 6:21, 22) and by qualifying Ezra's law book with the same divine title used of the temple (cf. 1:3); (2) the expression "all who tremble at the words of the God of Israel" (Ezra 9:4) alludes both to the Torah (7:6) and to that separation from foreigners appropriate to the context (cf. 9:1–3); and (3) Ezra's invocation (יהוה אלהי ישראל, 9:15), which reflects the language of Solomon's temple prayer (1 Kgs 8:23, 25, 26 = 2 Chr 6:14, 16, 17), befits his confession of the apostasy implicit in the marriages with foreigners (9:10–15; cf. 2 Chr 11:16; 29:7; 33:16).

the NM (Neh 1:1–7:5; 12:27–13:31) even in connection with Nehemiah's handling of mixed marriages (Neh 13:23–27; cf. 9:2), and the construction of the temple is not an issue in Nehemiah.

References to archival material. VanderKam's discussion of the books' different handling of their respective sources concerns two types of archival material: the official decrees of the Persian kings, and the one census list common to both books (Ezra 2:1–70; Neh 7:6–72a). Regarding the Achaemenid correspondence, he notes that the book of Ezra actually incorporates two forms of official documentation (royal edicts, in Hebrew [1:2–4] or Aramaic [6:3–5, 6–12; 7:12–26], and formal letters in Aramaic [Ezra 4:11–16, 17–22; 5:7–17; 6:2b–12]), whereas the book of Nehemiah refers only to the existence of letters certifying Nehemiah's mission without, however, quoting them in full (Neh 2:7–8, 9; 6:6–7, 8). Regarding the census lists and subsequent narrative parallels (e.g., the "seventh month" in Ezra 3:1 and Neh 7:72b–8:1), VanderKam asserts that the one list serves different purposes in diverse eras: in Ezra, it identifies those who returned shortly after 538 B.C.E., whereas in Nehemiah it serves to determine who is to inhabit Jerusalem during or after 445 B.C.E. (Neh 7:4–5).[104]

However, source criticism and historiography can account for the varying handling and arrangement of archival material in Ezra and Nehemiah. In the case of the Persian correspondence, Artaxerxes' edict (Ezra 7:12–26) might have been an original element of the EM, whereas Nehemiah's actual letters of recommendation (Neh 2:7–8) were not part of the NM. Moreover, the present arrangement of Ezra-Nehemiah suggests a sophisticated historiographical design by which the decree of Artaxerxes (Ezra 7:12–26) parallels that of Cyrus (1:2–4); just as the edict of Cyrus introduces the first major era, that is, the temple's construction (Ezra 1–6), so the edict of Artaxerxes prepares the second major era, that is, the mission of Ezra and Nehemiah (Ezra 7–Neh 13). Furthermore, the double quotation of the same census list provides continuity between two different eras since, in both cases, the list serves to identify the members of the true Israel of the postexilic era, whether as reentering the land and beginning to build the temple (Ezra 2:1–3:1) or as preparing to repopulate Jerusalem (Neh 7:6–72; 11:1).

Ideology. According to Kraemer, four categories of ideological distinctions differentiate the books of Ezra and Nehemiah. First, in terms of general orientation, priestly concerns predominate in Ezra, which focuses on the temple, its sacrifices, its personnel (priests and Levites), and its purity requirements, whereas a rather secular outlook permeates Nehemiah in its preoccupation with the city walls, its periodic criticism of the priesthood,

---

[104] VanderKam, "Ezra and Nehemiah?" 67–69.

and its comparative lack of interest in the temple and sacrifices.[105] Second, each book offers a distinctive portrait of Ezra: the book of Ezra presents him as a priest (Ezra 7:1–5; 10:10, 16), whereas the book of Nehemiah describes him as a scribe (Neh 8:1, 4, 5, 13; 12:37; cf. 8:2, 9; 12:26).[106] Third, the Torah also has a distinctive profile in each book: in Ezra, the Torah is the special possession of the priests and a resource for consultation about particular issues such as the standards for the altar, sacrifices, and temple personnel (Ezra 3:2; 6:18), whereas in Nehemiah the Torah is a text for public reading and the basis of education for the whole people (Neh 8:1–18).[107] Fourth, Kraemer identifies seven elements that the books of Ezra and Nehemiah share in common but that each treats distinctively.[108]

However, the distinctions between the two books are not as stark as Kraemer implies. First, his characterization of the book of Ezra as a more "priestly" document than the book of Nehemiah does not take into account the more numerous occurrences of the terms *priest* and *Levite* in the book of Nehemiah.[109] Similarly, his ascribing a relatively minor role to the

---

[105] Kraemer, "On the Relationship," 78–80.

[106] Ibid., 80–83.

[107] Ibid., 87–89.

[108] Ibid., 83–87. (1) The people weep in Ezra over the temple (3:12) and over their offense of mixed marriage (10:1) but in Nehemiah in reaction to hearing the Torah (8:9). (2) On the Festival of Booths in Ezra, the people offer sacrifices (3:4) but in Nehemiah they build shelters in accordance with the Torah (8:14–17). (3) The archival documents and lists in Ezra pertain to concerns about the temple (1:1–4, 9–11; 2:1–70; 5:3–6:12) but in Nehemiah to the building of the walls and the repopulating of the city according to the Torah (3:1–32; 7:6–72a; 10:2–28; 11:3–12:26). (4) The marriage reform arises in Ezra out of the priest's preoccupation with the "holy seed" (9:2) but in Nehemiah from the people's reading of the Torah (13:1–3). (5) The covenant in Ezra focuses exclusively on the purity of marriages (10:3), but in Nehemiah it encompasses observance of the Torah motivated by Israel's overall history (9:5–37; 10:1–40). (6) The sin that brought about the present hardship is, in Ezra, specifically mixed marriage (9:10–12) but in Nehemiah offenses of a more generic sort (1:6–9; 9:28; cf. 13:18). (7) In Ezra, the interests of the priest take precedence over those of the scribe (7:1–5; 10:10, 16; cf. 7:6) and determine the policy of governors (8:36), while in Nehemiah the priests follow the lead of the scribe (8:13) and serve the purposes of the governor (3:1–2; cf. 7:1). In addition to these elements, Kraemer also notes that in the book of Ezra the opponents protest the building of the temple, whereas in the book of Nehemiah they attempt to frustrate the construction of the city walls.

[109] כהן: 34x in Ezra; 44x in Nehemiah. לוי/לוים: 24x in Ezra; 45x in Nehemiah (this in spite of only two occurrences in Neh 1:1–7:5: 3:17; 7:1). Kraemer likewise fails to note that the more extensive lists of priests and Levites are in Nehemiah (11:10–18; 12:1–26; cf. Ezra 8:15–20).

temple in Nehemiah overlooks the fact that the covenant contract refers to "the house of God" eight times in seven verses (Neh 10:33–40), while the remainder of the book contains nine additional occurrences of the same term (בית [ה]אלהים: 11:11, 16, 22; 12:40; 13:4, 7, 9, 11, 14). Second, both books identify Ezra as priest and scribe.[110] Third, the transfer of the Torah from priests in Ezra to the people in Nehemiah can be understood as a significant development in the whole story (see below). Fourth, notwithstanding their variations in perspective, Ezra and Nehemiah are united by mutual interests: the people's weeping, the Festival of Booths, the census of the pioneers from exile, marriage reform, covenant commitment, sin, and the relationship between religion and public policy.

In sum, then, VanderKam and Kraemer fail to demonstrate that Ezra and Nehemiah are distinct books. Conversely, a positive consideration of the evidence confirms their unity.

The case for the unity of Ezra-Nehemiah

Three observations combine to support the unity of Ezra-Nehemiah: (1) the witness of tradition; (2) the narrative reciprocity of Ezra and Nehemiah as respectively the introduction to and conclusion of the full story; and (3) features of vocabulary and style that are unique to Ezra and Nehemiah in biblical literature.

First, in terms of tradition, the Masoretes provided a double indication that they regarded the two corpora as one book by placing their marginal indication of its midpoint between Neh 3:31 and 3:32 and by locating their statistics summarizing both at the end of Nehemiah. The LXX tradition similarly presents Ezra-Nehemiah as a single unit of twenty-three chapters (LXX 2 Esd 1–23). The Talmud makes reference only to the book of Ezra and subsumes the whole of MT Ezra-Nehemiah under this title.[111] According to Eusebius (ca. 260–ca. 339 C.E.), the list of OT books provided by Melito of Sardis (d. before 190 C.E.) mentions only Ezra (*Hist. eccl.* 4.26.14), whereas the list of Origen (ca. 185–254 C.E.) also provides the earliest indication of a partition into two books, 1 and 2 Esdras (*Hist.*

---

110 While the book of Ezra introduces Ezra with a long priestly pedigree (Ezra 7:1–5) and describes him exclusively as "the priest" on two occasions (10:10, 16), in three instances the designation "the scribe" accompanies the title "the priest" (7:11, 12, 21), once "scribe" is his exclusive title (7:6), and once a narrative portion concentrates exclusively on his activity as a scribe (7:10). The book of Nehemiah identifies Ezra once as "the priest" (Neh 8:2), twice as "the priest and scribe" (8:9; 12:26, in both instances alongside Nehemiah, "the governor"), and five times as "the scribe" (8:1, 4, 5, 13; 12:36). Cf. Kraemer ("On the Relationship," 79–83).

111 "Ezra wrote the book that is called by his name" (*b. B. Bat.* 15a). For the assertion that there was no book that bore the name of Nehemiah, see *b. Sanh.* 93b.

eccl. 6.25.2).[112] Perhaps Origen's influence prompted the Vulgate to divide the complex into two books (1 Esd 1–10 and 2 Esd 1–13) while attributing both to a single author, Ezra.

Second, Ezra and Nehemiah require each other for narrative completeness. The unqualified reference to the "twentieth year" in Neh 1:1 presumes that the reader can supply "of King Artaxerxes" from Ezra 7:7 (cf. 8:1; Neh 2:1).[113] The unadorned mention of "Ezra, the scribe" as the addressee of the people's request (Neh 8:2) requires the narrator's prior introduction of this important figure (Ezra 7:6, 10, 11).[114] The same holds true for the phrase "the book of the Torah" (Neh 8:1), which is never mentioned in Neh 1–7 and therefore requires the introduction provided by Ezra (7:6, 10, 11, 12, 21; 10:3; cf. 3:2; 6:18). The weeping of the people in reaction to Ezra's reading (Neh 8:9) makes no sense without a prior knowledge of his dealings with them over the matter of marriage reforms (Ezra 10:1). Likewise, the brief references to "separation" from foreigners in Neh 9:2; 10:29 presume a previous treatment of the issue (Ezra 9:1; 10:8, 11, 16: בדל *nipʿal*). Similarly, since concern for the temple is notoriously absent in Neh 1–9 (cf. 6:10; 8:16), the concentration on temple-related issues in the written oath of Neh 10:33–40 presupposes the prior attention to the temple found in Ezra (see, e.g., Ezra 1:2–4, 5–11; 2:68–3:13; 6:2b–12, 13–22; 7:15–20; 8:24–36). Lastly, Nehemiah's linking of the eras of Zerubbabel and Jeshua with the days of Ezra and Nehemiah by using lists (Neh 7:5–72a; 12:1–26) and narrative comment (12:47) presumes familiarity with Ezra's story of Zerubbabel and Jeshua (Ezra 2:1–5:2).

---

[112] But Origen qualifies that distinction by stating that these books were "in one, Ezra, that is 'Helper' [Ἔζδρας α΄β΄ἐν ἑνί, Ἔζρα, ὅ ἐστιν βοηθός]" (quoted in *Hist. eccl.* 6.25.2).

[113] E. J. Bickerman ("En Marge de L'Ecriture," *RB* 88 [1981]: 19–23) offers the best solution to the puzzling sequence of Chislev (the ninth month, Neh 1:1) before Nisan (the first month, Neh 2:1) by reading the "twentieth year" as a reference to the regnal year that began with the enthronement of Artaxerxes in the (fifth) month of Ab. This view is preferable to the alternative proposals: (1) that the original reading, i.e., "nineteenth year," was lost due either to haplography (so Rudolph, *Esra und Nehemia*, 102) or to a later correction by a Greek scribe (so D. J. A. Clines, "The Evidence for an Autumnal New Year in Preexilic Israel Reconsidered," *JBL* 93 [1974]: 25, 34–36); or (2) that the "twentieth year" refers to the period of absence of Nehemiah's brother, Hanani, from Jerusalem (so G. da Deliceto, "Epoca della partenza di Hanani per Gerusalemme e anno della petizione de Neemia ad Artasse: Neem. 1,1 e Neem. 2,1," *Laur* 4 [1963]: 431–68).

[114] Conversely, the elaborate introduction of Ezra as scribe of the Torah (Ezra 7:6, 10, 11) calls for the corresponding narrative of his scribal activities provided in Neh 8.

Third, certain basic shared elements of vocabulary and style distinguish Ezra and Nehemiah as a whole from the rest of the MT. Two lexical items are unique to these two books: (1) the designation "temple servants" (נְתִינִים);[115] and (2) the expression "the hand of God [was] upon..." (יַד אֱלֹהִים עַל).[116] Moreover, the books have in common an amalgam of diverse types of dating indicators. Note the similarities in specificity: (1) the month within the regnal year of Artaxerxes (Ezra 7:8; Neh 2:1; cf. 1:1); (2) the "seventh month" without specification (Ezra 3:1; Neh 8:1, 14); and (3) the day of the month (Ezra 3:6; 6:19; 7:9; 8:31; 10:16, 17; Neh 6:15; 8:2, 13; 9:1). In addition, the books are similar in their way of designating the months, that is, according to name (Ezra 6:15 [Adar]; Neh 1:1 [Chislev]; 2:1 [Nisan]; 6:15 [Elul]) and numerical sequence (Ezra 3:6; 6:19; 7:8, 9; 8:31; 10:16, 17; Neh 8:2, 13; 9:1).[117] Furthermore, various basic features of form and content respectively are unique to Ezra and Nehemiah in biblical literature: (1) the mixture of third-person autobiography and first-person narrative; and (2) the quantity of archival material incorporated into the narrative of each book.[118]

In sum, the external testimony of tradition and the internal demands of narrative integrity combine to sustain the unity of Ezra-Nehemiah.

---

[115] Ezra 2:43, 58, 70; 7:7, 24; 8:17, 20; Neh 3:26, 31; 7:46, 60, 72; 10:29; 11:3, 21. The one occurrence outside of Ezra-Nehemiah, 1 Chr 9:2, derives from Neh 11:3 since the list in 1 Chr 9:2–17 depends on Neh 11:3–9. See S. Japhet, *I and II Chronicles* (OTL; Louisville: Westminster/John Knox, 1993), 202–4, 206–8.

[116] Ezra 7:9; 8:18, 31; Neh 2:8, 18; cf. Ezra 7:6, 28; 8:22 and nowhere else in the MT.

[117] These names of months originated in the Babylonian calendar that the Persians adopted. The designation of months by ordinal numerals represents an earlier adaptation of the Babylonian calendar, which entailed the benefit of purging the Judean calendar of foreign nomenclature. See J. Morgenstern, "The Three Calendars of Ancient Israel," *HUCA* 1 (1924): 13–78; idem, "Supplementary Studies in the Calendars of Ancient Israel," *HUCA* 10 (1935): 1–148; J. Finegan, "The Principles of the Calendar and the Problems of Biblical Chronology," in *Light from the Ancient Past: The Archeological Background of Judaism and Christianity* (Princeton, N.J.: Princeton University Press, 1959), 552–87; J. C. VanderKam, "Calendars, Ancient Israelite and Jewish," *ABD* 1:814–20.

[118] Note the distribution of the eleven lists throughout Ezra-Nehemiah (cf. Eskenazi, *In an Age of Prose*, 180; idem, "The Structure of Ezra-Nehemiah and the Integrity of the Book," *JBL* 107 [1988]: 643): (1) Ezra 1:9–11 (inventory of temple utensils); (2) 2:1–70 (census of original returnees); (3) 8:1–14 (roster of those who returned with Ezra); (4) 10:18–44 (roster of those who terminated mixed marriages); (5) Neh 3:1–32 (enumeration of workers on the walls); (6) 7:6–72 (census of original returnees); (7) 10:2–29 (subscribers to the oath); (8) 11:3–24 (inhabitants of Jerusalem); (9) 11:25–36 (inhabitants of other places in Judah and Benjamin); (10) 12:1–26 (priests and Levites); and (11) 12:32–42 (participants in the dedication of the walls).

The Synchronic Approach

Scholars have devoted relatively scant attention to the synchronic study of Ezra-Nehemiah owing both to the purportedly meager literary quality of the work and to the comparatively recent emergence of literary criticism in application to biblical texts. The following survey of existing research from a synchronic perspective consists of two parts: first, it notes six scholars who at least have indicated the value of studying Ezra-Nehemiah as literature: Torrey, Talmon, Childs, Williamson, Japhet, and Eskenazi; and second, it evaluates Eskenazi's work in particular since her study has pioneered the exploration of Ezra-Nehemiah from a literary perspective and, therefore, provides a precedent for the present study.

One can trace the development of interest in a literary approach to Ezra-Nehemiah by surveying the work of the above-mentioned six scholars in historical sequence. Not all of them are equally enthusiastic about the literary approach to Ezra-Nehemiah. A concentration on the literary approach is more pronounced in the works of Talmon, Childs, and Eskenazi, who attend to the structural, stylistic, and semantic patterns within the text itself, almost prescinding from the relationship between text and event. Eskenazi's work is in a class of its own due to her extensive treatment of Ezra-Nehemiah from a synchronic perspective. By contrast to Talmon, Childs, and Eskenazi, who concentrate on synchronic analysis, Torrey, Williamson, and Japhet are primarily concerned with the correspondence between text and event and only secondarily with intra-textual balances, parallels, and contrasts. Nevertheless, they exhibit a derivative interest in historiography in their effort to uncover the ideological concerns of the author as mediated by his manner of shaping and presenting his material.

C. C. Torrey

Torrey emphatically directs attention to Ezra-Nehemiah as a literary work. Admittedly, he does this in view of his scathing critique of the Chronicler as a thoroughly unreliable historian whose Ezra narrative, in particular, is a prime example of counterfeit history. Torrey juxtaposes literature and history in asserting that the Chronicler's work is an ideological composition of negligible historical value.[119] Torrey summarizes the Chronicler's ideological purpose as providing legitimation for the Jerusalem temple and

---

[119] Torrey (*The Composition and Historical Value*, 52) states, "No fact of O. T. criticism is more firmly established than this; that the Chronicler, as a historian, is thoroughly untrustworthy. He distorts facts deliberately and habitually; invents chapter after chapter with the greatest freedom; and, what is most dangerous of all, his history is not written for its own sake, but in the interest of an extremely one-sided theory."

its cult and for the clans who had returned from the Babylonian exile as the authentic heirs to preexilic Israel against Samaritan claims on behalf of the indigenous populace and its sanctuary at Shechem.[120]

Torrey ascribes to the Chronicler a literary style distinguished by imaginative coloring, anachronistic staging, and fanciful dating. While on occasion Torrey concedes that the Chronicler can exhibit a refined touch, more often he judges the literary quality of the work to be poor.[121] By Torrey's estimation, Neh 8–10, as part of the Ezra narrative, constitutes a prime example of the Chronicler's approach.[122] In his earlier work, Torrey provided this evaluation of the literary quality of these chapters: "it might be possible, it would not be easy, to find a portion of Chr. of equal extent written more abominably than Neh 7,70–9,5; 10,1–40."[123] Such a comment alone begs for a literary study of these chapters.

S. Talmon

Within the vast scholarly consensus that opposes Torrey's denial of the historicity of the Chronistic work, Talmon in particular underlines the importance of interpreting Ezra-Nehemiah according to its genre as historiographical literature.[124] He notes that the work is composed of three major segments, each of which highlights a central figure of a particular era: (1) Zerubbabel (and Jeshua the high priest [538–515 B.C.E.], Ezra 1–6); (2) Ezra (beginning in 458 B.C.E., Ezra 7–10; Neh 8–9); and (3) Nehemiah (445/444–433/432 B.C.E. and 433/432–ca. 420 B.C.E., Neh 1–7; 10–13). These three pieces exhibit similar components: (1) Aramaic documents (in the first two segments: Ezra 4:17–23; 6:3–5, 6–12; 7:11–26; cf. 1:1–4); (2) letters

---

[120] Torrey, *Ezra Studies*, 153–57, 208–13.

[121] On the one hand, Torrey states, "[The Chronicler] is not merely a compiler and editor, selecting and shaping materials which lay before him; he is an original author, and possessed of some striking literary excellences, which appear in every part of his unaided work" (ibid., 208). On the other hand, in reference to the author's free compositions in Chronicles, Torrey provides this evaluation: "In constructing his narrative, he is often careless, sometimes extremely so; his language is inelegant, even for the time in which he lived; and his style is slovenly to the last degree" (ibid., 232).

[122] Torrey asserts, "There is no portion of the whole work Chron.-Ezr.-Neh. in which the Chronicler's literary peculiarities are more strongly marked, more abundant, more evenly and continuously distributed, and more easily recognizable, than in the Hebrew narrative of Ezr. 7–10 and Neh. 8–10" (ibid., 241).

[123] Torrey, *The Composition and Historical Value*, 28.

[124] S. Talmon, "Ezra and Nehemiah (Books and Men)," *IDBSup* 317–28; idem, "Ezra and Nehemiah," in *The Literary Guide to the Bible* (ed. R. Alter and F. Kermode; Cambridge, Mass.: Harvard University Press, 1987), 357–64; and, in particular, idem, "Historiographie oder Theologie?" 329–56.

(in the first and third segments: Ezra 4:8–16; 5:6–17; Neh 6:2–9); (3) a variety of inventory, census, and registration lists (in all three segments: Ezra 1:9–11 [cf. 8:24–28]; 2:2–64 = Neh 7:7–66 [cf. Ezra 8:1–14]; Ezra 10:18–44; Neh 3:1–32; 10:1–27; 11:3–24, 25–36); (4) major festivals in Jerusalem involving the whole people (in all three segments: Ezra 6:19–22a; Neh 8:1–18; 12:27–43); and (5) prayers (in the second and third segments: Ezra 9:6–15; Neh 1:5–11; 9:5–37).[125]

Talmon further points out that certain recurring literary features serve as editorial markers that designate subdivisions. In particular, he identifies three types of such markers: (1) Nehemiah's "closing invocations" ("Remember me/them, my God"), which define the end alternately of individual segments in the NM (Neh 5:19; 6:14; 13:14, 22, 29) and of the complete book (13:31); (2) "summary notations," which end individual sections by encapsulating their subject matter (Ezra 4:4–5a [for 3:1–4:3]; 6:14–15 [for 5:1–6:12]; Neh 12:26 [for 12:10–25]; 12:47 [for 12:44–46]; 13:29b–31 [for 10:1–13:29a]); and (3) "resumptive repetitions" at the beginning and end that frame some insertions (Ezra 4:5b and 24b enclose 4:6–24a; Ezra 2:1b and 70 [= Neh 7:6b and 73] enclose Ezra 2:2–69 [= Neh 7:7–72]).[126]

From a stylistic perspective, Talmon notes that prose narration represents the consistent literary mode used throughout Ezra-Nehemiah.[127] Echoes of epic poetry that occasionally crop up in preexilic histories are muted in postexilic historiography. Nevertheless, literary variation occurs when the third-person narrative in the opening segment about Zerubbabel (Ezra 1–6) moves to the first-person memoir in the concluding segment on Nehemiah (Neh 1–6; 10–13) via mixing narrative and autobiography in the middle segment dealing with Ezra (Ezra 7–10; Neh 7–9). Furthermore, the creative use of dialogue and emphasis on action produce a lively texture that distinguishes this narration from a flat reporting of events.

Historiography provides a narrative unity for events that are actually quite disparate. Talmon notes that Ezra-Nehemiah's depiction of a unified history is achieved by two contrasting literary means. For example, on the one hand, a generic temporal phrase ("After these things...," Ezra 7:1)

---

[125] Talmon, "Ezra and Nehemiah," in Alter and Kermode, *The Literary Guide to the Bible*, 358–59. By differentiating between festivals and prayers, I distinguish five categories of the material, whereas Talmon has only four.

[126] I cite Talmon's terminology: "Ezra and Nehemiah (Books and Men)," 312–22; and "Ezra and Nehemiah," in Alter and Kermode, *Literary Guide to the Bible*, 359–60. In the earlier of these two articles, Talmon notes two additional "resumptive repetitions": (1) Ezra 6:16b and 22b enclose 6:19–22a; and (2) Neh 7:4–5 and Neh 11:1 enclose 7:5b–10:40.

[127] This paragraph and the next summarize Talmon, "Ezra and Nehemiah," in Alter and Kermode, *Literary Guide to the Bible*, 361–64.

telescopes events by bridging a time gap of more than a half-century, while, on the other hand, specific references to days, months, and years (e.g., Neh 5:14; 7:72b; 9:1) maintain the impression of a sequential chronology. Two factors nonetheless militate against interpreting the work as a totally literary production: the variety and number of sources that are incorporated into the narrative; and the nearness of author and audience to the events narrated.

Historiography unifies events by interpreting them according to the author's concerns and ideology. In his more recent essay, Talmon identifies two such thematic principles that unify the originally disparate source material in Ezra-Nehemiah.[128] First, concern for the genealogical purity of the descendants of the Babylonian exiles, which is most evident in the marriage reforms of Ezra and Nehemiah (Ezra 9:2; Neh 9:2), is also reflected in the first segment of the history in the reference to the qualifications of those who celebrate the Passover following the dedication of the temple (Ezra 6:21). Second, the postexilic tradition of dual leadership by the Davidic descendant, Zerubbabel, and the high priest, Jeshua (also extant in the prophets, Hag 1:1, 12, 14; 2:2, 4, 20–23; Zech 3:1–5, 6–9; 4:6–10, 12–14; 6:9–15), appears in the first segment of Ezra-Nehemiah in the juxtaposition of these two figures (Ezra 2:2; 3:2, 8; 4:3; 5:2) with the historiographical portrayal of the dual leadership of Ezra and Nehemiah (Neh 7:72–8:18) in the remainder of the book.

B. S. CHILDS

Childs emphasizes the joining of the figures of Ezra and Nehemiah—not only in the reading of the law (Neh 8:1–18) but also in the dedication of the city walls (Neh 12:27–43)—as a climactic element of the text in its canonical form.[129] The historiographical sequence clusters all the material around four events: the reconstruction of the temple (Ezra 1–6); Ezra's marriage reform (Ezra 7–10); Nehemiah's rebuilding of the walls (Neh 1–6); and the reconstitution of the community (Neh 7–13). In the first and third sections, the narrative tension arises from the harassment of the returnees by the peoples of the land, while in the second and fourth sections it derives from the leaders' appeals for the people to separate themselves from foreigners. Both lines of narrative tension basically resolve in the solemn ratification of the new constitution (Neh 10:1–40; cf. 13:1–3). Locating Ezra's reading of the law, not at the beginning but at the end of his mission and after Nehemiah's reconstruction of the walls, reflects a theological vision of the place of the Torah in the community: hearing the law is not so much the seed as the ultimate fruit of reform.

---

128 Talmon, "Historiographie oder Theologie?" 343–54.

129 B. S. Childs, *Introduction to the Old Testament As Scripture* (Philadelphia: Fortress, 1979), 624–38.

H. G. M. WILLIAMSON

In light of his thorough diachronic investigation of the text, Williamson reaches a similar conclusion regarding the final configuration of the book, at least insofar as he asserts that Neh 8–10 constitutes the climax of Ezra-Nehemiah.[130] He notes that this climactic section constitutes a triptych in which the confessional prayer (Neh 9:6–37) occupies the central position between the exposition of the law (Neh 8:1–18) and the oath of allegiance to the law that the community signs (Neh 10:1–40).[131]

Williamson further suggests that the editors structured the missions of Ezra and Nehemiah in four parallel "panels" (Ezra 7–10; Neh 1–7; 8–10; 11–13) in order to present the work of these historically distinct individuals as a unity.[132] The introductory segment (Ezra 1–6) constitutes another panel, which is the latest addition to the work and therefore especially reflects the ideological concerns of the final editor.[133]

Thus, Ezra-Nehemiah is arranged so as to provide a cohesive vision of salvation history from the end of the exile through the missions of Nehemiah. The work of reconstruction that began under the leadership of Zerubbabel and Jeshua reaches its culmination under Ezra and Nehemiah. The book unfolds a divine program in successive stages beginning with the rebuilding of the temple (Ezra 1–6), continuing through the marriage reforms of Ezra (Ezra 7–10), the reconstruction of the walls under Nehemiah (Neh 1–7), the covenant renewal under Ezra (with the participation of Nehemiah [Neh 8–10]), and concluding with the dedication of the walls under Ezra and Nehemiah, supplemented by Nehemiah's final reforms (Neh 11–13).

---

[130] Williamson states, "There can be little doubt that Neh 8–10 is to be seen as the climax of the work in this form and that these chapters were intended by the editor to function paradigmatically within his own later community as it struggled to maintain its identity and sense of religious purpose" (*Ezra, Nehemiah,* xxxiv).

[131] H. G. M. Williamson, "Postexilic Historiography," in *The Future of Biblical Studies: The Hebrew Scriptures* (ed. R. E. Friedman and H. G. M. Williamson; Atlanta: Scholars Press, 1987), 189–207, esp. 199–201.

[132] One weakness in Williamson's judicious commentary (*Ezra, Nehemiah*) is its lack of a detailed analysis of the structure of Ezra-Nehemiah. He does not elaborate on what he means by a "panel" structure (cf. idem, "Postexilic Historiography," 203). Indeed, he exhibits a certain inconsistency on the matter since, when discussing the composition of the text (*Ezra, Nehemiah,* xxxiv–xxxv), he identifies the four panels as Ezra 7–10; Neh 1–7; 8–10; and 11–13 with Ezra 1–6 as an introduction. However, when considering the theology of the text (xlix–l), he outlines a salvation history in five chapters, i.e., Ezra 1:1–6:22; 7:1–10:44; Neh 1:1–7:72a; 7:72b–12:43; and 12:44–13:31. (Note the discrepancy in the delineation of the last two segments in these lists.)

[133] H. G. M. Williamson, "The Composition of Ezra i–vi," *JTS* 34 (1983): 1–30.

Diachronic analysis of the text highlights the historiographical artistry of this schema. Historical criticism establishes the fact that the events described represent distinct episodes of varying duration that occurred over the course of more than a century and which, for the most part, are quite unrelated. Consider the sporadic nature of the major events: (1) the reconstruction of the temple was undertaken almost immediately following Cyrus's decree in 538 B.C.E. but was aborted shortly thereafter; (2) the resumption of the temple project and its completion took place in the five-year period between 520 and 515 B.C.E.; (3) specific protests against Jerusalem projects were recorded in archival materials of the Achaemenid administration at a few particular points over the course of more than sixty years embracing the reigns of Xerxes I (486–465 B.C.E., Ezra 4:6) and Artaxerxes I (464–423 B.C.E., Ezra 4:7–22); (4) the mission of Ezra might have been limited to a single year beginning in 458 B.C.E.; and (5) the mission of Nehemiah extended to two terms, the first being of twelve-year duration (445–433 B.C.E.) and, following an interval away from Jerusalem to meet with Artaxerxes, a second one being of unknown length.

The historiographer's genius consists in bringing such disparate episodes into relationship with one another in a manner that discloses a divine plan. He employs a diversity of stylistic tools and archival ingredients to establish the connections that give meaning to history:[134] (1) the summary statement in Ezra 6:14 unifies the story under the aegis of the three Persian kings who ultimately promote and defend the interests of Judah; (2) the temporal transition in Ezra 7:1 ("After these things...") almost imperceptibly bridges a gap of practically half a century from the dedication of the temple to the commission of Ezra; (3) the presentation of Ezra and Nehemiah as partners theologically unifies their missions in the climax of the book (Neh 8–10); (4) the list of priests and Levites, beginning with Zerubbabel and Jeshua and ending with Nehemiah and Ezra (Neh 12:1–26), resumes the disclosure of the divine plan, which extends from the beginning to the end of the book; and (5) similarly, the concluding association of the era of Zerubbabel with that of Nehemiah (Neh 12:47) encompasses the history in a complete circle.[135]

---

[134] In the following résumé, the first five points come from H. G. M. Williamson, *Ezra and Nehemiah* (OTG; Sheffield: JSOT Press, 1987), 79–80, while the sixth is found in idem, *Ezra, Nehemiah*, 380.

[135] The final section of the book contains a number of temporal indicators: "On that day" (Neh 12:44; 13:1); "Now, before this" (Neh 13:4); and "In those days" (Neh 13:15, 23). However, Williamson views these indicators as markers that define narrative units (Neh 12:44–13:14; 13:15–31) that originate in different sources ("Postexilic Historiography," 202–3; and *Ezra, Nehemiah*, 380, 393). His primary allegiance to source criticism seems to prevent him from including these temporal indicators among the stylistic instruments that the redactor employed to unify the history. From

Employment of such devices produces a literary configuration that invites the reader to contemplate events in their relationship to one another rather than in terms of their objective chronology. The literary transposition of an event from its original chronological position into a context that better serves the ideological intent of the editor does not always result in a confusing sequence of dates; Ezra's reading of the Torah in "the seventh month" (Neh 7:72b) is a primary case in point.[136] However, when a decision had to be made between the two, the editor sacrificed chronological precision for the sake of ideological emphasis. Thus, for example, an editor inserted the archival material pertaining to the construction of the city walls from the reign of Artaxerxes I (Ezra 4:7–22) into the narration of the temple project during the reigns of Cyrus and Darius (Ezra 4:1–5, 24) in order to emphasize the rightness of the policy excluding the participation of those not from Judah and Benjamin. The latter-day Achaemenid correspondence (Ezra 4:7–22) demonstrates that, over the next half-century or more, Samaritan opposition continued to be the major source of frustration for the reconstruction not only of the temple but also of the city.[137] In summary, Williamson illustrates how the book of Ezra-Nehemiah represents the retailoring of available documents in such a fashion that the editor's historiographical concerns override and reshape the chronological preoccupations of his sources.[138]

S. Japhet

Japhet provides further insight into the historiography of Ezra-Nehemiah by devoting attention to the structure of the book in its

---

a narrative perspective, these temporal notations connect the supplementary material at the end of the book (Neh 12:44–13:31) with the culminating event that immediately precedes, namely, the dedication of the city walls (Neh 12:27–43).

[136] The "seventh month" fits best within the sequence of dates in the EM between Ezra 8 and 9 (therefore between 7:8, "the fifth month," and 10:9, "the ninth month"). However, the transposition of the reading of the Torah into its present context (in order to provide the climax for the whole work) establishes a new, but nevertheless reasonable, chronology in which this "seventh month" follows the prior notice on the (sixth) month of Elul during which the people completed the wall (Neh 6:15). See Williamson, "Postexilic Historiography," 202.

[137] Williamson, *Ezra, Nehemiah*, 56–60.

[138] For a study that complements Williamson's work and provides a detailed analysis of the difference between "real" chronology and "ostensible" chronology in the first part of Ezra-Nehemiah, see B. Halpern, "A Historiographic Commentary on Ezra 1–6: Achronological Narrative and Dual Chronology in Israelite Historiography," in *The Hebrew Bible and Its Interpreters* (ed. B. Halpern, W. H. Propp, and D. N. Freedman; Biblical and Judaic Studies from the University of California, San Diego 1; Winona Lake, Ind.: Eisenbrauns, 1990), 81–142.

completed form[139] and by examining the characters and events in the narrative of the temple's reconstruction both in terms of internal evidence within Ezra 1–6 and in comparison with the presentation of the same matter in the prophets Haggai and Zechariah.[140]

Japhet fills in the lacuna in Williamson's work by highlighting the structure of Ezra-Nehemiah as its primary historiographical feature. She outlines the apparent configuration of the book before presenting its actual historiographical structure. In terms of content and stylistic features, the book manifestly consists of three stories: Ezra 1–6, the history of the reconstruction of the temple; Ezra 7–10, the story of Ezra; and Neh 1–13, the story of Nehemiah.[141] Each of these sections exhibits stylistic peculiarities such as: (1) the combination of narrative and documents in two languages in Ezra 1–6 and Ezra 7–10; (2) the contrasting combinations of first-person memoir and third-person narrative in Ezra 7–10 (in which the narrative [7:1–26; 10:1–44] frames the memoir [7:27–9:15]) and in Neh 1–13 (in which the memoir [1:1–7:5; 13:4–31] frames the narrative [7:6–13:3; except for 12:27–43]); and (3) the interruption of narrative continuity by intrusive material especially in Ezra 1–6 (e.g., the archival letters in Ezra 4:8–22) and in Neh 1–13 (e.g., the lists in Neh 11:3–12:26).

In attempting to account for the arrangement of the material, Japhet boldly rejects the diachronic explanations that posit a series of editions and supplementary interventions. Instead, she conceives of the book as the work of a single author who is responsible for its design.[142]

According to Japhet, the author's historiographical achievement consists in reworking the apparent three-part arrangement into a configuration of two distinct periods that stand in chronographic balance:[143] Ezra 1–6

---

[139] S. Japhet, "Composition and Chronology in the Book of Ezra-Nehemiah," in *Second Temple Studies 2: Temple Community in the Persian Period* (ed. T. C. Eskenazi and K. H. Richards; JSOTSup 175; Sheffield: JSOT Press, 1994), 189–216.

[140] Japhet, "Sheshbazzar and Zerubbabel," 66–98; idem, "'History' and 'Literature' in the Persian Period; The Restoration of the Temple," in *Ah, Assyria ... Studies in Assyrian History and Ancient Near Eastern Historiography Presented to Hayim Tadmor* (ed. M. Cogan and I. Ephal; ScrHier 33; Jerusalem: Magnes, 1991), 174–88.

[141] Japhet, "Composition and Chronology," 190.

[142] Japhet states, "However, in full awareness of the dangers of this approach, with full recognition of the complexity of the material in the book, and despite the unpopularity of this approach, I wish to suggest that it is possible—and henceforth obligatory—to explain the composition of EN [Ezra-Nehemiah] precisely in that manner: as a book that was produced 'all at once', by an author, according to a clear plan" (ibid., 200–1).

[143] What follows is a summary of Japhet's "Composition and Chronology," 208–15.

embraces an actual time span of twenty-two years from the first year of Cyrus (Ezra 1:1, 538 B.C.E.) to the sixth year of Darius (Ezra 6:15, 517 B.C.E.);[144] and Ezra 7–Neh 13 spans twenty-six years from the seventh year of Artaxerxes (Ezra 7:7, 458 B.C.E.) to the thirty-third year of Artaxerxes (Neh 13:6–7, 432 B.C.E.).

Certain precise dates provide the key structural markers.[145] From a historiographical viewpoint, the two parts of the history exhibit several major similarities: (1) each period spans approximately one generation (twenty-two years in the first period and twenty-six years in the second); and (2) within each period, events cluster around the dates at specific points that define either a beginning or an end. In the first period (538–517 B.C.E.), the events converge around two points: (1) the beginning, "in the first year of Cyrus" (Ezra 1:1), and the time immediately thereafter when the people undertake the initial work on the temple (Ezra 1:1–4:23); and (2) the end, from "the second year of the reign of King Darius" (Ezra 4:24) until "the sixth year of the reign of King Darius" (Ezra 6:15), the last five years (522–517 B.C.E.) in which the reconstruction actually reaches completion (Ezra 5:1–6:22).

In the second period (458–432 B.C.E.), the events center around three points, two beginnings and an ending: (1) the beginning of Ezra's mission "in the seventh year of King Artaxerxes" (Ezra 7:7, 458 B.C.E.), from "the first day of the first month" (Ezra 7:9) until the "first day of the first month" of the following year" (Ezra 10:17), which encompasses all the events of the marriage reforms (Ezra 7:1–10:44); (2) the beginning of Nehemiah's mission "in the twentieth year of Artaxerxes" (Neh 2:1, 445 B.C.E.), during which the people complete the city walls (in the [sixth] month of Elul, 6:15), Ezra proclaims the Torah ("in the seventh month," 7:72b), and the people celebrate the dedication of the city walls (by implication in the same year, without mention of a date, 12:27–43); and (3) the final period of Nehemiah's mission more than twelve years later, upon his return to Jerusalem following his prior departure from the city "in the thirty-second year of King Artaxerxes of Babylon" (Neh 13:6–7,

---

[144] Japhet dates the rededication of the temple to 517 B.C.E., whereas others date it to 516 or 515 B.C.E.

[145] Japhet parts company with Williamson over the historiographical significance of these dates. Whereas Williamson views them as chronological indications that were primary in the sources but secondary in the final arrangement, Japhet considers them to be the markers that delineate the book in its ultimate form. Furthermore, while Williamson ("Postexilic Historiography," 202; *Ezra and Nehemiah*, 79–80) estimates the mention of the three Persian kings (Ezra 6:14) to be of major historiographical significance as a unifying element for the whole work, Japhet ("Composition and Chronology," 208–9) simply acknowledges that this verse contains significant chronological data, but not of the type that would determine the historiographical structure of the whole book.

433 B.C.E.), during which he implements reforms pertaining to the temple and marriage (Neh 13:4–31).

In terms of content, the above periods maintain a thematic balance without forfeiting their distinctive elements. Thus, for example, two leaders, a priest and a layman, stand at the head of the people in each period. Yet, the explicit titles of Ezra the priest and scribe (Ezra 7:11, 12; Neh 8:9; 12:26) and of Nehemiah the governor (Neh 5:14, 18; 12:26) contrast with the indirect designations for the offices of Jeshua (Ezra 3:2; 10:18) and Zerubbabel (Ezra 4:2). Furthermore, the temple project provides the constant factor throughout the first period, whereas the activities of the leaders constitute the bases of narrative continuity in the second period.

The author designed both periods by reshaping written sources that were available. For the second period (Ezra 7–Neh 13), his prime historiographical intervention consisted in his intentional splicing of the Ezra material (Neh 8) into the Nehemiah story (Neh 1–13), which effectively synchronized the missions of these two leaders and thereby reinterpreted history in contrast to his Ezra and Nehemiah sources, each of which had focused on one figure to the exclusion of the other. For the first period (Ezra 1–6), the author assembled a variety of documents for which he composed a narrative framework; the resultant complex theologically interprets history by exhibiting scant eschatological consciousness, portraying foreign kings as divine agents, and defining the people Israel in terms of the exile.

Japhet's observation that the portrait of Zerubbabel in Ezra 1–6 lacks two primary features that define the same figure in Haggai and Zechariah discloses two tenets of the historical worldview in Ezra-Nehemiah:[146] first, the lack of reference to Zerubbabel's Davidic lineage reflects an absence of messianic concern (Ezra 2:2; 3:2; cf. Hag 2:23; Zech 6:12–13); and, second, the silence about Zerubbabel's position as governor and the absence of tension with the Persian administration reflects a comparative lack of eschatological expectation and, indeed, a corresponding appreciation of the reigning political order as a divine provision for the exiles (Ezra 4:3; cf. Hag 2:21–22).[147] Moreover, in Ezra-Nehemiah, the lack of a distinguishing leadership profile for Zerubbabel (as well as for Jeshua and Sheshbazzar) corresponds with a tendency toward "democratization" whereby the people as a whole become the main participants in the history.[148]

---

[146] Japhet, "Sheshbazzar and Zerubbabel," 68–80.

[147] Japhet (ibid., 75) notes that the prayer in Neh 9 contrasts with the rest of the book insofar as it expresses dissatisfaction with the present order and implies a hope for change (esp. 9:36–37).

[148] Ibid., 80–89. Japhet (p. 86), however, asserts that this democratic emphasis in Ezra 1–6 does not apply to the remainder of the book (Ezra 7–Neh 13), in which the leaders, Ezra and Nehemiah, are the focus of attention.

The pictures of the community and of the Persian kings in their contribution to the reconstruction of the temple are markedly different in Ezra-Nehemiah than in Haggai and Zechariah.[149] According to Haggai, resistance to the temple project came from within the people of Judah themselves (Hag 1:2), whereas according to Ezra-Nehemiah the only resistance came from outsiders who attempted to frustrate the community's universal enthusiasm for the project dating from the earliest days of their restoration to the land (Ezra 2:68; 4:1–5). Haggai and, to a lesser degree, Zechariah speak to the people in Judah with little reference to the exile, whereas in Ezra-Nehemiah the returning exiles comprise the nucleus of the restored Israel (Ezra 2:1–68). Finally, the depiction of the Persian kings as agents through whom God works for the restoration of the temple and the protection of his people (Ezra 1:1; 4:3; 6:14) is unparalleled in Haggai and Zechariah.

T. C. ESKENAZI

Eskenazi inaugurated a new era in Ezra-Nehemiah studies with her analysis of the text from an exclusively synchronic perspective.[150] While recognizing the work as a piece of historiography, she investigates it as literature prescinding from its value as a historical resource. In other words, she focuses on the final text in search of its literary qualities as distinct from its putative merits as a witness to actual events and their tradition.

In view of the importance of Eskenazi's study, I shall discuss it in two parts by providing, first, a summary of her synchronic analysis of Ezra-Nehemiah, and second, an evaluation of her work.

SUMMARY OF ESKENAZI'S STUDY

Eskenazi's approach freshly interprets Ezra-Nehemiah in terms of structure, content, and characterization. The modern literary theory of the design of a story provides the basis for her structural analysis.[151] Thus, she outlines the book according to a three-part schema that commences with the phase of "potentiality" (in which the goal or "objective" is defined), passes through the "process of actualization," and concludes with the phase of "success" (in which the goal or "objective" is realized). Eskenazi limits the phase of "potentiality" to the presentation of Cyrus's edict for the reconstruction of the house of God (Ezra 1:1–4). She extends the "process of actualization" to embrace the work, not only on the temple, but also on

---

[149] Japhet, "'History' and 'Literature,'" 186–88.

[150] Eskenazi, *In an Age of Prose*.

[151] Discussion of the "Structure and Themes of Ezra-Nehemiah" constitutes the largest portion of her book (ibid., 37–126). For a more succinct presentation of her outline of the text, see Eskenazi, "Structure of Ezra-Nehemiah," 641–56.

the city walls (Ezra 1:5–Neh 7:72). Under the rubric of "success," she includes the remainder of the narrative following Ezra's reading of the law (Neh 8:1–13:31).

Moreover, she subdivides the second phase ("process of actualization") into three "movements" that basically correspond to conventional divisions: the building of the temple (Ezra 1:7–6:22); Ezra's marriage reform (Ezra 7:1–10:44); and the NM (Neh 1:1–7:5). She likewise segments the third phase ("success") into two major sections corresponding to the Torah ceremony (Neh 8:1–10:40) and the dedication of the walls (Neh 12:27–13:3), which are connected by the community roster (11:1–12:26) and followed by an ancillary "coda" comprised of Nehemiah's autobiographical notations (13:4–31).

The duplication of the census list (Ezra 2:1–67; Neh 7:6–72a) provides the key indicator for discerning the book's structure.[152] By virtue of its repetition, this list of returnees establishes the boundaries for the middle phase of the "process of actualization," which encompasses the building of both the temple and the city walls (Ezra 1:5–Neh 7:72). These census lists both divide and unite at the same time: they separate the phase of "actualization" (Ezra 1:5–Neh 7:72) from the phase of "potentiality" (Ezra 1:1–4), on the one hand, and from the phase of "success" (Neh 8:1–13:31), on the other; and they also serve as brackets that unite the middle phase of actualization (Ezra 1:5–Neh 7:72).

Literary unity is a major factor that Eskenazi emphasizes in her examination of the contents of Ezra-Nehemiah. Three elements in particular reinforce the overall unity of the book: summarizing devices, the repetition of movement in the "process of actualization," and consistent emphasis on three themes (the people, the house of God, and documentation) in every segment of the work. The summarizing devices are of two types: recapitulative lists and proleptic synopses. The repetition of the list of those who returned to Judah with Zerubbabel and Jeshua (Ezra 2:1–67), which follows the completion of the walls under Nehemiah (Neh 7:6–72), recapitulates the history and connects the two events.[153] Moreover, the list of priests and Levites (Neh 12:1–26), which is presented in the phase of "success" between the covenant renewal (Neh 8–10) and the dedication of the walls (Neh 12:27–43), recapitulates the history from beginning to end in two ways: first, by alluding to the first register of confreres who returned with Zerubbabel and Jeshua (Neh 12:1; cf. Ezra 2:1); and, second, by providing a résumé of the priestly and Levitical history that encompasses the whole period from Zerubbabel and Jeshua to Nehemiah and Ezra (Neh 12:1–26).[154]

---

[152] Eskenazi, *In an Age of Prose*, 39–40, 88–95, 182–83.
[153] Ibid., 88–95.
[154] Ibid., 115–16, 183–84.

Three proleptic synopses provide another type of unifying force within the narrative. The first proleptic synopsis is the verse that immediately follows the edict of Cyrus (Ezra 1:5) and offers a summary description of all that follows in the narration of the reconstruction.[155] Because Eskenazi contends that "the house of God" in Ezra-Nehemiah extends beyond the temple to embrace the whole city, she asserts that this first sentence in the phase of actualization encapsulates not only Ezra 1–6 but the whole story up to the completion of the walls (Ezra 1:5–Neh 7:72).

By Eskenazi's estimation, the most important proleptic summary in the book is the second one, which speaks of the completion of the reconstruction project: "They finished their building by the decree of the God of Israel and by the decree of Cyrus, Darius, and Artaxerxes, King of Persia" (Ezra 6:14).[156] Eskenazi underlines four elements of this verse: (1) the mention of the decree of Artaxerxes (which ensues in Ezra 7:12–26) testifies to the proleptic character of the verse and extends the horizon of reference to the remainder of Ezra-Nehemiah (Ezra 7–Neh 13), all of which takes place under the aegis of Artaxerxes; (2) however, the "building" alludes to more than the temple structure since the work that took place during the reign of Artaxerxes was not that of constructing the temple edifice but of restoring the city wall and of reforming the community; (3) mention of the three monarchs by name but with a single title ("king") and a single document ("decree") indicates that they act as one and that their joint oversight unites the diverse phases of the work and therefore of the whole story from beginning to end; and (4) the use of the same word (טעם) for the "decree" of God and the "decree" of the king equates them, thereby indicating that the royal edicts are divine instruments that promote the reconstruction of Jerusalem.

The third proleptic synopsis takes a different form, namely, the various epithets that both the narrator (Ezra 7:6, 11) and the king (Ezra 7:12) employ to designate Ezra as a scribe of the Torah.[157] These designations foreshadow the narration of Ezra's activities throughout the remainder of the book (Ezra 7–Neh 12).

The middle phase exhibits another unifying principle, that is, the threefold repetition of one basic story line. The "process of actualization" actually consists of three successive "movements" (Ezra 1–6; 7–10; Neh 1–7), each of which describes a journey of the people from exile to Jerusalem, where conflict ensues and is subsequently resolved in the

---

[155] Ibid., 45–46.

[156] An indication of the significance of this verse for Eskenazi is the number of times she cites it throughout her study: ibid., 41–42, 45, 48, 56, 59–60, 71–72, 77–78, 87–88, 176, 188, 190.

[157] Ibid., 62–65, 136–44.

process of rebuilding the community.¹⁵⁸ Because this same narrative process sustains each movement, it provides the bond between the initial stage of temple building (Ezra 1–6) and the subsequent stages of marriage reform (Ezra 7–10) and rebuilding the city walls (Neh 1–7).

The pervasive focus on three themes that Eskenazi has identified in every segment of the work reinforces her unifying conception of the whole: the protagonist from beginning to end is the people rather than a particular leader; the central concern is the house of God understood as extending beyond the temple to the walls encompassing the entire city and embracing the whole community; and the providential instruments propelling the building of this house are written documents.¹⁵⁹ In summary, "the book concentrates on how the people of God build the house of God in accordance with divinely ordained documents."¹⁶⁰

Three devices at the beginning cast the spotlight on the people:¹⁶¹ (1) the edict of Cyrus that addresses the exiles without concern for rank (Ezra 1:3–4); (2) the narrator's description of God stirring the spirit of those who will constitute the true Israel of the restoration (Ezra 1:5; namely, members of the tribes of Judah and Benjamin along with priests and Levites); and (3) the census list that introduces a cast of almost fifty thousand with only passing mention of leaders such as Zerubbabel and Jeshua (Ezra 2:1–67). The narration of Ezra's mission employs various means to direct attention away from this most important individual to the people: (1) the narrator has the people, priests, and Levites surround Ezra from the beginning of the journey (Ezra 7:7–8); (2) the lists of returning exiles (Ezra 8:1–24) and of subscribers to the marriage reform (Ezra 10:18–44) circumscribe the narrative; and (3) Ezra initiates the reform at the behest of the people (Ezra 10:2–4). The detailed list of those who worked on the walls (Neh 3:1–32) maintains the predominant profile of the people in spite of Nehemiah's tendency to take center stage. The repetition of the list of returnees (Neh 7:6–72) reinforces the focus on the people and prepares for their receiving direct possession of the Torah from Ezra (Neh 8:1–18), voicing the psalm of repentance (Neh 9:5–37), signing the oath (Neh 10:1–40), repopulating Jerusalem (Neh 11:1–12:26), and eventually participating in the dedication of the walls (Neh 12:27–43).

A basic tenet of Eskenazi's study is her assertion that Ezra-Nehemiah expands the "house of God" from the temple to the city.¹⁶² She offers

---

¹⁵⁸ Ibid., 39–40, 44–45.
¹⁵⁹ Ibid., 2, 40–41, 185–92.
¹⁶⁰ Ibid., 44.
¹⁶¹ Ibid., 48–53, 62–70, 79–83, 91–92, 97–104, 111–16, 117–19, 185–88.
¹⁶² Ibid., 2, 53–57, 71–73, 83–87, 119–21, 188–89.

various arguments to sustain her thesis, including: (1) establishing a fundamental distinction between the terms "temple" (היכל) and "house of God" (בית אלהים, e.g., Ezra 3:6–8); (2) noting in Ezra 4:1–24 that the narrative describes the people building "the house of God" (4:1–3, 24), whereas the archival documents refer to their constructing "the city" (4:12, 13, 16, 21), thereby equating these terms; (3) noting that the city walls are treated like temple precincts in descriptions both of the high priest's "consecrating" the Sheep Gate (Neh 3:1–2) and of Nehemiah's appointing singers and Levites at the city gates (Neh 7:1–4; cf. 13:22); and (4) pointing out that, at the beginning of the dedication ceremony, the priests and Levites "purified" not only themselves but also the people, the gates, and the walls (Neh 12:30), thus defining the boundaries of the sacred sphere as circumscribing the "holy city" (Neh 11:1, 18).

Eskenazi points out that a distinctive characteristic of Ezra-Nehemiah is the central role that documents play throughout the story.[163] To a large extent, the book represents a collection of archival materials in diverse forms, including edicts, letters, and lists. Historical-critical scholars estimate the purpose of such documents is to legitimize the status of the exilic descendants of Judah and Benjamin along with certain priests and Levites as the rightful heirs of preexilic Israel.[164] However, Eskenazi perceives that these documents exercise diverse narrative functions, such as propelling the story, personalizing the community, mediating dialogue, and defining the future vocation of the people.[165] Documents propel the narrative. The story of Ezra-Nehemiah concerns the actualization of authoritative pronouncements from word into reality. The decree of Cyrus (Ezra 1:1–4; cf. 6:2–5; 5:13–15), the edict of Artaxerxes (Ezra 7:12–26), and ultimately YHWH's Torah (cf. Ezra 7:26) are divine instruments that initiate and guide the restoration of the temple, the city, and the people. The census lists (e.g., Ezra 2:1–68; Neh 10:2–28) serve a descriptive function by mediating the personality of the community, not as an anonymous mass but as an assembly of unique individuals.

The dynamic interaction of documents (e.g., Ezra 4:9–22; cf. 5:8–17; 6:6–12) prompts Eskenazi to assert that written texts in Ezra-Nehemiah assume the role that the spoken word plays in other narratives. Finally, the climactic portrait of the community gathered around the open book of the Torah to seek direction for its life (Neh 8:2, 13; 9:2–3) suggests the

---

[163] Ibid., 43–44, 58–60, 73–77, 87–88, 109–11, 122, 180–82, 189–92.

[164] E.g., Williamson, *Ezra and Nehemiah*, 81–84.

[165] For a comprehensive treatment of the role of the written word in Ezra-Nehemiah, see: T. C. Eskenazi, "Ezra-Nehemiah: From Text to Actuality," in *Signs and Wonders: Biblical Texts in Literary Focus* (ed. J. C. Exum; SemeiaSt; n.p.: Society of Biblical Literature, 1989), 165–97.

vocation that will define this people for the future, according to Ezra-Nehemiah.[166] Eskenazi's study of the characterization of Ezra and Nehemiah[167] is an innovative contribution to synchronic research on the book. In particular, she opens new horizons by viewing the alternating forms of the first-person memoirs and third-person narratives as recounting the story from alternating subjective and objective perspectives. Thus, she probes the creative possibilities afforded by the autobiographical features that are distinctive of Ezra-Nehemiah within biblical literature. The narrator interacts with the characters in a dialogue that is established between the narratives and the memoirs. The omniscient narrator (speaking in the third person) tends to concur with the autobiographical account of Ezra while sometimes contradicting Nehemiah's first-person version of events.

The resulting depiction presents a contrast between the two main individuals in the book. On Eskenazi's reading, Ezra is the ideal leader who acts by consensus (Ezra 9:1; 10:1–4), transfers power to the people (Neh 8:13; 9:2–3), and quietly recedes into the background (Neh 8:18; cf. 9:1–4) so that the people can take their rightful place at center stage. So well does he accomplish his task of teaching the Torah of YHWH (Ezra 7:10) that he makes himself expendable since, in the end, the people can read the Torah without his mediation (Neh 9:2–3). Nehemiah, by contrast, pushes himself into the spotlight (Neh 5:14–19), presumes upon divine favor (Neh 13:14), passes over his own acts of injustice (Neh 5:7, 10), and arrogates to himself credit for the completion of the walls (Neh 6:1) in blatant contradiction to the narrator's crediting the accomplishment to the whole people (see the list in Neh 3:1–32). In summary, the story presents the figures of Ezra and Nehemiah symbiotically: Ezra is the champion, whereas Nehemiah is the pretender; Ezra is the prototype, Nehemiah the counterfeit.[168] However, ultimately, each of them must concede center stage to the people, whether graciously (Ezra) or reluctantly (Nehemiah).

EVALUATION OF ESKENAZI'S STUDY

Eskenazi's study underscores the value of Ezra-Nehemiah as a literary work that merits further investigation from a synchronic perspective. Her treatment demonstrates the benefits of applying to this book the interpretative methods of contemporary narrative theory. Two such benefits are her refreshing exposition of the multifaceted functioning of archival

---

[166] Eskenazi, *In an Age of Prose*, 191–92; idem, "From Text to Actuality," 193–94.
[167] Eskenazi, *In an Age of Prose*, 62–70, 136–54.
[168] Japhet differs markedly in her evaluation of the two leaders: "The figures of Ezra and Nehemiah differ considerably, and the passive character of Ezra pales before the active character of Nehemiah" ("Sheshbazzar and Zerubbabel," 86).

documents in the narration of the story and her illustrations of the impact of alternating narrative points of view on characterization.

The effort to conceptualize Ezra-Nehemiah as a unified whole pervades her approach to the text. One must admire the sense of cohesiveness that suffuses Eskenazi's reading of a book with a bewildering plethora of decrees, letters, lists, reports, memoirs, and financial statements. Amid a flood of documentation, her thematic schema provides a standard threefold ordering principle, which she claims is valid for every segment of the book: one protagonist (the community), one project (the house of God), and one divine instrument (documentation). Her illustration of the three parallel movements that constitute the "process of actualization" suggests a divinely inspired synergy pervading the restoration efforts of the people, who successively construct the temple (Ezra 1–6), participate in the marriage reform (Ezra 7–10), and erect the city walls (Neh 1–7). Perhaps her finest achievement conceptually is her perception that the building projects, first the temple and then the walls, are harmoniously aligned phases providing external coordinates for the interior construction of the community via the Torah.

However, the very tidiness of Eskenazi's work alerts the critic to its limitations, namely, of imposing a predetermined construct upon the text. Ezra-Nehemiah practically defies complete systematization. At certain junctures, Eskenazi's presentation of the material is too streamlined to account for all the evidence. Three examples of such streamlining are: her generic outline of the book; her focus on the same three themes in every segment of the book; and her identification of the "house of God" with the city of Jerusalem.

Eskenazi applies to Ezra-Nehemiah a generic structure from contemporary literary theory to trace the design of a story. Thus, her perception of the book's configuration derives not primarily from indications within the text itself but from the outside and, thereby, to a certain degree reflects the imposition of a modern mind on an ancient text. The effect is both positive and negative. The two beneficial results of applying such a generic structure to Ezra-Nehemiah are: first, it brings conceptual order to a perplexing amalgam of material; and, second, it diminishes the strangeness of the book by generically classifying it in the category of story.[169]

---

[169] By definition, a generic design is better able to distinguish what is common from what is unique about a particular text in comparison with others of the same category. One could apply the tripartite story design of "potentiality," "process of actualization," and "success" equally well to the major parts of the book (the building of the temple [Ezra 1:1–6:22: 1:1–4; 1:5–6:15; 6:16–22], the Ezra story [Ezra 7:1–10:44: 7:1–26; 7:27–10:17; 10:18–44], and the Nehemiah story [Neh 1:1–7:5: 1:1–2:8; 2:9–6:19; 7:1–5]) as to the whole of Ezra-Nehemiah.

However, the negative effect of such an application is the lack of a good match where ancient historiography does not correspond with contemporary storytelling. Thus, Eskenazi must overstate the case when she asserts that the major census lists (Ezra 2:1–67; Neh 7:6–72) provide the inclusion for the "process of actualization" since narrative material (Ezra 1:5–11) precedes the first list. Furthermore, while she includes the first list within the "first movement" of the process of actualization, she separates the second list from the "third movement" by placing this list in a category of its own under the heading "recapitulation," which identifies its function as the final section in the whole process of actualization (Ezra 1:5–Neh 7:72). Moreover, she delimits the lists differently in each case (Ezra 2:1–67; cf. Neh 7:1–72) because she perceives a dissimilarity in their respective relationships to the subsequent narratives.[170]

Eskenazi not only applies a tripartite generic outline to the book but also reads every segment according to a threefold thematic cluster comprised of "the people," "the house of God," and the "documents." This thematic approach views the book through a predefined lens, producing a distorted perception of the narrative landscape by reducing the variegations in content that constitute the distinguishing features of the diverse segments of the book. However, it does perform a legitimate function of coherence by indicating elements that are common throughout the book.

In this context, what Eskenazi omits is as vital as what she discusses. For example, while she highlights the importance of the edicts of the Persian monarchs, she fails to discuss the literary significance of the distinction between the first one being in Hebrew (Ezra 1:1–4) and the remainder being in Aramaic (Ezra 5:13–15; 6:2–6, 7–12; 7:12–27). Again, while she highlights the importance of the book of the law, she does not discuss the absence of the word *Torah* from the first-person memoir concerning Nehemiah's first mission up to the dedication of the walls (Neh 1:1–7:5; 12:27–43; cf. 12:44; 13:3).

---

[170] Eskenazi (*In an Age of Prose*, 46, cf. 88) treats Ezra 2:68–70 as part of the narrative that follows (Ezra 3:1–16), whereas she maintains the parallel material (Neh 7:69–72) as a continuation of the census list (Neh 7:6–68). One must challenge this inconsistency in her delimitations of the census list. Nevertheless, one can admit the validity of her perception that a more intimate relationship exists between the first list (Ezra 2:1–70) and the construction of the altar (Ezra 3:1–16) than between the second list (Neh 7:6–72) and the reading of the Torah (Neh 8:1–18). Given the variations in linkage, Eskenazi perceives a parallel between the story of the construction of the altar (Ezra 3:1–16) and the narrative of the proclamation of the Torah (Neh 8:1–18) on the basis of their identical positions relative to the census list. In light of this parallelism, she surmises, "One could postulate that here we find an earlier version of a view that later becomes normative, i.e., that the study of Torah replaces the offering of sacrifices" (pp. 92–93).

Moreover, while arguing that the "house of God" extends beyond the temple to the city walls, she neglects to mention that the same portion of Nehemiah's memoir contains only two occurrences of this term (Neh 6:10; 12:40; cf. 13:4, 7, 9, 11, 14), and, of these two, one comes from the mouth of an adversary of Nehemiah (Neh 6:10). The scarcity of (purportedly) central terms limits the weight of her interpretation.

Eskenazi's assertion that "Ezra-Nehemiah expands the concept of the house of God from temple to city"[171] touches upon a significant point but lacks sufficient nuance to account for all the evidence in the book. Of the fifty-seven occurrences of the term "house of God" in Ezra-Nehemiah, not a single one refers directly to the city or to the people.[172] Therefore, the text offers no lexical basis for equating the "house of God" with the city or with the assembly of the people in Jerusalem. Nevertheless, by means of narrative associations and connotations implicit in certain descriptive terminology, Ezra-Nehemiah does extend to the whole city and to the assembly therein the sacred quality that is emblematic of the temple precincts. In Ezra 4:1–24, the relationship between narrative and documentation establishes a connection between the "house of God," on the one hand (Ezra 4:1–3, 24), and the city and its walls, on the other (Ezra 4:11–22). Vocabulary otherwise distinctive of the temple and priesthood is evident in the "consecration" of city gates and walls (Neh 3:1–2), the "purification" of people, gates, and walls, and the concern for the "holy" seed (Ezra 9:2) and the "holy" city (Neh 11:1, 18). In summary, rather than equating the house of God with the city, as Eskenazi does, a more appropriate expression of the connection between the reconstruction of the temple and of the city in Ezra-Nehemiah might be this: "The fortification becomes the extension, or even the culmination of the temple-building."[173]

---

[171] Ibid., 2, cf. 53–57, 71–73, 83–87, 104–5, 119–21, 188–89.

[172] בית אלהים (39x): Ezra 1:7; 2:28; 4:24; 5:2, 8, 13, 14, 15, 16, 17; 6:3, 5 [bis], 7, 8, 12, 16, 17; 7:16, 17, 19, 20, 23, 24; 8:17, 25, 30, 33; 9:9; Neh 10:33, 34, 35, 37 [bis], 38, 39, 40; 13:4, 14; בית האלהים (18x): Ezra 1:4; 2:68; 3:8, 9; 6:22; 8:36; 10:1, 6, 9; Neh 6:10; 8:16; 11:11, 16, 22; 12:40; 13:7, 9, 11.

[173] Halpern, "A Historiographic Commentary on Ezra 1–6," 112. Therefore, Ezra 6:14 remains a proleptic statement that embraces the whole of Ezra-Nehemiah due to the narrative connection between the building of the temple and the building of the city but not, as Eskenazi would have it, due to the identification of the city with the "house of God." Cf. VanderKam ("Ezra and Nehemiah?" 70–74), who, in reaction against Eskenazi's extension of the "house of God" to embrace the city, insists that the prolepsis of Ezra 6:14 embraces only the book of Ezra.

The Synchronic Study of the Covenant Renewal (Nehemiah 7:72b–10:40)

Given the above qualifications, Eskenazi's study nevertheless succeeds in establishing the literary value of Ezra-Nehemiah. Her treatment contemplates the book as a literary whole. Her study of the Ezra-Nehemiah macrocosm invites analogous study of its microcosm to determine the applicability of a synchronic approach to a specific segment of the work. A detailed examination of a key segment of Ezra-Nehemiah will provide a more precise probing of the narrative landscape in search of literary features that elude a global study such as Eskenazi's.

I undertake a synchronic analysis of the covenant renewal (Neh 7:72b–10:40) for two reasons. First, until now no one has provided a detailed synchronic study of any portion of Ezra-Nehemiah; second, there has not been a monograph devoted exclusively to Neh 8–10 since that of M. Kegel in 1921.[174] Since the history of research demonstrates that the covenant renewal (Neh 7:72b–10:40) constitutes the narrative crux of the whole book, this passage stands out as prime potential subject matter for the first synchronic analysis of a particular segment of Ezra-Nehemiah.

This study of the covenant renewal in Ezra-Nehemiah proceeds in six more chapters. In the next chapter, I provide an outline of Ezra-Nehemiah in order to locate the covenant-renewal passage within its context. In the same chapter, after providing a delimitation of the covenant-renewal account, I describe the structure and note the subdivisions of this portion of Ezra-Nehemiah (Neh 7:72b–10:40). In the subsequent four chapters, I focus on each portion of the covenant-renewal account: (1) Ezra's reading of the law (7:72b–8:12) and the Festival of Booths (8:13–18); (2) the penitential rites (9:1–5); (3) the Levites' psalm (9:1–37); and (4) the signing of the agreement and the legal stipulations (10:1–40). I examine each section according to a five-part format: a fresh translation of the text; discussion of significant matters of textual criticism; an outline and literary analysis highlighting the narrative features within the covenant renewal; an examination of terminology within the broader context of Ezra-Nehemiah and related biblical and extrabiblical material; and a thematic summary of the results. A concluding chapter draws together the literary and theological findings of the study.

---

[174] Kegel, *Die Kultusreformation des Esra.*

2

The Context and Structure of the Covenant-Renewal Account (Nehemiah 7:72b–10:40)

The covenant-renewal account[1] (Neh 7:72b–10:40) constitutes a central but distinct unit within the complex of Ezra-Nehemiah. In order to show both its function within the narrative whole and its distinctiveness as a literary unit, I provide in this chapter the following three-part synchronic analysis of the context and structure of the covenant-renewal account: an outline of the whole book; a delimitation of the boundaries of the covenant-renewal account; and a detailed analysis of the literary structure of the account.

OUTLINE OF EZRA-NEHEMIAH

Ezra-Nehemiah presents a remarkably cohesive portrait of the foundation of postexilic Judaism. The following discussion progressively focuses on the covenant-renewal account itself through a four-stage examination of the book's contents: (1) the foundational two-part historiographical structure of the whole work; (2) the unifying features of Ezra 1–6; (3) the unifying features of Ezra 7–Neh 13; and (4) the function of the covenant renewal-account within the whole complex.

---

[1] I employ the expression "covenant-renewal account" for Neh 7:72b–10:40 because it represents the common nomenclature for the overall contents of this portion of Ezra-Nehemiah. As noted above (pp. 21–22), Baltzer (*Covenant Formulary*, 44–47), Kellermann (*Nehemia*, 90–92), and McCarthy ("Covenant and Law," 101–11) designate the event described in Neh 7:72b–10:40 as a "covenant renewal." Williamson (*Ezra, Nehemiah*, 275–76) subscribes to their thesis. Blenkinsopp (*Ezra-Nehemiah*, 312) notes similarities between Neh 9–10 and the covenant ceremony at Qumran (1QS). However, in contrast to their diachronic analyses, I will examine Neh 7:72b–10:40 purely as a literary construct, prescinding from issues of historicity. Therefore, in my study, "covenant renewal" designates a narrative theme independent of concern for its historical occurrence.

Table 2.1—The Book of Ezra-Nehemiah
I. Ezra 1–6: Construction of the temple after the exile (538–515 B.C.E.)
   A. 1:1–4: Cyrus's decree for the construction of the temple
   B. 1:5–11: Journey of the people and temple vessels to Jerusalem
   C. 2:1–70: Census of the returning exiles
   D. 3:1–13: Reestablishment of foundations at the temple site
   E. 4:1–24: Opposition from outsiders
   F. 5:1–6:15: Completion of the temple
   G. 6:16–22: Dedication of the temple and the festival of Passover
II. Ezra 7–Neh 13: Ezra and Nehemiah build the community (458–432 B.C.E.)
   A. Ezra 7:1–10:44 Ezra's journey to Jerusalem and marriage reform
      1. 7:1–10: Introduction: Ezra, priest and scribe of the Torah
      2. 7:11–26: Artaxerxes' decree regarding the temple and the Torah
      3. 7:27–8:36: Ezra's journey to Jerusalem
      4. 9:1–10:44: Ezra's marriage reform
   B. Neh 1:1–7:72a: Nehemiah's wall project and social reform
      1. 1:1–2:8: Introduction: Nehemiah, cupbearer for the king
      2. 2:9–20: Inspection of the walls
      3. 3:1–32: Initial phase of the work: laborers on the walls
      4. 3:33–4:23: Dealing with opposition
      5. 5:1–19: Economic, social, and political reform
      6. 6:1–7:4: Further opposition and completion of the walls
      7. 7:5–72a: Census of the returning exiles
   C. Neh 7:72b–10:40: Covenant renewal with Ezra and Nehemiah
      1. 7:72b–8:12: Ezra's introductory reading of the Torah
      2. 8:13–18: The leaders' study of the Torah
      3. 9:1–10:40: The people's reading of the Torah
         a. 9:1–5: Penitential rites
         b. 9:6–37: Penitential psalm
         c. 10:1–40: Commitment to the Torah
   D. Neh 11:1–12:43: Repopulation of Jerusalem under Ezra and Nehemiah
      1. 11:1–12:26: The inhabitants of Jerusalem and surrounding areas
      2. 12:27–43: Dedication of the walls with Ezra and Nehemiah
   E. Neh 12:44–13:31: Nehemiah's application of the Torah
      1. 12:44–13:3: Decisions concerning service and membership
      2. 13:4–31: Nehemiah's governance according to the Torah

THE OVERALL STRUCTURE OF EZRA-NEHEMIAH

In terms of subject-matter, Ezra-Nehemiah contains six major sections: (1) the reconstruction of the temple (Ezra 1:1–6:22); (2) Ezra's marriage reform (Ezra 7:1–10:44); (3) the reconstruction of the city walls (Neh 1:1–7:72a); (4) the renewal of the covenant (Neh 7:72b–10:40); (5) the repopulating of Jerusalem and the dedication of the city walls (Neh 11:1–12:43); and (6) Nehemiah's subsequent reforms (Neh 12:44–13:31).[2] Various boundary markers define the limits of each section: (1) Ezra 7:1 elaborately introduces a new protagonist, Ezra (7:1–6); (2) Neh 1:1 has the title (דברי נחמיה בן־חכליה: "the words of Nehemiah, son of Hacaliah"); (3) Neh 7:72b (ובני ישראל בעריהם: "the Israelites being in their towns") repeats a nominal phrase (cf. 7:72a: וכל ישראל בעריהם: "all Israel being in their towns"); (4) Neh 11:1 has the formal transition from first-person speech (Neh 10:40) to third-person narrative; and (5) Neh 12:44 shifts from first-person memoir (cf. 12:40) to third-person narrative and changes the subject matter from the dedication of the city walls (Neh 12:27–43) to more long-term administrative concerns (Neh 12:44–13:4).

However, as Japhet has demonstrated,[3] temporal indicators frame all this activity within two historical periods of approximately a quarter-century each: first, from the first year of Cyrus (Ezra 1:1, 538 B.C.E.) until the sixth year of Darius (Ezra 6:15, 515 B.C.E.) and, second, from the seventh year of Artaxerxes (Ezra 7:7, 458 B.C.E.) until the period immediately following the thirty-second year of Artaxerxes (Neh 13:6, ca. 432 B.C.E.). Thus, the primary division within Ezra-Nehemiah is between Ezra 1–6, which recounts the construction of the temple between 538 and 515 B.C.E., and Ezra 7–Neh 13, which narrates the activities of Ezra and Nehemiah from 458 to ca. 432 B.C.E.

Each era is defined by the initiatives of a Persian king whose name surfaces at various points from beginning to end: Cyrus in the first period (Ezra 1:1–4, 7, 8; 3:7; 5:13–15; 6:2b–5, 14; cf. 4:3, 5), and Artaxerxes in the second (Ezra 7:1, 7, 11–26; 8:1; Neh 2:1; 5:14; 13:6; cf. Ezra 4:7, 8, 11, 23; 6:14). The self-initiated edicts[4] of each of these kings provide parallel introductions to the above sections by setting in motion the events that follow. Thus, the edict of Cyrus (Ezra 1:2–4) launches the construction of the temple (Ezra 1:5–6:22), while the edict of Artaxerxes (Ezra 7:12–26) directly propels the mission of Ezra from his journey to Jerusalem to his reading of the Torah (Ezra 7:1–Neh 8:18) and, via its directive to implement the law in Judah (Ezra 7:14, 25–26), indirectly sustains the application of the Torah to the community's life, which continues to the conclusion of the book (Neh 12:44–13:31; cf. 10:29–40).

---

[2] This generic division of the text reflects the distribution of the major sources: Ezra 1–6 (archival documents of the Achaemenid administration); Ezra 7–10 (EM); Neh 1–7 (NM); Neh 8–10 (EM and other sources); Neh 11:1–12:43 (personnel lists and NM); and Neh 12:44–13:31 (two narrative fragments concerning the assembly for worship and the NM).

[3] Japhet, "Composition and Chronology," 208–15. See above pp. 44–47.

[4] Written inquiries from provincial officials prompt the book's two other royal ordinances from Artaxerxes (Ezra 4:17–22) and Darius (6:2b–12), respectively.

A dozen common thematic devices provide further parallels between Ezra 1–6 and Ezra 7–Neh 13: (1) a narrative portrayal of the Persian king as a divine instrument (Ezra 1:1; cf. Neh 2:4–6); (2) journeys from exile to Jerusalem (Ezra 1:5, 11; cf. 7:6, 7–9; 8:15–32; Neh 2:7–11); (3) a major reconstruction project in Jerusalem certified by the king (Ezra 1:2–4; 3:7–10; 4:24–6:15; cf. Neh 2:1–8; 2:9–6:15); (4) opposition from outsiders, who instill fear in the builders (Ezra 4:1–5; cf. Neh 2:10, 19–20; 3:33–4:17; 6:1–19); (5) the opponents' interpretation of the wall project as an act of rebellion (Ezra 4:11–16; cf. Neh 2:19; 6:6–7); (6) the guidance of the Torah (Ezra 3:2; 6:18; cf. 7:6, 10; 10:3; Neh 8:1–18; 9:3, 13–14, 26, 29, 34; 10:29–30, 35, 37; 12:44; 13:3); (7) the census list of the exiles who returned (Ezra 2:1–70; cf. Neh 7:6–72a); (8) two liturgical celebrations, the first characterized by a mixture of joy and sorrow (Ezra 3:10–13; cf. Neh 8:1–12), the second suffused with undiluted joy at the climax of the section (Ezra 6:16–22; cf. Neh 12:27–43); (9) the climactic celebration as a dedication (חנכה) of the completed edifice (Ezra 6:16; cf. Neh 12:27); (10) the Festival of Booths (Ezra 3:4–6; cf. Neh 8:13–18); (11) the transport of temple vessels from Babylon to Jerusalem (Ezra 1:7–11; cf. 8:19, 26–27, 33); and (12) focus on priests and Levites: the appointment of Levites for construction work on the temple (Ezra 3:8–9; cf. Neh 11:16), the purification of priests and Levites during the climactic celebration (Ezra 6:20; cf. Neh 12:30), and their undertaking regular duties at the temple (Ezra 6:18; cf. Neh 13:30).

Such parallels indicate that the reforms accomplished during the approximate quarter-century spanning the missions of Ezra and Nehemiah (Ezra 7–Neh 13, 458–ca.432 B.C.E.) continued the restoration that began with the reconstruction of the temple in the equivalent time span immediately after the exile (Ezra 1–6, 538–515 B.C.E.). The narrative thus blends these chronologically distinct eras into a theological continuum that presents the reforms under Ezra and Nehemiah as the divinely ordered sequel to the reconstruction of the temple. Just as YHWH "stirred up the spirit of King Cyrus" (Ezra 1:1) and kept "[his] eye ... upon the elders of the Jews" (5:5) to bring about the reconstruction of the temple, so his "hand was upon" Ezra and Nehemiah to accomplish their missions (Ezra 7:6, 9; 8:18, 22, 31; Neh 2:8, 18).

Three literary devices further meld the two eras into a continuous sequence of salvation history: (1) in Ezra 7:1, the temporal transition (ואחר הדברים האלה) bridges more than a half-century from the sixth year of Darius to the seventh year of Artaxerxes; (2) in Ezra 6:14, the summary statement embraces all of Ezra-Nehemiah, owing to the inclusion of Artaxerxes with Cyrus and Darius in their combined role as "king of Persia" responsible for completing the temple;[5] and (3) in the three major royal decrees (Ezra

---

[5] Mention of Artaxerxes here is a proleptic reference primarily to his decree mandating contributions to the temple via Ezra (Ezra 7:15–20; 8:25–26, 33–34, 35)

The Context and Structure of the Covenant Renewal Account

1:2–4; 6:2b–12; 7:12–26), a distinctive theological coloring reinforces the narrator's equating these with a singular divine edict (טעם/מטעם, Ezra 6:14).[6] Narrative continuity overrides the disjunctions in the chronological sequences throughout the remainder of Ezra-Nehemiah.[7] Thus, the narrative unfolds the story of the definitive reshaping of Judaism in the postexilic era and the reestablishment of its normative expression in Jerusalem.

UNIFYING FEATURES OF EZRA 1–6

The theme of building the temple provides the *inclusio* for the first era: the story begins with Cyrus's decree mandating the project (Ezra 1:1–4)

---

and secondarily to his permitting Nehemiah to rebuild the walls insofar as they represent an extension of the holiness associated with the temple (cf. Neh 3:1–2; 7:1–2; 11:1, 18; 12:30).

[6] In the decree that begins the story, Cyrus mentions God five times in three verses (Ezra 1:2–4). Darius follows suit by mandating not only the completion of the temple but also the provisions for sacrifices, while invoking divine retribution on anyone opposing God's temple (Ezra 6:9, 12). Artaxerxes, for his part, speaks of God in ten of eleven verses in the decree he addresses directly to Ezra (Ezra 7:12–20, 25–26). By comparison, such a theological aspect is notably lacking in Artaxerxes' letter to Rehum (Ezra 4:17–22; cf. 1:2–4; 6:2b–12; 7:12–26).

[7] The dating notations concentrate all activity at only five points of time within a span of some 106 years: (1) from the first year of Cyrus through the second year after the arrival of the exiles (Ezra 1:1; 3:8, 538–ca. 536 B.C.E. [Ezra 1:1–4:24]); (2) from the second year of Darius to the sixth year of Darius (Ezra 4:24; 6:15, 520–515 B.C.E. [Ezra 5:1–6:22]); (3) the seventh year of Artaxerxes (Ezra 7:7–8, 458 B.C.E. [Ezra 7:1–10:44]); (4) the twentieth year of Artaxerxes (Neh 2:1; cf. 1:1; 5:14, 445 B.C.E. [Neh 1:1–13:3]); and (5) just after the thirty-second year of Artaxerxes (Neh 13:6, ca. 432 B.C.E. [Neh 13:4–31]). Taken in isolation, these dates would convey the impression of chronological fragmentation as if the history recorded occurred in bits and pieces following a pattern of fits and starts. However, four transitional notations link the five segments: (1) Ezra 4:24 (cf. 4:5) mentions the duration of the work stoppage on the temple project (באדין ... בטלא עד שנת תרתין למלכות דריוש מלך־פרס: "at that time [the work on the temple stopped] ... and was discontinued until the second year of reign of Darius, king of Persia") and establishes a transition between the reigns of Cyrus and Darius; (2) Ezra 7:1 is the temporal transition (ואחר הדברים האלה: "after these events") covering more than a half-century from the sixth year of Darius to the seventh year of Artaxerxes; (3) Neh 1:1 has the temporal notice (בחדש כסלו שנת עשרים: "in the month of Chislev, in the twentieth year"), with a merely implied reference to Artaxerxes, joining the following account with the preceding narrative, which began with mention of the king's regnal year (Ezra 7:7–8); and (4) Neh 12:44 and 13:1 have the identical temporal indications (ביום ההוא: "on that day"), connecting temple regulations (12:44–13:3) to the dedication of the walls (12:27–43) and, thereby, linking Nehemiah's activities after the thirty-second year of Artaxerxes (Neh 13:4–31) with the culminating event in the king's twentieth year.

and concludes with the summary description of its completion (Ezra 6:13–15) and dedication (6:16–18), followed by the celebration of Passover (6:19–22). The account of the completion of the temple recalls the presentation of the introductory decree via the initial and final references to Cyrus in the book (1:1; 6:14) as well as via allusions to the prophetic word, namely, to Jeremiah in the beginning (1:1)[8] and to Haggai and Zechariah at the end (6:14). The subsequent celebration of the temple dedication (6:16–18) recalls the setting up of the altar and laying of the temple foundations (3:1–13), given the following common elements: the "children of Israel" (בני ישראל, 6:16; cf. 3:1); the "house of God" (6:16; cf. 3:9); the appointment of Levites (6:18; cf. 3:8b–9); and conformity with the law of Moses (6:18; cf. 3:2).[9] Moreover, mention of joy (שמחה/חדוה) and references to both priests and Levites connect the dedication festival (6:16–18) to the following narrative of the Festivals of Passover and Unleavened Bread (6:19–22), while also relating this latter episode to the laying of the foundations of the temple (3:10–13).

Between the decree of Cyrus (1:1–4) and the dedication of the temple (6:16–22), the story of Ezra 1–6 unfolds in five segments: (1) the journey of the people (with the temple vessels) to Jerusalem (1:5–11); (2) the settlement of the exiles from Babylon in Judah and Jerusalem (2:1–70); (3) the beginning of the construction project (3:1–13); (4) delay due to opposition by outsiders (4:1–24); and (5) the resolution of the crisis by royal mandate to complete the construction (5:1–6:15).

The journey from exile to Jerusalem and the construction of the temple take on a dramatic quality, given their implications for defining postexilic Israel. The narrative *ab initio* clearly establishes that those who return from exile—including the families of Judah and Benjamin, along with the priests and Levites—constitute the authentic community (1:5). The census list provides the names of those people whom God personally "stirred up" to return to the land (2:1–70; cf. 1:5). Building the temple affords the occasion for defining the community; the crisis evolves

---

[8] In Ezra 1:1, the phrase העיר יהוה את־רוח כרש ("YHWH stirred up the spirit of Cyrus") recalls Jer 51:11 ("YHWH has stirred up the spirit [העיר יהוה את־רוח] of the kings of the Medes because his purpose against Babylon is to destroy it, for this is the vengeance of YHWH, vengeance for his temple") as well as irenic texts in Deutero-Isaiah concerning Cyrus, such as Isa 45:13 ("I have stirred him up [העירתהו] in righteousness, and all his paths I will make straight; he shall build my city and send forth my exiles"; cf. 41:2, 25). A reference to Jeremiah's prophecies that speak of "seventy years" of exile (Jer 29:10; cf. 25:11–12) is evident in 2 Chr 36:22 (cf. 36:20–21) but less likely in Ezra 1:1. See Williamson, *Ezra, Nehemiah*, 9–10; idem, "Did the Author of Chronicles Also Write the Books of Ezra and Nehemiah?" *BRev* 3 (Spring 1987): 59 n. 6; cf. Blenkinsopp, *Ezra-Nehemiah*, 74–75.

[9] Blenkinsopp, *Ezra-Nehemiah*, 130.

precisely because Zerubbabel and Jeshua reject the outsiders' claim to membership and therefore to participation in the project (4:2–3). The narrator balances this episode of exclusion (4:1–3) with the description of the inclusion of proselytes at the Passover (6:21). Thus, the community expands from beginning (1:5) to end (6:21) but nevertheless defines itself in terms of separation (בדל‎ *nipʿal*) from the nations in the land and attachment to "YHWH, the God of Israel" (6:21).

Citation of the Persian correspondence in Aramaic demonstrates that such Judahite exclusivism, while generating controversy, ultimately has imperial support. The drama of the interruption and recommencement of work on the temple (4:4–6:12) provides the setting for a firsthand illustration of the debate among Gentile officials regarding the emergence of Judaism. Rehum's description of Jerusalem as "rebellious and wicked" (מרדתא ובאישתא‎, 4:12) and his viewing its previous destruction as a justified military response to sedition in Judah (4:15) contrast with Tattenai's observation of Judahite "diligence" and "effectiveness" in the work on the "house of the great God" (cf. 5:8, ועבידתא דך אספרנא מתעבדא ומצלח בידהם‎: "this work is being done diligently and prospers in their hands") and his quoting of the Judahite vision of Jerusalem's destruction as a manifestation of God's retributive justice (5:12). Should then an outsider view the Judahites[10] with suspicion or admiration? Ultimately, the edicts of the foreign kings Cyrus and Darius (6:2b–12) adjudicate the debate in favor of the latter.

UNIFYING FEATURES OF EZRA 7–NEHEMIAH 13

The interweaving of the careers of Ezra and Nehemiah is the foundational feature uniting the five parts of Ezra 7–Neh 13: (1) Ezra's marriage reform (Ezra 7:1–10:44); (2) Nehemiah's building of the walls and social reform (Neh 1:1–7:72a); (3) the covenant-renewal ceremony initiated by Ezra with the participation of Nehemiah (Neh 7:72b–10:40); (4) the repopulation of Jerusalem and the dedication of the walls under Nehemiah with the participation of Ezra (Neh 11:1–12:43); and (5) Nehemiah's initiatives following the covenant renewal (Neh 12:44–13:31).[11]

Abundant parallels in the descriptions of Ezra and Nehemiah reinforce the impression that they work with providential synergy. Some of the

---

[10] The term "the Judahites" (or "the Jews": יהודים/יהודיא‎) occurs only in the Aramaic portion of Ezra (Ezra 4:8–6:18, 8x: 4:12, 23; 5:1, 5; 6:7 [bis], 8, 14) and in the NM (Neh 1–7, 9x: 1:2; 2:16; 3:33, 34; 4:6; 5:1, 8, 17; 6:6; Neh 12:27–13:31, 1x: 13:23).

[11] A stylistic feature further contributes to the unity of Ezra 7–Neh 13: the autobiographical form links the first two parts (Ezra 7–10; Neh 1–7) and, at the end, ties them to the last part (Neh 12:44–13:31).

features common to the portrayal of both figures are: (1) personal sponsorship by Artaxerxes attested to in a letter (Ezra 7:12–26; cf. Neh 2:7–8); (2) official status within the Persian administration (Ezra 7:12, 21, 25–26 [scribe]; Neh 5:14 [governor]); (3) "the good hand of his God was upon [him]" (Ezra 7:6, 9; 8:18, 22, 31; cf. Neh 2:8, 18); (4) utterance of a penitential prayer on behalf of the people (Ezra 9:6–15; cf. Neh 1:5–11); (5) devotional practices of "weeping" (Ezra 10:1; Neh 1:4), "fasting" (Ezra 8:21, 23; cf. Neh 1:4), and "mourning" (Ezra 10:6; cf. Neh 1:4); (6) a decision made about a military escort for the journey to Jerusalem (Ezra 8:22; cf. Neh 2:9b); (7) a three-day hiatus after arriving in Jerusalem before undertaking activity there (Ezra 8:32; cf. Neh 2:11); (8) formal presentation of the letters of recommendation from the king (Ezra 8:36; cf. Neh 2:9); and (9) confrontation with priest(s) concerning mixed marriages (Ezra 10:18–19; cf. Neh 13:28).[12]

The objective that unites the efforts of Ezra and Nehemiah is the defining of the community by separating the people from outsiders.[13] Each leader establishes the separation primarily by activity that characterizes him: Ezra as teacher of the Torah, Nehemiah as builder of the city walls. The narrative portrays them working in tandem.[14] At the beginning of their missions in Jerusalem, each one must confront the foreign nemesis: in his marriage reform, Ezra expels the foreign wives and children (Ezra 9:1–10:44); in reconstructing the city walls, Nehemiah counteracts the hostile threats of outsiders (Neh 2:17–4:17; 6:1–19). In turn, the reconstruction of the walls becomes a symbol of the redefinition of the community. Nehemiah must complete the walls (7:1–4) before Ezra can initiate the people into the full community life as defined by the Torah (Neh 7:72b–10:40). Conversely, only after defining themselves by signing their allegiance to the precepts of the Torah are the people qualified to repopulate "the holy city" (Neh 11:1, 18) and to dedicate the city walls in solemn procession with Ezra and Nehemiah (12:27–43). Only in the end is there a convergence of the protagonists' roles as Nehemiah assumes the mantle of the advocate of the Torah who enforces the precepts of the covenant pledge

---

[12] Cf. Kellermann, *Nehemia*, 94–95.

[13] For Ezra and Nehemiah, the families, priests, and Levites who have come from exile constitute the nucleus of the community (see Ezra 8:1–14, 15–20; Neh 7:6–72a).

[14] Initially, the narrative presents the missions of Ezra and Nehemiah in sequential sections (Ezra 7:1–10:44; Neh 1:1–7:72a) that, at least in part, share in common the autobiographical form (Ezra 7:27–9:15; Neh 1:1–7:5). The partnership between the two protagonists becomes explicit at the reading of the Torah (Neh 8:9), in the conclusion of the priestly and Levitical genealogies (Neh 12:26), and at the dedication of the walls (Neh 12:33, 36; cf. 12:31–43).

(12:44–13:31; cf. 10:29–40), which includes reforming marriages to foreigners, a task reminiscent of the one that had confronted Ezra at the beginning of his mission in Jerusalem (13:23–27; cf. Ezra 9:1–10:44).

THE COVENANT-RENEWAL ACCOUNT WITHIN EZRA-NEHEMIAH

Against the background of the above consideration of the unifying features of Ezra 1–6 and Ezra 7–Neh 13, we can now appreciate the pivotal role that the covenant-renewal account plays in the Ezra-Nehemiah story. The narrative of the covenant renewal (Neh 7:72b–10:40) constitutes the climax of Ezra-Nehemiah because it represents the defining moment for the postexilic community. The missions of Ezra and Nehemiah converge precisely at this point when they are mentioned together for the first time (8:9). The function of this intersection of the narrative lines of the whole story is evident from a variety of motifs, including: (1) the assembly of the people, (2) focus on the Torah, (3) prayer, and (4) the temple.

The assembly of "all the people" in front of the Water Gate (8:1–18) represents the summit of a series of earlier gatherings that shape the community: the foundation of the temple (Ezra 3:1–13), the dedication of the temple and the Festival of Passover (6:16–22); Ezra's preparation at Ahava for the *aliyah* to Jerusalem (8:21–30); his expulsion of foreign wives and children (10:1–17); and Nehemiah's socioeconomic reform (Neh 5:1–13). Furthermore, the subsequent procession of the community around the walls (12:27–43) is a sequel to the plenary assembly at the Water Gate (8:1–10:40). Ezra's proclamation of the Torah (Neh 8:1–18) actualizes the promise cited in the narrator's introduction of him as "a scribe skilled in the Torah of Moses" (Ezra 7:6; cf. 7:10, 11) and in Artaxerxes' commissioning him to teach "the laws of your God" (7:25–26; cf. 7:14). The communal recitation of the psalm (Neh 9:6–37) echoes Ezra's confessional prayer in Jerusalem (Ezra 9:6–15) and that of Nehemiah in Susa (Neh 1:5–11). Concern for the affairs of the temple (Neh 10:33–40) foreshadows the book's closing note (Neh 13:30–31), which serves as an *inclusio* for the whole work (Ezra 1:1–4).[15]

---

[15] The concluding section that describes the follow-up work of Nehemiah (Neh 12:44–13:31) relates back to the covenant signing (Neh 10:1–40), given its references to the stipulations of the oath enumerated there: (1) contributions and tithes (Neh 12:44; cf. 10:36–40); (2) separation from foreigners (13:1–3; cf. 10:29); (3) the chambers for storage at the temple (13:4–5; cf. 10:38–40); (4) the tithes for the Levites (13:10–14; cf. 10:38); (5) Sabbath observance (13:15–22; cf. 10:32a); (6) marriage to foreigners (13:23–29; cf. 10:31); and (7) the wood offering (13:31; cf. 10:35). From a narrative perspective, Nehemiah's final activities are the practical implementation of the covenant stipulations and thereby testify to the centrality of the covenant renewal for the whole book.

The Delimitation of the Covenant-Renewal Account

With regard to the precise boundaries of the covenant-renewal account, debate centers more on where the section begins than on where it ends. The nearly unanimous consensus is that, from a narrative viewpoint, the covenant-renewal account ends at Neh 10:40.[16] Features of both form and content define Neh 11:1–2 as the beginning of a new section. The narrator's voice in the third person (Neh 11:1–2) here replaces the utterances in the first person, which began with the Levites' praying of the psalm (9:6–37) and continued with the people's declaration of commitment to the stipulations of the oath (10:1, 31–40). A shift in subject matter is also evident, as the major concern for repopulating Jerusalem (11:1–2) supplants preoccupation with spiritual renewal, which had predominated throughout the reading of the Torah (Neh 8:1–12), the Festival of Booths (8:13–18), the penitential service (9:1–37), and the signing of the pledge (10:1–40). The lists in Neh 10 and 11, respectively, further reflect this diversity of concern: Neh 10:2–27 provides the names of the officials, priests, and Levites who signed the pledge, whereas Neh 11:3–36 identifies the leaders, priests, and Levites (11:3–24) as well as the people (11:25–36) according to the location of their residences.[17]

The debate over the precise beginning of the covenant-renewal account concerns whether or not the census list of those who returned after the exile (Neh 7:6–72a) should be included as part of that account. The alternative proposals on the matter are: (1) the covenant-renewal account begins with Nehemiah's introduction to the census list (Neh 7:5b); or (2) it starts afresh with the narrator's description of the assembly in the seventh month (7:72b) subsequent to the census list (7:6–72a).

Four arguments seem to favor the proposal that the covenant-renewal account embraces Neh 7:5b–10:40.[18] First, Neh 11:1 resumes the narrative

---

[16] Even Clines—who separates Neh 8–9 from Neh 10 on the basis of his source-critical hypothesis that Neh 10 originally followed Neh 13—grants that, in the final arrangement of the book, Neh 8–10 is a unit: "It ... seems that the present position of Neh. 10, along with the link verse (9:38 [10:1]), is due to the post-Chronicler editor's sense that the pledge document formed an appropriate conclusion to a ceremony of national repentance" (*Ezra, Nehemiah, Esther*, 180–99, 200). Cf. Batten, *Ezra and Nehemiah*, 352–53, 372–73.

[17] At the same time, three elements in Neh 11:1–2 do provide linkage between the covenant-renewal account and the narrative of the repopulating of Jerusalem: the leaders (שרים, 11:1; cf. 10:1; 9:32, 34), the tithe (10:39–40, מעשר; cf. 11:1, אחד מן־העשרה), and the casting of lots (נפל גורלות [*hip'il*], 11:1; cf. 10:35).

[18] Two main advocates of this position are Gunneweg (*Esra*, 103–39, 140–41), who entitles Neh 7:4–10:40 "Die Konstituierung der Gemeinde," and Blenkinsopp (*Ezra-Nehemiah*, 277, 278–319, 322–23), who considers 7:5b–10:40 to be a cohesive unit.

preoccupation with the repopulation of Jerusalem that begins in 7:4. Nehemiah 7:4 relates to 11:1 via two factors: concern over the sparse habitation of the city; and employment of the term "city" to designate Jerusalem (העיר, 7:4; cf. עיר הקדש, 11:1).[19] Moreover, the threefold mention of Jerusalem in Neh 11:1–2 markedly contrasts with Neh 8–10, which contains only a single reference to Jerusalem (8:15). Such concentration on Jerusalem previously occurs in its twofold mention (7:2, 3) in Nehemiah's instructions concerning the city following the completion of the walls and gates (7:1–3).

Second, Nehemiah's discourse in the first person breaks off at Neh 7:5. Blenkinsopp discusses this verse from a source-critical perspective and makes two assertions: (1) 7:5a exhibits the distinctive vocabulary of the NM; and (2) 11:1–2 reflects the content (if not the autobiographical form) that would have provided the appropriate continuation of Neh 7:5a in the NM.[20] Moreover, the lists in Neh 11:3–19, 20–24 correspond better with Nehemiah's intention of repopulating Jerusalem as articulated in 7:5 than does the citation of the census list of the exiles who returned in the previous century (7:6–72a).[21] Therefore, Neh 7:5b–72a belongs with 7:72b–10:40 as part of the insertion that interrupts the flow of the original NM from 7:5a to 11:1–2.

---

[19] Of its fourteen occurrences throughout Ezra-Nehemiah, the term *city* in the singular (עיר) refers to Jerusalem ten times (Neh 2:3, 5, 8; 3:15; 7:4; 11:1, 9, 18; 12:37; 13:18; cf. Ezra 2:1; 10:14 [bis]; Neh 7:6).

[20] Blenkinsopp (*Ezra-Nehemiah*, 277) ascribes 7:5a to the NM on the basis of its use of three expressions: (1) "the nobles, the officials, and the people" (cf. 2:16; 4:8, 13, [14, 19]; 5:7); (2) "my God" (see 2:8, 12, 18; 5:19; 6:14); and (3) "my God put it into my mind" (see 2:12). He admits that Neh 11:1–2 deviates from the NM in both its third-person form and vocabulary (e.g., שרים [11:1] instead of חרים or סגנים [7:5]), but he accounts for the differences by proposing that the present form of 11:1–2 derives from a parallel source that contained the same material as the original NM (ibid., 322–23; so also, Batten, *Ezra and Nehemiah*, 265; and Clines, *Ezra, Nehemiah, Esther*, 201). By contrast, Kellermann (*Nehemia*, 23–26, 44–45) asserts that the NM, which is interrupted at 7:5, continues again only with the resumption of Nehemiah's first-person discourse in the account of the dedication of the walls (12:31–32, 37–40). However, Kellermann fails to show how Nehemiah's finding of the genealogical record (7:5) could link directly with the description of the dedication (12:31).

[21] Neh 11:3–36 contains two lists: (1) the residents of Jerusalem (11:1–20; cf. 1 Chr 9:2–17); and (2) the settlements in Judah and Benjamin (11:25–36). Nehemiah 11:21–24 is a secondary expansion of the first list. The subsequent list of priests and Levites (12:1–26) further develops the subject matter of 11:10–24. This list exhibits a distinctive chronological concern (cf. 12:7, 12, 22, 23, 26) and composite texture. Cf. Williamson, *Ezra, Nehemiah*, 344–53, 358–62; Blenkinsopp, *Ezra-Nehemiah*, 322–34.

Third, the parallels between the census lists in Ezra 2:1–70 and Neh 7:6–72a extend into the respective narrative continuations (e.g., Ezra 3:1 and Neh 7:72b–8:1a). Therefore, by analogy with the continuity between Ezra 2:1–70 and 3:1–13, the census list in Neh 7:6–72a belongs more with the subsequent narrative (Neh 7:72b–8:18) than with the preceding material (Neh 1:1–7:5a).

Fourth, the census list of early returnees from exile (Neh 7:6–72a) functions purposefully in leading into the narrative by explicitly naming those included among "all the people" who gather at the Water Gate (8:1). Although this list functions as a prelude to what follows, it does not serve a vital function vis-à-vis what precedes it.

However, a close reading of the text argues against viewing Neh 7:5b and the list of early returnees (7:6–72a) as the beginning of the covenant-renewal account. The plain sense of the text contradicts the arguments from source criticism advanced by Blenkinsopp. First, Neh 11:1–2 does not actually connect directly with Neh 7:4–5a. While the description of repopulating Jerusalem (11:1) does reflect the concern for the sparseness of the city's population (7:4), there is no comparable follow-up in 11:1–2 to the editor's remark that no houses had been constructed (7:4). Second, whereas Nehemiah plans to resolve the population problem by registering the people according to their familial lineages (7:5a), in fact the people decide the issue in another way, namely, by casting lots (11:1).[22] Third, the difference in the designation of the leaders (חרים or סגנים [7:5] rather than שׂרים [11:1]) further accentuates the disjunction between Neh 7:5a and 11:1. Fourth, the list of those who originally returned after the exile (7:6–72a) corresponds better with Nehemiah's stated concern for genealogies (7:5a) than do the lists of the inhabitants of Jerusalem and the towns of Judah (11:3–19, 20–24, 25–36). Therefore, the list of returnees (7:6–72a) does follow logically the narrative that precedes it (7:1–5).

Furthermore, two arguments favor separating the census list from the following covenant-renewal account. First, the first-person discourse of Nehemiah (7:5) cannot extend to the narrative of Ezra's reading of the Torah (7:72b–8:18; see esp. 8:9); it must therefore conclude at the end of the census list (7:6–72a). Second, the list in Neh 7:6–72a does not blend into the subsequent narrative of the Torah reading and the Festival of Booths (7:72b–8:18) with the same finesse that the list in Ezra 2:1–70 flows into the narrative of the laying of the temple foundations (Ezra 3:1–13).[23]

---

[22] Williamson, *Ezra, Nehemiah*, 345.

[23] Ezra 2:68–69 leads directly into the following narrative (3:1–13) via five elements: (1) the people's arriving at the house of YHWH (2:68; cf. 3:8); (2) the presentation of freewill offerings (נדב *hitpaᶜel*, 2:68; cf. 3:5); (3) the intention of building the house of God (2:68; cf. 3:3, 10); (4) the fund for building (מלאכה, 2:69;

Three arguments help establish Neh 7:72b as the beginning of the covenant-renewal account. First, 11:1 provides the narrative sequel to 7:72a. These verses have in common their introductory verb describing the "dwelling" (וישבו) of the leaders as well as mention of "the people" (העם).[24] Moreover, Neh 11:3 reflects the vocabulary and concern of 7:72a with references to the "towns" (בעריהם) in which "Israel" (ישראל), "the priests" (הכהנים), "the Levites" (הלוים), and "the temple servants" (הנתינים) "lived" (ישבו).[25] Since the narrative continues from 7:72a to 11:1–3, the intervening account of the covenant renewal must extend from 7:72b to 10:40.

Second, 7:72a constitutes a summary statement of the preceding census list, which, at the same time, relates this material to the preceding narrative by indirectly reinforcing Nehemiah's concern about the sparseness of the population of Jerusalem (7:4). All of the personnel cited in 7:72a are mentioned in the census list: the priests (הכהנים, 7:72a; cf. 7:39), the Levites (הלוים, 7:72a; cf. 7:43), the gatekeepers (השוערים, 7:72a; cf. 7:45), the singers (המשררים, 7:72a; cf. 7:67), and the temple servants (הנתינים, 7:72a; cf. 7:60). "All Israel" (כל־ישראל, 7:72a) comprises "the whole assembly" (כל־הקהל, 7:66) who returned from Babylon to Judah. The fact that these settled in "their towns" (העריהם, 7:72a) underlines the assertion that "the people" (העם, 7:4; cf. 7:72a) were few in "the city" (העיר, 7:4) of Jerusalem.[26]

---

cf. 3:8) the house of God; and (5) the priestly robes (2:69; cf. 3:10). By contrast, the parallel in Neh 7:69–71 has practically no connection with the account of the covenant renewal that follows (7:72b–10:40). Indeed, reference to the "work" (מלאכה, 7:69, 70) that requires funding links the census list more to the preceding narrative than to the following account since, within this context, the construction of the city wall constitutes this "work" (מלאכה, 2:16; 4:5, 9, 10, 11, 13, 15, 16; 5:16; 6:3, 9, 16; cf. 10:34).

[24] Williamson, *Ezra, Nehemiah*, 273.

[25] Neh 10:29a connects 7:72a and 11:1, 3 via vocabulary it has in common with all three verses: (1) 10:29a and 7:72a: ... הכהנים ו[ה]לוים ו[ה]שוערים ו[ה]משררים [ו]הנתינים ("the priests, Levites, gatekeepers, singers ... and temple servants"); (2) 10:29a and 11:1: שאר העם ("the remainder of the people"); and (3) 10:29a and 11:3: ... הכהנים ו[ה]לוים [ו]הנתינים ("the priests, Levites ... and the temple servants"). Moreover, 10:40 sustains the transition from 7:72a to 11:1 insofar as the officials mentioned in 10:40 recall 7:72a: הלוים/בני לוי ("the Levites"); הכהנים ... והשוערים ומשררים ("the priests ... the gatekeepers, the singers").

[26] Note that Neh 7:72a does not refer to Jerusalem, whereas the parallel in Ezra 2:70 could read, "The priests, the Levites, and some of the people settled in Jerusalem [and its vicinity]," according to an emendation based on LXX 1 Esd 5:45 (καὶ κατῳκίσθησαν οἱ ἱερεῖς καὶ οἱ Λευῖται καὶ οἱ ἐκ τοῦ λαοῦ ἐν Ιερουσαλημ καὶ τῇ χώρᾳ). See Blenkinsopp, *Ezra-Nehemiah*, 94; NAB; NJB; cf. NRSV.

Third, Neh 7:72b begins a new section while, at the same time, linking this with preceding material. The repetition of the phrase regarding the Israelites' living in their towns (וכל/ובני ישראל בעריהם, 7:72b; cf. 7:72a) signals the start of a new narrative portion. This phrase also ties the following account to the foregoing section via use of the same subject, that is, "Israel." However, the transition from "all Israel" (כל־ישראל, 7:72a) to "the children of Israel" (בני ישראל, 7:72b) reflects a leap across generations from the ancestors who arrived immediately after the exile (7:6–72a) to their descendants who gathered some eighty years later to hear Ezra read the Torah (7:72b–8:18).[27] This large chronological gap marks a disjunction between 7:72a and 7:72b.

Moreover, the temporal notice of the "seventh month" (ויגע החדש השביעי: "When the seventh month arrived...," 7:72b) indicates a new beginning, consistent with other dating notices elsewhere in Ezra-Nehemiah (cf. Ezra 3:1, 6; 6:19; 8:31; 10:9; Neh 1:1; 2:1; 8:13; 9:1). In summary, both elements of Neh 7:72b—the date and the description of the Israelites settled in their towns—establish this half-verse as the beginning of the covenant-renewal account that extends to Neh 10:40.

Having established the delimitation of the covenant-renewal account as extending from Neh 7:72b to 10:40, we can proceed to contemplate this section within its immediate context. The covenant-renewal account constitutes the center of a chiasm:

  A   The completion of the city walls (6:1–7:5a)
      B   The list of ancestral inhabitants of Jerusalem and Judah (7:5b–72a)
          C   The covenant renewal (7:72b–10:40)
      B' The repopulating of Jerusalem (11:1–12:26)
  A' The dedication of the city walls (12:27–43).

The story of the repopulating of Jerusalem (11:1–2) picks up the narrative thread from the description of "all Israel" living in the outlying towns (7:72a), which, in turn, seems to underscore the emptiness of the city newly endowed with reconstructed walls (7:4). Nehemiah's designating the list of exiles who returned in the early days (Neh 7:6–72a; cf. Ezra 2:1–70) as a "genealogical record" (ספר היחש, 7:5; cf. Ezra 2:62; 8:1, 3; Neh 7:64)

---

[27] The context in Nehemiah demands the transition from one century to the next. In Nehemiah, the census list is an archival document (ספר היחש: "the book of the genealogy") that Nehemiah "found" (Neh 7:5b) and that identifies "all Israel" as those who returned immediately after the exile. However, the narrative that begins in 7:72b describes events of the mission of Ezra during the reign of Artaxerxes (Ezra 7:7; Neh 6:15). By contrast, in Ezra 2:70–3:1, the terms "all Israel" and "the children of Israel" refer to the same generation, i.e., those who returned to Judah following the edict of Cyrus.

The Context and Structure of the Covenant Renewal Account

suggests the list's purpose as the standard for determining the legitimate members of the community. This list (7:6–72a) goes together with the lists of those who ultimately inhabit the land (11:3–36) and serve at the temple (12:1–26). The descendants of the exiles who returned (7:6–72a) make up the pool of candidates for selection as inhabitants of the "holy city" (11:1, 18; cf. 11:1–20). The covenant renewal intervenes between these lists as the event that definitively reconstitutes "the children of Israel" (7:72b) and thus serves as the necessary prerequisite for resettlement in Jerusalem (11:1–20) and in the outlying regions (11:25–36) as well as for service at the temple (12:1–26).

The dedication of the city walls (12:27–43) ties the narrative to the events that precede the covenant renewal. The focus on the city walls carries over from the description of their completion (6:15–7:5a) to the account of their dedication, and the first-person memoir (12:31–43) surfaces for the first time since 7:5.

In summary, the narrative of the covenant renewal (7:72b–10:40) provides the major transition from the account of the rebuilding of the city walls to that of the reemergence of the renewed Israel in the postexilic era. The narrative of the covenant renewal is intimately related to the subsequent repopulating of Jerusalem and dedication of the city walls (11:1–12:43) in that only these sections present Ezra and Nehemiah as contemporaries working in direct partnership with each other (8:9; 10:2; cf. 12:26, 31–36). Furthermore, the covenant-renewal account is the prerequisite for these subsequent events. The community that defined itself in the renewal of the covenant manifests its new identity, first by providing the candidates for inhabiting Jerusalem (11:1–12:26), and subsequently by celebrating its newly established distinctiveness with the dedication of the walls (12:27–43).

THE STRUCTURE OF THE COVENANT-RENEWAL ACCOUNT (NEHEMIAH 7:72B–10:40)

The covenant-renewal account consists of three parts, each of which involves an assembly for the reading or studying of the Torah: on the first day of the seventh month (8:1–12); on the second day (8:13–18); and on the twenty-fourth day (9:1–10:40).[28] These three parts exhibit commonalities of vocabulary and structure: (1) specification of date (ביום אחד: "on the first day," 8:3; ביום השני: "on the second day," 8:13; ביום עשרים וארבעה: "on the twenty-fourth day," 9:1); (2) the "gathering" (אסף nipʿal: 8:1, 13; 9:1); (3) of the people or their representatives (כל־העם: "all the people," 8:1; ראשי האבות לכל־העם: "the heads of the families of all the

---

[28] Cf. Eskenazi, *In an Age of Prose*, 96–97; M. A. Throntveit, *Ezra-Nehemiah* (IBC; Louisville: John Knox, 1992), 95.

people," 8:13; בני־ישראל: "the Israelites," 9:1); (4) the "reading" (קרא, 8:3, 8, 18; 9:3) or "study" (שכל, 8:13); (5) of "the book, the law of God/YHWH their God" (בספר בתורת יהוה אלהיהם/בספר בתורת האלהים, 8:8, 18; 9:3; cf. 8:2, 3, 13); (6) an exhortation to action ([ו]ויאמר, 8:9, 10; 9:5; cf. לאמר, 8:11, 15); and (7) the people's carrying out of the exhortation (8:12, 16–17; 9:6–37).

Table 2.2—Parallels in Vocabulary and Structure (Neh 7:72b–9:5)

	7:72b–8:12	8:13–18	9:1–5
1. Date	ביום אחד לחדש השביעי	ביום השני	ביום עשרים וארבעה לחדש הזה
2. Assembly	ויאספו	נאספו	נאספו
3. People	בני ישראל כל־העם	בני ישראל ראשי האבות לכל־העם הכהנים והלוים	בני ישראל
4. Reading/ Studying	ויקרא ויקראו	להשכיל ויקרא	ויקראו
5. The Law	בספר בתורת האלהים	אל־דברי התורה בספר תורת האלהים	בספר תורת יהוה אלהיהם
6. Exhortation	ויאמר ויאמר לאמר	לאמר	ויאמרו

Due to the diversity of the material in each part, verbal commonalities are absent from the portions describing the people's carrying out of the exhortation. However, there are formal similarities insofar as, in each instance, the people implement the instructions immediately after they receive them. In the first part, the people heed the admonitions not to grieve but to "go, eat, drink, and send a portion to those who have none" (8:10, 12). In the second, they observe the instruction of the Torah to "go out, bring [branches], and make booths" (8:15, 16).[29] In the third part, by

---

[29] The first and second parts exhibit formal similarities insofar as, in each case, the vocabulary describing the compliance repeats the vocabulary of the exhortation:

(A) Neh 8:10: לכו אכלו ... ושתו ... ושלחו מנות
    Neh 8:12: וילכו ... לאכל ולשתות ולשלח מנות
(B) Neh 8:15: צאו ... והביאו ... לעשת סכת
    Neh 8:16: ויצאו ... ויביאו ויעשו ... סכת.

implication, they adhere to the recitation of the psalm in compliance with the Levites' exhortation to "bless YHWH, your God" (9:5).

However, the third assembly differs from the previous two inasmuch as it does not conclude with mention of the people's simple compliance with the exhortation. Rather, this gathering on the twenty-fourth day culminates uniquely in the people's swearing an oath of commitment to observance of the Torah (10:1–40). The signing of the pledge and the oath of allegiance to the Torah constitute the climax of the covenant-renewal account and the defining moment for postexilic Israel.[30]

The similarities in the descriptions of the activities on each of the three days provide the basic structural framework for the covenant-renewal account.

Table 2.3—Structure of the Covenant Renewal Account (Neh 7:72b–10:40)[31]
A. The first day: Ezra reads the Torah (7:72b–8:12)
 1. Assembly (7:72b–8:1a)
 2. Reading the Torah (8:1b–8)
 3. Exhortation (8:9–11)
 4. Execution (8:12)
B. The second day: The leaders study the Torah (8:13–18)
 1. Assembly (8:13a)
 2. Studying the Torah (8:13b)
 3. Exhortation (8:14–15)
 4. Execution (8:16–18)
C. The twenty-fourth day (9:1–10:40)
 1. The people read the Torah (9:1–37)
  a. Assembly (9:1–2)
  b. Reading the Torah (9:3)
  c. Exhortation (9:4–5)
  d. Execution (penitential psalm) (9:6–37)
 2. The people express their commitment to the Torah (10:1–40)
  a. The signatories of the pledge (10:1–28)
  b. The oath of commitment to the Torah (10:29–30)
  c. The stipulations of the pledge (10:31–40)

A closer inspection of the material reveals that the three major sections are not equally distinct. Ezra's reading of the Torah on the first day (7:72b–8:12) and the leaders' study on the second day, which culminates in the Festival of Booths (8:13–18), exhibit a cohesiveness that sets them

---

[30] The *inclusio* בני ישראל supplies another delimitation of the covenant-renewal account (7:72b; 10:40).

[31] Cf. Eskenazi, *In an Age of Prose*, 96–97; Throntveit, *Ezra-Nehemiah*, 95.

apart from the penitential rites and expression of commitment on the twenty-fourth day (9:1–10:40).³² Five elements bind these episodes together: (1) the temporal notice referring to "the second day" (8:13), implying a direct sequel to the events that preceded on the "first day of the month" (8:2); (2) continual preoccupation with "the words of law" (דברי התורה, 8:9, 13); (3) mention of Ezra (8:1; cf. 8:13) and the square at the Water Gate (8:3; cf. 8:16), confined to these two episodes in the covenant-renewal account; (4) the people's reaction of "great joy" (שמחה גדולה, 8:12, 17); and (5) the expressions "he read" (ויקרא, 8:3, 18) and "the book of the law" (ספר תורה, 8:1, 18) providing an *inclusio* between the two sections (7:72b–8:18).³³

At the same time, the internal unity of Ezra's introductory reading (7:72b–8:12) and the leaders' subsequent studying (8:13–18) of the Torah highlights the distinctiveness of the climactic section, which comprises both the penitential rites (9:1–37) and the oath of allegiance to the Torah (10:1–40). Four elements define the boundary between the second (8:13–18) and third (9:1–10:40) major sections: the summary notice concluding the Festival of Booths (8:18); the date indicating a time lapse (9:1, "the twenty-fourth day"); mention of a new assembly (אסף *nipʿal*, 9:1; cf. 8:1, 13); and the change in purpose of the assembly from celebration (8:17) to confession (9:1–2).

The transition from the recitation of the psalm (9:6–37) to the declaration of commitment (10:1–40) establishes the fundamental unity of the third section. Three elements of 10:1 help bind these portions together: (1) the conjunctive phrase ובכל־זאת ("For all this..."); (2) the continuity of subject (אנחנו, 10:1; cf. 9:33, 36, 37); and, therefore, (3) the continuity of narrative voice in the first-person plural.

The last element indicates a significant feature of the covenant-renewal account overall. Nehemiah 7:72b–9:5 is a third-person narrative, whereas

---

³² Williamson (*Ezra, Nehemiah*, 279–81) treats 7:72b–8:18 as a single unit on the basis of temporal continuity (Neh 8:2: "On the first day..."; Neh 8:13: "on the second day") and thematic consistency (a constant focus on the law, 8:1, 2, 3, 7, 8, 9, 13, 14, 16, 18), which combine to unify Ezra's initial reading of the Torah (8:1–12) with the subsequent Festival of Booths (8:13–18). However, most commentators (Rudolph, *Esra und Nehemia*, 141–53; Myers, *Ezra, Nehemiah*, 155–57; Fensham, *Ezra and Nehemiah*, 219–21; Clines, *Ezra, Nehemiah, Esther*, 186–89; and Blenkinsopp, *Ezra-Nehemiah*, 279–81) regard them as distinct segments that are intimately linked by Ezra's presence in both episodes.

³³ Nevertheless, four elements distinguish the Festival of Booths (8:13–18) from Ezra's initial reading of the Torah (8:1–12): (1) the temporal indicator (8:13); (2) the verbal notice of a new assembly (אסף *nipʿal*, 8:13; cf. 8:1); (3) the new cast of participants (8:13; cf. 8:1); and (4) the self-contained nature of both narratives, the second of which consistently focuses on the Festival of Booths (8:14; cf. 8:17).

9:6–10:40 is a first-person plural account. In other words, while the narrator recounts Ezra's presentation of the Torah (7:72b–8:12), the Festival of Booths (8:13–18), and the penitential rites (9:1–5), the Levites declaim the confessional psalm (9:6–37), and the community voices its commitment to a written pledge (10:1–28), its oath of obedience to the Torah (10:29–30), and the stipulations of the contract (10:31–40).[34]

The nature of the speech forms used, that is, prayer (9:6–37) and declaration (10:29–40), respectively, indicates that the discourses culminate all the solemn pronouncements in the book. The Levites' psalm is the spiritual zenith that subsumes the earlier penitential prayers of Ezra and Nehemiah (Ezra 9:6–15; Neh 1:5–11). Moreover, the community's declaration of commitment to the Torah (10:29–40) parallels the royal decrees (Ezra 1:2–4; 6:2–12; 7:12–26) as the final authoritative pronouncement that actualizes God's word in history.[35] In the end, it is fitting, from a narrative perspective, that Artaxerxes does not give Nehemiah explicit authorization for his activities upon his return, since now the community's proclamation of the Torah, rather than an edict from the Persian king, provides the mandate for the reformer's subsequent mission (Neh 13:4–31; cf. 10:29–40).

Through its participation in the covenant renewal, the community assumes a new and vigorous posture. The literary shift from the third-person narration (7:72b–9:5) to the first-person declaration (9:6–10:40) represents a transition in congregational participation from reception to expression. In the narrative section, the people quietly obey (7:72b–9:5), whereas in the declarative section they attend to the blessing (9:5b–37) and then pronounce their commitment (10:1–40). The reconstituted Israel not only hears but also responds to and announces the Torah. In terms of

---

[34] The transition from narration to declaration occurs in the Levites' address in 9:5. The Levites make two statements: first, a command ("Arise and bless YHWH, your God..."), which they direct toward the assembly, and, second, an invocation ("May they bless your glorious name..."), which they direct toward God. This invocation introduces the confessional psalm that follows. The change in speaker from the Levites to the whole congregation occurs almost imperceptibly in the first line of the pledge (10:1). The equivalence between the pronouns "we" (אנחנו) at the end of 9:37 and at the beginning of 10:1 provides for a smooth transition. However, two factors indicate that the congregation begins speaking at this point: (1) the transitional phrase, "For all this" (ובכל־זאת, 10:1) and (2) the perdurance of the first-person plural as subject ("we") and possessive adjective ("our") throughout 10:1–40.

[35] In particular, five features associate the decrees of the Persian kings with the community's oath: (1) on a literary level, their common employment of first-person direct speech; (2) their explicit theological dimension; (3) their legally-binding contractual character; (4) their equation with God's decree (טעם, Ezra 6:14); and (5) the concern for the Torah in the final royal decree (Ezra 7:14, 25–26).

content, the discourses of the Levites and the community provide a synthesis of the history of Israel (9:6–37) and a résumé of the book of the Torah (10:29–40).

This chapter has demonstrated that Ezra-Nehemiah is a unified work that cohesively portrays the establishment of the community in Jerusalem and Judah as the genuine heir of preexilic Israel. The covenant renewal is the defining event of this postexilic community. The nuances uncovered in this overview of the context and structure of the covenant renewal indicate the need to examine its individual sections more precisely from an exegetical, literary, and theological perspective. This is the task of the next four chapters, in which I will discuss each segment of the covenant-renewal account: (1) Ezra's reading of the Torah on the first day (7:72b–8:12) and the leaders' study of the Torah on the second day, which leads into the Festival of Booths (8:13–18); (2) the people's reading of the Torah on the twenty-fourth day with the attendant penitential rites (9:1–5); (3) the Levites' prayer (9:6–37); and (4) the people's subsequent expression of commitment to the Torah (10:1–40).

3

The Reading of the Law and the Festival of Booths (Nehemiah 7:72b–8:18)

Nehemiah 8 recounts two major episodes: Ezra's introductory reading of the law to the plenary assembly at the Water Gate (8:1–12) and the leaders' studying of the law that prompts the promulgation of the Festival of Booths (8:13–18). I develop a synchronic study of these sections in sequence by examining their contents in five parts: (1) a literal translation of the material; (2) notes on text-critical issues; (3) an outline and literary analysis that will treat the narrative interplay of the various lexical components within the immediate context of the present passage and of the covenant-renewal account; (4) a lexical examination of the most significant terms in view of their occurrences elsewhere in Ezra-Nehemiah and in the remainder of OT literature; and (5) a thematic summary that highlights the implications of the study.

THE FIRST READING OF THE LAW (NEHEMIAH 7:72b–8:12)

TRANSLATION

7:72 When the seventh month arrived [a]and the Israelites were in their towns,[a] 8:1 all the people gathered as one at the square that is in front of the Water Gate. They told Ezra the scribe to bring the book of the law of Moses with which YHWH had charged Israel. 2 Consequently, on the first day of the seventh month, Ezra the priest brought the law before the assembly comprising men as well as women, and everyone who could understand by hearing. 3 Then he read from it facing the square that is in front of the Water Gate from daybreak until noonday, in front of the men, the women, and the ones who could understand. Indeed, the ears of all the people were on the book of the law.

4 Ezra the scribe stood on a wooden platform that they had made for the purpose. At his side stood Mattithiah, Shema, Anaiah, Uriah, Hilkiah, and Maaseiah on his right; and on his left, Pedaiah, Mishael, Malchijah, Hashum, Hashbaddanah, Zechariah, and Meshullam.[b] 5 Ezra opened the book in the sight of all the people (for he was above all the people), and

when he opened it all the people stood up. ⁶ Then Ezra blessed YHWH, the great God, and all the people, while raising their hands, responded, "Amen. Amen." Then they bowed down and worshiped YHWH with their faces to the ground.

⁷ Jeshua, Bani, Sherebiah, Jamin, Akkub, Shabbethai, Hodiah, Maaseiah, Kelitah, Azariah, Jozabad, Hanan, Pelaiah, ᶜthe Levites,ᶜ were helping the people understand the law as the people were at their place. ⁸ They read from the book, from the law of God, distinctly and presented the meaning so that they understood what was being read.

⁹ ᵈNehemiah (he was the governor),ᵈ Ezra the priest and scribe, and the Levites who helped the people understand, said to all the people, "This day is holy to YHWH your God. Do not mourn and do not weep." (For all the people had been weeping as they heard the words of the law.) ¹⁰ Then he said to them, "Go, eat rich food, drink sweet libations, and send a portion to the one for whom none is provided, for this day is holy to our Lord; and do not be grieved, because ᵉthe joy ofᵉ YHWH is your refuge." ¹¹ Also the Levites were calming all the people, saying, "Hush! for this day is holy; do not be grieved." ¹² So all the people went to eat, to drink, to send portions, and to make great joy because they had understood the matters that they had made known to them.

TEXTUAL CRITICISM

a–a ובני ישראל בעריהם is maintained in view of solid textual witnesses. The phrase is absent from only two Greek MSS (11th and 13th centuries C.E.), one Latin MS (11th century C.E.), and the Ethiopic text (16th and 17th centuries C.E.). Cf. L. F. Hartman et al., eds., *Textual Notes on the New American Bible* (Paterson, N.J.: St. Anthony's Guild, n.d.), 365.

b משלם is maintained in spite of its absence from 1 Esd 9:44.

c–c הלוים. Omit the copula (ו) with the Vg and 1 Esd 9:48.

d–d נחמיה הוא התרשתא. This phrase is maintained because it represents the *lectio difficilior* and textual evidence is lacking for removing it. נחמיה הוא is omitted in 1 Esd 9:49, which reads התרשתא as a personal name, that is, Ἀτθαράτης. Nehemiah's name was probably missing from the Hebrew *Vorlage* of 1 Esdras due to a copyist's error. נחמיה would have appeared in an earlier version in this manuscript tradition since, in the context, the title התרשתא does not make sense unless the name of one who bears it accompanies it (cf. 10:2). LXX 2 Esd 18:9 confirms the reading of Nehemiah's name but omits הוא התרשתא. A verb in the singular can have more than one subject (Neh 9:4; GKC §146f; GBH §150q).[1] Probably

---

[1] See Fensham, *Ezra and Nehemiah*, 218. Williamson excludes the phrase from the original version of the text in view of the identical third-person singular verb form (ויאמר) in 8:10 as in 8:9 (*Ezra, Nehemiah*, 279). He notes that making Nehemiah

נחמיה הוא התרשתא was inserted at some point after the establishment of the rest of the narrative (perhaps in view of 10:2 and 12:26). However, the manuscript evidence indicates that the phrase is an authentic component of the canonical text.

e–e חדות is maintained due to its attestation in all Heb MSS. It is lacking in 1 Esd 9:52 (ὁ γὰρ κύριος δοξάσει ὑμᾶς) and in LXX 2 Esd 18:10 (ὅτι ἐστὶν ἰσχὺς ἡμῶν) due to interpretative alterations.

LITERARY ANALYSIS

My literary analysis consists of an outline of the whole, and a discussion of each subunit.

OUTLINE

In the previous chapter[2] I indicated that, within the overall structure of the covenant renewal (Neh 7:72b–10:40), the account of Ezra's reading of the law (7:72b–8:12) follows a pattern that it shares in common with the two following segments, the celebration of Booths (8:13–18) and the expression of covenant commitment (9:1–10:40). This pattern is: assembly (7:72b–8:1a); reading of the law (8:1b–8); exhortation (8:9–11); and execution (8:12). However, at this point a more precise analysis of the account of events on the first day (7:72b–8:12) will help disclose its distinctive substructure beneath the generic framework.

Table 3.1—Outline of the Reading of the Law Narrative (Neh 7:72b–8:12)
A. Ezra introduces the book of the law to all the people (7:72b–8:3)
  1. Setting: gathering at the square in front of the Water Gate (7:72b–8:1a)
  2. Action: procession with the book of the law (8:1b–3a)
    a. The people request Ezra to bring the book of the law (8:1b)
    b. Ezra brings the law (8:2)
    c. Ezra reads from the law (8:3a)
  3. Response: the people are attentive to the book of the law (8:3b)

---

the primary subject (due to his name preceding Ezra's) violates the narrative flow that highlights Ezra as the predominant subject. Williamson's claim that Nehemiah's title is more often פחה than התרשתא is unconvincing, since each title occurs alongside his name only once elsewhere (התרשתא, 10:2; הפחה, 12:26) while in his autobiographical account Nehemiah's self-designations as פחה are confined to a restricted context (5:14, 15, 18). התרשתא in 8:9 is more likely due to harmonization with 10:2 than to a supposed influence of 7:69 (*pace* Williamson). Blenkinsopp is inconsistent: in his textual note (*Ezra-Nehemiah*, 284), he regards התרשתא as original and נחמיה as an addition, apparently on the basis of 1 Esd 9:48 (LXX); however, in his commentary (288), presumably in view of the third-person singular verbs in 8:9, 10 (ויאמר), he views as secondary additions both "Nehemiah, the governor" and "the Levites."

[2] Pp. 73–75.

B. Ezra leads all the people in worship (8:4–6)
  1. Setting: Ezra and thirteen leaders stand on the platform (8:4)
  2. Action and response: liturgical rites (8:5–6)
     a. Opening the book (8:5)
        i. Action: Ezra opens the book (8:5a)
        ii. Response: the people stand (8:5b)
     b. Blessing YHWH (8:6)
        i. Action: Ezra blesses YHWH (8:6a)
        ii. Response: the people worship (8:6b)
C. The Levites interpret the law to the people (8:7–8)
  1. Setting: the thirteen Levites (8:7aα)
  2. Action: the Levites read and interpret the law to the people (8:7aβ–8bα)
  3. Response: the people understand the reading (8:8bβ)
D. Nehemiah, Ezra, and the Levites counsel all the people (8:9–12)
  1. Action: the leaders speak to the people (8:9–11)
     a. The united counsel of all the leaders (8:9)
     b. The counsel of Ezra (8:10)
     c. The counsel of the Levites (8:11)
  2. Response: all the people depart (8:12)
     a. Departure to partake of the meal (8:12a)
     b. They have joy because of understanding (8:12b)

The limits of the narrative are defined by the gathering of "all the people" at the beginning and the departure of "all the people" at the end (ויאספו כל־העם, 8:1; וילכו כל־העם, 8:12).³ Three lists of multiple names subdivide the whole into four major subunits: the thirteen lay leaders who accompany Ezra on the platform (8:4); the thirteen Levites who teach the law (8:7); and Nehemiah, Ezra, and the Levites who provide counsel (8:9). These lists, which introduce three subunits (8:4–6, 7–8, 9–12), focus attention on the leaders. However, the first subunit (7:72b–8:3) does not begin with a list. Furthermore, each subunit concludes with a description of the people's response to what took place in the unit: (1) "the ears of all the people were on the book of the law" (8:3); (2) "all the people, while raising their hands, responded, 'Amen. Amen.' Then they bowed down and worshiped..." (8:6); (3) "they understood what was being read" (8:8); and (4) "they had understood the matters that had been made known to them"

---

³ Nehemiah 7:72b provides the background setting in space ("the children of Israel in their towns") and time ("the seventh month") not only for the first part of the covenant renewal (8:1–12) but also for its subsequent two parts (8:13–18; 9:1–10:40). In the terminology of R. Alter, this half-verse provides the "initial exposition" for the whole story that follows (*The Art of Biblical Narrative* [New York: Basic Books, 1981], 80).

(8:12). In three out of four cases, the subject of these concluding statements is "all the people" (כל־העם, 8:3, 6, 12), while in the fourth case it is simply "the people" (העם, 8:8). The first three of the four subunits (7:72b–8:3; 8:4–6; and 8:7–8) could each stand alone as a self-contained story consisting of: (1) an introductory setting (7:72b–8:1a; 8:4; 8:7); (2) initiating action (8:1b–3a; 8:5a, 6a; 8:7–8b); and (3) subsequent response to the initiative (8:3b; 8:5b, 6b; 8:8c).[4] The fourth subunit, by contrast, lacks an introductory setting of its own; thus, it requires the background of either the first or the third subunit for its comprehension. In summary, this whole segment of the covenant-renewal account (Neh 7:72b–8:12) consists of three self-contained subunits (7:72b–8:3; 8:4–6; 8:7–8) and a fourth (8:9–12), dependent, subunit.

Each of the four parts narrates the activity of a different subject or group performing a distinctive action: first, Ezra carries the book to the front of the assembly at the Water Gate (7:72b–8:3); second, a company of thirteen lay leaders stand with Ezra on a platform as he leads the people in worship (8:4–6); third, a group of thirteen Levites interprets the law for the people (8:7–8); and fourth, Nehemiah, Ezra, and the Levites encourage the people to return home in order to partake in a festive meal (8:9–12).

The constant subject through all the subunits is "the people" (העם). Of the thirteen occurrences of the term, ten appear in the expression "all the people" (כל־העם, 8:1, 3, 5 [3x], 6, 9 [bis], 11, 12; cf. העם, 8:7 [bis], 9). Nevertheless, this term is not evenly distributed throughout the four subunits: while כל־העם occurs in the first, second, and fourth parts (7:72b–8:3; 8:4–6; 8:9–12), the noun occurs alone in the account of the Levites interpreting the law (העם, 8:7–8).

The name *Ezra* and the designation "all the people" (כל־העם) occur in the same subunits and are absent from the same subunit. Ezra is not mentioned in the third part, where the Levites occupy center stage (8:7–8), but is the primary figure in the other three subunits.

One must look elsewhere for a term that complements "the people" (העם) as the constant factor in all three self-contained subunits (7:72b–8:3; 8:4–6; 8:7–9). The only other word that recurs throughout all the subunits is "book" (ספר, 8:1, 3, 5 [bis], 8). The "book of the law" (ה[סםר] [ה]תורה], 8:1, 3, 8) or "the law" (התורה, 8:2, 7) is the focus of attention in the first and third subunits (7:72b–8:3; 8:7–8), whereas the second subunit speaks only of "the book" (הספר, 8:5).[5]

---

[4] The second subunit is distinctive insofar as it exhibits a twofold action-response sequence (8:5a–5b; 8:6a–6b).

[5] It is noteworthy that the fourth subunit (8:9–12) does not mention "the book" (הספר) or "the law" (התורה). At this point, the narrative preoccupation shifts from

The above evidence suggests that the topic of this whole portion of the covenant renewal is the people's encounter with the book. Ezra (along with the Levites and other leaders) acts as a mediator in the relationship between all the people (כל־העם) and the book (הספר).

The following, more detailed analysis of the structure and vocabulary of each subunit will disclose its unique contribution to the articulation of the whole segment of the covenant renewal (7:72b–8:12).

EXAMINATION OF THE UNITS

Ezra introduces the book of the law to all the people (7:72b–8:3)

The first subunit (7:72b–8:3) describes the people's initial encounter with the book of the law. The correspondence between the opening epithets for the community (בני ישראל: "the Israelites," 7:72b) and for the law (ספר תורת משה אשר־צוה יהוה את־ישראל: "the book of the law of Moses with which YHWH had charged Israel," 8:1) suggests the appropriateness of their being united. The *inclusio* for the first subunit indicates the prime subject matter: כל־העם ("all the people," 8:1a, 3b) and ספר [ה]תורה (the "book of the law," 8:1b, 3b).

Repetition is the predominant literary feature of this subunit. Eight words or expressions occur twice: [ה]חדש שביעי ("the seventh month," 7:72b; 8:2), ישראל ("Israel," 7:72b; 8:1); כל־העם ("all the people," 8:1, 3); הרחוב אשר לפני שער־המים ("the square that is in front of the Water Gate," 8:1, 2); עזרא ("Ezra," 8:1, 2); בוא (*hip'il*, "to bring," 8:1, 2); ספר תורת משה ("the book of the law of Moses," 8:1; cf. ספר התורה, "the book of the law," 8:3); and האנשים והנשים והמבינים ("the men, the women, and the ones who could understand," 8:3; cf. מאיש ועד־אשה וכל מבין לשמע, "men as well as women, and everyone who could understand by hearing," 8:2).

Of particular significance is the diversity of the nouns highlighting the five main components of this story segment: time, place, the community, the book of the law, and Ezra. First, this subunit's three temporal referents point to a progressive narrowing of the time frame from the broad to the narrow: (1) the seventh month (7:72b); (2) the first day of the month (8:2); (3) from daybreak until noon (8:3).

Second, the initial mention of two different places governed by prepositions involves the movement of the people from within their towns (בעריהם, 7:72b) to "the square that is in front of the Water Gate" (הרחוב אשר לפני שער־המים, 8:1). Moreover, אל הרחוב אשר לפני שער־המים is mentioned twice, once (from outside) as the location for this communal

---

the written text to the instruction the people had received ("the matters that had been made known to them": [ה]דברים אשר הודיעו להם, 8:12).

gathering (8:1), and once (from inside) as the space before which Ezra stands to perform the reading (8:3). This twofold reference conveys an emphatic distinction between this location and other environs (i.e., the temple area; see Ezra 3:1–6; 10:9).

Third, the community receives the most attention due to its being mentioned seven times with five expressions: בני ישראל ("the Israelites," 7:72b); כל־העם ("all the people," 8:1, 3); כאיש אחד ("as one," 8:1: a simile); הקהל ("the assembly," 8:2); מאיש ועד־אשה וכל מבין לשמע ("men as well as women, and everyone who could understand by hearing," 8:2); and האנשים והנשים והמבינים ("the men, the women, and the ones who could understand," 8:3). Throughout Neh 7:72b–10:40, the term "the children of Israel" (בני ישראל) functions as a thematic element. Four of its five occurrences are at strategic junctures: at the beginning of each of the three major sections (7:72b; 8:14 [cf. 8:17]; 9:1) and at the end of the whole narrative (10:40). This expression, therefore, exercises two roles in the narrative: first, by its recurrences in the introduction to each major section (7:72b–8:12; 8:13–18; 9:1–10:40), it maintains the continuity of subject throughout Neh 7:72b–10:40; and, second, as the *inclusio* of the whole (7:72b; 10:40), it delimits the covenant renewal from the rest of the book.

Fourth, in the first subunit, the book of the law (ספר [ה]תורה, 8:1, 3) occurs twice, while the term התורה stands alone once (8:2) as an additional reference to the same book. Within the covenant-renewal account, the "book" (ספר) from which Ezra, the Levites, and eventually the people read is mentioned six times, with a variety of titles: "the book of the law of Moses" (8:1), "the book of the law" (8:3), "the book" (8:5), "the book of the law of God" (8:8, 18), and "the book of the law of YHWH their God" (9:3).

Fifth, Ezra's name appears only twice, first as the priest (הכהן, 8:1) and second as the scribe (הספר, 8:2). The sparse descriptions of Ezra at this point in the covenant renewal are remarkable in contrast to his prior absence from the book of Nehemiah (Neh 1:1–7:72b) and in comparison to the elaborate introduction of him in Ezra 7:1–10.

The seven references to the community suggest that it, rather than Ezra, is the focus of attention at this point. The verbs used confirm this surmise. Both figure as the subject of two distinct verbs: all the people "gather" (ויאספו, 8:1a) and they "speak" (ויאמרו, 8:1b); Ezra "brings" (ויבא, 8:2) the law and "reads from it" (ויקרא־בו, 8:3). However, in addition to these explicit verbs, the people are also the subject of two implied verbs in the nominal clauses at the beginning (ובני ישראל בעריהם: "and the Israelites were in their towns," 7:72b) and at the end (ואזני כל־העם אל־ספר התורה: "the ears of all the people were on the book of the law," 8:3b) of the subunit. Moreover, the people direct Ezra's activity. "All the people" take the initiative by requesting that Ezra perform the appropriate introductions (8:1). The correspondence between their spoken request and the narration of the subsequent action highlights Ezra's literal compliance with their demand:

8:1: ויאמרו לעזרא הספר להביא את־ספר תורת משה
8:2: ⁶ויביא עזרא הכהן את־התורה

The similarities between the people's directive and Ezra's action indicate that Ezra is the servant who mediates the introduction of the book of the law to the community.

Regarding כל־העם, the segment's main subject, the first subunit establishes its primary dimensions, namely, unity and inclusivity. Unity is underlined by the simile "as one" (כאיש אחד, 8:1), while inclusivity is stressed in the double enumeration of the various participants, "men, women, and the ones who could understand" (האנשים והנשים והמבינים, 8:3; cf. מאיש ועד־אשה וכל מבין לשמע, 8:2).

Ezra leads all the people in worship (8:4–6)

Repetition continues to be a feature in the second subunit: עמד (8:4 [bis], 5); פתח (8:5a, 5b); עזרא (8:4, 5, 6); כל־העם (8:5 [3x], 6); יהוה (8:6 [bis]); אמן (8:6 [bis]). In addition, assonance generates one couplet: מעל/ויפתח (8:5, 6) as well as clause parallelism: ויעמד עזרא הספר (8:4)/עזרא הספר(8:5). The mention of עזרא three times (8:4, 5, 6) and כל־העם four times (8:5 [3x], 6) draws attention to them as the two main subjects.

While nouns predominate in the first subunit, verbs become the focus of attention in the second. Ezra is the subject of five verbs (ויעמד: "[he] stood," 8:4; פתח: "[he] opened," 8:5a, 5b; הוה: "he was," 8:5; and ויברך: "[he] blessed," 8:6), the thirteen leaders of one (ויעמד: "[they] stood," 8:4), and "all the people" of five (עשו: "they had made," 8:4; עמדו: "[they] stood," 8:5; ויענו: "[they] answered," 8:6; ויקדו: "[they] bowed down," 8:6; and וישתחו: "[they] worshiped," 8:6).⁷ The use of the same singular verb (ויעמד, 8:4) for both Ezra and the thirteen leaders indicates that the latter support the former's activity. This subunit focuses on the interaction between Ezra and "all the people" in which Ezra initiates an action and the people respond. This sequence occurs twice in succession: first, when Ezra opens the book, the people respond by standing up (8:5); second, when Ezra blesses God, the people respond by worshiping (8:6).

Ezra has priority not only in initiative but also in position. While the first subunit is concerned with horizontal space (הרחוב אשר לפני שער־המים:

---

⁶ 8:1: "They told Ezra the scribe to bring the book of the law of Moses."
8:2: "Ezra the priest brought the law."

⁷ In the second subunit, the community is designated only by the expression כל־העם (in continuity with 8:3b) rather than by other terms (cf. the first subunit).

"the square that is in front of the Water Gate," 8:1, 2), the second subunit is preoccupied with vertical space. The narrative focus moves from a double mention of the broad square (הרחוב, 8:1b, 3a) in which Ezra comes before (לפני) the assembly, to a twofold allusion to height in the term for the platform (מגדל, 8:4a) and in Ezra's standing above (מעל, 8:5b; cf. 3:28) the people. The flanking of Ezra by thirteen leaders enhances his profile as leader and may suggest his welcoming of lay participation in preparation for 9:3a.

The presence of the thirteen indicates, at least, that Ezra acts in union with others from the populace. Moreover, three factors suggest that these thirteen are laymen: (1) this list of thirteen is clearly distinct from the subsequent list of thirteen Levites (8:7); (2) none of these names appears in any of the three subsequent lists of Levites (8:7; 9:4, 5); and (3) they are not designated as either priests or Levites (as would be customary in Ezra-Nehemiah).[8] Admittedly, in the absence of conclusive evidence, my designation of the individuals in Neh 8:4 as "laymen" is somewhat conjectural.[9] The listing of thirteen leaders in this untitled group prior to the same number of Levites (8:7) militates against the idea of clerical supremacy.[10]

In spite of Ezra's precedence in location and action, a verse-by-verse analysis discloses that, in the second subunit, the dramatic weight continues to fall upon "all the people" (כל־העם). First, the initial description (8:4a) suggests that the very possibility of Ezra taking up his position depends on the prior provision by "all the people" (כל־העם, 8:3b), that is,

---

[8] Williamson, *Ezra, Nehemiah*, 288–89; Blenkinsopp, *Ezra-Nehemiah*, 286.

[9] Comparisons with other lists are inconclusive, since the same name in two lists can refer to a different person in each one. Moreover, the name of a single individual can appear in alternate forms. Six names in Neh 8:4 appear on the signed document under the heading "leaders of the people" (10:15–28: Hashum [10:19], Meshullam [10:21], Anaiah [10:23], Hashabnah [10:26; = Hashbadanah], Maaseiah [10:25], and Malluch [10:28; = Malchijah]). Two of these names also appear among the priests (10:2–9: Malchijah [10:4], Meshullam [10:8]). Again, five of the names in Neh 8:4 occur also among the laity ("of Israel," Ezra 10:25) who separated from their foreign wives (Ezra 10:25–44): Mattithiah (10:31), Maaseiah (10:30), Malchijah (10:31), Hashum (10:33), and Zechariah (10:30). However, other lists associate the name Hilkiah with the priesthood in different generations (Neh 11:11; 12:7, 21; Ezra 7:1).

[10] The attempt to reduce the number of leaders to twelve violates the integrity of the MT (cf. Myers, *Ezra, Nehemiah*, 150–51). Thirteen appears "disappointing" on two counts: (1) it portrays a lack of symmetrical arrangement of the leaders on Ezra's right and those on his left; and (2) it lacks the symbolism of twelve. However, the unusual quality of thirteen confirms the parallelism between this group of leaders who stand with Ezra (8:4) and the Levites who read the law (8:7).

their "making" (עָשׂוּ, 8:4a) of the platform upon which Ezra and the thirteen leaders stand.

Second, Neh 8:5 consists of three statements linked by the phrase כל־העם that exhibit an a:b::b::a:b pattern in an ABA' structure:

A   ויפתח עזרא הספר לעיני כל־העם

B   כי־מעל כל־העם היה

A'   וכפתחו עמדו כל־העם

Ezra's position is defined in relationship to the people (8:5b), and his singular action of opening the book is described twice (ויפתח עזרא הספר/ וכפתחו): first, in reference to the people's seeing (לעיני כל־העם) and, second, in view of their response (עמדו כל־העם). The people respond not to Ezra but to his action (וכפתחו), since they attend not so much to him as to the book (הספר).

Third, the three self-contained statements of Neh 8:6 comprise an ABA' pattern:

A   ויברך עזרא את־יהוה האלהים הגדול

B   ויענו כל־העם אמן אמן במעל ידיהם

A'   ויקדו וישתחו ליהוה אפים ארצה

However, in contrast to 8:5, these three statements relate continuous actions without any intervening explanatory clause. This verse transfers attention from "Ezra" to "all the people." Whereas Ezra was the subject of three of the four verbs in 8:5, "all the people" are the subject of three of the four verbs and of one noun with verbal force (מעל) in 8:6. In the former verse, Ezra's actions involve both posture (ויעמד) and gesture (ויפתח), while the people express their response by a change in posture (עמדו). But in the latter verse, Ezra's activity is limited to speech (ויברך), while the people's responses consist of speech (ויענו), gesture (במעל ידיהם), and a change in posture (ויקדו וישתחו). Regarding speech, the exact words of Ezra are not quoted, whereas the response of all the people is (אמן אמן). Moreover, in the covenant-renewal account, Ezra's blessing of YHWH (8:6) is the precedent for the people's blessing of YHWH in response to the exhortation of the Levites (9:5).

Although the first subunit concludes with mention of Ezra's reading from the book of the law, the narrative says nothing about what he actually reads. Liturgical concerns override preoccupation with the book's content at this point. Seven verbal expressions in the second subunit describe liturgical actions: Ezra's opening the book (ויפתח); the people's standing up (עמדו); Ezra's blessing (ויברך) God; the people's responding (ויענו), raising their hands (במעל ידיהם), bowing (ויקדו), and prostrating to the ground (וישתחו). In the final analysis, all of these verbal expressions direct attention to the objects of such effusive veneration, namely, "the book" (הספר, 8:5) and YHWH (יהוה, 8:6 [bis]). The sequence of the verbs is significant: opening the book leads ultimately to worship of YHWH. The respect accorded the book reflected by all the people's standing leads to their veneration of YHWH in an elaborate sequence of speech and gestures.

Exaltation is the common denominator linking the treatment of the book (8:5) with worship of YHWH (8:6). Positioning the book with Ezra on the towerlike platform (מגדול, 8:4) above (מעל, 8:5) all the people provides the setting for all the people's raising (במעל) their hands in acclamation of "YHWH, the great God" (8:6). Resonance is established between the middle components of the rhetorical patterns in 8:5 and 8:6 by means of their common mention of כל־העם and by the occurrence of the consonants מעל twice in an echo that moves from preposition (8:5) to gerund (8:6):

8:5 כי־מעל כל־העם היה
8:6 ויענו כל־העם אמן אמן במעל ידיהם

I noted above that a transition occurs from the first subunit to the second via the spatial concern from the horizontal to the vertical. A transition also occurs with the category of time. The second subunit is a retrospection in time from the end of the first subunit, which describes Ezra's reading from the book from daybreak until noonday (8:3). In the second subunit (8:4–6), Ezra does not yet read from the book. This subunit describes events prior to Ezra's reading from the book (8:3), namely, the first solemn moments after his procession in front of the assembly with the book (8:2). The worship begins with his opening of the book and his blessing YHWH (8:5–6). All of the verbs, whether in the converted imperfect (*wayyiqtol*), simple perfect (*qatal:* עמד), or infinitive construct (כפתחו), indicate completed single actions in the past (GBH §112c, §118c, §124s). Thus, already in the second subunit, the account exhibits a nonlinear temporal flow, which suggests a sophisticated narration: after the summary description of the morning's activity at the end of the first subunit (8:3), the next subunit's account is a retrospective portrayal of the introduction to the community's worship that began the day (8:4–5).

The Levites interpret the law to the people (8:7–8)

Repetition is not as pronounced in the third subunit as in the previous two, being confined to two terms: תורה (8:7, 8) and העם (8:7b [bis]). However, two other expressions are linked by assonance: ויבינו/מבינים (8:7, 8) and במקרא/ויקראו (8:8a, b).

Four elements connect the third subunit to the second: (1) an introductory list of thirteen individuals (8:7a; cf. 8:4), (2) העם (8:7b; cf.

כל־העם, 8:5, 6), (3) the people standing in their places (והעם על־עמדם, 8:7b; cf. עמדו כל־עם, 8:5b), and (4) the book (בספר, 8:8a; cf. הספר, 8:5a).

The most significant aspect of the mention of the Levites in the third subunit is their number (thirteen), which corresponds to that of the lay leaders who stood on the platform with Ezra (Neh 8:4). The names of the first three Levites, Jeshua, Bani, and Sherebiah, along with the later-mentioned Hodiah (8:4; 9:4, 5), serve to relate the present episode to the third segment of the covenant renewal in which the Levites will lead the people in blessing YHWH in Ezra's absence.

Seven of the Levitical names link this episode with the signing of the pledge (10:1–28). Jeshua—whose name appears first in each of the four lists of Levites in the covenant-renewal account (8:7; 9:4, 5; 10:10–14)—resurfaces in the list of the Levites who will sign the agreement (10:10). Six of the other thirteen Levitical names here resurface in the list of the associates (אחים) of the Levites in the pledge: Bani (10:14), Sherebiah (10:13), Hodiah (10:12), Kelita (10:11), Hanan (10:11), and Pelaiah (10:11).

In contrast to the comparative passivity of the thirteen laymen in the second subunit, the thirteen Levites in the third subunit replace Ezra as the ones who interact with the people. Here Ezra is noteworthy by his absence. The Levites are the subjects of four verbs (מבינים: "causing to understand," 8:7; ויקראו: "they read," 8:8; מפרש: "distinctly," 8:8; ושום: "[they] presented [the meaning]," 8:8), whereas the people are the subject of only one explicit verb (ויבינו, 8:8) and one implied verb (in the nominal clause והעם על־עמדם, 8:7b). Thus, the dramatic emphasis falls on the activity of the Levites.

All the above verbs that have the Levites as their subject also have the law (תורה) as their explicit or implied direct object, and the people (העם) as their explicit or implied indirect object. Thus, attention is redirected away from the visual appearance of "the book" (הספר, 8:5) to its content (תורה). (Note that in the second subunit הספר occurs alone without any mention of תורה.)

In the third subunit, the action of the Levites and the response of the people recall the interaction between Ezra and the people in the first subunit. Four central lexemes establish the linkage: (1) ויקראו בספר (8:8a; cf. ויקרא בו, 8:3a); (2) בספר בתורת האלהים (8:8; cf. ספר תורת משה, 8:1b; ספר התורה, 8:3b; (3) מבינים (8:7) and ויבינו (8:8b; cf. הבינים, 8:3; מבין, 8:2); and (4) לתורה (8:7b; cf. התורה, 8:2a). Moreover, the use of additional verbs and phrases indicates that the Levites engage in more complex activity than did Ezra in mediating the law to the people. Not only do they (like Ezra) read from the book of the law; they also read "distinctly" (מפרש), presenting the meaning (שום שכל), thereby helping the people understand

(מבינים) the law. The success of their work is confirmed by the people's response (ויבינו במקרא).[11]

The description of the people standing at their places (והעם על־עמדם, 8:7b) recalls the people's rising to their feet when Ezra opened the book (כפתחו עמדו כל־העם, 8:5b) and thereby suggests their having continued in this posture.

The third subunit spans an extensive time frame similar to that of the first subunit (8:3). The absence of an introductory verb (*wayyiqtol*) at the beginning of 8:7b dissociates the third subunit from the consecutive verbal sequence of the second. The participle מבינים—which is the first verb form in this subunit—confers a durative aspect on the Levites' action ("they were helping the people understand," GBH §121f). The converted perfect ויקראו (8:8a) in this case suggests an extended action, given its congruity with ויקרא (8:3a), which described Ezra's reading during the course of half the daylight hours.[12]

Nehemiah, Ezra, and the Levites counsel all the people (8:9–12)

As in the previous three subunits, repetitions of particular words and expressions characterize the fourth subunit, such as ויאמר (8:9, 10; cf. לאמר, 8:11); הלוים (8:9, 11); המבינים (8:9; cf. הבינו, 8:12); כל־העם (8:9 [bis], 11, 12) and [דברי]ם (8:9, 12). However, in contrast to the previous three subunits, the repetitions in the fourth extend to complete statements, such as קדש היום ("this day is holy," 8:9, 12; cf. קדוש היום [8:10]) and אל־תעצבו ("do not be grieved," 8:10, 11).

The fourth subunit shares a variety of lexical elements with the previous three: עזרא (8:9; cf. 8:1, 2, 4, 5); הכהן (8:9; cf. 8:2); הספר (8:9; cf. 8:1, 4); הלוים [ה]מבינים את־העם (8:9; cf. 8:7); כל־העם (8:9–12 [4x]; cf. 8:1–8 [6x]); יהוה אלהיכם (8:9); cf. יהוה האלהים, 8:6); כשמעם (8:9; cf. לשמע, 8:2); and הבינו (8:12; cf. ויבינו, 8:8). However, closer inspection indicates that six of these eight items occur only in 8:9. Thus, the lexical range of 8:10–12 is distinctive vis-à-vis the rest of the segment (7:72b–8:9).

In fact, the naming of the personnel (Nehemiah, Ezra, and the Levites[13]) and their audience (כל־העם) in 8:9a provides the linkage with the previous subunits, while the remainder (8:9b–12) represents a new

---

11 The people's response to the Levites (ויבינו במקרא, 8:8b) is parallel to their response to Ezra's reading from the first subunit (ויאזני כל־העם אל־ספר התורה, 8:3b).

12 The *puʿal* participle (מפרש) functions virtually as an adverb qualifying ויקראו. The infinitive absolute (שום שכל) in this case is equivalent to the dominant preceding verbal form, i.e., ויקראו (*wayyiqtol*, GBH §123x).

13 The description of the Levites in 8:9 (והלוים המבינים את־העם: "the Levites who helped the people understand") repeats 8:7ab (הלוים מבינים את־העם לתורה: "the Levites were helping the people understand the law").

concern compared to what has preceded. Attention now turns from the reading of the law to its immediate application for the people. More precisely, these verses portray the leaders correcting the people's initial misapprehension of the law (as indicated in the explanatory clause in 8:9b, כי בוכים כל־העם כשמעם את־דברי התורה: "For all the people had been weeping as they heard the words of the law").

Various leaders exhort the people three times in succession. First, Nehemiah, Ezra, and the Levites speak in unison (8:9); second, Ezra speaks (8:10),[14] and, finally, the Levites add their voice (8:11). The declarations of the various speakers have in common a pronouncement of the day's holiness and resultant prohibition(s):

8:9   היום קדש־הוא ליהוה אלהיכם אל־תתאבלו ואל־תבכו
8:10 כי קדוש היום לאדנינו ואל־תעצבו
8:11 [15]כי היום קדש ואל־תעצבו

The closest parallels in vocabulary here are between the statements of Ezra (8:10) and of the Levites (8:11), both of which contain a motive clause (introduced by כי) for a preceding exhortation. However, the difference in the respective preliminary exhortations is enormous: the Levites' exhortation is only one word (הסו),[16] whereas Ezra's comprises a complete instruction on how to celebrate the day. Syntax confirms the impression that the Levites here play a subsidiary role to Ezra: Neh 8:11 is unique in this subunit in having the subject precede the verb (הלוים מחשים, "the Levites were calming"), thereby indicating a break in the narrative

---

[14] In 8:10, Ezra alone is the speaker despite the fact that the verse begins with the same verb form (ויאמר) as does 8:9 (cf. Williamson, *Ezra, Nehemiah*, 279). Three factors determine this identification: (1) the sequence of statements in the immediate context; i.e., the speaker in 8:10 must be different from 8:9; otherwise the close similarity in the rationale of the two statements ("this day is holy to YHWH [or: to our Lord].... Do not mourn [or: do not be grieved]") would be redundant; (2) the order of speakers in the broader context; Ezra's talking prior to the Levites (8:11) corresponds with their sequence in 8:9 and 8:3, 6 (cf. 8:7–8); and (3) consistency with the leader's profile in the preceding subunits: Ezra—rather than Nehemiah—is the individual who has stood in front of (לפני, 8:3) and above (מעל, 8:5) the assembly as the main speaker from the beginning (8:3).

[15] 8:9: "This day is holy to YHWH your God. Do not mourn and do not weep."
8:10: "for this day is holy to our Lord; and do not be grieved."
8:11: "for this day is holy; do not be grieved."

[16] The interjection הסו is onomatopoeic ("Hush"; cf. Judg 3:19; Amos 6:10; 8:3; Hab 2:20; Zeph 1:7; Zech 2:13). The instructions of the Levites (8:11) are notably more succinct than the previous words both of Ezra (8:10) and of the combined leadership (8:9). Their brevity reinforces the impression that the Levites are echoing the words that the other leaders already spoke.

sequence. Furthermore, the participle (מַחְשִׁים) bespeaks an enduring activity that is subordinate to what precedes (cf. GBH §121f).

Moreover, in terms of style, the subunit's second statement is more elaborate and contains more instruction than either the first or third. Specifically, in addition to its pronouncement of the day's holiness and subsequent prohibition(s), Ezra's statement (8:10) features two unique elements: (1) an extensive command concerning the proper response to the morning's reading through a festive meal; and (2) an explanatory clause (כִּי־חֶדְוַת יהוה הִיא מָעֻזְּכֶם): "because the joy of YHWH is your refuge," GBH §170d).

The above two literary components that are unique to Ezra's speech (8:10) provide the basic content for the following narration of the people's response (8:12). Compare (1) the command and the narrative and (2) the explanatory clause and the narrative:

8:10 לְכוּ אִכְלוּ מַשְׁמַנִּים וּשְׁתוּ מַמְתַקִּים וְשִׁלְחוּ מָנוֹת לְאֵין נָכוֹן לוֹ
8:12 ¹⁷וַיֵּלְכוּ כָל־הָעָם לֶאֱכֹל וְלִשְׁתּוֹת וּלְשַׁלַּח מָנוֹת

8:10 כִּי־חֶדְוַת יהוה הִיא מָעֻזְּכֶם
8:12 וְלַעֲשׂוֹת שִׂמְחָה גְדוֹלָה.¹⁸

Obviously, literal correspondence occurs only in the command and the narrative, while thematic correspondence through synonymous expressions (חֶדְוַת יהוה; cf. שִׂמְחָה גְדוֹלָה) is present in the explanatory clause and the narrative.

Thus, in the end, the narrative describes the response of "all the people" (כָּל־הָעָם, 8:12) in words that reflect Ezra's commands (8:10), just as, at the beginning, the description of Ezra's bringing the law reflects the request of "all the people" (כָּל־הָעָם, 8:1b–2a) to him. In other words, the narrative of events in the square begins with Ezra's responding to all the people's request and ends with all the people obeying Ezra.

The concluding explanatory clause narrates the successful accomplishment of the morning's activities: the people understand what the various leaders had taught them (8:12). This clause contrasts with that at the beginning of the subunit that notes the people's weeping as a consequence of their hearing the words of the law (8:9). The contrasting parallelism between these clauses is noteworthy: they feature alternate reactions (weeping versus joy) of "all the people" to "words" they have heard:

---

17 8:10: "Go, eat rich food, drink sweet libations, and send a portion to the one for whom none is provided."
    8:12: "So all the people went to eat, to drink, to send portions."
18 8:10: "because the joy of YHWH is your refuge."
    8:12: "and to make great joy."

8:9 בוכים כָל־הָעָם כְּשָׁמְעָם אֶת־דִּבְרֵי הַתּוֹרָה
8:12 ‎19‎ כָל־הָעָם ... וְלַעֲשׂוֹת שִׂמְחָה גְדוֹלָה כִּי הֵבִינוּ בַּדְּבָרִים אֲשֶׁר הוֹדִיעוּ לָהֶם

The story reaches its climax in the community's "understanding" (הֵבִינוּ) of the matters (הַ[דְּבָרִים]) that Ezra (8:10; cf. 8:3) and the Levites (8:11; cf. 8:7–8) have taught (הוֹדִיעוּ) them. This "understanding" was precisely what was missing in the people's immediate reaction to the "words of the law" (דִּבְרֵי הַתּוֹרָה, 8:9). The initial description of the community's makeup established the importance of communal comprehension: "understanding by hearing" (מֵבִין לִשְׁמֹעַ, 8:2) was the prerequisite for participation in the assembly. The "hearing" (כְּשָׁמְעָם) of the people that prompts their weeping (8:9) recalls the importance of this hearing with understanding (מֵבִין לִשְׁמֹעַ, 8:2).

The whole segment (7:72b–8:12) dramatizes the community's formation through understanding (בין). The root בין occurs six times, twice in each of three subunits: the first (8:2, 3), the third (8:7, 8), and the fourth (8:9, 12). The only children qualified for membership in the assembly are those capable of understanding (הַמְּבִינִים, 8:3; cf. מֵבִין לִשְׁמֹעַ, 8:2) the reading of the law.[20] The Levites actualize this capability of the congregation: they "helped the people understand the law" (מְבִינִים אֶת־הָעָם לַתּוֹרָה, 8:7), and their work resulted in the people "understanding the reading" (וַיָּבִינוּ בַּמִּקְרָא, 8:8). However, the final subunit indicates that the people's understanding mediated by the Levites (הַלְוִיִּם הַמְּבִינִים, 8:9) was only provisional. The people require final instructions from Ezra (supported by the Levites) to correct their immediate misapprehension of the law so that they can truly understand (הֵבִינוּ, 8:12) what they had been taught.

The content of the people's understanding is significant, namely, "the matters that were taught them," rather than merely "the words of the law." The distinction between these two contents is evident in the contrast between the clauses describing their initial misunderstanding (כְּשָׁמְעָם אֶת־דִּבְרֵי הַתּוֹרָה: "as they heard the words of the law," 8:9) and their subsequent understanding after correction (הֵבִינוּ בַּדְּבָרִים אֲשֶׁר הוֹדִיעוּ לָהֶם: "they understood the matters that had been made known to them," 8:12). Thus, the determinative factor is not the content of the book but rather its interpretation through the teaching of Ezra and the Levites.

At the same time, the verb הוֹדִיעוּ—which summarizes the work of Ezra and the Levites inculcating the law on the congregation—intimately bonds the law (תּוֹרָה) with its proclamation (וַיִּקְרָא[וּ], 8:3, 7;

---

[19] 8:9: "all the people had been weeping as they heard the words of the law."

8:12: "all the people [went] ... to make great joy because they had understood the matters that they had made known to them."

[20] For discussion of הַמְּבִינִים (8:3) as referring to children, see pp. 105–6.

מקרא, 8:8). In Ezra-Nehemiah, the only other occurrence of the *hip'il* of ידע involves a similar concern, that is, in the psalm's description of God's instructing the people about the Sabbath while giving them the law (Neh 9:14).

In a temporal aspect, the fourth subunit narrates the final phase of the morning's activities (cf. 8:3). Its content recounts events that follow the reading of the law. Three of its four verses begin with the converted imperfect (*wayyiqtol*) verbal form descriptive of completed actions in the past (GBH §112c). The remaining verse (8:11) begins with a subject followed by a participle (הלוים מחשים, 8:11), indicating durative action contemporaneous with what precedes (GBH §121f).[21] Thus, content, verb forms, and narrative position all suggest that the fourth subunit describes the conclusion of the assembly around noon (cf. 8:3).

Therefore in temporal sequence and relative duration, the four subunits feature the interlocking of alternating time frames:
 a. A comprehensive overview of the morning-long reading (7:72b–8:3)
 b. A retrospective focus on the initial solemn events (8:4–6)
 c. A comprehensive overview of the morning-long instruction (8:7–8)
 d. A concluding focus on the final critical events (8:9–12).

LEXICAL EXAMINATION

In order to provide an adequate context for discussing particular issues, I begin this section with a survey of the pentateuchal legislation governing the Festival of Booths in view of its influence on the composition of Neh 7:72b–8:18. I follow this introductory analysis of Booths with a treatment of the lexical elements in the description of Ezra's reading of the law (7:72b–8:12).

THE FESTIVAL OF BOOTHS AND NEHEMIAH 7:72b–8:18

The Pentateuch contains seven prescriptions governing the Festival of Booths, which I shall collate under three categories of tradition: pre-Deuteronomic (Exod 23:16b; 34:22b), Deuteronomic (Deut 16:13–17; 31:9–13), and Priestly (Num 29:12–38; Lev 23:33–36, 39–42).[22] These texts

---

[21] Note the similarity in both tense and subject-verb sequence.
8:11: והלוים מחשים לכל־העם.
8:7: הלוים מבינים את־העם.
Regarding 8:11, the *hip'il* חשה generally denotes silence or a lack of responsiveness (see, e.g., Judg 18:9; 1 Kgs 22:3; 2 Kgs 2:3, 5; 7:9). However, in Neh 8:11 the Levites' initial command (הסו) demands a causative sense for חשה.

[22] My synchronic study prescinds from the debate over further distinctions, e.g., (1) between early Deuteronomic (D¹: Deut 16:13–17) and late Deuteronomic (D²: Deut 31:9–13) laws (cf. M. Noth, *The Deuteronomistic History* [trans. D. J. A. Clines

without exception identify Booths as a "festival" (חג). The traditions also specify Booths as the major autumn festival in Israel (Exod 23:16b; 34:22b; Lev 23:34, 39; Deut 16:13).[23] According to all these traditions as well, pilgrimage is at least an implied dimension of the Festival of Booths.[24]

However, while the various traditions agree on the timing and importance of Booths as a pilgrimage celebration, they diverge over the precise character of the festival. A comparative reading of the texts discloses a tension among three dimensions of the celebration: agricultural, sacrificial, and catechetical. The agricultural aspect, which derives from the autumn harvest, is manifest in the pre-Deuteronomic (Exod 23:16b; 34:22b) and Deuteronomic legislation (Deut 16:13, 15b) but is only implied in the Priestly laws (Lev 23:39–40 [the four kinds of boughs]). By contrast, the sacrificial dimension comes to the fore in the Priestly texts (Num 29:12–38; Lev 23:36) but is absent from the other traditions. The catechetical thrust is muted in the Priestly interpretation of the booths as symbolizing Israel's wilderness era (Lev 23:43: "so that your generations may know") but predominates in the Deuteronomic injunction to proclaim the law during the Festival of Booths in the year of remission (Deut 31:10–13: "so that they may hear and learn").[25]

---

et al.; 2d ed.; JSOTSup 15; Sheffield: Sheffield Press, 1991], 28–29); and (2) between Priestly (P: Num 29:12–38; Lev 23:33–36) and Holiness (H: Lev 23:39–43) texts (cf. I. Knohl, "The Priestly Torah versus the Holiness School: Sabbath and Festivals," *HUCA* 58 [1987]: 65–117; idem, *The Sanctuary of Silence: The Priestly Torah and the Holiness School* [Minneapolis: Fortress, 1995]; and J. Milgrom, *Leviticus 1–16* [AB 3; New York: Doubleday, 1991], 35–42).

[23] The Pentateuch treats the Festival of Booths subsequent to Passover/Unleavened Bread (in spring) and Weeks (in summer), thereby identifying it as one of the three major "festivals" of the year (Exod 23:14–17; 34:18–24; Num 28:16–29:38; Lev 23:1–44; Deut 16:1–13). Deut 31:9–13 does not mention other festivals.

[24] The pre-Deuteronomic laws suggest a pilgrimage to a sanctuary by designating the Festival of Booths as one of the three times annually when "all your males shall appear before YHWH" (Exod 34:23; cf. 23:17). Similarly, the Priestly tradition enjoins the people to "rejoice before YHWH, your God" (Lev 23:40) and to offer sacrifices over a seven-day period (Num 29:12–38; Lev 23:34). The Deuteronomic tradition is more explicit in its prescription that the people celebrate the festival "at the place YHWH will choose" (Deut 16:15; 31:11).

[25] For a discussion of various theories regarding the origin and evolution of the Festival of Booths, see J. L. Rubenstein, "The History of Sukkot during the Second Temple and Rabbinic Periods: Studies in the Continuity and Change of a Festival" (Ph.D. diss., Columbia University, 1992), 36–61. According to the classical hypothesis, the Israelites adopted an originally Canaanite harvest feast (אסף, Exod 23:16b; 34:22; cf. Judg 9:27), which they subsequently centralized at a particular sanctuary (Deut 16:15; cf. Judg 21:19 [Shiloh]) and eventually historicized as a commemoration of the

The Reading of the Law and the Festival of Booths

The legislation governing the Festival of Booths has many points of contact with the account of the celebration of Booths under Ezra (Neh 8:13–18) and in the narrative of Ezra's reading of the law (Neh 7:72b–8:12).

Table 3.2—Neb 7:72b–8:18 and Laws Governing the Festival of Booths

Neh 7:72b–8:18	Exod 23:16b	Exod 34:22b	Num 29:12-38	Lev 23:33-36	Lev 23:39-43	Deut 16:13-17	Deut 31:9-13
Seventh month			x	x	x		
Children of Israel				x	x		
All							x
The people							x
Reading the law							x
Men and women							x
Levites							x
The words of the law							x
Joy					x	x	
The festival (חג)	x	x	x	x	x	x	x
Dwelling in booths					x		
Trees					x		
Seven days			x	x	x	x	
Eighth day			x	x	x		
Solemnity עצרת			x	x			

---

exodus. This perspective views the proclamation of the law as a late innovation. (See, e.g., G. W. MacRae, "The Meaning and Evolution of the Feast of Tabernacles," *CBQ* 22 [1960]: 251–76; R. de Vaux, *Ancient Israel: Its Life and Institutions* [trans. John McHugh; London: Darton, Longman & Todd, 1961], 495–502; cf. J. Wellhausen, *Prolegomena to the History of Ancient Israel* [Cleveland: World Publishing, 1957], 83–120.) An alternative hypothesis pictures the festival as originating as a covenant-renewal pilgrimage among the seminomadic ancestors of the Israelites who eventually settled in Canaan (Josh 8:30–35; 24:1–28) and, thereupon, incorporated the indigenous harvest feast into their celebration. This proposal considers the proclamation of the law as an original element of the feast. (See H.-J. Kraus, *Gottesdienst in Israel: Studien zur Geschichte des Laubenhüttenfestes* [BEvT 19; Munich: Kaiser, 1954], esp. 18–42; idem, *Worship in Israel: A Cultic History of the Old Testament* [trans. G. Buswell; Richmond: John Knox, 1966], 61–66, 131–32, 144–45; cf. G. von Rad, "The Form-Critical Problem of the Hexateuch," in *The Problem of the Hexateuch and Other Essays* [trans. E. W. Trueman Dicken; New York: McGraw-Hill, 1966], 34–38.)

In Neh 8:1–18, the term חג (8:14, 18) indistinctly echoes the pre-Deuteronomic tradition (Exod 34:23b; 23:16b), whereas the term is common to the entire legislation on Booths. The harvest motif that is the essence of the festival in this tradition (אָסִיף: "ingathering," Exod 34:22b; 23:16b) is absent in Neh 8:1–18.

The Priestly laws regulate the date (in the seventh month, Neh 7:72b; 8:14; cf. Num 29:12; Lev 23:34, 39) and the duration of the festival (seven days with an additional eighth day [עצרת], Neh 8:18; cf. Num 29:12–32; Lev 23:34, 36). The prescriptions in Lev 23:39–42 parallel three elements of Neh 8:13–18: the proclamation that the Israelites should dwell in booths during the festival (Neh 8:14; cf. Lev 23:41–43); the narrative fulfillment of that injunction (Neh 8:16–17; cf. Lev 23:42–43); and the listing of the various boughs associated with Booths (Neh 8:15; cf. Lev 23:40). Moreover, Lev 23:40 coincides with Deut 16:14–15 in ordaining the disposition of joy at the festival (Neh 8:12, 17b).[26]

For its part, Deut 16:13–17 corresponds with Num 29:12–32 and Lev 23:34, 36 in specifying a seven-day duration for the festival (Deut 16:13, 15; cf. Neh 8:18).

Nevertheless, Deut 31:9–13 exercises a greater influence than Deut 16:13–17 throughout Neh 7:72b–8:18, particularly in the account of Ezra's reading the law (Neh 7:72b–8:12). The legislation of Deut 31:9–13 contributes six distinctive elements to the narrative: (1) the term "the people" (העם, Deut 31:12; cf. the fifteen occurrences in Neh 7:72b–8:18); (2) the adjective "all" to designate the inclusiveness of the assembly (כל: "all," Deut 31:11 [qualifying ישראל]; cf. Neh 7:72b–8:18 [eleven times qualifying עם, once qualifying קהל]); (3) the specification of "men and women" (Deut 31:12; cf. Neh 8:2, 3); (4) specific mention of the Levites (Deut 31:9; cf. Neh 8:7, 9, 11, 13); (5) most importantly, the reading of the law during the Festival of Booths (Deut 31:11; Neh 8:18; cf. 8:3); and (6) the expression "the words of [the] law" (דברי התורה הזאת, Deut 31:12; cf. דברי התותה, Neh 8:9, 14).

In summary, Neh 7:72b–8:18 derives characteristics from the legislation regarding Booths in both the Deuteronomic and Priestly traditions. However, of these legal texts, Deut 31:9–13 and Lev 23:39–42 exert the strongest influence on Ezra's reading of the law (Neh 7:72b–8:12) and the subsequent celebration of Booths (Neh 8:13–18).

---

[26] Among the legal texts, Lev 23:34 and Deut 16:13, 16; 31:10 employ the title "the Festival of Booths" (חג הסכות). This designation occurs also in Ezra 3:4 but not in Neh 8:13–18, although Neh 8:13 does cite the words in reverse order when speaking of the Israelites dwelling "in booths on the festival of the seventh month" (בסכות בחג בחדש השביעי).

Lexical Analysis

My lexical examination proceeds according to the subunits I identified in the outline and literary analysis. My interpretation of each subunit involves studying its primary subject matter in view of its background in the rest of biblical literature and its significance elsewhere in Ezra-Nehemiah.

Ezra introduces the book of the law to all the people (7:72b–8:3)

The exegetical analysis of the first subunit focuses on its five main components: (1) time, (2) place, (3) the community, (4) the book of the law, and (5) Ezra.

Time. The introductory sentence (7:72b), which provides the setting in terms of date and place, is identical to Ezra 3:1a.²⁷ Both verses introduce a narrative that recounts a celebration of the Festival of Booths (Neh 8:13–18; cf. Ezra 3:4–6).

The seventh month (החדש השביעי, i.e., Tishri: September/October) maintains the chronological sequence, following as it does mention of Elul (the sixth month) during which the construction of the wall is completed (Neh 6:15). According to the narrative, these events take place in the twentieth year of Artaxerxes' reign (Neh 2:1, Nisan being the first month of the year).

The phrase "the seventh month" follows the numeration of the Babylonian calendar, which began the New Year in springtime. The Priestly tradition assigns three festivals to this month: the acclamation on the first day, the Day of Atonement on the tenth, and the Festival of Booths from the fifteenth to the twenty-second followed by an additional day of assembly (Lev 23:24–25, 27–32, 33–36; Num 29:1–6, 7–11, 12–38).

Against the background of the pentateuchal legislation on the festivals, the unit's progressive narrowing of the time frame from the seventh month (7:72b) to the first day (8:2) to the hours from sunrise until noon (8:3) successively clarifies the nature of the event. The first two indications point directly to the law codes: the seventh month, indicating the autumn festival (Exod 23:16b; 34:22a; Lev 23:23–43; Num 29:1–39; Deut 16:13–15); and the first day, pointing to the day of acclamation (Num 29:1–6; Lev 23:23–25). However, the third indication (i.e., the span of the morning hours devoted to the reading) signals an unprecedented event akin to the proclamation of the law in the year of remission (Deut 31:9–13).

The second reference to time ("on the first day of the seventh month," 8:2) raises an exegetical difficulty over the precise nature of the assembly. Within Ezra-Nehemiah, this day also marks the beginning of sacrificial

---

²⁷ In Ezra 3:1a, read בעריהם for בערים with several versions. The noun חדש as the subject of the verb נגע occurs only here and in Ezra 3:1a in the MT.

offerings at the temple by the exiles who first returned to Jerusalem (Ezra 3:6). The critical issue here is whether or not the "first day of the seventh month" was New Year's Day in Judah. Mowinckel views Ezra's proclamation of the Torah on this day as the centerpiece of a postexilic New Year's festival on the first of Tishri.[28]

However, the biblical and archaeological evidence militates against Mowinckel's thesis. The evidence favoring an autumn date as the beginning of the new year even in preexilic Israel is scant and ambiguous. The ancient traditions that situate the autumn festival of "ingathering" (אסיף) at the "turning of the year" (תקופת השנה, Exod 34:22) or at the "going forth of the year" (בצאת השנה, Exod 23:16) refer to the end of the agricultural season, which might not have been coterminus with the calendar year.[29] Similarly, the Gezer Calendar (ca. 925 B.C.E.), which begins the year with the autumn olive harvest, is concerned with the schedule of harvesting, planting, and tending, not with the calculations of days and months according to solar and lunar phenomena.[30] The only biblical reference to the "new year" (ראש השנה, Ezek 40:1) may actually point to Nisan rather than to Tishri. In any case, ראש השנה here refers to the month, not to the day, since the new year would not begin on the tenth day of the month.[31]

The fact that throughout the Pentateuch the calendar of the three great festivals begins with the spring festival and ends in the autumn further strengthens the case against associating the Festival of Booths with the new year (Exod 23:14–17; 34:18, 22–24; Lev 23:5–8, 15–22, 33–36; Num 28:16–25, 26–31; 29:12–39; Deut 16:1–17). The Priestly tradition prescribes the first day of the seventh month as "a memorial, an acclamation, and a proclamation of holiness" (זכרון תרועה מקרא־קדש, Lev 23:24–25). Elsewhere the same

---

[28] S. Mowinckel, *Studien III,* 44–59. Morgenstern offers a similar account of the events in Neh 7:72b–8:18 ("The Three Calendars of Ancient Israel," 28–35). Mowinckel's understanding of Neh 8 is an extension of his hypothesis that, beginning in the era of the monarchy, Israel celebrated an annual New Year's festival that centered on the enthronement of YHWH as king over his people. See S. Mowinckel, *Psalmenstudien II: Das Thronbesteigungsfest Jahwäs und der Ursprung der Eschatologie* (repr., Amsterdam: P. Schippers, 1961); idem, *Zum israelitischen Neujahr und zur Deutung der Thronbesteigungspsalmen* (AUNVAO 2; Oslo: Dybwad, 1952); idem, *The Psalms in Israel's Worship* (trans. D. R. Ap-Thomas; Nashville: Abingdon, 1962), 106–92.

[29] See D. J. A. Clines, "The Evidence for an Autumnal New Year in Pre-exilic Israel Reconsidered," *JBL* 93 (1974): 22–40.

[30] VanderKam, "Calendars," 817; cf. Finegan, "Principles of the Calendar," 570–73.

[31] De Vaux, *Ancient Israel,* 502–4; W. Eichrodt, *Ezekiel* (trans. C. Quin; OTL; Philadelphia: Westminster, 1970), 540–41; cf. W. Zimmerli, *Ezekiel 2* (trans. R. E. Clements; Hermeneia; Philadelphia: Fortress, 1983), 345–46.

tradition calls this "a day of acclamation" (יום תרועה, Num 29:1). However, while mention of this "acclamation" (תרועה) indicates that there was a special celebration of the monthly new moon in the seventh month (cf. Num 28:11–15), it does not suggest that this was also the beginning of the new year.³² In sum, incontestable biblical evidence is lacking that the celebration of the new year was a major event in Israel.³³ Furthermore, nothing in the Nehemiah account suggests that Ezra's reading of the law on the first day of the seventh month was part of a New Year's Day ritual.

The time span for the reading (מן־האור עד־מחצית היום): "from daybreak until noonday," 8:3) comes to some six and a half hours.³⁴ The construction "from ... to" (עד ... מן), expressing a temporal span, occurs seventeen times in the MT.³⁵ The three occurrences in the covenant-renewal account that mark a duration of activity (Neh 8:3, 18; 9:5; cf. 8:17) create a noteworthy parallelism that I shall discuss in connection with 9:5.

Place. On the place of assembly, Neh 8:1 departs from Ezra 3:1 by specifying a precise location rather than Jerusalem in general. The repetition of "the square that is in front of the Water Gate" (הרחוב אשר לפני שער־המים, 8:1, 3) indicates that the site is significant for the ensuing narrative.

The Water Gate was situated on the east side of Jerusalem. Its name suggests proximity to the Gihon Spring. However, its precise location relative to Nehemiah's wall is an archaeological puzzle.³⁶ Nevertheless, from a narrative perspective, Ezra-Nehemiah suggests that the Water Gate was

---

³² The Year of Jubilee begins with the sounding of the shofar (שפר תרועה, Lev 25:9) on the tenth day of the seventh month, a ritual that differs from the simple "acclamation" (תרועה, Lev 23:24) on the first day of the seventh month.

³³ D. J. A. Clines, "New Year," *IDBSup* 625–29.

³⁴ For a similar expression of time, see 1 Kgs 18:26 ("from morning until noon": מהבקר ועד־הצהרים). According to the U. S. Naval Observatory ("Jerusalem, Rise and Set for the Sun for Any Year," personal correspondence), on the day of the autumn equinox in 1995 (September 23, at 2:13 P.M.), sunrise in Jerusalem occurred at 5:28 A.M.

³⁵ Exod 18:13, 14; Judg 13:7; 2 Sam 21:10; 24:15; Jer 7:7; 25:5; Pss 41:14; 90:2; 103:17; 106:48; Dan 2:20; Ezra 5:16; Neh 8:3, 18; 9:5; 1 Chr 16:36. Nine of these instances involve the expression "from everlasting to everlasting" (מן־עולם עד־עולם and orthographic variations: Jer 7:7; 25:5; Pss 41:14; 90:2; 103:17; 106:48; Dan 2:20 [מן־עלמא ועד־עלמא]; 1 Chr 16:36; Neh 9:5), while the remaining eight indicate a measurable span of time.

³⁶ Nehemiah 12:37 suggests that the Water Gate was part of the restored walls since, at the dedication, the procession went "as far as the Water Gate on the east" (המים למזרח עד שער). However, Neh 3:26 indicates that the Water Gate was rather east of the wall since, in the construction, the temple servants repaired "as far as a point opposite the Water Gate on the east" (עד נגד שער המים למזרח); see Rudolph, *Esra und Nehemia,* 119). Primarily on the basis of this latter text, Williamson locates

part of Jerusalem but not part of the temple precincts. First, at least in terms of the ideology of Ezra-Nehemiah, the Water Gate is integral to Jerusalem. As an essential landmark, it defines the boundaries of Jerusalem both in the reconstruction of its walls and in their rededication (Neh 3:26; 12:37). Mention of the square at the Water Gate (along with the square at the Gate of Ephraim [cf. 12:39]) immediately after the temple courts as a location for the booths confirms its significance as a festival site (8:16).

Second, the Water Gate does not belong to the temple precincts. The square in front of the Water Gate is not the same as "the square in front of the house of God" (Ezra 10:9), nor is it equivalent to the temple site where the first returning exiles set up the altar, offered sacrifices, and celebrated the Festival of Booths (Ezra 3:1–6).[37] Locating Ezra's reading of the law in the square before the Water Gate thus differentiates this event from previous ones, notably those that took place in the environs of the temple (Ezra 3:1–7, 8–13; 10:9).

The community. In its first subunit, the narrative presents an introductory portrait of the community via three primary designations: (1) "the children of Israel" (7:72b); (2) "all the people" (8:1, 3); and (3) "the assembly" (8:2). I will discuss these terms in conjunction with other related expressions in the first subunit.

In Ezra-Nehemiah, the term בני ישראל has in view the generations that journeyed with Moses (Neh 13:2) and Joshua (8:17). The designation

---

the Water Gate outside the city wall down the slope of the Kidron Valley, near the Gihon Spring (*Ezra, Nehemiah,* 287, cf. 209, 374–75). However, one wonders whether such a locale is compatible with the fact that in front of the Water Gate there was a level "square" (רחוב) large enough to accommodate all the people (Neh 8:1, 3) and serve as a place for the booths (8:16).

[37] S. Mowinckel (*Studien zu dem Buche Ezra-Nehemia I: Die nachchronistiche Redaktion des Buches. Die Listen* [SUNVAO 3; Oslo: Universitetsforlaget, 1964], 36–40) and Pohlmann (*Dritten Esra,* 151–54) argue that the site of Neh 8 is identical to that of Ezra 3 so as to maintain that Ezra's reading of the law is part of a New Year's temple ritual. Mowinckel's evidence is conjectural: (1) the temple square would have been the only location large enough to accommodate an assembly of all the people (Ezra 10:9); (2) the name "Water Gate" may derive from the transportation of water to the temple precincts in early liturgical processions (cf. Isa 12:3); and (3) even the mistaken identification of the East Gate with the Water Gate in 1 Esdras (Neh 8:1 = 1 Esd 9:38: πρὸς ἀνατολὰς ἱεροῦ; cf. 1 Esd 5:46: πρὸς τῇ ἀνατολῇ) supports the claim that both gates belonged to the temple precincts and sustains the possibility that Ezra 3 was written from the viewpoint of the East Gate while Neh 8 reflects rather the perspective of the Water Gate. Pohlmann's further contention that the East Gate (1 Esd 5:46 = Ezra 3:1) could be another name for the Water Gate (1 Esd 9:48 = Neh 8:1) is dubious due to his (and Mowinckel's) disregard of the MT in both Ezra 3:1 and Neh 8:1.

applies more immediately to "those who had returned from the exile" (הַשָּׁבִים מֵהַגּוֹלָה, Ezra 6:21; cf. 2:1; 8:35; Neh 7:6) along with "those who had separated themselves from the impurity of the Gentiles of the land" (הַנִּבְדָּל מִטֻּמְאַת גּוֹיֵי־הָאָרֶץ, Ezra 6:21). The first generation of returnees were the people who rebuilt and dedicated the temple (Ezra 3:1; 6:16, 21). Over fifty years later, they were the comrades of Ezra and Nehemiah (Ezra 7:7; Neh 1:6; 2:10; 7:72; 8:14, 17; 9:1; 10:40). The title בְּנֵי יִשְׂרָאֵל identifies them as the rightful heirs of the ancient Israelites who first took possession of the land under the direction of Moses and Joshua.

The term בְּנֵי יִשְׂרָאֵל occurs in liturgical settings in ten of its thirteen uses within Ezra-Nehemiah: in the preparations for the initial rites at the temple site (Ezra 3:1); at the dedication of the temple (6:16); during the celebration of Passover (6:21); in the prayer of Nehemiah (1:6 [bis]); and the covenant-renewal account (Neh 7:72; 8:14, 17; 9:1; 10:40).[38] Particularly significant is the link that the term establishes between the covenant renewal and the three earlier celebrations.

Nehemiah 7:72b–8:18 contains eleven of the sixteen occurrences of the second designation, "all the people" (כָּל־הָעָם), in Ezra-Nehemiah.[39] The other four instances in Hebrew fall into two categories according to whether or not they are modified by a possessive adjective.[40] The two unqualified expressions (כָּל־הָעָם) appear in the accounts of other assemblies in Jerusalem: (1) at the temple site for the laying of the foundations (Ezra 3:11); and (2) in the square before the temple for the marriage reform (Ezra 10:9).[41] The two instances in which a possessive adjective modifies the expression exhibit a pronounced theological aspect, asserting that "all the people" belong to God: "all his people" (כָּל־עַמּוֹ, Ezra 1:3), and "all your people" (כָּל־עַמְּךָ, Neh 9:32). These two expressions occur at strategic locations in relationship to Ezra's reading of the law (Neh 7:72b–8:18): the first establishing the theme in the opening lines of the book that quote

---

[38] The contexts of the other occurrences are: (1) the introduction of those who accompanied Ezra from Babylon to Jerusalem (Ezra 7:7); (2) the initial description of the hostility toward Nehemiah on the part of Sanballat the Horonite and Tobiah the Ammonite (Neh 2:10); and (3) the recollection of Ammon's and Moab's refusing hospitality to the Israelites during the wilderness era (Neh 13:2).

[39] Ezra 1:3; 3:11; 7:25 [Aramaic]; 10:9; Neh 8:1, 3, 5 [3x], 6, 9 [bis], 11, 12, 13; 9:32.

[40] The remaining instance in Aramaic is an element in Artaxerxes' commissioning Ezra to appoint magistrates to judge "all the people" (כָּל־עַמָּה, Ezra 7:25).

[41] Each of these assemblies contains narrative links to the assembly for the reading of the law (Neh 7:72b–8:12): (1) via the liturgical action and the people's reactions of joy and weeping (Neh 8:5–6, 9–12; cf. Ezra 3:10–11, 12–13); and (2) via the profile of Ezra as leader and the mention of another square in Jerusalem (Neh 8:3; cf. Ezra 10:9–12).

the edict of Cyrus (Ezra 1:2–4); the second carrying the theme forward into the penitential psalm that the people recite subsequent to their learning the Torah (Neh 9:6–37).

In terms of background, it is noteworthy that כל־העם designates the audience Joshua addresses when he renews the covenant at Shechem (Josh 24:2, 27).[42] Similarly, toward the end of the Deuteronomistic History, "all the people" (כל־העם) ratify the covenant after hearing Josiah read from the book that had been discovered during the renovation of the temple (2 Kgs 23:1–3; cf. 2 Chr 34:30).

The verb אסף (nip'al), which describes the initial movement of "all the people," occurs six times in Ezra-Nehemiah, always within the context of a transforming event for the community: the initial offering of sacrifices at the temple site (Ezra 3:1); the marriage reform (9:4); the reading of the law (Neh 8:1); the Festival of Booths (8:13); the rites of repentance (9:1); and the dedication of the walls (12:28). In four of these instances (Ezra 3:1; Neh 8:1, 13; 9:1), the total population is the subject.[43] In Neh 7:72b–10:40, the threefold repetition of the third-person plural subdivides the covenant-renewal account into three major constituents by successively introducing each of the plenary assemblies (יאספו [8:1]; נאספו [8:13; 9:1]).

The simile that describes the people's gathering "as one" (כאיש אחד, 8:1) suggests unity among the populace for decision making and action (cf. 1 Sam 11:7; 2 Sam 19:15). The expression recurs in the account of the assembly of the tribes at Mizpah to take action against the Benjaminites (Judg 20:11; cf. 20:1, 8). The simile appears to be a Deuteronomistic expression (see Judg 6:16; 20:1, 8, 11; 1 Sam 11:7; 19:14; cf. Num 14:15; Ezra 3:1).

The third designation, "assembly" (קהל), occurs ten times in Ezra-Nehemiah. It designates the congregation of Israel as distinct from other nations (Neh 13:1). In Ezra-Nehemiah, this is "the assembly of the exile" (קהל הגולה, Ezra 10:8) or "the assembly of those who had returned from captivity" (הקהל השבים מן־השבי, Neh 8:17), that is, those who returned to Jerusalem from Babylon (Ezra 2:64 = Neh 7:66). Seven times קהל occurs within the context of gatherings for the reformation of the community: marriage reform under Ezra (Ezra 10:1, 8, 12, 14 in 10:1–17); social reform under Nehemiah (Neh 5:13 in 5:1–13), and covenant renewal under Ezra and other leaders (Neh 8:2, 17 in 7:72b–8:18). The two uses of the term

---

[42] The term provides an *inclusio* insofar as "all this people" (כל־העם הזה) designates the assembly that YHWH commissioned Joshua to lead across the Jordan in the opening lines of the book (Josh 1:2).

[43] In the remaining two instances, the subject of אסף is a significant subgroup: "those who tremble at the word" (Ezra 9:4) and the singers who live outside Jerusalem (Neh 12:28).

during the reading of the law unite Ezra's initial proclamation (Neh 7:72b–8:12) and the celebration of Booths (8:13–18).

Participants in the assembly are "men as well as women, and everyone who could understand by hearing" (מאיש עד־אשה וכל מבין לשמע, 8:2) or "the men, the women, and those who could understand" (האנשים והנשים והמבינים, 8:3). Who are "those who could understand" (לשמע כל מבין/ המבינים)? Viewing them as a third group of listeners (in addition to "men and women") is preferable to the alternative proposals that would take המבינים/כל מבין לשמע as either (1) an apposition to "the men and the women";[44] or (2) a reference to the teachers "who bring understanding to what one hears" (i.e., the Levites [cf. 8:8]).[45] In Neh 8:2, the *hipʿil* participle מבין is intransitive.[46] Moreover, the *hipʿil* of בין, which here conveys a noncausative sense (i.e., "to understand"), corresponds with the subsequent employment of the verb in the converted *qal* imperfect (ויבינו, 8:8) and then in the *hipʿil* perfect (הבינו, 8:12). By contrast, the causative sense denotes the activity of the Levites who enable the people to understand (מבינים, 8:7, 9).[47]

"Those who could understand" (וכל מבין, 8:2; ומבינים, 8:3) are the children. The parallelism between Ezra 10:1 and Neh 8:2 and 8:3 makes clear that the expression in the latter two cases is an alternative way of speaking of "the men, the women, and the children."[48] Moreover, Neh 10:29 confirms

---

[44] H. C. M. Vogt argues that in 8:2 the expression וכל מבין לשמע is a summarizing apposition for "the men and the women" (*Studie zur nachexilischen Gemeinde in Esra-Nehemia* [Werl: Dietrich Coelde, 1966], 80–81). His thesis presupposes that the phrase begins with a "waw colligans" (וכל); none of his examples, however, offers evidence for such a construction in Ezra-Nehemiah (cf. Ezra 1:5; 3:8; Neh 9:32; 10:29).

[45] C. Wiéner suggests this as a tentative proposal, given his ascribing a causative sense to all the six instances of the *hipʿil* בין (8:2, 3, 7, 8, 9, 12) in the account ("Des enfants à l'Assemblée? Note brève sur Néhémie 8," in *La Vie de la Parole: De l'Ancien au Nouveau Testament* [Mélanges Pierre Grelot; ed. Département des Etudes Bibliques de l'Institut Catholique de Paris; Paris: Desclée, 1987], 151–54). However, this reading would be uncharacteristically elliptical given the explicit mention of the Levites as subjects of the *hipʿil* in the remainder of the account (8:7, 9, 11). Moreover, Wiéner admits that Dan 8:16–17 provides evidence for taking the *hipʿil* of בין alternatively as causative and noncausative in two occurrences that stand in close proximity to one another.

[46] BDB, 106: מבין is "one who has understanding" (Prov 8:9; 17:10, 24; 28:2, 7, 11).

[47] In Ezra-Nehemiah, six of the seven uses of the *hipʿil* form of בין occur in the covenant-renewal account (Neh 7:72b–10:40): Ezra 8:16; Neh 8:2, 3, 7, 8, 9; 10:29.

[48] Like Neh 8:2, Ezra 10:1 describes a large assembly (קהל).
Ezra 10:1: אנשים ונשים וילדים.
Neh 8:3: האנשים והנשים ומבינים.

this identification by employing the phrase "all who knew how to understand" in apposition to "their wives, their sons, and their daughters."[49]

However, no one has yet answered why the expression "those who could understand" is used in Neh 8:2, 3 instead of the more conventional terms "children" (ילדים, Ezra 10:1) or "sons and daughters" (בנים ובנתים, Neh 10:29). I suggest the solution lies in the association between understanding (מבין) and observance of the law in a traditional definition of the ideal child: "One who keeps the law is a son who understands" (נוצר תורה בן מבין, Prov 28:7). Given this usage, employment of the more pointed term מבינים (in preference to the conventional ילדים or בנים ובנות) coincides with the focus on the law that dominates Neh 7:72b–8:18. Since מבינים is a term of discrimination, not all children are included, only those who are intent on keeping the law.[50]

The book of the law. The complete title of the book ("the book of the law of Moses with which YHWH had charged Israel") in Neh 8:1 is almost identical to that used in the introduction of Ezra (Ezra 7:6)[51] and closely resembles its designation in Neh 8:14. This title exhibits an affinity to the language of

---

Neh 8:2: מאיש עד־אשה וכל מבין לשמע.
Each of these expressions is unique to Ezra-Nehemiah. None of them occurs elsewhere in the Bible.

[49] Neh 10:29: נשיהם בניהם ובנתיהם כל יודע מבין ("their wives, their sons, their daughters, everyone who knows how to understand"). The explicit mention of these categories ("their women, their sons, and their daughters") who, along with the men, comprise the "people" (עם) corresponds up to a point with the Deuteronomic legislation on the reading of the law during the Festival of Booths in the year of remission (Deut 31:9–13). However, the designations in Deut 31:12 vary, not only from Neh 8:2, 3, but also from Ezra 10:1 and Neh 10:29. Like the texts in Ezra and Nehemiah, Deuteronomy speaks of "men and women," but, for "children," Deuteronomy employs the term הטף (cf. ילדים, Ezra 10:1; בניהם ובנתיהם, Neh 10:28). In addition, Deut 31:12 includes in its list of participants "your alien in your gates" (וגרך אשר בשעריך), a category that would be excluded a priori in Ezra-Nehemiah. The Deuteronomic categories recur in the covenant renewal at Mount Ebal and Mount Gerizim: "the whole congregation of Israel" (כל־קהל ישראל) to whom Joshua reads the law includes "the women, the children, and the aliens who walk in their midst" (הנשים והטף והגר ההלך בקרבם, Josh 8:35).

[50] In Neh 10:29, "the sons and daughters" who are "capable of understanding" (יודע מבין) belong to families that have separated themselves from the people of the land on account of the former's allegiance to the law (תורה). Ezra describes as "learned" (מבינים, Ezra 8:16) two delegates whom he sends to Iddo at Casiphia.

[51] Neh 8:1: ספר תורת משה אשר־צוה יהוה את־ישראל.
Ezra 7:6: תורת משה אשר־נתן יהוה אלהי ישראל.

Chronicles (cf. 1 Chr 16:40).⁵² Indeed, the expression in Neh 8:1 partially echoes expressions associated with the Davidic covenant in Chronicles.⁵³

Moreover, the above terminology reflects Deuteronomic origins. "The law with which YHWH charged Israel" expresses the Deuteronomic standard for the covenant relationship (2 Kgs 17:13, 34). A similar expression that explicitly mentions the role of Moses summarizes the covenant that the Israelites renewed on the plains of Moab (Deut 28:69; cf. Num 36:13).⁵⁴

None of these texts mentions "the book of the law" (ספר תורה). Neh 8:1 does, however, share this feature with another Deuteronomic text, Josh 8:31. Moreover, all the vocabulary in the title of the book that the people request Ezra to bring occurs in Josh 8:31.⁵⁵ Thus, the title of the book in Neh 8:1 alludes to Joshua's reading of the law book at Mount Ebal and Mount Gerizim upon entering the land (Josh 8:30–35). Furthermore, in his farewell discourse, Joshua instructs the Israelites to obey "the book of the law of Moses" (Josh 23:6).⁵⁶ The manner in which mention of the "book" associates Ezra with Joshua foreshadows the comparison between their respective generations in observing the Festival of Booths (Neh 8:17).

Of the twenty-five occurrences of תורה in Ezra-Nehemiah, nineteen are in the covenant-renewal account (Neh 7:72b–10:40).⁵⁷ Its significance as a primary theme within this context corresponds with the emphasis it receives in the introduction of Ezra (Ezra 7:6–10). In the Hebrew text, תורה occurs only once in the narrative between the introduction of Ezra and the covenant-renewal account (Ezra 7:27–Neh 7:72a), that is, in reference to the legislation on marriage (Ezra 10:3). Thus, the emphasis on the law in the introduction of Ezra (Ezra 7:6–10) dramatically foreshadows its exposition by the priest-scribe in the square in front of the Water Gate (Neh 7:72b–8:18).

---

52 However, 1 Chr 16:40, which describes the regular offerings in Jerusalem, does not mention Moses.
Neh 8:1: ספר תורת משה אשר־צוה יהוה את־ישראל.
1 Chr 16:40: תורת יהוה אשר צוה על ישראל.

53 David's farewell speech to Solomon contains two expressions whose elements occur as a single phrase in Neh 8:1: "the law of YHWH, your God" (1 Chr 22:12, תורת יהוה אלהיך) and "[the statutes and ordinances] that YHWH commanded Moses for Israel" (1 Chr 22:13, אשר צוה יהוה את משה על ישראל).

54 Neh 8:1: ספר תורת משה אשר־צוה יהוה את־ישראל.
Deut 28:69: אלה דברי הברית אשר־צוה יהוה את־משה לכרת את־בני ישראל.

55 Neh 8:1: ספר תורת משה אשר־צוה יהוה את־ישראל.
Josh 8:31: צוה משה עבד־יהוה את־בני ישראל ככתוב בספר תורת משה.

56 ספר תורת משה occurs only four times in the MT (Josh 8:31; 23:6; 2 Kgs 14:6; Neh 8:1).

57 Ezra 3:2; 7:6, 10; 10:3; Neh 8:1, 2, 3, 7, 8, 9, 13, 14, 18; 9:3, 13, 14, 26, 29, 34; 10:29, 30, 35, 37; 12:44; 13:3. Cf. Aramaic, דתא: Ezra 7:12, 21, 26 [bis].

The description of Ezra's reading of and the people's attentive response to the law (8:3) echoes the Deuteronomic precept ordaining the reading of the law on the Festival of Booths in the year of remission (Deut 31:11):

Deut 31:11   תקרא את־התורה הזאת נגד כל־ישראל באזניהם
Neh 8:3   ויקרא־בו ... נגד האנשים והנשים והמבינים ואזני כל־העם אל־ספר התורה

Moreover, the correspondence with Deut 31:11 explains why Neh 8:3 repeats mention of the site: "[before] the square that is in front of the Water Gate" (cf. Neh 8:1). This specification parallels the Deuteronomic mention of the location for the gathering of "all Israel ... in the place that [YHWH, your God] will choose" (Deut 31:11), that is, in Jerusalem.[58]

Outside the book of Nehemiah, the MT recounts four episodes of public book reading: (1) Moses' proclamation of the book of the covenant at Mount Sinai (Exod 24:7); (2) Joshua's reading of the book of the law at Mount Ebal and Mount Gerizim (Josh 8:34); (3) Baruch's reading of Jeremiah's scroll at the entrance to the New Gate of the temple (Jer 36:10; cf. Baruch's private reading of the same document to the officials [36:13] and Jehudi's subsequent reading of it to the king [36:21]); and (4) Josiah's reading of the newly discovered Deuteronomic scroll in Jerusalem (2 Kgs 23:2 = 2 Chr 34:30). Nehemiah alone features the same number of such episodes: (1) Ezra's reading at the Water Gate (Neh 8:3, 8); (2) his subsequent reading throughout the seven days of the festival (Neh 8:18); (3) the people's reading at the penitential gathering (9:3); and (4) their reading in the wake of the dedication of the walls (13:1).

The expression ויקרא־בו ("and he read from it," 8:3, 8) suggests that Ezra did not read the whole book but only portions of it. By contrast, Josiah read the entire book that had been discovered in the temple (ויקרא את־כל־דברי ספר הברית, 2 Chr 34:30; 2 Kgs 23:2).[59]

The people's ears' being attuned to the law (ואזני כל־העם אל־ספר התורה, 8:3) is a positive contrast to the proverb that warns against "turning one's ear from hearing the law" (מסיר אזנו משמע התורה, Prov 28:9). The term אזנים (literally, "ears") for "hearing" echoes the Deuteronomic legislation that prescribes the reading of the law during Booths in the year of remission (Deut 31:11, תקרא את־התורה הזאת נגד כל־ישראל באזניהם).

Ezra. Nehemiah 8:1 reintroduces Ezra for the first time since Ezra 10:16. This is the first time since his initial introduction (Ezra 7:6) that he

---

[58] S. R. Driver, *A Critical and Exegetical Commentary on Deuteronomy* (3d ed.; ICC; Edinburgh: T&T Clark, 1986), 140.

[59] Williamson, *Ezra, Nehemiah,* 288.

is designated simply as "the scribe." "Ezra the scribe" (עזרא הספר) occurs subsequently only in the description of his reading and teaching the law (Neh 8:1, 4, 5, 13) and in the mention of his leading half the people in the procession around the walls (12:36).

While the people ask "Ezra the scribe" to bring the book of the law (8:1), the narrator describes "Ezra the priest" acceding to their wishes (8:2). Elsewhere, Ezra is called simply "the priest" only when he implements his marriage reforms (עזרא הכהן, Ezra 10:10, 16). The title corresponds to the extended genealogy in Ezra 7:1–6, which traces Ezra's heritage back to Aaron, the chief priest (הכהן הראש).

The verb "to bring" (בוא *hipʿil*), which describes Ezra's action, occurs eleven times in Neh 7:72b–10:40 out of its twenty-four occurrences in Ezra-Nehemiah.[60] Of particular note are the occurrences in which the verb alludes to a solemn presentation of gifts at the temple (Ezra 8:30; Neh 10:32, 35, 36, 37, 38, 40; 13:12).[61] In terms of background, David's "bringing" of the ark to Jerusalem and ultimately Solomon's bringing of it to the temple (בוא *hipʿil*, 1 Chr 16:1; 2 Chr 5:7) seems an apt analogy for the solemnity of Ezra's "bringing" the law before the people (Neh 8:1).

Ezra leads all the people in worship (8:4–6)

The following exegetical discussion calls attention to the precedents for and the significance of the liturgical action recounted in this subunit with regard to setting and gestures.

Setting. Mention of Ezra's "standing" (ויעמד, 8:4) on a platform is reminiscent of Josiah's "standing" (beside a pillar) when he makes the covenant after reading the book to the people (ויעמד המלך על־העמוד, 2 Kgs 23:3; cf. 2 Chr 34:31, על־עמדו). Insofar as the platform upon which Ezra (as well as the thirteen men) stands elevates him above the ground, it serves a purpose similar to that of the dais Solomon used at the dedication of the First Temple (2 Chr 6:13). A comparison of the two structures highlights the unique features of Ezra's platform: (1) in appearance Ezra's was a makeshift "tower" (מגדל; cf. Isa 5:2) rather than a carefully measured dais (כיור, 2 Chr 6:13); (2) it was made from wood (עץ) rather than bronze (נחשת); and (3) the people, not the leader, "made" (עשו, Neh 8:4; cf. שלמה עשה, 2 Chr 6:13) it. The description thus suggests that Ezra's platform was a type of scaffolding.

The placing of the six men on Ezra's right and seven on his left (8:4) serves a double function: on the one hand, it heightens Ezra's profile as a

---

[60] Ezra 3:7; 8:17, 18, 30; Neh 1:9; 3:5; 8:1, 2, 15, 16; 9:23; 10:32, 35, 36, 37, 38, 40; Neh 11:1; 12:27; 13:12, 15 [bis], 16, 18.

[61] Cf., e.g., Lev 23:10, 14, 15, 17; Deut 26:2, 9, 10; Mal 1:13 [bis]; 3:10; 2 Chr 29:31–32; 31:5–6, 10, 12.

leader (cf. 2 Sam 16:6; 1 Kgs 22:19 = 2 Chr 18:18) while, on the other, it suggests that others support his exercise of authority.

Gestures. The narrative describes various gestures that suggest a communal worship service with liturgical and instructional dimensions: (1) the priest-scribe in solemn procession with the Torah scroll (8:2); (2) his position at the forefront and above the assembly (8:4); (3) the stationing of other leaders on either side of him (8:4); (4) the unrolling of the scroll before the assembly (8:5); (5) the people's rising to their feet in response (8:5); (6) the presider's invocation of a blessing (8:6); (7) the people's responding in unison with "Amen," while raising their hands and worshiping (8:6); (8) the presider's reading of the text to the assembly (8:3); (9) the Levites' interpreting the text to the people (8:7–8); and (10) the leaders' instructing the people concerning the celebration of a subsequent festive meal (8:9–12).[62] Mention of such gestures is concentrated in 8:5–6.

The position of the people vis-à-vis the book when Ezra opens it underscores the solemnity of the event. In its only other occurrences in the MT, the expression לעיני כל־העם describes the setting of a covenantal revelation of God (Exod 19:11) and of a prophetic announcement (Jer 28:5, 11).[63]

Ezra's physical opening (פתח, 8:4) of the book implies a disclosing of wisdom that had previously been hidden from view. Daybreak (האור, 8:3) has a similar implication. This is the hour for giving understanding (מבין, 8:2, 3, 7, 9, 12) of the words of the law (דברי התורה, 8:9). Combining these elements within the narrative suggests an underlying meditation, that is, "The disclosing of your words gives light; it imparts understanding to the simple" (פתח דבריך יאיר מבין פתיים, Ps 119:130).

The statement that "Ezra blessed YHWH" (ויברך עזרא את־יהוה, 8:6) is cultic language. Its two occurrences in the Pentateuch indicate that such an activity is a response to God's prior action in favor of the speaker or of the people (Gen 24:48; Deut 8:10; cf. also Josh 22:33 [ויברכו אלהים]). Elsewhere, the expression ברך את יהוה occurs only in Chronicles and

---

[62] Cf. Kellermann (*Nehemia*, 29–30), who, along with other commentators, suggests that Ezra's reading of the law reflects an early synagogue service. See, e.g., K. Galling, *Die Bücher der Chronik, Esra, Nehemia* (ATD 12; Göttingen: Vandenhoeck & Ruprecht, 1954), 233–34; Pohlmann, *Dritten Esra*, 136; W. Th. In der Smitten, *Esra: Quellen, Überlieferung und Geschichte* (SSN 15; Assen: Van Gorcum, 1973), 39–46; R. Rendtorff, "Esra und das 'Gesetz'," *ZAW* 96 (1984): 178–79; A. H. J. Gunneweg, *Nehemia* (KAT; Gütersloh: Gerd Mohn, 1987), 110–12. However, the hypothesis is speculative due to the lack of evidence about synagogue ritual in the late Persian and early Hellenistic eras.

[63] לעיני does not occur anywhere else in Ezra-Nehemiah.

Psalms, always within cultic settings and generally (as in Ezra 8:6) without a motivating clause (1 Chr 29:10, 20; 2 Chr 20:26; cf. Pss 16:7; 34:1; 134:1, 2; 135:19, 20).[64]

The title "YHWH, the great God" (יהוה האלהים הגדול, 8:6) does not occur anywhere else in the MT. However, a related appellation, "the God who is great [and awesome]" (האל הגדול [והנורא]), does appear within prayers of confession (Neh 1:5; 9:32; Dan 9:4; cf. Jer 32:18).[65] Particularly worthy of note is the resonance within the covenant-renewal account between the title יהוה האלהים הגדול (8:6) in this narrative portion and the expression האל הגדול at the turning point of the people's penitential psalm (9:32).

The people's response, "Amen" (8:6), carries both liturgical and covenantal connotations. The liturgical dimension is evident in Chronicles, in the public response to the psalm of blessing at the transportation of the ark into Jerusalem (1 Chr 16:36; cf. Pss 89:53; 106:48).[66] The association with covenant procedure is evident in Moses' demanding that "all the people" say "Amen" to each of the twelve covenant curses that the Levites will pronounce at Mount Gerizim (Deut 27:15–26, ואמר כל־העם אמן [12x]; cf. Num 5:22). Within Ezra-Nehemiah, the response of the community echoes their consent to Nehemiah's social reform: "And all the assembly said, 'Amen'" (Neh 5:13, ויאמרו כל־הקהל אמן).[67]

The precise expression for "lifting their hands" (במעל ידיהם) is unique to Neh 8:6; however, a more conventional expression describes the same gesture in prayer, namely, נשא ידים (Pss 28:2; 134:2). Related gestures are Ezra's hand movements at the introduction to his prayer of intercession (פרש כפים, Ezra 9:5).

The verbs קדד and חוה (hištapʿel) practically form a hendiadys meaning "to bow down and worship" (Neh 8:6; cf. Gen 24:48; 43:28; Exod 4:31; Num 22:31; 1 Chr 29:20; 2 Chr 29:30). In two of these instances, this gesture accompanies the action of blessing YHWH: in the expression of thanksgiving by Abraham's servant (Gen 24:48), and in the congregation's response to David's directive (1 Chr 29:20). The latter instance exhibits

---

[64] J. Scharbert, "ברך," *TDOT* 2:292–93.

[65] Cf. also Deut 10:17: האל הגדל הגבר והנורא.

[66] Note the common vocabulary in 1 Chr 16:36 and Neh 8:6: after the acclamation of blessing (ברוך יהוה אלהי ישראל) that concludes the psalm, "all the people say, 'Amen'" (ויאמרו כל־העם אמן). Moreover, 1 Chr 16:36 is a quotation of Ps 106:48, the statement that concludes the fourth book of the Psalter. The concluding line of the third book of the Psalter is similar: ברוך יהוה לעולם אמן ואמן (Ps 89:53).

[67] As in Deut 27:15–26, the community response in Neh 5:13 involves consenting to the binding power of a curse.

notable parallels with Neh 8:6: either by word (David) or gesture (Ezra), the leader directs the people to "bless YHWH" (ברך יהוה, 1 Chr 29:20; Neh 8:6) and the people respond by "bowing and worshiping YHWH" (ויקדו וישתחוו] ליהוה, 1 Chr 29:20; Neh 8:6).

The additional phrase "with their faces to the ground" (אפים ארצה) denotes a posture of servitude toward a superior (Gen 42:6; 1 Sam 25:41; 1 Kgs 1:3; Isa 49:23; 1 Chr 21:21; cf. Gen 19:1; 1 Sam 28:14). In Chronicles, YHWH is the one who receives such veneration (2 Chr 7:3; 20:18; cf. Gen 19:1 [Lot's veneration of the two messengers]). Thus, the expression in Neh 8:6 echoes the people's reaction to the manifestation of divine glory at the dedication of the First Temple (2 Chr 7:3) and Judah's response to the prophetic oracle that announced victory in the battle for Jehoshaphat and his forces (2 Chr 20:18).[68]

The Levites interpret the law to the people (8:7–8)

Mention of names of the Levites directs attention away from Ezra. From a narrative perspective, the Levites' activity in Neh 8:7 extends the mandate that Artaxerxes issued to Ezra, whom the king had charged to teach the laws of his God (Ezra 7:25). The Levites here assume a central role comparable to that which Ezra gave them at Ahiva (Ezra 8:16–17, 30).

The instructional activity of the Levites (8:7b–8) corresponds with the tradition that endowed the Levitical priests with responsibility for teaching the law (Deut 33:10; cf. 17:8–13; 21:5; 24:8). That the Levites rather than the priests fulfill this task is noteworthy in view of the widespread association of the priest with the law (see Jer 18:18; Ezek 7:26; Hag 2:11; Mal 2:7; cf. Lev 10:11 ["statutes": החקים]). However, the distinction between priests and Levites is much sharper in Chronicles and Ezra-Nehemiah than in earlier literature.[69] Chronicles also presents the Levites as teachers of the law. The most remarkable parallel to Neh 8:7–8 is the account of nine Levites designated by name (along with five lay officials and two priests) traveling throughout the cities of Judah with "the book of the law of YHWH" (ספר תורה יהוה) "teach[ing] the people" (וילמדו בעם) in 2 Chr 17:7–9. Furthermore, the verb describing the teaching activity of the Levites

---

[68] Only in Neh 8:6 does the phrase אפים ארצה modify both verbs (קדד and חוה [hištap'el]). In its ten other occurrences, אפים ארצה modifies חוה (hištap'el) five times (Gen 19:1; 42:6; 1 Sam 25:41; Isa 49:23; 1 Chr 21:21), קדד four times (1 Sam 24:9; 28:14; 1 Kgs 1:31; 2 Chr 20:18), and כרע once (2 Chr 7:3).

[69] For discussion of the historical evolution of the Levites, see Y. Kaufmann, *The Religion of Israel from Its Beginnings to the Babylonian Exile* (trans. M. Greenberg; Chicago: University of Chicago Press, 1960), 154–55, 193–200; de Vaux, *Ancient Israel*, 358–405; R. Abba, "Priests and Levites," *IDB* 3:876–89; M. D. Rehm, "Levites and Priests," *ABD* 4:297–310.

(מבינים) in 2 Chr 35:3 (Qere) is the same as in Neh 8:7, while the construction here is identical with that of Neh 8:9 (הלוים המבינים).

The Levites' "helping the people understand the law" (Neh 8:7) corresponds with the uses of בין (*hipʿil*) with the same object or a synonym in Psalm 119: "give me understanding that I may keep your law" (הבינני ואצרה תורתך, Ps 119:34; cf. 119:73 [הבינני ואלמדה מצותיך], 119:125 [הבינני ואדעה עדתיך]). These examples emphasize the aptness of this verb (בין *hipʿil*) to describe instruction in the law. Furthermore, Ps 119:34 indicates that the object of such instruction is not merely mental comprehension but observance of the law.

Outside the covenant-renewal account (8:7; 9:3), the noun for a "standing place" (עמד) in Chronicles and Ezra-Nehemiah refers to an official station for authorities (Neh 13:11), priests and Levites (2 Chr 30:16; 35:10), and the king (2 Chr 34:31).

The title "the book of the law of God" (ב]סספר [ב]תורת האלהים, 8:8, 18) recalls the covenant renewal at Shechem, at the end of which Joshua writes in "the book of the law of God" (בספר תורת אלהים, Josh 24:26).

Scholars agree that מפרש qualifies the manner in which the Levites read (ויקרא) from the book. However, there are three diverging opinions regarding the rendering of מפרש here: (1) "in translation," (2) "section by section," or (3) "distinctly." The first alternative involves interpreting מפרש in Ezra 4:18 (Aramaic) as referring to an official extemporaneous translation of an Aramaic document into Persian.[70] However two factors militate against understanding מפרש as "in translation": (1) the Aramaic term מפרש in Ezra 4:18 more likely refers to a reading "with precision" rather than "in translation"; and (2) in a contemporary Aramaic text (CAP 17:3), מפרש means "plainly [or exactly] set forth."[71] Once one recognizes that מפרש in Ezra 4:18 is not referring to "translation," one must also reject the further proposal based on this that Neh 8:8 offers an early precedent for the Targumim.[72]

---

[70] By analogy with this view of Ezra 4:18, H. H. Schaeder argues that in Neh 8:8 Ezra would be rendering the Hebrew text of the law into the Aramaic vernacular of those who returned with him from Babylon (*Iranische Beiträge I* [Halle: Max Niemeyer, 1930], 6–7). (Schaeder reads the singular ויקרא in Neh 8:8 and thereby identifies Ezra as the reader.) His interpretation of Neh 8:8 reflects his portrayal of Ezra as an official scribe of the Achaemenid administration.

[71] Cowley identifies CAP 17 as a commercial letter dating to 428 B.C.E. (*Aramaic Papyri*, 53–54). The pertinent line reads, "plainly set forth, each item month by month they were sending to me" (מפרש זן זן ירח בירח הוו שלחן עלי, CAP 17:3).

[72] R. Le Déaut proposes that, in view of ושום שכל ("to present the meaning," Neh 8:8), מפרש describes an expository manner of translating the Torah from Hebrew into Aramaic that subsequently entered the synagogue and eventually generated the Targumim (*Introduction à la Littérature Targumique* [Rome: Pontifical

The second proposal views the reading of the book as taking place "section by section" (מפרש). This rendering derives from understanding the root פרש as meaning "to separate," "to divide" (cf. Aramaic פרוש, "Pharisee").[73] The primary difficulty with this thesis is the absence of supporting evidence elsewhere in the MT.

The third proposal, which interprets מפרש as referring to the clarity of pronunciation, is consistent with two occurrences of the root פרש in the Pentateuch. In both Lev 24:12 (*qal* infinitive construct) and Num 15:34 (*pu'al* perfect), פרש refers to a legal judgment that was awaiting a "distinct" decision. Against this background, מפרש in Neh 8:8 would have in view both the accuracy of the Levites' enunciation of the text and the clarity of their vocal projection to the large assembly. Rendering מפרש as "distinctly" encompasses both of these connotations.[74]

In the expression שום שכל, the noun שכל denotes personal qualities of sound judgment (Prov 12:8; 19:11) and discretion (Prov 16:22; 1 Chr 22:12; 2 Chr 2:12). When used to communicate a text in public and governed by the verb שום, the noun שכל refers to "meaning." In two occurrences, שכל is associated with the Levites: (1) Hezekiah encourages the Levites, who demonstrated "good skill [in serving] YHWH" (כל־הלוים המשכילים שכל־טוב ליהוה) during the Festival of Unleavened Bread (2 Chr 30:22); and (2) Ezra describes the first of the Levites from Iddo who joined him as "a person of discretion" (איש שכל, Ezra 8:18). Note too that the Levites to whom Hezekiah refers exercised a vocal ministry, namely, praising YHWH (2 Chr 30:21).

Biblical Institute, 1966], 22–32). However, G. Veltri ("Der aramäische Targumvortrag zur Zeit Esras: Eine sprachgeschichtliche und historische Frage," *Laur* 34 [1993]: 187–207) argues that there is no evidence in Ezra-Nehemiah (including Neh 13:23–24 and Ezra 4:7 [מתרגם]) to support the contention that Neh 8:8 describes the Levites' translating the reading into Aramaic. For an extensive discussion of the issue, see A. van der Kooij, "Nehemiah 8:8 and the Question of the 'Targum' Tradition," in *Tradition of the Text: Studies offered to Dominique Barthélemy in Celebration of His 70th Birthday* (ed. G. J. Norton and S. Pisano; OBO 109; Göttingen: Vandenhoeck & Ruprecht, 1991), 79–90. Van der Kooij (88) concludes, "there is no linguistic basis at all for the interpretation of מפרש in the sense of 'translated'."

[73] L. Koehler, *Lexicon in Veteris Testamenti Libros* (2 vols.; Grand Rapids, Mich.: Eerdmans, 1953), 2:782–83 (cf. *HAL*, 918: "vom Blatt weg [extempore] übersetzen"); Z. W. Falk, "Hebrew Legal Terms: III," *JSS* 14 (1969): 42–43.

[74] In defense of rendering מפרש as "distinctly," see W. Weinberg, "Language Consciousness in the OT," *ZAW* 92 (1980): 188–89. M. Fishbane offers this vivid description of the type of reading described in Neh 8:8: "Such a lection undoubtedly involved care for the exact pronunciations, intonation, and phrasing, so as to make the units of the piece and its traditional sense readily comprehensible" (*Biblical Interpretation*, 109).

The *hipʿil* of בין, which describes the Levites' "helping [the people] to understand" (ויבינו במקרא, 8:7), occurs three times as a participle in Chronicles in reference to the Levites who "were skilled" in singing and music (ה[מבין], 1 Chr 15:22; 25:7; 2 Chr 34:12). Such evidence suggests that the Levites' activities of "presenting the meaning" (ושום שכל, 8:7a) and "helping [the people] understand" (ויבינו) are intimately connected with the enunciation of the text.[75]

Nevertheless, contextual indications suggest that the Levites' contribution extended beyond proclamation to instruction. Their activity (ויבינו במקרא, 8:8; המבינים את־העם, 8:9) has its counterpart in the capacity of the people "to understand" (מבין, 8:2; המבינים, 8:3; המבינו, 8:12). The people's "understanding" went beyond an appreciation of the clarity of the Levites' proclamation to include a correct perception of the reading's application to their lives (see below on 8:9–12).

Nehemiah, Ezra, and the Levites counsel all the people (8:9–12)

My lexical analysis of the fourth subunit considers four elements: (1) the official titles of Nehemiah and Ezra; (2) the lexical elements that are common to the three exhortations as well as the description of the people's weeping (8:9, 10, 11); (3) the unique components of Ezra's exhortation (8:10); and (4) the narration of the people's response (8:12).

The titles of Nehemiah and Ezra. The words הוא התרשתא constitute a noun clause ("he was the governor") in apposition to נחמיה (GKC §141a; GBH §154j; cf. Neh 9:6, אתה־הוא יהוה לבדך: "you are YHWH, you alone"; 9:7, אתה־הוא יהוה האלהים: "you are YHWH, the God"; Gen 42:6, ויוסף הוא השליט על־הארץ: "Now Joseph was governor over the land"). The noun התרשתא is the title for the chief administrative official over the Judahites (Ezra 2:63 = Neh 7:65; 7:69), but the precise nature of his office is a matter of conjecture.[76] In Nehemiah's case, התרשתא (8:9; 10:2) is

---

[75] S. Levin suggests that recitation of Aramaic documents was a refined art in the Achaemenid court ("The Traditional Chironomy of the Hebrew Scriptures," *JBL* 87 [1968]: 70). A. Cody mentions that the Levites' activity might have consisted in singing the text, a practice carried on in the present-day declamation of the Qur'an in Islam and in the singing of lectionary readings in Eastern Christian churches (*A History of the Old Testament Priesthood* [AnBib 35; Rome: Pontifical Biblical Institute, 1969], 189). M. Gertner extends the discussion beyond the biblical evidence when he focuses on the rabbinic tradition that views each component of Neh 8:8 in terms of its interpretative function: מפרש referring to the simple "reading," ויקראו בספר בתורת האלהים to the targumic "explanation," ושום שכל to "accentuation" and "intonation," and ויבינו במקרא to the Masorah ("The Masorah and the Levites," *VT* 10 [1960]: 248).

[76] See, e.g., W. Th. In der Smitten, "Der Tirschātāʾ in Esra-Nehemia," *VT* 21 (1971): 618–20.

apparently equivalent to הפחה (12:26; cf. 5:14, 15, 18). Within the covenant-renewal account (7:72b–10:40), reference to "Nehemiah the governor" (נחמיה [הוא] התרשתא) links the instruction in the law (היום קדש־הוא ליהוה אלהיכם, 8:9) with the pledge signing (10:2). In the broader context, mention of Nehemiah connects the covenant renewal with the totality of Nehemiah's mission (Neh 1:1–7:72a; 11:1–13:31). The combined reference to both events and to Nehemiah represents a landmark in history (see 12:26) and establishes a special narrative tie between the covenant renewal and the dedication of the walls (12:31, 33, 36, 38).

Ezra is identified by the double title "priest and scribe" in two contexts: first, in the introduction to the two rescripts Artaxerxes issues on his behalf to the general public (Ezra 7:12; cf. 7:12–20, 25–26) and to the provincial treasurers (Ezra 7:21; cf. 7:21–24); and, second, when his name occurs alongside Nehemiah, who bears the title "governor" (התרשתא, Neh 8:9; הפחה, 12:26). The contexts suggest that the double title "priest and scribe" is an official designation that the Persian administration accorded to Ezra.

The elements common to the three exhortations. The statements of the threefold group (8:9), of Ezra (8:10), and of the Levites (8:11) all consist of two components: a pronouncement of the day's holiness and consequent prohibitions. "Holy to YHWH" (קדש ליהוה; cf. היום קדש־הוא ליהוה אלהיכם, 8:9; קדש היום לאדנינו, 8:10; היום קדש, 8:11) is a traditional formula that solemnly removes its subject from the mundane to the sacred. The formula can apply to people (Deut 26:19; Ezra 8:28), utensils (Exod 28:36; 39:30; Ezra 8:28; Zech 14:20, 21), offerings (Lev 27:30, 32; cf. Isa 23:18), spaces (Lev 27:14 [house]; 27:21, 23 [field]; Jer 31:40 [Jerusalem]), and time (Exod 16:23; 31:15). In relation to Neh 8:9, 10, 11, the last category is most significant: in both occurrences, the Sabbath is the time "holy to YHWH" (Exod 16:23; 31:15; cf. Neh 10:32).

However, the three declarations of the day's holiness in Neh 8:9, 10, 11 are more directly related to the Priestly laws that identify the first day of the seventh month as a day that is proclaimed holy (מקרא קדש, Lev 23:24; Num 29:1).[77] The various statements of the leaders that "the day is

---

[77] With the exception of Exod 12:16 [bis], the term מקרא קדש occurs exclusively in the Priestly festival calendars (Lev 23:2, 3, 4, 7, 8, 21, 24, 27, 35, 36, 37; Num 28:18, 25, 26; 29:1, 7, 12). Various translations of the term include "a holy convocation" (RSV), and "a sacred assembly" (NAB, NJB, REB). However, E. Kutsch asserts that, in the various occurrences of the term, emphasis falls on the proclamation of the festival, not on the act of assembly ("מקרא," *ZAW* 65 [1953]: 247–53). Moreover, M. Noth makes the crucial observation that each occurrence involves "a public 'proclamation' ... of the day of rest" (*Leviticus* [trans. J. E. Anderson; OTL; Philadelphia: Westminster, 1965], 168). Milgrom translates מקרא קדש most appropriately as a "proclamation of [a day's] holiness" (*Leviticus 1–16*, 21).

holy" (היום קדש, 8:11; cf. 8:9, 10) echo the Priestly proclamation of the day as holy (מקרא קדש, Lev 23:24; Num 29:1).

Nehemiah, Ezra, and the Levites admonish the people not to mourn or weep (8:9). "Mourning" (אבל) and "weeping" (בכה) together comprise an established expression for despondency (Job 30:31), particularly over a death (Gen 37:35; Deut 34:8; 2 Sam 19:1). In reverse order, the verbs describe Nehemiah's reaction to the news of Jerusalem's desolate condition (Neh 1:4, ואבכה ואתאבלה: "I wept and mourned"). By itself, the verb אבל (*hitpaʿel*) recalls Ezra's reaction to the unfaithfulness of the exiles in the matter of mixed marriages (Ezra 10:6). The latter case in particular suggests that in Neh 8:9 the audience has been overwhelmed by their awareness of their unfaithfulness in light of the reading of the law.

Similarly, weeping can express repentance (2 Sam 12:21–22; cf. Num 25:6; Deut 1:45; Judg 20:23). Within Ezra-Nehemiah, the audience's weeping (Neh 8:9) recalls the leaders' weeping at the placement of the temple foundations (Ezra 3:12). Moreover, it harks back to Ezra's weeping when he confessed the sins of the people (Ezra 10:1). In sum, the "mourning" (אבל *hitpaʿel:* Neh 8:9; cf. Ezra 10:6) and "weeping" (בכה *qal:* Neh 8:9; cf. Ezra 10:1) provide a narrative indication that the leaders' admonition derives from the personal experience of one of their own, namely, Ezra. His counsel to the people in the square at the Water Gate (Neh 8:10) directly contrasts with his own response to the exiles' faithlessness prior to the assembly in the square before the temple (Ezra 10:6).

The verb עצב (*nipʿal*, 8:10, 11) is sometimes interchangeable with אבל (*hitpaʿel*) for describing mourning over a death (2 Sam 19:2–3; cf. Gen 37:34; 2 Sam 13:37; 14:2; 19:2) The *nipʿal* עצב more directly refers to personal anguish (1 Sam 20:3), including the anguish over wrongdoing (Gen 45:5).

From another perspective, the audience's reaction of weeping upon hearing the words of the law (כי בוכים כל־העם כשמעם את־דברי תורה, Neh 8:9) recalls Josiah's weeping when he heard the reading of the book of the law (2 Chr 34:27 par. 2 Kgs 22:19). While the narrative in Neh 8:9 describes the people's contrition in terms of weeping, it does not indicate the precise nature of the trespasses that evoke it. From a literary perspective, the weeping of the people is a manifestation of their misunderstanding of the law, which indicates their need for further counsel (8:9).[78]

---

[78] Any attempt to account for their weeping in terms of particular trespasses or ceremonial demands exceeds the evidence. For instance, according to Rudolph, the weeping indicates the people's consciousness of having violated the law by entering into marriages with foreigners (*Esra und Nehemia*, 149). However, his proposal views Neh 8 more in light of Ezra 9–10 than of its current immediate context. Again, Mowinckel (*Studien III*, 56–59) and Pohlmann (*Dritten Esra*, 136–37) view the

The unique components of Ezra's exhortation. Ezra alone offers a positive instruction about how the people are to react to the law by celebrating the holiness of the day, that is, by partaking of a festive meal (8:11). The festive meal developed from ancient tradition. "Eating and drinking" were constitutive elements of the Canaanite celebration at the grape harvest, antecedent to the Israelite festival of the "Ingathering" (Judg 9:27; cf. 21:21; Exod 23:16b; 34:22b). Such activity was part of a complex of events, including a covenant ceremony (cf. Exod 24:11), pilgrimage (1 Sam 1:9), royal enthronement (1 Chr 29:22), and household celebrations (Eccl 2:24; 3:13; 5:19; 8:15; 9:7; cf. Isa 22:13). Of these, especially relevant are the celebrations accompanied by joy (שמחה, Eccl 9:7; 1 Chr 29:22).

The noun משמנים, literally "fatty delicacies," does not occur anywhere else in the MT. However, its root שמן reappears in Neh 9:25 both as an adjective in the phrase "a rich land" (אדמה שמנה) and as a *hipʿil* verb meaning "to grow fat" (וישמינו). The noun ממתקים, literally "sweets," occurs elsewhere only in Song 5:16 describing something appealing to the palate. The root מתק occurs as a verb meaning "to become sweet" (e.g., Exod 15:25) and as an adjective (מתוק) describing the taste of honey (e.g., Ps 19:11).

The Deuteronomic prescriptions for distributing tithes of produce to the poor every third year provide the legal analogues for sharing benefits with others at harvest time (Deut 14:28–29; 26:12–15; cf. Neh 8:10). The book of Esther offers the most explicit witness to the custom of actually "sending portions" (שלח מנות) from a joyful (שמחה) festive meal to neighbors and to the poor (Esth 2:9; 9:19 [a gloss]; 9:22; cf. 1 Sam 1:4; 2 Sam 6:19). Hence, Ezra's admonition to send "a portion to the one for whom none is provided" (8:10) refers to a practice that might have become customary in the fifth or fourth centuries B.C.E.[79]

Notwithstanding Ezra's alluding to the Priestly legislation by his declaration, "the day is holy to our Lord" (כי־קדש היום לאדנינו), he does not prescribe its observance in terms of the Priestly injunction of "rest" (שבתון, Lev 23:24; cf. מקרא־קדש, Lev 23:24; Num 29:1). Instead, he calls for joy (כי־חדות יהוה היא מעזכם: "because the joy of YHWH is your refuge"), thereby reflecting a more Deuteronomic conception of the feast (cf. שמח, Deut 12:7, 18; 14:26). However, this allusion to Deuteronomy applies only to the atmosphere of the festival, not to the details of its observance. For

---

weeping (over past infidelity to the covenant) followed by the rejoicing in a festive meal (due to the gracious renewal of the covenant) as constitutive elements of their putative New Year festival.

[79] C. A. Moore notes the affinity of Esther to Chronicles in terms of language and dates Esther to the end of the Persian or the beginning of the Hellenistic era (*Esther* [AB 7B; Garden City, N.Y.: Doubleday, 1971], lvii–lx).

instance, while Ezra tells the people to depart (לכו, Neh 8:10), Deuteronomy insists that they partake of the festive meal at the sanctuary (see Deut 12:18).

In Neh 8:10, the term for "joy" (חדוה) is unrelated to the root שמח, which denotes "rejoicing" in Deuteronomy. The Chronistic History accounts for all three instances of חדוה in the MT (1 Chr 16:27; Ezra 6:16 [Aramaic]; Neh 8:10). The expression "the joy of YHWH is your refuge" (חדות יהוה היא מעזכם, Neh 8:10) recalls the phrase "strength and joy in his place" (עז וחדוה במקמו, 1 Chr 16:27).[80] However, Neh 8:10 lacks any reference to a physical place (cf. 1 Chr 16:27; Ps 96:6), though it does speak of an ethos whereby one is protected (מעוז). The phrase "the joy of YHWH is your refuge" is an elaboration of biblical references to YHWH as "a refuge" (מעוז, Pss 27:1; 28:8; 37:39; Prov 10:29; Nah 1:7).[81] Employment of the term חדוה links assembling for reading the law with dedicating the reconstructed temple (Neh 8:10; cf. Ezra 6:16 [Aramaic]).

The people's response (8:12). In the literary analysis, I noted that the description of the people's response mirrors the unique exhortations of Ezra (8:12; cf. 8:10). Within Ezra-Nehemiah, the people's move from "weeping" (בוכים, 8:9) to "joy" (שמחה, 8:12) recalls the mixture of "weeping" and "the joyful shout" with which the leaders reacted to the laying of the temple foundation (תרועת שמחה בכים, Ezra 3:12–13). In Neh 8:12, the term for "joy" (שמחה, 8:12; cf. חדוה, 8:11) is more suggestive of Deuteronomic legislation than of other legal traditions.[82] Nevertheless, the expression "great joy" (שמחה גדולה) is emblematic of the Chronistic

---

[80] Chronicles alters Psalm 96 to accommodate it to the narrative context:
1 Chr 16:27: הוד והדר לפניו עז וחדוה במקמו;
Ps 96:6: הוד והדר לפניו עז ותפארת במקדשו.
The two changes in 1 Chr 16:27 derive from the fact that the narrative describes the pretemple era. Thus, "in his place" (במקמו) does not indicate a temple setting (cf. "in his sanctuary," במקדשו, Ps 96:6), and "strength and joy" (עז וחדוה) do not allude to a structure as do "strength and beauty" (עז ותפארת). Cf. Japhet, *I and II Chronicles*, 317–18.

[81] In the clause חדות יהוה היא מעזכם (Neh 8:10), יהוה is an objective genitive (i.e., "[Your] joy in YHWH is your strength"). As an alternative, G. C. I. Wong ("A Note on 'Joy' in Nehemiah VIII 10," *VT* 45 [1995]: 383–86) proposes reading "the joy of YHWH" as a subjective genitive ("YHWH's joy [in you] is your strength"). However, the evidence favors the objective genitive since, in all other instances in Ezra-Nehemiah, "joy" (חדות, Ezra 6:16 [Aramaic]; and שמחה, Ezra 3:12, 13; Neh 8:17; 12:27, 43 [bis], 44) is an attribute of the people, not of YHWH.

[82] Deuteronomy accounts for eleven of thirteen occurrences of the verb שמח in the Pentateuch: Exod 4:14; Lev 23:40; Deut 12:7, 12, 18; 14:26; 16:11, 14, 15; 24:5; 26:11; 27:7; 33:18 (cf. שמחה, Gen 31:27; Num 10:10; Deut 28:47).

History, where it figures in the descriptions of major festivals, namely, the accession of Solomon (1 Chr 29:22; cf. 29:9), Hezekiah's Festival of Unleavened Bread (2 Chr 30:21, 26), and the dedication of the city walls (Neh 12:43), as well as the celebration of the Festival of Booths under Ezra (Neh 8:17).[83] In contrast to all other cases in the Chronistic History, the basis for the people's "great joy" (שמחה גדולה, 8:12; cf. 1 Chr 29:9, 22; 2 Chr 30:21, 26; Neh 8:17; 12:43) is not the celebration of a festival but rather their personal understanding (כי הבינו) of the matters that Ezra and the Levites had taught them.

THEMATIC SUMMARY

The account of events on the first day of the seventh month (Neh 7:72b–8:12) proceeds via an intricate web of repetitions within the framework of narrative sketches alternating between summary descriptions of the whole affair (8:3, 7–8) and detailed portrayals of the initial and final moments (8:4–6, 9–12). In four scenes, the narrative depicts the people's initial encounter with the book of the law and their growth in understanding. The agents who facilitate the process are Ezra and the Levites. My summary focuses on the characterization of the two principals (the people and the book) and the two agents (Ezra and the Levites), as well as the depiction of the dramatic issue (the pursuit of understanding).

As the narrative progresses within the first segment (7:72b–8:12), the people exhibit an increasing range of exemplary traits, including: initiative (8:1 [in requesting Ezra to bring the law]); unity (8:1 ["as one"]); attentiveness (8:3b); foresight (8:4 [in constructing the platform]); reverence (8:6); endurance (8:7 [by remaining in their places]); contrition (8:9 [in their weeping]); obedience (8:12; cf. 8:10); understanding (8:12); and ultimately joy (8:12). In contrast to the two previous assemblies under Ezra (10:9–17) and Nehemiah (5:7b–13), respectively, the people here do not need admonition. Their former recalcitrance has given way to zeal for the law (8:1, 9). The positioning of this episode long after the introduction of Ezra (Ezra 7:1–10) suggests that the people required extensive formation prior to their hearing the law.

The book (הספר) exhibits a threefold aspect as a text for proclamation (8:3, 7), an object of veneration (8:4–6), and a resource for instruction (8:7–8, 9–12). Ezra brings forth this book as the focal point for the assembly, for which it supplies a resource for worship (8:4–6) and instruction (8:7b–8).

The account evokes awe and veneration for the book in the mind of the reader for whom the book remains a mysterious presence that one sees

---

[83] Chronicles and Nehemiah together account for seven of the nine instances of the expression שמחה גדולה: 1 Kgs 1:40; Jonah 4:6; Neh 8:12, 17; 12:43; 1 Chr 29:9, 22; 2 Chr 30:21, 26.

but does not hear. The gestures of Ezra and the Levites (bringing the book before the whole assembly [8:2], opening it [8:4], reading from it [8:3, 7], and interpreting it [8:8]) and the reactions of the people (8:3, 5–6, 8, 9–12) provide the only indications about the nature of the book. The reader does not hear a word of the morning-long proclamation. Apparently, it is sufficient to appreciate that the initial opening of the book is a matter of worship (8:4–6) and that being privileged to hear its contents depends on one's participation in the assembly of those who can understand by hearing (8:3). In a sense, the account treats the reader as an outsider who must learn respect for the book of the law through the witness of the Israelites.

Ezra and the Levites are not the main actors in the account but agents facilitating the relationship between the people and the book. The narrative blurs any potential distinction between Ezra's offices as priest and scribe. As scribe and priest, he presents (8:1–2) and proclaims (8:3) the law and counsels the people (8:9–10). However, as scribe (rather than as priest), he is the leader in worship (8:4–6).

Moreover, Ezra's comportment tends to diminish his supremacy over others. He functions as the servant who responds to the people's desire for the law (8:1). Even on the platform, he stands in the midst of laymen (8:4). Furthermore, in his capacities as reader (8:3) and counselor (8:10) of the people, his actions coordinate with those of the Levites (8:7–8, 11). In almost every instance, his activity reflects solidarity both with other leaders and with the people.

The Levites, for their part, here exercise their most active role since their confreres first joined Ezra's company (Ezra 8:16–20). While Ezra alone presents the book (Neh 8:2) and opens it while beckoning the people to worship (8:4–5), the Levites share in the remainder of his activities, reading from the book (8:7; cf. 8:3), providing the people with understanding (8:7–8; cf. 8:12), and subsequently counseling them (8:10–11).

The activities of Ezra and the Levites demonstrate that, at this point, the law requires mediation in order for the people to gain correct understanding of it. Under the direction of Ezra and the Levites, the people's contact with the law develops in the following stages: from worship (8:4–6), to hearing (8:3, 7), to provisional understanding (8:8; cf. 8:9), and finally, through correction (8:9), to understanding marked by great joy (8:12).

Thus, understanding (בין) is a multidimensional process that develops through the interaction of the congregation with its leaders. Moreover, such understanding involves a communal aspect as it emerges within the gathering of all the people (כל־העם). The assembly's pursuit of understanding constitutes the narrative tension in the story. The basic requirement for participation in the assembly is the capacity to understand (8:2, 3). The service of the leaders consists in actualizing this capacity through proclamation and explanation (8:3, 7–8). The people, for their part, are responsible for being attentive (8:3) and persevering in the endeavor. Understanding does not occur all at once but requires correction of initial misconceptions (8:9–11).

In the end, the people understand, not so much "the words of the law" (8:9), as the instruction Ezra and the Levites give them (8:12). Oral proclamation rather than the written text is the element that brings understanding to the people upon their first encounter with the law. And the effect of understanding is great joy.

A Deuteronomic texture suffuses the account, first in the preoccupation with public reading (cf. Deut 31:9–13; Josh 8:34; 2 Kgs 23:2; Jer 36:10; cf. Exod 24:7) and then in at least six specific ingredients of the story: "the people," "the law," gathering "as one," "Amen," "ears" attentive to the law, and "joy." Especially noteworthy is the variety of allusions to Joshua's covenant renewals at Shechem (Josh 8:30–35; 24:1–28) in four primary elements of the text: "the children of Israel," "all the people," "the book of the law," and the participation of men, women, and children. Thus, the narrative anchors the events in the square in front of the Water Gate in the covenant renewals of the first "Israelites" who, upon occupying the land, pledged their obedience to the law of God.

THE STUDY OF THE LAW AND THE FESTIVAL OF BOOTHS (NEHEMIAH 8:13–18)

My analysis of Neh 8:13–18, the segment describing the leaders gathering with Ezra to study the law and of the subsequent Festival of Booths, proceeds in five steps: (1) a fresh translation; (2) textual criticism; (3) an outline and literary analysis of the segment's contents within the overall setting of the covenant-renewal account (7:72b–10:40); (4) lexical examination of the text's significant expressions as these occur in the rest of Ezra-Nehemiah and elsewhere in biblical literature; and (5) a thematic summary.

TRANSLATION

13 On the second day, the heads of the families of all the people as well as the priests and Levites gathered around Ezra the scribe [a]in order to study[a] [b]the words of the law.[b] 14 They found written in the law, which YHWH had commanded by the hand of Moses, that the children of Israel should dwell in booths on the festival of the seventh month 15 [c]and that[c] they should make it known and circulate a proclamation in all their towns and in Jerusalem, saying, "Go out to the hill country and bring olive branches, wild olive tree branches, myrtle branches, palm branches, and branches of leafy trees to make booths as it is written." 16 So the people went out and brought them and made for themselves booths, each one on his roof, in their courtyards, in the courtyards of the house of God, in the square of the Water Gate, and in the square of the Gate of Ephraim. 17 The

whole assembly of those who had returned from captivity made booths, and they dwelt in the booths as the Israelites had not done from the days of Jeshua son of Nun until that day. And there was very great joy. 18 ᵈHe readᵈ from the book of the law of God day by day from the first day until the last day. They kept the festival seven days, and on the eighth day a solemnity according to the ordinance.

TEXTUAL CRITICISM

a-a ולהשכיל. Maintain ו; the infinitive construct following ו and ל expresses intention in continuity with the finite verb that precedes (GKC §114p).

b-b אל־דברי התורה is to be maintained in view of the similar construction in Ps 41:2 (משכיל אל־דל).

c-c ואשר is to be maintained since there is no textual evidence for removing it.⁸⁴ The construction provides the beginning of a syndetic object clause (GBH §157c).

d-d ויקרא is to be maintained with the majority of manuscripts (cf. Syr). This reading squares with the preceding identification of Ezra as the custodian of the law: (1) the leaders congregate around him because he is responsible for the law (אל־עזרא הספר ולהשכיל אל־דברי התורה, 8:14); and (2) the previous narrative section presented him similarly as the custodian and primary reader of the law (8:1–3).

LITERARY ANALYSIS

My literary analysis of the narration (8:13–18) consists of three parts: (1) delimitation of the passage within its context; (2) an outline of the section; and (3) a discussion of each of the component units within the setting of the covenant renewal (Neh 7:72b–10:40).

DELIMITATION

The account of Ezra's reading of the law to all the people on the first day of the seventh month (7:72b–8:12) concludes with the description of their departure from the square in front of the Water Gate and with mention of their understanding the matters they had been taught (8:12). The verse that introduces the account of the celebration of Booths (8:13) constitutes a new beginning exhibiting five links to the previous segment: (1) "the second day" (ביום השני), which presumes "the seventh month," החדש השביעי [7:72b]) represents a fresh start in sequence after "the first day" (ביום אחד, 8:2); (2) "[they] gathered" describes a new assembly (נאספו, cf.

---

⁸⁴ Cf. Batten (*Ezra and Nehemiah*, 361) and Myers (*Ezra, Nehemiah*, 155), who apparently omit אשר and read וישמיעו in order to separate the command for the proclamation throughout the land (8:15) from the ordinance of the law (8:14).

ויאספו, 8:1) subsequent to the account of departure that concludes the previous segment (וילכו, 8:12); (3) "the heads of the families of all the people" (ראשי האבות לכל־העם) relates the first category of participants to the main subject throughout the previous segment, that is, כל־העם (ten times in 7:72b–8:12); (4) "the Levites" (cf. 8:7, 9, 11) and "Ezra" (cf. 8:1, 2, 4, 5, 6, 9) afford continuity of subject; and (5) the phrase "words of the law" (דברי התורה; cf. 8:9) supplies a thematic commonality.

Nehemiah 8:18 is a characteristic summarizing conclusion insofar as it succinctly encapsulates the activities of the preceding eight days. The subsequent description of another assembly on the twenty-fourth day introduces a distinct segment (9:1).

OUTLINE

The segment that recounts the Festival of Booths (8:13–18) begins with a one-day assembly to study the law (8:13) and concludes with eight days of reading the book of the law (8:18). Three elements parallel the introductory (8:13) and concluding verses (8:18): the individual leader, Ezra; specification of time by an ordinal enumeration of days (ביום השני, 8:13; cf. מן־היום הראשון עד היום האחרון, 8:18; וביום השמיני, 8:18); and preoccupation with the law (דברי התורה, 8:13; cf. ספר תורת האלהים, 8:18).

The intervening verses feature correspondences between the prescriptions that the leaders find in the law and the activities that the people undertake, including: (1) living in booths (ישבו בני־ישראל בסכות, 8:14; cf. וישבו בסכות, 8:17); (2) going out and bringing back boughs (צאו ... והביאו, 8:15; cf. ויצאו העם ויביאו, 8:16); and (c) constructing booths (לעשת סכת, 8:15; cf. ויעשו כל־הקהל השבים מן־השבי סכות, 8:16; ויעשו להם סכות, 8:17a).

In summary, the account (8:13–18) exhibits a basic chiastic structure:

A   8:13 The leaders study the law
   B   8:14–15 The prescriptions they find written in the law
   B' 8:16–17 The people's implementation of the prescriptions
A' 8:18 Ezra reads from the book of the law

A more detailed sketch notes the contents at the center of the account.

Table 3.3—Outline of the Festival of Booths (8:13–18)
A The assembly of leaders to study the law (8:13)
  B The prescriptions of the law (8:14–15)
    1. The command to live in booths (8:14)
    2. The command to gather branches for making booths (8:15)
  B' The people implement the prescriptions (8:16–17)
    1. The people gather branches and make booths (8:16)
    2. The comparative evaluation of their accomplishment (8:17)
A' Ezra reads from the book of the law of God (8:18)

In surveying the material, I find that three aspects comprising the central two parts of the chiasm (8:14–17) immediately stand out. First, a pattern of speech and response carries over here from the final subunit of the previous segment (8:9–12). However, there is a significant distinction between the subjects who issue the respective directives: in the earlier subunit, the leaders (Nehemiah, Ezra, and the Levites) give the exhortations to which the people respond (8:9–12), whereas in the present unit, the written text of law (התורה) makes demands that the people implement (8:14–17).

Second, the demand for the making of booths is highlighted beyond the previous demands by a twofold description of its implementation (לעשׂת סכת, 8:15; cf. ויעשׂו להם סכות, 8:16; ויעשׂו כל־הקהל השׁבים מן־השׁבי סכות, 8:17a).

Third, a difference in concern is evident between the attention to the five species of boughs in the prescriptions (8:15) and the preoccupation with the five locations for the booths in the implementation (8:16).

The following, more detailed analysis highlights the unique contribution of each subunit to the whole segment.

The assembly of leaders to study the law (8:13)

The second portion of the covenant renewal (8:13–18) is distinguished from both the first (7:72b–8:12) and the third (9:1–10:40) insofar as it begins with communal "study" (להשׂכיל) by the leaders rather than public "reading" to the whole assembly (ויקראו, 8:3, 8; 9:3; cf. 8:18). Nevertheless, the opening verse (8:13) maintains the narrative continuity from the previous segment (7:72b–8:12). While the specification of time (וביום השׁני) marks a new beginning (cf. ביום אחד, 8:2), it also establishes continuity with the preceding section (ו) and thereby indicates that Ezra's reading of the law (7:72b–8:12) prompts a renewal in the celebration of the Festival of Booths (8:13–18).

A new set of leaders now steps to the fore: Nehemiah recedes from view while the heads of all the ancestral families and the priests join the Levites and Ezra (8:13; cf. 8:9). Nevertheless, the focus on leadership (8:13) emerges from the prior account of leaders advising the people (8:9–11). Moreover, the purpose of the leaders' gathering "to study the words of the law" bespeaks continued concern for the most critical issue at the climax of the previous segment, namely, the proper understanding of the law. Note too the parallelism between the occasion for the people's distress (8:9) and the purpose of the leaders' meeting (8:13):

8:9   כשׁמעם את־דברי התורה
8:13   ולהשׂכיל אל־דברי התורה[85]

---

[85] 8:9: "[For all the people] had been weeping as they heard the words of the law."
8:13: "[They gathered] in order to study the words of the law."

The prescriptions of the law (8:14–15)

As in the first segment of the covenant-renewal account, so here, those who assemble exhibit initiative regarding the law. The sequence of verbs describing the leaders' gathering (נאספו) and then finding (וימצאו) a text in the law (8:13–14) recalls all the people's gathering (ויאספו) and requesting (ויאמרו) Ezra to bring forth the law book (8:1). Moreover, two other elements relate 8:14 to the opening lines of the first segment: (1) the elaborate description of the law:

8:1   ספר תורת משה אשר־צוה יהוה את־ישראל
8:14 תורה אשר צוה יהוה ביד־משה[86]

and (2) the identification of the people as בני־ישראל (8:14; cf. 7:72b).

The passive participle כתוב directs attention to the written text of the law for the first time in Neh 7:72b–8:18. Up to this point, the narrative presented the law as oral proclamation (ויקרא, 8:3; ויקראו, 8:8), and all the people endeavored to apprehend the "the words of the law" (דברי התורה) by hearing (כשמעם, 8:9). Now their leaders strive to appropriate "the words of the law" (דברי התורה) by studying (להשכיל, 8:13). The significance of the written text is underlined by the *inclusio* (כתוב[ם]) in the recounting of the law's prescriptions (8:14–15).

The material quoted from the law consists of two parts, each of which begins with אשר (8:14, 15). Each part communicates a prescription: first, for the people's dwelling in booths (8:14), and, second, for their making booths (8:15). In the first part, the term חג suggests for the first time that the previous assembly (7:72b–8:12) should be related to a traditional festival. The second part has a more complex structure than the first insofar as indirect speech expresses the command for the proclamation of the injunction, whereas the preceding injunction uses a direct quotation for the commanding of the gathering of boughs and constructing of booths.

The proclamation has a universal aspect embracing the whole community, since the expression "in their towns and in Jerusalem" is a variation on the expression "in Judah and in Jerusalem" (Ezra 5:1; 9:9; cf. Neh 13:16), given the mention of "their towns" (בעריהם) in Neh 7:72b. Moreover, while Ezra-Nehemiah speaks of Jerusalem (ירושלם) eighty-six times, this is the city's only mention in the covenant-renewal account (Neh 7:72b–10:40). Locations *in* Jerusalem (8:16) seem more important.

The written law speaks directly to the people for the first time in the quotation introduced by לאמר (8:15; cf. 8:11).

---

[86] 8:1: "the book of the law of Moses with which YHWH had charged Israel."
8:14: "the law, which YHWH had commanded by the hand of Moses."

The people implement the prescriptions (8:16–17)

The narrative recounts the people's literal compliance with three specific prescriptions: (1) dwelling in booths; (2) going out and bringing branches; and (3) making booths:

8:14 יֵשְׁבוּ בְנֵי־יִשְׂרָאֵל בַּסֻּכּוֹת
8:17 [87]וַיֵּשְׁבוּ בַסֻּכּוֹת

8:15 צְאוּ הָהָר וְהָבִיאוּ עֲלֵי־זַיִת
8:16 [88]וַיֵּצְאוּ הָעָם וַיָּבִיאוּ

8:15 לַעֲשֹׂת סֻכֹּת
8:16 וַיַּעֲשׂוּ לָהֶם סֻכּוֹת
8:17 וַיַּעֲשׂוּ כָל־הַקָּהָל הַשָּׁבִים מִן־הַשְּׁבִי סֻכּוֹת.[89]

The people's compliance prolongs their analogous docility to the exhortations of Ezra and the other leaders in the concluding subunit of the previous segment (8:12; cf. 8:10).

The description of the booths is a further link with the previous segment (7:72b–8:12). The *hipʿil* בוא in command and response (8:15–16) recalls the narrative exchange that initiated the events of the first day (8:1–2). There the people told Ezra "to bring [לְהָבִיא] the book of the law of Moses," and "Ezra brought [וַיָּבִיא] the law" (Neh 8:1–2). Here the law demands, "Go out and bring [וְהָבִיאוּ] [branches]," so "the people went out and brought [וַיָּבִיאוּ] them" (Neh 8:15–16). Thus, the celebration of the Festival of Booths echoes the beginning of the first day; that is, the people's bringing of the branches in response to the law resonates with Ezra's bringing of the law in response to the people's request.

Moreover, the material and artisans associated with the booths relate the booths to the platform upon which Ezra stood with the thirteen others (8:4). Both are temporary wooden structures (עֲלֵי עֵץ שָׁמֶן ... וְעֲלֵי עֵץ עָבֹת, 8:15; cf. עֵץ, 8:4)[90] that "they [i.e., the people] make" (עָשׂוּ, 8:4, 16, 17; cf. לַעֲשֹׂה, 8:15).

---

[87] 8:14: "the Israelites should dwell in booths."
8:17: "they dwelt in booths."
[88] 8:15: "Go out to the hill country and bring olive branches."
8:16: "So the people went out and brought."
[89] 8:15: "to make booths."
8:16: "[the people] made for themselves booths."
8:17: "The whole assembly of those who had returned from captivity made booths."
[90] Elsewhere, Ezra-Nehemiah mentions wood (עֵץ) for the construction of two permanent structures: (1) the reconstructed temple (Ezra 3:7 [cedar wood]), and (2) the city gates (Neh 2:8).

The locations for the booths involve a combination of environs: familial (one's roof and courtyard), sacred (the temple courtyard [cf. 13:7]), and communal (the square of the Water Gate and the square of the Gate of Ephraim). The last three locales, being in Jerusalem, underscore the city's character as the point of assembly for the whole people (cf. Ezra 3:1; 10:9). The square before the Water Gate maintains connection with the previous assembly (8:16; cf. 8:2, 3).

The expression כל־הקהל (8:17) conveys an inclusivity that characterized the prior assembly (הקהל מאיש עד־אשה וכל מבין לשמע, 8:2). The adjective *all* recalls as well the phrase כל־העם, which expressed both the representativeness of the leadership in the introduction to this segment (8:13) and the comprehensiveness of the community throughout the prior segment (כל־העם, ten times in Neh 7:72b–8:12). Nevertheless, the subjective genitive defines the community's boundaries, restricting the assembly to "those who had returned from captivity" (השבים מן־השבי, 8:17).

The comparative evaluation (8:17) expresses a judgment on the assembly's work in view of an ancient precedent that Joshua and his peers set. In 8:17, the title בני־ישראל ("the Israelites") designates both Joshua's generation and Ezra's contemporaries. In 8:14, בני־ישראל is a scriptural title. The manner of their constructing and living in booths for the festival certifies that the assembly of those who returned from captivity are the authentic heirs to the children of Israel who first inhabited the land. Literary structure underlines the significance of בני־ישראל in 8:17 insofar as this title provides a double *inclusio*: (1) in the present segment (8:13–18), for the central portions of the chiasm (B–B', 8:14–17) and (2) in the whole narrative from the beginning (7:72b).

The evaluation concludes with a phrase in the superlative concerning "joy" that is without parallel elsewhere in the MT (8:17, שמחה גדולה מאד). The adjective מאד indicates a level beyond שמחה גדולה (8:12) and therefore an intensification of the benefits the people had experienced at the end of the assembly on the first day.

Ezra reads from the book of the law (8:18)

The conclusion summarizing the eight-day Festival of Booths contains three lexical links with the preceding evaluation (8:17), which focus on other aspects of the festival: (1) יום ביום echoes [ההוא] היום but refers to each day of the festival rather than to the whole era of Ezra; (2) מן־היום הראשון עד היום האחרון, which marks a passage of time during the Festival of Booths (i.e., for Ezra's reading), is the same grammatical construction as מימי ישוע בן־נון כן בני ישראל עד היום ההוא ("as the Israelites had not done from the days of Jeshua son of Nun until that day"), which specifies a gap in time between the two optimal observances of the festival; (3) ויעשו־חג resonates with סכות ... ויעשו but refers more directly to the daily reading of the law book throughout the festival than to the construction of booths.

Ezra's daily reading of the law throughout the Festival of Booths is his last activity as a solitary leader in Ezra-Nehemiah (Neh 8:18; cf. 12:26, 33, 36). After this point, he disappears from the covenant-renewal account (9:1–10:40). The description of his activity here repeats the vocabulary depicting the Levites' efforts (ויקראו] בספר [ב]תורת האלהים, 8:18; cf. 8:8) and recalls Ezra's initial reading on the first day of the month (ויקרא בו, 8:3). The seven-day duration of Ezra's reading (מן־היום הראשון עד היום האחרון, 8:18) extends beyond the half-day time span of his proclamation at the beginning (מן־האור עד־מחצית היום, 8:3). The law (תורה, 8:18; cf. 8:13, 14) provides an *inclusio* for the segment (8:13–18).

The final word confirms the people's adherence to the law; that is, their observance of the seven days of the festival and the solemnity on the eighth day "according to the ordinance" (כמשפט) underlines their commitment to the law, which had been evident in their gathering branches to make booths "as it is written" (ככתוב, 8:15). Thus, the dedication of Ezra and the people to the law is manifest both in the duration of his reading (8:18a) and in their observing the festival according to the prescriptions for the number of days (8:18b) and for the construction of booths (8:15).

LEXICAL EXAMINATION

My lexical analysis follows the above outline of the account of the Festival of Booths (8:13–18).

THE ASSEMBLY OF LEADERS TO STUDY THE LAW (8:13)

The legal codes do not mention the "second day" (ביום השני, 8:13) of the seventh month. The expression ראשי האבות occurs frequently in Chronicles and Ezra-Nehemiah.[91] Its term האבות represents a shortened form of בית־אבות, a designation for ancestral families in earlier literature (Exod 6:14; 12:3; Num 1:2, 18–43). In the expression לכל־העם, the ל denotes a genitive (GBH §130a). The lack of the conjunctive ו before הכהנים in a list of multiple subjects is noticeable elsewhere in Ezra 3:8; Neh 10:29; 11:3, 20.

In Ezra-Nehemiah, the "heads of families, the priests, and the Levites" (ראשי האבות לכל־העם הכהנים והלוים) are mentioned at two other significant points: those who responded immediately to the decree of Cyrus and returned to Jerusalem (Ezra 1:5); and the elderly people who were

---

[91] ראשי האבות occurs twenty-nine times in the MT: (1) sixteen in Chronicles (1 Chr 7:11; 8:13; 9:34; 15:12; 23:9, 24; 24:6, 31; 26:21, 26, 32; 27:1; 2 Chr 1:2; 19:8; 23:2; 26:12); (2) eleven in Ezra-Nehemiah (Ezra 1:5; 2:68; 3:12; 4:2, 3; 10:16; Neh 7:69, 70; 8:13; 12:12, 23); and (3) twice elsewhere (Num 36:1; Josh 19:51).

present when the foundation of the temple was laid (Ezra 3:12). Their role as subjects here in Neh 8:13–14 suggests that their studying the law is of equal magnitude to both the initial restoration of the people to the land and the reestablishment of the temple.

The *hip'il* of שכל can mean "to ponder" (e.g., Deut 32:29; Ps 106:7; Isa 41:20); however, Neh 8:13 is the only instance in which the verb takes the law (התורה) as its object.[92] The context indicates that in this verse שכל means "to study" (since Neh 8:14 implies a researching of the written text).

The Prescriptions of the Law (8:14–15)

The leaders did not simply happen upon the relevant passage by chance. The specification בחג בחדש השביעי (8:14) indicates that they were looking for prescriptions outlining the proper manner of observing the seventh month (cf. [ה]חדש השביעי, 7:72b; 8:2). The expression וימצאו כתוב ("they found written," 8:14) describes the result of their perusing the text in search of a passage appropriate to the community's circumstances (cf. 7:5, ואמצא כתוב בו). At the end of Nehemiah, the same language describes the process of researching "the book of Moses" that results in the expulsion of foreigners from the assembly (ונמצא כתוב בו, 13:1; cf. Esth 6:2; Dan 12:1).

The expression כתוב בתורה אשר צוה יהוה ביד־משה (ביד־משה, 8:14) denotes agency (see, e.g., 2 Chr 33:8; 35:6); all three occurrences in Ezra-Nehemiah are in the covenant-renewal account (8:14; 9:14; 10:29).

The prescription that "the children of Israel should dwell in booths on the festival of the seventh month" is not an exact quotation of a biblical text. Of the various legal prescriptions for the Festival of Booths, only Lev 23:42 stipulates that the people should dwell in booths. However, the only words that are identical in Lev 23:42 and Neh 8:14 are: ישבו בסכו[ו]ת ("they should dwell in booths"). The phrase בחג בחדש השביעי ("on the festival of the seventh month") represents an amalgam of vocabulary from the legislation's introductory verse (Lev 23:39; cf. 23:34). The title "Festival of Booths" (חג הסכות) occurs also in Ezra 3:4 and elsewhere (Lev 23:34; Deut 16:13, 16; 31:10; Zech 14:16, 18, 19; 2 Chr 8:13).

None of the pentateuchal laws prescribes an announcement of the Festival of Booths (cf. Neh 8:15, ואשר ישמיעו ויעבירו קול בכל־עריהם ובירושלם לאמר: "and that they should make it known and circulate a proclamation in all their towns and in Jerusalem, saying..."). In the MT, five of six instances of עבר קול (*hip'il*) are in Chronicles and Ezra-Nehemiah, where the expression describes respectively the publication of: (1) Cyrus's

---

[92] In Prov 16:20, דבר is the object of [על]משכיל, but there דבר more likely refers to the prophetic word than to the word of the law. See W. McKane, *Proverbs* (OTL; Philadelphia: Westminster, 1970), 498.

decree of liberation (2 Chr 36:22; Ezra 1:1); (2) Hezekiah's Passover (2 Chr 30:5); and (3) the assembly for Ezra's marriage reform (Ezra 10:7; cf. Neh 8:15).[93] It is noteworthy that the latter two instances explicitly call for a gathering of the people in Jerusalem, whereas Neh 8:15 speaks only of the proclamation's taking place in Jerusalem as well as in all the towns.

The proclamation about going into the hills and gathering five species of boughs for constructing booths (8:15) similarly does not correspond precisely with any of the legal texts governing the Festival of Booths. However, it does reflect the two distinctive requirements of the Priestly legislation (Lev 23:39–43): the people's taking various species of branches for use in the Festival of Booths (Lev 23:40); and the use of booths (Lev 23:42–43). Nevertheless, Neh 8:15 has three variations from the directives for the festival in Lev 23:39–43: (1) Leviticus describes two ceremonies (one, a festive procession with the branches and fruit [23:40]; the other, the people's inhabiting booths [23:42]), whereas Nehemiah prescribes a single undertaking (the construction of booths out of the branches); (2) Leviticus lists four species of branches, but Nehemiah lists five and, of these, they agree only on two (תמרים [palm] and עץ עבת [leafy trees]);[94] and (3) Neh 8:15 prescribes the "making" (עשׂה) of booths, whereas Lev 23:42–43 speaks only of "dwelling" in booths (ישׁב, cf. Neh 8:17).[95]

The discrepancies between Neh 8:14–15 and the pentateuchal legislation on Booths raise questions about the meaning of "as it is written" (ככתוב) in 8:15. The two basic alternatives that scholars have proposed to account for the differences are either that Ezra's pentateuchal text was different from the MT[96] or that Ezra and the leaders were engaged in a halakic interpretation of Lev 23:39–43.[97] However, from a narrative perspective, the central issue is observance of the law, not the degree of literal correspondence between Neh 8:14–15 and Lev 23:39–43.

Elsewhere in Ezra-Nehemiah, the phrase "as it is written" (ככתוב, Ezra 3:2, 4; 6:18 [Aramaic, כתב]; Neh 10:35; 10:37) does not indicate a direct quotation of the law but rather an allusion to a legal injunction that

---

[93] The remaining instance of the phrase is in Exod 36:6.

[94] Using tree boughs is especially appropriate for the autumn harvest of trees as distinct from the summer harvest of grains. However, in view of the fact that Booths celebrates also the olive harvest, the absence of olive branches in Lev 23:40 is remarkable (cf. Neh 8:15, עלי־זית ועלי־עץ שמן).

[95] For an extensive comparison of Neh 8:14–15 with Lev 23:39–43 and various proposals to account for their differences, see Rubenstein, "History of Sukkot," 72–80.

[96] See, e.g., Mowinckel, *Studien III*, 166–75; Houtman, "Ezra and the Law," 104–5; 108–9.

[97] See, e.g., Fishbane, *Biblical Interpretation*, 109–10; Blenkinsopp, *Ezra-Nehemiah*, 291–92.

underscores the rectitude of the community's action or commitment. In three cases, the allusion suggests a norm in the extant Pentateuch that has similarities in theme (Ezra 3:4; cf. Num 29:12–38 [daily sacrifices during the Festival of Booths]; Neh 10:37; cf. Num 18:15 [the firstborn of the children and of the livestock]) and in vocabulary (Ezra 3:2; cf. Deut 27:6).[98] However, the other two instances are more conjectural: (1) supplying the wood offering is not stipulated as such but is presumed in the injunction to maintain the fire on the altar (Neh 10:35; cf. Lev 6:5–6); and (2) the ordering of priests and Levites in Jerusalem does not correspond directly to pentateuchal law but may have a generic relationship to its legislation on priests (Ezra 6:18; cf. Exod 29:1–30; Lev 8:1–36). In summary, within Ezra-Nehemiah, the phrase ככתוב underscores the role of the law in stimulating the renewal of community life without any overriding preoccupation with literal equivalence.

THE PEOPLE IMPLEMENT THE PRESCRIPTIONS (8:16–17)

In contrast to the mention of the five locations for the structures in Neh 8:16, Lev 23:42–43 does not indicate a precise location for the booths. Even in view of the specified locations in Jerusalem (Neh 8:16), some commentators contend that in Neh 8:13–18 the Festival of Booths was not confined to the city alone in light of these indications: (1) the proclamation circulated throughout the towns as well as in Jerusalem; (2) an indication is lacking that building on one's roof would be limited to citizens of Jerusalem; (3) the booths in the public squares are not designated for visitors from rural areas; and (4) everyone in the community celebrates the festival (8:17).[99] However, these arguments do not take sufficient account of the following literary factors: (1) the only locations named for the booths are in Jerusalem; (2) the verb בוא (*hip'il*, "to bring," 8:15, 16) suggests the transportation of the branches to a central location; and (3) Ezra's reading from the first until the last day presumes an audience of "the whole assembly" (כל־הקהל, 8:17–18), corresponding to "all the people" (כל־העם) on the first day of the month (8:3). Moreover, celebrating the festival in Jerusalem corresponds to the Deuteronomic prescriptions for the Festival of Booths as these would have been understood in the postexilic era (Deut 16:15; 31:11). In summary, the broader context indicates that Neh 8:14–18 portrays the festival as a gathering of the whole community in Jerusalem.

---

[98] Deut 27:6: תבנה את־מזבח יהוה אלהיך והעלית עליו עולת
Ezra 3:2: ויבנו את־מזבח אלהי ישראל להעלות עליו עלות

[99] Thus Fishbane, *Biblical Interpretation*, 111; Rubenstein, "History of Sukkot," 79–80; W. R. Scott, "The Booths of Ancient Israel's Autumn Festival" (Ph.D. diss., Johns Hopkins University, 1993), 116–17, 120.

In the description of the returned exiles who practiced living in booths, the phrase "the whole assembly" (כל־הקהל) is distinctive of Chronicles and Ezra-Nehemiah.[100] Among its many other occurrences in Chronicles, the term denotes the congregation that celebrated Hezekiah's Passover (2 Chr 30:25). In Ezra-Nehemiah, it refers alternately to two groups: those who originally returned to Jerusalem from Babylon (Ezra 2:64 = Neh 7:66); and those in gatherings who voice consent to the reforms that a leader proposes (Ezra 10:12; Neh 5:13). In Neh 8:17, the expression reflects the second usage since here כל־הקהל are those who obey the dictates of the law (cf. 8:14–15). At the same time, the subsequent qualifier "of those who had returned from captivity" (השבים מן־השבי) recalls the first group (cf. Ezra 2:64 = Neh 7:66). Furthermore, "those who had returned" (השבים, *qal* participle) occurs only once elsewhere in Ezra-Nehemiah: to define a segment of people who partook of the Passover following the reconstruction of the temple (Ezra 6:21, השבים מהגולה). Therefore, from a literary perspective, the expression כל־הקהל השבים מן־השבי ("the whole assembly of those who had returned from captivity") links the gathering for the Festival of Booths with four earlier episodes: the original return from Babylon (Ezra 2:64 = Neh 7:66); the celebration of Passover after the completion of the temple (Ezra 6:21); Ezra's marriage reform (Ezra 10:12; cf. 10:14); and Nehemiah's social reform (Neh 5:13).

The statement that "they dwelt in the booths" (וישבו בסכות) corresponds with "You shall dwell in booths" (בסכות תשבו, Lev 23:42).

The observation comparing the present festival with the standard set in the early days of Israel's establishment (Neh 8:17b) is consistent with the Chronicler's evaluations of the Passover celebrations under both Hezekiah (2 Chr 30:26) and Josiah (2 Chr 35:18). The central question here concerns the precise feature that makes this Festival of Booths unprecedented since the time of Joshua. Commentators have offered seven proposals: (1) no previous festival conformed to the standards of Ezra's law;[101] (2) the spirit of Ezra's celebration was unequaled since the settlement era;[102] (3) a new theocracy was being inaugurated;[103] (4) this was the first celebration of Booths that was centralized in Jerusalem;[104] (5) this was the first time

---

100 כל־הקהל occurs twenty-one times in the MT: (1) thirteen in Chronicles (1 Chr 13:4; 29:1, 10, 20 [bis]; 2 Chr 1:3; 23:3; 28:14, 28; 30:2, 4, 23, 25); (2) six in Ezra-Nehemiah (Ezra 2:64; 10:12, 14; Neh 5:13; 7:66; 8:17); and twice elsewhere (Exod 16:3; 1 Sam 17:47).

101 Batten, *Ezra and Nehemiah*, 362.

102 Fensham, *Ezra and Nehemiah*, 221.

103 In der Smitten, *Esra*, 44–47.

104 Rudolph, *Esra und Nehemia*, 152–53.

people actually dwelt in booths;[105] (6) for the first time, the booths were symbolic of the exodus rather than merely of the harvest;[106] and (7) the law of Moses was the centerpiece of this festival just as it had been when Joshua renewed the covenant at Shechem.[107]

The last of these proposals is the one that corresponds the most adequately to the literary indications within the account. Mention of the "children of Israel" (בני ישראל) identifies the people who gathered at the square in front of the Water Gate (Neh 7:72b) as the authentic descendants of those who first entered the land under "Joshua, son of Nun" (Deut 31:23; 34:9). Moreover, I note five lexical elements that relate the reading of the law in Neh 8 to the covenant renewals at Mount Ebal and Mount Gerizim (Josh 8:32–35) and at Shechem in the valley between the two mountains (24:1–28; cf. 23:1–16): (1) כל־העם (Neh 8:1; cf. Josh 24:2, 27); (2) ספר תורת משה (8:1; cf. Josh 8:31; 23:6); (3) public reading (קרא, 8:3; cf. Josh 8:34); (4) inclusion of women and children in the assembly (קהל) for the reading (8:2–3; cf. Josh 8:35); and (5) ספר תורת [ה]אלהים (8:8, 18; cf. Josh 24:26). The comparison with Joshua and his generation in 8:17 thus indicates that those who dwell in booths are the new "Israelites" who are undertaking a new settlement of the land by subscribing to the law of Moses in a manner that surpasses their forebears.[108]

The evaluation of the festival concludes with the description of the people's "very great joy" (שמחה גדולה מאד, 8:17). While this mention of "rejoicing" (שמח) reflects the influence of both the Priestly (Lev 23:40) and Deuteronomic (Deut 16:14–15) injunctions for the Festival of Booths, Lev 23:40 is more likely the primary referent in view of its influence on other elements of the account (i.e., the naming of boughs [8:15] and the dwelling in booths [8:17; cf. Lev 23:42]). Within Ezra-Nehemiah itself, the emphasis on joy (שמחה, 8:17) connects the Festival of Booths with the dedication of the temple (Ezra 6:16 [Aramaic], חדוה), on the one hand, and with the dedication of the city walls (12:43, שמחה גדולה), on the other hand.

Ezra Reads from the Book of the Law of God (8:18)

Ezra's reading of the law corresponds with Joshua's actions on behalf of the Israelites (8:18; cf. Josh 8:32–35; 24:1–28) after their settling in the

---

[105] Scott, "The Booths," 118–20.

[106] Myers, *Ezra, Nehemiah*, 157; Williamson, *Ezra, Nehemiah*, 296.

[107] Blenkinsopp, *Ezra-Nehemiah*, 292–93; cf. Gunneweg, *Nehemia*, 117.

[108] These allusions to the settlement under Joshua complement the allusions elsewhere in Ezra-Nehemiah to the journey from Babylon to Jerusalem as a new exodus. See Williamson, *Ezra, Nehemiah*, 16–19; K. Koch, "Ezra and The Origins of Judaism," *JSS* 19 (1974): 184–89; also, J. G. McConville, "Ezra-Nehemiah and the Fulfillment of Prophecy," *VT* 36 (1986): 205–24.

land (cf. Neh 7:6–72a). The book's title (ספר תורת ה[א]להים) is almost identical with that of the book in which Joshua inscribes the words of the covenant at Shechem (Josh 24:26). As the one responsible for the book of the law (ספר ה[תורה]), Ezra assumes the identity of Joshua (Josh 1:7–8; cf. Deut 32:44–47).

At this point, one can perceive the significant connection between Ezra's celebration of Booths and the rites at Mount Ebal and Mount Gerizim insofar as reading the law is central to each (Neh 8:18; cf. Josh 8:34–35). Furthermore, Deuteronomy inspires both of these events: the account of Joshua's ceremony at Mount Gerizim and Mount Ebal (Josh 8:30–35) reflects the injunctions of Deut 27:1–8, while Ezra's celebration corresponds, in part, with the Deuteronomic prescription for the Festival of Booths during the year of remission (8:18; cf. Deut 31:9–13).

The description of Ezra's daily reading over seven days reflects a combination of two traditions: the Priestly laws that specify a duration of seven days for the Booths festival, followed by an eighth day of rest (Lev 23:34–36, 39; cf. Deut 16:13–15 [seven days]); and the Deuteronomic prescription for the reading of the law (Deut 31:9–13). Given Nehemiah's explicit compliance with Lev 23:33–36, 39–43 in the matter of temporal duration, one must acknowledge that Neh 8:13–18 does not specify the exact day in the seventh month when the festival actually began. The text notes only that the leaders undertook their study on the second day (8:13) and that the festival lasted eight days (8:18). However, the text does not indicate the interval required to prepare for the festival between the leaders' studying and the community's celebration (8:14–16).[109]

Within the context of the note on the duration of the festival, the "ordinance" (משפט) must refer to the Priestly injunction concerning the concluding solemnity (עצרת, Lev 23:36; Num 29:35), which does not occur in the other legal codes governing the Festival of Booths. The noun עצרת designates a day of solemnity to be observed by resting from work (Lev 23:36; Num 29:35; Deut 16:8).[110]

---

[109] According to the Priestly tradition, the Festival of Booths began on the fifteenth day of the month and extended for eight days (i.e., to the twenty-second day of the seventh month; Lev 23:34, 39; cf. Num 29:12–38). Ezekiel identifies the same date for beginning the festival but indicates a seven-day duration (Ezek 45:25). The two accounts of the temple dedication under Solomon reflect this discrepancy in duration of the "festival of the seventh month": the Deuteronomistic History indicates a seven-day duration (1 Kgs 8:2, 65; cf. Deut 16:13–15). However, the Chronicler separates the dedication of the temple from the Festival of Booths and, furthermore, describes an additional eighth day at the end of the festival (2 Chr 5:3; 7:8–9; cf. Lev 23:36, 39).

[110] E. Kutsch, "Die Wurzel עצר im Hebräischen," *VT* 2 (1952): 65–67.

Thematic Summary

The account of the Festival of Booths (Neh 8:13–18) is a narrative intersection with avenues to all the other major assemblies in Jerusalem in Ezra-Nehemiah. Various features establish the connections: (1) "the whole assembly" (8:17) recalls Ezra's marriage reform (10:12) and Nehemiah's social reform (Neh 5:13); (2) "those who had returned from captivity" (8:17) earlier designated both the original arrivals (Ezra 2:64 = Neh 7:66) and the participants in the Passover following the temple dedication (Ezra 6:21); (3) the leadership of "priests and Levites" in a celebration marked by "joy" characterizes the dedications of the temple (Ezra 6:16–18) and the city walls (Neh 12:27–43); and (4) the Festival of Booths recalls the celebration of the original returnees (Ezra 3:4–6). This wealth of connections highlights the Festival of Booths as a literary centerpiece of Ezra-Nehemiah.

Moreover, the written text of the law provides the fulcrum around which this narrative portion turns. Therefore, this theological reflection will focus on the implications and attributes of the law in the account of the Festival of Booths (8:13–18).

The transition from the previous segment is noteworthy. The law passes into the hands of a wider circle as the heads of the families and the priests join Ezra and the Levites (8:13; cf. 8:9). Here emphasis shifts from what is proclaimed (מקרא, 8:8) to what is written (כתוב, 8:14, 15). The law that had been the object of proclamation and veneration (קרא, 8:3, 8; 8:4–5) now becomes the focus of study (השכיל, 8:13). Concern shifts from the leaders' teachings (הודיעו, 8:12) to the words of the law (דברי התורה, 8:13; cf. 8:9).

While the focus is on content and the narrative quotes the law for the first time (8:14–15), comparative analysis discloses a lack of preoccupation with literal fulfillment. The text's directives for the Israelites to live in booths, to promulgate the injunction, and to make booths (8:14–15) are not exact reproductions but rather adaptations of the pentateuchal legislation. These adaptations evoke the people's compliance (8:15–16). Thus, "as it is written" (ככתוב, 8:15) reflects a preoccupation with genuine observance in life rather than with literal reproduction of a text's commands.

Focus on the book of the law (8:13, 18) aligns this celebration of Booths with the events of Joshua's generation. Adherence to "the book of the law" (8:13, 18; cf. Josh 8:34–35) provides a common denominator between the "children of Israel" who entered the land and renewed the covenant at Shechem under Joshua (Josh 8:30–35; 24:1–28) and "the children of Israel" who returned to the land from exile and celebrated the Festival of Booths under Ezra and the other leaders (Neh 8:13–18).

However, the book of the law from which Ezra reads is even more extensive than Joshua's book, since Joshua was able to complete his reading during a single ceremony (Josh 8:35), while there is no indication that

The Reading of the Law and the Festival of Booths

Ezra exhausted his material even over the course of seven days (cf. ויקרא בספר, 8:18).

In retrospect, one should consider the character of Ezra's law book. On strictly exegetical grounds, the evidence is too limited to ascertain the precise contents of the book. Indications in Neh 8:13–18 suggest that the text contained elements at least of the Priestly and Deuteronomic traditions. In addition, from a literary perspective, the following features of the book are significant: (1) it evokes a procession (8:2) and reverence (8:4), which lead to the blessing of YHWH (8:5); (2) its titles manifest its authority as "the law that YHWH commanded for Israel" (8:1, 14); (3) seven days (let alone "from daybreak until noonday," 8:3) are insufficient to complete its reading (ויקרא בספר, 8:18); moreover, (4) the understanding of it requires skillful reading (ויקראו, 8:3, 7), enunciation (מפרש, 8:8), interpretation (שום שכל, 8:8), and study (להשכיל, 8:13) by the leaders as well as attentive hearing by the people (8:3). Such a book is far from a mere collection of laws that Artaxerxes might have had compiled for maintaining peace in the Persian empire (7:25–26). From a literary perspective, Ezra's book exhibits the character of the Torah as revered in later tradition (see, e.g., Sir 24:23–29).

4

The Penitential Rites (Nehemiah 9:1–5)

The events of the twenty-fourth day (9:1–10:40) comprise the third segment of the covenant renewal (Neh 7:72b–10:40). I shall treat this unit in three chapters: in the present one, I discuss the narrative account of the penitential rites (9:1–5); in the next chapter, I examine the Levites' prayer (9:6–37); and, in the subsequent chapter, I investigate the people's expression of commitment to the law (10:1–40). The bond between the present chapter and the next one is particularly strong due to the fundamental unity between the third-person description of the penitential rites (9:1–5) and the first-person declamation of the prayer (9:6–37).

The discussion of the penitential rites follows the same five-part development used in the treatment of the two preceding segments: (1) a literal translation; (2) textual criticism; (3) an outline and literary analysis of the lexical components as they interact within both the immediate confines of this portion and the covenant renewal (Neh 7:72b–10:40); (4) an examination of the essential terminology within the broader context of the remainder of Ezra-Nehemiah and of biblical literature; and (5) a thematic summary of the implications of the material.

TRANSLATION

9:1 On the twenty-fourth day of this month, the Israelites gathered fasting and in sackcloth with earth on them. 2 Thus the offspring of Israel separated themselves from all foreigners. They stood and confessed their sins and the guilt of their ancestors. 3 They stood up in their place and read from the book of the law of YHWH their God for a quarter of the day, while for another quarter they were confessing and worshiping YHWH their God. 4 Then, Jeshua, Binnui,[a] Kadmiel, Shebaniah, Bunni, Sherebiah, Bani, and Chenani stood up on the stairs of the Levites and cried out in a loud voice to YHWH their God. 5 The Levites, Jeshua, Kadmiel, Bani, Hashabneiah, Sherebiah, Hodiah, Shebaniah, and Pethahiah said, "Stand up and bless YHWH, your God[b] from everlasting to everlasting; [c]and may they bless[c] your glorious name that is exalted above all blessing and praise."

Textual Criticism

^a Emend בני to בנוי.¹ The error was due to haplography. Three reasons support the emendation: (1) this correction corresponds to the order of 10:10: Jeshua, Binnui, Kadmiel, and Shebaniah; (2) the repetition of five of these names in the subsequent verse (9:5) is likely to include a rearrangement; and (3) it is unlikely that a list of eight names would contain two identical names (בני). (Nevertheless, in both cases, LXX 2 Esd 19:4 reads υἱοι, indicative of a *Vorlage* in which בני occurred twice.²)

^b Maintain the text without emendation. The literary analysis will demonstrate that the transition from narration to quotation corresponds with the setting. Respecting the integrity of the text is preferable to a conjectural insertion of ברוך אתה יהוה אלהינו ("Blessed are you YHWH, our God"), which MSS do not support.³

^{c-c} Maintain ויברכו ("and may they bless") rather than reading ברוך ("blessed") in its place in view of Syr.⁴ Moreover, reading the *puʿal* וַיְבֹרַךְ instead of וִיבָרְכוּ in order to emphasize the passive meaning is an unnecessary emendation, since even the impersonal plural can serve as a passive (GKC §144g).⁵

Furthermore, textual evidence does not support the introduction of ברוך ("blessed") after ויברכו in an attempt to clarify the narration: "And they blessed [saying], 'Blessed is your glorious name'" (cf. *Textual Notes on the New American Bible*, 365; and NAB). In summary, there is no narrative transition between two forms of quoted speech: from admonition ("Arise and bless YHWH, your God") to prayer ("Blessed is your glorious name").

Literary Analysis

My literary analysis of the penitential rites consists of three parts: (1) a delimitation of the whole segment (9:1–10:40) and of the narration of the

---

¹ Rudolph (*Esra und Nehemia*, 152) and *Textual Notes on the New American Bible*, 365.

² See Williamson, *Ezra, Nehemiah*, 303. Cf. Torrey (*Ezra Studies*, 279), who reads ו[בני קדמיאל] as either "sons of Kadmiel" (cf. Ezra 2:40), or "son of Kadmiel" (cf. Neh 12:24). However, Williamson provides two decisive observations against Torrey's rendering: (1) ו precedes the second name in each list in Neh 9:4, 5, thereby indicating that בני is someone's name; and (2) the term "sons of" does not occur in the other related lists (8:7; 9:5; 10:10–14).

³ Torrey, *Ezra Studies*, 280–81; Williamson, *Ezra, Nehemiah*, 303–4.

⁴ G. R. Driver, "Forgotten Hebrew Idioms," *ZAW* 78 (1976): 6–7.

⁵ Cf. Myers, *Ezra, Nehemiah*, 164; Fensham, *Ezra and Nehemiah*, 223.

penitential rites (9:1–5); (2) an outline of the penitential-rites narrative (9:1–5); and (3) an examination of its components within the setting of the covenant renewal.

DELIMITATION

The indications of time, subject, and initial activity define the beginning of the third segment.[6] The "twenty-fourth day" represents a temporal point subsequent to the "second day" (8:13), the following preparations for Booths (cf. 8:14–16), and the eight days of the festival (8:18). The introductory temporal phrase וביום עשרים וארבעה ("on the twenty-fourth day," 9:1) mirrors וביום השני ("on the second day," 8:13), which introduced the second segment and also recalls ביום אחד ("on the first day," 8:2) of the first segment. "This month" (לחדש הזה, 9:1) points back to the "seventh month" (החדש השביעי) of the initial exposition (7:72b) and the first segment (8:3). The subject בני ישראל (the "Israelites") also recalls the initial exposition (7:72b) and provides continuity with the previous segment (8:14, 17). The verb used is the same as at the beginning of the previous two segments (נאספו: "[they] gathered," 9:1; 8:13; cf. ויאספו: "[they] gathered," 8:1).

The events of the twenty-fourth day conclude at the end of the people's expression of commitment (10:40). The viewpoint changes from third-person narration (9:1–5a) to first-person discourse with the Levites' exhortation to the people (9:5). The discourse in the first person continues throughout the psalm (9:6–37) and the expression of commitment (10:1–40). Another change in narrative voice and subject matter marks the end of the segment (9:1–10:40) and the conclusion of the covenant renewal (7:72b–10:40), since the subsequent third-person narrative describes the repopulating of Jerusalem (11:1–2).

Within the third segment (9:1–10:40), the transition from narration to discourse begins with the quotation of the Levites' exhortation, "Stand up and bless YHWH, your God" (9:5). The first-person discourse continues with three phrases of acclamation (9:5b, "from everlasting to everlasting," "and may your glorious name be blessed," "and exalted over all blessing and praise"). The actual psalm begins with the confession אתה־הוא יהוה לבדך ("You are YHWH, you alone," 9:6) and concludes with the description of the community's plight (9:37).

The transition from the acclamations (9:5b) to the psalm (9:6–37) provides the most obvious demarcation between the penitential rites and the confessional prayer. Therefore, I include the initial acclamations within the penitential rites (9:1–5) and subsequently discuss the psalm as a cohesive unit (9:6–37).

---

[6] However, in contrast to the two previous segments, there is no mention of "the square [that is in front] of the Water Gate" (cf. 8:1, 2, 16) in the third segment.

OUTLINE

The third-person narrative begins with the description of the people assembling (9:1) and concludes with the command that the Levites address to the people ("Stand up and bless YHWH, your God from everlasting to everlasting," 9:5b–c) and with the subsequent acclamation that they address to YHWH ("and may they bless your glorious name that is exalted above all blessing and praise," 9:5d–e).

Therefore, this narrative portion consists of two parts distinguished by their respective main subjects: first, the people assemble and perform acts of penance (9:1–3); second, the Levites take up their position and direct the congregation in prayer (9:4–5).

Table 4.1—Outline of the Penitential Narrative (9:1–5)
A. The Israelites perform penitential rites (9:1–3)
   1. The Israelites assemble with penitential comportment (9:1–3a)
      a. The Israelites assemble (9:1)
      b. The seed of Israel separates itself from foreigners (9:2a)
      c. They confess sin and guilt (9:2b)
      d. They read from the book of the law (9:3a)
   2. They worship YHWH (9:3b)
B. The Levites lead the people in prayer (9:4–5)
   1. Eight stand on the stairs of the Levites and cry to YHWH (9:4)
   2. Eight exhort the people to bless YHWH (9:5)

EXAMINATION OF THE UNITS

My general outline of the whole covenant-renewal account (p. 75) illustrates that, in the third segment (9:1–10:40), the narrative section (9:1–5) contains six lexical parallels that align this segment with the previous two: (1) the date (לחדש ... ביום [day ... month]: 9:1; cf. 7:72b; 8:3, 13); (2) the verb "to assemble" (אסף, 9:1; cf. 8:1, 13); (3) the "Israelites" (בני ישראל, 9:1; cf. 7:72b; 8:13); (4) the activity of "reading" (קרא, 9:3; cf. 8:3, 7, 18); (5) the title "the book of the law of [YHWH] their God" (בספר תורת [יהוה] אלהיהם, 9:3; cf. 8:8, 18); and (6) the introduction to an exhortation (אמר [to say], 9:5; cf. 8:9, 10, 11, 15).

To these six, one can add an additional eleven lexical connections that further establish the close relationship between this narrative portion (9:1–5) and the two prior segments (7:72b–8:12; 8:13–18): (a) "standing" as a liturgical posture (עמד, 9:2; cf. 8:4, 5); (2) reference to the "ancestors" (אבתיהם, 9:2; cf. אבות, 8:13); (3) the people's "[standing] place" (עמדם, 9:3; cf. 8:7); (4) the duration of the reading according to portions of the day ("for a quarter of the day," 9:3; cf. "from daybreak until noonday," 8:3); (5) worship expressed through "prostration before YHWH" (משתחוים ליהוה, 9:3; cf. וישתחו ליהוה, 8:6); (6) the central role of the Levites (הלוים,

9:4, 5; cf. 8:7–8, 9, 11); (7) the listings of the Levites' names (9:4, 5; cf. 8:7); (8) the assonance between "stairs" (מעלה, 9:4) and "above" (מעל, 8:5) in the position of the leaders vis-à-vis the assembly; (9) the similarity between the titles of YHWH in Ezra's blessing (יהוה אלהים הגדול: "YHWH, the great God," 8:6), in the cry of the Levites (יהוה אלהיהם: "YHWH, their God," 9:4), and in the Levites' command (יהוה אלהיכם: "YHWH, your God," 9:5); (10) the primacy of "blessing YHWH" in the Levites' exhortation to the people (ברכו את־יהוה: "bless YHWH, your God," 9:5) and in the description of Ezra's initiating the people's worship (ויברך את־יהוה: "[he] blessed YHWH," 8:6); and (11) the preoccupation with the duration of time expressed by the formula מן ... עד ("from ... to," 9:5; cf. 8:3, 17, 18).

The significance of these similarities will become more apparent in the following literary analysis of the three major parts of this narrative portion.

The Israelites Perform Penitential Rites (9:1–3)

The "Israelites" (בני־ישראל, 9:1) provide continuity of subject with the final designation of the community in the second segment (8:17; cf. 8:14) and with the initial exposition (7:72b). The "twenty-fourth day" of the month marks the temporal location of the third segment relative to the first two segments. This indicator signals a temporal gap between the second and third segments in contrast to the continuity of the first two segments that occurred on the first (8:2) and second (8:13) days of the month, respectively.

The distinctiveness of the third segment relative to the first two extends beyond a gap in time to an affective alteration in the assembly from "very great joy" (8:17; cf. 8:12) to sobriety, indicated by "fasting and ... sackcloth with earth on them" (9:1). This threefold demonstration of repentance is reminiscent of the people's earlier reaction of weeping upon their first hearing of the Torah (8:9b). However, this reminiscence also highlights the contrast between the people's considered response on the twenty-fourth day (9:1) and their initial, compulsive reaction on the first day (8:9b). In both cases, from a narrative perspective, the Torah prompts the respective responses (8:18; cf. 8:9b). The time gap between Ezra's seven-day reading (8:18) and the people's expressing repentance on the twenty-fourth day (9:1) coincides with the change in atmosphere (from joy to contrition) and thereby implies an interval of deliberation on the part of "the children of Israel" (9:1; cf. 8:17).

Separation from foreigners (9:2a) is the purpose of the penitential rites.[7] The distinctive location, style, and content of 9:2a suggests the primacy of this issue vis-à-vis the other clauses describing the people's

---

[7] Williamson confirms this estimation from a diachronic perspective when he identifies 9:2 as a "summary heading" (*Ezra, Nehemiah*, 311).

actions. In 9:2–3, the verb "they separated themselves" (וַיִּבָּדְלוּ) is the first in a sequence of five converted imperfects (*wayyiqtol*) that depict the people's conduct (cf. "they stood" [וַיַּעַמְדוּ]; "they confessed" [וַיִּתְוַדּוּ]; "they stood up" [וַיָּקֻמוּ]; and "they read" [וַיִּקְרְאוּ]). The verb וַיִּבָּדְלוּ occurs by itself, whereas the others appear in pairs with a reference to posture preceding a liturgical activity (וַיַּעַמְדוּ וַיִּתְוַדּוּ: "they stood and confessed," 9:2b; וַיָּקֻמוּ ... וַיִּקְרְאוּ: "they stood up ... and read," 9:3). Furthermore, the verb בדל (*nip'al*: "to separate oneself [from others]") represents an existential reorientation, whereas the other verbs describe specific, observable actions.

The congregation's confessing of their own sins and the guilt of their ancestors foreshadows the content of the psalm (9:16–17b, 18, 26, 28a, 29, 30a, 33, 35).[8]

The penitential discipline (fasting), attire (sackcloth and earth), and actions (confession, reading, and prostration [וּמִשְׁתַּחֲוִים]) provide the setting for the subsequent introduction of the proselytes as "all who separated themselves from the peoples of the lands to the law of God" (10:29). The people's activities (9:2–3) attain a specific focus in the witness of these proselytes (10:29). This becomes apparent in the parallels between 10:29 and 9:2–3 in terms of: (1) separation from foreigners and (2) attachment to the law:

10:29   כָּל־הַנִּבְדָּל מֵעַמֵּי הָאֲרָצוֹת
9:2a   [9]וַיִּבָּדְלוּ זֶרַע יִשְׂרָאֵל מִבְּנֵי נֵכָר

10:29   [כָּל־הַנִּבְדָּל] אֶל־תּוֹרַת הָאֱלֹהִים
9:3   [10]וַיִּקְרְאוּ בְּסֵפֶר תּוֹרַת יְהוָה הָאֱלֹהִים

The people's reading from the "book of the law of YHWH, their God" (9:3) culminates the book's transmission into the hands of an ever-widening circle: from Ezra (8:2–3, 4–5), to the Levites (8:7–8), to the more inclusive group of leaders (embracing also family heads and priests, 8:13), via Ezra (8:18), to the whole community (9:3). At the beginning of the third segment (9:1–3), the leaders are noteworthy by their absence. Thus, the assembly has direct access to the book without requiring the mediation of Ezra's proclamation (cf. 8:3), the Levites' interpretation (cf. 8:7–8), or the leaders' study (cf. 8:13).

Moreover, on their own initiative, the people perform the liturgical actions that they had previously done in response to the leaders' promptings:

---

[8] Ibid.

[9] 10:29: "all who had separated themselves from the peoples of the lands."
9:2a: "Thus the offspring of Israel separated themselves from all foreigners."

[10] 10:29: "[all who had separated themselves] to the law of God."
9:3: "They read from the book of YHWH their God."

they "stand" (עמד, 9:3; cf. 8:5), and, while "in their place" (על־עמדם, 9:3; cf. 8:7), they "read" (קרא, 9:3; cf. 8:3, 8, 18) and "worship YHWH" (חוה ליהוה [hištap̄ʿel], 9:3; cf. 8:6). A further indication of the people's development is the duration of their combined reading and penitential worship: two quarters of the day (רבעית היום ורבעית): "for a quarter of the day while for another quarter," 9:3) equals half the daylight hours, that is, the duration of Ezra's initial reading (מן־האור עד־מחצית היום): "from daybreak until noonday," 8:3).

Confession (ויתודו, 9:2b; cf. מתודים, 9:3b) frames the reading of the law (9:3a). The congregation's spending half its time in confession and worship shifts the emphasis from predominantly reading (8:3; cf. 8:6) to an equal balance with worship (9:3). The participles that conclude the description of the people's activity (מתודים ומשתחוים: "confessing and worshiping," 9:3) reinforce the durative aspect of the penitential worship on the twenty-fourth day in contrast to the punctual aspect that the converted imperfects (ויקדו וישתחו, 8:6) imply for the veneration on the first day.[11] These indications of extended worship provide the setting for the following exhortation to prayer.

The Levites Lead the People in Prayer (9:4–5)

Narrative cohesion is apparent through various structural devices. The two lists of eight Levites (9:4–5) link backward to the events of the first day and forward to the signing of the pledge later on the twenty-fourth day. In addition, aspects of narrative structure as well as some of the names recall the first segment of the covenant renewal (7:72b–8:12). The "standing up" (ויקם, 9:4a) of the eight men on the stairs of the Levites recalls the "standing" (ויעמד, 8:4) of the thirteen men on the platform with Ezra in two ways: (1) this is the first of two successive groups of an equivalent number of men listed by name (9:4a, 5a [eight names]; cf. 8:4, 7 [thirteen names]); and (2) this group is "above" (מעל, 8:5; cf. מעלה, 9:4a) the people. Regarding the actual names, four of the Levites who address the people directly (9:5: Jeshua, Bani, Sherebiah, and Hodiah) were among the thirteen who instructed the people in the law on the first day (9:5; cf. 8:7). Linkage with the narrative of commitment derives from the recurrence of five names in the two lists that appear also among the signatories of the pledge (Jeshua, Binnui, Kadmiel, Shebaniah, and Hodiah, 9:4–5; cf. 10:10–11).

Unlike every previous segment or subunit (8:1, 4, 7, 8, 13), this narrative portion (9:1–5a) does not introduce the leaders at the beginning. Therefore, these Levites function differently from previous leaders. Since

---

[11] The participle משתחוים ("they were worshiping") links the congregation's worship with that ascribed to the heavenly host at the beginning of the psalm that follows (9:3, 6).

the narrative focus turns to them following the description of the people's penitential activity, the Levites do not so much initiate as redirect the congregation's worship. The eight on the stairs unite themselves with the people's acts of worship by directing their outcry to "YHWH, their God" (יהוה אלהיהם, 9:4b; cf. 9:3b). This solidarity in worship provides the basis for the Levites' subsequent exhortation.

Five of the eight Levites on the stairs (Jeshua, Kadmiel, Bani, Sherebiah, and Shebaniah) join with three others (Hashabneiah, Hodiah, and Pethahiah) in voicing the exhortation (ויאמר, 9:5; cf. 8:9, 10; לאמר, 8:11, 15). Their appeal introduces the third reference to "YHWH, your [their] God" (יהוה אלהיכם, 9:5), and thereby culminates the intensifying devotion that began with the people's ongoing confession and worship (יהוה אלהיהם, 9:3) and increased with the Levites' crying out (יהוה אלהיהם, 9:4). Therefore, the Levites' exhortation does not so much invite worship as call for a vocal expression in keeping with the people's previous rites.

Moreover, their invitation for the people to "bless YHWH, your God" recalls the activity of Ezra after opening the book on the first day of the month:

9:5b   ברכו את־יהוה אלהיכם
8:6a   ¹²ויברך עזרא את־יהוה האלהים הגדול

This parallelism further suggests the people's growth in stature inasmuch as the Levites now invite them to do as Ezra did.

Following upon the Levites' command to the people, "Stand up and bless YHWH, your God," controversy envelopes the remainder of 9:5 regarding both its content and speakers. In terms of content, the first issue concerns the referent for the phrase "from everlasting to everlasting" (מן־העולם עד־העולם). Immediately prior to this phrase, various commentators and translations insert the standard acclamation "Blessed are you, YHWH, our God" in order to generate the statement ברוך אתה יהוה אלהינו מן־העולם עד־העולם ("Blessed are you, YHWH, our God, from everlasting to everlasting," cf. Pss 41:14; 106:48; and 1 Chr 16:27).¹³ However, this reading is not attested in any MS or ancient version, and it is unlikely that paraplepsis could account for such an omission.¹⁴

---

¹² 9:5b: "Bless YHWH, your God."
   8:6a: "Then Ezra blessed YHWH, the great God."

¹³ Torrey, *Ezra Studies*, 281; Rudolph, *Esra und Nehemia*, 152, 156–57; Williamson, *Ezra, Nehemiah*, 300, 303–4; NJB.

¹⁴ Contra Williamson (*Ezra, Nehemiah*, 303–4), who also proposes that a defective spelling of the pronoun (את: "you") would further the similarity with the preceding ברכו את־יהוה אלהיכם (Neh 9:5), and therefore enhance the possibility of paraplepsis.

Moreover, the argument that it would be absurd to consider the phrase "from everlasting to everlasting" (מן־העולם עד־העולם) as modifying the people's blessing of YHWH does not stand up to scrutiny.[15] In Ps 115:18, a similar temporal phrase follows a description of the human act of blessing: ואנחנו נברך יה מעתה ועד־עולם ("But we will bless YHWH from now and forevermore").

Moreover, the phrase מן־העולם עד־העולם ("from everlasting to everlasting") belongs with the preceding command rather than with the following clause. The strictures of syntax exclude a direct connection with the jussive, since the initial *waw* in ויברכו (9:5b) indicates the beginning of a new clause and therefore a separation from what precedes it.[16] Therefore, the phrase מן־העולם עד־העולם completes the exhortation ברכו את־יהוה אלהיכם ("bless YHWH, your God") as an indirect reflection, though not an exact duplication, of the standard liturgical acclamation (ברוך־יהוה אלהי ישראל מן־העולם עד־העולם: "Blessed be YHWH, the God of Israel, from everlasting to everlasting;" cf. Pss 41:14; 106:48; and 1 Chr 16:27).

As for the question of the speaker, most commentators and translations ascribe the command, the blessing, and the psalm to the Levites.[17] By contrast, Torrey ascribes only the command to the Levites but the blessing (and the psalm) to Ezra: "And the Levites ... said, 'Stand up and bless YHWH, your God.' And Ezra said, 'Blessed are you YHWH our God from everlasting to everlasting.'"[18] Furthermore, among the translations, the NAB is unique in its attribution of a response to the congregation. According to the NAB, the Levites speak the command, while the Israelites reply (and Ezra declaims the psalm): "The Levites ... said, / 'Arise, bless the Lord, your God / from eternity to eternity!' The Israelites answered with the

---

[15] Torrey (*Ezra Studies*, 280–81) asserts that common sense rules out the possibility of the phrase מן־העולם עד־העולם modifying the imperative ברכו, since it is nonsense to speak of people continuing to bless YHWH "forever" (cf. 9:5a). The JPSV seems to address this concern by inserting the relative pronoun into the Levites' command in order to relate the temporal phrase to YHWH rather than to the act of blessing: "Rise, bless the Lord your God who is from eternity to eternity."

[16] Cf. Blenkinsopp (*Ezra-Nehemiah*, 294) whose translation reads, "The Levites ... said, 'Arise and bless YHVH your God: From age to age / may they bless your glorious name / exalted beyond every blessing and praise!'" Similarly, the REB: "Then the Levites ... said, 'Stand up and bless the Lord your God in these words: From everlasting to everlasting may your glorious name be blessed.'"

[17] Williamson, *Ezra, Nehemiah*, 300; Blenkinsopp, *Ezra-Nehemiah*, 293–94; Myers, *Ezra, Nehemiah*, 158; NJB; REB; and JPSV.

[18] Torrey (*Ezra Studies*, 281). Rudolph tentatively accepts Torrey's proposal but maintains the possibility that the Levites might be the speakers throughout (*Esra und Nehemia*, 152, 154, 157).

blessing, / 'Blessed is your glorious name, / and exalted above all blessing and praise.' / Then Ezra said: 'It is you, O Lord, you are the only one.'"

However, evidence in the MSS and the versions fails to support the insertion of other voices into Neh 9:5. Torrey transposes the narrative portion of LXX 2 Esd 19:6 (καὶ εἶπεν Ἐσδρας) so that it follows the Levites' command instead of introducing the psalm. The NAB, for its part, fails to provide supporting evidence for its insertion of the congregational response.[19]

Therefore, I maintain that in Neh 9:5 the MT makes good sense. The Levites' command to bless YHWH and the attendant modifying phrase combine to form a parallelism with the following two clauses:

ברכו את־יהוה אלהיכם מן־העולם עד־העולם
ויברכו שם כבודך ומרומם על־כל־ברכה ותהלה[20]

The subject of the second line (שֵׁם כְּבוֹדֶךָ: "your glorious name") presumes the introduction of the divine name in the first line (אֶת־יהוה אֱלֹהֵיכֶם: "YHWH, your God"). The indirect volitive (וִיבָרְכוּ: "and may they bless") continues the mood following the initial imperative (בָּרְכוּ: "Bless").[21] Repetition, alliteration, and assonance also unite the two lines. Repetition occurs in the three forms of the root ברך: בָּרְכוּ ("bless"), וִיבָרְכוּ ("and may they bless"), and בְּרָכָה ("blessing"). Alliteration is manifest in the seven occurrences of כ: בָּרְכוּ, אֱלֹהֵיכֶם, וִיבָרְכוּ, כְּבוֹדֶךָ, and כָּל־בְּרָכָה. Assonance is found in three diverse sounds: (1) û in בָּרְכוּ and וִיבָרְכוּ (as well as in קוּמוּ); (2) m and ô in מִן־הָעוֹלָם עַד־הָעוֹלָם and in וּמְרוֹמַם; and (3) â in בְּרָכָה and וּתְהִלָּה.

The three successive occurrences of the construction עַד ... מִן ("from ... to") to express a positive duration of time (8:3, 18; 9:5; cf. 8:17)[22] signal a progressive expansion of the time frame. The temporal scope broadens according to the three gatherings for the reading or study of the law: first, Ezra reads the law "from sunrise to noon" (מִן־הָאוֹר עַד־מַחֲצִית, 8:3); next, during Booths, he reads "from the first until the last day" of the festival

---

[19] *The Textual Notes on the New American Bible* (p. 365) do not explain the origins of the insertion, "The Israelites answered with the blessing." The NAB adds ברוך after ויברכו, explaining its omission as due to haplography. Of course, in 9:6 the NAB follows the LXX when it inserts "And Ezra said."

[20] "[B]less YHWH, your God from everlasting to everlasting;
and may they bless your glorious name, which is exalted above all blessing and praise."

[21] The pointing distinguishes the jussive (or indirect volitive: וִיבָרְכוּ) from a *wāw* consecutive imperfect (וַיְבָרְכוּ, cf. Neh 11:2). See GKC §49c.

[22] The expression מִימֵי ... עַד הַיּוֹם (8:17) indicates a gap in the people's devotion. By contrast, the three other occurrences of מִן ... עַד mark durations of inspired activity (either by the community [8:3, 18] or by YHWH [9:5]).

(מִן־הַיּוֹם הָרִאשׁוֹן עַד הַיּוֹם הָאַחֲרוֹן, 8:18); finally, the Levites exhort the congregation to bless YHWH their God "from everlasting to everlasting" (מִן־הָעוֹלָם עַד־הָעוֹלָם, 9:5). The horizon for devotion has expanded from just over six hours (8:3) to an everlasting duration (9:5).

At the same time, "everlasting" alludes to the character of God and thereby provides the setting for the Levites' enunciation of God's activities and attributes throughout the psalm (9:6–37). This "everlasting" dimension of YHWH offers the ultimate temporal perspective for the recounting of Israel's history in the psalm.

LEXICAL EXAMINATION

THE CHILDREN OF ISRAEL PERFORM PENITENTIAL RITES (9:1–3)

The "twenty-fourth" day (בְּיוֹם עֶשְׂרִים וְאַרְבָּעָה, 9:1) of the seventh month is not mentioned anywhere else in the MT. However, in various postexilic books, the "twenty-fourth" is one of the days on which prophets had visions (Zech 1:7; Dan 10:4) or declared their messages (cf. Hag 2:10, 20).

Fasting accompanies prayer also in the two other episodes in Ezra-Nehemiah (צוּם, Ezra 8:21–23; Neh 1:4; cf. 9:1). As a public event of the whole community, the congregation's fast in Neh 9:1 recalls the comportment of the assembly at Ahava (Ezra 8:21, 23) but with distinctions both in purpose (in Ezra 8:21, 23 the fasting signifies supplication, not repentance, as in Neh 9:1) and in initiative (in Ezra 8:21, Ezra proclaims the fast, whereas in Neh 9:1 the community fasts on its own accord). For the community (Neh 9:1), as for Nehemiah himself (1:4), the fast indicates repentance. Yet another instance of the practice is Ezra's depriving himself of bread and water in response to the news of the exiles' marriages with foreigners (Ezra 10:6).

In the preexilic era, public fasts were not part of the liturgical cycle. Rather, fasting accompanied prayer in response to particular crises of the community (e.g., Judg 20:26; 1 Sam 7:6; 31:13; Jer 14:11–12) or of individuals (e.g., 2 Sam 12:15b–23).[23] In relation to Neh 9:1, the preexilic episode most worthy of note is Baruch's reading of Jeremiah's "book" to the assembly in Jerusalem on a day of fasting (Jer 36:6, 9). In the early postexilic period, fasts in the fifth and seventh months seem to have commemorated the destruction of Jerusalem and subsequent desolating events (Zech 7:3, 5; 8:19).[24] Apparently, the postexilic liturgical year also incorporated other

---

[23] J. Muddiman, "Fast, Fasting," *ABD* 2:773–74; H. H. Guthrie, "Fast," *IDB* 2:241–44.

[24] C. L. and E. M. Meyers (*Haggai, Zechariah 1–8* [AB 25B; New York: Doubleday, 1987], 388) view the fast in the fifth month as a commemoration of the destruction of Jerusalem (cf. 2 Kgs 25:8; Jer 52:12) and the fast in the seventh month as a subsequent memorial of the murder of Gedaliah (cf. 2 Kgs 25:25; Jer 41:1–3).

fasts (see Isa 58:3; Esth 9:31). While fasting was constitutive for the observance of the Day of Atonement (Lev 16:29, 31; 23:27, 29, 32; Num 29:7), there are no indications that would relate the fast in Neh 9:1 to that liturgical event. In summary, the fast that the people undertake on the twenty-fourth day of the seventh month (Neh 9:1) is a unique observance and not part of the liturgical calendar.

The wearing of sackcloth (שׂק, 9:1) accompanies fasting (צום, 9:1) to express repentance both by the community (Isa 58:5; Jonah 3:5; Esth 4:3) and by individuals (1 Kgs 21:27; Dan 9:3; Ps 35:13). However, the third component, "and earth on them" (ואדמה עליהם), is unusual. This precise expression does not occur anywhere else in the MT. Nevertheless, the related phrase "earth on his head" (אדמה על־ראשׁו) occurs three times, always in the description of a harbinger of bad news (1 Sam 4:12; 2 Sam 1:2; 15:32). An analogous phrase, "dust on their heads" (עפר על־ראשׁם/ראשׁיהם) occurs four times, always as an expression of grief in reaction to a catastrophe (Josh 7:6; Ezek 27:30; Job 2:12; Lam 2:10).[25] In six instances, "sackcloth and ashes" (שׂקים ואפר) represents virtually a standard phrase for expressing grief or repentance; here, however, the ashes are under the person, not on the head (Isa 58:5; Jer 6:26; Jonah 3:6; Esth 4:1, 3; Dan 9:3).[26] In Neh 9:1, the "earth on them" (אדמה עליהם) betokens death, the event in which human beings return to the "earth" (אדמה, Gen 3:19; Ps 146:4; Dan 12:2; cf. Gen 2:7).

What is the precise issue involved in the Israelites' separating themselves from foreigners (9:2a)? Three possibilities are: (1) the dissolving of mixed marriages (in view of Ezra 9–10);[27] (2) the dismissal of the strangers who would have participated in the Festival of Booths (according to Deut 16:14);[28] or (3) a general dissociation from non-Israelites (akin to Neh 13:1–3). Two factors seem to support the first alternative: the *nipʿal* of בדל ("to separate oneself") refers to the divorcing of foreign wives in Ezra 9:1; 10:11, and the expression "seed of Israel" (זרע ישׂראל, 9:1) recalls the reference to the "holy seed" (זרע הקדשׁ, Ezra 9:2) that became mixed with the peoples of the lands through intermarriage.[29]

---

[25] In Ezek 27:30–31 and Lam 2:10, those who cast dust on their heads also wear sackcloth (שׂקים).

[26] Fasting (צום), sackcloth (שׂק), and ashes (אפר) occur together in Isa 58:5; Esth 4:3; and Dan 9:3.

[27] Williamson (*Ezra, Nehemiah*, 310–11) and Rudolph (*Esra und Nehemia*, 154–55) interpret Neh 9:2a in view of Ezra 9–10, which they judge to be its original and proper context.

[28] Clines, *Ezra, Nehemiah, Esther*, 190; Blenkinsopp, *Ezra-Nehemiah*, 295–96.

[29] In the Isaian tradition, this "holy seed" is the remnant that will survive the impending desolation of the land and dispersion of its inhabitants (Isa 6:13).

However, further evidence renders these arguments untenable. First, within the more immediate setting of Neh 9:2, the two occurrences of the verb בדל (10:29; 13:3) describe separations of Israelites from foreigners that are not tied to the specific issue of mixed marriages. Second, זרע ישראל (the "offspring of Israel," 9:2) has a literary lineage of its own that dissociates it from an exclusive tie to זרע הקדש (the "holy seed," Ezra 9:2) and therefore to the issue of mixed marriages. Unlike זרע הקדש (which is unique in the MT), זרע ישראל occurs elsewhere, notably in the prophetic literature of the exile that promises a future for Israel (Isa 45:25; Jer 31:36–37; cf. 2 Kgs 17:20; Ps 22:23).

The second of the above proposals, which would identify the separation from foreigners with the dismissal of the "stranger" (גר) from the Festival of Booths, is untenable on three counts: (1) the time gap indicated by the "twenty-fourth day" as well as the description of a new assembly (נאספו, 9:1) distances the gathering in the third segment (9:1–10:40) from that of the second segment (8:13–18); (2) the previous assembly for the celebration of Booths under Ezra (Neh 8:13–18) does not even allude to the participation of foreigners; and (3) Neh 13:3 indicates that the *hipʿil* (rather than the *nipʿal*) בדל would be more appropriate for describing the dismissal of foreigners from the assembly.

In summary, Neh 9:2a refers to a liturgical action by which the Israelites express their commitment generally to dissociate themselves from foreigners. Five considerations sustain this view: (1) the introductory description of penitential discipline and garb (9:1) and the subsequent account of confession and reading provide a liturgical framework for the separation; (2) elsewhere in Nehemiah (10:29; 13:3), the verb בדל refers to a comprehensive dissociation from foreigners by the congregation; (3) זרע ישראל has its own distinctive history (vis-à-vis זרע הקדש, Ezra 9:2) and functions within its immediate context as a contrasting parallel to בני נכר ("foreigners");[30] (4) the term נכר is absent from Ezra but occurs in Neh 13:30 to designate everything foreign from which Nehemiah cleanses the people (מכל־נכר, Neh 13:30; cf. מכל־בני נכר, 9:2); and (5) the adjective כל ("all") is a global reference to all foreigners without qualification. Thus, Neh 9:2a describes a generic separation of the Israelites from foreigners.

The people's act of confessing (ויתודו, 9:2) corresponds to Ezra's response to mixed marriages (Ezra 10:1) and to Nehemiah's reaction to the news of Jerusalem's plight (Neh 1:6). However, two elements distinguish

---

O. Kaiser identifies Isa 6:13 as an editorial reference to the postexilic community in Judah (*Isaiah 1–12* [trans. R. A. Wilson; OTL; Philadelphia: Westminster, 1972], 85).

[30] Cf. 1 Chr 16:13: זרע ישראל [אברהם] עבדו בני יעקב בחיריו. Also, note the expression בן־נכר אשר לא מזרעך הוא ("the foreigner who is not of your offspring," Gen 17:12).

the precise setting of the people's confession from the confessions of the two leaders: (1) an explicit reference to "praying" (כהתפלל, Ezra 10:1; מתפלל, Neh 1:6) accompanies the confession of each of the leaders, but not that of the people (cf. Neh 9:2); and (2) mention of confession follows the quotation of Ezra's prayer (Ezra 10:1; cf. 9:10–15) and is part of Nehemiah's recitation (Neh 1:5–11), whereas it precedes the people's psalm (Neh 9:2; cf. 9:6–37). The comportment of the people here resembles that of Daniel, who—prior to reciting his penitential psalm (Dan 9:4–19)—used "fasting, sackcloth, and ashes" (בצום ושׂק ואפר, Dan 9:3; cf. בצום ובשׂקים ואדמה עליהם, Neh 9:1), prayed to "YHWH, my God" (ליהוה אלהי, Dan 9:4; cf. "YHWH, their God," ליהוה אלהיהם, Neh 9:3; אל־יהוה אלהיהם, 9:4; יהוה אלהיהם, 9:5), and "confessed" (אתודה, Dan 9:4 [מתודה], חטאתי, "I was confessing my sin," 9:20]; cf. ויתודו על־חטאתיהם, Neh 9:2 [מתודים, 9:3]). The people's confessing not only their sins but also the guilt of their ancestors reflects the sanction of the Holiness Code that advocates such a response for the people who have suffered exile (Neh 9:2; cf. Lev 26:40).[31]

The Levites Lead the People in Prayer (9:4–5)

The stairs of the Levites (מעלה הלוים, 9:4) are not attached to the wooden platform (מגדל־עץ, 8:4) on which Ezra stood. Ezra's platform was a temporary structure, whereas the title "the stairs of the Levites" suggests a permanent landmark, analogous to the "stairs of the city of David" (מעלות עיר דויד, 12:37; cf. 3:15).

Among the names of those on the stairs, Jeshua, Binnui, Kadmiel, and Sherebiah occur again in the list of Levites in Neh 12:8. The Levites' "crying out in a loud voice" (ויזעקו בקול גדול, 9:4) suggests both repentance and praise.[32] The aspect of repentance derives from the only other occurrence of the verb זעק in Ezra-Nehemiah, namely, in the psalm that follows (9:28), and thereby links the "outcry" of the Levites (9:4) with Israel's turning to YHWH in the midst of their affliction in order to experience his mercies. At the same time, the phrase בקול גדול ("in a loud voice") reflects the Levites' practice of praising YHWH in response to the promise of redemption (2 Chr 20:19).[33]

---

[31] Lev 26:40: והתודו את־עונם ואת־עון אבתם
Neh 9:2: ויתודו על־חטאתיהם ועונות אבתיהם

[32] The expression זעק [ב]קול גדול conveys a unique meaning in Neh 9:4 compared with its three other occurrences in the MT, each of which describes a reaction to bad news (1 Sam 28:12; 19:4; Ezek 11:13).

[33] Elsewhere in Ezra-Nehemiah, בקול גדול occurs twice: (1) as an accompaniment to the leaders' weeping at the laying of the temple foundation (Ezra 3:12); and (2) as an expression of the congregation's commitment to Ezra's marriage reform (10:12).

The command of the second group of Levites corresponds with David's admonition to the assembly following his prayer of thanksgiving (Neh 9:5; cf. 1 Chr 29:20, ברכו[־נא] את־יהוה אלהיכם: "bless YHWH, your God"). However, the sequences of command and worship are reversed: David's command prompts the congregation to worship YHWH (וישתחוו ליהוה: "and they worshiped YHWH," 1 Chr 29:20), whereas the Levites enjoin an end to the community's prostrations (קומו: "stand up," 9:5; cf. משתחוים ליהוה: "[they were] worshiping YHWH," 9:3) in preparation for their directive to "bless YHWH, your God."

The command of the Levites and the subsequent phrase combine to parallel the acclamations at the end of Pss 41 and 106 (= 1 Chr 16:36).[34]

Psalms 41:14 and 106:48 are doxologies that mark the end of the first (Pss 3–41) and fourth (Pss 90–106) books of the Psalter (cf. Pss 72:19; 89:53), respectively.[35] However, Chronicles treats this doxology (Ps 106:48) as the last verse of the psalm (1 Chr 16:36). By contrast, in Neh 9:5 the acclamation precedes the psalm (9:6–37). Thus, in terms of position, the Levites' command and acclamation resemble the opening statement of David's thanksgiving prayer.[36]

In all of the above instances, the phrase מן־עולם עד־העולם follows the formulaic blessing ברוך אתה יהוה אלהים (Pss 41:14; 106:48, 1 Chr 16:36; 29:10; cf. Neh 9:5). However, in its two other occurrences in prayer, the phrase modifies either God or a divine attribute: (1) "from everlasting to everlasting you are God" (מעולם עד־העולם אתה אל, Ps 90:2); and (2) "the love of YHWH is from everlasting to everlasting upon those who fear him" (חסד יהוה מעולם ועד־העולם על־יראיו, Ps 103:17).[37] In these two instances, "from everlasting to everlasting" refers to the boundless existence/activity of YHWH. These two occurrences suggest that, in Neh 9:5, the phrase מן־עולם עד־העולם transforms the act of blessing to reflect the limitless extension of YHWH.

Moreover, one should note that in Ps 106:48 and 1 Chr 16:36 the expression "from everlasting to everlasting" precedes the response by the

---

[34] Neh 9:5: ברכו את־יהוה אלהיכם מן־העולם עד־עולם
Ps 106:48: ברוך יהוה אלהי ישראל מן־העולם ועד העולם
1 Chr 16:36: ברוך יהוה אלהי ישראל מן־העולם ועד העולם
Ps 41:14: ברוך יהוה אלהי ישראל מהעולם ועד העולם

[35] H.-J. Kraus, *Psalms 1–59* (trans. H. C. Oswald; Minneapolis: Augsburg, 1988), 433; idem, *Psalms 60–150* (trans. H. C. Oswald; Minneapolis: Augsburg, 1988), 322.

[36] Blenkinsopp, *Ezra-Nehemiah*, 296–97.
Neh 9:5: ברכו את־יהוה אלהיכם מן־העולם עד־עולם
1 Chr 29:10: ברוך אתה יהוה אלהי ישראל אבינו מעולם ועד־עולם

[37] The phrase מן־עולם עד־העולם occurs twice elsewhere—both in Jeremiah—to describe the enduring nature of YHWH's gift of the land to Judah (Jer 7:7; 25:5).

congregation, namely, "Amen" and their rendering praise to YHWH.[38] According to such evidence, liturgical protocol practically demanded a response by the congregation to the proclamation blessing YHWH. During the assembly on the first day, "all the people" (כל־העם, Neh 8:6; cf. 1 Chr 16:36; Ps 106:48) follow habitual practice by declaring their "Amen." Given the unparalleled initiative and intensity of the congregation's worship during the third assembly (Neh 9:1–3) and the explicitness of the Levites' command that they bless YHWH, the absence of a vocal response on the part of the congregation is thus all the more noteworthy.[39] In fact, the people will voice their response, not here, but after the conclusion of the psalm (as in Pss 41:14 and 106:48). Their response will, however, consist of much more than a simple "Amen," since it will take the form of an extended declaration of commitment to the Torah (Neh 10:1–40).

The declaration "blessed be your glorious name" (Neh 9:5) resembles Ps 72:19a, which forms part of another doxological marker in the Psalter (concluding the second book).[40] The three other instances in which one "blesses" (ברך) the "name" (שם) of YHWH are also found in the Psalms (Pss 96:2; 100:4; 145:1).

The transition from one bicolon to the next in Neh 9:5d–e corresponds with the vocabulary in the only other instance of רום על כל in the MT that speaks of the exaltation (רום) of YHWH and of his "glory" (כבוד) in parallel bicola, Ps 113:4: רם על־כל־גוים יהוה על השמים כבודו ("YHWH is exalted above all nations, above the heavens is his glory"). Another instance of the po‛lal רום indicates that the "exaltation" in Neh 9:5 consists of the people's extolling God: "To him I called out, and he was extolled by my tongue" (אליו פי־קראתי ורומם תחת לשוני, Ps 66:17).

The expression "blessing and praise" (ברכה ותהלה, 9:5) is a hendiadys that does not occur anywhere else in the MT. The two nouns occur closest to each other in the Chronicler's narration of Jehoshaphat's victory over the Transjordanian invaders (2 Chr 20:20–30). Entering the battle, those who go in front of Judah's army "began to sing and praise" (החלו ברנה ותהלה, 20:22), while after collecting the booty the people gathered "in the Valley of Blessing" (נקהלו לעמק ברכה כי־שם ברכו את־יהוה, 20:26). Furthermore, three occurrences of the root ברך associate 2 Chr 20:26 (the noun twice

---

[38] Ps 106:48: ואמר כל־העם אמן הללו־יה

1 Chr 16:36: ויאמרו כל־העם אמן והלל ליהוה

Ps 41:14 cites the response "Amen, Amen" (but not "praise YHWH") without designating the speakers.

[39] This may explain why the NAB inserts into Neh 9:5 a responsorial blessing by the people; see pp. 147–48.

[40] Neh 9:5: ויברכו שם כבודך

Ps 72:19: וברוך שם כבודו לעולם

The Penitential Rites

[ברכה] and the verb once [ברכו]) with Neh 9:5 (two verbs [ויברכו, ברכו] plus the noun [ברכה]).[41]

The Levites' command and acclamation (9:5b) introduce the psalm that follows (9:6–37), but these declarations are not part of the psalm. Two factors distinguish their initial statements from the psalm itself: there is no psalm that contains the imperative of קום addressed to the congregation,[42] and the psalms speak rarely of "your God" (אלהיכם), but frequently of "our God" (אלהינו).[43] Nevertheless, while distinct from the psalm, Neh 9:5b is analogous to the first line in the descriptive psalms of praise that begin with an exhortation to praise (הלל) or to proclaim (ידה hip'il) God.[44] Moreover, the imperative "Bless YHWH" introduces psalms of both individuals (ברכי נפשי את־יהוה: "Bless YHWH, my soul," Pss 103:1–2; 104:1) and the community (ברכו את־יהוה: "Bless YHWH," Ps 134:1–2; cf. Neh 9:5).

THEMATIC SUMMARY

In the overall depiction of the final assembly in the seventh month (9:1–10:40), the third-person narrative (9:1–5) sets the stage for the first-person declamations of prayer (9:6–37) and commitment to the Torah (10:1–40). The narrative describes the community as redefining itself through liturgy. By its approach to Torah reading and worship, the community undergoes an increased democratization among its members and achieves a definitive separation from outsiders.

The democratic tendency is apparent in the absence of any reference to leaders in the opening verses, a factor that distinguishes this assembly from the previous ones (9:1–3; cf. 8:1–3, 13). The people undertake the rites of penance without prompting from the leadership (9:1–2; cf. 8:13–15). More significantly, the whole assembly assumes the task formerly reserved to Ezra and the Levites by reading in public from the book of the law (9:3; cf. 8:3, 4–6, 8). Furthermore, in comparison to Ezra's reading for

---

[41] The root ברך also occurs three times in Gen 49:28.

[42] In the Psalter, the imperative of קום occurs only in the singular (קומה), ten times in all, and each instance is an address to God (Pss 3:8; 7:7; 9:20; 10:12; 17:13; 35:2; 44:26; 74:22; 82:8; 132:8).

[43] In the Psalter, אלהיכם ("your God") occurs only once (Ps 76:11), whereas אלהינו ("our God") occurs thirty times (Pss 18:32; 20:6, 8; 40:3; 44:21; 48:2, 9, 15; 50:3; 66:8; 67:7; 90:17; 92:14; 94:23; 95:7; 98:3; 99:5, 8, 9 [bis]; 105:7; 106:47; 113:5; 115:3; 116:5; 122:9; 123:2; 135:2; 147:1, 7). Note in particular the instances of אלהינו in the opening lines of a psalm (48:2; 147:1).

[44] הלל: Pss 113:1; 117:1; 135:1; 146:1; 147; ידה hip'il: Ps 136:1. See C. Westermann, *Praise and Lament in the Psalms* (trans. Keith R. Crim and Richard N. Soulen; Atlanta: John Knox, 1981), 122–23.

a half-day, the people initiate a new balance between Torah reading and worship by doing each for a quarter of the day (9:3; cf. 8:3).

The separation from foreigners (9:2a) stands out as the objective of the penitential rites, since the description of the community's mourning garb (9:1b) introduces this initiative, while the account of their confession of sins (9:2b) follows it. Furthermore, the narrative sequence indicates that achieving such a separation is the prerequisite for the people's reading of the Torah (9:3).

In two ways, the Levites exercise a role in the third assembly different from the one assigned them in the first and second gatherings. First, since there is no participation by figures such as Ezra, Nehemiah, the priests, or the heads of families (cf. 8:9, 13), the Levites are the only functioning leaders in the events of the twenty-fourth day of the month. Second, they act as animators of worship rather than as mediators of the Torah (9:4–5; cf. 8:8). In contradistinction to the leaders of the assemblies on the first and second days, these Levites do not initiate liturgical activity; instead, they redirect the people's worship by giving voice to the prayer of the community.

Finally, the threefold mention of "YHWH, their God" (9:3 [bis]; cf. 9:5) directs attention throughout to the one to whom the community devotes its reading, worship, and praise.

5

The Levites' Prayer (Nehemiah 9:6–37)

My analysis of the Levites' prayer proceeds according to the five-stage sequence I used in the previous sections of the covenant renewal: (1) a fresh translation; (2) textual criticism; (3) an outline and literary analysis of the lexical components within the context of the psalm and of the covenant renewal (Neh 7:72b–10:40); (4) an examination of the language and form of the Levites' prayer in comparison with the remainder of Ezra-Nehemiah and with other related biblical texts and traditions; and (5) a thematic reflection on the results of the study.

TRANSLATION

9:6a   [a]You are YHWH, you alone.[1]
9:6b   You[b] made the heavens,
        the highest heavens and all their host,
9:6c   the earth and all that is on it,
        the seas and all that is in them.
9:6d   Moreover, you make them all alive,
        and the host of the heavens worships you.
9:7a   You are YHWH, the God who chose Abram,
9:7b   brought him out of Ur of the Chaldeans,
        and named him Abraham.
9:8a   When you found his heart was faithful before you,
        you made the covenant with him
9:8b   to give [c]to his offspring[c] the land of the Canaanites,
        the Hittites, the Amorites,
9:8c   the Perizzites, the Jebusites, and the Girgashites;
9:8d   and you kept your word because you are righteous.
9:9   You saw the misery of our ancestors in Egypt,
        and their cry you heard at the Reed Sea.
9:10a You produced signs and wonders against Pharaoh,

---

[1] My translation follows the arrangement of lines in *BHS*. I designate each line within a verse according to alphabetical sequence (e.g., 9:6a, 6b, 6c).

	against all his servants, and against all the people of his land,
9:10b	for you knew that they had acted insolently toward them.
	Thus, you made a name for yourself as it is even to this day.
9:11a	The sea you split before them,
	and they passed through the midst of the sea on dry ground;
9:11b	but their pursuers you cast into the depths
	like a rock into mighty waters.
9:12a	By a column of cloud you led them during the day
	and by a column of fire during the night
9:12b	to light up for them
	the way in which they should go.
9:13a	Upon Mount Sinai you descended,
	and you spoke with them from heaven;
9:13b	you gave them just ordinances
9:13c	and true laws, good statutes and commandments.
9:14a	Your holy Sabbath you made known to them;
9:14b	also, commandments, statutes, and a law you commanded for them
	by the hand of Moses your servant.
9:15a	You gave them bread from heaven for their hunger,
9:15b	and you brought forth water from rock for their thirst.
9:15c	Then you told them to go and take possession of the land
9:15d	that you had sworn to give to them.
9:16	But they, our ancestors, acted insolently, they stiffened their necks,
	and did not obey your commandments.
9:17a	Indeed, they refused to obey.
	They did not remember the wonders that you accomplished with them,
9:17b	they stiffened their necks, and appointed a leader
	in order to return to their slavery ᵈin Egypt.ᵈ
9:17c	But you are God, forgiving, gracious, and merciful,
9:17d	slow to anger and ᵉbountiful in loyalty,ᵉ
	so you did not abandon them.
9:18a	Even when they made a molten calf for themselves,
9:18b	and said, "This is your god who brought you up out of Egypt,"
9:18c	and committed great infamies,
9:19a	you, in your abundant mercies,
	did not abandon them in the wilderness.
9:19b	The column of cloud in the day did not cease to guide them on the way,
9:19c	and the column of fire in the night did not cease to light up for them ᶠthe wayᶠ in which they should go.
9:20a	Moreover, your good spirit you gave to instruct them.
9:20b	Also, your manna you did not withhold from their mouths,

The Levites' Prayer

	and water you gave them for their thirst.
9:21a	For forty years you sustained them;
	in the wilderness they lacked nothing.
9:21b	Their clothes did not wear out
	and their feet did not swell.
9:22a	Moreover, you gave them kingdoms and peoples,
	and you allotted them as a boundary;
9:22b	so they took possession of the land of Sihon, ᵍking of Heshbon,
9:22c	and the land of Og, king of Bashan.
9:23a	You had multiplied their children like the stars of heaven;
9:23b	thus you brought them to the land
	that you had told their ancestors to enter and possess.
9:24a	The children entered and possessed the land.
	You subdued before them
9:24b	the inhabitants of the land, the Canaanites,
	and you delivered into their hand
9:24c	their kings and the peoples of the land
	to do with them as they pleased.
9:25a	They captured fortified cities and fertile land,
9:25b	and they took possession of houses filled with all good things:
9:25c	cisterns hewn out, vineyards, and olive orchards,
	and fruit trees in abundance.
9:25d	They ate, became filled, grew fat,
	and delighted themselves in your great goodness.
9:26a	But they resisted and rebelled against you;
	they cast your law behind their backs.
9:26b	They killed your prophets,
	who had warned them in order to turn them back to you,
9:26c	but they committed great infamies.
9:27a	So you gave them into the hand of their oppressors,
	and they oppressed them.
9:27b	Then, in the time of their oppression, they cried out to you.
	And you heard from heaven
9:27c	and, ʰaccording toʰ your many mercies, you gave them saviors,
	and they saved them from the hand of their oppressors.
9:28a	But once they had recuperated, they turned again to do evil before you.
9:28b	Then you abandoned them into the hand of their enemies so that they had dominion over them. But they turned back and cried out to you.
9:28c	And you heard from heaven and delivered them
	ⁱaccording to your merciesⁱ ʲmany times.ʲ
9:29a	Moreover, you warned them in order to turn them back to your law,

9:29a but they acted insolently and did not obey your commandments.
9:29b Rather, they sinned against your ordinances,
   which one must carry out and thereby live.
9:29c They gave you a stubborn shoulder, stiffened their necks,
   and did not obey.
9:30a But you bore with them for many years,
9:30b and you warned them through your spirit by the hand of your prophets.
9:30c However, when they would not give ear,
   you gave them into the hand of the peoples of the lands.
9:31a Yet, in your abundant mercies you did not make an end of them;
9:31b you did not abandon them because you are a God of grace and mercy.
9:32a And now, our God, the great, mighty, and awesome God,
9:32b who keeps the covenant with loyalty,
   do not consider as too little before you all the hardship
9:32c that has befallen us, our kings, ^{k}our princes^k, our priests,
   our prophets, our ancestors, and all your people,
9:32d from the days of the Assyrian kings until this day.
9:33a You are righteous
   with regard to all that has come upon us,
9:33b since you have practiced faithfulness,
   but we have behaved wickedly.
9:34a Our kings, our princes, our priests, and our ancestors
   have not kept your law;
9:34b they have not paid attention to your commandments
   and to your warnings by which you warned them.
9:35a Indeed they—even in their kingdom, and amid the abundant goodness
   that you presented for them,
9:35b and on the broad and fertile land
   that you presented before them—
9:35c did not serve you, and did not turn back from their evil deeds.
9:36a Look, we are slaves this day,
9:36b and the land that you gave to our ancestors
   to eat of its fruit and of its goodness—
9:36c look, we are slaves upon it.
9:37a Moreover, its abundant yield belongs to kings
   whom you have set over us because of our sins;
9:37b they rule over our bodies and over our livestock as they please.
   Thus, we are in great distress.

TEXTUAL CRITICISM

a Disregard LXX 2 Esd 19:6, "And Ezra said" (καὶ εἶπεν Ἔσδρας), an insertion that erroneously attempts to resolve the uncertainty concerning the identity of the speaker. The Syr and Vg follow the MT.

b Read אתה (Qere) instead of את, which is a defective spelling.

c-c The expression לתת (ל + infinitive construct, expressing purpose) occurs twice in the verse, before and after the list of prior occupants of the land. However, one indirect object (לזרעו) is sufficient. The emendation in LXX 2 Esd 19:8 (αὐτῷ [i.e., לו]) is unnecessary.

d-d With LXX 2 Esd 19:17 (ἐν Αἰγύπτῳ), read במצרים, which is supported by the allusion to Num 14:4.

e-e With LXX 2 Esd 19:17 and Vg, read the Qere חסד instead of וחסד.

f-f With LXX 2 Esd 19:19, Syr, and Vg, read את rather than ואת.

g With LXX 2 Esd 19:22, omit ואת־ארץ as due to dittography.

h-h Maintain וכרחמיך rather than ברחמיך, which is found in many MSS and in the LXX (ἐν οἰκτιρμοῖς σου τοῖς μεγάλοις). The phrase ברחמיך occurs rather in 9:31a.

i-i Maintain כרחמיך rather than ברחמיך, which occurs in many MSS and in the LXX (ἐν οἰκτιρμοῖς σου), corresponding with the same word in 9:27.

j-j Maintain רבות in spite of some Heb MSS and the LXX (ἐν οἰκτιρμοῖς σου πολλοῖς), which read ברבים and thereby take the word as an adjective modifying כרחמיך in conformity with 9:27.

k-k With LXX, Syr, and Vg, read ולשרינו for לשרינו; haplography accounts for the loss of the initial ו.

LITERARY ANALYSIS

My literary analysis consists of two parts: an outline of the whole psalm and a detailed discussion of each unit.

OUTLINE

With the majority of commentators and translations, I follow the MT, which does not indicate a change in speaker and thereby designates the Levites as the speakers of the psalm.[2] The lack of an introduction for Ezra at the beginning of the narrative (9:1–5) would be uncharacteristic of Ezra-Nehemiah (cf. Ezra 7:1–10; 8:15, 21, 31; 9:1, 5; 10:1, 6, 10, 16; Neh 8:1, 13) and thereby constitutes a definitive argument against viewing him as the speaker of the psalm, as does the LXX.[3]

---

[2] See Myers, *Ezra, Nehemiah*, 158; Williamson, *Ezra, Nehemiah*, 300, 304; Blenkinsopp, *Ezra-Nehemiah*, 297; NJB, REB, and JPSV.

[3] Cf. Torrey, *Ezra Studies*, 280–81; Rudolph, *Esra und Nehemia*, 152–57; NRSV; NAB.

Eskenazi, however, posits no alteration in the text in order to identify rather the community as the speakers of the psalm. In her estimation, the MT does not specify whether the Levites or the people voice the psalm. She argues that the community declaims the psalm on the basis of two pieces of evidence: "antiphonal recitation" is constitutive of previous assemblies in Ezra-Nehemiah (Ezra 3:11; Neh 8:5–7), and the first line of the pledge account emphasizes the community (Neh 10:1).[4] In addition to her observations, one should note the continuity of the first-person plural throughout 9:6–37 and 10:1–40, which are united by the repetition of the pronoun "we" (אנחנו) in the last line of the psalm (9:37) and the first line of the pledge account (10:1). Moreover, an immediate response of the people to an exhortation by their leaders (9:5b) would be consistent with their behavior in the previous two segments: initially, in their prompt reply to Ezra's blessing of YHWH (8:6) and subsequently in their ready obedience to the demands of their leaders (8:12; cf. 8:9–11) and of the law (8:16–17a; cf. 8:14–15).[5]

Such evidence leaves open the possibility that the people join the Levites in speaking the psalm. However, all these arguments are inferential. The narrative affords no explicit indication that the people do speak the psalm. In the absence of clear evidence to the contrary, one must acquiesce to custom. In other literature of the period and elsewhere in Ezra-Nehemiah, the speakers of such extended prayers are either individuals or leaders of the community (see Ezra 9:6–15; Neh 1:5–11; cf. 1 Chr 16:7–36; 29:10–19; 2 Chr 6:14–42; 20:5–15). In sum, the evidence clearly points to the Levites as the speakers of the psalm but leaves open the possibility that the community joins in its recitation. From a literary standpoint, the matter is subject to the reader's conjecture. In any case, the subsequent declarations of the people (Neh 10:1–40) indicate their identification with the confessional psalm, if not by their speaking, then at least by their hearing it.

In literary format, Neh 9:6–37 exhibits alternately the characteristics of prose (e.g., 9:8, 24, 32)[6] and poetry (e.g., 9:6,15a–b, 20b, 33b). *BHK* displays the prayer in prose format, whereas *BHS* offers a poetic arrangement.[7] While my commentary follows the sequence of lines according to *BHS*, I

---

[4] Eskenazi, *In an Age of Prose*, 100.

[5] The people's responsiveness to the Levites' instruction would accord especially with their previous following of the instruction that four of these Levites (Jeshua, Banni, Sherebiah, and Hodiah) had given them on the first day (9:5; cf. 8:7–8).

[6] See S. Segert, "History and Poetry: Poetic Patterns in Nehemiah 9:5–37," in *Storia e Tradizioni di Israele: Scritti in Onore di J. Alberto Soggin* (ed. D. Garrone and F. Israel; Brescia: Paideia, 1991), 255–65.

[7] H. H. Schaeder and J. Begrich, "Libros Esrae et Nehemiae," in *Biblia Hebraica* (ed. R. Kittel and P. Kahle; Stuttgart: Württembergische Bibelanstalt, 1937), 1314–16;

refrain from subscribing to the *BHS* subdivisions into a single colon, a bicolon, or a tricolon.[8] I will make note of the most evident poetic lines as they occur in the prayer.

The psalm begins and ends with pronouns designating the parties involved: its first word is "you" (אתה, 9:6), in reference to God, and its last word is "us" (אנחנו, 9:37), in reference to the community. The psalm begins with a declaration of God's supremacy over creation (9:6) and concludes with a description of his people's subjection in the land he gave them (9:36–37). In summary, the psalm consists of a confession that elaborates on the contrast between God's acts and Israel's lack of response in the past (9:6–31), which accounts for the contrast between the greatness of God and the misery of his people in the present (9:32–37).[9]

The petition in 9:32 stands out as a unique statement that occurs precisely at the transition point from recollection of the past (9:6–31) to meditation on the present (9:32–37). The expression "And now" (ועתה), which introduces the petition, is a constitutive element in various biblical examples of the confession of sins. In these texts, ועתה provides the turning point from the acknowledgment of past guilt to an appeal for forgiveness and deliverance in the present (e.g., Exod 10:16–17; 32:30, 31–32; 1 Sam 12:10; Ezra 10:2–3, 10–11; cf. Num 22:34).[10]

Within Neh 9:6–37, verse 32 marks the transition from third-person to first-person speech concerning the people. The third person ("they," "them," "their"), which suffuses the account of Israel's history from the exodus to the most recent past (Neh 9:9–31), designates the previous generations (Neh 9:9–31). However, the present generation speaks in the first person ("we," "us," "our") in the remainder of the psalm (9:32–37).[11] Such evidence suggests that the petition in Neh 9:32 represents the primary demarcation point

---

W. Rudolph, "Libros Esrae et Nehemiae," *Biblia Hebraica Stuttgartensia* (ed. K. Elliger and W. Rudolph; Stuttgart: Deutsche Bibelstiftung, 1977), 1446–49. J. Kugel warns against applying anachronistic distinctions between prose and poetry to Hebrew literature (*The Idea of Biblical Poetry: Parallelism and Its History* [New Haven, Conn.: Yale University Press, 1981], esp. 76–84).

[8] Rudolph's editorial arrangement in *BHS* corresponds with that given in his commentary (*Esra und Nehemia*, 157).

[9] Clines (*Ezra, Nehemiah, Esther*, 192) astutely points out that the distinction between these two major parts corresponds with two steps in the prior liturgical rites: first, the "confession" of the people (9:3; cf. 9:6–31) and, second, the "cry" of the Levites (9:4; cf. 9:32–37).

[10] M. Gilbert, "La place de la Loi dans la prière de Néhémie 9," in *De la Tôrah au Messie: Mélanges Henri Cazelles* (ed. J. Doré, P. Grelot, and M. Carrez; Paris: Desclée, 1981), 307–10; cf. idem, "Notes sur Néhémie 9" (TMs [photocopy] 1995), 2–4.

[11] Outside 9:32–37, the first person occurs only twice, in the expression "our ancestors" (אבתינו, 9:9, 16).

between the two major parts of the prayer. The first part (9:6–31) recounts the history of God's dealings with Israel from creation (9:6) to the recent past (9:31). The second part (9:32–37) takes the form of an intercessory appeal that proceeds to describe the present distress of the people in their own land.

Stylistic devices of *inclusio* and repetition complement the partitioning of the prayer into its two major parts. The recitation of past history (9:6–31) begins and ends with the second-person pronoun (אתה) in a confessional statement (אתה־הוא יהוה לבדך: "You are YHWH, you alone," 9:6; cf. [כי] אל־חנון ורחום אתה: "[because] you are a God of grace and mercy," 9:31b). Furthermore, the intercessory appeal in the present (9:32–27) begins in an analogous fashion with a credal pronouncement in the vocative case (9:32, "Our God, the great, mighty, and awesome God observing the covenant and loyalty").[12]

Similar indicators mark the boundaries of the first segment of the past history, which embraces both the account of creation and the call of Abraham (9:6–8). Here, again, אתה provides the *inclusio* (אתה־הוא, 9:6a; cf. כי צדיק אתה: "because you are righteous," 9:8d). Similar introductory lines unify the accounts of the creation of the universe (אתה־הוא יהוה לבדך, 9:6a) and the election of Abraham (אתה־הוא יהוה האלהים: "You are YHWH, the God," 9:7a).

The remainder of the history (9:9–31) consists of two major segments, the first of which recounts the exodus and the wilderness era (9:9–21), while the second describes the occupation of the land and the subsequent settlement era (9:22–31). These two segments exhibit a variety of parallels. Each begins with a description of God's concern for his people in the face of their foreign opponents (ותרא את־עני אבתינו במצרים: "You saw the misery of our ancestors in Egypt," 9:9; cf. ותתן להם ממלכות ועממים: "Moreover, you gave them kingdoms and peoples," 9:22a) and concludes with negative statements that describe the people's survival (במדבר לא חסרו שלמתיהם לא בלו ורגליהם לא בצקו: "in the wilderness they lacked nothing. Their clothes did not wear out and their feet did not swell," 9:21; cf. לא־עשיתם כלה ולא עזבתם: "you did not make an end of them; you did not abandon them," 9:31).

The descriptions of both periods fall into two parts, the first of which recounts God's powerful actions and generous provisions for his people (9:9–15, 22–25); the second, the people's subsequent rebellion against God and his consequent demonstration of mercy (9:16–21, 26–31). The negatives (לא) occur only in the second parts (9:16–21, 26–31), never in the first parts (9:9–15, 22–25) of each era. Thus, in each period, the initial account of harmony between God and his people (9:9–15, 22–25) contrasts with the description of discord between them that follows (9:16–21, 26–31).

---

[12] 9:32: אלהינו האל הגדול הגבור והנורא שומר הברית והחסד.

In the account of the wilderness era (9:9–21), the introduction of the third-person plural pronoun (וְהֵם: "But they," 9:16) and the renewed reference to "our ancestors" (אֲבֹתֵינוּ, 9:16; cf. 9:9) mark the narrative transition from the section of harmony (9:9–15) to that of discord (9:16–21).[13] Up to this juncture, the account emphasizes God's activity and gives only passing notice to the people's movements.[14] By contrast, in the remainder of the segment (9:16–21), the people's activities are juxtaposed to God's responses as the subject alternates four times between "them" (וְהֵם, 9:16a; עָשׂוּ לָהֶם, 9:18a) and "you" (וְאַתָּה, 9:17c, 19a). These alternations, in turn, consist of two instances of the same sequence that recount the people's rebellion and God's response of mercy (9:16–17, 18–21). The first description of their interaction is rather generic (9:16–17), whereas the second (introduced by אַף־כִּי: "even when," 9:18a) mentions specific actions on the part of both the people and God (9:18–21).

Moreover, the demonstrations of God's mercy in the second cycle of their exchange (9:18–20) parallel the gifts that he had initially provided his people following their crossing of the sea (9:12–15): the columns of cloud and fire (9:19; cf. 9:12); his good spirit that he "gives" (נֹתֵן, 9:20a; cf. the ordinances and laws that he "gave" [וַתִּתֵּן], 9:13–14); and bread and water (9:15a–b; cf. 9:20b). Thus, the manifestation of divine mercy consists of God's restoration of his gifts to the people. A summary description of the effect of God's sustaining his people for forty years in the wilderness (9:21) concludes the whole section.

The introduction of the command to possess the land (9:15c–d) immediately after the description of God's gifts (9:12–15b) and before the account of the people's rebellion (9:16–17b) links the wilderness era and the period of the settlement (9:22–31).[15] The command to "possess" the land (9:15c–d) is specifically fulfilled in the description of the occupation (9:22–25), since the verb יָרַשׁ occurs only in these verses (9:15c, 22b, 23b, 24a, 25b).

Cycles of human rebellion and divine mercy, reminiscent of the wilderness era (9:16–21), characterize the period of settlement in the land (9:26–31). However, in the latter period, the cycles of history are more intricate and extensive than in the earlier period. In the wilderness era, the cycles follow a two-sided format describing first the people's sinning (9:16–17b, 18) and then God's displaying mercy (9:17c–d, 19–21). However, for the settlement period, the cycles follow a four-stage pattern:

---

[13] Outside the final major section pertaining to the present (9:32–37), אֲבֹתֵינוּ occurs only in 9:9, 16 (cf. 9:32, 34, 36).

[14] In Neh 9:9–15, God is the subject of seventeen verbs (including וַדַּבֵּר in 9:13a), whereas the people are the subject of only two (עָבְרוּ, 9:11a; וַיֵּלְכוּ, 9:12b), and Pharaoh and his servants of one (הֵזִידוּ, 9:10b).

[15] Williamson, *Ezra, Nehemiah*, 313–14.

(1) the people turn away from God and his commandments (9:26, 28a, 29–30cα); (2) God gives them "into the hand" of their enemies (ביד, 9:27a, 28b, 30cβ); (3) the people cry out to God (יצעקו אליך, 9:27b; ויזעקוך, 9:28b); and (4) God hears from heaven (ואתה משמים תשמע, 9:27bβ, 28cα) and mercifully (כרחמיך, 9:27c, 28cβ; ברחמיך, 9:31a) rescues them (9:27c, 28c). Whereas the two-sided format occurred twice in the wilderness era (9:16–17, 18–21), the four-stage pattern recurs two and a half times in the settlement period (9:26–27, 28, 29–31).

The third cycle of the settlement pattern recounts only the first two of the above four stages. At the same time, the description of these two initial stages in the third cycle exhibits four differences with the equivalent accounts in the first and second cycles: (1) the unparalleled abundance of clauses describing the people's rebellion (9:29, 30cα; cf. 9:26, 28a); (2) the repetition of God's "warning" (עוד *hipʿil*, 9:29a, 30b; cf. 9:26b); (3) the mention of God's mercies in the second, rather than in the fourth, stage of the cycle (רחמיך, 9:31a; cf. 9:27c, 28c); and (4) the insistence that God "did not abandon them" (ולא עזבתם, 9:31b; cf. ותעזבם, 9:28b), although he "gave [his people] into the hand" (ותתנם ביד, 9:30c; cf. 9:27a) of their enemies. All of these factors suggest that the third cycle represents, on the one hand, the culmination of the people's rebellion, but, on the other, an unprecedented hopefulness regarding the future—this, even at the (second) stage of God's handing his people over to their adversaries.

The absence of the last two stages in the third recurrence of the cycle in the settlement era provides the setting for the appeal to God in the present (9:32–37), which occupies the place of the third stage of the incomplete pattern (i.e., the people's crying out to God; cf. 9:27b, 28b). The fourth stage, that is, the event of deliverance (cf. 9:27c, 28c), remains in the future as a potential consequence of the people's prayer. Thus the psalm locates Israel's present distressful situation (9:32–37) within the broader context of its history in the land (9:22–31) and, prior to that, of its experience in the wilderness (9:9–21).

In the description of the present moment (9:32–37), firsthand experience replaces historical reminiscence as the focus turns to first-person narration. The pronoun "we" (אנחנו) occurs exclusively within this description of the present situation (9:33, 36 [bis], 37). Moreover, the first-person possessive pronoun "our" occurs seventeen times in the description of Israel's present condition (9:32–37) but only twice elsewhere (9:9, 16).[16]

Various literary features delimit and define the structure of this final part of the prayer (9:32–37). This segment begins with God (אלהינו, 9:32a)

---

[16] Both occurrences are in the expression "our ancestors" (אבתינו, 9:9, 16). This same expression occurs three times in the final segment (9:32, 34, 36). The noun occurs one other time (אבתיהם, 9:23).

as the subject and concludes with "we" (אנחנו, 9:37b) as the subject. "Great" (גדול) provides an *inclusio:* at the beginning, in reference to the character of God (אלהינו האל הגדול: "our God, the great God," 9:32a), and at the end, in reference to the people's distress (ובצרה הגדולה אנחנו, "Thus, we are in great distress," 9:37b).

In literary form, this segment consists of a petition (9:32), a confession (9:33–35), and a description of distress (9:36–37). Distinctive markers define the beginning of each subunit: the introductory adverb and address to God (ועתה אלהינו: "And now, our God," 9:32a), the confessional statement (ואתה צדיק: "You are righteous," 9:33a; cf. כי צדיק אתה: "because you are righteous," 9:8d), and an interjection followed by the first-person pronoun (הנה אנחנו: "Look, we..." 9:36a). The markers in the concluding subunit (9:36–37) form a structural pattern analogous to that in the opening unit of the psalm (9:6–8): two of the final five lines repeat the people's status as slaves (הנה אנחנו היום עבדים: "Look, we are slaves this day," 9:36a; cf. הנה אנחנו עבדים עליה: "Look, we are slaves upon it," 9:36c) in a manner that recalls the underscoring of the status of YHWH as God in two of the initial five lines of the psalm (אתה־הוא יהוה לבדך, 9:6a; אתה־הוא יהוה האלהים, 9:7a).

Table 4.2—The Structure of the Confessional Psalm (Neh 9:6–37)
A. God and Israel throughout the past (9:6–31)
  1. YHWH's foundational activity (9:6–8)
     a. The creation of the universe (9:6)
     b. The election of Abraham (9:7–8)
  2. The wilderness period (9:9–21)
     a. The era of harmony (9:9–15)
        (1) The exodus (9:9–11)
        (2) God's gifts in the wilderness (9:12–15)
           (a) The columns of cloud and fire (9:12)
           (b) The commandments (9:13–14)
           (c) Bread and water (9:15a)
           (d) The mandate to possess the land (9:15b)
     b. The people's rebellion and God's mercy (9:16–21)
        (1) The people's rebellion (9:16–17b)
        (2) God's mercy (9:17c–d)
        (3) The people's rebellion (9:18)
        (4) God's demonstrations of mercy (9:19–21)
           (a) The columns of cloud and fire (9:19)
           (b) The spirit for instruction (9:20a)
           (c) Bread and water (9:20b)
           (d) Summary: sustenance for forty years (9:21)
  3. The occupation and subsequent life in the land (9:22–31)
     a. The era of harmony: the occupation of the land (9:22–25)

    b. Rebellion and mercy: life in the land (9:26–31)
        (1) Rebellion, oppression, outcry, deliverance (9:26–27)
        (2) Rebellion, oppression, outcry, deliverance (9:28)
        (3) Rebellion, oppression (9:29–31)
B. God and Israel in the present (9:32–37)
    1. Petition (9:32)
    2. Confession (9:33–35)
    3. The present distress (9:36–37)

The most evident stylistic feature throughout the psalm is repetition, which generates its thematic consistency. At various points, the prayer repeats whole statements as well as significant vocabulary. Three types of statements recur in the prayer: credal professions; narrative illustrations of divine benevolence; and descriptions of the people's resistance to God. In addition to the three credal statements at the opening and end of the first major part (9:6, 31) and at the beginning of the second part (9:32), three other professions of faith are interspersed throughout the prayer: "You are righteous" (twice: 9:8; cf. 9:33) and "You are God, forgiving, gracious, and merciful, slow to anger, and bountiful in loyalty" (9:17).[17] The mention of God's benevolence occurs in the first lines describing the wilderness experience and again after the description of the people's apostasy: "By a column of cloud you led them during the day and by a column of fire during the night to light up for them the path in which they should go" (9:12; cf. 9:19). Two statements recur that describe the people's resistance to God: (1) "they committed great infamies" (9:18c, 26c); and (2) "they did not obey your commandments" (9:16, 29a).[18] In sum, the repetitions of these statements throughout the prayer reinforces its confessional tone, which emphasizes both God's fidelity and the people's infidelity.

Repetition of key words highlights both the themes that persist throughout the prayer and those that are distinctive of particular sections. Four words serve as leitmotifs running through the whole prayer: the noun אֶרֶץ ("land"), the verbs נתן ("to give") and עשׂה ("to do"), and the pronoun אתה ("you"). The "land" (אֶרֶץ), which occurs more frequently than any other noun, is the psalm's primary focus.[19] The specific application of this

---

[17] 9:8d: אתה צדיק (cf. 9:33a: ואתה צדיק).
9:17: ואתה אלוה סליחות חנון ורחום ארך־אפים ורב־חסד
[18] 9:16: ולא־שמעו אל־מצותיך (cf. 9:29a: ולא שמעו למצותיך).
[19] Of the thirteen instances of אֶרֶץ, the most significant are the eight that refer to the promised land (9:8b, 15c, 22b [bis], 23b, 24a, 35b, 36b). The remaining references are to: "peoples [or inhabitants] of the land[s]" (9:24b, 24c, 30c), the "earth" (9:6c), and Egypt (9:10a).

noun to the promised land links the eras of Abraham (9:8b), the wilderness (9:15c), the settlement (9:22b [bis], 23b, 24a–c), and the present (9:35b, 36b). The most-repeated verb is "to give" (נתן), which has God for its subject seventeen times and Israel twice.[20] The land (ארץ) is foremost among God's many gifts (9:8b–c, 22b–c, 35b, 36b). The verb נתן expresses God's generosity to Israel at every stage of its history, beginning with the call of Abraham, but also denotes his retributive justice both during the time of the settlement and in the present (9:27a, 30c, 37a). The verb "to do" (עשה) also occurs from beginning to end, figuring in every significant portion except the call of Abraham (9:7–8).[21] The occurrences of עשה suggest a contrast between God's performing deeds of faithfulness (9:6a, 10b, 17a, 31a, 33b) and the people's doing evil (9:18a, 18c, 26c, 28a, 34a; cf. 9:24c, 29b). The pronoun "you" (אתה) keeps a continual focus on God throughout the prayer.[22] The six credal statements account for more than half of its occurrences (9:6a, 7a, 8d, 17c, 31b, 33a), while the remaining five emphasize God's solicitude for creation (9:6b, 6d) and for his people even in their rebellion and consequent affliction (9:19a, 27b, 28c).

Various additional words link the psalm's diverse segments. The fourfold mention of "heaven" (שמים) at the beginning (9:6b [3x], 6d) establishes the priority of God's realm from which he provides for the people in the wilderness (9:13a; cf. 9:15a) and in the land (9:23a, 27b, 28c). References to God's mercy (רחמים/רחום) occur exclusively in descriptions of God's responses to the people's rebellion during both the wilderness era (9:17c, 19a) and the settlement (9:27c, 28c, 31a).[23] The law (תורה/תורות) is God's gift to his people at Sinai (9:14b; cf. 9:13c), which they rejected at various times during their life in the land (9:26a, 29a) with dire consequences for the present (9:34). Similarly, God gave the commandments (מצות) at Sinai (9:13b, 14b), but the people disobeyed them both in the wilderness (9:16a) and in the land (9:29a, 34b). The term טוב serves as both an adjective ("good") modifying various divine gifts and as a noun

---

[20] With God as subject, נתן bespeaks divine liberality in fourteen occurrences (9:8b, 8c, 13b, 15a, 15d, 20a, 20b, 22a, 24b, 27a, 27c, 35a, 35b, 36b) but divine retribution twice (9:30c, 37a). In both occurrences when Israel is the subject, נתן describes acts of rebellion (9:17b, 29c). Cf. Gilbert, "Notes," 25.

[21] Of the twelve occurrences of עשה, God is the subject in 9:6b, 10b, 17a, 31a, 33b and the people in 9:18a, 18c, 24c, 26c, 28a, 29b, 34a. Cf. Gilbert, "Notes," 25.

[22] אתה (or את, 9:6) occurs eleven times: 9:6a, 6b, 6d, 7a, 8d, 17c, 19a, 27b, 28c, 31b, 33a.

[23] The statement "You did not abandon them" (לא עזבתם) follows shortly after three of these references to God's mercy (9:17d, 19a, 31b). In its one other occurrence, the verb "to abandon" (עזב) describes God's retributive action in view of the people's offenses and therefore precedes the reference to his mercy (9:28b).

denoting a divine attribute ("goodness"), which links the eras of the wilderness (9:13c, 20a), the settlement (9:25b), and the present (9:35a, 36b). The verb "to turn back" (שׁוּב) refers alternately to Israel's apostasies and to its conversion during both the wilderness era (9:17b) and the settlement (9:26b, 28a, 28b, 29a) up to the present (9:35c).

Some lexemes are characteristic of particular sections. The verb "to possess" (ירשׁ), which always has Israel as its subject and the land as its object, occurs four times in the account of the occupation (9:22b, 23b, 24a, 25b) and once in the wilderness segment (as part of God's command for the people to seize the land, 9:15c). The verb "to warn" (עוד hip'il) refers to the unsuccessful attempts by God and his delegates to correct the people at the times of their rebellion in the land (9:26b, 29a, 30b) up to the recent past (9:34b).

Finally, two terms offer subsidiary studies in contrast. The verb "to hear" (שׁמע) is affirmative when its subject is God (תשׁמע/שׁמעת: "You heard," 9:9, 27b, 28b) but negative when the subject is the people (ימאנו לשׁמע/לא שׁמעו: "They did not [or 'refused to'] obey," 9:16a, 17a, 29a, 29c). God's heeding the cries of his people contrasts with their refusing to heed the divine precepts. The references to various "kings" (מלך) suggest an opposition between "their kings" (מלכיהם, 9:24c; cf. 9:22b [מלך חשׁבון], 9:22c [מלך־הבשׁן], 32d [מלכי אשׁור], 37a [מלכים]) and "our kings" (מלכינו, 9:32c, 34a). During the occupation, God enabled his people to subdue other kings and their kingdoms (ממלכות, 9:22a; cf. 9:24c), whereas, due to the disobedience of Israel's monarchs, their kingdom (מלכותם, 9:35a) is now under foreign kings (9:34–37). This opposition between kings enhances the paradox with regard to the "land" (ארץ) inasmuch as it was the gift of God (9:15c-d, 22–24), but, at the present moment, it is a place of servitude for his people, since it remains under foreign rule (9:36–37).

The following literary analysis presents a more detailed examination of the vocabulary and style of the prayer.

EXAMINATION OF THE UNITS

My literary analysis now focuses on each line according to the major sections distinguished in the outline.

GOD AND ISRAEL THROUGHOUT THE PAST (9:6–31)

YHWH's foundational activity (9:6–8)

The creation of the universe (9:6). Three features link the first verse of the psalm (9:6) to the previous commands and acclamations (9:5b): (1) direct discourse addressed to YHWH (אתה־הוא יהוה: "You are YHWH") in response to the command (ברכו את־יהוה: "Bless YHWH"); (2) the second-person singular possessive adjective referring to YHWH (כבודך: "your glory"; cf. לְבַדְּךָ: "you alone"); and (3) an emphasis on height (שְׁמֵי הַשָּׁמַיִם: "the highest heavens") analogous to the exaltation (מְרוֹמָם) of YHWH's name as affirmed by the Levites.

The description of YHWH's acts of creation (9:6a–d) consists of four poetic lines. The pronoun אַתָּה at the beginning of the first, second, and fourth lines (9:6a, 6b, 6d) supplies a unifying anaphora. The sequence of verbs suggests a development in aspect: from the absent copula (the nominal sentence in 9:6a) to the perfect (suggestive of action in the past: עָשִׂיתָ governing 9:6b, 6c) to the participles (indicating enduring activity in the present: מִשְׁתַּחֲוִים and מְחַיֶּה in 9:6d).

Nehemiah 9:6b–c forms a unit by virtue of two factors: (1) the subject (אַתָּה) and verb (עָשִׂיתָ) in 9:6ba are in ellipsis in verses 6bβ, 6cα, and 6cβ,[24] and (2) the expression וְכָל ("and all") links 9:6bβ with verses 6cα and 6cβ. Also, in 9:6b–c, the conventional merism, "the heavens and the earth" (e.g., Gen 1:1; cf. הַשָּׁמַיִם, 9:6ba; הָאָרֶץ, 9:6cα), is interrupted by mention of the "highest heavens and all their host" (שְׁמֵי הַשָּׁמַיִם וְכָל־צְבָאָם, 9:6bβ), which, in turn, has a parallel in "the seas and all that is in them" (וְכָל־אֲשֶׁר בָּהֶם הַיַּמִּים, 9:6cb). Thus, the sovereignty of YHWH extends from the greatest heights to the most profound depths of creation.

The third line, 9:6c, is a bicolon that exhibits synonymous parallelism: a:b:c::a':b:c':

הָאָרֶץ וְכָל־אֲשֶׁר עָלֶיהָ
הַיַּמִּים וְכָל־אֲשֶׁר בָּהֶם

the earth and all that [is] on it
the seas and all that [is] in them.

The fourth line (9:6d) is a bicolon that encapsulates the previous three lines by its connections to each of them. Its first colon is a parallel for the first colon of the second line (second-person pronoun + verb + object marker + object).[25] The expression כֻּלָּם (9:6dα) recalls the adjective כָּל in the previous three cola (9:6bβ, 6cα, 6cβ). The subject of the second colon ("the host of heaven": צְבָא הַשָּׁמַיִם, 9:6dβ) refers to the objects of the verb in the second line (כָּל־צְבָאָם, 9:6bβ). Finally, the reference to YHWH in the second-person singular pronoun governed by the preposition (לְ, 9:6db) recalls the first line (לְבַדְּךָ, 9:6a).

The participles (מְחַיֶּה: "make alive"; מִשְׁתַּחֲוִים: "worships") in 9:6d extend the focus from YHWH's past action (עָשִׂיתָ, perfect) to his ongoing activities. The pattern of action and response connects the two cola: YHWH

---

[24] "You made the heaven, [you made] the highest heavens and all their host/ [you made] the earth and all that is on it, [you made] the seas and all that is in them."

[25] 9:6ba: אַתָּה עָשִׂיתָ אֶת־הַשָּׁמַיִם
9:6da: אַתָּה מְחַיֶּה אֶת־כֻּלָּם

gives life (9:6dα), and the celestial host worships him (9:6dβ). Therefore, this line sets the stage for the action-and-response pattern in the remainder of the psalm. Emphasis on the positive nature of YHWH's work in creation prepares for the subsequent account of his gracious interventions in history on behalf of Israel. The worship of the highest realm of creation recalls the people's previous veneration in their penitential rites (חוה [hištapʿel], 9:6d; cf. 8:6; 9:3) and suggests the ideal standard for Israel's response to the initiatives of YHWH throughout the remainder of the prayer.

The election of Abraham (9:7–8). The prayer recounts in six lines (9:7a–8d) the call of Abraham. The first and last clauses are confessional statements, while the pronoun אתה (9:7a, 8d) provides the *inclusio* for the section. The opening clause echoes the first line of the prayer.[26] These represent the only two occurrences of the divine name (יהוה) in the whole psalm. Mention of "YHWH, the God" (יהוה האלהים) recalls Ezra's blessing "YHWH, the great God" (Neh 9:7a; cf. 8:6).

The confessional statements at the beginning and end are nominal clauses (אתה־הוא יהוה האלהים: "You are YHWH, the God," 9:7a; and צדיק אתה: "you are righteous," 9:8d). In between these clauses, eight verbs portray YHWH's cumulative activity in Abraham's life in a manner that suggests divine persistence and purposefulness over time.[27] By comparison with Genesis, the changing of Abraham's name (cf. Gen 17:5) is out of sequence in the midst of all the other events in the unfolding of YHWH's dealings with him (cf. Gen 15:1–21). However, this allows the bestowal of the land to form the climax of the narrative buildup.

In the psalm, YHWH's covenant with Abraham focuses not so much on the provision of descendants (cf. Gen 15:1–6) as on the promise of the land for his offspring (cf. Gen 15:7–21).[28] YHWH keeps his word (ותקם את־דבריך, 9:8d) by bestowing the land of other peoples upon Abraham's progeny. Thus, the psalm speaks of his "offspring" (זרעו) as the recipients of the land (ארץ). Within the covenant renewal, "his offspring" (זרעו) is equivalent to the "seed of Israel" (זרע ישראל) who separated

---

[26] 9:6aα: אתה־הוא יהוה לבדך
9:7aα: אתה־הוא יהוה אלהים

[27] The eight verbs in this section do not follow a regular pattern: the perfect (בחרת), three in the form of *w-qataltī* (והוצאתו, ושמת, and ומצאת), the infinitive absolute (וכרות), the repeated infinitive construct (לתת), and the *wayyiqtol* form (ותקם). See GBH §119za.

[28] However, the change of name (in Neh 9:7bβ) alludes to the concern for multiplying Abraham's descendants (cf. Gen 15:1–5; 17:1–18:15; 21:1–7). This theme surfaces explicitly in Neh 9:23a ובניהם הרבית ככבי השמים: "you had multiplied their children like the stars of heaven").

themselves from the foreigners in the penitential rites (9:2). Moreover, the repetition of the infinitive construct (לתת, 9:8c, 8d) emphasizes that the land is the gift of YHWH to the heirs of Abraham.

The one verb with Abraham as its subject is the *nip'al* participle (נאמן, 9:8a) that refers to his fidelity. This participle represents an indirect accusative subordinated to the main verb (ומצאת: "you found").[29] The prepositional phrase "before you" (לפניך, 9:8a) defines not only the context of Abraham's faithfulness but also the setting of Israel's past evil and present intercession (לפניך, 9:8a; cf. 9:28a, 32b). Thus, Abraham's faithfulness provides the standard for Israel's responding to YHWH in the remainder of the prayer.

Moreover, within the covenant renewal, the highlighting of Abraham's "faithfulness" (נאמן, 9:8a) as the basis for making the covenant (כרות ברית) provides the background for the people's "making a firm agreement" (כרתים אמנה, 10:1) immediately after the prayer.

The explanatory clause that concludes the section establishes the basis for Israel's history: "because you are righteous" (כי צדיק אתה, 9:8d). God ratifies the covenant in view of Abraham's faithfulness, but he subsequently gives the land of the foreigners to Abraham's offspring on account of his own justice. Divine justice (צדק, 9:8d) and human faithfulness (אמונה, 9:8a) are the essential attributes of the respective parties in the covenant relationship and form the basis for Israel's possessing the land. The confession, "you are righteous," which accounts for God's gift of the land to Abraham's offspring (9:8d, כי צדיק אתה) also explains why Israel does not rule the land (9:33a, ואתה צדיק). In the first case, God's righteousness consists in fidelity to his promise to Abraham (9:8), whereas, in the second, God's righteousness refers to his retribution for Israel's wickedness (9:33).

Thus, Israel's life in the land is an experience of God's righteousness from the beginning (9:8) until the present moment (9:33). The line that concludes the era of Abraham also encapsulates the whole of Israel's history that follows by drawing attention, not to the eras of the exodus (9:9–11) and the wilderness (9:12–21), but to the occupation and settlement in the land (הארץ, 9:8b) that endures to the present (9:15c–d, 22–24, 35–36).

The wilderness period (9:9–21)

The era of harmony (9:9–15). This section highlights YHWH's beneficence by recounting his intervention on Israel's behalf at the Sea of Reeds (9:9–11) and his provision of gifts in the wilderness (9:12–15).

---

[29] GBH §126 a–b. See also C. Giraudo, *La Struttura Letteraria della Preghiera Eucaristica: Saggio sulla genesi letteraria di una forma: Toda Veterotestamentaria, Beraka Giudaica, Anafora Cristiana* (AnBib 92; Rome: Biblical Institute, 1981), 96.

The psalm's recounting of the events at the Sea of Reeds consists of five lines (9:9–11b). The first two lines follow the pattern of the previous line insofar as each begins with a converted imperfect (וַתֵּרֶא: "you saw," 9:9a; וַתִּתֵּן: "you produced," 9:10a; cf. וַתָּקֶם: "you kept," 9:8d). While the first two lines begin with a verb, the last two begin with an accusative (וְהַיָּם: the "sea," 9:11a; וְאֶת־רֹדְפֵיהֶם: "their pursuers," 9:11b), and the middle (third) line with an explanatory conjunction (כִּי, 9:10b).

The first (9:9) and fourth lines (9:11a) are the only two that employ parallelism. In each case, the second colon transposes the position of the verb and its object vis-à-vis the first colon. Nehemiah 9:9 follows an a:b:c:d::b':a':d' structure:

וַתֵּרֶא אֶת־עֳנִי אֲבֹתֵינוּ בְּמִצְרָיִם
וְאֶת־זַעֲקָתָם שָׁמַעְתָּ עַל־יַם־סוּף

You saw the misery of our ancestors in Egypt,
and their cry you heard at the Reed Sea.

Nehemiah 9:11a has an a:b:c::b':a:c' structure:

וְהַיָּם בָּקַעְתָּ לִפְנֵיהֶם
וַיַּעַבְרוּ בְתוֹךְ־הַיָּם בַּיַּבָּשָׁה

The sea you split before them,
and they passed through the midst of the sea on dry ground.

Within the setting of the whole psalm, this account of the exodus introduces YHWH's manner of intervening on behalf of his people that perdures even to the present day. The first line (9:9) provides a paradigm of his salvific interaction with them that offers hope for the present: the people cry out (זעק, 9:9, 28b; צעק, 9:27b), and YHWH hears (שמע, 9:9, 27b, 28c).

This pattern, once established at the Reed Sea, later is doubly emphasized as constitutive of Israel's history in the land (9:27, 28). The phrase "our ancestors" forms a lexical connection between the first line of the exodus account and the concerns of the present era (אֲבֹתֵינוּ, 9:9; cf. 9:32c, 34a, 36b). Thus, the line that describes the origins of liberation from Egypt (9:9) ultimately suggests the motive for praying the psalm (9:32–37): YHWH hears the cry of the people and looks upon the misery of "our ancestors" (אֲבֹתֵינוּ). The same root (זעק) designates both the activity of the people in Egypt (זַעֲקָתָם: "their cry," 9:9) and the contribution of the Levites to the prior penitential rites (וַיִּזְעֲקוּ: "[they] cried out," 9:4). Thus, the prayer is the "cry" of the Levites on behalf of their contemporaries for deliverance from their present slavery (cf. 9:36a: הִנֵּה אֲנַחְנוּ הַיּוֹם עֲבָדִים: "Look, we are slaves this day").

Nehemiah 9:10 also relates the events in Egypt to the current situation in the land. The initial verb (וַתִּתֵּן, 9:10a), describing YHWH's producing signs and wonders, echoes his promising "to give" (לתת, 9:8b, 8c) the land to Abraham's offspring. "All the people of his land" (כל־עם ארצו, 9:10a) at least alludes to the subsequent expressions "the peoples of the land" (עמי הארץ, 9:24c; cf. 10:31, 32) and "the peoples of the lands" (עמי הארצת, 9:30c; 10:29) who are Israel's opponents even in the present day. The fact that YHWH directs his prodigious works against such people augurs well for Israel's future.

The final statement in 9:10b ("Thus you made a name for yourself as it is even to this day" [כהיום הזה]) asserts the paradigmatic nature of YHWH's actions in Egypt: as YHWH acted in the exodus, so he acts in the present. However, the question arises as to how YHWH has "made a name for [himself in] this day." One must decide whether the comparison (כהיום הזה) refers to the immediate past (i.e., "You made a name for yourself") or to the present and immediate future (i.e., "You are making a name for yourself").

Pointing to the immediate past is the reference to the Egyptians' insolent behavior (זיד *hipʿil*, 9:10c) in the previous colon. YHWH acts against human insolence (זיד *hipʿil*) on two other occasions: first in the wilderness era (9:16) and, second, after the settlement in the land (9:29). However, in both these later cases, he acts against the insolence of Israel, not against its foes. According to this interpretation, YHWH made a name for himself insofar as he demonstrated his retributive justice against Israel by allowing foreigners to dominate their land (cf. 9:33).

By contrast, two factors favor the alternative interpretation that looks to the present and immediate future with hope. First, the plain meaning of 9:10d is that YHWH makes a name for himself by saving his people from their oppressors. Second, "this day" (כהיום הזה, 9:10b) occurs again in the descriptions of both Israel's long experience of oppression (עד היום, 9:32d) and its present state of enslavement (היום, 9:36a). In both settings, the expression is a component of a prayer for deliverance, whether explicit (9:32) or implied (9:36). According to this evidence, YHWH is about to make a name for himself by delivering his people from their present state of servitude in their own land (9:36).

Both the lexical evidence and the structure of the prayer favor the second alternative. Clearly, 9:10 speaks of YHWH's intervention to save rather than to discipline Israel. Moreover, the intercessory appeal (9:32) occurs immediately after the third description of Israel's turning from God (9:30) as a cry for salvation equivalent to the cries that gained a response of deliverance in the prior two instances (cf. 9:27b, 28b).

In Neh 9:11, the successive designations of the sea in each of the four cola convey an increased dramatic quality. The "sea" (הים), its "midst" (בתוך־הים), "the depths" (מצולת), and the "mighty waters" (מים עזים) suggest initially the enormity of the obstacle that YHWH overcame in delivering his people (9:11a) and subsequently the magnitude of the power by which he vanquished his people's oppressors (9:11b). Both aspects of the event at the Reed Sea bolster the hope for his salvific intervention against those who exercise tyranny over God's people in the present (cf. 9:32, 36–37).

Of the four demonstrations of God's generosity in the wilderness (9:12–15), two are out of place vis-à-vis the contexts in which they occur in the Pentateuch. The book of Exodus introduces the pillars of cloud and fire (Neh 9:12) prior to the crossing of the sea (Exod 13:21–22). Furthermore, Exodus recounts the miracles of bread and water (Neh 9:15a) prior to the people's arrival at Sinai (Exod 16:1–17:8). The Levites' psalm rearranges these episodes so that they frame the longer account of the divine lawgiving at Sinai (Neh 9:13–14).

The description of the columns of cloud and fire takes the form of two poetic lines (9:12a, 12b). The first line (9:12a), a bicolon, exhibits parallelism with an ellipsis of the verb in the second colon (a:b:c:d::a:b':d'):

ובעמוד ענן הנחיתם יומם
ובעמוד אש לילה

By a column of cloud you led them during the day,
and by a column of fire during the night.

The noun בעמוד ("by a column," 9:12a) is the first word in each colon. In the first colon, there is the repetition of *n* and *ām* in עָנָן הִנְחִיתָם יוֹמָם.

Contextually, the subunit redirects attention from the depths of the sea (9:11) to the cloud and fire in the sky (9:12).

In terms of content, the subunit introduces the symbiosis of divine solicitude and human response that will shape Israel's history. The first line and a half (9:12a–bα) emphasizes God's initiative in providing cloud and fire to guide and give light to his people. The final half-line (9:12bβ) represents the first allusion in the psalm to Israel's responsibility for its future. The expression, "the way in which they should go" (הדרך אשר ילכו־בה, 9:12bβ) conveys ethical as well as geographical nuances. This language conveys a moral depth in anticipation of the following account of the giving of the law, which will replace cloud and fire as Israel's definitive guide through history.

The account of events at Sinai takes the form of an initial presentation in four lines (9:13–14a) and a summarizing conclusion (9:14b) that offer alternate perspectives on the same event, namely, the giving of the law. The first four lines present the view "from above," while the final line offers rather the view "from below." The difference in perspective becomes apparent by comparing the final words of the first and the last lines, respectively. The first line begins by noting the heavenly origins of the precepts (מִשָּׁמַיִם, 9:13a), whereas the last line concludes by focusing on the human agent, Moses (ביד משה עבדך: "by the hand of Moses your servant," 9:14b). This contrast extends to the distinction between the immediacy of God's communication with the people in the first four lines (9:13–14a) and the mediation of the law by his servant in the final line (9:14b).

The first line (9:13a) highlights both the transcendence of God and the intimacy of his communication with the people. Mention of his descent upon Mount Sinai provides a smooth transition from the descriptions of the phenomena of cloud and fire in the sky (9:12). God's speaking "from heaven" (משמים, 9:13a) recalls the first moment of his creative work (השמים, 9:6b–d [3x]). Moreover, mention of "heaven" (משמים, 9:13a) at Sinai provides a distant contrast with the "sea" (הים, 9:11a [bis]) of the exodus in a manner that echoes the polarity between "the highest heaven" (שמי משמים, 9:6b) and "the seas" (הימים, 9:6c) in creation.

The indirect and direct objects of the verbs constitute the subject matter that the first three lines (9:13a–c) and the fifth line (9:14b) have in common. The indirect pronominal objects, which always refer to the people, invariably follow verbs of communication in four of the five lines: "you spoke with them" (דבר עמהם),[30] "you gave them" (תתן להם), "you made known to them" (הודעת להם), and "you commanded them" (צוית להם). The plethora of these constructions suggests that God entered into a unique intimacy with his people at Sinai. Two rarely used verbs in Ezra-Nehemiah (דבר עמהם, 9:13a; הודעת להם, 9:14a) frame the account of his "giving" the precepts to them (תתן להם, 9:13b–c). His "speaking" with them (9:13a) is the only instance of the verb דבר in the covenant-renewal account (7:72b–10:40; cf. Ezra 8:17; Neh 6:12; 13:24). The *hip͑il* of ידע occurs one other time in Ezra-Nehemiah: to describe the leaders' work of instructing the people in the Torah (8:12). This framework, which highlights discourse, indicates that God's "giving" (נתן *qal*) the precepts to the people is a matter of personal communication. Moreover, the verb נתן links the precepts with the previous objects, namely, the land (9:8b–c) and the signs and wonders (9:10a).

The accusatives occur in two series: first in two pairs (משפטים ישרים ותורות אמת: "just ordinances and true laws," 9:13b–c; חקים ומצות טובים: "good statutes and commandments," 9:13c), then in a row of three (מצוות וחקים ותורה: "commandments, statutes, and a law," 9:14b). The last three terms of the first list (9:13b–c) occur in reverse sequence in the second list (9:14b): "law[s]" (תורת/תורות), "statutes" (חקים), and "commandments" (מצוות/מצות). These three general terms frame the Sabbath commandment (9:14a), which is the only specific precept mentioned in Neh 9:13–14. The centrality of the Sabbath commandment at Sinai corresponds with its

---

[30] The infinitive absolute (דַּבֵּר) has the same aspect as the preceding verb (i.e., *qatal*); see GBH 123x.

subsequent importance both in the community's pledge (10:32, 34) and ultimately in Nehemiah's enforcement of the pledge (13:15–22 [6x]; cf. 10:32).

Moreover, in terms of syntax, the Sabbath occupies an emphatic position parallel to that of the juridical terms in the second list insofar as these direct objects precede their respective (perfect) verbs and subsequent indirect objects (9:14a; cf. 9:14b).

The various juridical nouns are the most significant links within the psalm and beyond it to the commitment that follows. The "ordinances" (משפטים), "law[s]" (תורות), and "commandments" (מצות) that God gives at Sinai (9:13b–c) are precisely those items that the people reject in the land (9:29a–b). Conversely, following the prayer, the participants in the covenant renewal pledge themselves anew to the observance of all four categories of precepts (9:13a–c; cf. 10:30): the "law" (תורה), the "commandments" (מצות), the "ordinances" (משפטים), and the "statutes" (חקים). The latter verse contains further reflections of the Sinai account (9:13–14) in the people's reference to the "law of God that was given by the hand of Moses, the servant of God" (תורת האלהים אשר נתנה ביד משה עבד־האלהים, 10:30; cf. 9:14b). Thus, the description of the law giving at Sinai (9:13–14) is the reference point for the people's oath taking (10:30).

The adjectives אמת and טוב (9:13c) link the precepts to the descriptions of God and his gifts elsewhere in the prayer. The "true laws" (תורות אמת, 9:13c) correspond with the "faithful" actions (כי־אמת עשית, 9:33) that distinguish God's behavior from that of his disobedient people. The term "good" defines not only the statutes and commandments (חקים ומצות טובים, 9:13c) but also God's gifts of his spirit (רוחך הטובה, 9:20a), the contents of the captured houses (מלאים כל־טוב, 9:25b), God's character (טובך, 9:35a), and the produce of the land (טובה, 9:36b).

The Torah (תורה) is the seventh and last of the accumulated juridical terms in 9:13–14. Its association with YHWH's "command" (צוה) and Moses' "hand" (ביד משה) establishes links not only to the previous celebration of Booths (8:14) but also to the commitment that follows (10:30).[31] The book that Ezra had studied with the leaders (8:14) and the law that the people promise to observe (10:30) is the Torah that YHWH communicates at Sinai (9:13). It is noteworthy that Moses and Abraham are the only two human figures mentioned in the psalm.

The description of God's provision of bread and water in the wilderness takes the form of two poetic bicola that exhibit word-for-word parallelism.[32]

---

[31] Neh 9:14: [ו]תורה צוית להם ביד משה עבדך
Neh 8:14: [ב]תורה אשר צוה יהוה ביד־משה
Neh 10:30: [ב]תורת האלהים אשר נתנה ביד משה עבד־האלהים

[32] I maintain Rudolph's format against Segert ("History and Poetry," 259–60), who places the verb in the second colon of each line.

Assonance unites the lines via threefold repetition in both the first and second cola of the respective lines: (1) in the first colon *mayîm* (מים/שמים); the preposition *m* (מסלע/משמים); and the second-person ending of the verb, that is, *tâ, tā* (הוצאת/נתתה); and (2) in the second colon the identical first word להם; the identical form of a noun introduced by the preposition ל (לצמאם/לרעבם); and the ending furnished by the third-person plural possessive adjective, that is, *ām* (לצמאם/לרבם).

The parallel nouns are merisms for nutritional needs (hunger and thirst) and provisions (bread and water) that are essential for existence. The sources of the provisions ("from heaven" and "from the rock") implicitly carry forward the allusion to the merism "heaven and earth" in the account of creation (9:6). Just as mention of "the sea" and "heaven," respectively, in the events of the exodus (9:11a) and at Sinai (9:13a) alluded to God's making everything from "the highest heaven" to "the seas" (9:6b–c), so here mention of "heaven" and the "rock" alludes to God's having made "heaven" (9:6b) and "earth" (or "ground," 9:6c).[33] In other words, the fact that God brings forth the essential provisions both "from above" and "from below" (9:15a–b) reflects his sovereignty over the universe that the portrayal of creation established at the beginning of the prayer (9:6).

YHWH's direct conversation with the people, which was emblematic of the events at Sinai, resurfaces in his command for the people to enter and take possession of the land (ותאמר להם: "Then, you told them," 9:15c; cf. ודבר עמהם: "and you spoke with them," 9:13a). The latter is, however, the first precise directive he gives to the people. In terms of content, the command (לרשת את־הארץ: "to go and take possession of the land," 9:15c) actualizes the promise implicit in the covenant with Abraham (לתת את־ארץ: "to give the land," 9:8b). Within the context of the psalm, Moses' generation thus represents the "offspring" of Abraham to whom YHWH gives the land (לתת להם: "to give to them," 9:15d; cf. לתת לזרעו: "to give to his offspring," 9:8c). However, the next generation (הבנים: "the children," 9:24a) will carry out the command.

The people's rebellion and God's mercy (9:16–21). The twofold description of the people's rebellion and YHWH's merciful responses (9:16–17, 18–21) presents these not simply as isolated episodes but rather

---

[33] Through these parallels, the account of creation is echoed in the description of the wilderness period:

	The heavens	The earth	The sea
9:6:	השמים	הארץ	הימים
9:11:			הים
9:13:	משמים		
9:15:	משמים	מסלע	

as the powers that shape Israel's history. The first description of both rebellion and mercy is general (9:16–17), whereas the second features specific episodes (9:18–21). Thus, the general statements of the people's rebellion and YHWH's forgiveness that comprise the first account (9:16–17) acquire specificity in the most radical illustrations (אף־כי, 9:18a) of these behavior patterns in the second account (9:18–21).

In the first account, the pronouns designating the contrasting subjects introduce the respective eras of rebellion and mercy (והם: "but they," 9:16a; cf. ואתה: "but you," 9:17c). In the second account, an intensive particle introduces the era of rebellion (אף־כי: "even when," 9:18a), whereas the second-person singular pronoun introduces the era of mercy (ואתה, "you," 9:19a). Use of the pronoun אתה to generate parallel introductions for the two eras of mercy (9:17c, 19a) recalls the fourfold occurrence of the same term as an anaphora at the beginning of the psalm (9:6a, 6b, 6d, 7a).

The first account of rebellion (9:16a–17b) consists of seven clauses that form an a:b:c:d:c':b:a' structure.[34] The first and last clauses describe the hold of the Israelites' former life in Egypt upon them: the verb הזידו ("they acted insolently," 9:16a [a]) in the first clause attributes to the Israelites an insolence reminiscent of that of the Egyptians (9:10b), which corresponds with their decision to return to Egypt in the last clause (9:17b [a']). The second and sixth clauses (9:16a [b], 17b [b]) are identical descriptions of the Israelites' stiffening their necks. The third (c) and fifth (c') clauses are the only two that begin with לא. The central component of the structure is the shortest clause: "they refused to obey" (9:17a [d]).

Within the broader setting of the covenant-renewal account, the centrality of the people's refusal to obey (וימאנו לשמע, 9:17a) in the list of rebellious actions corresponds with the urgency of the capacity "to understand by hearing" (מבין לשמע, 8:2) as the prerequisite for participating in the assembly on the first day.

The three verbs that describe the rebellion of the people afford an ironic reflection on the description of the exodus in 9:9–10: (1) the verb הזידו ("to act insolently," 9:16a; cf. 9:10b) indicates that the Israelites treat YHWH as their Egyptian overlords had treated them (9:16a); (2) the Israelites' refusal to obey the commandments (לא שמע אל־מצותיך, 9:16a) contrasts with YHWH's heeding their cry from slavery (ואת זעקתם שמעת,

---

[34] a   והם ואבתינו הזידו
b   ויקשו את־ערפם
c   ולא שמעו אל־מצותיך
d   וימאנו לשמע
c' ולא זכרו נפלאתיך אשר עשית עמהם
b   ויקשו את־ערפם
a' ויתנו־ראש לשוב לעבדתם במצרים

9:9a); and (3) their providing (נתן, 9:17b) themselves with a leader contrasts with YHWH's giving (נתן, 9:10a) signs and wonders against Pharaoh.

Moreover, four expressions subsequently describe the behavior of the people in the land that brought about their present difficulties (9:29): (1) "they acted insolently" (הזידו, 9:16a, 29a); (2) "they did not obey your commandments" (לא שמע אל־מצותיך, 9:16a, 29a); (3) "they stiffened their necks" (ויקשו את־ערפם, 9:16a; cf. וערפם הקשו, 9:29c); and (4) their refusal to obey intensified (ולא שמעו): "they did not obey," 9:29c; cf. וימאנו לשמע: "they refused to obey," 9:17a, in each case, following לא שמע אל־מצותיך: "they did not obey your commandments," 9:16a, 29a).

The explicative *wāw* (ואבתינו, 9:16a) at the beginning of the account of rebellion clarifies the identity of those designated by the third-person pronoun ("they, our ancestors").[35] References to "our ancestors" (אבתינו, 9:16a) and "slavery" (עבדה, 9:17b) link this description of rebellion (9:16–17b) with the account of the present state of the people (9:32–36). While the term "our ancestors" also recalls those who were oppressed in Egypt (9:9), in the present context it more emphatically prepares the attribution of responsibility for the present plight of the people to "our ancestors" (אבתינו, 9:16a; 9:34a) who did not keep the law.

The ancestors' preference for slavery (ויתנו־ראש לשוב לעבדתם במצרים: "[they] appointed a leader in order to return to their slavery in Egypt," 9:17b) helps explain why the people are slaves (עבדים, 9:36a, 36c) in their own land at the present time. The position of this clause at the end of the series of seven descriptions of the ancestral rebellion in 9:17b indicates that slavery was a state that the people consciously chose in outright rejection of YHWH's gifts. By "giving" (נתן) themselves a leader (9:17b), the people gave themselves slavery in blatant contradiction to what YHWH had "given" (נתן) them up to this point: the promise of the land (9:8b–c, 15c), signs and wonders (9:10a), ordinances (9:13a–c), and food (9:15a).

The predominance of verbs in the sevenfold series of clauses describing the people's rebellion (9:16–17b) gives way to an accumulation of five nouns describing the character of God in the psalm's most elaborate confessional statement (9:17c–d). Only the credal declaration that introduces the second major portion of the psalm is comparable in extent (9:32a–b). The confessional statement, in turn, prepares for the singular description of God's response: "You did not abandon them." Therefore, the accent falls on the attributes of God (9:17c–d), which contrast with the actions of the people (9:16–17b).

The introductory phrase ואתה ("But you," 9:17c), referring to God, contrasts with והם ("But they," 9:16), referring to the people. The first two

---

35 On the explicative *wāw*, see GKC §154a n. 1(b).

words ואתה אלוה ("But you are God," 9:17c) recall the psalm's earlier confession אתה־הוא יהוה האלהים ("You are YHWH, the God," 9:7a). Moreover, use of the pronoun אתה ("you") to introduce a confessional statement comprised of godly attributes (9:17c) provides continuity with the previous occurrence of the pronoun in the clause כי צדיק אתה ("because you are righteous," 9:8d).

The final clause ("You did not abandon them") serves a twofold function: its singularity contrasts with the sevenfold series of the people's rebellious actions, and its employment of the negative to describe God's reaction bespeaks his restraint but leaves open the possibility for further rebellion by the people. The statement ולא עזבתם ("you did not abandon them," 9:17d) occurs three times in the psalm (9:17d, 19a, 31b), in contrast to the one instance of the opposite expression ותעזבם ("you abandoned them," 9:28b).

The intensive adverb (אף־כי: "Even when," 9:18a) directs attention to the fabricating of the molten calf as the prime example of the people's rebelliousness. The reflexive pronoun להם ("for themselves," 9:18a) recalls והם ("But they," 9:16). The people's statement, "This is your god" (זה אלהיך, 9:18b), contradicts the confessional invocation "But you are God" (ואתה אלוה, 9:17c). The people's attribution of their exodus from "Egypt" (9:18b) to the idol recalls their prior rebellion in their determination to return to "Egypt" (9:17b).

The description of apostasy concludes with a summary statement suggesting that the making of the molten calf was only the foremost among Israel's "great infamies." The repetition of the verb עשה (ויעשו: "they committed," 9:18c; cf. עשׂו: "they made," 9:18a) links the particular episode and the summary. The summary statement, "they commited great infamies" (ויעשו נאצות גדלות), recurs as a résumé of the people's rebellious activity in the first cycle concerning their troubled life in the land (9:26c).

In the second sequence, the description of God's mercies (9:19–21) is over three times longer than the account of the people's apostasy (9:18). The second-person pronoun repeats the introduction to the first description of divine mercy (ואתה: "you," 9:19a; cf. 9:17c). Mention of God's "abundant mercies" (ברחמיך הרבים, 9:19a) recalls the third of his five attributes previously listed (רחום, 9:17c). Moreover, one has here the first of four instances in which God's "abundant mercies" ([רבות] רחמים רבים, 9:19a, 27c, 28c, 31a) account for the preservation of the people in spite of their rebellion.

However, in contrast to the first description of God's forgiving response (9:17c–d), the emphasis here falls not on the nouns designating the divine attributes but rather on the verbs describing a series of providential actions (9:19–21). The initial verb לא עזבתם ("you did not abandon them," 9:19a; cf. 9:17c) echoes the conclusion of the first phase of the divine response.

The subsequent descriptions elaborate on the precise meaning of God's "not abandoning" his people. Six verbs reiterate the negative introductory phrase (לא עזבתם: "you did not abandon them," 9:19a; cf. לא־סר: "[it] did not cease," 9:19b; לא־מנעת: "you did not withhold," 9:20b; לא חסרו: "they lacked nothing," 9:21a; לא בלו: "[they] did not wear out," 9:21b; לא בצקו: "[they] did not swell," 9:21b). These six are twice the number of positive verbs denoting divine provision (נתת: "you gave," 9:20a; נתתה: "you gave," 9:20b; כלכלתם: "you sustained them," 9:21a). The expression "in the wilderness" (במדבר, 9:19a, 21a) provides an *inclusio* for the second phase of God's mercy.

The mercies of God consist precisely in his not withdrawing the gifts he had bestowed upon the people following their passage through the sea: the columns of cloud and fire (9:19b–c; cf. 9:12); instruction (9:20a; cf. 9:13–14); and bread and water (9:20b; cf. 9:15a–b). These gifts stand in the emphatic position at the beginning of each clause in which they are mentioned (את־עמוד הענן: the "column of cloud," 9:19b; ואת־עמוד האש: the "column of fire," 9:19b; ורוחך הטובה: "your good spirit," 9:20a; ומנך: "your manna," 9:20bα; ומים: "and water," 9:20bβ).

The portrayal of the columns of cloud and fire (9:19b–c) is both an elaboration of 9:12a and an identical repetition of 9:12b. The following elements constitute variations on 9:12a: (1) the syntagm את־עמוד [bis]);[36] (2) the definite articles in הענן ("the cloud") and האש ("the fire"); (3) the clause describing God's nonwithdrawal of the columns (לא־סר מעליהם: "[it] did not cease [from above them]"); (4) the change in the form of the verb and the reversal of its position vis-à-vis the temporal qualifier (ביומם להנחתם: "in the day to guide them," 9:19; cf. הנחיתם יומם: "you led them during the day," 9:12a); (5) the insertion of the prepositions in the expressions ביומם ("in the day") and בלילה ("in the night");[37] and (6) the addition of בהדרך ("on the way," 9:19a) as a parallel for את־הדרך ("the way," 9:12b).

The description of God's endowment with his spirit (9:20a) occurs within the same context as the previous account of the events at Sinai (9:13–14), that is, after the columns of cloud and fire (9:12; cf. 9:19b–c) and before the episodes of manna and water (9:15a–b; cf. 9:20b). The verb נתן describing God's activity, first in providing (ותתן, 9:13b) correct ordinances

---

[36] J. Hoftijzer, "Remarks concerning the Use of the Particle ʾT in Classical Hebrew," *OtSt* 14 (1965): 1–99. This nonaccusative את occurs four times in the psalm (את־עמוד: "the column," 9:19 [bis]; את כל־התלאה: "all the hardship," 9:32b; ואת־מלכינו: "our kings," 9:34a) and nowhere else in Nehemiah. Cf. GBH §127j(7).

[37] Note the oddity of the expression ביומם, which does not occur anywhere else among the other fifty-two MT instances of יומם.

and then in bequeathing (נתת, 9:20a) his good spirit, further links the two episodes. Moreover, these two passages contain the sole occurrences of the adjective טוב in the psalm (רוחך הטובה: "your good spirit," 9:20a; cf. חקים ומצות טובים: "good statutes and commandments," 9:13c).[38] The purpose of God's spirit, namely, "to instruct them" (להשכילם, 9:20a), is consistent with God's activity at Sinai, that is, "making known" (הודעת להם, 9:14a) the Sabbath to them and "commanding" (צוית להם: 9:14b) the law for them.

Within the broader context of the covenant-renewal account, the instructional purpose of the spirit (להשכילם, 9:20a) immediately recalls the leaders' studying (להשכיל, 8:13) the words of the law on the second day and, more indirectly, the Levites' giving the sense (שום שכל, 8:8) of the law on the first day.

Nehemiah 9:20a and 9:30b provide the only references to God's spirit in Ezra-Nehemiah (cf. Ezra 1:1, 5). Thus, in the wilderness God provides the means (רוחך: "your spirit," 9:20a) by which he will admonish the people through his prophets when rebellion stirs in the land (ברוחך: "through your spirit," 9:30b).

The description of God's continuing provision of manna and water (9:20b) takes the form of a poetic line but lacks the tight parallelism of the original account (9:15a–b). The term "your manna" (מנך, 9:20b) takes the place of "bread" (לחם, 9:15a) and maintains the personal nature of the divine gift that the previous noun, "your spirit" (רוחך, 9:20a), indicated. Paronomasia is evident in the clause מנך לא־מנעת ("your manna you did not withhold," 9:20b).[39] The verbs maintain continuity with previous elements in the section: (1) the negative לא־מנעת ("you did not withhold," 9:20b) recalls לא עזבתם ("you did not abandon them," 9:19a) and לא־סר ("[it] did not cease," 9:19b); and (2) the positive נתתה ("you gave," 9:20b) reinforces נתת ("you gave," 9:20a). The concluding phrase להם לצמאם ("to them for their thirst," 9:20b) repeats the ending of 9:15b.

The account of God's provisions for the people in the wilderness concludes with a summary of their survival over the course of the forty years (9:21). The description consists of two poetic lines. The parallelism of the second bicolon (9:21b) is evident in: (1) the word order in each colon (noun - negation - verb); (2) the repetition of the negative לא; and (3) the endings of the nouns (-*hem*) and the verbs (-*û*).[40] The verbs in the two lines (9:21a, 21b) maintain continuity with earlier verbs in the section: (1) the positive כלכלתם ("you sustained them," 9:21a) carries over from the

---

[38] The substantive טוב occurs in 9:25b, 25d, 35a, 36b.

[39] C. R. Anderson, "The Formation of the Levitical Prayer of Nehemiah 9" (Th.D. diss.; Dallas Theological Seminary, 1987), 171.

[40] Neh 9:21b: שלמתיהם לא בלו ורגליהם לא בצקו

previous נתתה ("you gave," 9:20b) and נתת ("you gave," 9:20a); and (2) the negatives לא חסרו ("they lacked nothing," 9:21b), לא בלו ("[they] did not wear out," 9:21b) and לא בצקו ("they did not swell," 9:21b)—with assonance (*û*) in their final syllables—echo לא־מנעת ("you did not withhold," 9:20b), לא־סר ("[it] did not cease," 9:19b), and לא עזבתם ("you did not abandon them," 9:19a).

The occupation and subsequent life in the land (9:22–31)

The era of harmony: the occupation of the land (9:22–25). The account of the occupation of the land (9:22–25) is intimately related to the command for it that YHWH decreed in the wilderness (9:15c–d). Four key words of that decree (9:15c–d) recur more than once in the description of the conquest (9:22–25): (1) בוא ("to come," 9:15c, 23b [bis], 24a); (2) ירש ("to take possession," 9:22b, 23b, 24a, 25b); (3) נתן ("to give," 9:22a, 24b); and (4) ארץ ("land," 9:22b, 22c, 23b, 24a, 24b, 24c).[41] Moreover, the last words of 9:15d (לתת להם: "to give to them") recur at the beginning of 9:22a (ותתן להם: "you gave them"), and the vocabulary of 9:15c provides the content of the subordinate clause describing the land (הארץ) in 9:23b.[42] In summary, the only words from 9:15c–d that do not recur in 9:22–25 are those of the subordinate clause, אשר־נשאת את־ידך ("which you had sworn," 9:15d).

In terms of structure, the account of the occupation (9:22–25) consists of two major parts: the story of the capture of the territory (9:22–24), and the description of the seizure of the land's goods (9:25). The *inclusio* that delimits the first part consists of the two summary descriptions of God's "giving kingdoms [or kings] and peoples" into the power of his people.[43] Moreover, except for a single word (ירש: "they took possession," 9:25b), all the vocabulary from 9:15c–d recurs in 9:22–24 but not in 9:25. The first major part (9:22–24) further divides into two subunits: the first describing the conquest of the Transjordan by the "ancestors" (אבותיהם, 9:22) who left Egypt, the second recounting the conquest of Canaan by "their children" (הבנים, 9:23–24). The identical clause (ויירשו את־הארץ: "they possessed the land," 9:22b, 24a) near the beginning of each subunit establishes a parallelism between these two narrative portions.

---

[41] Williamson notes the repetitions of ירש, נתן, and ארץ from 9:15 in 9:22–25 (*Ezra, Nehemiah*, 316).

[42] 9:15c: ותאמר להם לבוא לרשת את־הארץ
9:23b: הארץ אשר אמרת לאבתיהם לבוא לרשת

[43] 9:22a: ותתן להם ממלכות ועממים
9:24c: ותתנם בידם ואת־מלכיהם ואת־עממי הארץ

Table 4.3—Outline of the Occupation of the Land (9:22–25)
1. The capture of the territory (9:22–24)
   a. The ancestors capture the lands of Kings Sihon and Og (9:22–23)
   b. The children capture the land of the Canaanites (9:24)
2. The seizure of the territory, properties, and produce of the land (9:25)

The summary descriptions of YHWH's giving his own people "kingdoms [or kings] and peoples" (9:22a, 24c–d) provide the background for the portrayal of the power struggle that will characterize Israel's life in the land up to the present. The "kingdoms" (ממלכות, 9:22a) that YHWH gives his people become "their kingdom" (מלכותם, 9:35a) over which "our kings" (מלכינו, 9:32c, 34a) rule until YHWH permits foreign "kings" (מלכים, 9:37a) to oversee the land. References to "peoples" (עממים, 9:22a), especially "the peoples of the land" (עממי הארץ, 9:24b), introduce the population with whom the covenant community must neither intermarry (עמי הארץ, 10:31) nor do business on the Sabbath (10:32). As outsiders to the community committed to the covenant, these "peoples of the land" (עממי הארץ, 9:24b) overlap with "the peoples of the lands" (עמי הארצת, 9:30c) into whose power YHWH will give his own people when they refuse to heed his warnings.

The parallel descriptions of "the land of Sihon, King of Heshbon," and "the land of Og, King of Bashan" (9:22b–c), immediately exemplify the plurality of "kingdoms and peoples" that YHWH bequeaths to his own (9:22a). Moreover, mention of the territories of these kings shifts the emphasis from "kingdoms" to "land" (ארץ, 9:22c–d [bis]), which in turn becomes the major theme in 9:23–24 (הארץ [4x]).

The emphatic positioning of the expression "their children" (ובניהם) at the beginning of 9:23a directs attention to the new generation. The *w . . . qatal* (ובניהם הרבית: "You had multiplied their children," 9:23a) construction following the *wayyiqtol* (ויירשו: "so they took possession," 9:22b) indicates the pluperfect tense of this introductory clause (9:23a).[44] Within the broader context of the covenant-renewal account, mention of "the children" (בניהם, 9:23a; הבנים, 9:24a) also prepares for the participation of the children in the declaration of commitment (בניהם: "their sons," 10:29; בנינו: "our sons," 10:31).

The allusion to YHWH's promise to Abraham in the multiplication of children (9:23a) indirectly recalls his commitment to give "the land of the Canaanites" (ארץ הכנעני) to Abraham's offspring (לזרעו, 9:8b–c).

The infinitives at the end of 9:23b (לבוא לרשת: "to enter and possess," 9:15c) are repeated in the perfects (ויבאו . . . ויירשו) of 9:24a to describe the people's entrance into and possession of the land. The children act on

---

[44] Gilbert, "Notes," 16; GBH §118d.

the command against which their ancestors had rebelled (ויבאו הבנים
וירשו: "the children entered and possessed," 9:24a; cf. 9:16a: והם ואבתינו
הזידו: "But they, our ancestors, acted insolently").

Paronomasia is evident between the verb [ותכנע ("you subdued,"
9:24a) and the noun הכנענים ("the Canaanites," 9:24b).

Two elements at the conclusion of the conquest account are ironic:
(1) just as YHWH gave the kings and peoples of the land into the power
of his people in the conquest, so in response to the latter's rebellions he
will give his own people into the power of their oppressors (ותתנם
בידם: "you delivered into their hand," 9:24b; cf. ותתנם ביד: "you gave
them into the hand," 9:27a, 30c; ותעזבם ביד: "you abandoned them into
the hand," 9:28b); and (2) in the conquest YHWH's people treated the
vanquished "as they please[d]," but in the present time the foreign
regents reign over God's people and cattle "as they please" (כרצונם,
9:24c; cf. 9:37b).

A change in subject occurs with the description of the seizure of the
properties (9:25). Whereas in the account of the occupation (9:22–24)
mention of YHWH's activities (ותתן להם: "you gave them," 9:22a; ובניהם
הרבית: "You had multiplied their children," 9:23a; ותביאם אל־הארץ: "you
brought them to the land," 9:23b; ותכנע לפניהם: "you subdued before
them," 9:24a; ותתנם בידם: "you delivered into their hand," 9:24b) precedes mention of those of his people (ויירש את־הארץ: "so they took
possession of the land," 9:22b, 24a; ויבאו הבנים: "the children entered,"
9:24a), in the description of the capture of the goods (9:25) the people are
the only subjects of the verbs. The latter account subdivides into two
parts: the seizure of the properties (9:25a–c), and the consumption of the
produce (9:25d).

Nouns predominate in the first part, whereas verbs are most prominent
in the second. The list of captured goods includes seven items: two referring to the territory in general (cities and land, 9:25a) and five to various
forms of property (houses, wells, vineyards, olive orchards, and fruit trees,
9:25b–c). Reference to the trees is particularly appropriate within the context of the autumn harvest of trees (9:25c; cf. 8:15). The indications of
plenitude following the first and last property items (מלאים־כל־טוב: "filled
with all good things," 9:25b; לרב: "in abundance," 9:25b) prepare for the
attribution of everything to God's "great goodness" (טובך הגדול: "your
great goodness," 9:25c).

The sequence of four verbs that describe the people's consumption of
goods (eating, becoming full, growing fat, and delighting themselves)
suggests a movement toward unbridled excess (9:25d). The "rich land"
(אדמה שמנה, 9:25a) becomes the occasion for the people's "becoming fat"
(וישמינו, 9:25d). The people's self-indulgent consumption contrasts with
the concluding reference to God's goodness, which is manifested in the

abundant resources he gave them (ויתעדנו בטובך הגדול: "[they] delighted themselves in your great goodness," 9:25d).

Rebellion and mercy: life in the land (9:26–31). A detailed inspection of the cycles of rebellion and mercy that portray life in the land discloses consistency in the first two complete cycles (9:26–27, 28) and comparative inconsistency in the last half-cycle (9:29–31). As noted above,[45] each of the first two cycles consists of four stages in which the people and God are alternating subjects: (1) the people offend God (9:26, 28a); (2) God hands them over to their adversaries (9:27a, 28b); (3) the people cry out to God (9:27b, 28b); and (4) God rescues them (9:27b–c, 28c). The parallels between the last three stages of these two cycles are remarkably close: (1) the verb עשׂה provides the common factor in the first stages (9:26c, 28a); (2) God's consequent discipline is the subject of two statements, that is, a three-word depiction of his placing them in the hand of their foes, and a two-word summary of the adversaries' rule (9:27a, 28b);[46] (3) the people's outcry to God is cited succinctly (9:27b, 28b);[47] (4) God's rescuing them involves two statements: identical mentions of his hearing them from heaven (אתה משמים תשמע, 9:27c, 28c) and a highlighting of his mercy (9:27c, 28c).[48]

The third cycle (9:29–31) differs from the first two (9:26–27, 28), not only in its mentioning only the first two stages, but also in its depiction of God acting on behalf of his people in both those stages. The first stage of this cycle contains two descriptions of God "warning" the people (ותעד בהם, 9:29a; ותעד בם, 9:30b) and one of him "bearing with them" (ותמשך עלהם, 9:30a), interspersed among references to seven actions expressive of the people's rebellion (9:29a–30c).

The second stage of this cycle is notably more elaborate than its equivalents in the first two cycles. The initial statement of this stage closely parallels the corresponding depictions of God handing his own into the power of their adversaries (9:30c; cf. 9:27a, 28b).[49] However, the following reference to God's abundant mercy and the subsequent two clauses

---

[45] Pp. 165–66.
[46] 9:27a: ותתנם ביד צריהם ויצרו להם
9:28b: ותעזבם ביד איביהם וירדו בהם
[47] 9:27b: ובעת צרתם יצעקו אליך
9:28b: וישובו ויזעקוך
[48] 9:27c: וכרחמיך הרבים תתן להם מושיעים ויושיעום מיד צריהם
9:28c: ותצילם כרחמיך רבות עתים
[49] 9:27a: ותתנם ביד צריהם
9:28b: ותעזבם ביד איביהם
9:30c: ותתנם ביד עמי הארצת

describing his not abandoning the people somewhat resemble the second statements in the fourth stage of the previous cycles, which recount his rescuing the people (9:31a–b; cf. 9:27c, 28c).[50]

The emphasis on God's mercy in the final lines of all three cycles (9:27c, 28c, 31a) provides the basis for the confessional statement that concludes the section (כי אל חנון ורחום אתה: "because you are a God of grace and mercy," 9:31b).

The depiction of the people's rebellion, which begins the first cycle (9:26a–c), consists of four statements, the first and last of which are less specific than the middle two. The opening clause exhibits paronomasia in the verbs for "resisting and rebelling" (וימרו וימרדו, 9:26a). The concluding clause repeats the summary notation of the great infamies that brought to a close the previous era of rebellion in the wilderness (ויעשו נאצות גדולת, 9:26c; cf. 9:18c). The repetition of the clause here indicates that the gift of the land does not fundamentally change the people: once in the land, they return to the same infamous behavior they had exhibited in the wilderness.

The two middle clauses describe the people's rejection of the law and the prophets (9:26a–b). The main clauses form a partial grammatical chiasm a:b:c::b':a', verb:object:modifier::object:verb:

   a'   b'   c   b   a
וישלכו את־תורתך אחרי גום ואת־נביאיך הרגו.
They cast your law behind their backs; your prophets they killed.

"Your law" (תורתך) here refers not simply to the various commandments God gave at Sinai (תורות, 9:13c) but to the whole content of God's instruction (cf. תורה, 9:14b).[51] The parallelism between the descriptions of the divine admonitions in the initial stage of the first and third cycles (9:26a, 29a) equates turning to God with turning to his law.[52] Therefore, "your law" (תורתך, 9:26a, 29a) is the complete instruction of God and has the same character as the Torah or "the book of the law" in the prior narrative (8:1, 2, 3, 7, 8, 9, 13, 14, 18; 9:3).

There is irony in the people's treatment of the Torah insofar as their "casting" it away recalls God's casting away the people's adversaries at the Reed Sea (שלך, 9:26a; cf. 9:11b). Moreover, this rejection of the Torah by former generations provides the setting for the present generation's

---

[50] 9:27c: וכרחמיך הרבים תתן להם מושיעים ויושיעום מיד צריהם
    9:28c: ותצילם כרחמיך רבות עתים
    9:31a–b: וברחמיך הרבים לא־עשיתם כלה ולא עזבתם

[51] Cf. Gilbert ("La place de la Loi," 313), who views התורה in 9:26a as more comprehensive than תורה in 9:14b.

[52] 9:26b: אשר־העידו בם להשיבם אליך
    9:29a: ותעד בהם להשיבם אל תורתך

pledging themselves to walk in "the law of God [תורה אלהים] that was given through the hand of Moses, the servant of God" (10:30; cf. 9:26b).

The only references to the prophets in the covenant-renewal account (7:72b–10:40) occur in the psalm's descriptions of the people's rebellion in the land (9:26b, 30b) and in the intercession that lists their leaders (9:32c). Both references to the prophets in the cycles of rebellion are modified by the possessive adjective (נביאיך) to highlight their role as God's agents who admonish the people (9:26b, 30b; cf. 9:29a).[53] In both cases, the prophets experience rejection either in the form of martyrdom (הרגו: "they killed," 9:26b) or of inattentiveness (לא האזינו: "they would not give ear," 9:30c). In the first instance, rejection of "your prophets" (נביאיך, 9:26b) parallels rejection of "your law" (תורתך, 9:26a).

The expression "the hand of their oppressors" (יד צריהם, 9:27a, 27c) provides the *inclusio* that brackets the following three stages in the first cycle of life in the land. Moreover, one notes a verbal correspondence between God's initially "giving" (ותתנם, 9:27a) the rebellious people into the power of their adversaries and his finally "giving" (תתן, 9:27c) them saviors to rescue them from that same power. The whole account develops through a root play on צר/צרר, which occurs in each of the three stages: (1) oppression (ביד צריהם ויצרו): "into the hand of their oppressors and they oppressed them," 9:27a); (2) outcry (בעת צרתם: "in the time of their oppression," 9:27b); and (3) rescue (מיד צריהם: "from the hand of their oppressors," 9:27c). Another form of wordplay with a noun and subsequent verb is evident in both the first and last lines: צריהם ויצרו ("their oppressors and they oppressed them," 9:27a); מושיעים יושיעום ("saviors and they saved them," 9:27c).

Within the broader context of the psalm, the people's "crying out" (יצעקו, 9:27b) recalls, at least by assonance, the ancestors' outcry in Egypt (זעקתם, 9:9) and, ultimately, the Levites' action in the introductory rites (ויזעקו, 9:4; cf. ויזעקוך: "they cried out to you," 9:28b). Similarly, God's "hearing" the people's cry recalls his initial response to their affliction in Egypt (שמע, 9:27b; cf. 9:9a). His responding "from heaven" (משמים, 9:27b; cf. 9:13a) recalls the location from which he spoke with them at Sinai. Furthermore, just as the description of Israel's infamies (ויעשו נאצות גדולת, 9:26c; cf. 9:18c) links the second cycle of rebellion in the wilderness to the first cycle in the land, so also mention of God's "many mercies" (רחמיך הרבים, 9:27c; cf. 9:19a) provides continuity between the final stage of restoration in the wilderness and the initial stage of redemption in the land.

---

[53] 9:26b: ואת־נביאיך הרגו אשר־העידו בם להשיבם אליך
9:29a: ותעד בהם להשיבם אל תורתך
9:30b: ותעד בם ברוחך ביד נביאיך

The presentation of the second cycle of history in the land (9:28) is more succinct than that of the first (9:26–27) or third (9:29–31). While the first and third cycles cite YHWH's admonition to repentance (להשיבם, 9:26b, 29a), only the second cycle depicts the people as actually repenting (וישובו, 9:28b). Indeed, the first and third stages of the second cycle involve a contrast in the direction of the people's "turning," first (ישובו, 9:28a) to evil and later (וישובו, 9:28b) to YHWH. In the initial stage, their returning to do evil "before" YHWH (לפניך, 9:28a) suggests a stark contrast to Abraham, whose heart was faithful "before" YHWH (לפניך, 9:8a). YHWH's "abandoning" (ותעזבם, 9:28b) his people to their enemies in this case is not definitive, since the expression contrasts with his "not abandoning" (ולא תעזבם) them either in the last cycle of the wilderness era (9:19a) or in the third cycle of the settlement period (9:31b). The concluding phrase (רבות עתים, 9:28c) underscores the multitude of YHWH's merciful interventions and thereby supplies the second cycle with a temporal extension.

The account of the initial stage of the third cycle (9:29a–30c) differs from its equivalents in the first two cycles (9:26, 27a) insofar as God's action precedes that of the people and subsequently interrupts the list of their rebellious activities. His first and last specific initiatives in this stage consist of admonition (ותעד בה[ם], 9:29a, 30b). Furthermore, the more generic description of his "bearing with them for many years" (ותמשך עליהם שנים רבות, 9:30a) suggests the extension of his mercy (cf. כרחמיך רבות עתים, 9:28c) in terms of forbearance throughout this era of rebellion.

The seven rebellious activities of the people (9:29a–30c) equal the number of their fractious deeds in the initial description of their disobedience in the wilderness (9:16–17b). Three of these activities are identical: (1) their insolent deeds (והמה הזידו, 9:29a; cf. 9:16a); (2) their disobedience to the commandments (ולא־שמעו למצותיך, 9:29a; cf. 9:16a); and (3) their stiffening their necks (וערפם הקשו, 9:29c; cf. ויקשו את־ערפם, 9:16a, 17b). Moreover, mention of their disobedience occurs in both settings (ולא שמעו, 9:29c; cf. וימאנו לשמע, 9:17a).[54] The repetition of these behavior patterns indicates a lack of fundamental change over the course of generations from the ancestors who journeyed in the wilderness to their descendants who live in the land.

Each of the three rebellious activities that is unique to the period of the settlement intensifies one of the activities carried over from the wilderness

---

[54] Another correspondence between the two lists of Israel's rebellious activities is the occurrence of one subordinate clause modifying a gift of God in each list (9:29b: [משפטיך] אשר־יעשה אדם וחיה בהם: "[against your ordinances] that one must carry out and thereby live"; cf. 9:17a: נפלאתיך אשר עשית עמהם: "the wonders that you accomplished with them").

era: (1) the people's sinning against the ordinances (ובמשפטיך חטאו־בם, 9:29b) is practically a synonym for their disobeying the commandments (ולא־שמעו למצותיך, 9:29a); (2) their giving a stubborn shoulder (ויתנו כתף סוררת, 9:29c) corresponds to stiffening their neck (ועָרפם הקשׁו, 9:29c); and (3) their not giving an ear (ולא האזינו, 9:30c) is equivalent to their not obeying (ולא שמעו, 9:29c).

More so than any of the prior descriptions of Israel's unfaithfulness, the account in the final cycle of life in the land underlines rejection of instruction as the core of the people's rebellion (9:29–30; cf. 9:16–17b, 18, 26, 28a). The initial references to the Torah (תורה), the commandments (מצות), and the ordinances (משפטים) recall the gifts that YHWH bestowed at Sinai (9:29a–b; cf. 9:13–14). Mention of "your spirit" (רוחך) harks back to the source of instruction that God bestowed on his people in the wilderness (9:30b; cf. 9:20a), which, in turn, restored the gifts he had given (נתן) at Sinai (9:20a; cf. 9:13–14). Moreover, the people's refusal to return to the Torah and to heed the admonitions of the prophets indicates the persistence of their rejection of "your law" (תורתך, 9:29a; cf. 9:26a) and "your prophets" (נביאיך, 9:30b; cf. 9:26b) throughout the era of their life in the land.

The consequence of Israel's rebellion in the second stage is particularly pointed within the broader setting of Ezra-Nehemiah. In this third cycle, YHWH gives his people into the power of "the peoples of the lands" (עמי הארצת, 9:30c) as distinct from "their enemies" (איביהם, 9:28b) or "their oppressors" (צריהם, 9:27a) in the previous cycles. Within the covenant renewal, the "peoples of the lands" are the social and religious category from whom proselytes must separate themselves in order to become part of the covenant community (cf. Neh 10:29). Therefore, in this final cycle of history in the land, the retribution is most poignant since it involves the people's subjugation to those who represent the most persistent political, social, and religious threat to the integrity of the community.

In the third cycle, the stage of rebellion concludes with a double reference to God's mercy that provides the *inclusio* (ברחמיך: "in your mercies," 9:31a; רחום: "[a God of ...] mercy," 9:31b) for this final verse describing past times in the land. The emphasis on God's mercy brings the third cycle to the threshold of redemption, since the other four mentions of divine "mercy" all introduce the eras of salvation (רחום, 9:17c–d; כ/ברחמיך, 19a, 27c, 28c). For the most part, the content of 9:31 reprises—in inverted order—the two accounts of God's mercy in the wilderness: (1) "you, in your abundant mercies, did not abandon them" (9:19a; cf. 9:31a–b); and (2) "you, God, are ... gracious, and merciful ... so you did not abandon them" (9:17c–d; cf. 9:31b).[55] In summary, just as the people's

---

[55] 9:31a–b: ברחמיך הרבים ... לא עזבתם
9:19a: ואתה ברחמיך הרבים לא עזבתם במדבר

rebellion in the land reflects their behavior in the wilderness (9:29; cf. 9:16–17b), so YHWH's forbearing mercy in the land extends the disposition he manifested in the wilderness.

The only clause that is unique to 9:31 provides for the continuity of the people's history into the present: "you did not make an end of them" (לא־עשיתם כלה, 9:31a). This is the only phrase in the prayer that might afford even a slight allusion to the exile.

GOD AND ISRAEL IN THE PRESENT SITUATION (9:32–37)

The conjunctive adverb ועתה ("And now") provides the transition from the recollection (9:6–31) of the past to the description of the present (9:32–37). The intercessory plea (9:32), which introduces this final section, basically consists of three parts: an address to God (אלהינו: "our God," 9:32a); a request that he not neglect the plight of his people (9:32bβ–c); and an adverbial phrase indicating the temporal extension of their affliction (9:32d). However, the emphasis shifts from the actual request to the character of the protagonists by the insertion of two lists: the first elaborating on the attributes of God (9:32a–bα), and the second detailing the composition of the people (9:32c).

The addition of the possessive adjective (אלהינו, 9:32a) is the most personal reference to God in the prayer and anticipates mention of the covenant (שומר הברית: "[who] keeps the covenant," 9:32b) in the confessional statement. Calling on "our God" (אלהינו, 9:32a) is an appropriate response to the Levites' command for the people to bless "your God" (אלהיכם, 9:5). The expression "our God" recurs in the stipulations of the covenant renewal to identify the one who reigns over the temple and the altar (אלהינו, 10:33, 34, 36, 37, 39, 40).

The elaboration of the vocative (אלהינו) via a listing of godly attributes allows confessional statements (9:31b, 32a–bα) to provide the transition from the past to the present. The identical term for "God" (אל, 9:31b; cf. האל, 9:32a) at the beginning of the two statements establishes the link between them. Thus, the continuity of the people's history from past to present is due to the character of God rather than to any trait within the people.

However, the absence of the definite article in the former confession (9:31b) and its presence in the latter (9:32a–b) suggests a transition from viewing God in terms of his compassion for his rebellious people in the wilderness and in the land (9:31b; cf. 9:17c–d) to seeing him in terms of his original election of Abraham (9:32a–b; cf. 9:7). The definite article precedes "God" only in 9:32a (האל) and 9:7a (האלהים). Two other confessional

---

9:31b: לא עזבתם כי אל־חנון ורחום
9:17c–d: אתה אלוה סליחות חנון ורחום ארך־אפים ורב־חסד לא עזבתם

elements link the final section to the earlier remembrance of Abraham: (1) reference to "the covenant" (הברית, 9:32b; cf. 9:8a); and (2) the confession "you are righteous" (ואתה צדיק, 9:33a; cf. צדיק אתה, 9:8d).

The definite article preceding six of the seven words in the confession provides alliteration (האל הגדול הגבור והנורא שומר הברית והחסד), while assonance is apparent in the *ḥōlem* in four successive words (הגדול הגבור והנורא שומר). The term, "the great God" (האל הגדול, 9:32a) recalls the apposition used of YHWH (האלהים הגדול, 8:6), whom Ezra blessed in the liturgy of the first day. חסד is the only attribute that the credal statement in 9:32a–b has in common with 9:17c–d. Mention of God's "keeping the covenant with loyalty" (שומר הברית והחסד, 9:32b) combines allusions to his covenant with Abraham (הברית, 9:8a) and to his relationship to the people in the wilderness era (רב־חסד, 9:17d).

In the petition regarding the present situation, the occurrence of the first-person plural direct object (אשר־מצאתנו: "that has befallen us," 9:32c) constitutes a transition from the third-person plural that characterized the psalm's recounting of the past (cf., e.g., ולא עזבתם: "you did not abandon them," 9:31b). The shift in concern from past generations to the present becomes evident in the possessive adjectives governing the list of officials; for example, references to "their ancestors" (לאבתיהם, 9:23b) now gives way to mention of "our ancestors" (אבתינו, 9:32c).

The list of leaders (9:32c)—civic (kings and princes), religious (priests and prophets), and familial (ancestors)—emphasizes the pervasiveness of the present hardship, which transcends social distinctions and perhaps also suggests a consequent solidarity among its victims.

A notable change in the possessive adjective occurs in the final category "all your people" (לכל־עמך, 9:32c; cf. the alliteration in the prefixes and the assonance in the endings of למלכינו לשרינו ולכהנינו ולנביאנו ולאבתינו). The expression "your people" (עמך, 9:32c) reflects covenant language, complementing the vocative "our God" (אלהינו, 9:32a). Moreover, the comprehensive expression "all [your] people" (כל־עמך, 9:32c) recalls the inclusivity of the assembly on the first day of the seventh month (כל־העם, 8:1, 3, 5 [3x], 6, 9 [bis], 11, 12).

Contextualizing the present situation within a time span extending from the distant past is a literary device that the psalm shares in common with the account of the celebration of Booths (9:32d; cf. 8:17).[56]

The confession of sin (9:33–35) provides the explanation for the hardship that has befallen the people. This confession consists of two parts distinguished by the pronouns identifying the people: initially the first-person plural (אנחנו: "we," 9:33b) and subsequently the third-person

---

[56] 9:32d: מימי מלכי אשור עד היום הזה
8:17: מימי ישוע בן־נון ... עד היום הזה

plural (והם: "they," 9:35a). Thus, the first subunit expresses the sentiment of the whole people in the present generation (9:33a–b), whereas the second subunit redirects attention to the leaders in previous generations (9:34–35).

The first subunit (9:33a–b) consists of two lines in which the first half of each line focuses on God and the second on the people. The pronominal subjects establish a contrast between God (ואתה: "you," 9:33a) and the people (ואנחנו: "we," 9:33b). These pronouns constitute a narrative juncture, since this is the final occurrence of אתה (eleven times in 9:6–37) and the first instance of אנחנו (four times in 9:33–37) in the psalm.

The first line of the subunit (9:33a) announces the vindication of God vis-à-vis the hardship experienced by his people. The declaration "you are righteous" (ואתה צדיק, 9:33a) here refers to his exercising retributive justice and to his practicing faithfulness (כי־אמת עשית, 9:33a) rather than to his fulfilling a promise (cf. צדיק אתה: "you are righteous," 9:8d). "All that has come upon us" (כל־הבא עלינו, 9:33a) is a synonym for "all the hardship that has befallen us" (כל־התלאה אשר־מצאתנו, 9:32b–c).

The second line of the subunit is a bicolon that concentrates on patterns of action in declaring contrasting verdicts of God's innocence and his people's guilt: "you have practiced faithfulness, but we have behaved wickedly" (9:33b).

Having included the present generation in the corporate confession of guilt (ואנחנו הרשענו: "but we have behaved wickedly," 9:33b), the psalm then ascribes the blame specifically to the leaders in the past (9:34–35).[57] Assonance in the form of six first-person plural (nû) endings provides a smooth literary transition from the community to its authorities (ואנחנו הרשענו ואת־מלכינו שרינו כהנינו ואבתינו: "we have behaved wickedly, our kings, our princes, our priests, and our ancestors," 9:33b–34a). Conversely, the particle את serves as a demarcation between the "we" (ואנחנו, 9:33b) and the subsequent four categories of leaders (9:34a).[58]

In summary, 9:34–35 attributes to the leaders the previously mentioned patterns of rebellion during the settlement (9:34a–b, 35c; cf. 9:26–30) while recalling the benefits of the land that God had originally bestowed in the

---

[57] W. Chrostowski reads 9:34a as the continuation of the sentence that begins in 9:33bβ: "Also we condemn both our kings, our princes, our priests, and our fathers" ("An Examination of Conscience by God's People As Exemplified in Neh 9,6–37," *BZ* 34 [1990]: 255–57). However, his reading does not take account of the *wāw* preceding את (which he considers to be the marker for the objects of the verb רשע [*hipʿil*]).

[58] P. P. Saydon views the construction את + nominative as a means of emphasizing the subject(s) ("Meanings and Uses of the Particle את," *VT* 14 [1964]: 192–210).

occupation (9:35a–b; cf. 9:22–25). The resulting portrait contrasts the leaders' infidelity with God's beneficence.

The list of leaders in 9:34a repeats the one in 9:32c except for the omission of "our prophets," the one category of leaders who had cooperated with God during the settlement era (נביאנו, 9:32c; cf. נביאיך: 9:26b, 30b). Indeed, the prophets' role had been "to warn" the people, the very activity recalled by the final words of the verse (תעידת בהם: "you warned them," 9:34b; cf. העידו בם, 9:26b; תעד בם, 9:30b).

It is noteworthy that, contrary to other lists of leaders in the covenant renewal, the Levites who declaim the psalm are not cited among those who trespassed the Torah and refused to heed the prophets (9:34; cf. 8:9, 13).

Assonance is evident throughout 9:34 in: (1) the four subjects (ending in *nû*: [ואת־מלכינו שרינו כהנינו ואבתינו]); (2) the two main verbs (ending in *û*, preceded by לא [לא הקשיבו; לא עשו]); and (3) the three objects (ending in *kā* [עדותיך; מצותיך; תורתך]).

In terms of content, 9:34 alludes back to the stages of rebellion that initiated each of the three cycles of history in the land. Mention of Israel's lack of compliance with the "Torah" and of adherence to the "commandments" recalls the beginning of the third cycle in particular (תורתך; מצותיך, 9:34a–b; cf. 9:29a). The third object, "your warnings" (עדותיך), introduces the subordinate clause that alludes to God's responding to the people's rebellion by "warning them" in every cycle of history in the land (תעידת בהם, 9:34b; cf. העידו בם, 9:26b; ותעד בהם, 9:29a; תעד בם, 9:30b).

The emphatic pronoun והם ("they," 9:35a) recalls the initial rebellion in the wilderness (9:16a) as well as the final cycle of rebellion in the land (והמה: "but they," 9:29a). Note that the latter pronoun also followed upon the account of God's warning (תעידת בהם, 9:34b; cf. תעד בהם, 9:29a). The distinguishing feature of 9:35 is the interruption introduced by the three expressions of location between the subject (והם: "they," 9:35a) and the verbs (לא עבדוך ולא־שבו: "[they] did not serve you and did not turn back," 9:35c). In the intervening section, alliteration in the prefixes links the three descriptions of the surroundings (*be*: ובארץ ... במלכותם ובטובך). Repetition in the adjectival clauses (אשר־נתת להם: "that you presented for them," 9:35a; אשר־נתת לפניהם: "that you presented before them," 9:35b) provides parallelism between "their kingdom" (מלכות, 9:35a) and "the land" (הארץ, 9:35b). Moreover, the two negative verbs that follow their respective subjects balance the closing and opening lines of 9:34–35 (לא עבדוך ולא־שבו: "[they] did not serve you and did not turn back," 9:35c; cf. לא עשו ... ולא הקשיבו: "[they] have not kept ... and they have not paid attention," 9:34a–b).

The description that intervenes between the subject (הם, 9:35a) and the verbs (9:35c) directs attention to the land. Almost all the vocabulary in this depiction of the landscape derives from the account of the settlement (9:22–25): (1) מלכותם ("their kingdom," 9:35a; cf. ממלכות: "kingdoms," 9:22a); (2) בטובך הרב ("amid your abundant goodness," 9:35a; cf. בטובך הגדול: "in your great goodness," 9:25d); (3) נתת להם ("you presented for them," 9:35a, b; cf. ותתן להם: "you gave them," 9:22a); (4) ארץ ("land," 9:35b; cf. 9:22b [bis], 23b, 24a, 24b, 24c); and (5) ארץ ... השמנה ("the fertile land," 9:35b; cf. אדמה שמנה: "fertile land," 9:25a). Thus, the monstrous nature of the leaders' offenses is accentuated by their commission within the environs that bespeak a three-dimensional blessing: (1) political sovereignty (מלכותם: "their kingdom," 35a); (2) divine benevolence (טובך הרב: "your abundant goodness," 9:35a); and (3) material abundance (בארץ הרחבה והשמנה: "on the broad and fertile land," 9:35b).

The leaders' refusal to turn from evil reinforces the earlier description of the people's resistance to God's warnings (לא שׁוב: "[they] did not turn back," 9:35c; cf. עוד ... להשיבם [hip'il]: "to warn ... in order to turn them back," 9:26b, 29a; also, עוד [hip'il]: "to warn," 9:34b).

The description of the present distress (9:36–37) is marked by the reintroduction of the pronoun "we" (אנחנו, 9:36a; cf. 9:33b) and by the reference to "today" (היום, 9:36a; cf. היום הזה, 9:32d). The linkage between 9:35c and 9:36a is ironic: because the leaders in the past would not "serve" (לא עבדוך, 9:35c), the people now are "slaves" (עבדים, 9:36a). Bridging the gap from past to present is the abiding preoccupation with "the land that you gave to our ancestors" (הארץ אשר־נתתה לאבתינו, 9:36b; cf. ארץ ... אשר־נתת לפניהם, 9:35b).

The structural integrity of 9:36 is remarkable. The parallel assertions of the people's slavery (9:36a, 36c) frame the recollection of the gift of the land (9:36b; cf. 9:35b). Nevertheless, the one difference between the two parallel assertions is significant: the opening statement specifies the time of slavery (הנה אנחנו היום עבדים: "Look, we are slaves this day," 9:36a), whereas the concluding statement highlights the place of slavery (הנה אנחנו עבדים עליה: "look, we are slaves upon it," 9:36a). The transfer of emphasis from time to place reflects the concern for the land (הארץ) in the intervening line (9:36b). The language here alludes—in reverse order—to the second and third designations of the leaders' environs in the previous verse: (1) "the land that you gave" (הארץ אשר־נתתה [לאבתינו], 9:36b; cf. [לפניהם] אשר־נתת ... בארץ, 9:35b); and (2) "its [your] goodness" (טובה, 9:36b; cf. בטובך, 9:35a). The allusions to these two designations set the stage for the contrast between the land as the "kingdom" of the past leaders (במלכותם, 9:35a) and as the place in which the present generation are "slaves" (עבדים, 9:36a, 36c).

The vocabulary describing God's objective in providing the ancestors with the land (9:36bβ) recalls the last line depicting the occupation: (1) לאכל ("to eat," 9:36b; cf. ויאכלו: "They ate," 9:25d); and (2) טובה ("its goodness," 9:36b; cf. טובך: "your ... goodness," 9:25d; cf. also בתים מלאים־כל־טוב: "houses filled with all good things," 9:25b).

The absence of a main verb in 9:36 is noteworthy. Insofar as the principal statements take the form of parallel nominal clauses (הנה אנחנו היום עבדים: "Look, we are slaves this day," 9:36a; הנה אנחנו עבדים עליה: "look, we are slaves upon it," 9:36c), they grammatically resemble the confessional statements at the beginning of the psalm (אתה־הוא יהוה לבדך: "You are YHWH, you alone," 9:6a; אתה־הוא יהוה האלהים: "You are YHWH, the God," 9:7a). Such similarity in construction calls attention to the contrast between the psalm's initial confessions that declare the sovereignty of YHWH (9:6a, 7a) and its final declarations that announce the slavery of his people (9:36a, 36c).

The repetition of the prepositional phrase "upon it" (עליה, 9:36c; cf. 9:6c), referring to the land, further links this description of the people's status as slaves to the sovereignty of YHWH as creator. If YHWH made "the earth and all that is upon it" (הארץ וכל־אשר עליה, 9:6c), then, even now, he must reign over "the land" (הארץ, 9:36b) and his people who are slaves "upon it" (עליה, 9:36c).

The final verse, which describes the people's plight (9:37), reflects syntactical similarity to the previous verse insofar as nominal clauses stand at the beginning (ותבואתה מרבה למלכים: "Moreover, its abundant yield belongs to kings," 9:37a) and at the end (ובצרה גדולה אנחינו: "Thus, we are in great distress," 9:37b). The section between these main clauses consists of an adjectival clause modifying "kings" (מלכים) with subsidiary elaborations on the manner in which these monarchs exercise their hegemony. These "kings" (מלכים) are counterpoised to "our kings" (מלכינו, 9:32c, 34a) and continue the tradition of foreign rule begun by the "kings of Assyria" (מלכי אשור, 9:32d). The fact that the same adjectival clause that was earlier used of the land here modifies these kings (אשר־נתתה עלינו: "whom you have set over us," 9:37a; cf. אשר־נתתה לאבתינו: "which you gave to our ancestors," 9:36b) indicates that their rule is providential: God "gave" them as regents over the people just as he gave the land to their ancestors (cf. also אשר־נתת להם, 9:35a; אשר־נתת לפניהם, 9:35b).

The preposition על links 9:37a with 9:36b and thereby alludes to a state of domination: as the slaves are "upon" the land (עליה, 9:36b), so the kings are "over" the people (עליה, 9:37a). The explanatory addition accentuates the nuance of oppression: the kings "rule over [על] our bodies." Here the participle for the kings' ruling (משלים) implies duration, while the noun for the people's bodies (גויתינו) suggests more a corpse than a vital physique.

The extension of the kings' power to using the livestock "as they please" hints at an ironic reversal of fortunes, since this expression earlier described the people's treatment of the previous kings and people of the land at the time of occupation (כרצונם: "as they please," 9:37b; cf. 9:24c). Nevertheless, it is noteworthy that while the psalm describes the foreign monarchs as reaping the produce and dominating the populace and the livestock, it does not speak of these kings taking possession of the land (הארץ, 9:36b). Thus, the psalm implies that the land is an irrevocable gift from God to his people (אשר־נתתה לאבתינו: "which you gave to our ancestors," 9:36b).

The expression "because of our sins" (בחטאותינו, 9:37a) represents the only explanation in the final lines for God's installing foreign rulers over the people. Moreover, its first-person possessive pronoun corresponds with the earlier first-person confession (אנחנו הרשענו: "we have behaved wickedly," 9:33b). Hence, in the end, the present generation assumes a share of the sin that they had attributed primarily to their ancestors (cf. במשפטיך חטאו־בם: "they sinned against your ordinances," 9:29b; 9:34–35). This concluding of the psalm with the people's attributing the present distress to their own "sins" (חטאתינו, 9:37a) after describing their ancestors' misdeeds (9:34–35) corresponds with the introductory narrative description of the assembly's confessing "their sins [חטאתיהם] and the guilt of their ancestors" (9:2).

The final clause locates the present situation within the broad scope of history. The term "distress" (צרה, 9:37b) recalls the triple occurrence of the root in the first settlement cycle (בצרתם, ויצרו, צריהם, 9:27a–b) and thereby indicates that the present day (היום, 9:36a) is the stage for experiencing retribution for previous crimes. Moreover, this allusion to 9:27b suggests the reason for reciting the psalm: just as the people cried out at the time of distress (ובעת צרתם, 9:27b), so, through the leadership of the Levites, they now voice this prayer when they are "in great distress" (בצרה גדולה, 9:37b). In so doing, they have reason for hope, since history teaches that God hears the cry of his people (9:9a, 27b, 28c); in addition, the "greatness" of their distress (צרה גדולה, 9:37b) recalls the "greatness" of their God (האל הגדול, 9:32a). The emphatic position of the pronoun at the end of the prayer (אנחנו: "we," 9:37b), designating the people in the statement of distress, is the counterpoint to the emphatic position of the pronoun at its beginning (אתה: "you," 9:6a), designating God in the confession of faith.

THE LANGUAGE AND FORM OF THE PRAYER

In this section, I locate the Levites' prayer within the broader spectrum of biblical tradition by identifying those texts to which it is related most closely in content and form. My investigation consists of two parts: first, in a line-by-line analysis, I trace the derivation of every significant expression in the prayer; second, in a summary overview of form and content, I compare the Levites' prayer with both historical psalms and penitential confessions elsewhere in the MT in order to highlight the uniqueness of this prayer within biblical literature and its function within Ezra-Nehemiah.

THE EXPRESSIONS IN THE LEVITES' PRAYER

In order to point out the diverse origins of the material that comprise the different parts of the prayer, I will examine the expressions used in each line under the same headings employed in the literary analysis. For the sake of clarity, I identify in parentheses the number of the verse under discussion.

GOD AND ISRAEL THROUGHOUT THE PAST (9:6–31)

YHWH's foundational activity (9:6–8)

The creation of the universe (9:6). Deuteronomic vocabulary provides the essential substructure for the description of creation (9:6a–c). The first line of the prayer declares the uniqueness of YHWH.[59] The proclamation resembles similar expressions in the prayer of Hezekiah (2 Kgs 19:15, 19 = Isa 37:16, 20) and in Ps 86:10.[60] The similarity with the beginning of Hezekiah's prayer extends to the king's assertion, "You have made the heavens and the earth" (2 Kgs 19:15 = Isa 37:16; also, Jer 32:17; cf. Neh 9:6b–c). However, the Levites' psalm elaborates on the merism "the heavens and the earth." The "highest heavens" (שׁמי השׁמים) occurs elsewhere in prayer to emphasize God's transcendence and sovereignty (1 Kgs 8:27 = 2 Chr 6:18; 2 Chr 2:6; Ps 148:4). Nevertheless, the phrasing of the Levites' prayer is closest to the Deuteronomic assertion that provides the context for God's election of Israel: "Behold, to YHWH your God belong the heavens and the highest heavens, the earth and all that is in it" (הן ליהוה אלהיך השׁמים ושׁמי השׁמים הארץ וכל־אשׁר־בה, Deut 10:14). Nehemiah 9:6 exhibits similarities in vocabulary to this verse that extend from YHWH (יהוה) and "the heavens ... the highest heavens" (השׁמים [ו]שׁמי השׁמים) to "the earth" (הארץ). In addition, the Levites' prayer provides a variation on

---

[59] For the intrabiblical parallels of Neh 9:6–37, I have consulted Myers, *Ezra, Nehemiah,* 167–69; Anderson, "The Levitical Prayer," 145–200; and Gilbert, "Notes," 7–24.

[60] Neh 9:6:   לבדך   יהוה   אתה־הוא
    2 Kgs 19:15: לבדך   האלהים   אתה־הוא
    2 Kgs 19:19: לבדך   אלהים   יהוה   אתה
    Isa 37:16:   לבדך   האלהים   אתה־הוא
    Isa 37:20:   לבדך   יהוה   אתה
    Ps 86:10:   לבדך   אלהים   אתה

this verse's final phrase (וְכָל־אֲשֶׁר־בָּהּ, Deut 10:14; cf. וְכָל־אֲשֶׁר עָלֶיהָ, Neh 9:6cα). A virtual duplicate of the final phrase in Deut 10:14 occurs not in reference to the earth but in connection with its parallel, the seas (הַיַּמִּים וְכָל־אֲשֶׁר־בָּהֶם): "the seas and all that is in them," Neh 9:6cβ; cf. וְכָל־אֲשֶׁר־בָּהּ: "and all that is in it [the earth]," Deut 10:14).

Vocabulary from the Tetrateuch, the Prophets, and the Psalms elaborates on the Deuteronomic portrait of creation (Neh 9:6c–d). Extending the creation of the heavens to mention of "all their host" (כָּל־צְבָאָם) represents a variation on such a diversity of texts.[61] Genesis 2:1 refers to "the heavens and the earth" in the same order as Neh 9:6b–c but relates "all their host" to both the heavens and the earth. Isaiah 45:12 speaks of the earth, then the heavens, and—as in Neh 9:6b—associates "all their host" only with the heavens. Psalm 33:6 exhibits two lexical affinities with Neh 9:6b in describing the "making" (עָשָׂה) of the heavens and the creation of "all their host" (כָּל־צְבָאָם).

Moreover, the description of YHWH's "making ... the heavens ... the earth ... the seas and all that is them" resonates with Exod 20:11 and Ps 146:6.[62]

The assertion that YHWH gives life to all (מְחַיֶּה אֶת־כֻּלָּם, Neh 9:6d) summarizes the verse's previous recounting of his creative activities. Job 33:4 is the only other MT text in which עשׂה and חוה (*pi'el*) occur in parallelism: "The spirit of God made me, and the breath of the Almighty gives me life" (רוּחַ־אֵל עָשָׂתְנִי וְנִשְׁמַת שַׁדַּי תְּחַיֵּנִי). The witness of this text suggests that מְחַיֶּה describes God's acting not only to sustain but also to bring forth life.[63] Elsewhere, with God as subject the *pi'el* of חיה generally denotes his action of preserving or restoring human beings in the face of impending or actual disaster (e.g., Pss 33:19; 41:3; 71:20; 138:7; 143:11; Hos 6:2). This action represents God's twofold power to "put to death and to bring to life" (cf. Deut 32:39; 1 Sam 2:6), of which the Levites focus only on the latter (Neh 9:6d). Due to its association with God's work of redeeming Israel (cf. Deut 32:39; 1 Sam 2:6; Pss 80:19; 85:7; Hos 6:2), the *pi'el* חיה provides a remarkable transition from creation (Neh 9:6) to salvation history (Neh 9:7–37).

---

61 The "host" (צָבָא) of the heavens is the totality of extraterrestrial cosmic bodies. Alternatively, in biblical literature the "host of heaven" (צְבָא הַשָּׁמַיִם) designates either (1) the cosmic forces personified as YHWH's army (e.g., Josh 5:14–15; Isa 13:4), or (2) the council of heaven gathered around YHWH (1 Kgs 22:19–23). See E. T. Mullen Jr., "Hosts, Host of Heaven," *ABD* 3:301–4.

62 Note the similarities in expression:
Neh 9:6b–c: יהוה ... עֹשֵׂה אֶת־הַשָּׁמַיִם ... הָאָרֶץ ... הַיַּמִּים וְכָל־אֲשֶׁר בָּהֶם
Exod 20:11: עָשָׂה יְהוָה אֶת־הַשָּׁמַיִם וְאֶת־הָאָרֶץ אֶת־הַיָּם וְאֶת כָּל־אֲשֶׁר־בָּם
Ps 146:6: [יהוה] עֹשֶׂה שָׁמַיִם וָאָרֶץ אֶת־הַיָּם וְאֶת כָּל־אֲשֶׁר־בָּם

63 Cf. Williamson, *Ezra, Nehemiah*, 300; Blenkinsopp, *Ezra-Nehemiah*, 297.

Mention of the host of heaven worshiping YHWH sharply contrasts with the Deuteronomistic descriptions of Israel's apostasy, which consisted precisely in the people worshiping the host of heaven (וישתחו לכל־צבא השמים: "they worshiped all the host of heaven," 2 Kgs 21:3 = 2 Chr 33:3; cf. Deut 4:19; 17:3; Jer 8:2; Zeph 1:5).

The election of Abraham (9:7–8). The account of the covenant with Abraham (9:7–8) takes the form of a meditation on Gen 15:6–21 (and 17:5), which is supplemented primarily by Deuteronomistic elements.

(9:7) The first colon approximates a complete credal statement, "You, YHWH, are God" (אתה יהוה האלהים, 1 Kgs 18:37). The most succinct form of this statement is found in the third person: "YHWH is God" (יהוה האלהים, Josh 22:34; cf. 1 Kgs 18:21). In Chronicles, this same expression serves as a divine title, "YHWH God" (1 Chr 22:1, 19; 2 Chr 32:16). In Neh 9:7, this confession of faith (cf. 1 Kgs 18:37) becomes the subject of the verbs that follow in the next three cola.

Nowhere else does the MT speak of God "choosing" (בחר) Abraham (Neh 9:7a). The use of the verb in this case seems to originate in its frequent application to Israel in the Deuteronomic tradition (e.g., Deut 4:37; 7:7; 10:15; 14:2; 1 Kgs 3:8). In prayers and prophetic texts, the verb is applied to Jacob in view of his identification with Israel (Pss 47:4; 135:4; Isa 14:1; 41:8; 44:1–2; Ezek 20:5). Isaiah 41:8 may account for the transfer of the verb from Jacob to Abraham: "You, Israel, my servant, Jacob whom I have chosen [בחרתיך], the offspring of Abraham, my friend." In this statement, Deutero-Isaiah identifies his audience of exiles as the true Israel, the "offspring of Abraham" (זרע אברהם, 41:8–9; cf. 51:1–2). Such a declaration indicates that the covenant with Abraham was particularly vital to defining the authentic Israel in exilic controversies. Evidence in Ezekiel discloses the roots of the debate. Ezekiel quotes those who remained in Judah during the exile as asserting that they regarded themselves as the genuine descendants of Abraham and therefore the rightful inheritors of the land (Ezek 33:24). Furthermore, in the estimation of those who remained in the land, the exiles—by the very fact of their deportation—had lost any claim to the land (11:15). In the face of such assertions, the prophet sides with the exiles in declaring that they will return to possess the land (11:16–21; cf. 33:25–29).[64]

Up to this point, the Ezra-Nehemiah narrative emphasizes that the legitimate Israel of the postexilic era is comprised of the exiles of Benjamin

---

[64] S. Japhet, "People and Land in the Restoration Period," in *Das Land Israel in biblischer Zeit* (ed. G. Strecker; Jerusalem Symposium 1983; GTA 25; Göttingen: Vandenhoeck & Ruprecht, 1983), 106–9.

and Judah who returned to the land (e.g., Ezra 1:5; 2:1–70; 6:16; 9:4; 10:6–8, 9; Neh 7:6–72a; 8:17). However, the Levites' prayer does not explicitly mention the exile (cf. 9:30–31) and therefore does not enter into the polemics regarding the claims of the exiles.[65] In summary, while the focus on the covenant with Abraham in the Levites' prayer might derive from the exilic and postexilic controversies over legitimate rights to the land, the prayer does not strive to support the claims of the exiles, as does the preceding narrative in Ezra-Nehemiah.

The first half of 9:7b is practically a transposition of Gen 15:7.[66]

The expression "to change the name" (שׂוּם שֵׁם) occurs also in 2 Kgs 17:34 in reference to YHWH's changing Jacob's name to Israel (cf. Dan 5:12 [Aramaic]).[67] Otherwise, the expression is found in the Deuteronomistic descriptions of YHWH's "putting" his name in his chosen place (Deut 12:21; 14:24; 1 Kgs 8:21; 9:3; 11:36; 2 Chr 6:20). Nehemiah 9:7b here refers to Gen 17:5, which recounts God's renaming of Abraham. However, unlike the text in Genesis, the prayer does not mention the significance of this name change.

(9:8) The first three lines of Neh 9:8 refer to Gen 15:6–21. In Neh 9:8aα, mention of "faithfulness" (נאמן) alludes to Gen 15:6, which describes Abraham's "belief" (האמן) in YHWH. The uniqueness of God's discovering (מצא) fidelity (אמן) in someone is apparent in light of the proverbial question, "Who can find one who is faithful?" (ואיש אמונים מי ימצא, Prov 20:6).

In the same vein, Jeremiah challenges his contemporaries to search throughout Jerusalem to find (מצא) one person who "seeks truthfulness" (מבקש אמונה, Jer 5:1). Later tradition relates Abraham's faithfulness to his passing the test of his willingness to sacrifice Isaac (Sir 44:20; 1 Macc 2:52). Two of the three words in the final colon of Sir 44:20 occur in Neh 9:8: ובניסוי נמצא נאמן ("and when tested, he was found faithful").[68] The evidence of Prov 20:6; Jer 5:1; and Sir 44:20 shows that the verb "to find" (מצא) in 9:8a connotes the discovery of another person's character within the context of a long-standing relationship.

---

[65] Cf. Williamson ("Structure and Historiography in Nehemiah 9," in *Proceedings of the Ninth World Congress of Jewish Studies [1985]. Panel Sessions: Bible Studies and Ancient Near East* [ed. M. Goshen-Gottstein. Jerusalem: Magnes, Hebrew University, 1988], 129–30), who asserts that both the reference to Abraham and the absence of reference to the exile suggest that Neh 9:6–37 originated among the people who remained in Judah during the exile and whose convictions are quoted in Ezek 11:15 and 33:24.

[66] Neh 9:7: והוצאתו מאור כשדים
Gen 15:7: אני יהוה אשר הוצאתיך מאור כשדים

[67] The analogous expression in Aramaic describes the king's renaming Daniel (שׂם־שׁמה, Dan 5:12).

[68] M. H. Segal, ספר בן סירא השלם (2d ed.; Jerusalem: Bialik Institute, 1958), 306.

The description of YHWH's making the covenant with Abraham (Neh 9:8a) refers to Gen 15:18, "On that day, YHWH made a covenant with Abram."[69] Sirach 44:20 also speaks of the Most High's entering into covenant with Abraham (ובא בברית עמו) but does so before mentioning the test that manifested Abraham's faithfulness.

Nehemiah 9:8b–c continues the reference to the covenant narrated in Gen 15:18–21.[70] The six peoples in Neh 9:8 occur among the list of ten in Gen 15:19–21. However, the order of the first four is identical with Exod 3:8, 17, although, in contrast to Neh 9:8, both of these texts mention the Hivites rather than the Girgashites. Within Ezra-Nehemiah, the list recalls Ezra 9:1, which mentions five of the peoples in Neh 9:8b–c but in a different order.[71]

In the final part of 9:8b–c, the phrase "to give to his offspring [the land]" recalls the language of Gen 15:18.[72] Moreover, mention of "his offspring" (זרעו, Neh 9:8c) also reflects the concern in the postexilic era to identify the true "offspring of Abraham (cf. זרעו: "his offspring," Neh 9:8c).

The expression that describes YHWH's fulfilling his word (קום את־דבר [*hipʿil*]) occurs primarily in Deuteronomistic literature.[73] The text exhibiting the closest kinship to Neh 9:8dα is Deut 9:5, which explains YHWH's bringing the people into the land as the fulfillment of the word he spoke to Abraham, Isaac, and Jacob. Within Ezra-Nehemiah, the same expression occurs in the curse upon anyone who "does not keep the word" of Nehemiah's social reform (Neh 5:13).

The final confession of YHWH's righteousness (כי צדיק אתה, 9:8dβ) relates to his fidelity to his promise to provide the land for the offspring of Abraham. Insofar as YHWH's justice is manifest in his election of and covenant with Abraham (9:7–8), it is akin to the righteousness that he

---

[69] Neh 9:8: וכרות עמו הברית
Gen 15:18: ביום ההוא כרת יהוה את־אברם הברית

[70] At first sight, the introductory verbal construction (לתת) seems to reflect Gen 15:7 (cf. the first colon of Neh 9:8). This would account for the LXX reading δοῦναι αὐτῷ (cf. לתת לך: "to give him"). However, the list of peoples suggests that Neh 9:8 is rather a reflection on Gen 15:18. The verbal construction is repeated, and its indirect object is clarified (לתת לזרעו: "to give to his offspring") after the list of the peoples.

[71] Ezra 9:1: "the Canaanites, the Hittites, the Perizzites, the Jebusites ... and the Amorites."

[72] Neh 9:8b–c: לתת לזרעו [את־הארץ]
Gen 15:18: לזרעך נתתי את־הארץ הזאת

[73] Deut 9:5; 1 Sam 1:23; 2 Sam 7:25; 1 Kgs 2:4; 6:12; 8:20 (= 2 Chr 6:10); 12:15 (= 2 Chr 10:15); Jer 28:6; 29:10; cf. Dan 9:12.

displayed in calling forth Israel (בצדק: "in righteousness," Isa 42:6) and in raising up Cyrus (בצדק: "in righteousness," Isa 45:13).[74]

The wilderness period (9:9–21)

The era of harmony (9:9–15). In the first part of this section (9:9–11), the portrayal of God's activities in Egypt (9:9–10) is fundamentally a reflection on the narrative in Exodus that incorporates established expressions from Deuteronomic and liturgical traditions. The account of the passage through the Reed Sea (9:11) reflects the language of hymns as well as the narrative of the event in Exodus.

(9:9) The parallelism of verbs and their objects in 9:9a reflects Exod 3:7: "I have see the affliction of my people in Egypt, and I have heard their cry."[75] However, in Neh 9:9a, "their cry" arises, not within the setting of their life in Egypt (Exod 3:7), but rather in their reaction to Pharaoh's army at the Reed Sea (cf. Exod 14:10). Mention of the "ancestors" (אבות) reflects traditional language regarding the exodus.[76]

(9:10) Mention of the "signs and wonders" that YHWH accomplished in Egypt (9:10a) occurs in other historical prayers (Jer 32:20–21; Pss 78:43; 105:27; 135:9). The expression seems emblematic of Deuteronomic tradition (Deut 4:34; 6:22; 7:19; 13:1, 2; 26:8; 28:46; 29:3; 34:11; cf. Exod 7:3; Isa 8:18; 20:3).[77] In terms of vocabulary, Neh 9:10a is a pastiche of texts. All the language of its first colon occurs in Deut 6:22: "YHWH produced [נתן] signs and wonders [אותת ומפתים], great and serious, against Egypt, against Pharaoh [בפרעה], and against all his household." However, the list of recipients in 9:10a is closer to Deut 34:11 ("Pharaoh," "all his servants," and "all his land") and to Ps 135:9 ("Pharaoh and all his servants").

The one element of Neh 9:10a that is unparalleled in any other text is the final category: "all the people of his land" (ובכל־עם ארצו). The distinctiveness of this expression underscores its link with similar expressions in the poem, that is, "peoples" (עמים, 9:22), "peoples of the land" (עמי הארץ,

---

[74] Both these texts follow upon descriptions of YHWH as creator (Isa 42:5; 45:11–12; cf. Neh 9:6). J. J. Scullion, "Righteousness: Old Testament," *ABD* 5:733.

[75] Neh 9:9: ותרא את־עני אבתינו במצרים ואת־זעקתם שמעת
Exod 3:7: ראה ראיתי את־עני עמי אשר במצרים ואת־צעקתם שמעתי

[76] Num 20:15; Deut 29:25; Josh 24:6, 14, 17; Judg 2:12; 6:13; 1 Sam 12:6, 8; 1 Kgs 8:21, 53; 9:9; 2 Kgs 21:15; Jer 7:22, 25; 11:4, 7; 31:32; 34:13; Ezek 20:36; Pss 78:12; 106:7. In relation to Neh 9:9, 1 Sam 12:8 is especially worth noting: "your fathers cried to YHWH" (ויזעקו אבותיכם אל־יהוה).

[77] F. J. Helfmyer, "אות," *TDOT* 1:168.

9:24), and "peoples of the lands" (עמי הארצת, 9:30). Moreover, YHWH's action against such groups provides the basis for the community's subsequently pledging their separation from them, which extends to renunciation of intermarriage as well as doing commerce on the Sabbath (10:29, 31, 32).

In 9:10bα, the verb זוד (*hipʿil*) suggests an allusion to Exod 18:11 (זוד *qal*), which is the only other text in the MT that describes the Egyptians' acting insolently toward the Israelites.

Nehemiah 9:10bβ is practically identical to Jer 32:20 and Dan 9:15: "You made a name for yourself as in this day" (ותעש[ה]־לך שם כיום הזה). Thus, the expression occurs only in penitential prayers and exclusively in reference to God's activities in the exodus (cf. also Isa 63:12). Viewing the activities of Israel's past as extending to the present links this psalm with Ezra's confessional prayer (כיום הזה, Neh 9:10bβ; cf. Ezra 9:7, 15). Note, however, the distinction between the two forms of activity that endure to the present: the Levites speak of YHWH's wonders, whereas Ezra reflects on Israel's guilt.

(9:11) Nehemiah 9:11a is a pastiche of Exod 14:16, 21–22a (narrative) and Exod 15:19b (poetry).[78] The theme of YHWH's "parting" (בקע) the sea also occurs in other historical psalms (e.g., Ps 78:13; cf. Isa 63:12). The verb describing the people's "passing through" (עבר) reflects Exod 15:16b and occurs with "the midst of the sea" in a traditional phrase (ויעברו בתוך־הים, Num 33:8). Nehemiah 9:11b reflects the content of Exod 15:4–5, although only the final words of the latter text (במצולת כמו־אבן) afford linguistically identical vocabulary. However, "their pursuers" (רדפיהם, Neh 9:11) also reflects the language of Exodus since, in that book, the verb "to pursue" refers exclusively to the movement of the Egyptians against the Israelites at the Reed Sea (רדף, Exod 14:4, 8, 9, 23; 15:9). Nehemiah 9:11b makes two alterations in connection with the expression for YHWH's "throwing [the enemy] into the sea" (ירה בים, Exod 15:4): (1) the verb שלך ("to cast") takes the place of ירה ("to throw"); and (2) במצולת ("into the depths," Exod 15:5) replaces בים ("into the sea"). Moreover, the expression "mighty waters" (במים עזים) occurs elsewhere only in Isa 43:16, where it describes the same sea event. Apparently, the phrase developed as a traditional variation of במים אדירים ("in the mighty waters," Exod 15:10).[79]

---

[78] Neh 9:11a: והים בקעת לפניהם
Exod 14:16: ואתה הרם את־מטך ונטה את־ידך על־הים ובקעהו
Exod 14:21b: ויבקעו המים

Neh 9:11a: ויעברו בתוך־הים ביבשה
Exod 14:22a: ויבאו בני־ישראל בתוך־הים ביבשה
Exod 15:19b: בני־ישראל הלכו ביבשה בתוך־הים

[79] Cf. Anderson, "The Levitical Prayer," 155–56.

After addressing the events associated with the exodus, the psalm turns to God's gifts in the wilderness (Neh 9:12–15). The description of God's provisions of the columns of cloud and fire, the commandments, and bread and water (9:12–15b) constitutes a distinctive reflection on these episodes in the Exodus narratives. Hymnic traditions (especially Pss 78 and 105) influence the descriptions of the first and third endowments (the cloud and fire; the bread and water). This material exhibits few specifically Deuteronomic characteristics. By contrast, God's command for the people to take possession of the land (Neh 9:15c–d) manifests both Deuteronomic and Priestly characteristics.

(9:12) Apart from Neh 9:12, 19, the "column of cloud" (עמוד ענן) and the "column of fire" (עמוד אש) are mentioned only four times in the MT (Exod 13:21, 22; 14:24; Num 14:14). Furthermore, the Levites' prayer is unique insofar as it describes the columns of cloud and fire themselves leading the people, whereas the pentateuchal texts invariably speak of YHWH's presence "in" these columns. Nehemiah 9:12a–bα represents a rearrangement of Exod 13:21, which supplies all the vocabulary except the object marker (את־הדרך: "the way," 9:12bα).[80] However, the context is different in each case: Exod 13:21 describes the scene prior to the crossing of the Reed Sea, whereas Neh 9:12a–bα concerns the period following the crossing. In Neh 9:12a the preposition ב (in בעמוד [bis]) has an instrumental sense, whereas in Exod 13:21 it exhibits the aspect of locality.[81]

Mention of YHWH's providing a cloud during the day and a fire to light the night occurs in two other historical psalms (Pss 78:14; 105:39). Nehemiah 9:12bβ echoes the content of Deut 1:33, which describes YHWH's going before the people in cloud and fire to show them the way through the wilderness.[82] The phrase "the way in which [they] should go" occurs most often in Deuteronomistic literature.[83] Both in that tradition and

---

[80] Neh 9:12a: ובעמוד ענן הנחיתם יומם
Exod 13:21a: ויהוה הלך לפניהם יומם ובעמוד ענן לנחתם הדרך

Neh 9:12b: ובעמוד אש לילה
Exod 13:21b: ולילה בעמוד אש

Neh 9:12c: להאיר להם את־הדרך
Exod 13:21c: להאיר להם ללכת יומם ולילה

[81] GKC §119q; cf. §102c.
[82] Neh 9:12b: להאיר להם את־הדרך אשר ילכו־בה
Deut 1:33: לראתכם בדרך אשר תלכו־בה ובענן יומם
[83] Deut 1:33; 5:33; 8:2; 13:5; Josh 3:4; 24:17; Judg 2:22; 4:9; 18:6; 1 Kgs 8:36 (= 2 Chr 6:27); 13:17; cf. Gen 42:38; Exod 8:27; 18:20; Jer 42:3; Neh 9:12, 19; 2 Chr 6:16.

elsewhere, the spatial language functions as an ethical metaphor for the orientation of one's life in relationship to God (e.g., Exod 18:20; Deut 5:33; 13:5; Judg 2:22; 1 Kgs 8:36 [= 2 Chr 6:27]; 2 Chr 6:16).

(9:13) The portrait of YHWH descending on Mount Sinai (Neh 9:13aα) mirrors Exod 19:20a (prior to the giving of the commandments).[84] The description of YHWH speaking directly with the people (Neh 9:13aβ) reflects Exod 20:22 (following the Decalogue).[85] Only in Neh 9:13 and nowhere else does Ezra-Nehemiah describe God speaking directly to his people.[86]

The juridical terms, which link the psalm to the pledge, are relatively distinctive for the covenant renewal in the MT. Outside Neh 9:13 and 10:29, the four legal terms (משפט [ordinance], תורה [law], חק [statute], and מצוה [commandment]) occur together only in 2 Kgs 17:37 and 2 Chr 19:10.[87] Moreover, three of the four terms (תורה, חק, and מצוה) occur together only in these texts and in Neh 9:14b. Another three of the four terms occur together on two other occasions in Ezra-Nehemiah: in the introduction of Ezra (Ezra 7:10, תורה, חק, and משפט) and in Nehemiah's prayer (Neh 1:7, מצוה, חקים, and משפטים).

The "good statutes" (טובים ... חקים, 9:13c) that YHWH gives his people at Sinai apparently contrast with the statutes that were "not good" (חקים לא טובים) of which Ezekiel speaks (Ezek 20:25). However, the general rarity of the legal terms in combination with their modifiers (משפטים ישרים: "just ordinances," 9:13b; cf. Ps 119:137; תורות אמת: "true laws," 9:13c; cf. תורתך אמת: "your law is truth," Ps 119:142; תורת אמת: "true instruction," Mal 2:6) suggests the purposefulness of the links that אמת ("true") and טוב ("good") establish with other verses in the prayer.[88]

(9:14) In the Decalogue, the Sabbath commandment (cf. 9:14a) takes the form of an imperative followed by the accusative and an infinitive construct (Exod 20:8; Deut 5:12).[89] However, the periphrasis of the genitive

---

[84] Neh 9:13: ועל הר־סיני ירדת
Exod 19:20: וירד יהוה על־הר סיני

[85] Neh 9:13: דבר עמהם משמים
Exod 20:22: מן־השמים דברתי עמכם

[86] The verb דבר ("to speak") occurs elsewhere only in Ezra 8:17; Neh 6:12; 13:24.

[87] Chronicles associates the four terms with the Levites, who, along with other leaders, receive the commission to adjudicate disputes (2 Chr 19:10).

[88] On these and other parallels to Neh 9:13–14, see Gilbert, "La place de la Loi," 310–11.

[89] Exod 20:8: זכור את־יום השבת לקדשו
Deut 5:12: שמור את־יום השבת לקדשו

following the noun in the construct state (שַׁבַּת קָדְשְׁךָ: "your holy Sabbath," Neh 9:14a) resembles instead the phrase "the holy sabbath to YHWH" (שַׁבַּת־קֹדֶשׁ לַיהוה): Exod 16:23), which occurs in the instructions regarding the manna.[90] The manna event is the topic of the subsequent verse of the psalm (Neh 9:15a).

The concluding phrase of Neh 9:14, which speaks of the "law" (תּוֹרָה) that YHWH "commanded" (צִוָּה) by the hand of "Moses the servant" (מֹשֶׁה עַבְדּ[וֹ]), reflects the language of two exhortations: Joshua's words to the Transjordanian tribes (Josh 22:5), and the final admonition in the prophetic corpus (Mal 3:22). Within Ezra-Nehemiah, the mediation of "the commandments" (מִצְוֹת) that YHWH "commands" (צִוָּה) through his "servant[s]" (עֶבֶד) links the Levites' psalm with the prayers of Ezra (Ezra 9:6–15) and Nehemiah (Neh 1:5–11). Ezra speaks of the people forsaking "the commandments that you commanded through your servants the prophets" (Ezra 9:9–10), whereas Nehemiah confesses their not observing "the commandments, statutes, and ordinances that you commanded through your servant Moses" (Neh 1:7).[91]

(9:15) The description of God providing bread and water in the wilderness (Neh 9:15a–b) is a reworking of the Exodus narratives (Exod 16:4–36; 17:1–6) on two counts: first, the prayer narrates the events after rather than before the giving of the law at Sinai; and second, the similarities in vocabulary are minimal.[92] The term סֶלַע ("rock") occurs not in Exodus but in the episode at Meribah, which follows Israel's departure from Sinai (Num 20:8; cf. Exod 17:6, צוּר).

The parallelism between the provisions of food and water occurs also in Ps 105:40–41 but with vocabulary that is different from Neh 9:15a–b. The same events provide the content for disparate segments of Ps 78 (vv. 15, 20, 24).

Within Ezra-Nehemiah, the pairing of eating bread and drinking water occurs in the description of Ezra's fast (Ezra 10:6; cf. Deut 9:9, 18). The scriptural basis for excluding foreigners from the assembly suggests that the providing of bread and water is a sign of goodwill (Neh 13:2; cf. Deut 23:4).

---

[90] GKC §135n.; Gilbert, "La place de la Loi," 311.

[91] Neh 9:14b: וּמִצְוֹת ... צִוִּיתָ לָהֶם בְּיַד מֹשֶׁה עַבְדֶּךָ
Ezra 9:10–11: וּמִצְוֹתֶיךָ אֲשֶׁר צִוִּיתָ בְּיַד עֲבָדֶיךָ הַנְּבִיאִים
Neh 1:7: אֶת־הַמִּצְוֹת וְ... אֲשֶׁר צִוִּיתָ אֶת־מֹשֶׁה עַבְדֶּךָ

[92] Only two words are common to the accounts of the bread, on the one hand (Neh 9:15a, וְלַחְמָם מִשָּׁמַיִם: "for them from heaven"; cf. Exod 16:4, לֶחֶם מִן הַשָּׁמָיִם: "for them from heaven"), and of the water, on the other (מַיִם and יָצָא [hip'il]: Neh 9:15b; cf. Exod 17:6).

YHWH's command to settle the land (9:15c–d) contains a mixture of Deuteronomistic and Priestly elements. The expression to "go to take possession of the land" (לבוא לרשת את־הארץ) in Neh 9:15c and 24a occurs elsewhere only in Deuteronomistic literature (Deut 1:8; 4:1; 6:18; 8:1; 9:4; 10:11; 11:8, 31; Josh 1:11; 18:3, 9). However, the expression concerning YHWH "swearing to give" (נשא את־יד, cf. 9:15d) the land to the people reflects the Priestly description of his oath to the patriarchs (Exod 6:8), as well as Ezekiel's account of the entrance into the land at the conquest in the past (Ezek 20:28) and following the exile in the future (Ezek 20:42).[93]

The people's rebellion and God's mercy (9:16–21). The vocabulary of Deuteronomistic tradition and of Jeremiah predominates in the description of the people's rejection of YHWH's command (Neh 9:16–17b).

(9:16) The Israelites' acting insolently (זיד *hipʿil*, 9:16a) reflects the Deuteronomic description of their rebellion at Kadesh (Deut 1:43; cf. Num 14:39–45). However, the application of the term is distinctive of the psalm. In Deuteronomy, the Israelites' insolence refers to their attempting to take the land after they had initially disobeyed the command of YHWH. By contrast, in the psalm their insolence refers to their initial refusal to take the land.

The reference to the Israelites "stiffening their necks" (קשה ערפם [*hipʿil*]), which appears three times in the psalm (9:16a, 17b, 29c), occurs in the Deuteronomistic History (Deut 10:16; 2 Kgs 17:14), Jeremiah (7:26; 17:23; 19:15), Chronicles (2 Chr 30:8; 36:13), and Proverbs (29:1). The occurrences in Neh 9:16, 17b, and 29c most closely parallel those texts in which this expression accompanies the clause "they did not listen" (לא שמעו), that is, 2 Kgs 17:14; Jer 7:26; 17:23; 19:15.[94]

The description of the Israelites not obeying YHWH's commandments (Neh 9:16, 29a) approximates the protasis for the Deuteronomic curse, "if you do not obey the commandments of YHWH your God" (אם־לא תשמעו אל־מצות יהוה אלהיכם, Deut 11:28).

---

[93] Neh 9:15:   להם   הארץ אשר נשאת את־ידך לתת
      Exod 6:8:   לאבדהם   הארץ אשר נשאתי את־ידי לתת אתה
      Ezek 20:28: להם   הארץ אשר נשאתי את־ידי לתת אותה
      Ezek 20:42: לאבותיכם   הארץ אשר נשאתי את־ידי לתת אותה

The expression "to swear" translates an idiom (נשא את־יד; literally, "to raise the hand," Neh 9:15d), which occurs elsewhere in the MT exclusively in Priestly texts (Exod 6:8; Num 14:30) and in Ezekiel (20:23, 28, 42; 36:7; 47:14).

[94] B. Couroyer interprets "stiffening the neck" as a human reaction that is the opposite of inclining the ear to listen ("'Avoir la nuque raide': ne pas incliner l'oreille," *RB* 88 [1981]: 216–25).

(9:17a–b) Their refusal to obey (וימאנו לשמע, 9:17a) reflects the language of Jeremiah, who views such behavior as the root of idolatry (מאן לשמוע את־דברי: "they refused to obey my words," Jer 11:10; 13:10; cf. 1 Sam 8:19).

Mention of YHWH's wonders echoes a concern in certain historical psalms. In Pss 78 (vv. 11, 32) and 106 (vv. 7, 22), the wonders (נפלאות) refer in particular to the events in Egypt and at the Reed Sea. The Israelites' "not remembering" the wonders (ולא־זכרו נפלאתיך אשר עשית עמהם, 9:17a) contrasts with the admonition in Ps 105:5 (זכרו נפלאותיו אשר עשה: "remember the wonderful works he has done" [=1 Chr 16:12]).

The people's decision to appoint one to lead them back to Egypt reflects the language of Num 14:4.[95] This episode provides an appropriate finale to the psalm's seven descriptions of rebellion, since it directs attention to the people's refusal to enter the land from Kadesh, as YHWH had commanded (Num 13:1–33; cf. Neh 9:15b–c).

(9:17c–d) Moving beyond the report of the people's rebellion, the initial assertion of God's mercy consists of a standard credal formula supplemented by a standard description of divine forebearance. Numbers 14 inspires this depiction of God's merciful response to the people's disobedience.

The noun "forgiveness" occurs in only three MT texts, each of which attributes it to God: Neh 9:17c (סליחות), Ps 130:4 (הסליחה), and Dan 9:9 (הסלחות). However, the tradition that most likely influenced the emphasis on forgiveness in Neh 9:17c is found in Num 14:18–20, which speaks of God forgiving (סלח, Num 14:19–20) the people for refusing to take possession of the land. The introductory confessional statement, which mentions two attributes of YHWH (יהוה ארך אפים ורב־חסד: "YHWH [is] slow to anger and bountiful in loyalty," 14:18), confirms the significance of this text for Neh 9:17c.

The four divine attributes that follow "forgiveness" in Neh 9:17c–d apparently reflect a common credal or liturgical formula, since they occur in precisely the same sequence in Jonah 4:2 and have a near equivalent in Joel 2:13. They also appear in a slightly different order in Exod 34:6 and Pss 86:15; 103:8.[96] Ultimately, these four attributes recall the self-

---

[95] Neh 9:17: ויתנו־ראש לשוב לעבדתם במצרים
    Num 14:4: נתנה ראש ונשובה מצרימה

[96] Neh 9:17: ארך אפים רב־חסד   חנון ורחום
    Exod 34:6: וחנון ארך אפים רב־חסד ואמת   רחום   אל־
    Ps 86:15: וחנון ארך אפים רב־חסד ואמת   רחום   אל־
    Ps 103:8: רחום וחנון יהוה ארך אפים רב־חסד
    Joel 2:13: הוא ארך אפים רב־חסד   כי־חנון ורחום
    Jonah 4:2: ארך אפים רב־חסד   אל־חנון ורחום

revelation of YHWH in the reestablishment of the covenant at Sinai (Exod 34:6–7).[97]

The statement that YHWH "did not abandon" (לא עזב, 9:17d) his people suggests his faithfulness to promises as expressed in both the Deuteronomistic History (Deut 31:6, 8; Josh 1:5; 1 Kgs 6:13) and in Deutero-Isaiah (Isa 41:17; 42:16). The conviction that YHWH will not abandon his own is also expressed in the Psalter (Pss 37:28, 33; 94:14). The above statement in direct address occurs only in Neh 9:17d and Ps 9:10 (לא־עזבת). However, the content of Neh 9:17d recalls Ezra's statement in prayer: "Our God has not abandoned us in our bondage" (לא עזבנו, Ezra 9:9).

(9:18) Having recalled God's mercy, the psalm once again returns to a report of the people's rebellion. The portrait of apostasy here is a meditation on the narrative in Exod 32.

Because the making of the molten calf (Neh 9:18a–b) represents the height of apostasy, the Levites in their psalm transpose this episode from its location in the Exodus narrative, where it follows upon the giving of the law at Sinai, to later in the wilderness era (Exod 19:1–24:18; 32:1–35; cf. Neh 9:13–14). The actual description of the event in Neh 9:18a–b is a quotation of Exod 32:4, 8 with significant variations.[98] The wording in the prayer is distinctly monotheistic due to the replacement of the ambiguous plural (אשר העלוך ... אלה אלהיך: "these are your gods ... who brought you up [out of the land of Egypt]," Exod 32:4, 8) with the singular (זה אלהיך אשר העלך: "This is your god who brought you up out of Egypt," Neh 9:18b). The plural forms in Exod 32:4, 8 (אלה ... העלוך: "these brought you up out") allude to the two calf images that Jeroboam erected in Dan and Bethel, respectively (1 Kgs 12:28).[99] The psalm replaces these plurals (אלה ... העלוך) with the singular (זה ... העלך: "this is ... the one who brought you up out," Neh 9:18b) and thereby plays down the clear reference to the schism of the northern kingdom implied in the Exodus version.

---

[97] See J. Scharbert, "Formgeschichte und Exegese von Ex 34,6f und seiner Parallelen," *Bib* 38 (1957): 130–50. R. C. Dentan views Exod 34:6–7 as the product of a wisdom school ("The Literary Affinities of Exodus XXXIV 6f.," *VT* 13 [1963]: 34–51).

[98] Neh 9:18a: אף כי־עשׂו להם עגל מסכה
    Exod 32:4: ויעשׂהו עגל מסכה
    Exod 32:8: עשׂו להם עגל מסכה

Neh 9:18b: ממצרים אשר העלך זה אלהיך ויאמרו
    Exod 32:4: ויאמרו אלה אלהיך ישׂראל אשר העלוך מארץ ממצרים
    Exod 32:8: ויאמרו אלה אלהיך ישׂראל אשר העלוך מארץ ממצרים

[99] B. S. Childs, *The Book of Exodus* (OTL; Philadelphia: Westminster, 1974), 566.

Moreover, the psalm omits the vocative "Israel" of Exod 32:4, 8, since this term does not occur anywhere in the psalm. The psalm does not include the specification of "land" (ארץ) prior to "Egypt" in Exodus, perhaps out of concern to reserve this term for the territory God gives to his people (Neh 9:8b, 15d, 22b [bis], 23b, 24a, 24b, 24c, 35b, 36b; cf. 9:10a).

In the only occurrence of "infamies" (נאצות) outside the psalm (Neh 9:18c, 26c), the term is the object of the verb "to hear" (שמע), indicating that it refers to contemptuous speech (Ezek 35:12). However, in Neh 9:18c, 26c, the noun, as the object of the verb "to do" (עשה), points to more global forms of behavior that reflect contempt for YHWH (cf. נאץ, Num 14:11, 23).[100]

(9:19) Once again discussion of the people's rebellion leads to a recounting of God's demonstrations of mercy (Neh 9:19–21). The depiction of God's restoration of his gifts in the wilderness is a meditation on the pertinent narratives in Numbers. The final statement (9:21), which summarizes the people's experience in the wilderness, is thoroughly Deuteronomic.

Outside Neh 9:19a, 27c, 28c, 31a, only Ps 119:156 and Dan 9:18 use the expression "your abundant mercies" (רחמיך [ה]רבים).

For the background regarding the columns of cloud and fire, see the exegetical commentary on Neh 9:12.[101] The additional expression describing the position of the cloud "over them" (מעליהם, 9:19) reflects the statement in Num 14:14 that "your cloud stands over them" (ועננך עמד עלהם).

(9:20) God's provision of his spirit (Neh 9:20a) alludes to the episode of his distributing the spirit of Moses upon the seventy elders at the tent of meeting and upon the two who remained in the camp (Num 11:16–30). The vocabulary of God's "giving" (נתן) his "spirit" (רוח) reflects Moses' expressed wish that YHWH would "give his spirit" to all the people (כי־יתן יהוה את־רוחו עליהם, Num 11:29).

The episode Neh 9:20a describes is unique: God bestows his "good spirit" apparently on all the people rather than merely on the leaders.[102] This is similar to the note in Isa 63:11 of God putting his "holy spirit" (רוח קדש) in the midst of the people after they had rebelled in the wilderness.[103] The precise

---

[100] Blenkinsopp translates נאצות גדולת (Neh 9:18, 26) as "great contempt" (*Ezra, Nehemiah*, 306). Anderson proposes an allusion to Num 14:11, 23 ("The Levitical Prayer," 169).

[101] Pp. 207–8 above.

[102] Gilbert, "Notes," 15.

[103] H. G. M. Williamson states, "Only at Neh 9,20 and Isa 63,11 in the Old Testament is there a reference to God's Spirit in association with the wilderness traditions" ("Isaiah 63,7–64,11. Exilic Lament or Post-Exilic Protest?" *ZAW* 102 [1990]:

phrase "your good spirit" (רוחך טובה) occurs elsewhere only in Ps 143:10, where the phrase has a tutorial function consistent with Neh 9:20a.[104]

The reference to manna and water for the second time (Neh 9:20b; cf. 9:15a–b) corresponds with the narratives in Num 11:4–9 and 20:1–13, which mirror Exod 16:1–36 and 17:1–7, respectively. The description of the perdurance of the manna (Num 11:4–9; cf. Neh 9:20b) occurs in proximity to the account of God distributing his spirit from Moses to the elders (Num 11:16–30; cf. Neh 9:20a).

(9:21) A distinctly Deuteronomic texture suffuses the psalm's summary description of the forty years in the wilderness. The first verse of Moses' covenant speech in Moab (Deut 29:4) provides the overarching content of Neh 9:21a–b.[105] Nehemiah 9:21a reflects Moses' statement in his introductory speech: "these forty years [זה ארבעים שנה], YHWH your God has been with you; you have lacked nothing [לא חסרת דבר]" (Deut 2:7). Nehemiah 9:21b reflects Moses' description of Israel's survival in the wilderness: "Your clothing did not wear out on you, and your foot did not swell these forty years" (Deut. 8:4).[106]

The occupation and subsequent life in the land (9:22–31)

The era of harmony: the occupation of the land (9:22–25). Traditional expressions from hymns and narratives supplement the Deuteronomic expressions that predominate in the depiction of the conquests of the land on both sides of the Jordan.

(9:22) The sequence describing the people's survival in the wilderness (Neh 9:21) and their conquest of the lands of Sihon and Og (9:22b) has a counterpart in Deut 29:4, 6.[107] The summary description in 9:22a is

---

56). This observation contributes to his thesis that Isa 63:7–64:11 and Neh 9:6–37 (as well as Ps 106) have kindred origins as prayers composed in Judah during the exile. See also idem, "Laments at the Destroyed Temple: Excavating the Biblical Text Reveals Ancient Jewish Prayers," *BRev* 6 (Aug 1990): 12–17, 44.

[104] Ps 143:10: למדני לעשות רצונך כי־אתה אלוהי
רוחך טובה תנחני בדרך מישור
"Teach me to do your will, for you are my God.
Let your good spirit guide me on a level path."

[105] Deut 29:4: ואולך אתכם ארבעים שנה במדבר לא־בלו שלמתיכם מעליכם ונעלך
לא־בלתה מעל רגלך ("I led you in the wilderness for forty years; the clothes on your back did not wear out, and the sandals on your feet did not wear out").

[106] Deut 8:4: שמלתך לא בלתה מעליך ורגלך לא בצקה זה ארבעים שנה
Neh 9:21b: שמלתיהם לא בלו ורגליהם לא בצקו

[107] Gilbert, "Notes," 15.

without parallel in vocabulary, although its content reflects the account of the conquest of the Transjordan in Pss 135:12 and 136:21 (ויתן ארצם לנחלה]). In Ps 135:11, the term "kingdoms" (ממלכות, Neh 9:22a) refers to subdivisions within Canaan. The noun פאה otherwise designates a "corner" of a field (Lev 19:9; 23:22) or a "side" (Num 35:5; Josh 15:5; 18:14–15) that marks the boundary line of a parcel of land or territory.

Three MT narratives recount the conquest of the lands of Sihon and Og (Num 21:21–35; Deut 2:24–3:7; Judg 11:18–22; cf. Neh 9:22c–d). The language of the psalm most nearly reflects the summary notice in Deut 4:47 (ויירשו את־ארצו ואת־ארץ עוג מלך־הבשן: "they took possession of his [Sihon's] land and of the land of Og, king of Bashan").

(9:23) Mention of YHWH's having multiplied his people "like the stars of heaven" (Neh 9:23a) recalls Deut 1:10.[108] At the same time, the description evokes the fulfillment of his promise to Abraham (Gen 22:17) and the patriarchs (Gen 26:4; Exod 32:13).[109]

The summary of the second generation's entrance into the land (Neh 9:23b) does not correspond to any other text in the MT except 9:15c–d.

(9:24) The description of the second generation's entering and taking possession of the land reflects the Deuteronomic formulation of the objective for the community assembled on the plains of Moab: "to enter and take possession of the land" (Neh 9:24a; cf. Deut 1:8; 4:1; 6:18; 8:1; 10:11; 11:8). The accent on YHWH's activity in "subduing" (כנע hip'il, Neh 9:24a) the inhabitants of the land recalls Deut 9:3. The wordplay (כנע hip'il and כנען ["Canaan"], Neh 9:24a–b) occurs also in Judg 4:23. YHWH's giving of "kings" into the hands of his people (Neh 9:24b–c) reflects the language of Deut 7:24. The expression "to do as they pleased" (עשה כרצון, 9:24c) occurs elsewhere only in Esther (1:8; 9:5) and Daniel (8:4; 11:3, 16, 36) and generally refers to domination over others.[110]

The description of YHWH's giving "the peoples of the land" (עממי הארץ, 9:24c) into the power of his own people is most significant within the broader context of Ezra-Nehemiah. These "peoples of the land" are the adversaries of the community that had returned from exile (cf. Ezra 4:4; עם־הארץ [singular]). Moreover, Ezra's reform consists precisely in separating the community from these peoples of the land through his

---

[108] Deut 1:10: יהוה אלהיכם הרבה אתכם והנכם היום ככוכבי השמים לרב Neh 9:23a: ובניהם הרבית ככוכבי השמים

[109] The simile "as the stars of heaven" for the multitude of the Israelites occurs eight times in the MT (Gen 22:17; 26:4; 32:13; Deut 1:10; 10:22; 28:62; Neh 9:23; 1 Chr 27:23).

[110] Clines, *Ezra, Nehemiah, Esther,* 196.

dissolving of marriages contracted with them (Ezra 10:2, 11, עמי הארץ [plural]).[111]

(9:25) Summaries of the abundant resources of the land are characteristic of Deuteronomy (Deut 6:10–11; 8:7–10; 11:10–15; 28:3–8; cf. Neh 9:25). It is noteworthy that in Deuteronomy each of these summaries is followed by a warning to the people against turning away from YHWH once they have enjoyed the benefits of the land (Deut 6:12–13; 8:11–13; 11:16–17; 28:15–46; cf. Neh 9:26).

The psalm's enumeration of the land's resources basically consists of standard expressions. The first two elements occur in the pentateuchal narrative about the spies inspecting the land from the south (Num 13:1–33): "fortified cities" (ערים בצרות[ה], Neh 9:25a; cf. Num 13:28) and "fertile land" (אדמה שמנה, Neh 9:25a; cf. הארץ השמנה, Num 13:20). Deuteronomistic accounts of the conquest also refer to "fortified cities" (ערים בצרות, Neh 9:25a; cf. Deut 1:28; 3:5; 9:1; Josh 14:12). Moreover, the subsequent three phrases in Neh 9:25b–c reflect Deut 6:11.[112] The "trees for food" (עץ מאכל, Neh 9:25c) recall both Ezekiel's vision of the land (Ezek 47:12; cf. Lev 19:23; Deut 20:20) and the Eden narrative (Gen 2:9).

The expression "they ate and became full" (ויאכלו וישבעו, Neh 9:25c) reflects the Deuteronomic description of the people's satiating themselves with the resources of the land and thereby becoming vulnerable to the temptation of turning away from YHWH to serve other gods (Deut 6:11; 8:10, 12; 11:15; 31:20). The additional verb "to grow fat" (שמן *hipʿil*, Neh 9:25c) intensifies the suggestion of apostasy, since it bears this connotation in Deut 32:15 (*qal*) as well as in its two occurrences in the prophets (Isa 6:10 [*hipʿil*]; Jer 5:28 [*qal*]).

Both the verb (עדן) and the expression "your great goodness" (טובך הגדול) are unique to Neh 9:25d in the MT.[113]

---

[111] A. H. J. Gunneweg, "עם הארץ—A Semantic Revolution," *ZAW* 95 (1983): 437–40; Japhet, "People and Land," 112–18.

[112] Deut 6:11: בתים מלאים כל־טוב אשר לא־מלאת
Neh 9:25b: בתים מלאים כל־טוב

Deut 6:11: וברת חצובים אשר לא־חצבת כרמים וזיתים אשר לא־נטעת
Neh 9:25c: ברות חצובים כרמים וזיתים

[113] Gilbert ("Notes," 17) raises the possibility that a paradisial motif reflected in Ezekiel may be implied by two components in Neh 9:25c–d: (1) the noun עץ מאכל ("fruit tree"), which is central to Ezekiel's vision of the land (Neh 9:25c; cf. Ezek 47:12); and (2) the verbal root עדן (Neh 9:25d), which resonates with the name of the garden to which the prophet compares the land (כגן־עדן: "like the garden of Eden," Ezek 36:35). However, the suggestion is unlikely on both counts: (1) Neh 9:25c lacks the totalizing adjective of the paradisial accounts (עץ מאכל לרב: "fruit

Rebellion and mercy: life in the land (9:26–31). In rough outline, the cycles of rebellion and restoration in the land (Neh 9:26–31) are an adaptation of the historical schema that introduces the stories of the judges (Judg 2:11–23): (1) the Israelites rebel against YHWH (2:11–13); (2) YHWH surrenders them to the power of their enemies (2:14–15); (3) YHWH sends judges as saviors to deliver them (2:16, 18); but (4) after the death of each judge, Israel relapses into apostasy and the cycle begins again (2:17, 19).

In contrast to this Deuteronomistic construct, the Levites' psalm offers these changes in emphasis: (1) saviors are a feature only of the first cycle but not of the second (9:27c; cf. 9:28c); (2) the people's outcry and YHWH's hearing it are constant factors in each cycle (9:27b, 28b–c; cf. Judg 3:9; 4:3); and (3) YHWH's mercy is highlighted as the basis for his redemptive intervention (9:27c, 28c, 31a–b). While the cyclical schema of history is Deuteronomistic, the vocabulary describing life in the land reflects Priestly and prophetic as well as Deuteronomistic traditions.

(9:26) The combining of מרה and מרד (Neh 9:26a) is unique in the MT. Furthermore, the verb מרה does not occur elsewhere in Ezra-Nehemiah or Chronicles. However, מרה is used in other historical psalms to describe Israel's rebellion against YHWH (Pss 78:8, 17, 40, 56; 106:7, 33, 43; Isa 63:10; cf. Deut 9:7, 23, 24; Ezek 20:8, 13, 21). Its usage in Ps 106:43 is most closely related to that of Neh 9:26a on two counts: (1) the verb refers to Israel's rebellion after entering the land rather than in the wilderness (also Ps 78:56); and (2) in both cases, the following verse describes YHWH's looking upon their "distress" (צר להם) and "hearing" (שמע) their appeal (Ps 106:44; cf. Neh 9:27b). The verb מרד occurs in prayer elsewhere only in the confessional statements in Dan 9:5, 9.

The people's casting of the Torah behind their backs (Neh 9:26a) reflects the prophetic accusation "you have cast me behind your back" (Ezek 23:35; cf. 1 Kgs 14:9). Thus, in Neh 9:26a, the Torah takes the place of YHWH in the prophetic expression.[114] An emphasis on the word is

---

trees in abundance," Neh 9:25c; cf. כל־עץ־מאכל: "every tree for food," Ezek 47:12; כל־עץ ... למאכל: "every tree ... for food," Gen 2:9); and (2) the *hitpaᶜel* verb (ויתערנו: "and they delighted themselves," Neh 9:25d) affords only a very loose allusion to the noun עדן (Eden).

114 Gilbert, "La place de la Loi," 313. The word order in Neh 9:26a reflects Ezek 23:35 rather than 1 Kgs 14:9.

Neh 9:26a: וישלכו את־תורתך אחרי גום
Ezek 23:35: ותשליכי אותי אחרי גוך
1 Kgs 14:9: אותי ותשליכי אחרי גוך
Ps 50:17: ותשלך דברי אחריך

evident in the divine declaration in the second-person singular of Ps 50:17: "You cast my words behind you."

The killing of the prophets represents a general summary of a variety of biblical episodes (1 Kgs 18:4, 13; 19:10, 14; Jer 2:30; 26:20–23; 2 Chr 24:20–22). Chronicles recounts the only episode in which the people (rather than a king or queen) actually kill a (priest) prophet (2 Chr 24:20–22; cf. Jer 2:30). The verse immediately prior to this account of the stoning of Zechariah the priest is reminiscent of the psalm's description of the prophets' mission to admonish the people to turn back to God (2 Chr 24:19; cf. Neh 9:26b).[115] An equally significant parallel occurs in the Deuteronomistic interpretation of the fall of Samaria (2 Kgs 17:13; cf. Neh 9:26b).[116]

However, in the remainder of Ezra-Nehemiah, the people's treatment of the prophets contrasts with the description in Neh 9:26b and 9:30c. The former generations who returned from exile heeded the prophecies of Haggai and Zechariah to rebuild the temple (Ezra 5:1–2; 6:14). Moreover, Ezra's peers who subscribed to the marriage reform conformed to the message of earlier "prophets" (Ezra 9:10–12; cf. 10:9–44). The psalm's portrayal of the prophets as honorable servants of God (Neh 9:26b, 30c) contrasts with the mention of Nodiah and "the rest of the prophets" who threatened Nehemiah (6:14).

(9:27) YHWH's giving of his people into the power of their oppressors (Neh 9:27a) reflects the language of Ezek 39:23, while recalling the second stage of the Deuteronomistic schema of history (Judg 2:14).[117] The people's crying out from their oppression (Neh 9:27b) reflects the vocabulary of Ps 107:6, 28 (ויצעקו אל־יהוה בצר להם): "And they cried to YHWH in their trouble"). Such an appeal (צעק) also sets the stage for the providential leadership of Deborah (Judg 4:3).

YHWH's hearing from heaven (Neh 9:27b, 28c) echoes the repeated prayerful request of Solomon at the dedication of the temple: אתה תשמע מן־השמים ("may you hear from heaven," 2 Chr 6:23, 25, 27, 33, 39; cf. 1 Kgs 8:32, 34, 36, 43, 49).

---

[115] 2 Chr 24:19: וישלח בהם נבאים להשיבם אל־יהוה ויעידו בם ולא האזינו ("Yet he sent among them prophets to turn them back to YHWH. They warned them, but they would not give ear").

[116] 2 Kgs 17:13: ויעד יהוה בישראל וביהודה ביד כל־נביאו כל־חזה לאמר שבו ("YHWH warned Israel and Judah by the hand of every prophet and every seer, saying, 'Turn back'").

[117] Neh 9:27a: ותתנם ביד צריהם
Ezek 39:23: ואתנם ביד צריהם
Judg 2:14: ויתנם ביד־שסים

The attribution of God's intervention to his "mercies" (Neh 9:19a, 27c, 28c, 31a) is distinctive of the Levites' psalm vis-à-vis the Deuteronomistic schema of Israel's history (cf. Judg 2:11–18; 2 Kgs 17:7–18). However, his providing saviors or judges (שפט/מושיע) to save (ישע hip'il) his people from the hand (מיד) of their adversaries corresponds to the final stage of the Deuteronomistic cycle (Neh 9:27c; cf. Judg 2:18; 3:9, 15).

(9:28) At the beginning of the second cycle of life in the land, the description of the people being "at rest" reflects the Deuteronomistic description of the periods when adversaries did not pose a threat to Israel's security (Neh 9:28a; cf. Deut 3:20; 12:10; 25:19; Josh 1:13, 15; 21:44; 22:4, 23; 23:1; 2 Sam 7:1, 11; 1 Kgs 5:18).

The people's "returning" to do evil is a noteworthy contrast to the thrust of Ezra's rhetorical question, which suggests that retribution for previous sins should have prevented the people from "returning" to trespass the commandments by marrying foreigners (שוב + infinitive construct, Neh 9:28a; cf. Ezra 9:14).

YHWH's "abandoning" the people to "the hand" of their enemies (Neh 9:28b) reflects the vocabulary of the prophet Shemaiah in his judgment against Rehoboam's unfaithfulness (ואף־אני עזבתי אתכם ביד־שישק: "so I have abandoned you to the hand of Shishak," 2 Chr 12:5; cf. Ps 37:33). The foes' "exercising of dominion" over the people echoes the sanction for the people's disobedience in the Holiness Code (רדה, Neh 9:28b; cf. Lev 26:17).

The account of YHWH "delivering" (נצל hip'il) his rebellious people from oppression "many times" (רבות עתים, Neh 9:28c) approximates the description in Ps 106:43a (פעמים רבות יצילם: "many times he delivered them"). YHWH's "delivering" (נצל hip'il) his people from their adversaries in the land is a theme in diverse Deuteronomistic locutions (Judg 6:9; 1 Sam 7:3; 10:18; 12:10–11; 2 Kgs 17:39).

(9:29) The subordinate clause of 9:29b, which states that observance of the ordinances gives one life, derives from the command in Lev 18:5: "You shall observe my statutes and ordinances; by doing them one shall live."[118] However, the formulation in the prayer is closer to Ezekiel's repeated accusations that, throughout its history, Israel did not observe these ordinances (9:29b; cf. Ezek 20:11, 13, 21).

(9:29–30) Two expressions in Neh 9:29–30 reflect the vocabulary of Zechariah's description of the people's resistance to YHWH's word that

---

[118] Lev 18:5: שמרתם את־חקתי ואת־משפטי אשר יעשה אתם האדם וחי בהם ("You shall keep my statutes and my ordinances, which one must carry out and thereby live").

resulted in YHWH exiling them from the land (Zech 7:8–14): (1) "giving a stubborn shoulder" (ויתנו כתף סו[ו]ררת, Neh 9:29c) describes the people's refusal to heed YHWH's admonitions in Zech 7:9; and (2) YHWH's speaking to them "through [his] spirit by the hand of [his] prophets" (ברוחך ביד־נביאיך, 9:30b) represents his final attempt to communicate with them prior to revealing his wrath in Zech 7:12.

(9:30) Mention of the people's lack of response to the mission of the prophets (ולא האזינו: "they would not give ear," 9:30c) provides another link with 2 Chr 24:19, in addition to its links with Neh 9:26b.[119]

In Ezra-Nehemiah, by definition "the peoples of the lands" (עמי הארצת, Neh 9:30c; cf. Ezra 3:3; 9:1, 2, 11) are those living in the region of Yehud who do not belong to the authentic community comprised of the families of Judah and Benjamin who had returned from exile (Ezra 1:5; 2:1; 9:4; 10:6, 8).[120] Throughout the story, these "peoples of the lands" persistently threaten to undermine the authentic Israel: first externally, through intimidation (Ezra 3:3), and later internally, through intermarriage (Ezra 9:1–2, 11). Thus, God's surrender of his community into the power of the "peoples of the land" realizes their greatest fear and is a most extreme form of retribution (Neh 9:30c).

(9:31) In the concluding verse, the clause that does not occur anywhere else in the psalm—"you did not make an end of them" (Neh 9:31a)—has a counterpart in Jeremiah's prophecy regarding Israel's future (Jer 5:18; 30:11; 46:28) and in Ezekiel's account of the people's history in the wilderness period (Ezek 20:17). Jeremiah's words express YHWH's promise that his people will survive the exile. This promise echoes in the statement that "you did not make an end of them" (Neh 9:31a), which, therefore, represents the only allusion to the exile in the Levites' prayer.

GOD AND ISRAEL IN THE PRESENT (9:32–37)

The depiction of the present situation of the people exhibits the least traditional language of the whole prayer. The Deuteronomic tradition is manifest in both the initial credal statement (9:32a–b) and in the implied theology of retribution (9:35). However, the style and formulation throughout is most akin to that of other confessional prayers, notably those of Ezra (Ezra 9:6–15) and Daniel (Dan 9:4–19).

---

[119] 2 Chr 24:19: וישלח בהם נבאים להשיבם אל־יהוה ויעידו בם ולא האזינו ("Yet he sent among them prophets to turn them back to YHWH. They warned them but they would not give ear"). Cf. p. 218 above.

[120] Japhet, "People and Land," 114–15.

(9:32) The vocative "our God" (אלהינו) occurs in proximity to the conjunctive adverb ועתה ("And now") in the intercessory prayer of Ezra (Ezra 9:10; cf. Neh 9:32) in a location similar to its occurrence in the Levites' psalm, that is, at the point of transition from a recollection of the past (Ezra 9:6–9; cf. Neh 9:6–31) to a consideration of the present (Ezra 9:10–15; cf. Neh 9:32–37).

The attributes of God cited in Neh 9:32a–bα reflect Deuteronomistic theology and combine Deut 7:9 and 10:17. The confession in Neh 9:32 repeats, in part, the introductory appellations in Nehemiah's prayer (Neh 1:5; also Dan 9:4), while adding the designation "the mighty" (הגבור, 9:32a). Similar expressions appear also in the address of Solomon's blessing at the dedication of the temple (1 Kgs 8:23 = 2 Chr 6:14) and in Jeremiah's prayer after his buying of the field at Anathoth (Jer 32:18).[121] Moreover, within Ezra-Nehemiah, Ezra's prayer refers to God's demonstrating חסד (Ezra 9:9).

By analogy with the construction in Josh 22:17 (המעט־לנו את־עון פעור: "Is the guilt of Peor insufficient for us?"), the actual petition in Neh 9:32b–c (אל־ימעט לפניך את כל־התלאה) "do not consider as too little before you all the hardship") requests that God not consider the present plight of the people as insufficient retribution for their crimes in the past. In both Neh 9:32 and Josh 22:17, the particle את exercises an exceptional function by marking the subject of the verb מעט (hipʿil).[122]

In Neh 9:32b, the term "hardship" (תלאה) reflects its employment, first, in the Pentateuch, in reference to the trials that the Israelites endured in Egypt and in the wilderness (Exod 18:8; Num 20:14), and, second, in Lamentations, in reference to the affliction consequent upon the destruction of Jerusalem (Lam 3:5).[123]

The order of leaders who experience the hardship (Neh 9:32c) reflects Jeremiah's lists of those who offend YHWH (Jer 1:18; 2:26; cf. 44:17, 21).

---

[121] Neh 9:32: האל הגדול הגבור והנורא שומר הברית והחסד
Deut 7:9: האל הנאמן שמר הברית והחסד
Deut 10:17: האל הגדל הגבר והנורא
Neh 1:5: האל הגדול והנורא שמר הברית והחסד
Dan 9:4: האל הגדול והנורא שמר הברית והחסד
Jer 32:18: האל הגדול הגבור
1 Kgs 8:23: שמר הברית והחסד

[122] This proposal of J. Macdonald ("The Particle את in Classical Hebrew: Some New Data on Its Use with the Nominative," VT 14 [1964]: 275) is preferable to the suggestion that in Neh 9:32 את marks either (1) an "accusative of limitation" (GBH §125j[6]); or (2) a putative accusative of a verb referring to a deficiency (GKC §117aa).

[123] In its sole remaining occurrence, תלאה denotes the listlessness of those reluctant to offer proper sacrifices (Mal 1:13).

The list in the Levites' prayer (Neh 9:32c) expands the subjects of foreign oppression whom Ezra mentions: "we, our kings, and our priests" (Ezra 9:7). Similar lists also appear in Daniel's confession (Dan 9:6, 8).

According to the biblical record, hardship under the "Assyrian kings" extended for more than a century from the invasion by Tiglath-Pileser in 734 B.C.E. (2 Kgs 15:19–20) until the fall of Nineveh in 612 B.C.E. (cf. Nah 2:2–3:19). Within this time frame, the significant episodes under the respective kings would have included: (1) Tiglath-Pileser's invasion of the northern kingdom and deportation of its populace in 733 B.C.E. (2 Kgs 15:29); (2) the siege of Samaria by Shalmaneser V from 724 to 722 B.C.E. and its fall to Sargon II in 721 B.C.E. (2 Kgs 17:3–6, 24; 18:9–12); and (3) the invasion of Judah by Sennacherib in 701 B.C.E. (2 Kgs 18:13–19:37; Isa 36:1–37:38; 2 Chr 32:1–23). Moreover, the book of Ezra refers to the settlement of foreigners in Judah under King Esarhaddon (680–669 B.C.E., Ezra 4:2) and under Ashurbanipal (669–630 B.C.E., Ezra 4:10).[124] It is noteworthy that the temporal phrase in Neh 9:32d indicates that the era of the Assyrian kings lies in the remote past.[125]

(9:33) In the declaration of God's innocence, the sequence of a pronoun preceding the attribute (צדיק אתה: "You are righteous," Neh 9:33a) is unique in the MT. Such a confession to God by a plaintiff who suffers occurs in Jeremiah's first confession (צדיק אתה יהוה: "You [will be] right, YHWH," Jer 12:1). Ezra voices a similar declaration (צדיק אתה: "you are righteous," Ezra 9:15) at the conclusion of his prayer, but he attributes a redemptive as well as retributive dimension to God's justice insofar as he highlights the preservation of a remnant while confessing the people's guilt.[126] In his prayer, Daniel twice confesses that God is just while also employing the first-person plural ("we") in a confession of corporate guilt (Dan 9:7, 14).[127]

---

[124] Gilbert, "Notes," 21–22.

[125] Cf. A. C. Welch ("The Source of Nehemiah IX," *ZAW* 47 [1929]: 130–37; idem, "The Share of N. Israel in the Restoration of the Temple Worship," *ZAW* 48 [1930]: 175–87), who argues that Neh 9 is the composition of northerners who opposed the Josianic reforms.

[126] Ezra 9:15: יהוה אלהי ישראל צדיק אתה כי־נשארנו פליטה כהיום הזה הננו לפניך באשמתינו ("YHWH, God of Israel, you are righteous, for we are left here, a remnant, up to this day. Here we are before you in our guilt").

[127] Dan 9:7: לך אדני הצדקה ולנו בשת הפנים כיום הזה ("Righteousness belongs to you, Lord, but open shame to us as on this day").

Dan 9:14: כי־צדיק יהוה אלהינו על־כל־מעשיו אשר עשה ולא שמענו בקלו ("Indeed, YHWH, our God, is right in all that he has done; for we have disobeyed his voice").

The phrase "all that has come upon us" (כל־הבא עלינו) occurs only in the prayers of Ezra (Ezra 9:13) and the Levites (Neh 9:33a), in both cases to describe divine retribution for the people's offensive behavior. Nehemiah's correction of trespasses against the Sabbath legislation explicitly points to God's initiative in bringing about retributive calamity (כל־הרעה: "all the disaster," Neh 13:18).[128]

The key words in Neh 9:33 that define the behavior of God, on the one hand, and the people, on the other, are rare in Ezra-Nehemiah: (1) צדיק ("righteousness") occurs only in the prayers of Ezra (Ezra 9:15) and the Levites (Neh 9:8, 33); (2) אמת ("truth") occurs only once (Neh 7:2) outside the Levites' prayer (9:13, 33); and (3) רשע ("to act wickedly") occurs solely in Neh 9:33. In Neh 9:33a–b, the clauses that contain the contrasting pronouns together reflect the confession of Pharaoh: "YHWH is right, and I and my people are wrong" (Exod 9:27).[129]

(9:34) The rebelliousness of the "ancestors" (אבות, Neh 9:34a) constitutes an introductory theme in Psalm 78 (v. 8). Regarding the actual sins of past leaders in Neh 9:34, their not "observing the law" (לא עשה תורה, 9:34a) contrasts with the personal example of Ezra (Ezra 7:10) and with Shecaniah's appeal for the marriage reform (Ezra 10:3). The precise expression "to do the law" occurs elsewhere only in the Chronicler's summary of Asa's kingship (2 Chr 14:4) but nevertheless exhibits kinship with the Deuteronomic injunction "to do all the words of this law" (עשה את־כל־ דברי התורה, Deut 28:58; 29:29; 31:12; 32:46; cf. 27:26; Josh 1:7).

Moreover, their not "paying attention to the commandments" reflects the behavior that Deutero-Isaiah laments as the cause of the people's suffering in the past (קשב אל/למצות [*hipʿil*], Neh 9:34b; cf. Isa 48:18). Furthermore, the expression "the warnings by which you warned them" occurs elsewhere only in the explanation of the fall of Samaria in the Deuteronomistic History (עדות אשר העיד בהם, Neh 9:34b; cf. 2 Kgs 17:15).

(9:35) The former leaders' "not serving YHWH" indicates their disobedience to a basic Deuteronomic injunction (Deut 6:13; 10:12, 20; 11:13; 13:5). The irony evident in their being "slaves" to their foes as a consequence of

---

128 By comparison with Ezra 9:13 and Neh 9:33a (which do not mention רעה), Neh 13:18 (as well as Dan 9:12, 13) is more reminiscent of the Deuteronomic expression "Behold, I will bring evil upon" (הנני/הנה אנכי מביא רעה על, 1 Kgs 14:10; 21:21; 2 Kgs 21:12; 22:16; cf. 1 Kgs 9:9 [= 2 Chr 7:22]). See M. Weinfeld, *Deuteronomy and the Deuteronomic School* (Winona Lake, Ind.: Eisenbrauns, 1992), 350.

129 Gilbert, "Notes," 22.
Neh 9:33b: אתה צדיק ... ואנחנו הרשענו
Exod 9:27: יהוה הצדיק ואני ועמי הרשעים

their not "serving" YHWH (Neh 9:35c, 36a) reflects Deut 28:47–48 but is most explicit in Jer 5:19 and 2 Chr 12:8. The cycle of sin and retribution originating with their not serving (לא עבד) YHWH corresponds with the description of Israel's history in Judg 10:6–8.

Moreover, their not "turning back from their evil deeds" (לא־שבו ממעלליהם הרעים, Neh 9:35c) reflects variations on the language of Jeremiah (Jer 23:22; 25:5; 26:3; cf. 4:4; 21:12; 23:2; 44:22; cf. Zech 1:4).

(9:36) In the portrayal of the present (9:36b), the reference to God's intention that the people would "eat of [the land's] fruit and of its goodness" represents another instance of vocabulary drawn from Jeremiah (Jer 2:7).[130]

The pronouncement "we are slaves" is an element shared in common by the prayers of the Levites and of Ezra (אנחנו עבדים, 9:36a, c; cf. עבדים אנחנו, Ezra 9:9).

(9:37) In the final line of the prayer, the term for "body" (גויה, Neh 9:37b) generally refers either to a corpse (1 Sam 31:10, 12; Ps 110:6; Nah 3:3; cf. Judg 14:8, 9) or to a visionary figure (Ezek 1:11, 23; Dan 10:6). The instance that most closely approximates the meaning of the term in the psalm is the famished Egyptians' reference to their "bodies" when they appeal to Joseph for food (Gen 47:18).

In summary, the Levites' prayer is a mosaic of traditions. In the résumé of Israel's history (9:6–31), every key expression resonates with material elsewhere, whether in the Pentateuch, the Historical Books, the Prophets, or the Psalms. Nevertheless, one rarely meets an exact representation of the source text (e.g., 9:7bα; cf. Gen 15:7). The prayer is not comprised of quotations but of expressions that became standardized, probably through liturgical use.

Deuteronomistic vocabulary predominates in approximately half the verses of the prayer and is most evident in: (1) three credal statements (9:6a–c, 7a, 32a); (2) the elaborations of the people's recalcitrance (9:16–17b, 29); (3) the summary of the wilderness era (9:21); and (4) the material dealing with the occupation (9:15c–d, 22–25) and settlement in the land (9:26–31).

However, the Deuteronomistic element is muted throughout most of the story from Abraham through the wilderness era (9:7–20). The terminology in these sections reflects features of the narration of the relevant episodes in Genesis (15:6–21; 17:5; cf. Neh 9:7–8), Exodus (13:17–15:19; 19:1–20:21; 34:6–7; cf. Neh 9:9–15b, 18), and Numbers (11:16–30; 13:1–14:25; cf. Neh 9:19–20).

---

[130] Jer 2:7: ואביא אתכם אל־ארץ הכרמל לאכל פריה וטובה ("I brought you to a plentiful land to eat its fruits and good things").

The influence of the Priestly tradition is apparent in: (1) the making of "the heavens [and] ... the earth" (Neh 9:6b–d; cf. Gen 2:1); (2) the naming of Abraham (Neh 9:7b; cf. Gen 17:5); (3) the provision of bread and water (Neh 9:15a–b; cf. Exod 16:4–36; Num 20:8); (4) God's having sworn to give the land to the people (Neh 9:15d; Exod 6:8); (5) the ancestors' refusal to occupy the land (Neh 9:17; cf. Num 13–14);[131] (6) the provision of manna and water (Neh 9:20b; cf. Num 20:1–13); (7) the descriptions of hardship in the land (Neh 9:28b; cf. Lev 26:17); and (8) a portrait of the people's rebellion (Neh 9:29b; cf. Lev 18:5). Thus, the Priestly tradition exercised an impact at diverse points throughout the prayer.

Among the prophets, Ezekiel is the one who made the most distinctive contribution to the Levites' prayer. Ezekiel's vision of history (Ezek 20:1–31) has a certain kinship with the prayer insofar as it suggests that every positive historical development is due to God's providence, whereas every regressive step results from the people's rebellion (e.g., Neh 9:15c–d [cf. Ezek 20:28]; 9:26a [cf. Ezek 20:8]; 9:29b [cf. Ezek 20:11, 13, 21]; 9:31a [cf. Ezek 20:17]).

Jeremiah is the other prophet whose voice echoes in the prayer. The vocabulary of Jeremiah comes to the fore particularly in some descriptions of the people's rebellion (Neh 9:16–17; cf. Jer 7:26; 11:10; 13:10; 17:23), the accusation of killing the prophets (Neh 9:26b; cf. Jer 2:30), and the assertion that God "did not make an end of" his people (Neh 9:31a; cf. Jer 5:18; 30:11; 46:28).

Certain lexical ingredients are peculiar to the prayer, such as: (1) the verb בחר ("to choose," Neh 9:7a) to describe God's election of Abraham; (2) the references to "the peoples of the land" in prayer (9:10a, 22a, 24c, 30c); (3) the "committing of great infamies" (ויעשו נאצות גדלות, 9:18c, 26c); (4) the particle את related to the nominative case (9:19b, 19c, 32b, 34a); (5) the expression "they resisted and rebelled against you" (וימרו וימרדו, 9:26a); and (6) the list of leaders and people for whom the Levites make intercession (9:32c).

The Form and Content of the Levites' Prayer

In form and content, the uniqueness of the Levites' prayer consists in its exhibiting characteristics both of the historical psalms (Pss 78; 105; 106; 135; 136) and of certain penitential confessions (Jer 32:17–25; Ezra 9:6–15; Neh 1:5–11; Dan 9:4–19). Generally speaking, these two forms have their counterparts in the two major parts of the Levites' prayer: the review of the past takes the form of a historical psalm (Neh 9:6–31), whereas the description of

---

[131] The account in Num 13–14 is an amalgamation of J and P material. However, its present form is the product of Priestly redaction. See B. Levine, *Numbers 1–20* (AB 4; New York: Doubleday, 1993), 52–57, 64–68, 347–81.

the present situation has the form of a penitential confession (9:32–37). A detailed comparison with the texts that exemplify the two forms will illustrate how the Levites' prayer distinctively blends both.

THE HISTORICAL PSALMS

The historical psalms (78; 105; 106; 135; 136) are hymnic confessions that variously recount Israel's history of salvation. Their poetic form situates them in the tradition of the ancient Song of the Sea (Exod 15:1–18). Their confessional character similarly associates them with credal pronouncements (Deut 26:5–9; cf. 6:20–24).[132] Such creeds provide the nucleus of material that all the historical psalms share in common: (1) reference to life in Egypt; (2) description of the exodus; and (3) mention of Israel's entering or living in the land.

The following table illustrates the relationship between the Levites' prayer and the historical psalms in terms of content.

Table 4.4—The Content of The Historical Psalms

Neh 9:6–37	Psalm 78	Psalm 105	Psalm 106	Psalm 135	Psalm 136
Creation: 9:6					4–9
Abraham: 9:7–8		7–11			
Exodus: 9:9–11	12–13, 42–53	12–15	7–12	8–9	10–15
Egypt: 9:9–10	12, 42–51	16–36	7–8	8–9	10–12
Reed Sea: 9:11	13, 53		9–12		13–15
Wilderness: 9:12–21	14–41, 52	39–42	13–33		16
Fire/cloud: 9:12, 19	14		39		
Sinai: 9:13–14, 18			19 (molten calf)		
Manna/water: 9:15, 20	15–25		41 (water)		
Rebellion: 9:16, 18	8, 17–20, 32–37, 40–42		13–22, 24–25, 28–33		
Seizing the land: 9:22–25	53–55		43–45	10–11	21–22
Sihon/Og: 9:22				11	19–20
Life in the land: 9:26–37	56–72		34–39		

---

[132] Deut 26:5–9 and 6:20–24 are Deuteronomic compositions (see Weinfeld, *The Deuteronomic School*, 34) and not ancient liturgical texts (cf. G. von Rad, "The Form-Critical Problem of the Hexateuch," in *The Problem of the Hexateuch and Other Essays* [trans. E. W. Treuerman Dicken; New York: McGraw-Hill, 1966], 1–13).

This table demonstrates that the Levites' prayer (Neh 9:6–37) recounts the events of salvation according to a basic preexisting chronological schema, one that is common to all historical psalms. However, comparing this prayer with the other historical psalms in terms of theological outlook discloses its variable proximity to each of them and highlights its distinctive features.[133]

Most distant from the tenor of Neh 9:6–37 are Pss 135 and 136, inasmuch as they are hymns of praise that refer only to the works of God but never to the activities of his people. Differences in historical focus distance the Levites' prayer (Neh 9:6–37) from Ps 78, insofar as the latter directs attention to such matters as the plagues in Egypt (Ps 78:12, 42–51), the rejection of the northern kingdom (78:60–64), and the divine choice of David and Zion (78:67–72). Nevertheless, these prayers share a common theological concern in that each of them interprets history in terms of divine retribution (e.g., Ps 78:5, 8–11, 17–18, 20–22, 30–41, 56–66; Neh 9:26–37).

On the basis of content, the Levites' prayer exhibits closest kinship with Pss 105 and 106, which share a common preoccupation with the exodus. Of these two psalms, Ps 105 is a hymn of praise that describes a fully harmonious relationship between God and his people, whereas Ps 106 is a lament that presents similar content by contrasting God's benevolence with his people's obstinancy. This hermeneutics of retribution provides a common theological interest that links Neh 9:6–37 more closely with Ps 106 than with any other historical psalm.

While preoccupation with retributive theology associates Neh 9:6–37 with Pss 78 and 106, such an association otherwise highlights the distinctiveness of that theme's presentation in the Levites' prayer. In contrast with the two psalms, retribution in Neh 9:6–37 is limited in both time and intensity. According to the Levites' prayer, the wilderness era was remarkable for the fact that God did not exercise retribution when one would have expected: first in response to his people's disobedience (9:16–17), then to their apostasy (9:18–21). This scenario starkly contrasts with the graphic descriptions of the divine reprisals for rebellion in the wilderness as found in Pss 78 (vv. 21–22, 31, 32–34) and 106 (vv. 13–15, 17–18; cf. 23). Thus, in contrast to these two psalms, the Levites' prayer portrays retribution as occurring only in the era following the settlement in the land (Neh 9:26–37).

Moreover, in the Levites' prayer retribution in this final era is disproportionately less than the people's behavior would seem to have merited.

Von Rad views the historical psalms (78; 105; 106; 135; 136) as representing further developments of the liturgical tradition witnessed in these credal statements.

[133] Cf. F. C. Fensham, "Neh. 9 and Pss. 105, 106, 135, and 136: Post-exilic Historical Traditions in Poetic Form," *JNSL* 9 (1981): 35–51.

Its extensive descriptions of rebellion (9:26, 29; cf. 9:16–17b) markedly contrast with the succinct mentions of consequent divine sanctions (9:27a, 28b, 30c). Always in describing God's response, emphasis falls on divine mercy (9:27c, 28c, 31). Such a portrayal is wholly unlike the description of the exile and extermination of the northern kingdom in Ps 78 (vv. 59–64). Moreover, the subtle allusion to exile in the Levites' prayer (cf. Neh 9:31a) represents a major dissimilarity vis-à-vis the elaborate description of captivity and dispersion recounted at the end of Ps 106 (vv. 40–47; especially vv. 46–47).[134]

THE PENITENTIAL CONFESSIONS

A number of the elements that distinguish the Levites' prayer (Neh 9:6–37) from the historical psalms do have their counterparts in the penitential prayers of Jeremiah (Jer 32:17–25), Ezra (Ezra 9:6–15), Nehemiah (Neh 1:5–11), and Daniel (Dan 9:4–19).[135] Each of the following elements appears in at least two of these prayers but not in any of the historical psalms: (1) an introductory narrative describing penitential rites (Neh 9:1–3; cf. Ezra 9:5; Neh 1:4; Dan 9:3); (2) credal statements (Neh 9:6, 7a, 17c–d, 31b, 32a–b; cf. Jer 32:18; Neh 1:5; Dan 9:4, 15); (3) the summary evaluation of God's work in the exodus: "you made a name for yourself as it is even to this day" (Neh 9:10; cf. Jer 32:20; Dan 9:15); (4) the expression "but now" indicating a transition from recollection of the past to focus on the present (ועתה, Neh 9:32a; cf. Ezra 9:8, 10; Dan 9:15); (5) a description of the present distressful situation (Neh 9:32–33, 36–37; cf. Jer 32:24;

---

[134] The portrait of retribution in the Levites' prayer (Neh 9:6–37) differs not only from the depiction in Pss 78 and 106, respectively, but also the presentation in the Deuteronomistic History. The Levites' prayer departs from the Deuteronomistic theology of retribution on two counts: first, in the Levites' prayer, the emphasis falls more on the lack of retribution than on its all-encompassing extent (e.g., Neh 9:30–31; cf. 2 Kgs 23:26–27; 24:20); and, second, the people's history is not fractured by exile from the land but rather continues uninterrupted into the present (Neh 9:32–37; cf. 2 Kgs 25:21). The Levites' prayer further differentiates itself from Deuteronomistic retribution by making two adjustments in the cyclic schema of history as found in the book of Judges (2:11–23): first, by repeatedly pointing to God's "mercies" (ב/כרחמיך, Neh 9:27c, 28c, 31a; cf. כי־ינחם יהוה מנאקתם, Judg 2:18), and, second, by extending the application of the cycles beyond the era of the judges to the whole span of the people's life in the land so that there will be no doubt about their history continuing into the future. In summary, the Levites' prayer is an adaptation rather than an adoption of Deuteronomistic retributive theology.

[135] The prayer in Dan 9:4–19 predates the composition of Daniel. Its antiquity enhances its proximity to Neh 9:6–37. See L. F. Hartman and A. A. Di Lella, *The Book of Daniel* (AB 23; Garden City, N.Y.: Doubleday, 1978), 248–49; and M. Gilbert, "La prière de Daniel: Dn 9, 4–19," *RTL* 3 (1972): 284–310.

Ezra 9:8–9); (6) an explicit mention of kings and other leaders sharing in the people's shame (Neh 9:32, 34; cf. Ezra 9:7; Dan 9:7); and (7) a confession that God is just, while the people are guilty (Neh 9:33; cf. Ezra 9:15 [cf. 9:8]; Dan 9:14).[136] This summary listing illustrates that it is the final section of the Levites' prayer (Neh 9:32–37) that contains the majority of the correspondences with the other penitential prayers.

Unlike the historical psalms, the penitential prayers (Jer 32:17–25; Ezra 9:6–15; Neh 1:5–11; Dan 9:4–19) do not constitute a homogeneous literary genre. Nevertheless, they share a common character insofar as all of them are confessions that acknowledge the corporate guilt of the people. However, in terms of how they conclude, these four penitential prayers can be subdivided into two groups: (1) those of Jeremiah and Ezra that end with a description of the present distress (Jer 32:25; Ezra 9:15); and (2) those of Nehemiah and Daniel that conclude with intercessory appeals (Neh 1:11; Dan 9:16–19). The Levites' prayer incorporates both elements: intercession (Neh 9:32b–d) and a final mention of the present troubles (9:36–37).

Within the Ezra-Nehemiah story, the penitential component of the final section of the Levites' prayer (9:32–37) necessarily associates it with the earlier confessions of Ezra (Ezra 9:6–15) and Nehemiah (Neh 1:5–11). Nevertheless, while their common literary form provides continuity among these prayers, the distinctive content of the Levites' prayer vis-à-vis the two prior invocations shows a remarkable narrative development.

Specifically, the Levites' prayer expands the horizon of concern in six areas. First, the confession of guilt emanates from the whole people rather than from an individual leader (Neh 9:1–3, 5; cf. Ezra 9:6; Neh 1:5). Second, a more global concern for autonomy and self-determination in the land (Neh 9:15c–d, 22–37) replaces a preoccupation with the particular matter of mixed marriages (Ezra 9:11–14). Third, an adversarial attitude toward the Persian overlords replaces an appreciation of them as agents of providence (Neh 9:32, 37; cf. Ezra 9:9; Neh 1:11). Fourth, the geographical focus shifts from a fixation on Jerusalem to a concern for the whole land (Neh 9:8b, 15c–d, 23b–24c, 36b; cf. Ezra 9:8–9). Fifth, the historical memory reaches back beyond the origins of trouble in the land to the wilderness era, the exodus, the covenant with Abraham, and ultimately the beginning of creation (Neh 9:6–25; cf. Ezra 9:7). Sixth, the exile is no longer the central event for defining the people in terms of their history, past and present (Neh 9:30–31, 32–37; cf. Ezra 9:7–8, 14–15; Neh 1:8–10); the covenant with Abraham (9:8a; cf. 32b)—including its promise of the land (9:8b–d, cf. 9:15c–d, 22–25, 36b)—is now the focal point of history.

---

136 See: G. von Rad, "Gerichtsdoxologie," in *Gesammelte Studien zum Alten Testament* (2 vols.; TB 48; Munich: Kaiser, 1973), 2:245–54.

THEMATIC SUMMARY

The prayer of the Levites (Neh 9:6–37) is the theological summit of Ezra-Nehemiah. In the narrative unfolding of the whole book, this prayer represents a major reorientation of perspective on a variety of central issues, including: (1) the historical framework of the story; (2) the nature of God's involvement in history; (3) the characterization of the Persian administration; (4) the role of the exile in the people's self-understanding; (5) the significance of the land; and (6) the interpretation of the Torah.

THE FRAMEWORK OF HISTORY

The Levites' prayer portrays Israel's history as a cohesive whole that provides the ultimate context for interpreting the Ezra-Nehemiah story. Its review of history extends from creation to the present and represents the only mention in the book of the covenant with Abraham, the exodus, the wilderness era, and the occupation of the land (9:6–25). Furthermore, this conception of history as a totality extends into the present situation as the critical point where the forces of the historical struggle now converge (9:32–37). While there is no pragmatic evidence of imminent political change, the recollection of the past in terms of the cycles of rebellion and correction excludes all doubt that the people will survive and affords the hope that they will enter into a time of deliverance.

Moreover, the prayer's conceiving of history in terms of successive cycles of rebellion, retribution, mercy, and renewed life ultimately makes sense of the manner in which the book ends—not with a resolution of all tension but with mention of much that still requires amendment. The conclusion to the book (13:4–31) is analogous to the conclusion of the psalm (9:32–37) insofar as each describes the present time more in terms of the people's shortcomings than of their having fully attained a new level of integrity. The prayer's depiction of history in terms of a continual interaction between divine mercy and human failure runs counter to any utopianism. Indeed, such a conception of historical dynamics relativizes rather than absolutizes the covenant renewal that follows (10:1–40). The book's final episodes (13:4–31) illustrate a variety of failures to keep the covenant commitment (cf. 10:29–40) and thereby confirm the necessity of history's continuing to unfold under the aegis of God's justice and mercy as depicted in the Levites' prayer.

GOD'S INVOLVEMENT IN HISTORY

The prayer stands out from the remainder of Ezra-Nehemiah insofar as it portrays God's direct participation in history. While the prayer depicts history as a concatenation of divine interventions, the book otherwise describes God acting indirectly, primarily through interior persuasion (cf., e.g., Ezra 1:1–2, 5; 6:14; 7:6; Neh 1:8).

Furthermore, the prayer certifies that the history recounted in the narrative is, indeed, salvation history. The prayer highlights a theme that is implicit throughout the narrative, namely, the contrast between God's actions and those of his people. According to the prayer, God's interventions account for the positive side of history, whereas the actions of his people (with the exception of his servants such as Abraham, Moses, and the prophets) are almost entirely negative. Thus, the very survival of the people testifies to the sovereignty of God. Hence, the recounting of their history occasions a series of credal statements (9:6a, 7a, 8d, 17c–d, 31b, 32a–b) and an additional liturgical formula (9:33) that are unprecedented among the historical psalms.

The two divine attributes that determine the course of history in particular are God's justice and mercy. Confessions of his justice appear in the two contexts of the psalm that mention "covenant" (הברית, 9:8a, 32b): (1) in the description of the call of Abraham (צדיק אתה: 9:8d); and (2) in the account of the present distress (אתה צדיק, 9:33). This justice, which bespeaks faithfulness on the one hand (9:8d) and retribution on the other (9:33), governs the first and last periods of history, respectively: the time of Abraham (9:7–8) and the present era (9:32–37).

God's mercy (רחם), for its part, governs history in the intervening span from the wilderness era to the last of the former generations (9:9–31). The lessons of the past provide hope for the present, since history demonstrates that divine mercy becomes manifest in response to the people's rebellion and accounts for their survival in the wilderness (9:17c; 19a) and in the land (9:27c, 28b, 31b). Furthermore, this history provides a reason for voicing the prayer at this time: invariably, God reveals his mercy as deliverance when his people "cry out" from their oppression (9:9, 27b–c, 28b; cf. 9:4).

THE PERSIAN ADMINISTRATION

The prayer's allusion to the Persian kings as perpetrators of the people's enslavement (9:36; cf. Ezra 9:8–9) and oppression (9:32, 37) contrasts with the earlier portraits of them as both the providential sponsors of the temple's reconstruction (Ezra 1:1–4; 6:14) and as patrons of Ezra (Ezra 7:11–26) and Nehemiah (Neh 2:1–8). In the remainder of Ezra-Nehemiah following the Levites' prayer, the narrative does not ascribe any credit to the Persian authorities for developments in Judah.[137] The negative light that the psalm casts on the Persian authorities endows the covenant

---

[137] In the account of Nehemiah's final visit to Artaxerxes, the Persian king is not given any active role in the affairs of Judah (13:6).

commitment that follows (10:1–40) with a political dimension. Within this context, the people's pronouncement of allegiance to YHWH and the temple represents, to some degree, an implied declaration of independence from their current political overlords.

Moreover, the foreign "peoples of the lands" who currently rule (9:30c) are sociological kindred of the "offspring of foreigners" from whom the people separate themselves (9:2). Dissociation from such people is a step toward liberation rather than a matter of self-segregation.

THE EXILE AND THE PEOPLE

The minimal allusion to the exile in the prayer is remarkable in view of the manner in which this event had defined the community throughout the preceding narrative. Prior to the prayer, Ezra-Nehemiah had designated the authentic Israel variously as "the children of the exile" (בני הגולה, Ezra 4:1; 6:19, 20, [cf. 21]; 8:35; 10:7, 16), "the assembly of the exile" (קהל הגולה, Ezra 10:8), and "those who had escaped captivity" (הנשארים אשר־נשארו מן־השבי, Neh 1:3; cf. 1:2; 7:6; Ezra 2:1; 3:8; 8:35). The last explicit reference to the exile in Ezra-Nehemiah occurs in the expression "the whole assembly of those who had returned from captivity" (כל־הקהל השבים מן־השבי, Neh 8:17) in the summary evaluation of the Festival of Booths celebrated under Ezra. Thus, the Levites' prayer represents a transition in the manner of the community's defining itself: no longer in terms of the exile (cf. Neh 7:6–72a), but rather of commitment to the Torah (Neh 10:29–40; cf. 9:13–14).

THE LAND

By avoiding explicit reference to the exile, the Levites' prayer implies that the land (הארץ) is an irrevocable gift of God to the people. The land represents the main thematic concern that extends from the beginning to the end of the prayer, linking the eras of Abraham (9:8), the wilderness (9:15), the occupation (9:22–24), and the present (9:35–36). In the present time, foreign kings might have control over the land's produce, livestock, and populace; nevertheless, they do not possess the land.

Furthermore, the prayer's depiction of the land as the focus of God's ancient promises provides the necessary context for interpreting the concern for rebuilding the temple and the city, which pervades the remainder of Ezra-Nehemiah. Whereas the book elsewhere persistently highlights the centrality of Jerusalem, the prayer underlines the importance of the whole land. By directing attention to the broader landscape beyond the city, the prayer also points toward the life setting of the whole community as depicted both within the covenant renewal (7:72b; 8:15) and in its immediate context (11:1–36).

THE TORAH

Finally, the Levites' prayer enhances the characterization of the Torah in Ezra-Nehemiah. Throughout the book, the Torah is portrayed as the compendium of normative legal texts that God communicated through Moses.[138] The Levites' prayer broadens this conception in two ways: first by locating the origins of the Torah within the historical context of Israel's formative years,[139] and second by emphasizing its original character as the radically personal word that God spoke at Sinai (9:13, 14). The setting and vocabulary in the prayer underline the nature of the Torah as a gift (ותתן להם, 9:13b) akin to the cloud and fire that provided direction (9:12) and the food and water that offered sustenance (9:15a–b) in the wilderness.

Moreover, the prayer's broad historical survey connects the divine realities associated with the only two persons whom the prayer cites by name: the Torah, which was in the hand of Moses, and the covenant, which is synonymous with Abraham. The prayer features the only two occurrences of the term "covenant" (ברית, 9:8a, 32b) in the covenant-renewal account. The association of the covenant with "faithful" (נאמן, 9:8a) Abraham prepares for the people's signing of the "agreement" (אמנה, 10:1) immediately after the prayer.

In summary, the Levites' prayer reflects the canonical tradition by locating the legislation of the Torah within the narrative of the Pentateuch and of subsequent biblical history.

---

[138] Ezra 3:2; 7:6, 10; 10:3; Neh 8:1–3, 7–9, 13–14, 18; 9:3, 13–14, 26, 29, 34; 10:29–30, 35, 37; 12:44; 13:3.

[139] According to von Rad ("Hexateuch," 12–13), Neh 9:6–37 presents a new synthesis of traditions insofar as it is the only historical psalm to incorporate the Sinai event into the salvation story.

6

The Covenant Commitment (Nehemiah 10:1–40)

The community's declaration of commitment to the covenant (Neh 10:1–40) completes the activities of the assembly on the twenty-fourth day of the seventh month (9:1). Furthermore, the communal oath taking during this third assembly is the climax of the covenant-renewal account, which began with all the people gathering on the first day of the month (7:72b–8:1).

My study of the covenant commitment follows the same five stages as my discussion of the prior segments of the covenant renewal: (1) a fresh translation; (2) textual criticism; (3) an outline of the text followed by a literary analysis of its style and contents in light of its setting within the covenant renewal; (4) a lexical examination of this material in view of related texts both in Ezra-Nehemiah and elsewhere in the MT; and (5) a concluding thematic summary.

TRANSLATION

10:1 For all this, we are making a firm agreement, and we are writing it; and on the sealed document are our princes, our Levites, and our priests.

2 [a]And on the sealed document[a]: Nehemiah, [b]the governor,[b] son of Hacaliah, and Zedekiah; 3 Seraiah[a], Azariah, Jeremiah, 4 Pashhur, Amariah, Malchijah, 5 Hattush, Shebaniah,[c] Malluch, 6 Harim, Meremoth, Obadiah, 7 Daniel, Ginnethon, Baruch, 8 Meshullam, Abijah, Mijamin, 9 Maaziah, Bilgai, Shemaiah. These are the priests.

10 And the Levites: [d]Jeshua, son of Azaniah, Binnui of the sons of Henadad, Kadmiel; 11 and their brothers: Shebaniah,[e] Hodiah,[f] Kelita, Pelaiah, Hanan, 12 Mica, Rehob, Hashabiah, 13 Zaccur, Sherebiah, Shebaniah,[g] 14 Hodiah, Bani, Beninu.[h]

15 The leaders of the people: Parosh, Pahath-moab, Elam, Zattu, Bani, 16 Bunni, Azgad, Bebai, 17 Adonijah, Bigvai, Adin, 18 Ater, Hezekiah, Azzur, 19 Hodiah, Hashum, Bezai, 20 Hariph, Anathoth, Nebai,[i] 21 Magpiash, Meshullam, Hezir, 22 Meshezabel, Zadok, Jaddua, 23 Pelatiah, Hanan, Anaiah, 24 Hoshea, Hananiah, Hasshub, 25 Hallohesh, Pilha, Shobek, 26 Rehum, Hashabnah, Maaseiah, 27 Ahiah, Hanan, Anan, 28 Malluch, Harim, Baanah.

²⁹ The remainder of the people, the priests, the Levites, the gatekeepers, the singers, the temple servants, and all who had separated themselves from the peoples of the lands to the law of God, including their wives, their sons, and their daughters, everyone who knows how to understand, ³⁰ are joining their noble kindred by entering into an oath with sanctions to walk in the law of God that was given through the hand of Moses, the servant of God, to observe and to do all the commandments of YHWH our Lord as well as his ordinances and his statutes.

³¹ Specifically, we will not give our daughters to the peoples of the land, nor their daughters will we take for our sons.

³² If the peoples of the land bring merchandise or grain to sell on the Sabbath day, we will not take it from them on the Sabbath or on a holy day.

We will forego the seventh year and the pledge in every hand.

³³ We take upon ourselves the obligations to give[j] a third of the shekel annually for the service at the house of our God: ³⁴ for the bread arrangement, for the regular grain offering, for the regular burnt offering, the Sabbaths, the new moons, for the appointed festivals, for the sacred things, and for the sin offerings, to make atonement for Israel, and for all the work at the house of our God.

³⁵ We—the priests, the Levites, and the people—have cast lots in order to bring the donation of wood to the house of our God, according to our ancestral families, at specified times year by year, for burning on the altar of YHWH our God, as it is written in the law.

³⁶ We take it upon ourselves to bring to the house of YHWH the firstfruits of our soil and the firstfruits of all the fruit of every tree year by year; ³⁷ also, the firstborn of our sons and of our livestock, as it is written in the law; and to bring the firstborn of our herds and of our flocks to the house of our God, to the priests who are ministering in the house of our God.

³⁸ And we will bring to the priests at the storerooms of the house of our God the choicest of our dough, of our contributions,[k] of the fruit of every tree, of wine, and of oil.

But the tithe of our soil we will bring to the Levites, since the Levites are the ones who collect the tithes in all the towns where we work. ³⁹ Yet when the Levites collect the tithe, the priest, the son of Aaron, must be with the Levites. And the Levites must carry up a tenth of the tithe to the house of our God, to the storerooms at the storehouse. ⁴⁰ For the Israelites and the Levites must bring the contribution of the grain, the wine, and the oil to the storerooms, since the vessels of the sanctuary, the ministering priests, the gatekeepers, and the singers are there.

We will not abandon the house of our God.

Textual Criticism

a–a Read the singular (וְעַל הֶחָתוּם) in accordance with 10:1 as in one Hebrew MS. Syntax and contemporary legal protocol confirm this reading. In terms of syntax, the whole of 10:2–28 is an apposition to 10:1b. The names in 10:2–28 take the place of the categories of leaders in 10:1b ("our princes, our Levites, and our priests"). Thus, both verses must refer to the identical document that bears the names of these leaders. Therefore, the expression that introduces the categories of those who signed the document in 10:1b (וְעַל הֶחָתוּם) is the most appropriate one for introducing the list of names in 10:2a. Moreover, legal convention demanded that there be only one sealed copy to serve as the official text in resolving subsequent disputes.[1]

Admittedly, all the versions support the plural. However, their various attempts at correction—while reflecting a general dissatisfaction with the MT (וְעַל הַחֲתוּמִים: "and on the sealed documents")—ultimately fail to account for the initial preposition (וְעַל). The Vg, Syr, and Arabic indicate the plural but read the term as a participle (הַחוֹתְמִים: "those who sealed it"). Furthermore, these versions find the preposition (עַל) problematic. LXX 2 Esd 20:1 (καὶ ἐπὶ τῶν σφραγιζόντων) testifies to the presence of the preposition עַל in the *Vorlage*—hence, the likelihood that the Syr and Arabic emended עַל to אֵלֶּה, while the Vg ignored the preposition.

b–b Maintain הַתִּרְשָׁתָא given its universal occurrence in the Hebrew MSS and its attestation in the Vg, although it is missing from LXX 2 Esd 20:1.

c Maintain "Shebaniah" although many Hebrew MSS and the Syr read "Shecaniah." "Shebaniah" also occurs in 10:11, 13.

d Omit the *wāw* before "Jeshu" in accordance with correct syntax and the Hebrew MSS as well as LXX 2 Esd 20:9, Syr, and Vg.

e Maintain "Shebaniah" although a number of Hebrew MSS as well as the Syr and Vg read "Shecaniah." The repetition of the same order "Shebaniah, Hodiah" in 10:11, 13–14 raises the possibility of a scribal error. However, Shebaniah occurs as the fourth name on the list in 9:4 (cf. 10:11) and as the seventh name on the list in 9:5 (cf. 10:13), thereby suggesting the likelihood that the name refers to different individuals.

f Maintain "Hodiah" although LXX 2 Esd 20:9 reads Ὡδουιά, that is, "Hodaviah," as in Ezra 2:40.

g As in 10:11, maintain "Shebaniah" rather than "Shecaniah."

h Maintain "Beninu" (בְּנִינוּ) since it occurs in all MSS. The fact that the name does not occur anywhere else makes this the *lectio difficilior*. (Otherwise, the best emendation would be to the previously mentioned "Chenani" [כְּנָנִי: Neh 9:4]).

---

[1] Cf. Jer 32:10–11. See below, pp. 257–60.

ⁱ Follow the Qere (נִיבִי), whereas LXX 2 Esd 20:19 reads Νωβαί in line with the Kethib (נובי).

ʲ In accordance with a few MSS, the Syr, and the Vg, omit the second occurrence of עלינו as an unnecessary repetition.

ᵏ Maintain ותרומתינו, although it does not occur in the LXX.

LITERARY ANALYSIS

The first-person voice proceeds from the declamation of the psalm (9:6–37) to the communal oath taking (10:1–40) via the repetition of the pronominal subject "we" (אנחנו, 9:37; 10:1) at the juncture between these sections. This first-person plural form occurs next in the verb endings of the first specific stipulation (10:31: the renunciation of marriage to foreigners by the covenanters' children) and continues to the end of the commitment (10:40). Nevertheless, the same voice speaks also in the intervening section (10:2–30), since: (1) there are no verbs or pronouns in the list of signatories (10:2–28); and (2) the subsequent piece (10:29–30) continues directly from its narrative antecedent (10:1), using as verbs only a combination of plural participles and absolute infinitives (... מחזיקים ובאים ... ללכת ... ולשמור ... ולעשות).

Moreover, the first-person plural prevails throughout the commitment account (10:1–40) as the subject of the six main verbs in the stipulations (לא־נתן: "we will not give," 10:31; ונטש ... לא־נקח: "we will not take ... we will forego," 10:32; והעמדנו עלינו: "we take upon ourselves," 10:33; הפלנו: "we have cast lots," 10:35 [governing להביא: "to bring," 10:35, 36, 37]; לא נעזב: "we will not abandon," 10:40), which twenty-five possessive pronouns ("our") reinforce.²

Granted that the covenant commitment (10:1–40) takes the form of first-person discourse, the question remains: Who is the speaker—the Levites or the people? The continuity with the first-person from the psalm (9:6–37) immediately suggests the Levites. However, the content of the commitment decides the issue in favor of the people. The Levites would not speak of "our Levites" (לויינו, 10:1) in the opening line. Moreover, the people rather than the Levites must declare their commitment to bring offerings and tithes to the priests and Levites (Neh 10:36–39). Thus, the content of Neh 10 indicates that it is the people

---

² "Our officials" (שרינו, 10:1); "our Levites" (לויינו, 10:1); "our priests" (כהנינו, 10:1); "our Lord" (אדנינו, 10:30); "our daughters" (בנתינו, 10:31); "our sons" (בנינו, 10:31, 37); "our God" (אלהינו, 10:33, 34 [bis], 35, 37 [bis], 38, 39, 40); "our ancestors" (אבתינו, 10:35); "our ground" (אדמתנו, 10:36, 38); "our cattle" (בהמתינו, 10:37); "our herds" (בקרינו, 10:37); "our flocks" (צאנינו, 10:37); "our dough" (עריסתינו, 10:38); "our contributions" (תרומתינו, 10:38); "our labor" (עבדתנו, 10:38).

The Covenant Commitment (Nehemiah 10:1–40)

who recount the signing of the document (10:1, 2–28) and also announce the stipulations (10:29–40).[3]

The transfer of voice from the Levites to the assembly is possible in view of the ambiguity of speaker that I indicated in connection with 9:5. At that point, the text does not make clear whether the people respond to the Levites' exhortations by simply listening to the prayer or by actually declaiming it with the Levites. In either case, the liturgical activities of the people recounted in 9:1–3 indicate their active participation. The covenant commitment occurs precisely at the juncture where one would expect a congregational response to the Levites' psalm (cf. Pss 41:14; 106:48; 1 Chr 16:36).[4] Moreover, such a response corresponds with the activity of the assembly on the first day, when they declared their "Amen" to Ezra's blessing of YHWH (8:6; cf. 9:5–10:1). The community's referring to the Torah at this point (10:31–40) is consistent with their reading "from the book of the law of YHWH, their God" at the beginning of this assembly on the twenty-fourth day of the seventh month (9:3).

OUTLINE

The first-person account of the covenant commitment consists of two major parts: the signing of the document (10:1–28); and the pronouncement of the stipulations (10:29–40). The opening line recounts the signing of the document (10:1), while the subsequent list of signatories is subdivided into four groups according to office: (1) the governor (10:2a); (2) the priests (10:2b–9); (3) the Levites (10:10–14); and (4) the leaders of the people (10:15–28).

The announcement of the stipulations consists of two major sections: affirmation of a general adherence to the Torah (10:29–30); and the pronouncement of specific stipulations (10:31–40). The six specific stipulations in turn fall into two categories: (1) three pertaining to societal concerns (10:31–32); and (2) three pertaining to temple affairs (10:33–40). The new introductory clause, "We take upon ourselves the obligation" (והעמדנו עלינו מצות, 10:33a) demarcates the two categories of stipulations. The

---

[3] Williamson, REB, and JPSV place quotation marks around the whole of Neh 10:1–40 (*Ezra, Nehemiah*, 320–23). D. Kidner emphasizes the continuity between the prayer and the covenant commitment: "The inverted commas should not have been closed at 9:37, for this passage [10:1–40] (including the list of names) is as definitely a 'we'-passage as the prayer which has led up to it" (*Ezra and Nehemiah* [TOTC; Leicester: Inter-Varsity Press, 1979], 114). The voice of the community in 10:1 is the primary evidence that Eskenazi (*In an Age of Prose*, 100) invokes for her identification of the community as the speaker of the preceding psalm (see above p. 162).

[4] See pp. 153–54.

concluding statement ("We will not abandon the house of our God," 10:40b) generally expresses allegiance to the temple, unifying the second category of precepts (10:33–40a).

Table 6.1—The Structure of the Covenant Commitment (Neh 10:1–40)
A. The signatures (10:1–28)
   1. Narrative introduction (10:1)
   2. The signatories (10:2–28)
     a. The governor (10:2a)
     b. The priests (10:2b–9)
     c. The Levites (10:10–14)
       (1) Levites (10:10)
       (2) Fellow Levites (10:11–14)
     d. The leaders of the people (10:15–28)
B. The stipulations (10:29–40)
   1. General principle: commitment to the Torah (10:29–30)
   2. Specific stipulations (10:31–40)
     a. Societal commitments (10:31–32)
       (1) Renunciation of marriage to foreigners (10:31)
       (2) Sabbath observance (10:32a)
       (3) The seventh year and the release of pledges (10:32b)
     b. Obligations to the temple (10:33–40)
       (1) Temple tax (10:33–34)
       (2) Donation of wood (10:35)
       (3) Contributions (10:36–40a)
         (a) Firstfruits and firstborn (10:36–37)
         (b) The choicest harvest products (10:38a)
         (c) The tithe of the soil (10:38b–40a)
       (4) Summary promise of support for the temple (10:40b)

The foremost structural components that unify the account are the references to the categories of leaders that occur at the beginning (10:1, שָׂרֵינוּ לְוִיֵּנוּ כֹּהֲנֵינוּ: "our princes, our Levites, and our priests"), middle (10:29, הַכֹּהֲנִים לְוִיִּם הַשּׁוֹעֲרִים הַמְשֹׁרְרִים הַנְּתִינִים: "the priests, the Levites, the gatekeepers, the singers, the temple servants"), and end (10:40, הַכֹּהֲנִים הַמְשָׁרְתִים וְהַשּׁוֹעֲרִים וְהַמְשֹׁרְרִים: "the ministering priests, the gatekeepers, and the singers"). The latter two lists provide an *inclusio* for the major section that recounts the community's commitment (10:29–40). Two leadership categories in particular are the subjects of recurring attention: (1) the priests (כֹּהֲנִים, 10:1, 9, 29, 35, 37, 38, 40; cf. כֹּהֵן, 10:39); and (2) the Levites (לְוִיִּם, 10:1, 10, 29, 35, 38 [bis], 39 [3x], 40).

Attention to the priests and Levites coincides with a preoccupation with the temple that unifies the second set of specific stipulations

(10:33–40). This section contains nine references to the temple (בית אלהינו: the "house of our God," 10:33, 34, 35, 37 [bis], 38, 39, 40; בית יהוה: the "house of YHWH," 10:36) and one reference to the altar (מזבח יהוה אלהינו: the "altar of YHWH our God," 10:36).

LITERARY ANALYSIS

In the following examination of style and syntax, I follow the categories of the above outline.

THE SIGNATURES (10:1–28)

Narrative Introduction (10:1)

The first three words of Neh 10:1 provide a link with the preceding prayer (9:6–37). "For all this" (ובכל זאת, 10:1) indicates the motive for the people's making the agreement. The expression encompasses the complete (כל) history that the Levites recounted in the psalm (9:6–37). The comprehensive nature of the expression prohibits focusing on a particular episode. However, the subsequent descriptions of the signing of the agreement (10:1a), the listing of leaders (10:1b–28), and the expression of their commitment to the Torah (10:29–30) highlight, respectively, the psalm's account of the covenant with Abraham (9:8a), the former leaders' infidelity to the Torah (9:34a), and the people's rejection of the Torah (9:26a; cf. 9:16–17b, 18, 28a, 29–30). Thus the expression "for all this" (ובכל זאת, 10:1) indicates that the people commit themselves because they have recognized the dynamics of history recounted in the prayer. Specifically, their recognition of God's fidelity and their own guilt prompts them to renew their commitment to the Abrahamic covenant (9:8a, 32b) and the Mosaic law (9:13–14; cf. 9:26a, 29a, 34a).

The first-person pronoun in 10:1 provides a strong link with the final segment of the prayer, which describes the present situation of the people (אנחנו; "we," 10:1; cf. 9:33b, 36a, 36c, 37b). At the same time, this pronoun emphasizes that it is the people who proclaim the covenant commitment that follows. As the Levites declaimed the psalm and proclaimed its final "we" (אנחנו, 9:37b), the people now follow their lead and immediately apply the same pronoun to themselves in introducing the covenant commitment.

The people's "making a firm agreement" (כרתים אמנה, 10:1) recalls YHWH's "making the covenant" with Abraham (כרות עמו הברית: "you made the covenant with him," 9:8a). The word used for "firm agreement" (אמנה, 10:1) resonates with the "faithfulness" (נאמן, 9:8a) of Abraham due to their common derivation from the root אמן. Moreover, within the book of Nehemiah, the verb כרת occurs only in these two verses (cf. Ezra 10:3). Therefore, the agreement that the people make (10:1) actualizes in their day the covenant that YHWH had made with Abraham (9:8a). The description of God as "keeping the covenant with loyalty" (שׁוֹמֵר הַבְּרִית וְהַחֶסֶד, 9:32b) provides the theological horizon before which the people make this agreement.[5]

The people's establishing the agreement "in writing" (כְּתָבִים, 10:1) parallels this with the "written" character of the Torah noted elsewhere in the covenant renewal: previously, concerning the Festival of Booths, and subsequently in connection with the precepts (כתוב[כ], 8:14, 15; 10:35, 37). The appropriate response to the written text of the Torah is a written agreement by the people.

Specification of the categories of leaders (שָׂרֵינוּ לְוִיֵּנוּ כֹּהֲנֵינוּ: "our princes, our Levites, and our priests," 10:1) whose names appear on the sealed document refers back to the two listings of authorities, respectively, in the intercessory (9:32b) and confessional (9:34a) subunits of the final segment of the Levites' prayer (9:32–37). In each of those lists, "our princes" are mentioned immediately before "our priests" (שָׂרֵינוּ כֹּהֲנֵינוּ, 9:34a; cf. 9:32b). In 10:1, the "Levites" come between these previously mentioned categories due to their role in the covenant renewal, both as leaders of the prayer (9:4–5) and as interpreters of the Torah (8:7–8, 9, 11). Mention of the categories of leaders who sign the agreement introduces a contrast with the previous list of authorities who "[had] not kept your law" (לֹא עָשׂוּ תוֹרָתֶךָ, 9:34a). Therefore, the leaders' signing the agreement constitutes that "turning" toward God and the Torah that divine warnings had sought to produce in prior eras following Israel's settlement in the land (תָּעַד בָּהֶם לַהֲשִׁיבָם אֶל־תּוֹרָתֶךָ: "you warned them in order to turn them back to your law," 9:29a; cf. 9:26b, 30b).

The Signatories (10:2–28)

Introducing the names of the contracting parties at the beginning corresponds with the normative format for contemporary legal documents.[6] Moreover, listing the names prior to the stipulations provides for narrative consistency, since, within the covenant renewal, each major section begins with an introduction of the main characters prior to the description of their activities (7:72b–8:1: "the children of Israel," "the whole people," "Ezra, the scribe"; 8:13: "the heads of the families of all the people," "the priests and Levites," "Ezra, the scribe"; 9:1: "the children of Israel").

---

[5] F. C. Holmgren ("Faithful Abraham and the ᵓamānâ Covenant: Nehemiah 9,6–10,1," *ZAW* 104 [1992]: 249–53) correctly underlines the semantic relationship between the people's agreement (10:1) and the covenant with Abraham (9:8). However, I disagree with his views that 9:6–37 (1) exhibits a "loose chiastic structure," (2) suggests that the exile was determinative, and (3) implies that the land was "taken away" from Israel.

[6] See below pp. 258–60.

The Covenant Commitment (Nehemiah 10:1–40)

The extensive list of names (10:2–28) highlights the importance of the individual within the community. From the general mass there now emerge the unique personalities that comprise the community. Listing the names prior to the covenant commitment provides a narrative contrast to the absence of any names for those who initiated the penitential rites on the twenty-fourth day (9:1–3). The lack of individual names at that point (9:1–3) underscored the democratic nature of the event as a grass-roots initiative. The insertion of an abundance of names at this point (10:2–28) confirms the same democratic tendency from another perspective by illustrating that the reformation of the community results from the unified commitment of various personalities.[7]

The various categories in the list itself (10:2–28: the governor, the priests, the Levites and their brothers, and the leaders of the people) differ from those in the summary (10:1: princes, Levites, and priests). Nevertheless, in both cases, remarkable emphasis falls on the laypeople insofar as the secular officials (שָׂרֵינוּ: "our princes," 10:1; cf. נְחֶמְיָה הַתִּרְשָׁתָא: "Nehemiah, the governor," 10:2) are mentioned before the clerics (לְוִיֵּנוּ כֹהֲנֵינוּ: "our Levites and our priests," 10:1; cf. הַכֹּהֲנִים: "the priests," 10:3–9; וַאֲחֵיהֶם ... הַלְוִיִּם: "the Levites ... and their brothers," 10:10–14). Furthermore, the forty-four "leaders of the people" (רָאשֵׁי הָעָם, 10:15–28) outnumber the combined sum of twenty-one priests (הַכֹּהֲנִים, 10:3–9) and seventeen Levites (וַאֲחֵיהֶם ... הַלְוִיִּם, 10:10–14) in the list of names (10:2–28).

The eighty-four names on the document reflect a symbolic number for all Israel (seven times twelve).[8] This number suggests that "the whole people" (כָּל־הָעָם, ten times in 8:1–12) who heard the reading of the law on the first day now enter into the covenant agreement.

The Governor (10:2a). Mention of "Nehemiah the governor" (נְחֶמְיָה הַתִּרְשָׁתָא, 10:2) as the first name on the list recalls the reference to him at the head of the list of officials who spoke to the people on the first day of the month (נְחֶמְיָה הוּא הַתִּרְשָׁתָא, 8:9). Moreover, his position in the list as the highest political authority in the community suggests that, as the first to sign the agreement, he represents a reversal of the behavior of "our kings and princes" who head the list of those who had not complied with the Torah (cf. 9:34) and thereby were responsible for the present distress.

The *wāw* that links Zedekiah with Nehemiah suggests that Zedekiah was a civil official who assisted the governor.

---

7 Eskenazi, *In an Age of Prose*, 103–4.

8 Torrey, *Ezra Studies*, 284. The number eighty-four presumes that the sequence "Shebaniah, Hodiah" occurs twice in the list of the Levites (Neh 10:11, 13–14; see textual notes above, p. 237).

The Priests (10:2b–9). Up to this point in the covenant renewal, references to priests have alternated between a concentration on the individual, Ezra (הכהן, 8:2, 9), and summary references to "the priests" (הכהנים, 8:13; 9:32, 34; 10:1) as an anonymous group. Within the covenant renewal, the list of twenty-one priestly names serves four purposes: (1) the absence of Ezra's name combines with the extensive list of twenty-one to signal a democratic shift from individual to collegial leadership; (2) the priestly commitment to the Torah explicitly reverses past clerical infidelities (cf. 9:34); (3) the names reverse the previous anonymity of the priestly group (cf. 8:9, 13); and (4) the introduction of the priestly names prepares for the subsequent highlighting of the priestly service in the temple reforms announced in the stipulations (10:35, 37, 38, 39, 40).

The Levites (10:10–14). The list subdivides the Levites into two groups: (1) the first three who are called "Levites" (הלוים, 10:9–10) and (2) the remaining fourteen designated as "their brothers" (אחיהם, 10:11–14). The complete list recalls the three groups of the Levites previously mentioned in the covenant renewal: (1) those who read the Torah on the first day of the month (8:7); (2) those who stood on the stairs of the Levites and cried out to YHWH (9:4); and (3) those who encouraged the people to bless YHWH (9:5).

Table 6.2—The Levites in the Covenant Renewal (Neh 7:72b–10:40)[9]

Neh 10:10–14	Neh 8:7	Neh 9:4	Neh 9:5
1. Jeshua, son of Azaniah	Jeshua [1]	Jeshua [1]	Jeshua [1]
2. Binnui of the sons of Henadad		Binnui [2]	
3. Kadmiel		Kadmiel [3]	Kadmiel [2]
4. Shebaniah		Shebaniah [4]	
5. Hodiah			
6. Kelita	Kelita [9]		Hodiah [6]
7. Pelaiah	Pelaiah [13]		
8. Hanan	Hanan [12]		
9. Mica			
10. Rehob			
11. Hashabiah			Hashabneiah [4]
12. Zaccur			
13. Sherebiah	Sherebiah [3]	Sherebiah [6]	Sherebiah [5]
14. Shebaniah			Shebaniah [7]
15. Hodiah			
16. Bani	Bani [2]	Bani [7]	Bani [3]
17. Beninu			

[9] The numbers in brackets refer to the position of the name in the respective lists.

The names of the three Levites (Jeshua, Sherebiah, and Bani) that occur in all four Levitical lists (8:7; 9:4, 5; 10:10–14) are the only ones to recur in each of the three chapters of the covenant-renewal account. From a narrative perspective, the names of the Levites in the list of signatories (10:10–14) connect the community agreement (10:1–40) with the reading of the law on the first day (8:1–12) and with the penitential rites at the beginning of the twenty-fourth day (9:1–5). The Levites' signing of the document in union with the people (10:29–30) culminates the service that they rendered to the community by reading the Torah (8:8) and leading the prayer (9:4–5). Moreover, their signatures (10:10–14) prepare for the further expansion of their activities to include the supplying of wood and the tithing of their tithes in support of the temple (10:35, 38–40).

The Leaders of the People (10:15–28). The "leaders of the people" (ראשׁי העם, 10:15) recall the "heads of the families of all the people" (ראשׁי האבות לכל־העם, 8:13) who gathered on the second day to study the words of the law with Ezra. The title "the heads of the families" might apply more directly to the first twenty-one names (10:15–21a: Parosh to Magpiash) than to the last twenty-three (10:21b–28: Meshullam to Baanah) insofar as the first part of the list seems to refer to families whose roots go back to the first wave of exiles to return to Judah (Ezra 2:1–70; Neh 7:6–72a).[10] In any case, dedication to the Torah (דברי התורה: the "words of the law," 8:13; cf. תורת האלהים: "the law of God," 10:29, 30) provides a common feature for the two passages of the covenant-renewal account that mention the laypeople who are "heads" (ראשׁים, 8:13; 10:15) of the community. The two references to these "heads of the people" link the community commitment on the twenty-fourth day (10:15) to the study of the law on the second day of the seventh month (8:13).

Of the final twenty-three names in the list, six occur in the enumeration of the thirteen men who stood on the platform with Ezra when he opened the book of the law (8:4): Hashum (10:19), Meshullam (10:21), Anaiah (10:23), Hashabnah (10:26; Hashbaddanah, 8:4), Maaseiah (10:25), and Malluch (10:28; Malchijah, 8:4). Their names link the covenant commitment on the twenty-fourth day (10:1–40) to the initial assembly that took place on the first day of the seventh month (8:1–12).

The Stipulations (10:29–40)

General Principle: Commitment to the Torah (10:29–30). The participial verb forms provide grammatical continuity between the opening announcement of the written agreement (10:1, וכתבים ... וכרתים) and the

---

[10] See below, pp. 264–65.

community's oath of allegiance to the Torah (10:29–30: מחזיקים ... ובאים). The making of the firm agreement (וכרתים אמנה, 10:1) involves the people "entering into an oath with sanctions" (באים באלה ובשבועה, 10:30) to conform their lives to the Torah.

All the members of the community not listed among the signatories (אחיהם אדיריהם: "their noble kindred," 10:30) are subsumed under eleven categories that fall into four groupings: (1) "the remainder of the people"; (2) the temple personnel ("the priests, the Levites, the gatekeepers, the singers, the temple servants"); (3) "all who had separated themselves from the peoples of the lands to the law of God"; and (4) the families of all the men ("their wives, their sons, and their daughters," i.e., "all who know how to understand").

The "remainder of the people" (שאר העם, 10:29) are distinct from the "leaders of the people" (ראשי העם, 10:15). Mention of this majority of the populace reflects a continuing concern for the "whole people" that suffused the description of the events on the first day (כל־העם, 8:1–12 [10x]) and extended to the account of the Festival of Booths (כל־העם, 8:13; כל־הקהל, 8:17).

"The priests" and "the Levites" (10:29) refer to those clergy whose names do not appear among the signatories (cf. 10:3–9, "the priests"; 10:10–14, "the Levites"). Mention of these two groups in 10:29 indicates that the list of signatories (10:2–28) does not encompass all the leaders.

"The gatekeepers," "the singers," and "the temple servants" (10:29) are mentioned for the first time at this point in the covenant renewal. Reference to these offices provides an introductory allusion to the concern for the temple that will characterize the last five stipulations (10:33–40).[11]

"All who had separated themselves from the peoples of the lands to the law of God" (כל־הנבדל מעמי הארצות אל־תורת האלהים, 10:29) here designates only one category among the eleven groups comprising the body of the reformed community. Therefore, the act of separation mentioned here is more specific than the foundational activity of the whole assembly at the beginning of the twenty-fourth day whereby the offspring of Israel separated themselves from foreigners (ויבדלו זרע ישראל מכל בני נכר, 9:2a). There the decision for separation at the beginning of the day belonged to those who were Israelites by birth (זרע ישראל, 9:2a), whereas here the separation "from the peoples of the lands to the law of God" serves as a designation for proselytes.

---

[11] The absence of any reference to specific categories of lay leaders is unique to this list (10:29) vis-à-vis the prior listings of lay offices in the covenant renewal (cf. 8:9: the governor, the priest and scribe, and the Levites; 8:13: the heads of families, the priests, and the Levites; 9:32: our kings, our princes, our priests, our prophets, our ancestors; 9:34: our kings, our princes, our priests, and our ancestors).

The Covenant Commitment (Nehemiah 10:1–40)

Nevertheless, the language that defines these proselytes resonates with previous vocabulary in the covenant renewal. Separation from the "peoples of the lands" (עמי הארצות, 10:29) constitutes an act of liberation insofar as these "peoples of the lands" (עמי הארצת, 9:30c) are those into whose hands God gave his people in punishment for their refusal to obey him. Moreover, the separation to "the law of God" (תורת האלהים) recalls the book from which the Levites read on the first day (8:8) and from which Ezra read every day during the Festival of Booths (8:18).

The mention of "their wives" (נשיהם, 10:29) echoes the only other references to "the women" (הנשים, 8:3; cf. אשה, 8:2) in the covenant renewal, that is, as part of the audience who gathered to hear the Torah on the first day.

The reference to "their sons" (בניהם, 10:29) suggests a recognition of the importance of the next generation in view of the psalm's description of "the children" entering to possess the land (בניהם, 9:23; הבנים, 9:24a).

The reference to "their daughters" (בנתיהם, 10:29) in addition to "their sons" (בניהם, 10:29) prepares for the first stipulation, namely, the one by which the parents renounce the betrothal of their children to foreigners (10:31).

"Everyone who knows how to understand" (כל יודע מבין, 10:29) is a summary category that stands in apposition to "their sons and their daughters" and defines the youngest group who could take part in the community commitment. "Everyone who knows how to understand" is equivalent to "everyone who could understand by hearing" (כל מבין לשמע, 8:2), a group that was integral to the assembly on the first day.

In summary, the familial categories of "their wives," "their sons," and "everyone who knows how to understand" (10:29) serve a recollective function by alluding to the inclusivity of the initial assembly that had listened to the reading of the Torah (8:2–3).

The description of the signatories as "their noble kindred" (אחיהם אדיריהם, 10:30) extends the familial terminology ("their wives, their sons, and their daughters," 10:29) to embrace the leadership as well. Furthermore, the term "kindred" (את) replaces the various official titles (cf. 10:1b, 2, 9, 10, 11, 15, 29a) and thereby recalls the trend toward democratization implied in the populist initiative that gave rise to the events of the day (9:1–3).

The pronouncement of "an oath with sanctions" (באים באלה ובשבועה, 10:30) by the remainder of the people is equivalent to the signatures of the leaders insofar as it constitutes the means for making the agreement (כרתים אמנה, 10:1).[12] The statement of the general principle is elaborate,

---

[12] The nouns אלה ("curse") and שבועה ("oath," Neh 10:30; Dan 9:11) form a hendiadys. I adopt the JPSV translation. H. C. Brichto renders the expression

consisting of four verbs (a governing participle [באים], three dependent absolute infinitives [ללכת, לשמור, ל[ע]שות]), and four nouns referring to legislation (חקיו, משפטיו, מצות יהוה אדנינו, התורת האלהים). Such language recalls four segments of the psalm, the first being the description of God's communication of his precepts at Sinai (9:13–14) and the subsequent three being the successive portrayals of rebellion by the people or their leaders (9:26, 29–30, 34). The extensive description of the Torah recalls its mention at Sinai (10:30; cf. 9:14b).[13] Furthermore, in both settings, references to the commandments (מצות), ordinances (משפטים), and statutes (חקים) supplement the primary concentration on the Torah (10:30; cf. 9:13b–14b). The community's profession of allegiance to these legislative norms (10:30) contrasts with their ancestors' previous disregard for God's law (תורתך, 9:29a; cf. 9:26a, 34a), commandments (מצותיך, 9:29a; cf. 9:16; 9:34b), and ordinances (משפטיך, 9:29b). Therefore, in principle (10:30) the people pledge their allegiance to the Sinaitic legislation (cf. 9:13–14) and thereby renounce their ancestors' repeated disobedience to this essential instruction (cf. 9:26, 29–30, 34).

Furthermore, the elaborate description of the Torah (10:30) recalls the designation of the book that the people requested Ezra to bring on the first day (8:1) and that the leaders consulted on the second day (8:14).[14] Thus, the full title of the Torah occurs in each of the three major segments of the covenant renewal (7:72b–8:12; 8:13–18; 9:1–10:40). Such evidence indicates that the people's ultimate commitment to the Torah (10:30) is the product of their developing familiarity with it over the course of the successive assemblies in the seventh month.

The expression "our Lord" (אדנינו, 10:30) recalls its only other occurrence in Ezra-Nehemiah (8:10) and thereby provides another link between the covenant commitment and the events of the first day. Moreover, this expression (אדנינו) reinforces the first-person narrative voice by providing a continuation of the first-person possessive adjectives from the introduction (שרינו לוינו כהנינו): "our princes, our Levites, and our priests," 10:1).

Specific Stipulations (10:31–40). The specific stipulations address both societal commitments (10:31–32) and obligations to the temple (10:33–40). More specifically, the societal commitments entail renunciation of marriage

---

אלה ושבועה as "a penalty-fraught oath" (*The Problem of "Curse" in the Hebrew Bible* [JBLMS 13; Philadelphia: Society of Biblical Literature, 1963], 32–34).

[13] 10:30: תורת האלהים אשר נתנה ביד־משה עבד־האלהים
9:14b: תורה צוית להם ביד־משה עבדך

[14] 10:30: תורת האלהים אשר נתנה ביד־משה עבד־האלהים
8:1: ספר תורת משה אשר־צוה יהוה את־ישראל
8:14: תורת אשר־צוה יהוה ביד־משה

to foreigners (10:31), Sabbath observance (10:32a), and obligations related to the seventh year and the release of pledges (10:32b), while the temple obligations concern the temple tax (10:33–34), the donation of wood (10:35), and various contributions (10:36–40a).

The stipulations specify the content of the "oath with sanctions," since the expression ואשר ("specifically") follows from the hendiadys ב[אלה ‏וב[שבועה (10:30).[15] Three nouns link the parents' refusal to allow their children to marry foreigners (10:31) to the general principle (10:29–30): daughters (בנתינו, 10:31; cf. בנתיהם, 10:30), peoples of the land[s] (עמי הארץ, 10:31; cf. עמי הארצות, 10:29), and sons (בנינו, 10:31; cf. בניהם, 10:30).

The renunciation of future marriages to the "peoples of the land" (עמי הארץ, 10:31) is most appropriate as the first stipulation because it—more so than the following five (10:32–40a)—maintains a thematic continuity extending back to the beginning of this final day of assembly (9:1–10:40).

First, mention of the "peoples of the land" (עמי הארץ, 10:31) unites this commitment by the Judahite families to the decision of the proselytes to separate themselves from the "peoples of the lands" (עמי הארצות, 10:29).

Second, reference to the "peoples of the land" (עמי הארץ, 10:31) links this stipulation to the psalm by recalling how God brought the Israelite "children" (בניהם, 9:23a) into the land and gave "the peoples of the land" (עממי הארץ, 9:24c) into their hands. By focusing on the issue of betrothal, the stipulation involves two generations (the parents and their children) and thereby recalls the historical transition from the generation that left Egypt and passed through the wilderness (9:9–22) to the next generation, which entered the land (9:23–25). The parents' refusal to betroth their children to foreigners implies their desire to bequeath to the next generation a heritage of fidelity (10:31). This contrasts with the legacy of infidelity that carried over from the parents of the wilderness era (9:16–17b, 18) to their children who conquered the land (9:26, 28a, 29a–30c).

Third, the refusal to betroth Judahite children to the offspring of the people of the land corresponds with the initial activity of the day (9:2) whereby "the offspring of Israel" (זרע ישראל) separated themselves from "all foreign children" (בני נכר). Moreover, the familial dimension implied in the parents' announcing their stance regarding the betrothal of their children (10:31) maintains the sociological focus on the family suggested by the mention of men, women, and children participating in the assemblies on the first (8:2, 3) and last (10:29) days of the covenant renewal.

The first stipulation thus serves as a bridge from the preceding narrative to the remaining stipulations. Its vocabulary links this stipulation—more

---

[15] The word אשר similarly introduces oral or written pronouncements elsewhere in Nehemiah: 2:5; 7:65; 8:14; 13:1, 19, 22. Moreover, the expression ואשר fulfills this function earlier in the covenant-renewal account (8:15). See BDB, 83.

than the rest—to the prior account of the covenant renewal. Its sociological concern to maintain the integrity of the community through the exclusion of foreigners provides the context for the preoccupation with economic issues in the remaining stipulations. The parents' refusal to allow their children to marry foreigners is the only nonfiscal stipulation. Each of the remaining five has an explicit financial dimension (10:32–40a).

Ongoing preoccupation with the "peoples of the land" (עמי הארץ, 10:31, 32a) and the identical verbal expression לא נקח ("we will not take") link the second stipulation to the first (10:31, 32a).[16] The people's commitment to Sabbath observance (10:32a) recalls the centrality of this precept in the presentation of the Sinai event in the Levites' prayer (9:14a). According to the preceding psalm, the sanctity of the Sabbath is the only specific stipulation that God "made known" (ידע hipʿil) amid all the laws, commandments, precepts, and statutes that he "gave" (נתן) or "commanded" (צוה) at Sinai (9:13–14).

The people's extending their commitment to include not only the Sabbath but also every "holy day" evokes the memory of the threefold declaration by various leaders that the first day of assembly was holy to YHWH (ביום קדש, 10:32a; cf. היום קדש: "this day is holy," 8:11; היום קדש־הוא ליהוה אלהיכם: "this day is holy to YHWH your God," 8:9; קדוש היום לאדנינו: "for this day is holy to our Lord," 8:10).

In summary, the second stipulation attests to the community's appropriation of the instruction they received from two sources: their leaders (cf. 8:9–11); and their history as a people (cf. 9:13–14).

The third stipulation, concerning the seventh year and the release of pledges, is immediately addressed in Neh 10:32b. The terseness of the statement in 10:32b implies an intimate connection between its two components. The first portion ("We will forgo the seventh year": ונטש את־השנה השביעית) presumes an accusative designating the produce of the land.[17] Moreover, in the second portion ("and the pledge in every hand": ומשא כל־יד), there is an ellipsis of the initial verb (נטש: "we will forgo").[18]

---

[16] These are the only occurrences of the verb לקח ("to take") in the covenant renewal. Their respective applications correspond to the two uses of the verb elsewhere in Ezra-Nehemiah, i.e., to describe: (1) the "taking" of a person in marriage (Ezra 2:61 = Neh 7:63; Neh 6:18; 10:31); and (2) the acquisition of goods (Neh 5:2, 3, 15; 10:32a).

[17] BHS notes a possible emendation of תבואת ("yield") after the object-marker (את־) in view of the occurrence of את־תבואת in Exod 23:10. However, such a proposal lacks support from either MSS or from the versions.

[18] BHS notes the conjecture of supplying the verb נשא ("we will dispense with") to govern the accusative משא ("pledge"). However, the lack of supporting textual witnesses precludes this hypothesis.

Thus, the people's commitment to observe the seventh year (10:32b) encompasses a twofold renunciation: first, of the crops, and second, of the pledges held in repayment for loans. These forms of renunciation are on behalf of the poor and the indebted, who would be the beneficiaries of this double initiative in the seventh year.[19] The poor would glean the produce from the fallow land, while debtors would regain possession of the pledges that they had handed over to their creditors.

Thus, this third stipulation provides for the social welfare of the economically disadvantaged. It addresses the issues of poverty and gross economic disparity by focusing on both the management of agricultural resources and the provision for personal indemnity. In summary, this declaration is a commitment on the part of the wealthy for the sake of the impoverished members of the community.

As such, this commitment marks a reorientation in the focus of the agreement (אמנה, 10:1) insofar as this stipulation and the remaining three (10:32b–40a) treat relationships within the community (10:32b–40a), whereas the first two stipulations dealt with relationships to outsiders (the "peoples of the land," 10:31–32a).

In the fourth stipulation (which is the first of the temple obligations, 10:33–40), the community announces an annual tax to supply the offerings at the temple. Their commitment to "give" (לתת, 10:33) a third of the shekel marks the only instance in the covenant renewal in which the verb נתן ("to give") describes a positive action by the people. As such, נתן suggests a contrast with the rebellious behavior of earlier generations: initially of those who "appointed a leader" (ויתנו־ראש, 9:17b) in the wilderness, and later of those who "gave God a stubborn shoulder" (ויתנו כתף סוררת, 9:29c) after the settlement. Moreover, the people's "giving" (נתן) of the tax implies their ultimate responsiveness to God's "giving" them his diverse gifts throughout their history (נתן, 9:8a, 8c, 10a, 13b, 15a, 15d, 20a, 20b, 22a, 24b, 27c, 35a, 35b) and, more immediately, the Torah (10:30).

The first two occurrences of the expression the "house of our God" (בית אלהינו, 10:33, 34) in the covenant renewal provide an *inclusio* that frames the list of provisions. Moreover, these occurrences appear in analogous phrases describing the purpose of the tax: "for the service of the house of our God" (לעבדת בית אלהינו, 10:33) or for "all the work at the house of our God" (כל מלאכת בית אלהינו, 10:34).

The fifth stipulation disrupts the syntax of the fourth and sixth stipulations, which begin with ל plus the infinitive construct, in dependence on the introductory phrase "we take upon ourselves the obligations" (והעמדנו

---

[19] See below pp. 275–79.

עלינו מצות, 10:33).²⁰ Nevertheless, two factors make this prescription an appropriate sequel to the previous one: the focus on "the house of our God" (בית אלהינו, 10:35; cf. 10:33, 34); and the concern for wood after mention of burnt offerings (10:35; cf. 10:34).

Moreover, this stipulation introduces four elements that are absent in the prior four stipulations but that recur in the next one: (1) "the priests" and "the Levites" (הכהנים: "the priests," 10:35, 37, 38; cf. 10:39 [הכהן: "the priest"]; הלוים: "the Levites," 10:35, 38 [bis], 39 [bis]); (2) "bringing" offerings to the temple (להביא לבית אלהינו: "to bring to the house of our God," 10:35, 37; cf. 10:36: להביא ... לבית יהוה: "to bring to the house of YHWH"); (3) "year by year" (שנה בשנה, 10:35, 36); and (4) "as it is written in the law" (ככתוב בתורה, 10:35, 37).²¹

The three parties who cast lots ("the priests, the Levites, and the people," 10:35) are mentioned in the same sequence as the titles of the signatories ("the priests," 10:3–9; "the Levites," 10:10–14, and "the leaders of the people," 10:15–28). However, the designations in the fifth stipulation suggest a greater degree of democracy insofar as "the people" (העם)—and not only their leaders—take part in the event. This final occurrence of the term העם in the covenant renewal (7:72b–10:40) suggests an advancement in their role: from recipients of instruction (8:3, 16) to providers for the temple (10:35).

Nevertheless, while the noun "the people" (העם) refers to the whole community, the term "our ancestral houses" (בית־אבתינו, 10:35) might allude to the family names among the signatories: the priestly subgroups (10:3–9), the Levitical families (Jeshua, Binnui, Kadmiel, 10:10), and the first twenty-one names of the laity (10:15–21a). Therefore, the combination of titles for those who provide the wood donation could recall both the leaders (10:2–28) and "the remainder of the people" (שאר העם, 10:29).

Mention of "the wood" (העצים, 10:35) for the temple sacrifices recalls the "trees" for constructing booths (עץ, 8:15 [bis]) and the "wood" of Ezra's platform (מגדל־עץ, 8:4). Thus, the term *wood* occurs once in each of the three major segments of the covenant renewal (7:72b–8:12; 8:13–18; 9:1–10:40).

The phrase "the altar of YHWH our God" (מזבח יהוה אלהינו, 10:35) is the only instance in the covenant renewal in which the people actually call

---

²⁰ Note the constructions used: לתת ("to give," 10:33); להביא ("to bring," 10:36); להביא ("to bring," 10:37). Because 10:35 does not conform to this pattern, Rudolph (*Esra und Nehemia*, 176) transposes the stipulation on the wood offering to the end of the series (after 10:40a).

²¹ Within Ezra-Nehemiah, the following expressions occur only in Neh 10:35, 36–37: שנה בשנה (10:35, 36); and ככתוב בתורה (10:35, 37; cf. ככתוב בתורת משה, Ezra 3:2).

YHWH "our God." In all the related instances, the title occurs either in statements of Ezra and the Levites (יהוה אלהיכם: "YHWH, your God," Neh 8:9; 9:4, 5) or in the narrator's description (יהוה אלהיהם: "YHWH, their God," 9:3 [bis]). In summary, in their designation of the altar, the people implicitly confess the creed that Ezra and the Levites taught them: "YHWH [is] our God."

The sixth clause of the community's oath (10:36–40a) is the most complex. It lists four categories of items that the people are to present at the temple: (1) the firstfruits of the soil (10:36); (2) the firstborn of families and livestock (10:37); (3) the choicest harvest products (10:38a); and (4) the tithes (10:38b). This sixth stipulation concludes by outlining the protocol for collecting the tithes (10:39) and consigning them to the storerooms (10:40a). The recurrence of the verb "to bring" (בוא *hip'il*) provides continuity throughout the stipulation (להביא, 10:36, 37; נביא, 10:38; יביאו, 10:40).

The verbal expression "to bring" (להביא, 10:36), which introduces the sixth clause, is dependent on the introductory assertion, "We take upon ourselves the obligations" (10:33). Various parallels link the presentation of the firstfruits (10:36) with the bringing of the firstborn (10:37): (1) the verb "to bring" (להביא, 10:36, 37); (2) the repetition of "firstfruits" (בִּכּוּרֵי: 10:36 [bis]), on the one hand, and of "firstborn" (בְּכוֹרֵי/בְּכֹרוֹת, 10:37), on the other; (3) the alliteration between בִּכּוּרֵי (10:36 [bis]) and בְּכוֹרֵי (10:37); and (4) the temple as the destination of the offerings (לבית יהוה: "to the house of YHWH," 10:36; cf. לבית אלהינו: "to the house of our God," 10:37).

Furthermore, the alternate names for the temple ("the house of YHWH," 10:36; "the house of our God," 10:37) reflect the two aspects of the altar's designation in the previous stipulation ("the altar of YHWH our God," 10:35) and therefore strengthen the connection between the stipulation governing the firstfruits and the firstborn and the stipulation that precedes it.

Two lexical elements recall the psalm's portrait of the land at the conquest: (1) "our land" (אדמתנו, 10:36) resonates with the "fertile land" (אדמה שמנה, 9:25); and (2) "all the fruit of every tree" (כל־פרי כל־עץ, 10:35) corresponds with "fruit trees in abundance" (עץ מאכל לרב, 9:25).[22]

Three items that the people will bring to the temple recall prior statements in the covenant renewal. First, the presentation of the firstfruits (10:36) symbolizes the people's acknowledgment that the land is a gift of YHWH (9:24a–b, 35a–b) and thereby represents a contrast to the self-indulgence of its original Israelite inhabitants (9:25). Second, the presentation of the firstborn of "our sons" (בנינו, 10:36; cf. 10:31) reflects the priority of YHWH in family life and is consistent with the parents' earlier pledge not to allow their sons to take foreign wives. Third, the bringing of the firstborn of "our

---

22 Moreover, the fruit trees (10:35) also recall the trees for making the booths (8:15).

livestock" (בהמתינו, 10:37) implies a sense of Judahite ownership that was lacking in the affirmation of Persian control of "our livestock" (בהמתנו, 9:37b) in the concluding line of the psalm.

The bringing of foodstuffs (i.e., the choicest harvest products, 10:38a) exhibits two linguistic links with the bringing of the firstfruits and of the firstborn: (1) the "fruit of every tree" (פרי כל־עץ, 10:38) corresponds with "all the fruit of every tree" (כל־פרי כל־עץ); and (2) the bringing of these goods "to the priests at the storerooms of the house of God" (לכהנים אל־לשכות בית־אלהינו, 10:38) parallels the bringing of the firstborn "to the priests who are ministering in the house of God" (לכהנים המשרתים בבית־אלהינו, 10:37). Whereas the firstfruits consist of the raw produce from the grain and tree harvests (10:36), these foodstuffs result from the processing of such crops, notably, dough, wine, and oil (10:37). These products that surround mention of the "fruit of every tree" (פרי כל־עץ, 10:38) suggest that the fruit here is in a processed form.[23] In any case, within the community's sixth stipulation, the qualification of the products shifts from the earliest ("firstfruits": בכורים, 10:36; "firstborn": בכורים, 10:37) to the best ("choicest": ראשית, 10:38). The temple storerooms were available for the depositing of such harvest products.

The statement on tithes (10:38b–39) extends into a summary directive on the handling of both tithes and contributions (10:40a). Elements of both syntax and content link the proviso on tithes (10:38b–39) to the previous one on harvest products (10:38a). There is a double syntactical bond consisting of the gapping of the verb "we will bring" (נביא, 10:38a) and the antithetical parallelism between "to the Levites" (ללוים, 10:38b) and "to the priests" (לכהנים, 10:38a). In terms of content, the summary directive (10:40a) connects the two articles by alluding to the tithes (i.e., what the "Levites" bring to the temple; cf. 10:39b) and by mentioning the "contribution" (תרומה, 10:40a; cf. 10:38a) of the "Israelites."

The community's statement on tithes consists of four parts: (1) the contractual clause ("But the tithes of our soil we will bring to the Levites," 10:38bα); (2) an explanation of the clause ("since the Levites are the ones who collect the tithes in all the towns where we work," 10:38bβ); (3) a proviso regarding the Levites' collecting of the tithes (i.e., a priest must accompany the Levites, 10:39a); and (4) a proviso regarding the Levites' depositing of the tithes (i.e., a tenth goes to the temple, 10:39b).

Thus, the Levites receive the tithes (10:38b), whereas the priests receive the firstborn and the harvest products (10:37–38a). Given the

---

[23] Cf. כל־פרי כל־עץ: "all the fruit of every tree" (10:36), which designates fruit in its raw form. By contrast, identifying the "fruit of every tree" (פרי כל־עץ, 10:38) with "all the fruit of every tree" (כל־פרי כל־עץ, 10:36) would suggest that such fruit requires no processing in order to become fit for consumption.

Levites' central role in the reception of the tithes, the two provisos protect the priests' authority by guaranteeing their right to supervise (10:39a) and to benefit from (10:39b) the collecting of tithes.

The summary directive (10:40a) highlights the temple as the focal point for the collection and storage of the tithes and contributions. Mention of the sanctuary vessels and the various temple personnel indicates what and whom the donations are to support.

From a literary perspective, the summary directive encapsulates the whole community by speaking of its various members: "the Israelites ... the Levites ... the priests, the gatekeepers, and the singers" (10:40a). Such a list recalls the roster of participants in the covenant renewal: "the remainder of the people, the priests, the Levites, the gatekeepers, the singers, the temple servants" (10:29). Coming at the end of the covenant renewal, the list also echoes the categories of the settlers whose mention immediately precedes the whole account: "the priests, the Levites, the gatekeepers, the singers, some of the people, the temple servants, and all Israel" (Neh 7:72a).

Moreover, the verb "to bring" (בוא *hipʿil*) provides an *inclusio* for the covenant-renewal account: the narrative that begins with Ezra "the priest" (הכהן, 8:2) "bringing" (ויביא, 8:2) the law before the assembly concludes with the people "bringing" (יביאו, 10:40a) their contributions to "the priests" (הכהנים, 10:40a) at the temple. Furthermore, the narrative begins with "all Israel" (כל־ישראל, 7:72b) settled in their towns and concludes with "the Israelites" (בני־ישראל, 10:40a) bringing contributions to the temple.

The community's concluding promise summarizes its commitment to "the house of our God" (בית אלהינו, 10:40b; cf. 10:33, 34, 35, 37 [bis], 38, 39, 40), which unifies the last three stipulations. The negative formulation of the promise (לא נעזב: "We will not abandon," 10:40b) recalls the first two stipulations (לא נתן: "we will not give," 10:31; לא נקח: "we will not take," 10:31, 32).

The verbal expression "we will not abandon [the house of our God]" ([לא נעזב [את־בית אלהינו, 10:40a) similarly echoes the repetition of the phrase "you did not abandon them" (לא עזבתם, 9:17, 19, 31) in the prayer. Thus, the people's refusal to abandon the temple constitutes their ultimate response to God's not abandoning their rebellious ancestors throughout their history.

Lexical Examination

The Signatures (10:1–28)

Narrative Introduction (10:1)

In Neh 10:1, the expression "for all this" (ובכל זאת) introduces a change in the people's behavior from infidelity to commitment. Insofar as the expression defines a turning point in history, it exhibits a unique meaning vis-à-vis its other occurrences in the MT. The three other instances in which the expression refers to the actions of the people underline the refusal of Israel (or Judah) to return to God in spite of the afflictions they experienced in punishment for their apostasy (Jer 3:10; Hos 7:10; Ps 78:32). The two occurrences in Job emphasize his perseverance in virtue in spite of losses of children, property, and health (Job 1:22; 2:10). The five occurrences of the expression in Isaiah are part of a refrain that describes the perdurance of God's anger against Judah (Isa 5:25; 9:12, 17, 21; 10:4).[24]

The word for "firm agreement" (אמנה, 10:1) occurs elsewhere in the MT only in Neh 11:23, where it designates a piece of legislation concerning the temple singers.

The term that definitively identifies the event as a covenant ceremony is the participle כרתים (lit., "we are cutting [it]"). The verb כרת immediately calls to mind the idiom כרת ברית ("to make a covenant"), which occurs more than seventy times in the MT.[25] The same verb governs alternate objects in at least two expressions: (1) in Deut 29:11, 13, the single verb כרת takes as its object אלה ("curse") as well as ברית ("covenant"); and (2) in Hag 2:5, the noun דבר ("promise") is the object of כרת. Moreover, in 1 Sam 22:8 and 2 Chr 7:18, the verb כרת alone, without an object, means "to make a covenant."[26]

The above expressions are variations analogous to the unique occurrence of כרת אמנה in Neh 10:1. At the same time, their common derivation from כרת ברית demonstrates the intimate relationship—within the last day of the covenant renewal (9:1–10:40)—between the description of God's "making the covenant with Abraham" (כרות עמו הברית, 9:8a) and the account of the people's subsequently "making a firm agreement" (כרתים אמנה, 10:1).

Earlier, Shechaniah used the technical expression כרת־ברית (Ezra 10:3). This occurrence exhibits affinity to כרת אמנה in Neh 10:1 insofar as both expressions refer to a pact that concentrates on specific stipulations. The "covenant" (ברית, Ezra 10:3) that Shecaniah advocates concerns only the dissolution of marriages with foreigners. Similarly, the "firm agreement" (אמנה, Neh 10:1) that the people make focuses on specific stipulations

---

[24] "[I]n all this, his anger has not turned away, and still his hand is stretched out" (בכל־זאת לא־שב אפו ועוד ידו נטויה).

[25] J. Barr states, "kārat bᵉrît is probably by far the most important and striking case of idiom in all biblical Hebrew" ("Some Semantic Notes on the Covenant," in Beiträge zur Alttestamentlichen Theologie: Festschrift für Walther Zimmerli zum 70. Geburtstag [ed. H. Donner, R. Hanhart, and R. Smend; Göttingen: Vandenhoeck & Ruprecht, 1977], 27).

[26] See G. F. Hasel, "כָּרַת ktl," TDOT 7:349; Barr, "Semantic Notes," 27–29.

(10:31–40). Nevertheless, in both cases, the concentration on these particular issues reflects a more global commitment to keep the whole Torah (כתורה, Ezra 10:3; cf. תורת האלהים, Neh 10:29, 30).²⁷

The people's setting of the agreement in writing (וכתבים, 10:1) gives it the character of both a contract and a solemn declaration. Within the biblical tradition, its written form identifies the agreement (אמנה, Neh 10:1) as a contract akin to other legal documents, such as the Deuteronomic bill of divorce (Deut 24:1, 3), Jeremiah's property deed (Jer 32:12), and Samuel's prescriptions for the monarchy (1 Sam 10:25).²⁸

Even within Ezra-Nehemiah itself, its writing (וכתבים, 10:1) gives the agreement (אמנה) the character of a legal declaration.²⁹ This is the only written pronouncement to emerge from Judahite hands in the whole book.³⁰ As a written statement, this agreement is analogous to the decrees (Ezra 1:1–4; 6:2–12; 6:14; 7:12–26) and letters (4:6–16, 17–22; 5:6–17) of the Persian administration insofar as each of these declarations addresses an immediate situation and determines the subsequent course of history within Jerusalem and Judah.³¹ Just as the written decrees of the Persian monarchs opened the way for the return of the exiles (Ezra 1:1–4), the completion of the temple (6:14), and the mission of Ezra (7:12–26), so the written agreement of the community sets the agenda for the subsequent reforms of Nehemiah (Neh 10:29–40; cf. 13:4–31).

The "sealed" document (החתום, 10:1) identifies the agreement as a legal record.³² The protocol for the transfer of property described in Jeremiah mentions two copies of the contract: one that is open (הגלוי) for

---

²⁷ Cf. McCarthy, "Covenant and Law," 32–33.

²⁸ H. Haag, "כָּתַב ktb," *TDOT* 7:375. However, Haag mistakenly describes the agreement in Neh 10:1 as "the obligation imposed upon the community by Nehemiah" and, therefore, fails to recognize its distinctiveness as a declaration that arises purely from the community's own initiative.

²⁹ In Ezra-Nehemiah, the root כתב applies to both Persian and Jewish documentation. Persian "writings" include: (1) the edict of Cyrus (מכתב, Ezra 1:1; cf. כתיב [Aramaic], 6:2); (2) the letters opposing the rebuilding of the temple (4:6, 7, 8); (3) Tattenai's report (5:7; cf. 5:10); and (4) Sanballat's letter to Nehemiah (Neh 6:6). Jewish "writings" include: (1) the Torah (ככתוב, Ezra 3:2, 4; 6:18 [כתב: Aramaic]; 8:14, 15; Neh 10:35, 37; 13:1 [כתוב]); (2) a temple receipt (Ezra 8:34); (3) genealogical records (Neh 7:5, 64 [= Ezra 2:62]); (4) the agreement (Neh 10:1); and (5) Levitical lists (Neh 12:22–23).

³⁰ The law (תורה), being a book, represents an entirely different category of publication (cf. Ezra 3:2; 7:6, 10; 10:3; Neh 12:44; 13:3).

³¹ Eskenazi shows how the official publications of the Persian administration are the determinative forces that shape history in Judah from the return of the exile through the mission of Ezra (*In an Age of Prose*, 42–44, 58–60, 76–77, 189–90).

³² S. Moscati, "I Sigilli nell'Antico Testamento," *Bib* 30 (1949): 320–23.

ready consultation, and the other that is sealed (הֶחָתוּם) for safekeeping (Jer 32:10–11, 14; cf. 32:44). However, since Neh 10:1 does not refer to an open copy, the reference to the "sealed" document (הֶחָתוּם, 10:1) indicates only the official nature of the contract without implying a distinction between this text and a putative open copy.³³

The three categories of "princes," "Levites," and "priests" occur exclusively in the Chronistic History (Neh 10:1; cf. 1 Chr 23:2; 24:6; 28:21; 2 Chr 35:8; Ezra 8:29; 9:1). The groups in Neh 10:1 correspond most closely to the audience that David assembled for his decree on the organization of the Levites (1 Chr 23:2: כָּל־שָׂרֵי יִשְׂרָאֵל וְהַכֹּהֲנִים וְהַלְוִיִּם: "all the princes of Israel, the priests, and the Levites"). Within Ezra-Nehemiah, reference to these three groups recalls, in particular, their involvement in Ezra's marriage reforms (Ezra 9:1; cf. 10:5 ["leading priests, Levites, and all Israel"]).

THE SIGNATORIES (10:2–28)

The individuals would have affixed their names to the sealed document (וְעַל הֶחָתוּם, 10:2) by signature rather than by the stamp of their personal seals.³⁴ It is difficult to conceive how scribes could have applied more than eighty seals to one document.³⁵ Archaeological evidence from the Achaemenid period demonstrates that the seal was impressed on clay to make a bulla, which secured the cord that wrapped the document.³⁶

---

³³ Cf. Mowinckel (*Studien I*, 135–36), who interprets Neh 10:1–2 in view of the protocol outlined in Jer 32:11, 14.

³⁴ Cf. Williamson (*Ezra-Nehemiah*, 323), who suggests reading וְעַל הַחוֹתָמִים ("and on the seals") instead of וְעַל הַחֲתוּמִים ("and on the sealed documents") in Neh 10:2. Furthermore, B. Otzen asserts that the officials who signed the agreement were distinguished from the rest of the community by the fact that they were of sufficient social status to possess a seal ("חָתַם κτλ," *TDOT* 5:266). The evidence from Elephantine (n. 36 below) indicates that such assertions fail to take sufficient account of the archaeological evidence pertaining to seals, bullae, and documents in the Achaemenid period. The Samaritan Papyrus 1 [SP 1] from Wâdī ed-Dâliyeh is an example of a document that the witnesses verified by applying their seals rather than their signatures, but the number of these witnesses was comparatively small. See nn. 35, 36, and 42 below.

³⁵ Blenkinsopp, *Ezra-Nehemiah*, 312. F. M. Cross provides this description of the plurality of seals on SP 1: "The papyrus was sealed with at least seven seals—seven remained attached to the rolled document—and there is no room for seven names [on the papyrus] even if we include the officials among the seven or more whose seals are attached" ("Samaria Papyrus 1: An Aramaic Slave Conveyance of 335 B.C.E. Found in the Wâdī ed-Dâliyeh," *ErIsr* 18 [1985]: 15*).

³⁶ N. Avigad gives this description of the seals and bullae that he examined: "The bullae themselves are small lumps of clay which had been used to seal letters and/or documents. They were pressed on the knotted cord or string tying the

Furthermore, the Elephantine documents testify to the importance of signatures and name lists for the certification of contracts. However, in the Elephantine legal corpus, the signatures of the witnesses far outweigh those of the contracting parties both in number and importance.[37] Among the Elephantine documents, the signature of a party is certain in only one contract (CAP 13:17–18), whereas the signatures of a plethora of witnesses appear in some twenty-nine agreements.[38]

Samaria Papyrus 1 from Wâdī ed-Dâliyeh further attests to the importance of the validation by witnesses at the end of the document.[39] The language of the validation is significant for the study of Neh 10:2. The final line uses the verb חתם: "[the witnesses] affix their seals, they being

---

rolled papyrus or leather scroll, then stamped with seals" (*Bullae and Seals from a Postexilic Judean Archive* [Qedem 4; Jerusalem: The Institute of Archaeology, The Hebrew University, 1976], 3). For a picture of sealed contracts from Elephantine, see *The Brooklyn Museum Aramaic Papyri: New Documents of the Fifth Century B.C. from the Jewish Colony at Elephantine* (ed. E. G. Kraeling; New Haven, Conn.: Yale University Press, 1953), plate xxi. For an introduction to the sealing of these documents, see J. D. Cooney's article in the same work, "The Papyri and Their Sealings, with a Brief Description of Their Unrolling" (123–27). For a more detailed presentation of how a papyrus was folded and sealed at Elephantine, see B. Porten, "A New Look: Aramaic Papyri and Parchments," *BA* 42 (1979): 74–104. For a further illustration of the impact of folding and binding on the text, see idem, "Aramaic Papyri in the Egyptian Museum: The Missing Endorsements," in *The Word of the Lord Shall Go Forth: Essays in Honor of David Noel Freedman in Celebration of His Sixtieth Birthday* (ed. C. L. Meyers and M. O'Connor; Winona Lake, Ind.: Eisenbrauns, 1983), 527–44). Moreover, Cross describes the appearance of SP 1 in these words: "SP1 came into my hands still tightly rolled, tied and sealed with seven bullae.... There was no evidence of folding. It was quite possible, however, that the papyrus had been folded in half, and that it broke apart along one side of the fold. The papyrus was rolled (and flattened) from top to bottom (the top inside, the lower margin outside)" ("Samaria Papyrus 1," 7*).

[37] See R. Yaron, "The Schema of the Aramaic Legal Documents," *JSS* 2 (1957) 44–54; and idem, *Introduction to the Law of the Aramaic Papyri* (Oxford: Oxford University Press, 1961), 16–24. Yaron states, "It was the signature of the witnesses that was of legal import, not that of the parties; the latter seems here [CAP 13] to be added for the sake of emphasis" (*Introduction*, 17).

[38] Yaron calculates the number of witnesses as varying between four and twelve but concludes that they ultimately fall into two categories of transactions: those that require four witnesses and those that require eight witnesses (*Introduction*, 17–24).

[39] This document dates to March 19, 335 B.C.E. F. M. Cross originally presented this document in "Samaria Papyrus 1," 7*–17* and subsequently updated his analysis of it in "A Report on the Samaria Papyri," *Congress Volume: Jerusalem, 1986* (ed. J. A. Emerton; VTSup 40; Leiden: Brill, 1988), 17–26.

trustworthy" (יחתמון המו מהימנן [Aramaic], SP 1:12; cf. ועל החתום: "and on the sealed document," Neh 10:1, 2).[40]

Therefore, the primary function of the signatures in Neh 10:2–28 differs from that of almost all the Elephantine and Samaritan Aramaic legal documents (cf. CAP 13:17–18). The narrative indicates that the leaders catalogued in Neh 10:2–28 sign their names as parties—rather than as witnesses— to the agreement (אמנה, 10:1), for they are the "noble kindred" (אחיהם אדיריהם, 10:30) whom the rest of the populace joins in voicing its commitment. At the same time, insofar as these signatures endow the sealed document with official status (10:2–28), they function in a manner analogous to that of the Elephantine and Samaritan documents.

The listing of the names at the beginning of the written agreement (Neh 10:2–28) corresponds with the format of legal documents at Elephantine inasmuch as the latter texts identify the parties before describing the terms of the contract.[41] However, the listing of these names as signatures at the beginning (Neh 10:2–28) is the feature that distinguishes the community agreement from the legal documents at Elephantine.[42]

The written agreement (Neh 10:1–40) is the only sealed (חתם) document in the MT that bears a multiplicity of signatures (cf. 1 Kgs 21:8; Jer 32:10–11, 14, 44; Esth 3:12; 8:8, 10). The number eighty-four, as the product of seven times twelve, corresponds with other texts in Ezra-Nehemiah that highlight the number twelve as symbolic of "all Israel" (כל־ישראל, Ezra 8:35; cf. 6:17 [the twelve tribes]; 8:24 [twelve leading priests]; Neh 7:7 [twelve leaders]).

The Governor (10:2a).

Nehemiah's leadership as governor in the signing of the agreement recalls the origins of his tenure as governor (התרשתא, 10:2; cf. הפחה, 5:14, 15). His being the first to enter into "an oath" (שבועה, 10:30) of obedience to the Torah is consistent with his previous initiative in making the men "take an oath" (שבע hip'il, 5:12) to cancel the debts of their Judahite kindred. Moreover, identifying Nehemiah by his patronymic (בן־חכליה: "son

---

[40] Cross, "Samaria Papyrus 1," 8*, 9*.

[41] In terms of the complete schema of Elephantine contracts, Yaron (*Introduction,* 55) distinguishes between two categories: Group A (the minority of the texts): (1) date; (2) parties; (3) operative part; (4) witnesses; (5) name of scribe; (6) dictation clause; and (7) endorsement; and Group B (the majority of texts): (1) date; (2) place of execution; (3) parties; (4) operative part; (5) name of scribe; (6) dictation clause; (7) witnesses; (8) endorsement. Yaron describes the differences between the alternative structures as "slight."

[42] Because the signatures belong to the witnesses, they occur at the end of the Elephantine documents (CAP 1:8–11; 2:19–21; 5:15–19; 6:17–21; 8:29–34; 9:17–22; 10:22; 11:10–14; 13:18–20; 14:12–13; 15:37–39; 18:4–5; 20:17–18; 25:18–19; 28:15–16; 43:12; 46:12–15).

The Covenant Commitment (Nehemiah 10:1–40)

of Hacaliah," 10:2) recalls his original introduction (1:1) and thereby suggests that his signing of the agreement culminates his activities that began when he was in Susa and heard of Jerusalem's sorry state.

The listing of the governor's name first among the signatories in Neh 10:2–28 corresponds with the position of the governor's name that heads the list of witnesses in SP 7:17 ("before Hananyah, governor of Samaria": קדם [ח]ניה פחת שמרין).[43]

The name Zedekiah does not occur anywhere else in Ezra-Nehemiah.[44] However, the uniqueness of his association with Nehemiah in the list suggests that he could be "Zadok, the scribe" who enjoyed Nehemiah's confidence (13:13).[45]

The Priests (10:2b–9).

The list of twenty-one priests who signed the agreement (10:3–9) exhibits noteworthy parallels with three other priestly rosters in the Chronistic History: (1) those who originally returned from exile (Neh 12:1–7); (2) those who were heads of families sometime thereafter in the days of Joiakim (Neh 12:12–21; cf. 12:10, 26); and (3) the twenty-four priestly courses established by David (1 Chr 24:7–18).

Table 6.3—The Lists of Priests[46]

Neh 10:3–9	Neh 12:1–7	Neh 12:12–21	1 Chr 24:7–18
1. Seraiah	Seraiah	of Seraiah, Meriah	
2. Azariah	Jeremiah	of Jeremiah, Hananiah	
3. Jeremiah	Ezra	of Ezra, Meshullam	
4. Pashhur			
5. Amariah	Amariah	of Amariah, Jehohanan	
6. Malchijah	Malluch	of Malluchi, Jonathan	Malchijah [5]
7. Hattush	Hattush		
8. Shebaniah	Shecaniah	of Shebaniah, Joseph	Shecaniah [10]

---

[43] Quoted in Cross, "Samaria Papyrus 1," 15*.

[44] For an analysis of the names listed in Neh 10:2–28, see R. Zadok, *The Pre-Hellenistic Israelite Anthroponymy and Prosopography* (OLA 28; Leuven: Peeters, 1988), 274–75.

[45] Blenkinsopp (*Ezra-Nehemiah,* 312) suggests a comparison between "Nehemiah, the governor ... and Zedekiah" (Neh 10:2) with "Rehum, the chancellor, and Shimshai, the scribe" (Ezra 4:8). The phrase in Neh 10:2 lacks only the last of the five components in the sequence of Ezra 4:8 (name of the main figure, his office, *wāw,* name, "the scribe").

[46] Adapted from Blenkinsopp, *Ezra-Nehemiah,* 337. The numbers in brackets refer to the position of the name in the respective lists.

9. Malluch			
10. Harim	Rehum	of Harim, Adna	Harim [3]
11. Meremoth	Meremoth	of Meraioth, Helkai	
12. Obadiah			
13. Daniel			
	Iddo	of Iddo, Zechariah	
14. Ginnethon	Ginnethoi	of Ginnethon, Meshullam	
15. Baruch			
16. Meshullam			
17. Abijah	Abijah	of Abijah, Zichri	Abijah [8]
18. Mijamin	Mijamin	of Miniamin	Mijamin [6]
19. Maaziah	Maadiah	of Maadiah, Piltai	Maaziah [24]
20. Bilgai	Bilgah	of Bilgah, Shammua	Bilgah [15]
21. Shemaiah	Shemaiah	of Shemaiah, Jehonathan	

The priestly names in the list of signatories (10:3–9) are not designations of individuals but of priestly families or subgroups. The correspondences between these names and those on the rosters both of the priests under Jeshua (12:1–7) and of the heads of priestly families under Joiakim (12:12–21) confirms that these names refer to divisions of the priesthood in the postexilic era.[47]

The variations in some names might be due to scribal errors or alternative traditions: (1) Ezra (עזרא, 12:1, 13; third in the lists) could be a short form of Azariah (עזריה, 10:3; second in the list); (2) Malluch (מלוך, 12:2; cf. מלוכי, 12:14) seems to be a variant of Malchijah (מלכיה, 10:4; cf. 1 Chr 24:9); (3) Shecaniah (שכניה, 12:3; 1 Chr 24:11) closely resembles Shebaniah (שבניה, 10:5; 12:14); and (4) metathesis probably transformed Harim (חרם, 10:6; 12:15) into Rehum (רחם, 12:3).[48]

The three lists in Nehemiah are linked by similarities not only in names but also in numbers. There are twenty-one priestly signatories (10:3–9), twenty-two priests who returned with Jeshua (12:1–7), and twenty-one heads of priestly families at the time of Joiakim (12:12–21).[49] Furthermore,

---

[47] Pashhur (10:4) and Harim (10:6) also occur as the names of priestly families in Ezra 2:38–39 (= Neh 7:41–42).

[48] A. Jepsen, "Nehemia 10," *ZAW* 66 (1954): 87–88.

[49] The list of signatories (10:3–9) contains five names that do not occur in either 12:1–7 or 12:12–21: Pashhur, Malluch, Obadiah, Daniel, Baruch, and Meshullam. One name (Hattush) occurs among the signatories (10:3–9) and in Jeshua's group (12:1–7) but not in Joiakim's group (12:12–21). Furthermore, the latter two lists conclude with an identical sequence of six names in addition to the ones they have in common with the signatories (10:3–9): Joiarib, Jedaiah, Sallu [Sallai], Amok, Hilkiah, and Jedaiah (12:6–7; cf. 12:19–21).

these numbers are close to the twenty-four priestly divisions (מחלקות) in Chronicles (1 Chr 24:7–18).[50] This numerical evidence suggests that the list of signatories (10:3–9) reflects the organizing of the priests to provide for regular services at the temple (cf. 1 Chr 24:1–6, 19).[51] Therefore, this listing of the twenty-one priests (10:3–9) corresponds with the summary commitment of the community: "We will not abandon the house of our God" (10:40).

Insofar as the names relate not to individuals but to the subdivisions of the priesthood while their number (twenty-one) closely approximates that of other rosters, the list of priestly signatories in Neh 10:3–9 appears to be comprehensive. Therefore, these twenty-one signatures might be emblematic of the unanimous consent of the whole priesthood to the written agreement. In that case, the subsequent participation of "the remainder of the priests" (הכהנים ... שאר, 10:29) confirms the universality of commitment already implied in the list of priestly signatories (10:3–9).

The Levites (10:10–14).

In the list of Levitical signatories, the separation of Jeshua, Binnui, and Kadmiel, the first three names ("the Levites," 10:10), from "their brothers" (10:11) corresponds with the priority of these three throughout Ezra-Nehemiah. Jeshua and Kadmiel designate families in the register of the first wave of those who returned from exile (Ezra 2:40 = Neh 7:43). The subsequent narrative depicts Jeshua and his sons cooperating with Kadmiel and his sons (one of whom is "Binnui") in supervising construction at the temple site (Ezra 3:9). Moreover, Jeshua, Binnui, and Kadmiel are mentioned first among the original Levitical returnees in the list that follows after the covenant-renewal account (Neh 12:8).

Hashabiah (10:12) and Sherebiah (10:13) might be the individuals who joined Ezra's entourage at Ahiva (Ezra 8:18–19 [note, however, the reverse order of the names]). Moreover, Hashabiah and Sherebiah (and "Jeshua, son of Kadmiel") are counted among the heads of the Levites at the time of Ezra (Neh 12:24).[52] The latter list (12:24; cf. 10:10, 11)

---

[50] In addition to the parallels noted in the chart, the names of the first two divisions, Jehoiarib and Jedaiah (1 Chr 24:7), correspond with the first two of the six names in 12:6–7 and 12:19–21 (Joiarib and Jedaiah), which extend beyond the list of signatories (cf. 10:3–9).

[51] For a diachronic examination of the narrative in Chronicles, see H. G. M. Williamson, "The Origins of the Twenty-Four Priestly Courses: A Study of 1 Chronicles xxiii–xxvii," in *Studies in the Historical Books of the Old Testament* (ed. J. A. Emerton; VTSup 30; Leiden: Brill, 1979), 251–68.

[52] I follow Blenkinsopp (*Ezra-Nehemiah*, 340–41) and Clines (*Ezra, Nehemiah, Esther*, 226–227), who understand the Levitical list in 12:24–25 to represent the

distinguishes between "the heads of the Levites" (ראשי הלוים) and "their brothers" (אחיהם).

Three Levitical names in the list of the signatories (10:10–14) also occur in the roster of those who repaired the wall (3:1–32): Bani (the father of Rehum: 3:17; cf. 10:14), Hashabiah (the prince of the half-district of Keilah: 3:17; cf. 10:12), and "Binnui, son of Henadad" (3:18 [reading בני rather than בוי]; cf. 10:10). The distinction between "the Levites" (הלוים) and "their brothers" (אחיהם) also occurs at this point in the roster of those who rebuilt the walls (3:17–18; cf. 10:10, 11).

In summary, the names of the Levites who signed the agreement apparently reflect both the traditional priority of the families of Jeshua, Binnui, and Kadmiel and the perduring influence of at least some individuals who returned to Jerusalem with Ezra (for example, Hashabiah and Sherebiah).

From a narrative perspective, these names reinforce the covenant agreement as the climax of the whole book. The names of the three leaders (Jeshua, Binnui, and Kadmiel) link the covenant commitment (10:1–40) to the original return and the beginnings of the temple reconstruction (Ezra 2:40; 3:9). Furthermore, the signatures of Hashabiah and Sherebiah suggest the possibility that this event represents the providential culmination of the lives of the Levites who had joined Ezra to make the journey from Ahiva (cf. Ezra 8:18: "for the good hand of our God was upon us").

The Leaders of the People (10:15–28).

The first twenty-one names of the lay leaders who signed the agreement have substantial parallels with the names of the original families who returned from exile (Ezra 2:1–70 = Neh 7:6–72a). Furthermore, a variety of these names also occur in the lists of those who accompanied Ezra on the journey from Babylon (Ezra 8:2–14) and of those who separated from their foreign wives (10:25–43).

---

situation "in the days of Joiakim" (12:26), that is, at the time of Ezra. Clines (*Ezra, Nehemiah, Esther*, 202, 227) suggests that Hashabiah and Sherebiah (10:12–13; 12:24) could be identical with the individuals mentioned in Ezra 8:18–19. Cf. Williamson (*Ezra, Nehemiah*, 358–62), who relates the list of Levites in 12:24–25 to the statement in 12:23 and identifies "the days of Johanan" (12:23) with the early fourth century B.C.E. Moreover, he asserts that the list of Levites in 12:24–25 consists of family names and provides the basis for the list in 12:8–9.

The Covenant Commitment (Nehemiah 10:1-40)

Table 6.4—The First Twenty-One Leaders of the People (Neh 10:15-21a)[53]

Neh 10:15-20	Ezra 2:1-70	Neh 7:6-72a	Ezra 8:2-14	Ezra 10:25-43
1. Parosh	Parosh [1]	Parosh [1]	Parosh [4]	Parosh [1]
2. Pahath-moab	Pahath-moab [4]	Pahath-moab [4]	Pahath-moab [5]	Pahath-moab [6]
3. Elam	Elam [5]	Elam [5]	Elam [8]	Elam [2]
4. Zattu	Zattu [6]	Zattu [6]	Zattu [6]	Zattu [3]
5. Bani	Bani [8]		Bani [11]	Bani [5] [9]
6. Bunni		Binnui [8]		Binnui [10]
7. Azgad	Azgad [10]	Azgad [10]	Azgad [13]	
8. Bebai	Bebai [9]	Bebai [9]	Bebai [12]	Bebai [4]
9. Adonijah	Adonikam [11]	Adonikam [11]	Adonikam [14]	
10. Bigvai	Bigvai [12]	Bigvai [12]	Bigvai [15]	
11. Adin	Adin [13]	Adin [13]	Adin [7]	
12. Ater	Ater [14]	Ater [14]		
13. Hezekiah	[Hezekiah]	[Hezekiah]		
14. Azzur				
15. Hodiah				
16. Hashum	Hashum [17]	Hashum [15]		Hashum [8]
17. Bezai	Bezai [15]	Bezai [16]		
18. Hariph		Hariph [17]		
19. Anathoth	Anathoth [21]	Anathoth [20]		
20. Nebai	Nebo [27]	Nebo [26]		Nebo [11]
21. Magpiash	Magbish [28]			

Of the twenty-one signatories, only two names (Azzur and Hodiah) clearly do not occur in either list of the exiles (Ezra 2:1-70; Neh 7:6-72a).[54] Furthermore, the sequence of the signatories generally reflects the order of the exiles' names. The parallels with the four other lists demonstrate that this list of signatories consists of family names. In the cases of Anathoth, Nebai, and Magpiash, the family name reflects a place name.

In sum, the majority of the first twenty-one names of lay signatories represents established families that could trace their origin back to the first wave of exiles who had returned to the land.

More than half of the last twenty-three names of lay signatories (Neh 10:21b-28) occurs also in the roster of those who worked on the city walls (3:1-32).

---

[53] The numbers in brackets refer to the position of the names within the respective lists.

[54] However, that Binnui (בנוי, Neh 7:15) is equivalent to Bunni (בני, 10:16) is a matter of conjecture.

Table 6.5—The Final Twenty-Three Leaders of the People (Neh 10:21b–28)

Neh 10:21–28	Neh 3:1–32
22. Meshullam	Meshullam [3:4, 6, 30]
23. Hezir	
24. Meshezabel	son of Meshezabel [3:4]
25. Zadok	Zadok [3:4, 29]
26. Jaddua	Joiada [3:6]
27. Pelatiah	Melatiah [3:7]
28. Hanan	
29. Anaiah	
30. Hoshea	
31. Hananiah	Hananiah [3:8, 30]
32. Hasshub	Hasshub [3:11, 23]
33. Hallohesh	son of Hallohesh [3:12]
34. Pilha	
35. Shobek	
36. Rehum	
37. Hashabnah	
38. Maaseiah	son of Maaseiah [3:23]
39. Ahiah	
40. Hanan	Hanun [3:30; cf. 3:13]
41. Anan	Hananiah [3:30; cf. 3:8]
42. Malluch	Malchijah [3:31]
43. Harim	son of Harim [3:11]
44. Baanah	son of Baana [3:4]

The order of the signatories generally corresponds with the sequence of the construction crews.[55] Fourteen names of the signatories occur in the construction roster (3:1–32). However, the following names occur more than once in the list of builders: Meshullam (3:4, 6, 30); Zadok (3:4, 29); Hananiah (3:8, 30); Hanun (3:13, 30); Hanaiah (3:8; 30); Malchijah (3:11, 14, 31). The correspondences between the lists presuppose alternative renditions for these names: (1) Pelatiah (10:23; cf. Melatiah, 3:7); (2) Malluch (10:28; cf. Malchijah, 3:31); and (c) Baanah (בענה, 10:28; cf. Baana [בעבא:], 3:4).

Among the builders, the names Rehum and Hashabiah (3:17) resemble Rehum and Hashabnah (10:26) insofar as they occur in proximity to each other and in the same relative position vis-à-vis the other names in their respective lists. However, among the builders, Rehum and Hashabiah (3:17) are numbered among the Levites, not the laity.

---

[55] The construction list differs from the order of signatories in the following names: (1) Baanah (3:4); (2) Hananiah precedes Hanun (3:30); (3) Malchijah occurs at the beginning (3:4) as well as at the end (3:31).

Finally, five names among the signatories do not occur elsewhere in Ezra-Nehemiah: Hezir (10:21), Hoshea (10:24), Pilha (10:25), Shobek (10:25), and Ahiah (10:27). From a narrative perspective, this evidence suggests that the final twenty-three signatures (10:21b–28) represent families who rose to prominence during the interval between the return of the exiles (Ezra 2:1–70; Neh 7:6–72a) and the renewal of the covenant. These are the more recently established families who attained sufficient distinction to follow the ranks of the first twenty-one (10:15–21a), who represent the more traditional families who could trace their roots back to the original returnees. The parallels between the signatories and the names of those who rebuilt the walls (3:1–32), on the one hand, and of those who stood with Ezra on the platform (8:4), on the other, suggests that association with the projects of Nehemiah and Ezra ultimately enhanced the status of these newer families.

In summary, the list of the "heads of families" who sign the agreement represents a blend of the old (10:15–21a) with the new (10:21b–28). The composite nature of the list suggests that this is a society that treasures its historical roots in the return from exile (cf. 10:15–21a) but that also values the contribution of more recent arrivals to the development of a new social fabric (cf. 10:21b–28).

THE STIPULATIONS (10:29–40)

General Principle: Commitment to the Torah (10:29–30)

The "remainder of the people" (שְׁאָר הָעָם) occurs twice in Ezra-Nehemiah: first to designate the general populace as distinct from the priests, Levites, and leaders of the people who signed the document (10:29); and second to denote the populace as distinct from the princes of the people who lived in Jerusalem (11:1). While the two groups vary in their definition and therefore in their extension, nevertheless, from a literary perspective, the one expression links the climax of the covenant renewal (10:1–40) with the following account that describes the repopulating of Jerusalem (11:1–24). The narrative focus on the populace continues from the "remainder of the people" who take the oath of fidelity to the Torah (10:29–30) to the "remainder of the people" who cast lots to identify who will live in Jerusalem (11:1).

The list of temple personnel that introduces the voicing of the commitment (10:29a) is almost identical to the list that concludes the roster of the people who returned from exile (7:72a).[56] Moreover, a comprehensive designation for the whole community accompanies each of these lists

---

[56] 10:29a: הכהנים הלוים השוערים המשררים הנתינים
7:72a: הכהנים והלוים והשוערים והמשררים ומן־העם והנתינים

שְׁאָר הָעָם ... כָּל־יוֹדֵעַ מֵבִין: "the remainder of the people ... everyone who knows how to understand," 10:29; cf. וּכָל־יִשְׂרָאֵל: "and all Israel," 7:72a). The similarity in these expressions indicates that the participants in the covenant renewal (10:29) constitute the authentic Israel of the post-exilic era (Ezra 2:70; cf. Neh 7:72a).[57] Their expression of commitment to the Torah (10:29–40) represents the full reconstitution of Israel that began with the return of the first wave of exiles to Jerusalem (Ezra 1:5; 2:1–70).

The expression "all who separated themselves from the people of the lands to the law of God" (Neh 10:29) is analogous in form to "all who separated themselves from the pollutions of the Gentiles to worship YHWH, the God of Israel" (Ezra 6:21).[58] The two-step separation "from" those outside the Judahite community and "to" God suggests that the expression in 10:29 refers to proselytes. While the descriptions of Ezra's marriage reform (Ezra 9:1; 10:11) assert the necessity of "separating" (בדל *nipʿal*) "from the peoples of the land[s]" (מֵעַמֵּי הָאָרֶץ/הָאֲרָצוֹת), they do not mention a corresponding movement "toward" God or his law (cf. Neh 10:29). Such evidence suggests that the separatists in Neh 10:29 are proselytes rather than the Judahites who had consented to Ezra's marriage reform. The liturgical setting provides a further correspondence between Neh 10:29 and Ezra 6:21: these separatists participate in the covenant renewal (10:29–40), just as those of the former era had joined in the Passover (Ezra 6:19–22).

The reference to wives, sons, and daughters among those who take the covenant oath (10:29) recalls the only other instance of their common mention, namely, in Nehemiah's encouragement of the workers to persevere with the wall project on behalf of their sons, daughters, and wives (Neh 4:8). Moreover, he there extends the familial categories by designating others who partake in the project as "brothers" (אֲחֵיכֶם: "your brothers," 4:8; cf. אֲחֵיהֶם: "their kindred," 10:30).

The mention of "their sons and their daughters" in particular recalls not only the crises of betrothal (Ezra 9:12; cf. Neh 10:31) and marriage (Ezra 9:12) but also the social emergency provoked by the practice of debt-

---

[57] Note the difference between Ezra 2:70 and Neh 7:72b regarding the order of "some of the people," "the singers," and "the gatekeepers." These same categories (in the order corresponding to Ezra 2:70) occur in the roster of those who returned from exile (Ezra 2:1–70 = Neh 7:6–72a): "the priests" (Ezra 2:36–39; Neh 7:39–42), "the Levites" (Ezra 2:40; Neh 7:43), "the singers" (Ezra 2:41; Neh 7:44), "the gatekeepers" (Ezra 4:42; Neh 7:45), and "the temple servants" (Ezra 2:43–54; Neh 7:46–56).

[58] Note the common structure of separation "from ... to":
Neh 10:29: כָּל־הַנִּבְדָּל מֵעַמֵּי הָאֲרָצוֹת אֶל־תּוֹרַת הָאֱלֹהִים
Ezra 6:21: כֹּל הַנִּבְדָּל מִטֻּמְאַת גּוֹיֵ־הָאָרֶץ אֲלֵהֶם לִדְרֹשׁ לַיהוָה אֱלֹהֵי יִשְׂרָאֵל

The Covenant Commitment (Nehemiah 10:1–40)

slavery (Neh 5:1–13). The participation of the daughters in the oath ceremony represents a transformation in the status of those who had experienced slavery in payment for household debts (10:29; cf. 5:5).

The description of the various categories of the populace "entering into an oath with sanctions" (באים באלה ובשבועה, 10:30) reflects the account of the covenant renewal in Deuteronomy (29:9–20) in which Moses invites the diverse segments of his community "to pass into the covenant of YHWH your God and into his curse" (לעברך בברית יהוה אלהיך באלתו, Deut 29:11). The noun אלה, which is a constitutive element of this covenant (ברית, 29:13, 20; cf. Ezek 17:16, 18, 19), designates the invocation of sanctions for violation of the pact. The priority of the sanctions in the covenant renewal corresponds with the invocation of them in the Deuteronomic covenant renewal (אלה, Neh 10:30; cf. Deut 29:18, 19).

The term שבועה (oath) originally pertained to the sphere of personal commitments.[59] However, in postexilic literature, שבועה sometimes serves as an alternative word for ברית ("covenant," 1 Chr 16:16 [= Ps 105:9]; 2 Chr 15:15). This association of שבועה with ברית provides the basis for its intimate connection with אלה in both Neh 10:30 (באלה ובשבועה: "an oath with sanctions") and Dan 9:11 (האלה והשבועה: "the oath with sanctions"). Furthermore, both in the account of the community commitment (Neh 10:30) and in the penitential prayer of Daniel (Dan 9:11), the oath with sanctions derives from the law of "Moses the servant of God."

The description of the people's "entering into an oath with sanctions" (באים באלה ובשבועה, Neh 10:30) has some similarities in vocabulary with the Chronicler's accounts of the covenant renewal under Asa (2 Chr 15:8–15) and of the discovery of the book of the law under Josiah (2 Chr 34:14–28). Under Asa, the people "entered into covenant" (ויבאו בברית, 2 Chr 15:12; cf. באים באלה ובשבועה, Neh 10:30) and subsequently rejoiced over "the oath" (השבועה, 2 Chr 15:15). Under Josiah, Huldah prophesies that "all the curses" (כל־האלות, 2 Chr 34:24)[60] of the book will fall upon Jerusalem.

The summary description of the commitment (Neh 10:30) exhibits a Deuteronomic texture. The expression "to walk in the law" (הלך בתורה, Neh 10:30) occurs in the Deuteronomistic sections of Jeremiah (Jer 26:4; 44:10, 23; cf. 2 Kgs 10:31) as well as in postexilic texts, including Daniel's prayer of repentance (Dan 9:10; Ps 119:1; 2 Chr 6:16).

Moreover, a Deuteronomistic character is manifest in the following combination of terms in Neh 10:30: "to observe and to do" (שמר ועשה)

---

[59] An oath (שבועה) can refer alternatively to: (1) a declaration of innocence (Exod 22:10; Num 5:21a); (2) a pact of friendship (2 Sam 21:7; Neh 6:18); (3) a vow (Num 30:3, 11, 14; Josh 9:20); (4) a curse (Num 5:21b; Isa 65:15); or (5) a promise (Gen 24:8; Josh 2:17, 20). See BDB, 989–90.

[60] The Deuteronomistic parallel reads: "all the words" (כל־דברים, 2 Kgs 22:16).

YHWH's "commandments" (מצות), "ordinances" (משפטים) and "statutes" (חקים).[61]

The expression "YHWH our Lord" (יהוה אדנינו, Neh 10:30) exhibits a liturgical tone insofar as it occurs elsewhere in the MT only in the refrain at the beginning and end of Ps 8 (vv. 2, 10; cf. יהוה אדון: "YHWH the Lord," Josh 3:13; 1 Sam 25:28; אדנינו: "our Lord," Pss 135:5; 147:5).[62]

In terms of a summary review of the vocabulary, the three infinitives (ללכת ... לשמור ... לעשות) and two of the three accusatives (מצוה and חקים) that describe the community's oath taking (Neh 10:30) also occur in the Chronicler's account of Josiah's covenant ceremony (2 Chr 34:31). Such evidence confirms that, although the term ברית does not occur in the narrative, the community's oath taking constitutes a renewal of the covenant.

Specific Stipulations (10:31–40)

The particular stipulations in the community's oath are intimately related to the various reforms Nehemiah undertakes. Of the six stipulations (10:31–40), four pertain to issues that Nehemiah addresses upon his return from meeting with Artaxerxes (13:4–31): (1) the betrothal of children to foreigners (10:31; cf. 13:23–27); (2) the prohibition of commercial transactions on the Sabbath (10:32a; cf. 13:15–22); (3) the provision of the wood offering (10:35); and (4) the contributions for the support of priests and Levites (10:36–40a; cf. 13:10–13). Furthermore, the observance of the year of release and the cancellation of debts represent the codification of Nehemiah's earlier reform of debt-slavery (10:32b; cf. 5:1–13). Finally, when Nehemiah acts on behalf of the Levites, he utters a rhetorical question ("Why is the house of God abandoned?") that echoes the community's concluding statement (10:40b; cf. 13:11).

In view of the intimate relationship between the stipulations (10:31–40) and Nehemiah's reforms (5:1–13; 13:4–31), my analysis of the terminological background for each stipulation proceeds by comparing the stipulation with other legal and prophetic texts and examining the connection between the stipulation and the narrative account of the pertinent reform Nehemiah undertakes (13:4–31). Examining the narrative relationship between the stipulations in 10:31–40 and the subsequent reforms in

---

[61] In Neh 10:30, לשמר ולעשה (lit., "to observe and to do") is a hendiadys (cf. Lev 25:18; 26:3; Deut 4:6; 6:12; 23:23; Ezek 11:20; 18:19; 20:19; 36:27; 37:24). In the MT, the verbs שמר and עשה occur together with various combinations of the nouns: (1) מצוה (sing.), משפטים, and חקים (Deut 7:11; 2 Kgs 17:37); (2) מצות and משפטים (1 Kgs 2:3; 6:12 [Deuteronomistic locutions]); (3) משפטים and חקים (Deut 5:1; 11:32; 12:1; 26:16; 1 Kgs 19:4); (4) מצות and חקים (Exod 15:26; 1 Chr 29:19; 2 Chr 34:31).

[62] Ps 8:2, 10: יהוה אדנינו מה־אדיר שמך בכל־הארץ ("YHWH, our Lord, how majestic is your name in all the earth").

The Covenant Commitment (Nehemiah 10:1–40)

13:4–31 is particularly necessary due to the propensity of commentators to treat the stipulations as historically subsequent to Nehemiah's reforms, thereby evidencing a lack of appreciation for the integrity of the book's literary format.[63]

Societal Commitments (10:31–32). The parents' pledge not to betroth their children to foreigners (10:31) is a reworking of Deut 7:3 (cf. Exod 34:15–16).[64] Allusions to Deut 7:3 occur four times in Ezra-Nehemiah, always in direct speech: in the leaders' description of the marriage crisis in Judah (Ezra 9:1–2); in Ezra's prayer (9:12); in the community's stipulation (Neh 10:31); and in the oath that Nehemiah imposes on the violators (13:25). However, the leaders' description (Ezra 9:1–2) is distinctive inasmuch as it is a narrative statement, whereas the remaining three occurrences exhibit the form of legislative pronouncements.

The above evidence calls for a three-step analysis: (1) comparing Neh 10:31 with Deut 7:3 will determine the degree of lexical proximity of the stipulation to the original precept; (2) examining the stipulation in light of the other two pronouncements (Ezra 9:12; Neh 13:25) will illustrate the legislative variations on Deut 7:3 in Ezra-Nehemiah; and (3) probing the narrative relationships between the four allusions to Deut 7:3 in Ezra-Nehemiah will illustrate the function of the community's stipulation vis-à-vis the marriage reforms of Ezra (Ezra 9:1–10:44) and Nehemiah (13:23–27).

---

[63] Williamson (*Ezra, Nehemiah*, 325, 330–31), Blenkinsopp (*Ezra-Nehemiah*, 311, 315), and Clines (*Ezra, Nehemiah, Esther*, 199–200, 205, 245) assert that the stipulations (10:31–40) should follow Nehemiah's reforms (13:4–31). By contrast, Eskenazi provides an insight that is fundamental to understanding the format of the book: "The arrangement in Ezra-Nehemiah ascribes the reforms to the community as a whole, making Nehemiah's activities essentially the administering of communally ordained regulations" (*In an Age of Prose*, 124–25).

[64] The pentateuchal legislation that prohibits betrothal to foreigners occurs in the renewal of the covenant at Sinai (Exod 34:11–16) and in the Deuteronomic instruction on the plains of Moab (Deut 7:1–6). In each case, the prohibition occurs as part of Moses' instructions on the conquest. Thus, in each case, the foreigners consist, not of the peoples beyond Israel's borders, but of the mixed populations who were the prior inhabitants of the land. The scope of application constitutes the primary difference between the respective laws: Exod 34:16 deals solely with the case of Israelite sons taking foreign wives, whereas Deut 7:3 also considers the converse, that is, Israelite daughters marrying the sons of foreigners. Nehemiah 10:31 takes account of both possibilities and thus refers specifically to Deut 7:3.

Table 6.6—Legislation on Mixed Marriage

Deut 7:3 לא תתחתן בם	Ezra 9:12	Neh 10:31	Neh 13:25
בתך לא־תתן לבנו	בנתיכם אל־תתן לבניהם	לא־נתן בנתינו לעמי הארץ	אם־תתנו בנתיכם לבניהם
ובתו לא־תקח לבנך	ובנתיהם אל־תשאו לבניכם	ואת־בנתיהם לא נקח לבנינו	ואם תשאו מבנתיהם לבניכם ולכם

Deuteronomy 7:3 employs the singular, whereas all three legislative allusions in Ezra-Nehemiah use the plural. Furthermore, the initial clause of Deut 7:3 ("Do not intermarry with them") does not appear in any of these allusions.

Of the three pronouncements in Ezra-Nehemiah, Neh 10:31 alone follows Deut 7:3 in two features: (1) by using the verb לקח ("to take"; cf. נשא, Ezra 9:12; Neh 13:25); and (2) by exhibiting the identical forms of the negative particle (לא נתן and לא לקח; cf. Ezra 9:12, אל נתן and אל נשא; Neh 13:25, אם־נתן and אם־לקח).

However, the community's stipulation is not a precise quotation. The expression לא נתן ("we will not give") introduces the stipulation (10:31) but follows the accusative (בתך: "your daughter") in the law (Deut 7:3). More important, in the stipulation, the "peoples of the land" (עמי הארץ, Neh 10:31a) take the place of the Deuteronomic "many nations" (גוים רבים) whom the Israelites were to conquer, namely, the Hittites, the Girgashites, the Amorites, the Canaanites, the Perizzites, the Hivites, and the Jebusites (Deut 7:1).[65] By means of this adaptation, the stipulation maintains the preoccupation with "the people[s] of the land[s]" that is emblematic of Ezra-Nehemiah (עם הארץ, Ezra 4:4; עמי הארץ, Ezra 10:2, 11; Neh 10:31, 32; עמי הארצות, Ezra 3:3; 9:1, 2, 11; Neh 9:30; 10:29; עממי הארץ, Neh 9:24).

The variations in the three legal pronouncements (Ezra 9:12; Neh 10:31; 13:25) demonstrate that there is no fixed rendering of Deut 7:3 in Ezra-Nehemiah. The pronouncement in Ezra's prayer (Ezra 9:12) corresponds with the word order of Deut 7:3 and thereby provides the closest approximation to the Deuteronomic precept in Ezra-Nehemiah.[66]

---

[65] The replacement of "many nations" (גוים רבים, Deut 7:1) by "peoples of the land[s]" (עמי הארצות, 9:1) originally took place in the leaders' portrayal of the situation that gave rise to Ezra's reform (Ezra 9:1–2).

[66] Ezra's statement (Ezra 9:12) makes only two adjustments to the Deuteronomic precept (Deut 7:3), i.e., by employing: (1) an alternative negative particle (אל); and (2) the verb נשא (in place of לקח).

Nevertheless, the identical word order in the second half of the community's stipulation (Neh 10:31b [regarding the marriages of Judahite sons]) establishes a strong link with Ezra's statement (Ezra 9:12; Deut 7:3). The "peoples of the land[s]" (עמי הארץ) reinforces this linkage insofar as the expression occurs explicitly in the community's stipulation (10:31a) and constitutes the referent for the possessive pronouns in Ezra's statement (בניהם, בנתיהם, 9:12; cf. עמי הארצות, 9:11).

Nehemiah's oath (Neh 13:25) alters the Deuteronomic precept (Deut 7:3) in three ways: (1) by taking the format of an oath (אם ... ואם); (2) by changing the word order; and (3) by including the men as well as their sons among those who might marry a foreigner (לבניכם ולכם: "for your sons and for yourselves," 13:25). The immediate context accounts for these changes. Nehemiah makes his people take the oath (Neh 13:25) in reaction to the Judahite men's marrying foreign wives (13:21–24, 28).[67]

However, the first half of the oath (concerning Judahite daughters marrying foreign sons) is irrelevant to the context. Therefore, the very fact that his oath (13:25) refers to both propositions (Judahite daughters marrying foreign sons and Judahite sons marrying foreign daughters) establishes a linkage to the community's stipulation (10:31) and to Deut 7:3. Thus, the community's stipulation constitutes a precedent that echoes in the oath that Nehemiah impresses upon the men and their sons who were tempted to marry foreign women.

In summary, the community's stipulation not to give their children in marriage to foreigners (Neh 10:31) serves a dual purpose vis-à-vis the other two pronouncements of the Deuteronomic precept (Ezra 9:12; Neh 13:25; cf. Deut 7:3). On the one hand, the community's stipulation codifies Ezra's marriage reform (Ezra 9:12; cf. 9:1–2; 10:11) as an article of public legislation, while, on the other, it provides the implied point of reference for Nehemiah's corrections of subsequent abuses (13:21–27).

Moreover, narrative descriptions before and after the covenant renewal suggest the importance of this stipulation for the development of autonomous community leadership. Nehemiah's nemesis, Tobiah the Ammonite, exercised personal influence within the community by virtue of his and his son's marriages to Judahite women (Neh 6:18; cf. 10:31a). His other adversary, Sanballat the Horonite, had access to Eliashib the high priest due to his daughter's marriage to Eliashib's son (13:28; cf. 10:31b). Thus, Nehemiah's two major adversaries (Neh 2:10, 19; 3:33; 4:1; 6:1–2, 12, 14) derived substantial power from the intermarriages of their children

---

[67] Nehemiah's preoccupation with foreign daughters marrying Judahite sons (13:25bβ) actually reflects the leaders' description of the crisis to Ezra (Ezra 9:2).
Neh 13:25: ואם־תשאו מבנתיהם לבניכם ולכם
Ezra 9:2: כי־נשאו מבנתיהם להם ולבניהם

with Judahites. The refusal by Judahite parents to permit such marriages would close this avenue of foreign influence on the community's internal affairs.

The community's pledge not to purchase merchandise or grain that the peoples of the land would bring to sell on the Sabbath is a specific application of the commandment to keep the day holy (Exod 20:8–11; Deut 5:12–15). However, no law or narrative in the Pentateuch explicitly prohibits buying or selling on the Sabbath. The stipulations in the Covenant Code (Exod 23:12) and in the renewed Sinaitic covenant (34:21) forbid agricultural work. The Priestly injunction against lighting a fire prohibits cooking (Exod 35:3; cf. 16:23). This injunction corresponds with the Priestly narrative that outlaws the gathering of firewood on the Sabbath (Num 15:32–36).

While the Pentateuch does not explicitly prohibit the purchasing of food on the Sabbath (cf. Neh 10:32a), such a prohibition might derive from Moses' injunction against gathering food on the Sabbath (Exod 16:22–30; especially 16:22, 26–27). Moreover, this Mosaic injunction is related to his forbidding the people to journey from their homes on the Sabbath (16:29), another precept that they might contravene by going to the market (cf. Neh 10:32a). In any case, this survey of pentateuchal legislation and narrative indicates that the community's pledge (10:32a) is more rigorous than the Mosaic law itself.

The prophetic tradition indirectly contributed to the Sabbath stipulation (Neh 10:32a) both by introducing a concern over commercial activity on the Sabbath and by linking Sabbath observance to the survival of Jerusalem. In the preexilic era, Amos chided merchants for their impatience with new moons and Sabbaths due to their pursuit of unjust profits (Amos 8:5). In the exilic period, Ezekiel (20:16, 24; 22:8, 26; 23:38) viewed the destruction of Jerusalem, in part, as retribution for the people's violation of the Sabbath.[68] Similarly, the postexilic Isaian tradition asserted that Sabbath observance was a prerequisite for the restoration of Jerusalem (Isa 56:1–8; 58:13–14). The community's pledge to observe the Sabbath (Neh 10:32a) implies a similar conviction.

The community's commitment not to purchase goods that foreigners bring (מביאים) to sell on the Sabbath (ביום השבת למכור, 10:32a) applies to the situation that Nehemiah subsequently encounters when the Tyrians bring (מביאים) their fish and merchandise to sell to the Judahites on the

---

[68] In Jer 17:19–27, the prophet also threatens Jerusalem with destruction for breaking the Sabbath. However, commentators generally view this passage as a late addition to Jeremiah. W. L. Holladay dates the passage to Nehemiah's era on the basis of the similarities between Jer 17:19–27 and Neh 13:15–22 (*Jeremiah 1* [Hermeneia; Philadelphia: Fortress, 1986], 509).

Sabbath (מכרים בשבת, 13:16). As noted in these parentheses, the vocabulary of the community's stipulation (10:32a) echoes once again in the description of the Tyrians' activities. Thus, from a literary perspective, the community's Sabbath stipulation (10:32a) suggests the need for Nehemiah's corrective measures.

Furthermore, in terms of content, the community's Sabbath stipulation provides a catalyst—but not a predetermined agenda—for Nehemiah's activities. Nehemiah's Sabbath reform (13:15–22) exceeds the bounds of the community's Sabbath stipulation (10:32a). Specifically, the stipulation does not address these activities that Nehemiah observes the Judahites performing on the Sabbath: treading grapes; selling grain and produce; and having their donkeys carry burdens (13:15; cf. Deut 5:14). The stipulation focuses on the Judahites who might buy (10:32a), whereas Nehemiah directs his concern to those who sell (whether Judahites or foreigners [cf. 13:15–16]). Moreover, Nehemiah not only prohibits the foreigners from selling at the gates but even prevents their entering the city during the Sabbath.

In summary, within Ezra-Nehemiah, the community's stipulation (10:32a) introduces the importance of Sabbath observance for the restoration of the community and thereby establishes this issue as a priority in Nehemiah's subsequent supervision of the city and its people (13:15–22).

The extension of the stipulation to the observance of holy days (ביום קדש, 10:32a) as well as Sabbaths (10:32a) reflects concerns similar to those of the Priestly calendar (Num 28:1–30:1). The prohibition of work applies to Passover (Num 28:18) and to the first day of the Festival of Weeks (Num 28:26). Moreover, of particular concern for the covenant renewal in the seventh month (Neh 7:72b) are the remaining labor-free holy days: (1) the first day of the seventh month (Num 29:1; cf. Neh 8:2, 9–11); (2) the tenth day of the seventh month (Num 29:7 [a fast]; cf. Neh 9:1–2 [fasting on the twenty-fourth day of the month]); and (3) the first and last days of the Festival of Booths (Num 29:12, 22; cf. Neh 8:18). The evidence thus suggests that the community's concern for holy days (Neh 10:32a) derives from a Priestly tradition but not from the codified legislation in the liturgical calendar (Num 28:1–30:1).

The people's commitment to observe the seventh year alludes to the pentateuchal laws that mandate, first, the fallow year for the land (Exod 23:10–11; Lev 25:1–8) and, second, the release of pledges (Deut 15:1–3). The introductory verb (נטש: "to forgo") echoes the prescription of the Covenant Code (Exod 23:10–11) calling for the land "to lie fallow" every seven years so that the poor can glean from it as well as from the vineyards and olive orchards.[69] The community's stipulation does not exhibit

---

[69] Exod 23:10: והשביעת תשמטנה ונטשתה ("but on the seventh year, you shall let it [the land] rest and lie fallow").

an equivalent connection with the parallel Priestly legislation (Lev 25:1–8). However, the Priestly designation of this year as "a Sabbath to YHWH" (שבת ליהוה, Lev 25:4) might account for the position of this stipulation following the one governing Sabbath observance in the community's oath (ב[יום השבת], Neh 10:32a).

The commitment to forgo "the pledge in every hand" (Neh 10:32b) reflects the vocabulary of the Deuteronomic precept: "every possessor of a pledge in hand shall release what he obtained as pledge from his neighbor" (Deut 15:2).[70] The noun משא is a technical term for a loan secured on the basis of a pledge (Deut 24:10). By extension, in Deut 15:2 the noun משא refers to the pledge. The corresponding verb נשא means "to loan against a pledge," while the participle נשא designates the creditor in such transactions.[71]

The pledges for securing a loan could vary from the garments of the poor (Exod 22:24–26) to the properties of financially strapped land owners (Neh 5:3–4). The pledging of oneself or one's children to work for the creditor was a last resort for securing a loan (see Lev 25:39–43; cf. 25:25–38).

The last of these is an antichretic pledge, by which I mean a person who amortizes a debt by working for the creditor. A preexilic illustration of this arrangement is the case of the insolvent widow dreading the arrival of the creditor (הנשא) who is coming to enslave the two sons she had pledged as security for a loan (2 Kgs 4:1). Within exilic literature, such a practice provides the basis for the metaphor in YHWH's rhetorical question: "To which of my creditors [מנושי] have I sold you?" (Isa 50:1).[72]

In the postexilic literature, Nehemiah refers to the Judahite children's servitude in payment for their families' debts (Neh 5:1–5). The account of Nehemiah's social reform (Neh 5:1–13) contains the nouns משא ("loan on pledge" or "pledge," 5:7, 10) and יד ("hand," 5:5), which are the subject matter of the community's stipulation (ומשא כל־יד: "the pledge of every hand," 10:32b). The noun יד is part of an idiom, "it is not in our power"

---

[70] Neh 10:32bb: [וננטש] ... ומשה כל־יד:
Deut 15:2: שמוט כל־בעל משה ידו אשר ישה ברעהו
R. North proposes this translation of Deut 15:2: "every holder of a pledge *at his disposition* (*yâdô*) shall release what he has received-by-pledge-loan-contract with his brother" [italics original] ("*Yâd* in the Shemitta-Law," *VT* 14 [1964]: 199).

[71] Cf. BDB (673–74): נשא: "lend on interest, or usury" (*qal:* 1 Sam 22:2; Isa 24:2; Neh 5:7; *hip'il:* Ps 89:23); משא: "lending on interest, or usury" (Neh 5:7, 10; 10:32); משאה: "loan" (Deut 24:10; Prov 22:26); נשה: "lend, become a creditor" (Exod 22:24; Deut 24:11; 2 Kgs 4:1; Neh 5:7 [Qere], 10, 11; Isa 24:2; 50:1; Jer 15:10; Ps 109:11; *hip'il:* Deut 15:2; 24:10).

[72] According to Deutero-Isaiah, the image of a father selling his children to a creditor is not apt for describing YHWH's treatment of Israel.

The Covenant Commitment (Nehemiah 10:1–40)

(אין לאל ידנו, 5:5)[73] and thereby connotes control, as in the stipulation (10:32b).

The precise meaning of מַשָּׁא (5:7, 10)[74] in the account of Nehemiah's social reform is particularly significant for the interpretation of the stipulation (10:32b). After pledging their fields, vineyards, and houses, parents had to hand their children over to servitude under fellow Judahites in order to secure loans for food and the payment of taxes (Neh 5:2–4). In response to their predicament, Nehemiah levels this charge against the creditors: "Each of you is contracting a loan on pledge with his brother" (מַשָּׁא איש־באחיו אתם נשאים, Neh 5:7). Subsequently, he urges the creditors, "Let us abandon this [holding of] pledge[s]" (נעזבה־נא את־המשא הזה, 5:10). Finally, he demands the restoration of all mortgaged properties to the debtors (5:11).

In Neh 5:7, the term מַשָּׁא designates the antichretic pledge in particular rather than other types of securities for loans. Nehemiah's reprimand of the nobles (5:7) refers to the complaints of the people (5:2–4), which culminate in the description of their sons and daughters becoming slaves to the creditors (5:5).[75] Nehemiah accuses the wealthy class of acting as "creditors" (נשאים, 5:7). Within this context, the participle conveys a meaning identical with הַנֹּשֶׁה ("the creditor") in 2 Kgs 4:1 and נֹשַׁי ("my creditors") in Isa 50:1: the one who enslaves the children to amortize the family debts. The subsequent description of the selling of the Judahite kindred into slavery (5:8) confirms this reading.

However, in Nehemiah's subsequent declaration, "Let us abandon this holding of pledges" (נעזבה־נא את־המשא הזה, 5:10), the same noun has a

---

[73] This idiom occurs elsewhere in Gen 31:29; Deut 28:32; Prov 3:27; Mic 2:1; see also Sir 5:1; 14:11. On the texts in Sirach, see P. W. Skehan and A. A. Di Lella, *The Wisdom of Ben Sira* (AB 39; New York: Doubleday, 1987), 181. They refer to W. G. E. Watson ("Reclustering Hebrew *l'yd-*," *Bib* 58 [1977]: 213–15), who argues that the correct form of the expression is אין לא ליד ("there is not power in the hand of"). In this case, the term לא means "power" (in view of Akkadian, Punic, and Ugaritic cognates).

[74] In Neh 5:11, read the MT מאת ("percentage") rather than the proposed emendation משאת ("pledge"). E. Neufeld proposes that the term refers to an interest rate of 1 percent per month or 12 percent per year ("The Rate of Interest and the Text of Nehemiah 5:11," *JQR* 44 [1953]: 194–204).

[75] Nehemiah 5:5 is a summary statement by all the indebted people that brings to a crescendo the successive complaints of the three particular groups of debtors (5:2, 3, 4, יש אשר אמרים: "there were those who said"). The outcry of the first group (5:2) might also refer to debt-slavery. In 5:2, the emendation of רבים ("many") to ערבים ("pledging"; cf. 5:3) makes for a more suitable reading within the context. "We are pledging our sons and daughters" affords a parallelism with the financial concerns in 5:3 and 5:4. By comparison, "Our sons and daughters are many" bespeaks an extraneous concern.

broader meaning. There, מַשָּׁא designates property pledges, that is, the fields, vineyards, olive groves, and houses that he mentions in the following statement (5:11).

The account of Nehemiah's social reform (Neh 5:1–13) does not make reference to pentateuchal legislation. The episode represents an ad hoc response to a particular situation.[76]

From a literary perspective, Nehemiah's making the nobles take an oath (שׁבע hipʿil, 5:12) to fulfill the requirements of his reform prepares for the community's "oath" (שְׁבוּעָה, 10:30) to release the pledges in the seventh year (10:32b). The assembly (5:7), rituals (5:12b–13a), and consent of the people (5:13b) foreshadow the more comprehensive covenant renewal (7:72b–10:40).

The allusion to the Deuteronomic release (Deut 15:2) in the third stipulation of the community's commitment (10:32b) supplies the legal referent that was absent in the social reform (5:1–13). In the prescription, the term מַשָּׁא (10:32b) provides a connection not only to the Deuteronomic precept but also to the social reform (5:7, 10). Therefore, the term מַשָּׁא has a more specific connotation in the community's commitment (10:32b) than in the Deuteronomic prescription (Deut 15:2). Within the setting of Ezra-Nehemiah, מַשָּׁא refers especially, but not exclusively, to antichretic pledges (live "gages," Neh 5:7) and to property pledges ("mortgages" [dead "gages"], 5:10). However, in the Deuteronomic mandate for the seventh-year release (Deut 15:2), מַשָּׁא designates all pledges without discrimination.[77]

---

[76] By contrast, in another ad hoc initiative to liberate Judean slaves (Jer 34:8–16), Jeremiah appeals to the Deuteronomic prescriptions about releasing slaves in the seventh year (Jer 34:14; cf. Deut 15:12–13).

[77] Cf. de Vaux (*Ancient Israel*, 172), who asserts, "Now in Dt 15:2 the *mashsheh* is a person who works for the creditor, and this is also the sense which must be given to *mashsha'* in Ne 10:32, referring to the sabbatical year, like Dt 15." This interpretation of מַשָּׁא originated with H. M. Weil, "Gage et cautionnement dans la Bible," *Archives d'Histoire du Droit Oriental* 2 (1938): 171–240 [page references are to the offprint edition, 1–68]. Weil restricted the meaning of מַשָּׁא to the antichretic pledge. He offers this description: "Par contre, l'institution que la Bible appelle *maššâ* et qui est, selon nous, un gage n'est pas une garantie pour renforcer le crédit du débiteur, mais un mode de satisfaction pour le créancier; c'est pourquoi, d'abord, ce gage ne droit être remis au créancier qu'au moment où le débiteur commence à amortir sa dette, ce que, pour simplifier, nous appellerons de façon approximative l'échéance de la dette; ensuite, ce gage attribue au créancier, à côté de la possession, surtout la jouissance de la chose remise en gage—gage à jouissance, antichrèse—; enfin, le créancier ne se fait pas payer, d'ordinaire, par la vente du gage *maššâ*, mais par le travail du *maššâ* qui consiste en un enfant ou en un esclave du débiteur" (pp. 1–2). (Weil's transcription *maššâ* equally encompasses three terms: *maššāʾ*, *maššāʾâ*, and *maššēh*.)

The question remains whether this release of pledges in the seventh year (Neh 10:32b) represented a full cancellation of the debt or merely a one-year suspension of it. Nehemiah's reform consisted in the cancellation of debts and the unqualified return of pledges (Neh 5:10–11). However, the community's stipulation links the return of pledges with the fallow year (10:32b). Moreover, the Deuteronomic prescription (15:2) more likely mandated a suspension of debt payments for a single year out of seven during which time the debtor would have use of the pledge (whether property or a family member) to enhance his long-term financial security.[78] Therefore, the community's stipulation (10:38b) mandates a one-year suspension of the debt payment in contrast to Nehemiah's universal cancellation of all debts (5:10–11). Nehemiah's dramatic reform worked as a one-time event, but this more restricted legislation would afford a more realistic possibility for the long-term future (10:32b).

Therefore, from a literary perspective, the community's third stipulation establishes an economic infrastructure to maintain the social transformation that began with Nehemiah's reform. The participation in the covenant renewal of those who had experienced oppression indicates the enfranchisement of these groups: "the people" (העם, 5:1; cf. 10:29), "their wives" (נשיהם, 5:1; cf. 10:29), the "sons" (בנינו ["our sons"], 5:5; cf. בניהם ["their sons"], 10:29), and the "daughters" (בנתינו ["our daughters"], 5:5; cf. בנתיהם ["their daughters"], 10:29). Thus, the third stipulation inaugurates a new social order by guaranteeing the abiding concern for the "remainder of the people" (10:29) on the part of the more privileged classes (cf. 10:1–28).

Obligations to the Temple (10:33–40). The tax of "a third of a shekel" (10:33) does not occur anywhere else in the MT. Nevertheless, this community stipulation exhibits two linguistic associations with the Priestly law of the half-shekel offering (Exod 30:11–16): (1) the donation is "to make atonement" (לכפר [על־נפשתיכם ["for your lives"], Exod 30:15; cf. לכפר [על־ישראל] ["for Israel"], Neh 10:34); and (2) the money is to pay for "the service" of the sanctuary (על־עבדת [אהל מועד]: "the service [of the tent of meeting"], Exod 30:16; cf. לעבדת [בית אלהינו]: "the service [at the house of our God]"). Moreover, a third of a shekel (Neh 10:33) is not far removed from the numerical value of a half-shekel (Exod 30:13).

---

[78] The outright cancellation of the debt prior to its full repayment would have discouraged creditors from making loans. R. North argues that the release was actually a year-long suspension and that the pledge (משא) that the creditor released during this time was the debtor, his family, and his property (*Sociology of the Biblical Jubilee* [AnBib 4; Rome: Biblical Institute, 1954], 184–87). By contrast, E. Neufeld insists that this legislation refers to the outright cancellation of all debts and the restoration of all pledges ("Socio-economic Background of Yōbēl and šᵉmiṭṭa," *RSO* 33 [1958]: 58–62).

However, the community's stipulation does not exactly reflect the Mosaic prescription. Both the reason for "atonement" (לכפר) and the meaning of the "service" (עבדה) are different in each case. In the Mosaic mandate (Exod 30:12), the people provide the money to atone for the potential of engendering divine wrath by the census (cf. 2 Sam 24:1–17). By contrast, the community speaks of "atonement for Israel" (Neh 10:34) without referring to a specific sin (Neh 10:33–34). Furthermore, in Moses' directive, "the service of the tent of meeting" apparently refers to the construction of the sanctuary (cf. Exod 38:25–28).[79] On the contrary, the community's stipulation (Neh 10:33) uses the same term (עבדה) to designate offerings made in the temple. Furthermore, the community's stipulation calls for a yearly collection of the tax, something that the Mosaic prescription does not mention.

In sum, the community's stipulation (Neh 10:33–34) alludes to the Mosaic prescription (Exod 30:11–16) but alters its orientation. Therefore, the stipulation in Nehemiah provides a "midrashic interpretation" of the Mosaic directive.[80]

The fact that the community alludes to the Mosaic prescription (Neh 10:33–34) echoes the Chronicler's account of King Joash calling for "the tax levied by Moses, the servant of YHWH, and the congregation" (משאת משה עבד־יהוה והקהל, 2 Chr 24:6).[81] A further similarity to the community's stipulation is the king's mandating that the collection take place "year by year" (מדי שנה בשנה, 2 Chr 24:5; cf. בשנה, Neh 10:33). The purpose of the respective taxes constitutes the major distinction between them: the community's levy is for the offerings (Neh 10:33–34), whereas Joash's tax is for the repairs to the temple structure (2 Chr 24:5). Nevertheless, both accounts of taxation allude to the same Mosaic prescription (Exod 30:11–16).

Within Ezra-Nehemiah, the community's taking up the temple tax (Neh 10:33) represents a move toward greater independence from the Persian administration. By assuming financial responsibility for the temple offerings, the people are taking control of a function that the narrative had

---

[79] Alternatively, in the Priestly tradition, the "service of the tent of meeting" (עבדת אהל מועד) designates the work of the Levites at the sanctuary (Num 4:30; 7:5; 8:24; 18:6, 21, 23). See J. Liver, "The Half-Shekel Offering in Biblical and Post-Biblical Literature," *HTR* 56 (1963): 176–77.

[80] M. Haran, "Behind the Scenes of History: Determining the Date of the Priestly Source," *JBL* 100 (1981): 323; Williamson, *Ezra, Nehemiah*, 335–36.

[81] In 2 Chr 24:6, read the MT (והקהל): Japhet, *I and II Chronicles*, 844. Cf. Liver ("The Half-Shekel Offering," 178–79), who argues that the "tax of Moses" (משאת משה, 2 Chr 24:6, 9) refers to the contributions for the building of the sanctuary (Exod 25:1–2).

previously associated with the three Achaemenid monarchs, Cyrus (cf. Ezra 1:4), Darius (cf. Ezra 6:9–10), and Artaxerxes (cf. Ezra 7:21–24).

The "bread arrangement" (לחם המערכת, Neh 10:34)[82] consisted of twelve cakes, stacked in two piles of six, that were placed on a golden table in the sanctuary (Lev 24:5–8; Exod 25:23–30). The priest burned incense over the bread as a "reminiscence by fire to YHWH" (לאזכרה אשה ליהוה, Lev 24:7). This was the "bread of presence" (לחם פנים, Exod 25:30).

The "regular grain offering" (מנחת תמיד) accompanied the "regular burnt offering" (עולת תמיד, Neh 10:34). The "regular grain offering" (מנחת תמיד) was the flour mixed with oil (Exod 29:40–41; Num 28:5), which went with the "regular burnt offering" (עולת תמיד) that consisted of one lamb in the morning and one in the evening of each day (Exod 29:38–42; Num 28:3–8).

The community's list of special occasions (Neh 10:34) follows the sequence of the Priestly calendar (Num 28:1–29:39), which prescribes the offerings for the "Sabbath" (שבת, 28:9–10), the beginnings of "months" (חדשים, 28:11–15), and the "festivals" (מועדים, 29:39). According to this calendar, the festivals (מועדים) include: Passover and Unleavened Bread (28:16–25), Weeks (28:26–31), the first day of the seventh month (29:1–6; cf. Neh 8:2), the Day of Atonement (the tenth day of the seventh month, Num 29:7–11), and the Festival of Booths (Num 29:12–38; cf. Neh 8:13–18).

The "sacred things" (קדשים, Neh 10:34) likely are the "sacred offerings" associated with unique events such as Hezekiah's restoration of the temple liturgy (2 Chr 29:33) and Josiah's Passover celebration (2 Chr 35:3).

"Sin offerings to make atonement for Israel" (חטאות לכפר על־ישראל, Neh 10:34) are those prescribed for particular situations (Lev 4:1–5:13; Num 15:22–29). In Ezra-Nehemiah, the people made such an offering on two previous occasions: at the dedication of the temple (Ezra 6:17), and at the presentation of the donations from Babylon (Ezra 8:35).

Although the community declares that the gift of wood will take place "as it is written in the law" (Neh 10:35), there is no precept in the Torah prescribing such a donation. The community's pledge is an adaptation of the Priestly injunction that the fire on the altar burn continually (Lev 6:2, 5–6). The community's declaration that "the wood [is] for burning on the altar" (Neh 10:35) corresponds most literally with a clause from the Priestly

---

[82] The phrase "bread arrangement" (לחם המערכת) occurs elsewhere only in Chronicles (1 Chr 9:32; 23:29; cf. המערכת לחם, 2 Chr 13:11). The term corresponds with Moses' "arranging the bread on [the table] in the presence of YHWH" (ויערך עליו ערך לחם לפני יהוה, Exod 40:23). See W. Dommershausen, "לֶחֶם," *TDOT* 7:525–27.

ordinance ("the priest shall burn the wood on it [i.e., the fire on the altar]," Lev 6:5).[83]

The mention of the "altar" (מזבח, 10:35) recalls the two other occurrences of the term within Ezra-Nehemiah in the narrative of its construction at the temple site (Ezra 3:2, 3). The description of the wood's purpose (Neh 10:35) reflects that of the original altar (Ezra 3:2) via three common elements: (1) "the altar of God" (מזבח יהוה אלהינו: "the altar of YHWH our God," Neh 10:35; cf. מזבח אלהי ישראל: "the altar of the God of Israel," Ezra 3:2); (2) the burning that takes place "upon" it [וקרבן העצים לבער על־מזבח]: "[the donation of wood] to burn upon the altar," Neh 10:35; cf. להעלות עליו עלות: "to offer burnt offerings upon it," Ezra 3:2); and (3) "as it is written in the law [of Moses]" (ככתוב בתורה, Neh 10:35; cf. ככתוב בתורת משה, Ezra 3:2). Thus, the fifth stipulation (Neh 10:35) assures the future continuity of the rituals that began immediately upon the return of the exiles to the temple site (Ezra 3:2–3).

In the phrase "the altar of YHWH, our God" (מזבח יהוה אלהינו, 10:35), the divine title occurs elsewhere in Ezra-Nehemiah only in Ezra's prayer (יהוה אלהינו, Ezra 9:8). From a narrative perspective, the people's use of the title suggests their appropriation of their leader's spirituality.

The book concludes with Nehemiah's declaration that he implemented the community's commitment to supplying the donation of wood (Neh 13:31). All of the terminology in Nehemiah's statement here derives from the community's oath, thereby indicating his respect for the prescription ("[I arranged] for the donation of wood at specified times," 13:31).[84]

The community's pledge to bring the firstfruits to the temple (Neh 10:36) uses the vocabulary of a precept in the Covenant Code and its parallel in the account of the covenant renewal at Sinai: "The choicest of the firstfruits of your soil you shall bring to the house of YHWH your God" (Exod 23:19a = 34:26a).[85] The Priestly legislation earmarks the firstfruits for the priests (Num 18:13). The Deuteronomic Code describes the liturgy for presenting the firstfruits (Deut 26:1–11).

The pentateuchal legislation mentions only the firstfruits of the crops ("of your soil": אדמתך, Exod 23:19a; 34:26a). Therefore, the community's reference to the "firstfruits of all the fruit of every tree" (10:36) is an expansion of the legal requirements. However, the reference to fruit trees is

---

[83] Neh 10:35: [וקרבן העצים] ... לבער על־מזבח
    Lev 6:5: ובער עליה הכהן עצים

[84] Neh 13:31: ולקרבן העצים בעתים מזמנות
    Neh 10:35: על־קרבן העצים ... לעתים מזמנים

[85] Neh 10:36: להביא את־בכורי אדמתנו ... לבית יהוה
    Exod 23:19a: ראשית בכורי אדמתך תביא בית יהוה אלהיך
    Exod 34:26a: ראשית בכורי אדמתך תביא בית יהוה אלהיך

The Covenant Commitment (Nehemiah 10:1–40)

particularly appropriate for the Festival of Booths in the seventh month (Neh 8:14–18; cf. Exod 23:16b; 34:22c), following the harvesting of summer fruit (August) and olives (September–October).[86]

The community's pledge to bring the firstfruits provides the background for Nehemiah's final activity, namely, providing the firstfruits (בכורים, Neh 13:31; cf. 10:36).

The community will bring the firstborn sons and livestock "as it is written in the law" (ככתוב בתורה, 10:37). The declaration is not a quotation but an allusion to the pentateuchal command to sanctify the firstborn of humans and of unclean livestock (Exod 13:2, 12–15).[87] The people had to redeem the firstborn of their sons and of their unclean animals by a substitutionary sacrifice (Exod 13:13; 34:19–20) or by a payment of money (Num 18:15–16; cf. Lev 27:27).[88]

The community's pledge to bring "the firstborn of our herds and of our flocks" to the priests corresponds with the Priestly ordinance that these firstborn of the clean animals are to be consumed by the priests (Num 18:17–18).[89]

The community's pledge to bring the "choicest of our dough ... to the priests" (את־ראשית ערסתינו ... לכהנים, Neh 10:38) corresponds with Ezekiel's command, "the choicest of your dough you shall give to the priest" (ראשית ערסותיכם תתנו לכהן, Ezek 44:30). However, both of these

---

[86] O. Borowski ("Harvests, Harvesting," *ABD* 3:63–64) notes that the Gezer Calendar (ca. 925 B.C.E.) lists five harvests: (1) barley (mid-March to mid-April; cf. Ruth 2:23); (2) wheat (up to mid-May; cf. Gen 30:14; Judg 15:1); (3) grapes (mid-May to mid-July; cf. Lev 26:5; Isa 24:13); (4) summer fruit (August; cf. Jer 40:10, 12; Amos 8:1–2) and (5) olives (September–October; cf. Exod 23:16b; 34:22c). Thus, the three pilgrimage festivals cited in the Pentateuch (Exod 23:14–17, 19; cf. 34:18–23; Lev 23:4–22; Deut 16:1–16) correspond with the conclusions of different harvests: (1) Passover (following the barley harvest); (2) Weeks (following the wheat harvest); and (3) Booths (following the harvests of trees [grapes, summer fruit, and olives]).

[87] Note these linguistic associations:
Neh 10:37: את־בכרות בנינו ובהמתינו
Exod 13:2: קדש־לי כל־בכור פטר כל־רחם בבני ישראל באדם ובבהמה

[88] G. Brin ("The Firstling of Unclean Animals," *JQR* 68 [1978]: 1–12) argues that Num 18:15–18 represents a broadening of the earlier laws of Exod 13:13 and 34:19–20 on two counts: (1) by referring to unclean animals in general (בהמה, Num 18:15) rather than to the ass in particular (חמור, Exod 13:13; 34:20); and (2) by providing for redemption by a monetary payment (Num 18:16) rather than by the sacrifice of a lamb (Exod 13:13; 34:20).

[89] By contrast, the Deuteronomic Code prescribes the firstborn of herds and flocks as food that the owner and his family eats while on pilgrimage at the sanctuary (Deut 15:19–20). The Covenant Code established the principle that the firstborn of the oxen and sheep belong to YHWH (Exod 22:30).

statements derive from the Priestly injunction to give to YHWH the "choicest of your dough" (ראשית ערסתיכם, Num 15:20–21). This dough is the highest quality "bread of the land" (לחם הארץ, 15:19) and thereby expresses thanksgiving to YHWH for the land.

The mention of "our contributions" (תרומתינו, Neh 10:38) appears somewhat out of place amid the list of harvest products (dough, fruit, wine, and oil). Its inclusion seems to reflect the influence of Ezek 44:30, which mentions both "your contributions" (ערסותיכם) and "the choicest of your dough" (ראשית ערסותיכם).

The presentation of the "choicest of our dough ... of wine and of oil" (את־ראשית עריסתינו ... תירוש ויצהר, Neh 10:38a) reflects the Deuteronomic injunction to present to YHWH "the choicest of your grain, your wine, and your oil" (ראשית דגנך תירושך ויצהרך, Deut 18:4). The presentation of these gifts "to the priests" (לכהנים, Neh 10:38a) in particular corresponds with the Priestly declaration that "all the best" (כל־חלב, Num 18:12 [3x]) of each of these belongs to the priests.

The commitment to bring "the tithe of our soil to the Levites" (מעשר אדמתנו ללוים, 10:38b) is an adaptation of the Priestly legislation in which YHWH states, "To the Levites I give every tithe in Israel" (לבני לוי הנה נתתי כל־מעשר בישראל, Num 18:21). Moreover, the same tradition enjoins the Levites to give "a tithe of [their] tithe" (מעשר המן־מעשר, 18:26; cf. מעשר המעשר: "a tenth of the tithe," Neh 10:39b) to the priests.[90]

However, the Priestly legislation (Num 18:25–32) does not offer any prescriptions regarding the manner in which the Levites should collect the tithes (cf. Neh 10:38b) or any stipulation that a priest should supervise the Levitical collection of tithes (cf. Neh 10:39a). The only reflection of the Priestly law in these provisions (Neh 10:38b–39a) might be the mention of "a priest, a son of Aaron" (הכהן בן־אהרן, Neh 10:39), which echoes "the priest, Aaron" (אהרן הכהן, Num 18:28). However, these figures function in a distinctive manner in the two texts: "a priest, a son of Aaron" accompanies the Levites who collect the tithes (Neh 10:39), whereas "the priest Aaron" receives the tenth of the tithe from the Levites (Num 18:28).

---

[90] The Deuteronomic Code describes a different protocol (Deut 14:22–29). In two of every three years, the tithes were for consumption by the owner and his household at the sanctuary during their annual pilgrimage (14:22–26). Nevertheless, this code makes two provisions for the Levites: (1) in the two years when the owner consumes the tithes at the sanctuary, the Levites are to receive some portion of the tithe (14:28); and (2) every third year, the Levites—along with the resident aliens, the orphans, and the widows—receive the full tithe that the owner must bring to the town (14:28–29). On the relationship between Num 18:21–28; Deut 14:27–29; and Neh 10:38b, see Z. Zevit, "Converging Lines of Evidence Bearing on the Date of P," *ZAW* 94 (1982): 487–93.

The mandate for the Levites to go to towns in order to collect the tithes (Neh 10:38b–39a) might derive from the Deuteronomic ordinance that, in every third year, the residents of a locality must bring their tithes to their towns for distribution to the Levites and the poor (Deut 14:28–29). Nevertheless, the description of the Levites going into the towns to collect tithes (Neh 10:38b–39a) represents a change vis-à-vis the previous system of the people's bringing their tithes to the temple (Neh 10:40a; Deut 14:23–26; Amos 4:4; Mal 3:10).[91]

The community's concern for the presentation of tithes and contributions to the priests and Levites (Neh 10:38b–40) has a number of affinities with the Chronicler's account of Hezekiah's temple reform (2 Chr 31:2–19). First, the priests and Levites receive the tithes (Neh 10:38b–39; cf. 2 Chr 31:4); and, second, there is explicit mention of: (1) the "tithe" (המעשר, Neh 10:38b; cf. 2 Chr 31:12); (2) the "Israelites" (בני ישראל, Neh 10:40; 2 Chr 31:5); (3) "bringing" (בוא hipʿil, Neh 10:40; 2 Chr 31:12); (4) the "contribution" (התרומה, Neh 10:40; cf. 2 Chr 31:12); and (5) "the grain, the wine, and the oil" (הדגן ה[ה]תירוש והיצהר, Neh 10:40; cf. 2 Chr 31:5). However, three elements of the community's stipulation (Neh 10:38b–40) are absent from the Chronicler's account: the Levites having primacy over the priests in the collecting of tithes (10:38b); the towns as locales for the collections (10:39a); and the Levites' donating a tenth to the priests (10:39b).

The Ezra-Nehemiah narrative indicates that the people initially adhered to their oaths pertaining to tithes and contributions (10:38a–40a). The account of the administration at the temple storerooms (Neh 12:44–47) has numerous lexical affinities with the community oath on tithes and contributions: (1) the "stores" (אוצרות, 12:44) or the "storehouse" (בית האוצר, 10:39b); (2) "contributions" (תרומות, 12:44; cf. 10:38); (3) the "choicest [portions]" (ראשית, 12:44; cf. 10:38); (4) "tithes" (מעשרות, 12:44; cf. מעשר, 10:38b); (5) "the priests" (הכהנים, 12:44; cf. 10:38a, 40a); (6) "the Levites" (הלוים, 12:44; cf. 10:38b); (7) "the singers" (המשררים, 12:45; cf. 10:40a); and (8) "gatekeepers" (השערים, 12:45; cf. 10:40a). Moreover, the collecting of the tithes "according to the fields of the towns" (לשדי הערים, 13:44) alludes to the practice of the Levites going outside Jerusalem to receive the tithes (Neh 10:38b–39). Finally, the summary evaluation describes the Levites' control over the tithes that went to the priests, while also testifying to the care for the temple personnel on the part of the whole community ("all Israel," 12:47).

In contrast to such observance, the account of the personnel removing the contents from the storeroom in preparation for its occupation by Tobiah (13:4–5) indicates a lack of adherence to the community's stipulation (cf.

---

91 For a sketch of the development of tithing practices, see H. Jagersma, "The Tithes in the Old Testament," *OtSt* 21 (1981): 116–28.

10:38–40a). The list of the room's former contents (13:5) features various lexical allusions to the community's summary directive (10:40a): (1) the "vessels" (הכלים, 13:5); (2) the "tithes for the Levites, singers, and gatekeepers" and (3) "the contributions for the priests" were no longer in the storerooms (Neh 13:5; cf. 10:40a). Indeed, from a narrative perspective, the description of the removed tithes as donated "by commandment" (מצות, 13:5) refers to the community's stipulation (10:38b–40a).

The subsequent description of the people not providing the portions for the Levites and singers (13:10–13) indicates a slackening of the community's adherence to the oath of renewal (10:38b–40). Nehemiah corrects this abuse in such a manner that the people return to an observance of the community's directive (13:12; cf. 10:40a).

The people's declaration not to abandon the house of God provides a basis for Nehemiah's inquiry upon returning to Jerusalem: "Why is the house of God forsaken?" (13:11; cf. 10:40b).[92] Thus, the last word in the community's covenant renewal becomes the first word in Nehemiah's reforms.

THEMATIC SUMMARY

Within Ezra-Nehemiah, the community's oath taking (10:1–40) is the central event of self-definition by postexilic Israel. By signing the agreement and by voicing the oath, the community identifies itself both internally, in terms of its membership, and externally, in terms of its relationship to outsiders. I shall highlight five themes in the commitment narrative: (1) the roots of the agreement in the Abrahamic covenant and the Mosaic law; (2) the articulation of the law as an interpretive reading of traditions; (3) unity as the commitment's internal effect on its members; (4) enhanced autonomy as the commitment's external impact on relationships to outsiders; and (5) the commitment event as a means of reorientation from past to future.

THE ROOTS OF THE AGREEMENT

Three terms in particular identify the commitment ceremony as a covenant renewal: (1) the verb כרת (lit., "to cut") in this context alludes to the expression כרת ברית ("to make a covenant") and thereby implies that the accompanying accusative אמנה ("firm agreement," 10:1) is a synonym for ברית ("covenant"); (2) the accusative אמנה ("firm agreement," 10:1) recalls the mention of Abraham's "faithfulness" (נאמן, 9:8a) in the preceding psalm; and (3) the noun "oath" (שבועה), on occasion, serves as a substitute for ברית ("covenant").

---

[92] Neh 10:40b: לא נעזב את־בית אלהינו
Neh 13:11: מדוע נעזב בית־האלהים

The preceding psalm (9:6–37) states that God established the "covenant" (ברית, 9:8a; cf. 9:32b) with Abraham while he communicated the "law" (תורה, 9:14b; cf. 8:1, 14; 10:30) through Moses. Thus, the community's agreement emerges as the confluence of these traditions. The "firm agreement" (אמנה, 10:1) of the community implies their imitation of Abraham's "faithfulness" (נאמן, 9:8a). Their swearing "to walk in the law of God that was given through the hand of Moses" (10:30) indicates their allegiance to the Sinaitic legislation (9:13–14).

THE LAW

The six stipulations that the people announce allude to the full range of legal traditions of the Pentateuch: pre-Deuteronomic, Deuteronomic, and Priestly.

Table 6.7—The Stipulations and the Pentateuchal Traditions[93]

Stipulation	Pre-Deuteronomic	D	P
1. 10:31 Marriage	(Exod 34:15–16)	Deut 7:3	
2. 10:32a Sabbath	Exod 20:8–11	Deut 5:12–15	
	Exod 23:12		Exod 35:3
	Exod 34:21		
Holy Day			Num 15:32–36
			Exod 16:22–30
			Num 28:1–30:1
3. 10:32b Seventh-Year Pledge	Exod 23:10–11	Deut 15:1–3	(Lev 25:1–8)
4. 10:33–34 Temple Tax			Exod 30:11–16
5. 10:35 Wood			Lev 6:2, 5–6
6. 10:36–40a			
Firstfruits	Exod 23:19a	(Deut 26:1–11)	Num 18:12–13
	Exod 34:26		
Firstborn			Num 18:17–18
Products		Deut 18:4	Num 15:20–21
Tithe		Deut 14:23–26	Num 18:21, 26

In terms of content, the Deuteronomic and Priestly traditions are the most predominant in the formulation of the community's stipulations. Nevertheless, the literary allusions pertain to the full diversity of legislative traditions. Such evidence suggests that "the law of God" (תורת אלהים, 10:30) to which the people pledge their allegiance approximates the complete Torah.

---

[93] Citations in parentheses are legal parallels that have little influence on the stipulation in Neh 10:31–40a.

However, none of the stipulations actually quotes verbatim a text in the Pentateuch. Each of them represents rather an interpretive reading of the legislation: (1) the prohibition of intermarriage exhibits a new application, namely, the contemporary concern with the "peoples of the land" (10:31); (2) the Sabbath stipulation is more specific than the legislation in its attention to detail (forbidding purchasing) and extends its application to holy days (10:32a); (3) the fallow year coincides with the release of pledges (10:32b); (4) the annual temple tax is an adaptation of an ancient census custom (10:33–34); (5) the wood donation derives from the injunction for maintaining the fire on the altar (10:35); and (6) the pledge of support for temple personnel is an amalgamation of legislation on the handling of livestock and crops (10:36–40a).

The stipulations reflect a flexible handling of the legislation and thereby represent halakic reinterpretations of the pentateuchal laws.[94]

UNITY: THE INTERNAL EFFECT

The commitment unifies the community and defines its boundaries. The forces of unity emerge from the grass roots rather than from the initiative of individual leaders. The contrast in social dynamics between the first assembly (7:72b–8:12) and the last (9:1–10:40) are remarkable: (1) on the first day, the people gather around Ezra (8:2–12), whereas on the last day they assemble and pray on their own initiative (9:1–3); and (2) on the first day, they listen to the law (8:3, 7–8), whereas on the last day they proclaim the law (10:31–40).

The process of democratization that was implicit in the people's gathering on their own (9:1–3) becomes explicit in the participation of the whole populace (10:1–30). The eighty-four signatories (10:2–28) take the place of the individual leader (cf. 8:1: Ezra) at the head of the community. Moreover, these eighty-four are intimately related to the rest of the populace as their "noble kindred" (10:30). Thus, Nehemiah is the "first among equals" in the list of signatories (cf. 10:2). The transformation in his position becomes apparent in a narrative reading: prior to the commitment, he determines his own agenda (Neh 1:1–7:72a), whereas afterward the stipulations of the community govern his reform activities (Neh 13:4–31; cf. 10:31–40).

The community expands due to the incorporation of the proselytes ("all who had separated themselves from the peoples of the lands to the law of God," 10:29). Moreover, the commitment ceremony indicates the enfranchisement of the women and children (10:29; cf. 8:2–3). The participation of the sons and daughters suggests their complete redemption from their prior status in which they could be and some actually were debt-slaves (cf. 5:5).

---

[94] See D. J. A. Clines, "Nehemiah 10 As an Example of Early Jewish Biblical Exegesis," *JSOT* 21 (1981): 111–17; and Fishbane, *Biblical Interpretation*, 114–34.

Finally, the stipulation's guarantee of social protection for the poor further solidifies the community. The observance of the fallow year and the release of pledges provides an infrastructure to care for the most economically disadvantaged in the community.

INCREASED AUTONOMY: THE EXTERNAL EFFECT

The commitment in writing (וכתבים, 10:1) provides the means for Israel to shape its own destiny. Up to this point in Ezra-Nehemiah, the documents of the Persian monarchs propelled developments in Jerusalem and Judah (cf. Ezra 1:1–4; 4:11–16, 17–22; 5:6–17; 6:2–12; 7:12–26; cf. Neh 2:7–10). The edicts of Cyrus, Darius, and Artaxerxes (cf. Ezra 6:14) opened the way for the reconstruction of the temple, the marriage reform, and the building of the wall, respectively.

However, from this point forward, the Persian kings do not issue edicts that determine the course of history in Judah (cf. Neh 13:6–7). Instead, the stipulations that the community proclaims provide the basis for Nehemiah's subsequent work of reform (10:31–40; cf. 13:4–31). Moreover, the fact that the book terminates with reference to these stipulations (13:30–31) suggests that the stipulations will continue to shape the community in the future.

Three stipulations in particular provide greater autonomy for the community. The injunctions against intermarriage (10:31) and commercial transactions on the Sabbath (10:32a) establish social boundaries that protect the community from intrusion on the part of the peoples of the lands (cf. 6:18–19; 13:4–5, 28). Furthermore, the commitment to the annual temple tax indicates that the Israelites are assuming fiscal responsibility for the temple, a domain for which previously their foreign overlords had provided support (cf. Ezra 1:4; 6:9–10; 7:21–24).

HISTORICAL REORIENTATION

The community's oath taking is a turning point that reorients the community from the past into the future. Their dedication to the law of God (10:30) constitutes their turning away from the rebellious patterns of their ancestors (cf. 9:29a). By making this commitment, the community is no longer the victim of historical effects stemming from past wickedness (cf. 9:33–35). The management of their livestock is symbolic of the new order: whereas the Levites had just declared that the Persians rule over "our livestock" (בהמתנו, 9:37b), now the people announce their decision to bring the firstborn "of our livestock" (בהמתינו, 10:37) to the temple.

Furthermore, in the oath taking, Israel demonstrates the capacity to shape its own future. The stipulations of the commitment become the agenda for Nehemiah's reforms at the conclusion of the book (10:31–40; cf. 13:4–31).

7

Conclusion

The foregoing analysis discloses that the covenant-renewal account (Neh 7:72b–10:40) is sophisticated literature. Singular literary features distinguish this segment as the climax of the Ezra-Nehemiah story. Moreover, the content of this segment makes a unique contribution to the message of the whole book.

In this summary, I highlight the results of the synchronic analysis that constitute the original contributions of this study to Ezra-Nehemiah research. The summary consists of two parts. First, I survey the primary literary features that characterize the covenant-renewal account: (1) the shift in narrative voice, (2) the structuring of particular sections, and (3) the repetition of significant vocabulary. Second, I offer an overview of content with a specific concern for dramatic development evident in: (1) the dynamic relationship between the people and the law; (2) the maturation of the people in terms of democracy, autonomy, and unity; (3) the changes in the identity and functioning of leadership; and (4) the role of the Levites' prayer as a hermeneutical key for the whole story.

LITERARY FEATURES

SHIFT IN NARRATIVE VOICE

The shift from third-person narrative (7:72b–9:5) to first-person discourse (9:6–10:40) is perhaps the most distinctive literary feature of the covenant-renewal account. Yet none of the commentaries has devoted particular attention to this remarkable feature.[1] The change in narrative voice serves three purposes: (1) it sustains the transition in the people's comportment from respondents to initiators of activity (9:1–3; cf. 7:72b–8:18); (2) it corresponds with the alternations between first-person memoir and third-person narration of the career of Ezra and the first-person memoir of Nehemiah elsewhere in the book; and (3) it enables the people to speak directly to the book's audience.

---

[1] Cf. Eskenazi, *In an Age of Prose*, 100.

The Levites declaim the psalm on behalf of the people (9:6–37), whereas the people recount the signing of the firm agreement (10:1–28) and announce their allegiance to the Torah in general (10:29–30) and to the stipulations in particular (10:31–40). The transition from third-person to first-person voice occurs just after the people demonstrate initiative in undertaking the penitential rites without the prompting of their leaders (9:1–3). The people's initial participation consists in allowing the Levites to declaim the psalm on their behalf (9:6–37) before they finally speak for themselves in announcing their commitment to the Torah (10:1–40). Moreover, the people's declaration of allegiance to the Torah (10:29–30) and their pronouncement of the stipulations (10:31–40a) go far beyond their brief statements of consent to the marriage reform of Ezra (Ezra 10:12–14) and the social reform of Nehemiah (Neh 5:12) during previous assemblies. Thus, the first-person speech of the people that concludes the covenant renewal climaxes the previous stages of community reform.

The alternation from third person (7:72b–9:5) to first person (9:6–10:40) reflects a unique stylistic feature of Ezra-Nehemiah vis-à-vis the rest of biblical literature. This alternation is most apparent in the account of Ezra's career, which moves from first-person memoir (Ezra 7:27–9:15) to third-person narrative (10:1–44). Furthermore, third-person narration (Neh 7:6–72a; 11:1–12:26; 12:44–13:3) interrupts the description of Nehemiah's work, which is related entirely in the first person (Neh 1:1–7:5a; 12:27–43; 13:4–31).[2] Thus, the alternation in narrative voice in the covenant renewal is consistent with the rest of the material in Ezra and Nehemiah.

Finally, the first-person declarations provide the book's audience with a firsthand encounter with the people. Here the audience can reassess its prior understanding of the people that had derived from the narrator's account of them. Moreover, the first-person pronouncements of commitment endow the covenant renewal with an aspect of immediacy for the book's audience.

Structure

Parallels in vocabulary and structure unify the narrative descriptions of the three assemblies that comprise the covenant renewal (7:72b–8:12; 8:13–18; 9:1–5). These parallels are: (1) date; (2) assembly; (3) description of the people; (4) reading or study of the law; (5) designations of the book of the law; and (6) leaders' exhortations.[3] The present study advances

---

[2] A distinctive feature of Eskenazi's study is her discussion of the shift in narrative viewpoint from first to third person in Ezra-Nehemiah and the impact of this alternation on the characterization of Ezra and Nehemiah, respectively. See ibid., 129–35.

[3] Ibid., 96–97; Throntveit, *Ezra-Nehemiah*, 95.

Conclusion 293

beyond previous research in its identification of the unique narrative development in each of these segments: (1) the four subunits with interlocking alternative time frames in the account of the first day (7:72b–8:12: 7:72b–8:3; 8:4–6, 7–8, 9–12); (2) the chiastic structure of the narrative of Booths (8:13–18: 8:13 [A], 14–15 [B], 16–17 [B'], 18 [A']); and (3) the two-part description of the penitential rites, which emphasizes the initiative of the Israelites (9:1–3) prior to the intervention of the Levites (9:4–5).

REPETITION

The repetition of words unifies the covenant-renewal account and highlights the distinctiveness of its individual sections. The designation "Israelites" (בני ישראל) provides the *inclusio* for the whole (7:72b; 10:40) and also introduces each major section (7:72b; 8:14; 9:1; cf. 8:17). "The law" (התורה) is the account's most pervasive noun (8:1, 2, 3, 7, 8, 9, 13, 14, 18; 9:3, 14b, 26a, 29a, 34a; 10:29, 30, 35, 37). The "book of the law" (ספר התורה) occurs only in the third-person narrative (8:1–12: 8:1, 3, 8, 18; 9:3), whereas the Levites and the people speak in the first person of "the law" (התורה, 10:29, 30, 35, 37). Thus, the third-person narrative concentrates on reading from the book (8:3, 8, 18; 9:3), whereas the first-person discourse emphasizes commitment to its principles and stipulations (10:29–30, 35, 37; cf. 9:14b, 26a, 29a, 34a).

The repetition of particular words also links individual sections. Reference to the day of the seventh month (ביום) and mention of the people's "gathering" (אסף *nipʿal*) introduce each major section (8:1–2, 13; 9:1). Focus on the "words of the law" (דברי התורה, 8:9, 13) provides the transition from the first to the second section. The people's reaction, progressing from "great joy" (שמחה גדולה, 8:12) to "very great joy" (שמחה גדולה מאד, 8:17), indicates a development from the first day to the end of the celebration of Booths. The mention of the half-day time span parallels the people's reading and worship on the twenty-fourth day (9:3) with Ezra's reading on the first day (8:3). Five words in particular link the description of the penitential rites with the Levites' prayer: (1) the confession of "their sins" (חטאתיהם, 9:2; cf. חטאתינו, 9:37a); (2) the guilt of their "ancestors" (אבתיהם, 9:2; cf. אבתינו, 9:9, 16, 32c, 34a, 36b); (3) worshiping YHWH (משתחוים, 9:3; cf. 9:6d); (4) the "crying out" in prayer to YHWH (זעק, 9:3; cf. זעק, 9:28b; צעק, 9:27b; זעקה, 9:9); and (5) the acknowledgment that YHWH is God (9:3, 4, 5; cf. 9:6a, 7a).

Finally, the repetition of the pronoun "we" (אנחנו, 9:37b; 10:1) provides the transition from the Levites' prayer to the people's commitment. Moreover, separation from the "peoples of the land[s]" (עמי הארצ(ו)ת) progresses from the penitential rites (9:2) through the historical recollections in the Levites' prayer (9:24c, 30c) to full expression in the community's stipulations (10:29, 30, 32). In conclusion, the people's declaration not to abandon the temple echoes the response in the psalm's description of YHWH's not abandoning the people (לא עזב, 10:40b; cf. 9:17d, 19a, 31b).

The repetition of particular words within each section highlights the theme that is specific to that portion of the covenant renewal. The recurrence of "all the people" (כל־העם) ten times in the account of the first day (8:1, 3, 5 [3x], 6, 9 [bis], 11, 12) calls attention to the unity and inclusivity of the assembly. Furthermore, the occurrence of the terms "the people" (העם) and "the book" (הספר) in every subunit (7:72b–8:3; 8:4–6, 7–8, 9–12) indicates that this section describes the encounter between the people and the book. The recurrence of the terms "the law" (התורה, 8:13, 14, 18) and "booths" (סכות, 8:14, 15, 16, 17) in the second section (8:13–18) suggests that celebration of the festival provides the people with the occasion for both observing the law (8:16) and hearing it for eight days (8:18). The threefold repetition of "YHWH, your [their] God" (9:3, 4, 5) highlights the theological focus of the penitential rites (9:1–5).

The interplay of various phrases and words throughout generates the rich texture of the Levites' prayer:

1. the confessional statements (9:6a, 8d, 17c–d, 31b, 32a–b, 33a);
2. "you" referring to God (אתה, 9:6a, 6b, 6d, 7a, 8d, 17c, 19a, 27b, 28c, 31b, 33a);
3. God's "mercy" (רחמים/רחום, 9:17c, 19a, 27c, 28c, 31a);
4. the "land" (ארץ, 9:8b, 15c, 22b [bis], 24a–b, 32b, 35b, 36b);
5. the "law/laws" (תורות/תורה, 9:13c, 14b, 26a, 29a, 34a);
6. the "commandments" (מצות, 9:13b, 14b, 16a, 29a, 34b);
7. "good" and "goodness" (טוב, 9:13c, 20a, 25b, 35a, 36b);
8. "king" (מלך, 9:22b–c, 24c, 32d, 37a; cf. 9:32c, 34a);
9. "heaven" (שמים, 9:6b [3x], 6d, 13a, 15a, 23a, 27b, 28c);
10. "to give" (נתן, 9:8b–c, 13b, 15a, 15d, 20a–b, 22a, 24b, 27a, 30c, 35a–b, 36b, 37a; cf. 9:17b, 29c);
11. "to do" (עשה, 9:6b, 10b, 17a, 31a, 33b; cf. 9:18a, 18c, 24c, 26a, 28a, 29b, 34a);
12. "to hear" (שמע, 9:9, 27b, 28b; cf. 16a, 17a, 29a, 29c);
13. "to possess" (ירש, 9:15c, 22b, 23b, 24a, 25b);
14. "to turn back" (שוב, 9:17b; 26b, 28a–b, 29a, 35c); and
15. "to warn" (עוד hip'il, 9:26b, 29a, 30b, 34b).

The final section (10:1–40) directs attention to the plethora of leaders at its beginning (10:1: "our princes, our Levites, and our priests"), middle (10:29: "the priests, the Levites, the gatekeepers, the singers, the temple servants"), and end (10:40: "the ministering priests, the gatekeepers, and the singers"). Moreover, the nine references to the temple (בית אלהינו: the "house of our God" [8x]: 10:33, 34, 35, 37 [bis], 38, 39, 40; בית יהוה, 10:36) indicate the theme of the final three stipulations.

An additional noteworthy feature of various sections is the preoccupation with numerical congruency, whether explicit or implied: (1) in the account of the first day (7:72b–8:12), thirteen lay leaders (8:4) and thirteen Levites (8:7); (2) for the Festival of Booths (8:13–18), five types of branches (8:15) and five locations for the booths (8:16); (3) in the penitential rites, eight Levites on the steps (9:4) and eight Levites exhorting the people to pray (9:5); and (4) in the psalm, seven juridical terms in reference to Sinai (9:13–14), seven rebellious actions in the wilderness (9:16a–17b), seven captured items (9:25a–c), and seven rebellious actions in the land (9:29a–30c). The numerical concern culminates in the eighty-four (seven times twelve) signatories who are emblematic of all Israel (10:2–28).

In summary, the repetition of terms is a consistent feature throughout the covenant-renewal account that both unifies the whole and manifests the uniqueness of each component section.

Dramatic Development of Content

The People and the Torah

The covenant-renewal account describes the people's developing acquaintance with the Torah. The third-person narrative recounts the people's advancement in understanding through three activities: (1) hearing on the first day (ואזני כל־העם על־ספר התורה: "and the ears of all the people were on the book of the law," 8:3; cf. כשמעם: "as they heard," 8:9); (2) studying (by the leaders) on the second day (8:13, להשכיל: "in order to study"); and (3) reading on the twenty-fourth day (ויקראו בספר תורת יהוה אלהיהם: "and [they] read from the book of the law of YHWH, their God," 9:3). However, it is the first-person pronouncements that evidence the completion of the process, when the people proclaim their allegiance in principle to the Torah (10:29–30) and announce the specific stipulations of the law whose objective is to reform their way of living (10:31–40).

Thus, each segment indicates an advance in the people's appropriation of the Torah: (1) their pursuit of "understanding" (בין, 8:2, 3, 7, 8, 9, 12) distinguishes the first day (7:72b–8:12); (2) the Festival of Booths (8:13–18) provides the first opportunity for them to put into practice written prescriptions of the Torah; (3) in the penitential rites (9:1–5), their reading of the Torah culminates in their definitive separation—as the offspring of Israel (זרע ישראל, 9:2)—from the influence of foreigners (מכל בני נכר, 9:2); and (4) their ultimate proclamation of commitment to the Torah (10:29–40) defines the future shape of the community in terms of communal and noncommunal relationships. Thus one can discern a four-step process in the people's appropriating the Torah: (1) initial hearing and understanding of the oral reading (8:12); (2) initial study by the leaders and application by the people (8:13–18); (3) reading by the people pursuant to their definitive step toward community self-definition (9:1–5); and (4) commitment by the people to the principles and stipulations (10:1–40).

THE GROWTH OF DEMOCRACY, UNITY, AND AUTONOMY

The Torah passes through the hands of an expanding circle: Ezra (8:2–6); the Levites (8:7–8); the heads of ancestral families, the priests, Levites, and Ezra (8:13); and the Israelites as a whole (9:3). This movement of the law into the hands of the people reflects a trend toward democratization that is evident in diverse aspects of the narrative.

From the beginning, the people take a certain initiative in the covenant renewal as they request Ezra to bring them the book of the law (8:1). However, the people are dependent on various leaders to direct their activities both on the first day (7:72b–8:12) and throughout the celebration of Booths (8:13–18). The final assembly (9:1–10:40) inaugurates a new order insofar as the people initiate their own penitential rites and reading of the Torah (9:1–3), which the Levites subsequently animate through their declamation of the psalm (9:4–5, 6–37). Nevertheless, the people's voice supersedes that of the Levites in the signing of the agreement (10:1–28) and in the declaration of allegiance to the Torah (10:29–40).

The successive assemblies that comprise the covenant renewal are characterized by unity and inclusivity. The people gather "as one" (כאיש אחד, 8:1) on the first day. Throughout the remainder of the account, there is no hint of division or tension among the people (compare, e.g., 5:1–5). The people always act in unison: weeping upon hearing the words of the Torah (8:9); going forth to prepare the festive meal (8:12); constructing booths according to the legal prescription (8:16); performing the penitential rites (9:1–3); and professing allegiance to the Torah (10:1–40).

Moreover, the major assemblies reflect a concern for the inclusivity of the whole community: the women and "everyone who could understand by hearing" take part with the men on the first day (8:2–3); the proclamation of the Festival of Booths extends to "all their towns" as well as to Jerusalem (8:15); the proselytes, as well as the wives, sons, and daughters, take part in the oath of commitment (10:29).

The participation of the sons and daughters reflects a concern for their enfranchisement that is especially poignant in view of the debt-slavery that some of their number had suffered (5:5). Similarly, the stipulation for the observance of the seventh year (10:32b) evidences a commitment to protect the poor members of the community.

The covenant renewal consolidates the community by defining its boundaries. Separation from "all foreigners" (בני נכר, 9:2) is a prerequisite for the community's self-determination. The Levites' psalm (9:24c, 30c) and the community's oath (10:29, 31, 32) designate such foreigners as "the peoples of the land[s]." Since the term in the psalm refers to the imperial overlords (9:30c; cf. 9:32b–d, 37), the people's oath of separation extends beyond the opponents who live in the immediate vicinity (cf. Ezra 3:3; 4:4; 9:1, 2, 11; 10:2, 11) to include the Persians as well. Thus, the community's oath indicates the people's determination that the Torah shape their future without foreign interference from any quarter.

Changes in Leadership

The covenant-renewal process entails a transition in the identity and functioning of leadership within the community. In terms of identity, single leadership gradually gives way to the leadership of many. Thus, in the beginning, Ezra functions alone with the book of the law (8:1–3). However, he gradually recedes from prominence as thirteen laymen accompany him on the platform (8:4) and thirteen Levites assist in his work of reading from the book of the law (8:7–8). Having introduced the blessing of YHWH (8:6), Ezra's voice becomes one among others who issue directives (8:9–12, 13–15).

The leadership of the heads of families, along with the priests and Levites who study the law with Ezra (8:13), prepares for the commingling of secular and clerical categories among the eighty-four signatories ("the governor," 10:2; "the priests," 10:3–9; "the Levites," 10:10–14;[4] and "the leaders of the people," 10:15–28). Overall, the covenant renewal describes the development of an increasingly collegial form of leadership, one that moves from the individual leader to the eighty-four signatories who represent the whole people. The designation of these leaders as the people's "noble kindred" (10:30) indicates that they derive their identity from their roots within the community rather than from an authoritative position above the community.

Moreover, the various leaders exercise their offices differently as a result of the covenant-renewal process. In the first two assemblies, the leaders issue directives with which the people comply (8:9–12, 14–16). However, in the final assembly, the people initiate the activities (9:1–3), and the Levites join them (9:4) prior to voicing their exhortation (9:5). Moreover, by announcing the stipulations, the people, in the end, provide directives for the priests and Levites (e.g., 10:38b–40a).

The example of Nehemiah indicates that, in the covenant renewal, the community provides the mandate for the activities of its leaders. Thus, the community stipulations determine the agenda for Nehemiah's reforms (10:31; cf. 13:23–27; 10:32a; cf. 13:15–22; 10:35; cf. 13:31; 10:36–40a; cf. 13:10–13; 10:40b; cf. 13:11).

---

[4] Among these categories, the group that takes the most active role throughout the covenant renewal is the Levites (8:7–8, 11, 13; 9:4–5, 6–37; 10:1, 10–14, 29; cf. 10:35, 38b–40a).

The community's written (וכתבים, 10:1) agreement thereby manifests its power to determine Israel's future. This time, the community rather than the Persian king (cf. 13:6) promulgates the written document. The "firm agreement" (אמנה, 10:1) assumes the role that the documents of the Persian monarchs had previously filled as the force that generates developments in Jerusalem and Judah (Ezra 1:1–4; 6:2–12, 14; 7:12–26). Thus, Israel begins to determine its own destiny as its leader Nehemiah (13:4–31) enforces the stipulations of the whole people (10:31–40).

The Levites' Prayer As a Hermeneutical Key to Ezra-Nehemiah

The Levites' prayer (9:6–37) is the theological centerpiece of the covenant renewal and the spiritual apex of the Ezra-Nehemiah story. This historical psalm unfolds a theology of history that provides the key for understanding various aspects of the whole book, as the following ten points indicate.

First, the Levites' prayer subsumes the penitential confessions of Ezra (Ezra 9:6–15) and Nehemiah (Neh 1:5–11) and thereby suggests that the devotion of these protagonists now pervades the community. Second, by extending the historical horizon from creation to the present moment, the psalm provides the appropriate context for interpreting the events immediately after the exile (Ezra 1–6) and during the reign of Artaxerxes (Ezra 7–Neh 13). Third, in view of the conflicts that characterized the construction of the temple (Ezra 2–6) and the city walls (Neh 1:1–7:72a), the psalm provides assurance that the land is God's irrevocable gift to his people. Fourth, emphasis on God's covenant with "faithful" (נאמן, 9:8a) Abraham and on the law Moses gave (9:14b) undergirds the people's "firm agreement" (אמנה, 10:1) and oath of commitment to "the law of God that was given through the hand of Moses" (10:30). Fifth, the psalm's lack of reference to the exile (cf. 9:30c) redefines the people in terms of their allegiance to the law (10:29–30; cf. 9:26a, 29a, 34a) rather than of their surviving the exile (cf. 8:17). Sixth, the description of the events at Sinai locates the law in its pentateuchal setting and, at the same time, portrays the law as the most intimate and personal communication of God to his people (9:13–14; cf. 10:29–30, 31–40a). Seventh, describing the present overlords as "peoples of the lands" (9:30c) who treat the Israelites as "slaves" (9:36–37) recasts the Persian administration in a negative light, which, in turn, bestows a political dimension on the community's subsequent separation from such "peoples of the land[s]" (10:31, 32a; cf. 10:29). Eighth, the cycles of peace, rebellion, prayerful outcry, and redemption throughout the era of the settlement (9:26–31) characterize the present distressful time as one of hope insofar as it inspires the people's outcry to God in prayer. Ninth, the recollection of the ancestors' rejection of the law (9:26a, 29a, 34a) contrasts with the positive commitment of the present leaders to the Torah (10:1–28, 29–30) and thus indicates that the covenant commitment marks the end of servitude to foreigners and a new beginning of service to God. Tenth, the recollection of the cycles of peace and rebellion in the land provide the basis for understanding the conclusion of the story in which Nehemiah acts like a prophet whom God sends to warn his rebellious people once again (13:4–31; cf. 9:30b).

In summary, the covenant renewal represents the determinative juncture in which Israel seizes control of its destiny. Insofar as the people remain loyal to the Torah, they need no longer be victims of the infidelities of past generations or slaves of present foreign overlords. From a narrative perspective, the covenant renewal provides a new beginning in the tradition of the Abrahamic covenant. However, the shape of the future depends on the people's remaining attentive to the Mosaic law that God gave them when he spoke to them from heaven at Sinai (9:13–14).

Works Consulted

PRIMARY SOURCES

Baars, W., and J. C. H. Lebram, eds. "1 (3) Esdras." In *Cantica sive Odae—Oratio Manasse—Psalmi Apocryphi—Psalmi Salomonis—Tobit—I (III) Ezrae*. Part 4, fascicle 6 of *Vetus Testamentum Syriace iuxta simplicem Syrorum versionem*. Leiden: Brill, 1972.

Bardy, G., ed. *Eusèbe de Césaré: Histoire Ecclésiastique Livres V–VII, Texte Grec, Traduction et Notes*. SC 41. Paris: Cerf, 1955.

Biblia Sacra iuxta latinam versionem: Libri Ezrae Tobiae Iudith. Rome: Typis Polyglottis Vaticanis, 1950.

Biblia Sacra iuxta versionem simplicem quae dicitur Pschitta. Beirut: Typis Typographiae Catholica, 1951.

Brooke, A. E., N. McLean, and H. St. J. Thackery, eds. *I Esdras, Ezra-Nehemiah*. Part 4 of *The Later Historical Books*. Vol. 2 of *The Old Testament in Greek*. Cambridge: Cambridge University Press, 1935.

Cowley, A. E. *Aramaic Papyri of the Fifth Century B.C.* Oxford: Clarendon, 1923.

Elliger, K., and W. Rudolph, eds. *Biblia Hebraica Stuttgartensia*. Stuttgart: Deutsche Bibelgesellschaft, 1977.

Hanhart, R., ed. *Esdrae liber I*. Vol. 8.1 of *Septuaginta, Vetus Testamentum Graecum auctoritate Academiae Scientiarum Gottingensis editum*. Göttingen: Vandenhoeck & Ruprecht, 1974.

―――. *Esdrae liber II*. Vol. 8.2 of *Septuaginta, Vetus Testamentum Graecum auctoritate Academiae Scientiarum Gottingensis editum*. Göttingen: Vandenhoeck & Ruprecht, 1993.

Josephus. *The Works of Josephus, Complete and Unabridged*. Translated by W. Whiston. Peabody, Mass.: Hendrickson, 1987.

Kittel, R., ed. *Biblia Hebraica*. Stuttgart: Württembergische Bibelanstalt, 1951.

Kraeling, E. G. *The Brooklyn Museum Aramaic Papyri: New Documents of the Fifth Century from the Jewish Colony at Elephantine.* New Haven, Conn.: Yale University Press, 1953.

Lapp, P. W., and N. L., eds. *Discoveries in the Wâdī ed-Dâliyeh.* Cambridge, Mass.: American Schools of Oriental Research, 1974.

Rudolph, W. "Esra Nehemia." Pages 1411–58 in *Biblia Hebraica Stuttgartensia.* Edited by K. Elliger and W. Rudolph. 3d ed. Stuttgart: Deutsche Bibelgesellschaft, 1987.

SECONDARY LITERATURE

Abba, R. "Priests and Levites." *IDB* 3:876–89.

Ackroyd, P. R. *The Chronicler in His Age.* JSOTSup 101. Sheffield: JSOT Press, 1991.

———. "The Death of Hezekiah—A Pointer to the Future?" Pages 219–26 in *De la Tôrah au Messie [Mélanges Henri Cazelles].* Edited by J. Doré, P. Grelot, and M. Carrez. Paris: Desclée, 1981.

———. "Faith and Its Reformulation in the Post-exilic Period: Prophetic Material." *TD* 27 (1979): 335–46.

———. "Faith and Its Reformulation in the Post-exilic Period: Sources." *TD* 27 (1979): 323–34.

———. "The Historical Literature." Pages 297–323 in *The Hebrew Bible and Its Modern Interpreters.* Edited by D. A. Knight and G. M. Tucker. Philadelphia: Fortress, 1985.

———. "The Jewish Community in Palestine in the Persian Period." Pages 130–61 in *Introduction; The Persian Period.* Vol. 1 of *The Cambridge History of Judaism.* Edited by W. D. Davies and L. Finkelstein. Cambridge: Cambridge University Press, 1984.

———. "The Temple Vessels—A Continuity Theme." Pages 166–81 in *Studies in the Religion of Ancient Israel.* Edited by G. W. Anderson. VTSup 23. Leiden: Brill, 1972.

Ahlemann, F. "Zur Esra-Quelle." *ZAW* 59 (1942–1943): 77–98.

Albright, W. F. *The Biblical Period from Abraham to Ezra.* New York: Harper & Row, 1963.

———. "The Date and Personality of the Chronicler." *JBL* 40 (1921): 104–24.

Alt, A. "The Origins of Israelite Law." Pages 101–71 in *Essays on Old Testament History and Religion*. Translated by R. A. Wilson. Garden City, N.Y.: Doubleday, 1967.

Alter, R. *The Art of Biblical Narrative*. New York: Basic Books, 1981.

Anderson, C. R. "The Formation of the Levitical Prayer of Nehemiah 9." Th.D. diss. Dallas Theological Seminary, 1987.

Auerbach, E. "Die Feste im alten Israel." *VT* 8 (1958): 1–18.

Avigad, N. *Bullae and Seals from a Post-exilic Judean Archive*. Qedem 4. Jerusalem: The Institute of Archaeology, Hebrew University, 1976.

———. "The Contribution of Hebrew Seals to an Understanding of Israelite Religion and Society." Pages 195–208 in *Ancient Israelite Religion: Essays in Honor of Frank Moore Cross*. Edited by P. D. Hanson, P. D. Miller Jr., and S. D. McBride. Philadelphia: Fortress, 1987.

———. "Hebrew Seals and Sealings and Their Significance for Biblical Research." Pp. 7–16 in *Congress Volume: Jerusalem, 1986*. Edited by J. A. Emerton. VTSup 40. Leiden: Brill, 1988.

———. "Seals and Sealings." *IEJ* 14 (1964): 190–94.

———. "Seals of the Exiles." *IEJ* 15 (1965): 222–32.

Baars, W. "Einige Bemerkungen zu einem Altlateinischen Text von Nehemia." *VT* 8 (1958): 425.

Baillet, M. "Un Recueil Liturgique de Qumrân, Grotte 4: 'Les Paroles des Luminaires.'" *RB* 68 (1961): 195–250.

Baltzer, K. *The Covenant Formulary in Old Testament, Jewish, and Early Christian Writings*. Translated by D. E. Green. Philadelphia: Fortress, 1971.

Barr, J. "Some Semantic Notes on Covenant." Pages 23–38 in *Beiträge zur alttestamentlichen Theologie: Festschrift für Walther Zimmerli zum 70. Geburtstag*. Edited by R. Hanhart, H. Donner, and R. Smend. Göttingen: Vandenhoeck & Ruprecht, 1977.

Batten, L. W. *The Books of Ezra and Nehemiah*. ICC. Edinburgh: T&T Clark, 1913.

Begg, C. T. "Ben Sirach's Non-mention of Ezra." *BN* 42 (1988): 14–18.

Berquist, J. L. *Judaism in Persia's Shadow: A Social and Historical Approach*. Minneapolis: Fortress, 1995.

Bickerman, E. J. "En marge de l'écriture." *RB* 88 (1981): 19–41.

———. "The Historical Foundations of Postbiblical Judaism." Pages 9–45 in *Emerging Judaism: Studies on the Fourth and Third Centuries B.C.E.* Edited by M. E. Stone and D. Satran. Minneapolis: Fortress, 1989.

Blenkinsopp, J. *Ezra-Nehemiah*. OTL. Philadelphia: Westminster, 1988.

———. "Interpretation and the Tendency to Sectarianism: An Aspect of Second Temple History." Pages 1–26 in vol. 2 of *Jewish and Christian Self-Definition*. Edited by E. P. Sanders. 2 vols. Philadelphia: Fortress, 1981.

———. "A Jewish Sect of the Persian Period." *CBQ* 52 (1990): 5–20.

———. "The Mission of Udjahorresnet and Those of Ezra and Nehemiah." *JBL* 106 (1987): 409–21.

———. "Temple and Society in Achaemenid Judah." Pages 22–53 in *Second Temple Studies 1: Persian Period*. Edited by P. R. Davies. JSOTSup 117. Sheffield: JSOT Press, 1991.

Bliese, L. F. "Chiastic Structures, Peaks and Cohesion in Nehemiah 9:6–37." *BT* 39 (1988): 208–15.

Boda, M. J. "The Use of Tôdôt in Nehemiah XII." *VT* 44 (1994): 387–93.

Bordreuil, P. "Sceaux Inscrits des Pays du Levant." *DBSup* 66: cols. 86–212.

Borowski, O. "Harvests, Harvesting." *ABD* 3:63–64.

Braun, R. "Chronicles, Ezra, and Nehemiah: Theology and Literary History." Pages 52–64 in *Studies in the Historical Books of the Old Testament*. Edited by J. A. Emerton. VTSup 30. Leiden: Brill, 1979.

———. *1 Chronicles*. WBC 14. Waco, Tex.: Word, 1986.

Brichto, H. C. *The Problem of "Curse" in the Hebrew Bible*. JBLMS 13. Philadelphia: Society of Biblical Literature, 1963.

Bright, J. *A History of Israel*. 3d ed. Philadelphia: Westminster, 1981.

Brin, G. "The Firstling of Unclean Animals." *JQR* 68 (1977/1978): 1–15.

Brongers, H. A. "Bemerkungen zum Gebrauch des Adverbialen $w^e att\bar{a}h$ im Alten Testament." *VT* 15 (1965): 289–99.

Brooke, G. J. "Psalms 105 and 106 at Qumran." *RevQ* 14 (1989): 267–92.

Brunet, A. M. "La Théologie du Chroniste: Théocratie et Messianisme." Pages 384–97 in *Sacra pagina: Miscellanea biblica Congressus Internationalis Catholici de Re Biblica*. Edited by J. Coppens, A. Descamps, and E. Massaux. 2 vols. BETL 12–13. Gembloux: J. Duculot, 1959.

Cameron, G. C. "Darius, Egypt and the 'Lands beyond the Sea.'" *JNES* 2 (1943): 307-13.

Carroll, R. P. "Coopting the Prophets: Nehemiah and Noadiah." Pages 87-99 in *Priests, Prophets and Scribes: Essays on the Formation and Heritage of Second Temple Judaism in Honour of Joseph Blenkinsopp.* Edited by E. Ulrich, J. W. Wright, R. P. Carroll, and P. R. Davies. JSOTSup 149. Sheffield: JSOT Press, 1992.

—————. "Textual Strategies and Ideology in the Second Temple Period." Pages 108-24 in *Second Temple Studies 1: Persian Period.* Edited by P. R. Davies. JSOTSup 117. Sheffield: JSOT Press, 1991.

Carter, C. E. "The Province of Yehud in the Post-exilic Period: Soundings in Site Distribution and Demography." Pages 106-45 in *Second Temple Studies 2: Temple Community in the Persian Period.* Edited by T. C. Eskenazi and K. H. Richards. JSOTSup 175. Sheffield: JSOT Press, 1994.

Cazelles, H. "La Mission d'Esdras." *VT* 4 (1954): 113-40.

—————. Review of H. G. M. Williamson, *Israel in the Books of Chronicles. VT* 29 (1979): 375-80.

Childs, B. S. *The Book of Exodus.* OTL. Philadelphia: Westminster, 1974.

—————. *Introduction to the Old Testament As Scripture.* Philadelphia: Fortress, 1979.

Chirichigno, G. C. *Debt-Slavery in Israel and the Ancient Near East.* JSOTSup 141. Sheffield: JSOT Press, 1993.

Chrostowski, W. "An Examination of Conscience by God's People As Exemplified in Neh 9,6-37." *BZ* 34 (1990): 253-61.

Clines, D. J. A. *Ezra, Nehemiah, Esther.* NCB. Grand Rapids. Mich.: Eerdmans, 1992.

—————. "The Force of the Text: A Response to Tamara C. Eskenazi's 'Ezra-Nehemiah: From Text to Actuality.'" Pages 198-215 in *Signs and Wonders: Biblical Texts in Literary Focus.* Edited by J. C. Exum. SemeiaSt. n.p.: Society of Biblical Literature, 1989.

—————. "Haggai's Temple, Constructed, Deconstructed and Reconstructed." Pages 60-87 in *Second Temple Studies 2: Temple Community in the Persian Period.* Edited by T. C. Eskenazi and K. H. Richards. JSOTSup 175. Sheffield: JSOT Press, 1994.

———. "The Nehemiah Memoir: The Perils of Autobiography." Pages 124–64 in *What Does Eve Do to Help? and Other Readerly Questions to the Old Testament*. JSOTSup 94. Sheffield: JSOT Press, 1990.

———. "Nehemiah 10 As an Example of Early Jewish Biblical Exegesis." *JSOT* 21 (1981): 111–17.

———, ed. *The Dictionary of Classical Hebrew*. Vol. 1. Sheffield: Sheffield Academic Press, 1993.

Cody, A. *A History of the Old Testament Priesthood*. AnBib 35. Rome: Pontifical Biblical Institute, 1969.

Coggins, R. J. *The Books of Ezra and Nehemiah*. CBC. Cambridge: Cambridge University Press, 1976.

———. "The Interpretation of Ezra IV. 4." *JTS* 16 (1965): 124–27.

Cohen, N. G. "Jewish Names As Cultural Indicators in Antiquity." *JSJ* 7 (1976): 97–128.

Coogan, M. D. *West Semitic Personal Names in the Murašû Documents*. HSM 7. Missoula, Mont.: Scholars Press, 1976.

Couroyer, B. "'Avoir la nuque raide': ne pas incliner l'oreille." *RB* 88 (1981): 216–25.

Coxon, P. W. "The 'List' Genre and Narrative Style in the Court Tales of Daniel." *JSOT* 35 (1986): 95–121.

Cross, F. M. "Aspects of Samaritan and Jewish History in Late Persian and Hellenistic Times." *HTR* 59 (1966): 201–11.

———. "The Discovery of the Samaria Papyri." *BA* 26 (1963): 110–21.

———. "The Papyri and Their Historical Implications." Pages 17–29 in *Discoveries in the Wâdī Ed-Dâliyeh*. Edited by P. W. and N. L. Lapp. AASOR 41. Cambridge, Mass.: American Schools of Oriental Research, 1974.

———. "Papyri of the Fourth Century B.C. from Dâliyeh." Pages 41–62 and figs. 34–39 in *New Directions in Biblical Archaeology*. Edited by D. N. Freedman and J. C. Greenfield. Garden City, N.Y.: Doubleday, 1969.

———. "A Reconstruction of the Judean Restoration." *JBL* 94 (1975): 4–18.

———. "A Report on the Samaria Papyri." Pages 17–26 in *Congress Volume: Jerusalem, 1986*. Edited by J. A. Emerton. VTSup 40. Leiden: Brill, 1988.

———. "Samaria Papyrus 1: An Aramaic Slave Conveyance of 335 B.C.E. Found in the Wâdī ed-Dâliyeh." *ErIsr* 18 (1985) 7*-17*.

Curtis, E. L., and A. A. Madsen. *The Books of Chronicles*. ICC. Edinburgh: T&T Clark, 1910.

da Deliceto, G. "Epoca della Partenza di Hanani per Gerusalemme e Anno della Petizione di Neemia ad Artaserse. Neem. 1,1 e Neem. 2,1." *Laur* 4 (1963): 431–68.

Daniels, D. R. "The Composition of the Ezra-Nehemiah Narrative." Pages 311–28 in *Ernten, was man sät: Festschrift für Klaus Koch zu seinem 65. Geburtstag*. Edited by D. R. Daniels, U. Gleßmer, and M. Rösel. Neukirchen-Vluyn: Neukirchener Verlag, 1992.

Davies, P. R. "Defending the Boundaries of Israel in the Second Temple Period: 2 Chronicles and the 'Salvation Army.'" Pages 43–54 in *Priests, Prophets and Scribes: Essays on the Formation and Heritage of Second Temple Judaism in Honour of Joseph Blenkinsopp*. Edited by E. Ulrich, J. W. Wright, R. P. Carroll, and P. R. Davies. JSOTSup 149. Sheffield: JSOT Press, 1992.

———. "The Society of Biblical Israel." Pages 22–33 in *Second Temple Studies 2: Temple Community in the Persian Period*. Edited by T. C. Eskenazi and K. H. Richards. JSOTSup 175. Sheffield: JSOT Press, 1994.

Davies, W. D., and L. Finkelstein, eds. *Introduction; The Persian Period*. Vol. 1 of *The Cambridge History of Judaism*. Cambridge: Cambridge University Press, 1984.

Demsky, A. "Who Came First, Ezra or Nehemiah? The Synchronistic Approach," *HUCA* 65 (1994): 1–19.

———. "Who Returned First—Ezra or Nehemiah?" *BRev* 12 (April 1996): 28–33, 46, 48.

Dentan, R. C. "The Literary Affinities of Exodus XXXIV 6f." *VT* 13 (1963): 34–51.

Di Lella, A. A., and L. F. Hartman. *The Book of Daniel*. AB 23. Garden City, N.Y.: Doubleday, 1978.

Di Lella, A. A., and P. W. Skehan. *The Wisdom of Ben Sira*. AB 39. New York: Doubleday, 1987.

Dillard, R. B. *2 Chronicles*. WBC 15. Waco, Tex.: Word, 1987.

Dionisio, F. "E Dario disse: 'Che sia ricostruito il Tempio…!' Storie di profeti, di funzionari regi, di mafia, di appalti e di 'lupara'." *BeO* 32 (1990) 81–94.

Dommershausen, W. "לֶקַח." *TDOT* 7:521–29.

Driver, G. R. "Forgotten Hebrew Idioms." *ZAW* 78 (1976): 1–7.

———. "Studies in the Vocabulary of the Old Testament II." *JTS* 32 (1931): 250–57.

Driver, S. R. *A Critical and Exegetical Commentary on Deuteronomy*. 3d ed. Edinburgh: T&T Clark, 1902.

———. *An Introduction to the Literature of the Old Testament*. Edinburgh: T&T Clark, 1898.

Dumbrell, W. J. "Malachi and the Ezra-Nehemiah Reforms." *RTR* 35 (1976): 42–52.

Dyke Parunak, H. van. "Oral Typesetting: Some Uses of Biblical Structure." *Bib* 62 (1981): 153–68.

Eerdmans, B. D. "Ezra and the Priestly Code." *The Expositor* 7th series 10 (1910): 306–26.

Eichrodt, W. *Ezekiel*. Translated by C. Quin. OTL. Philadelphia: Westminster, 1970.

Eissfeldt, O. *The Old Testament: An Introduction*. Translated by P. R. Ackroyd. Oxford: Blackwell, 1966.

Ellison, H. L. *From Babylon to Bethlehem: The People of God from Exile to the Messiah*. Atlanta: John Knox, 1976.

———. "The Importance of Ezra." *EvQ* 53 (1981): 48–53.

Emerton, J. A. "Did Ezra Go to Jerusalem in 428 B.C.?" *JTS* 17 (1966): 1–19.

———. Review of U. Kellermann, *Nehemia: Quellen, Überlieferung und Geschichte*. *JTS* 23 (1972): 171–85.

Eskenazi, T. C. "The Chronicler and the Composition of 1 Esdras." *CBQ* 48 (1986): 39–61.

———. "Current Perspectives on Ezra-Nehemiah and the Persian Period." *CurBS* 1 (1993): 59–86.

———. "Ezra-Nehemiah: From Text to Actuality." Pages 165–97 in *Signs and Wonders: Biblical Texts in Literary Focus*. Edited by J. C. Exum. SemeiaSt. n.p.: Society of Biblical Literature, 1989.

———. *In an Age of Prose: A Literary Approach to Ezra-Nehemiah*. SBLMS 36. Atlanta: Scholars Press, 1988.

———. "Out from the Shadows: Biblical Women in the Postexilic Era." *JSOT* 54 (1992): 25–43.

———. "The Structure of Ezra-Nehemiah and the Integrity of the Book." *JBL* 107 (1988): 641–56.

Eskenazi, T. C., and E. P. Judd. "Marriage to a Stranger in Ezra 9–10." Pages 266–85 in *Second Temple Studies 2: Temple Community in the Persian Period*. Edited by T. C. Eskenazi and K. H. Richards. JSOTSup 175. Sheffield: JSOT Press, 1994.

Eslinger, L. "Inner-Biblical Exegesis and Inner-Biblical Allusion: The Question of Category." *VT* 42 (1992): 47–58.

Eves, T. L. "The Role of Passover in the Book of Chronicles." Ph.D. diss. Annenberg Research Institute, 1992.

Falk, D. "4Q393: A Communal Confession." *JSS* 45 (1994): 184–207.

Falk, Z. W. "Hebrew Legal Terms: III." *JSS* 14 (1969): 39–44.

Feldman, L. H. "Josephus' Portrait of Ezra." *VT* 43 (1993): 190–214.

Fensham, F. C. *The Books of Ezra and Nehemiah*. NICOT. Grand Rapids, Mich.: Eerdmans, 1982.

———. "Mĕdînâ in Ezra and Nehemiah." *VT* 25 (1975): 795–97.

———. "Neh. 9 and Pss. 105, 106, and 135. Post-exilic Historical Traditions in Poetic Form." *JNSL* 9 (1981): 35–51.

———. "Some Theological and Religious Aspects in Ezra and Nehemiah." *JNSL* 11 (1983): 59–68.

Fernández, A. "Epoca de la Actividad de Esdras." *Bib* 2 (1921): 424–47.

Finegan, J. "The Principles of the Calendar and the Problems of Biblical Chronology." Pages 552–98 in *Light from the Ancient Past: The Archeological Background of Judaism and Christianity*. Princeton, N.J.: Princeton University Press, 1959.

Finkelstein, J. J. "Ammiṣaduqa's Edict and the Babylonian 'Law Codes.'" *JCS* 15 (1961): 91–104.

Fishbane, M. *Biblical Interpretation in Ancient Israel*. Oxford: Clarendon, 1985.

Fitzmyer, J. A. "Aramaic Epistolography." Pages 183–204 in *A Wandering Aramean: Collected Aramaic Essays*. SBLMS 25. Missoula, Mont.: Scholars Press, 1979.

Fox, M. V. "The Identification of Quotations in Biblical Literature." *ZAW* 92 (1980): 416–31.

Galling, K. *Die Bücher der Chronik, Esra, Nehemia.* ATD 12. Göttingen: Vandenhoeck & Ruprecht, 1954.

Garbini, G. "Hebrew Literature in the Persian Period." Pages 180–88 in *Second Temple Studies 2: Temple Community in the Persian Period.* Edited by T. C. Eskenazi and K. H. Richards. JSOTSup 175. Sheffield: JSOT Press, 1994.

Gertner, M. "Appendix: An Attempt at an Interpretation of Hosea XII." *VT* 10 (1960): 272–84.

———. "The Masorah and the Levites: An Essay in the History of a Concept." *VT* 10 (1960): 241–72.

Gilbert, M. "Notes sur Néhémie 9." TMs (photocopy) 1995.

———. "La place de la Loi dans la prière de Néhémie 9." Pages 307–16 in *De la Tôrah au Messie [Mélanges Henri Cazelles].* Edited by J. Doré, P. Grelot, and M. Carrez. Paris: Desclée, 1981.

———. "La prière de Daniel: Dn 9,4–19." *RTL* 3 (1972): 284–310.

Giraudo, C. *La Struttura Letteraria della Preghiera Eucaristica.* AnBib 92. Rome: Biblical Institute, 1981.

Goldingay, J. "The Chronicler As a Theologian." *BTB* 5 (1975): 99–126.

Grabbe, L. L. "Reconstructing History from the Book of Ezra." Pages 98–106 in *Second Temple Studies 1: Persian Period.* Edited by P. R. Davies. JSOTSup 117. Sheffield: JSOT Press, 1991.

———. "What Was Ezra's Mission?" Pages 286–99 in *Second Temple Studies 2: Temple Community in the Persian Period.* Edited by T. C. Eskenazi and K. H. Richards. JSOTSup 175. Sheffield: JSOT Press, 1994.

Green, A. R. W. "The Date of Nehemiah: A Reexamination." *AUSS* 28 (1990): 195–209.

Greenfield, J. C. "Studies in Aramaic Lexicography I." *JAOS* 82 (1962): 290–99.

Grelot, P. "La Dernière Étape de la Rédaction Sacerdotale." *VT* 6 (1956): 174–89.

Grol, H. W. M. van. "Ezra 7, 1–10: Een Literair-Stilistische Analyse." *Bijdr* 51 (1990): 21–37.

Gunneweg, A. H. J. "עם הארץ—A Semantic Revolution." *ZAW* 95 (1983): 437–40.

———. "Die aramäische und die hebräische Erzählung über die nachexilische Restauration—ein Vergleich." *ZAW* 94 (1982): 299–302.

———. *Esra*. KAT. Gütersloh: Gerd Mohn, 1985.

———. *Nehemia*. KAT. Gütersloh: Gerd Mohn, 1987.

———. "Zur Interpretation der Bücher Esra-Nehemia." Pages 146–61 in *Congress Volume: Vienna, 1980*. Edited by J. A. Emerton. VTSup 32. Leiden: Brill, 1981.

Guthrie, H. H. "Fast." *IDB* 2:241–44.

Haag, H. "כָּתַב κτλ." *TDOT* 7:371–82.

Halligan, J. M. "Nehemiah 5: By Way of a Response to Hoglund and Smith." Pages 146–53 in *Second Temple Studies 1: Persian Period*. Edited by P. R. Davies. JSOTSup 117. Sheffield: JSOT Press, 1991.

Halpern, B. "A Historiographic Commentary on Ezra 1–6: Achronological Narrative and Dual Chronology in Israelite Historiography." Pages 81–142 in *The Hebrew Bible and Its Interpreters*. Edited by B. Halpern, W. H. Propp, and D. N. Freedman. Biblical and Judaic Studies from the University of California, San Diego 1. Winona Lake, Ind.: Eisenbrauns, 1990.

Hamilton, M. W. "Who Was a Jew? Jewish Ethnicity during the Achaemenid Period." *ResQ* 37 (1995): 102–17.

Haran, M. "Behind the Scenes of History: Determining the Date of the Priestly Source." *JBL* 100 (1981): 321–33.

———. "Explaining the Identical Lines at the End of Chronicles and the Beginning of Ezra." *BRev* 2 (Fall 1986): 18–20.

———. "On the Diffusion of Literacy and Schools in Ancient Israel." Pages 81–95 in *Congress Volume: Jerusalem, 1986*. Edited by J. A. Emerton. VTSup 40. Leiden: Brill, 1988.

Hartman, L. F., et al., eds. *Textual Notes on the New American Bible*. Paterson, N.J.: St. Anthony's Guild, n.d.

Hasel, G. F. "כָּרַת κτλ." *TDOT* 7:339–52.

Helfmeyer, F. J. "אוֹת." *TDOT* 1:167–88.

Heltzer, M. "A propos des Banquets des Rois Archéménides et du Retour d'Exil sous Zorobabel." *RB* 86 (1979): 102–6.

Hensley, L. V. "The Official Persian Documents in the Book of Ezra." Ph.D. diss. Liverpool, 1977.

Höffken, P. "Warum schwieg Jesus Sirach über Esra?" *ZAW* 87 (1975): 184–202.

Hoftijzer, J. "Remarks Concerning the Use of the Particle ʾT in Classical Hebrew." *OtSt* 14 (1965): 1–99.

Hoglund, K. "The Achaemenid Context." Pages 54–72 in *Second Temple Studies 1: Persian Period*. Edited by P. R. Davies. JSOTSup 117. Sheffield: JSOT Press, 1991.

———. *Achaemenid Imperial Administration of Syria-Palestine and the Missions of Ezra and Nehemiah*. SBLDS 125. Atlanta: Scholars Press, 1992.

Holladay, W. L. *Jeremiah 1*. Hermeneia. Philadelphia: Fortress, 1986.

Holmgren, F. C. *Ezra and Nehemiah: Israel Alive Again*. ITC. Grand Rapids, Mich.: Eerdmans, 1987.

———. "Faithful Abraham and the ʾamānâ Covenant." *ZAW* 104 (1992): 249–54.

Hoonacker, A. van. "La Succession Chronologique. Néhémie-Esdras (Suite)." *RB* 33 (1924): 33–64.

Horbury, W. "Extirpation and Excommunication." *VT* 35 (1985): 13–38.

Houtman, C. "Ezra and the Law. Observations on the Supposed Relation between Ezra and the Pentateuch." *OtSt* 21 (1981): 91–115.

Ibáñez Arana, A. "Sobre la colocación original de Neh. 10." *EstBib* 10 (1951): 379–402.

In der Smitten, W. Th. *Esra: Quellen, Überlieferung und Geschichte*. SSN 15. Assen: Van Gorcum, 1973.

———. "Der Tirschātāʾ in Esra-Nehemia." *VT* 21 (1971): 618–20.

Irvine, S. A. "The Isaianic *Denkschrift*: Reconsidering an Old Hypothesis." *ZAW* 104 (1992): 216–31.

Ishida, T. "The Structure and Historical Implications of the Lists of Pre-Israelite Nations." *Bib* 60 (1979): 461–90.

Ivry, A. L. "Nehemiah 6,10: Politics and the Temple." *JSJ* 3 (1972): 35–45.

Jagersma, H. "The Tithes in the Old Testament." Pages 116–28 in *Remembering All the Way...* Edited by A. S. van der Woude. OTS 21. Leiden: Brill, 1981.

Japhet, S. "Composition and Chronology in the Book of Ezra-Nehemiah." Pages 189–216 in *Second Temple Studies 2: Temple Community in the Persian Period*. Edited by T. C. Eskenazi and K. H. Richards. JSOTSup 175. Sheffield: JSOT Press, 1994.

———. *I and II Chronicles*. OTL. Louisville: Westminster/John Knox, 1993.

———. "The Historical Reliability of Chronicles: The History of the Problem and Its Place in Biblical Research." *JSOT* 33 (1985): 83–107.

———. "'History' and 'Literature' in the Persian Period; The Restoration of the Temple." Pages 174–88 in *Ah, Assyria...: Studies in Assyrian History and Ancient Near Eastern Historiography Presented to Hayim Tadmor*. Edited by Mordechai Cogan and Israel Eph'al. ScrHier 33. Jerusalem: Magnes, 1991.

———. "The Israelite Legal and Social Reality As Reflected in Chronicles: A Case Study." Pages 79–91 in *"Sha'arei Talmon": Studies in the Bible, Qumran, and the Ancient Near East Presented to Shemaryahu Talmon*. Edited by M. Fishbane and E. Tov. Winona Lake, Ind.: Eisenbrauns, 1992.

———. "Law and 'The Law' in Ezra-Nehemiah." Pages 99–115 in *Proceedings of the Ninth World Congress of Jewish Studies*. Edited by M. Goshen-Gottstein. Jerusalem: Magnes, 1985.

———. "People and Land in the Restoration Period." Pages 103–25 in *Das Land Israel in biblischer Zeit*. Edited by G. Strecker. GTA 25. Göttingen: Vandenhoeck & Ruprecht, 1983.

———. "The Relationship between Chronicles and Ezra-Nehemiah." Pages 298–313 in *Congress Volume: Leuven, 1989*. Edited by J. A. Emerton. VTSup 43. Leiden: Brill, 1991.

———. "Sheshbazzar and Zerubbabel—Against the Background of the Historical and Religious Tendencies of Ezra-Nehemiah." *ZAW* 94 (1982): 66–98; 95 (1983): 218–29.

———. "The Supposed Common Authorship of Chronicles and Ezra-Nehemia Investigated Anew." *VT* 18 (1968): 330–71.

———. "The Temple in the Restoration Period: Reality and Ideology." *USQR* 44 (1991): 195–251.

Jensen, J. *Isaiah 1–12*. OTM 8. Wilmington, Del.: Glazier, 1984.

Jepsen, A. "Nehemia 10." *ZAW* 66 (1954): 87–106.

Johnson, J. H. "Demotic Chronicle." *ABD* 2:142–44.

Joüon, P. *Grammaire de L'Hébreu Biblique*. Rome: Biblical Institute, 1965.

Joüon, P., and T. Muraoka. *A Grammar of Biblical Hebrew*. 2 vols. Subsidia Biblica 14.1, 2. Rome: Biblical Institute, 1991.

Kaiser, O. *Isaiah 1–12*. Translated by. R. A. Wilson. OTL. Philadelphia: Westminster, 1972.

Kalimi, I. "Die Abfassungszeit der Chronik—Forschungsstand und Perspektiven." *ZAW* 105 (1993): 223–33.

———. *The Books of Chronicles, A Classified Bibliography*. Simor Bible Bibliographies. Jerusalem: Simor, 1990.

———. "Literary-Chronological Proximity in the Chronicler's Historiography." *VT* 43 (1993): 318–38.

———. *Zur Geschichtsschreibung des Chronisten: Literarischhistoriographische Abweichungen der Chronik von ihren Paralleltexten in den Samuel- und Königsbüchern*. BZAW 226. Berlin and New York: Walter de Gruyter, 1995.

Kalluveettil, P. *Declaration and Covenant: A Comprehensive Review of Covenant Formulae from the Old Testament and the Ancient Near East*. AnBib 88. Rome: Biblical Institute, 1982.

Kapelrud, A. S. *The Question of Authorship in the Ezra-Narrative: A Lexical Investigation*. SUNVAO 1. Oslo: Dybwad, 1944.

Kaplony, P. "Demotische Chronik." Pages 1056–60 in *Lexicon der Ägyptologie*. Vol. 1. Edited by W. Helck and E. Otto. Wiesbaden: Otto Harrassowitz, 1975.

Katz, P. "מקרא." *ZAW* 65 (1953): 253–55.

Kautzsch, E., ed. *Gesenius' Hebrew Grammar*. Revised and translated by A. E. Cowley. 2d ed. Oxford: Clarendon, 1910.

Kaufmann, Y. *From the Babylonian Captivity to the End of Prophecy*. Vol. 4 of *History of the Religion of Israel*. New York: Ktav, 1977.

———. *The Religion of Israel: From its Beginnings to the Babylonian Exile*. Translated and abridged by M. Greenberg. Chicago: University of Chicago Press, 1960.

Kegel, M. *Die Kultusreformation des Esra: Aufsagen moderner Kritik über Neh. 8–10 kritisch beleuchtet*. Gütersloh: Bertelsmann, 1921.

———. *The Religious Reformation of Ezra*. Aftermath 1.3. Nashville: Lamar & Barton, 1923.

Kegler, J., and M. Augustin. *Synopse zum Chronistischen Geschichtswerk*. 2d ed. New York: Peter Lang, 1991.

Kellermann, D. "לוי ktλ." *TDOT* 7:483–503.

Kellermann, U. "Erwägungen zum Problem der Esradatierung." *ZAW* 80 (1968): 55–87.

———. "Erwägungen zum Esragesetz." *ZAW* 80 (1968): 373–85.

———. *Nehemia: Quellen, Überlieferung und Geschichte*. BZAW 102. Berlin: Töpelmann, 1967.

Kidner, D. *Ezra and Nehemiah: An Introduction and Commentary*. TOTC. Leicester: Inter-Varsity, 1979.

Kippenberg, H. G. "Name and Person in Ancient Judaism and Christianity." Pages 103–24 in *Concepts of Person in Religion and Thought*. Edited by Y. B. Kuiper, H. G. Kippenberg, and A. F. Sanders. Religion and Reason 37. Berlin: Mouton de Gruyter, 1990.

Klein, R. W. "Ezra and Nehemiah in Recent Studies." Pages 361–76 in *Magnalia Dei: The Mighty Acts of God. Essays on the Bible and Archaeology in Memory of G. Ernest Wright*. Ed. F. M. Cross, W. E. Lemke, and P. D. Miller Jr. Garden City, N.Y.: Doubleday, 1976.

———. "Ezra-Nehemiah, Books of," *ABD* 2:731–42.

———. "Old Readings in I Esdras: The List of Returnees from Babylon (Ezra 2 // Nehemiah 7)." *HTR* 62 (1969): 99–107.

Klingbeil, G. A. "The Onomasticon of the Aramaic Inscriptions of Syro-Palestine during the Persian Period." *JNSL* 18 (1992): 67–94.

Knauf, E. A. "Zum Verhältnis von Esra 1,1 zu 2 Chronik 36,20–23." *BN* 78 (1995): 16–17.

Knohl, I. "The Priestly Torah versus the Holiness School: Sabbath and the Festivals." *HUCA* 58 (1987): 65–117.

———. *The Sanctuary of Silence: The Priestly Torah and the Holiness School*. Minneapolis: Fortress, 1995.

Knoppers, G. N. "Jehoshaphat's Judiciary and 'The Scroll of YHWH's Torah.'" *JBL* 113 (1994): 59–80.

Koch, K. "Ezra and Meremoth: Remarks on the History of the High Priesthood." Pages 105–10 in *"Sha'arei Talmon": Studies in the Bible, Qumran, and the Ancient Near East Presented to Shemaryahu Talmon*. Edited by M. Fishbane and E. Tov. Winona Lake, Ind.: Eisenbrauns, 1992.

———. "Ezra and the Origins of Judaism." *JSS* 19 (1974): 173–97.

Koehler, L. *Lexicon in Veteris Testamenti Libros*. 2 vols. Grand Rapids, Mich.: Eerdmans, 1953.

Koehler, L., and W. Baumgartner. ראה-נבט. Vol. 3 of *Hebräisches und Aramäisches Lexicon zum Alten Testament*. 3d ed. Leiden: Brill, 1983.

———. כספיא [Heb.]–תתני [Aram.]. Vol. 2 of *Lexicon in Veteris Testamenti Libros*. 2 vols. Leiden: Brill, 1953.

Kooij, A. van der. "Nehemiah 8:8 and the Question of the 'Targum'-Tradition." Pages 79–90 in *Tradition of the Text: Studies Offered to Dominique Barthélemy in Celebration of His 70th Birthday*. Edited by G. J. Norton and S. Pisano. OBO 109. Göttingen: Vandenhoeck & Ruprecht, 1991.

Kraemer, D. "On the Relationship of the Books of Ezra and Nehemiah." *JSOT* 59 (1993): 73–92.

Kraus, H.-J. *Gottesdienst in Israel: Studien zur Geschichte des Laubhüttenfestes*. BEvT 19. Munich: Chr. Kaiser Verlag, 1954.

———. *Psalms 1–59*. CC. Translated by H. C. Oswald. Minneapolis: Augsburg, 1988.

———. *Psalms 60–150*. CC. Translated by H. C. Oswald. Minneapolis: Augsburg, 1988.

———. *Worship in Israel: A Cultic History of the Old Testament*. Translated by G. Buswell. Richmond: John Knox, 1966.

Krüger, T. "Esra 1–6: Struktur und Konzept." *BN* 41 (1988): 65–75.

Kugel, J. L. *The Idea of Biblical Poetry: Parallelism and Its History*. New Haven, Conn.: Yale University Press, 1981.

Kühlewein, J. *Geschichte in den Psalmen*. Calwer Theologische Monographien 2. Stuttgart: Calwer, 1973.

Kutsch, E. "'...am Ende des Jahres' Zur Datierung des israelitische Herbstfestes in Ex 23:16." *ZAW* 83 (1971): 15–21.

———. "Gesetz und Gnade: Probleme des alttestamentlichen Bundesbegriffs." *ZAW* 79 (1967): 18–35.

———. "מקרא." *ZAW* 65 (1953): 247–53.

———. "Sukkot." Cols. 495–98 in vol. 15 of *Encyclopaedia Judaica*. Edited by C. Roth and G. Wigoder. Jerusalem: Keter, 1971.

———. "Die Wurzel עצר im Hebräischen." *VT* 2 (1952): 57–69.

Lacocque, A. "The Liturgical Prayer of Daniel 9." *HUCA* 47 (1976): 119–42.

Langlamet, F. "Israël et 'l'habitant du Pays.' Vocabulaire et formules d'Ex., XXXIV, 11–16." *RB* 76 (1969): 321–50, 481–507.

Lapp, P. "An Account of the Discovery." Pages 1–6 in *Discoveries in the Wâdī ed-Dâliyeh*. Edited by P. W. and N. L. Lapp. AASOR 41. Cambridge, Mass.: American Schools of Oriental Research, 1974.

Le Déaut, R. *Introduction à la Littérature Targumique*. Rome: Pontifical Biblical Institute, 1966.

Leeseberg, M. W. "Ezra and Nehemiah: A Review of the Return and Reform." *CTM* 33 (1982): 79–90.

Lefèvre, A. "Néhémie et Esdras." *DBSup* 6:393–424.

Lehmann, M. R. "Biblical Oaths." *ZAW* 81 (1969): 74–92.

Lemaire, A. "Populations et territoires de la Palestine à l'époque perse." *Transeu* 2 (1990): 31–74.

Lemche, N. P. "The 'Hebrew Slave.'" *VT* 25 (1975): 129–44.

———. "The Manumission of Slaves—The Fallow Year—The Sabbatical Year—The Jobel Year." *VT* 26 (1976): 38–59.

Levenson, J. D. "The Davidic Covenant and Its Modern Interpreters." *CBQ* 41 (1979): 205–19.

Levin, S. "The Traditional Chironomy of the Hebrew Scriptures." *JBL* 87 (1968): 59–70.

Levine, B. *Numbers 1–20*. AB 4. New York: Doubleday, 1993.

Liebreich, L. J. "The Impact of Nehemiah 9:5–37 on the Liturgy of the Synagogue." *HUCA* 32 (1961): 227–37.

Liver, J. "The Half-Shekel Offering in Biblical and Post-biblical Literature." *HTR* 56 (1963): 173–98.

Macdonald, J. "The Particle את in Classical Hebrew: Some New Data on Its Use with the Nominative." *VT* 14 (1964): 264–75.

MacRae, G. W. "The Meaning and Evolution of the Feast of Tabernacles." *CBQ* 22 (1960): 251–76.

Mantel, H. "The Dichotomy of Judaism during the Second Temple." *HUCA* 44 (1973): 55–87.

Margalith, O. "The Political Background of Zerubbabel's Mission and the Samaritan Schism." *VT* (1991): 312–23.

———. "The Political Role of Ezra As Persian Governor." *ZAW* 98 (1986): 110–12.

Marx, A. *Les Offrandes Végétales dans L'Ancien Testament: Du Tribut d'Homme au Repas Eschatologique*. VTSup 57. Leiden: Brill, 1994.

Mason, R. *Preaching the Tradition: Homily and Hermeneutics after the Exile*. Cambridge: Cambridge University Press, 1990.

———. "Some Chronistic Themes in the 'Speeches' in Ezra and Nehemiah." *ExpTim* 101 (1989): 72–76.

Mathys, H.-P. *Dichter und Beter: Theologen aus spätalttestamentlicher Zeit*. OBO 132. Göttingen: Vandenhoeck & Ruprecht, 1994.

McCarthy, D. J. "Covenant and Law in Chronicles-Nehemiah." *CBQ* 44 (1982): 25–44.

McConville, J. G. "Ezra-Nehemiah and the Fulfillment of Prophecy." *VT* 36 (1986): 205–24.

McEvenue, S. "The Political Structure in Judah from Cyrus to Nehemiah." *CBQ* 44 (1981): 353–64.

McFall, L. "Was Nehemiah Contemporary with Ezra in 458 BC?" *WTJ* 53 (1991): 263–93.

McKane, W. *Proverbs*. OTL. Philadelphia: Westminster, 1970.

McKenzie, S. L. *The Chronicler's Use of the Deuteronomistic History*. HSM 33. Atlanta: Scholars Press, 1984.

Mendels, D. "Hecataeus of Abdera and a Jewish 'patrios politeia' of the Persian Period (Diodorus Siculus XL, 3)." *ZAW* 95 (1983): 96–110.

Meyers, C. L., and E. M. Meyers. *Haggai, Zechariah 1–8*. AB 25B. New York: Doubleday, 1987.

Meyers, E. M. "The Persian Period and the Judean Restoration: From Zerubbabel to Nehemiah." Pages 509–21 in *Ancient Israelite Religion: Essays in Honor of Frank Moore Cross*. Edited by P. D. Hanson, P. D. Miller Jr., and S. D. McBride. Phildelphia: Fortress, 1987.

———. "The Use of tôrâ in Haggai 2:11 and the Role of the Prophet in the Restoration Community." Pages 69–76 in *The Word Shall Go Forth: Essays in Honor of David Noel Freedman in Celebration of His Sixtieth Birthday*. Edited by C. L. Meyers and M. O'Connor. Winona Lake, Ind.: Eisenbrauns, 1983.

Milgrom, J. *Leviticus 1–16*. AB 3. New York: Doubleday, 1991.

Moda, A. "Libri di Esdra e Neemia." *BeO* 32 (1990): 129–39.

Moore, C. A. *Esther*. AB 7B. Garden City, N.Y.: Doubleday, 1971.

Morgenstern, J. "Supplementary Studies in the Calendars of Ancient Israel." *HUCA* 10 (1935): 1–148.

———. "The Three Calendars of Ancient Israel." *HUCA* 1 (1924): 13–78.

Moscati, S. "I Sigilli nell'Antico Testamento: Studio Esegetico-Filogico." *Bib* 30 (1949): 314–38.

Mosis, R. *Untersuchungen zur Theologie des chronistischen Geschichtswerkes.* Freiberger Theologische Studien 92. Freiburg: Herder, 1973.

Mowinckel, S. "אשרנא Ezr. 5:3,9." *ST* 19 (1965): 130–35.

———. "'Ich' und 'Er' in der Esrageschichte." Pages 211–33 in *Verbannung und Heimkehr. Beiträge zur Geschichte und Theologie Israels im 6. und 5. Jahrundert v. Chr.: Wilhelm Rudolph zum 70. Geburtstage.* Edited by A. Kuschke. Tübingen: Mohr (Siebeck), 1961.

———. *Psalmenstudien II: Das Thronbesteigungsfest Jahwäs und der Ursprung der Eschatologie.* Repr., Amsterdam: P. Schippers, 1961.

———. *The Psalms in Israel's Worship.* Translated by D. R. Ap-Thomas. Nashville: Abingdon, 1962.

———. *The Question of Authorship in the Ezra-Narrative: A Lexical Investigation.* SUNVAO 1. Oslo: Dybwad, 1944.

———. *Studien zu dem Buche Ezra-Nehemia I: Die nachchronistiche Redaktion des Buches. Die Listen.* SUNVAO 3. Oslo: Universitetsforlaget, 1964.

———. *Studien zu dem Buche Ezra-Nehemia II: Die Nehemia-Denkshrift.* SUNVAO 5. Oslo: Universitetsforlaget, 1964.

———. *Studien zu dem Buche Ezra-Nehemia III: Die Ezrageschichte und das Gesetz Moses.* SUNVAO 7. Oslo: Universitetsforlaget, 1965.

———. *Zum israelitischen Neujahr und zur Deutung der Thron-besteigungspsalmen.* AUNVAO 2. Oslo: Dybwad, 1952.

Muddiman, J. "Fast, Fasting." *ABD* 2:773–76.

Muilenburg, J. "The Form and Structure of the Covenantal Formulations." *VT* 9 (1959): 347–65.

Mullen, E. T., Jr. "Hosts, Host of Heaven." *ABD* 3:301–4.

Muraoka, T. A *Greek-Hebrew/Aramaic Index to I Esdras.* SBLSCS 16. Chico, Calif.: Scholars Press, 1984.

Murray, D. F. "Dynasty, People, and the Future: The Message of Chronicles." *JSOT* 58 (1993): 71–92.

Myers, J. M. *Ezra, Nehemiah.* AB 14. Garden City, N.Y.: Doubleday, 1965.

———. *I Chronicles.* 2d ed. AB 12. Garden City, N.Y.: Doubleday, 1983.

———. "The Kerygma of the Chronicler." *Int* 20 (1966): 259–73.

———. *II Chronicles.* 2d ed. AB 13. Garden City, N.Y.: Doubleday, 1983.

Naveh, J., and J. C. Greenfield. "Hebrew and Aramaic in the Persian Period." Pages 115–29 in *Introduction; Persian Period.* Vol. 1 of *The Cambridge History of Judaism.* Edited by W. D. Davies and L. Finkelstein. Cambridge: Cambridge University Press, 1984.

Neufeld, E. "The Prohibitions against Loans at Interest in Ancient Hebrew Laws." *HUCA* 26 (1955): 355–412.

———. "The Rate of Interest and the Text of Nehemiah 5:11." *JQR* 44 (1953): 194–204.

———. "Socio-economic Background of Yōbēl and šᵉmiṭṭa," *RSO* 33 (1958): 53–124.

Newsome, J. D. "Toward a New Understanding of the Chronicler and His Purposes." *JBL* 94 (1975): 201–17.

North, R. *Sociology of the Biblical Jubilee.* AnBib 4. Rome: Biblical Institute, 1954.

———. "Theology of the Chronicler." *JBL* 82 (1963): 369–81.

———. "*Yâd* in the Shemitta-Law." *VT* 4 (1954): 196–99.

Noth, M. *The Chronicler's History.* Translated by H. G. M. Williamson. JSOTSup 50. Sheffield: JSOT Press, 1987.

———. *The Deuteronomistic History.* Translated by D. J. A. Clines et al. 2d ed. JSOTSup 15. Sheffield: Sheffield Press, 1991.

———. *The History of Israel.* Translated by P. R. Ackroyd. 2d ed. New York: Harper & Row, 1960

———. *Die israelitischen Personennamen im Rahmen der gemeinsemitischen Namengebung.* BWANT 10. Repr., Hildesheim: Olms, 1966.

———. *Leviticus.* OTL. Translated by J. E. Anderson. Philadelphia: Westminster, 1965.

O'Connor, M. *Hebrew Verse Structure.* Winona Lake, Ind.: Eisenbrauns, 1980.

Olmstead, A. T. "Darius As Lawgiver." *AJSL* 51 (1934–1935): 247–49.

Oorschot, J. van. "Nachkultische Psalmen und spätbiblische Rollendichtung." *ZAW* 106 (1994): 69–86.

Otzen, B. "םתח κτλ." *TDOT* 5:263–69.

Pavlovsky, V. "Die Chronologie der Tätigkeit Esdras. Versuch einer neuen Lösung." *Bib* 38 (1957): 278–305, 428–56.

Pelzl, B. "Philogisches zu Esra 8:27." *ZAW* 87 (1975): 221–24.

Petersen, D. L. "The Temple in Persian Period Prophetic Texts." *BTB* 21 (1991): 88–96.

―――. "The Temple in Persian Period Prophetic Texts." Pages 125–44 in *Second Temple Studies 1: Persian Period*. Edited by P. R. Davies. JSOTSup 117. Sheffield: JSOT Press, 1991.

Pfeiffer, R. H. *Introduction to the Old Testament*. New York: Harper & Brothers, 1948.

Phillips, A. "The Laws of Slavery: Exodus 21.2–11." *JSOT* 30 (1984): 51–66.

Plöger, O. "Reden und Gebete im deuteronomischen und chronistischen Geschichtswerk." Pages 50–66 in *Aus der Spätzeit des Alten Testaments*. Göttingen: Vandenhoeck & Ruprecht, 1971.

Pohlmann, K.-F. *Studien zum dritten Esra*. FRLANT 104. Göttingen: Vandenhoeck & Ruprecht, 1970.

―――. "Zur Frage von Korrespondenzen und Divergenzen zwichen den Chronikbüchern und dem Esra/Nehemia-Buch." Pages 314–30 in *Congress Volume: Leuven, 1989*. Edited by J. A. Emerton. VTSup 43. Leiden: Brill, 1991.

Polak, F. "Literary Design in Ezra-Nehemia." *Shnaton* 9 (1985): 127–43 (Hebrew); ix–x (English summary).

Polzin, R. *Late Biblical Hebrew. Toward an Historical Typology of Biblical Hebrew Prose*. HSM 12. Missoula, Mont.: Scholars Press, 1976.

Porten, B. "Aramaic Papyri in the Egyptian Museum: The Missing Endorsements." Pages 527–44 in *The Word Shall Go Forth: Essays in Honor of David Noel Freedman in Celebration of His Sixtieth Birthday*. Ed. C. L. Meyer and M. O'Connor. Winona Lake, Ind.: Eisenbrauns, 1983.

―――. *Archives from Elephantine: The Life of an Ancient Jewish Military Colony*. Berkeley and Los Angeles: University of California Press, 1968.

―――. "A New Look: Aramaic Papyri and Parchments." *BA* 42 (1979): 104.

Rabinowitz, Y. *Ezra: The Book of Ezra, Translation and Commentary.* Brooklyn: Mesorah, 1984.

———. *Nehemiah: The Book of Nehemiah, Translation, Commentary and Overview.* New York: Mesorah, 1990.

Rad, G. von. "The Form-Critical Problem of the Hexateuch." Pages 1–78 in *The Problem of the Hexateuch and Other Essays.* Translated by E. W. Trueman Dicken. New York: McGraw-Hill, 1966.

———. "Gerichtsdoxologie." Pages 245–54 in vol. 2 of *Gesammelte Studien zum Alten Testament.* TB 48. Munich: Kaiser, 1973.

———. *Das Geschichtsbild des Chronistischen Werkes.* BWANT 3. Stuttgart: Kohlhammer, 1930.

———. "The Levitical Sermon in I and II Chronicles." Pages 267–80 in *The Problem of the Hexateuch and Other Essays.* Translated by E. W. Trueman Dicken. New York: McGraw-Hill, 1966.

———. "Die Nehemia-Denkschrift." *ZAW* 76 (1964): 176–87.

———. *Studies in Deuteronomy.* Translated by D. Stalker. SBT 9. London: SCM Press, 1953.

———. *The Theology of Israel's Traditions.* Vol. 1 of *Old Testament Theology.* Translated by D. M. G. Stalker. Edinburgh: Oliver & Boyd, 1962.

Rehm, M. "Nehemias 9." *BZ* n.s. 1 (1957): 59–69.

Rehm, M. D. "Levites and Priests." *ABD* 4:297–310.

Reich, N. J. "The Codification of the Egyptian Laws by Darius and the Origin of the 'Demotic Chronicle.'" *Mizraim* 1 (1933): 178–85.

Rendsburg, G. A. "The Northern Origins of Nehemiah 9." *Bib* 72 (1991): 348–66.

Rendtorff, R. "Esra und das 'Gesetz.'" *ZAW* 96 (1984): 165–84.

Richards, K. H. "Reshaping Chronicles and Ezra-Nehemiah Interpretation." Pages 211–24 in *Old Testament Interpretation, Past, Present, and Future: Essays in Honor of Gene M. Tucker.* Edited by D. L. Petersen, J. L. Mays, and K. H. Richards. Nashville: Abingdon, 1995.

Rofé, A. "Isaiah 66:1–4: Judean Sects in the Persian Period As Viewed by Trito-Isaiah." Pages 205–17 in *Biblical and Related Studies Presented to Samuel Iwry.* Edited by A. Kort and S. Morschauser. Winona Lake, Ind.: Eisenbrauns, 1985.

Rowley, H. H. "The Chronological Order of Ezra and Nehemiah." Pages 137–68 in *The Servant of the Lord and Other Essays on the Old Testament*. 2d ed. Oxford: Blackwell, 1952.

———. "Nehemiah's Mission and Its Background." *BJRL* 37 (1954–1955): 528–61.

Rubenstein, J. L. "The History of Sukkot during the Second Temple and Rabbinic Periods: Studies in the Continuity and Change of a Festival." Ph.D. diss. Columbia, 1992.

Rudolph, W. *Esra und Nehemia*. HAT 20. Tübingen: Mohr (Siebeck), 1949.

———. "Problems of the Books of Chronicles." *VT* 4 (1954): 401–9.

Saebø, M. "Chronistische Theologie/Chronistisches Geschichtswerk." *TRE* 8 (1981): 74–87.

———. "Esra/Esraschriften." *TRE* 10 (1982): 374–86.

Saley, R. J. "The Date of Nehemiah Reconsidered." Pages 151–65 in *Biblical and Near Eastern Studies: Essays in Honor of William Sanford LaSor*. Edited by G. A. Tuttle. Grand Rapids, Mich.: Eerdmans, 1978.

Sanchez Caro, J. M. "Esdras, Nehemias y Los Origenes del Judaismo." *Salm* 32 (1985) 5–34.

Saydon, P. P. "Meanings and Uses of the Particle את." *VT* 14 (1964): 192–210.

Schaeder, H. H. *Esra der Schreiber*. BHT 5. Tübingen: Mohr (Siebeck), 1930.

———. *Iranische Beiträge I*. Halle: Max Niemeyer, 1930.

Scharbert, J. "'Běrît' im Pentateuch." Pages 163–70 in *De la Tôrah au Messie [Mélanges Henri Cazelles]*. Edited by J. Doré, P. Grelot, and M. Carrez. Paris: Desclée, 1981.

———. "ברך κτλ." *TDOT* 2:279–308.

———. "Formgeschichte und Exegese von Ex 34,6f und seiner Parallelen." *Bib* 38 (1950): 130–50.

Schenker, A. "La Relation d'Esdras A' au texte massorétique d'Esdras-Néhémie." Pages 218–48 in *Tradition of the Text: Studies Offered to Dominique Barthélemy in Celebration of His 70th Birthday*. Edited by G. J. Norton and S. Pisano. OBO 109. Göttingen: Vandenhoeck & Ruprecht, 1991.

Scherman, N. "An Overview/Ezra—Molder of a New Era." Pages xv–liv in *Ezra: The Book of Ezra, Translation and Commentary*, by Y. Rabinowitz. Brooklyn: Mesorah, 1984.

Schottroff, W. *'Gedenken' im Alten Orient und im Alten Testament. Die Wurzel zākar im semitischen Sprachkreis*. 2d ed. WMANT 15. Neukirchen-Vluyn: Neukirchener Verlag, 1967.

Schramm, B. *The Opponents of Third Isaiah: Reconstructing the Cultic History of the Restoration*. JSOTSup 193. Sheffield: Sheffield Academic Press, 1995.

Schultz, C. "The Political Tensions Reflected in Ezra-Nehemiah." Pages 221–44 in *Scripture in Context*. Edited by C. D. Evans, W. W. Hallo, and J. B. White. Pittsburgh: Pickwick, 1980.

Scott, W. R. "The Booths of Ancient Israel's Autumn Festival." Ph.D. diss. Johns Hopkins University, 1993.

Scullion, J. J. "Righteousness: Old Testament," *ABD* 5:724–36.

Segal, M. H. ספר בן־סירא השלם. 2d ed. Jerusalem: Bialik Institute, 1958.

Segert, S. "History and Poetry: Poetic Patterns in Nehemiah 9:5–37." Pages 255–65 in *Storia e Tradizioni di Israele: Scritti in Onore di J. Alberto Soggin*. Edited by D. Garrone and F. Israel. Brescia: Paideia, 1991.

Shaver, J. R. "Ezra and Nehemiah: On the Theological Significance of Making Them Contemporaries." Pages 76–86 in *Priests, Prophets and Scribes: Essays on the Formation and Heritage of Second Temple Judaism*. Edited by E. Ulrich, J. W. Wright, R. P. Carroll, and P. R. Davies. JSOTSup 149. Sheffield: JSOT Press, 1992.

———. "Torah and the Chronicler's History Work: An Inquiry into the Chronicler's References to Laws, Festivals and Cultic Institutions in Relation to the Pentateuchal Legislation." Ph.D. diss. University of Notre Dame, 1983.

Silverman, M. H. *Religious Values in the Jewish Proper Names at Elephantine*. AOAT 217. Neukirchen-Vluyn: Neukirchener Verlag, 1985.

Smith, D. L. "The Politics of Ezra: Sociological Indicators of Postexilic Judaean Society." Pages 73–97 in *Second Temple Studies 1: Persian Period*. Edited by P. R. Davies. JSOTSup 117. Sheffield: JSOT Press, 1991.

Smith, M. "Palestinian Judaism in the Persian Period." Pages 386–401 in *The Greeks and the Persians: From the Sixth to the Fourth Centuries*. Edited by H. Bengtson. New York: Delacorte, 1968.

———. *Palestinian Parties and Politics That Shaped the Old Testament*. 2d ed. London: SCM, 1987.

Smith-Christopher, D. L. "The Mixed Marriage Crisis in Ezra 9–10 and Nehemiah 13: A Study of the Sociology of the Post-exilic Judaean

Community." Pages 243–65 in *Second Temple Studies 2: Temple Community in the Persian Period.* Edited by T. C. Eskenazi and K. H. Richards. JSOTSup 175. Sheffield: JSOT Press, 1994.

Snaith, N. *The Jewish New Year Festival.* London: SPCK, 1947.

———. "A Note on Ezra viii. 35." *JTS* 22 (1971): 150–52.

Snell, D. C. "Why Is There Aramaic in the Bible?" *JSOT* 18 (1980): 32–51.

Sobb, J. A. "Israel in Transition." Ph.D. diss. Cambridge, 1980.

Spiegelberg, W. *Die sogennante demotische Chronik des Pap. 215 der Bibliothèque Nationale zu Paris nebst den auf der Rückseite des Papyrus stehenden Texten.* Demotische Studien 7. Leipzig: Hinrichs'sche Buchhandlung, 1914.

Sternberg, M. *The Poetics of Biblical Narrative: Ideological Literature and the Drama of Reading.* Bloomington: Indiana University Press, 1987.

Steuernagel, C. "Jahwe, der Gott Israels." Pages 329–49 in *Studien zur semitischen Philologie und Religionsgeschichte.* Fest. J. Wellhausen. Edited by K. Marti. BZAW 27. Gießen: Töpelmann, 1914.

Swete, H. B. *An Introduction to the Old Testament in Greek.* Revised by R. R. Ottley. Cambridge: Cambridge University Press, 1914. Repr., Peabody, Mass.: Hendrickson, 1989.

Talmon, S. "The Emergence of Jewish Sectarianism in the Early Second Temple Period." Pages 587–616 in *Ancient Israelite Religion: Essays in Honor of Frank Moore Cross.* Ed. P. D. Hanson, P. D. Miller Jr., and S. D. McBride. Philadelphia: Fortress, 1987.

———. "Esra-Nehemia: Historiographie oder Theologie?" Pages 329–56 in *Ernten, was man sät: Festschrift für Klaus Koch zu seinem 65. Geburtstag.* Edited by D. R. Daniels, U. Glessmer, and M. Rösel. Neukirchen-Vluyn: Neurkirchener, 1991.

———. "Ezra and Nehemiah." Pages 357–64 in *The Literary Guide to the Bible.* Edited by R. Alter and F. Kermode. Cambridge Mass.: Harvard University Press, 1987.

———. "Ezra and Nehemiah (Books and Men)." *IDBSup* 317–28.

———. "The Presentation of Synchroneity and Simultaneity in Biblical Nar-rative." Pages 9–26 in *Studies in Hebrew Narrative Art.* Edited by J. Heinemann and S. Weres. ScrHier 27. Jerusalem: Hebrew University, 1978.

———. "The Sectarian יחד—A Biblical Noun." *VT* 3 (1953): 133–40.

Talshir, D. "A Reinvestigation of the Linguistic Relationship between Chronicles and Ezra-Nehemiah." *VT* 38 (1988): 165–93.

Tångberg, A. "Nehemia/Nehemiabuch." *TRE* 24 (1994): 242–46.

Throntveit, M. A. *Ezra-Nehemiah*. IBC. Louisville: John Knox, 1992.

———. "Linguistic Analysis and the Question of Authorship in Chronicles, Ezra and Nehemiah." *VT* 32 (1982): 201–16.

Tigay, J. H. "Israelite Religion: The Onomastic Evidence." Pages 157–94 in *Ancient Israelite Religion: Essays in Honor of Frank Moore Cross*. Edited by P. D. Hanson, P. D. Miller Jr., and S. D. McBride. Philadelphia: Fortress, 1987.

Torrey, C. C. *The Composition and Historical Value of Ezra-Nehemiah*. BZAW 2. Gießen: Rickers'sche Buchhandlung, 1896.

———. *Ezra Studies*. Library of Biblical Studies. 1910. Repr., New York: Ktav, 1970.

Tucker, G. M. "Covenant Forms and Contract Forms." *VT* 15 (1965): 487–503.

Tuland, C. G. "Ezra-Nehemiah or Nehemiah-Ezra?" *AUSS* 12 (1974): 47–62.

VanderKam, J. C. "Ezra-Nehemiah or Ezra and Nehemiah?" Pages 55–75 in *Priests, Prophets and Scribes: Essays on the Formation and Heritage of Second Temple Judaism in Honour of Joseph Blenkinsopp*. Edited by E. Ulrich, J. W. Wright, R. P. Carroll, and P. R. Davies. JSOTSup 149. Sheffield: JSOT Press, 1992.

———. "Jewish High Priests of the Persian Period: Is the List Complete?" Pages 67–91 in *Priesthood and Cult in Ancient Israel*. Edited by G. A. Anderson and S. M. Olyan. JSOTSup 125. Sheffield: Sheffield Academic Press, 1991.

Vaux, R. de. *Ancient Israel: Its Life and Institutions*. Translated by John McHugh. London: Darton, Longman & Todd, 1961.

———. "Les Décrets de Cyrus et de Darius sur la Reconstruction du Temple," *RB* 46 (1937): 29–57.

———. "Israel (histoire d')." *DBSup* 4:764–69.

Veltri, G. "Der Aramäische Targumvortrag zur Zeit Esras: Eine sprachgeschichtliche und historische Frage." *Laur* 34 (1993): 187–207.

Venter, P. M. "Die aard van die geloofsgemeenskap in Nehemia 9." *HvTst* 51 (1995): 720–31.

Vicent, R. *La fiesta judía de las Cabañas (Sukkot). Interpretaciones midrásicas en la Biblia y en judaísmo antiguo.* Estella (Navarra): Verbo Divino, 1995.

Vink, J. G. "The Date and Origin of the Priestly Code in the Old Testament," Pages 1–144 in *The Priestly Code and Seven Other Studies*. Edited by P. A. H. de Boer. OTS 15. Leiden: Brill, 1969.

Vogt, H. C. M. *Studie zur nachexilischen Gemeinde in Esra-Nehemia.* Werl: Dietrich Coelde, 1966.

Wacholder, B. Z. "The Calendar of Sabbatical Cycles during the Second Temple and the Early Rabbinic Period." *HUCA* 44 (1973): 153–94.

Watson, W. G. E. *Classical Hebrew Poetry: A Guide to Its Techniques.* JSOTSup 26. Sheffield: JSOT Press, 1984.

———. "Reclustering Hebrew *l'yd*." *Bib* 58 (1977): 213–15.

Watts, J. W. *Psalm and Story, Inset Hymns in Hebrew Narrative.* JSOTSup 139. Sheffield: JSOT Press, 1992.

Weil, H. M. "Gage et cautionnement dans la Bible." *Archives d'Histoire du Droit Oriental* 2 (1938): 171–240 [offprint 1–68].

Weinberg, J. *The Citizen-Temple Community.* Translated by D. L. Smith-Christopher. JSOTSup 151. Sheffield: JSOT press, 1992.

Weinberg, W. "Language Consciousness in the OT." *ZAW* 92 (1980): 185–204.

Weinfeld, M. *Deuteronomy and the Deuteronomic School.* Winona Lake, Ind.: Eisenbrauns, 1992.

Welch, A. C. "The Share of N. Israel in the Restoration of the Temple Worship." *ZAW* 48 (1930): 175–87.

———. "The Source of Nehemiah IX." *ZAW* 47 (1929): 130–37.

Wellhausen, J. *Prolegomena to the History of Ancient Israel.* Cleveland: World Publishing, 1957.

Westbrook, R. *Property and the Family in Biblical Law.* JSOTSup 113. Sheffield: JSOT Press, 1991.

Westermann, C. *Praise and Lament in the Psalms.* Translated by K. R. Crim and R. N. Soulen. Atlanta: John Knox, 1981.

Widengren, G. "The Persian Period." Pages 489–538 in *Israelite and Judaean History.* Edited by J. H. Hayes and J. M. Miller. Philadelphia: Westminster, 1977.

Wiéner, C. "Des enfants à l'assemblée? Note brève sur Néhémie 8." Pages 151–54 in *La Vie de la Parole: De l'Ancien au Nouveau Testament. Mélanges P. Grelot.* Edited by Départment des Etudes Bibliques de l'Institut Catholique de Paris. Paris: Desclée, 1987.

Wildberger, H. *Isaiah 1–12. A Commentary.* Translated by T. H. Tropp. CC. Minneapolis: Fortress, 1991.

Williamson, H. G. M. "The Composition of Ezra i–vi." *JTS* 34 (1983): 1–30.

———. "Did the Author of Chronicles Also Write the Books of Ezra and Nehemiah?" *BRev* 3 (Spring 1987): 56–59.

———. *Ezra and Nehemiah.* OTG. Sheffield: JSOT Press, 1987.

———. *Ezra, Nehemiah.* WBC 16. Waco, Tex.: Word, 1985.

———. *1 and 2 Chronicles.* NCB. Grand Rapids, Mich.: Eerdmans, 1982.

———. "The Historical Value of Josephus' *Jewish Antiquities* XI. 297–301." *JTS* n.s. 28 (1977): 49–66.

———. "Isaiah 63,7–64,11. Exilic Lament or Post-exilic Protest?" *ZAW* 102 (1990): 48–58.

———. *Israel in the Books of Chronicles.* Cambridge: Cambridge University Press, 1977.

———. "Laments at the Destroyed Temple." *BRev* 6 (August 1990): 12–17, 44.

———. "The Origins of the Twenty-Four Priestly Courses: A Study of 1 Chronicles xxiii–xxvii." Pages 251–68 in *Studies in the Historical Books of the Old Testament.* Edited by J. A. Emerton. VTSup 30. Leiden: Brill, 1979.

———. "Post-exilic Historiography." Pages 189–207 in *The Future of Biblical Studies: The Hebrew Scriptures.* Edited by R. E. Friedman and H. G. M. Williamson. SemeiaSt. Atlanta: Scholars Press, 1987.

———. "Reliving the Death of Josiah: A Reply to C. T. Begg." *VT* 37 (1987): 9–15.

———. "Structure and Historiography in Nehemiah 9." Pages 117–31 in *Proceedings of the Ninth World Congress of Jewish Studies (1985). Panel Sessions: Bible Studies and Ancient Near East.* Edited by M. Goshen-Gottstein. Jerusalem: Magnes, Hebrew University, 1988.

Wong, G. C. I. "A Note on 'Joy' in Nehemiah VIII 10." *VT* 45 (1995): 383–86.

Wright, C. J. H. "Sabbatical Year." *ABD* 5:857–61.

Yamauchi, E. M. "The Archaeological Background of Ezra." *BSac* 37 (1980): 195–211.

———. "Was Nehemiah the Cupbearer a Eunuch?" *ZAW* 92 (1980): 132–42.

Yaron, R. *Introduction to the Law of the Aramaic Papyri*. Oxford: Oxford University Press, 1961.

———. "The Schema of the Aramaic Legal Documents." *JSS* 2 (1957): 33–61.

Zadok, R. *The Pre-Hellenistic Israelite Anthroponymy and Prosopography*. OLA 28. Leuven: Peeters, 1988.

———. "Remarks on Ezra and Nehemiah." *ZAW* 94 (1982): 296–98.

Zevit, Z. "A Chapter in the History of Israelite Personal Names." *BASOR* 250 (1983): 1–16.

———. "Converging Lines of Evidence Bearing on the Date of P." *ZAW* 94 (1982): 481–511.

Zimmerli, W. *Ezekiel 2*. Translated by R. E. CLements. Hermeneia. Philadelphia: Fortress, 1983.

Zunz, L. "Dibre hajamim oder die Bücher der Chronik." Pages 13–36 in *Die gottesdienstlichen Vorträge der Juden, historisch entwickelt. Ein Beitrag zur Alterthumskunde und biblischen Kritik, zur Literatur- und Religionsgeschichte*. 1832. Repr., Frankfurt: Kauffmann, 1892.

Index of Primary Sources

Genesis

Ref	Page
1:1	171
2:1	201, 225
2:7	150
2:9	216, 217 n. 113
3:19	150
15:1–5	172 n. 28
15:1–6	172
15:1–21	172
15:6	203
15:6–21	202, 203, 224
15:7	203, 203 n. 66, 204 n. 70, 224
15:7–21	172
15:18	204, 204 nn. 69–70 and 72
15:18–21	204
15:19–21	204
17:1–18:15	172 n. 28
17:5	172, 202, 203, 224, 225
17:12	151 n. 30
19:1	112, 112 n. 68
21:1–7	172 n. 28
22:17	215, 215 n. 109
24:8	269 n. 59
24:48	110, 111
26:4	215, 215 n. 109
30:14	283 n. 86
31:27	119 n. 82
31:29	277 n. 73
32:13	215 n. 109
37:34	117
37:35	117
42:6	112, 112 n. 68, 115
42:38	207 n. 83
43:28	111
45:5	117
47:18	224
49:28	155 n. 41

Exodus

Ref	Page
3:7	205, 205 n. 75
3:8	204
3:17	204
4:14	119 n. 82
4:31	111
6:8	210, 210 n. 93, 225
6:14	129
7:3	205
8:27	207 n. 83
9:27	223, 223 n. 129
10:16–17	163
12:3	129
12:16	116 n. 77
13:2	283, 283 n. 87
13:12–15	283
13:13	283, 283 n. 88
13:17–15:19	224
13:21	207, 207 n. 80
13:21–22	176
13:22	207
14:4	206
14:8	206
14:9	206
14:10	205
14:16	206, 206 n. 78
14:21–22a	206
14:21b	206 n. 78
14:22a	206 n. 78
14:23	206
14:24	207
15:1–18	226
15:4	206
15:4–5	206
15:5	206
15:9	206
15:10	206
15:16b	206
15:19b	206, 206 n. 78

15:25	118	25:30	281
15:26	270 n. 61	28:36	116
16:1–36	214	29:1–30	132
16:1–17:8	176	29:38–42	281
16:3	133 n. 100	29:40–41	281
16:4	209 n. 92	30:11–16	279, 280, 287
16:4–36	209, 225	30:12	280
16:22	274	30:13	279
16:22–30	274, 287	30:15	279
16:23	116, 209, 274	30:16	279
16:26–27	274	31:15	116
16:29	274	32	212
17:1–6	209	32:1–35	212
17:1–7	214	32:4	212, 212 n. 98, 213
17:6	209, 209 n. 92	32:13	215
18:8	221	32:8	212, 212 n. 98, 213
18:11	206	32:30	163
18:13	101 n. 35	32:31–32	163
18:14	101 n. 35	34	21
18:20	207 n. 83, 208	34:6	211, 211 n. 96
19–24	21	34:6–7	212, 212 n. 97, 224
19:1–20:21	224	34:11–16	271 n. 64
19:1–24:18	212	34:15–16	271, 287
19:11	110	34:16	271 n. 64
19:20	208, 208 n. 84	34:17–26	21 n. 60
20:8	208, 208 n. 89	34:18	100
20:8–11	274, 287	34:18–23	283 n. 86
20:11	201, 201 n. 62	34:18–24	96 n. 23
20:22	208, 208 n. 85	34:19–20	283, 283 n. 88
22:10	269 n. 59	34:20	283 n. 88
22:24	276 n. 71	34:21	274, 287
22:24–26	276	34:22	95, 96, 96 n. 25, 97, 98, 99, 100, 118, 283, 283 n. 86
22:30	283 n. 89		
23:10	250 n. 17, 275 n. 69		
23:10–11	275, 287	34:22–24	100
23:12	274, 287	34:23	96 n. 24, 98
23:14–17	96 n. 23, 100, 283 n. 86	34:26	282, 282 n. 85, 287
23:16	95, 96, 96 n. 25, 97, 98, 99, 100, 118, 283, 283 n. 86	35:3	274, 287
		36:6	131 n. 93
		38:25–28	280
23:17	96 n. 24	39:30	116
23:19	282, 282 n. 85, 283 n. 86, 287	40:23	281 n. 82
24:7	108, 122	**Leviticus**	
24:11	118	4:1–5:13	281
25:1–2	280 n. 81	6:2	281, 287
25:23–30	281	6:5	282, 282 n. 83

6:5–6	132, 281, 287	23:40	96 n. 24, 98, 119 n. 82, 131, 131 n. 94, 134
8:1–36	132		
10:11	112	23:41–43	98
16:29	150	23:42	130, 131, 133, 134
16:31	150	23:42–43	98, 131, 132
18:5	219, 219 n. 118, 225	23:43	96
19:9	215	24:5–8	281
19:23	216	24:7	281
23:1–44	96 n. 23	24:12	114
23:2	116 n. 77	25:1–8	275, 276, 287
23:3	116 n. 77	25:4	276
23:4	116 n. 77	25:9	101 n. 32
23:4–22	283 n. 86	25:18	270 n. 61
23:5–8	100	25:25–38	276
23:7	116 n. 77	25:39–43	276
23:8	116 n. 77	26:3	270 n. 61
23:10	109 n. 61	26:5	283 n. 86
23:14	109 n. 61	26:17	219, 225
23:15	109 n. 61	26:40	152, 152 n. 31
23:15–22	100	27:14	116
23:17	109 n. 61	27:21	116
23:21	116 n. 77	27:23	116
23:22	215	27:27	283
23:23–25	99	27:30	116
23:23–43	99	27:32	116
23:24	101 n. 32, 116, 116 n. 77, 117, 118	**Numbers**	
23:24–25	99, 100	1:2	129
23:27	116 n. 77, 150	1:53	10 n. 23
23:27–32	99	4:30	280 n. 79
23:29	150	5:21	269 n. 59
23:32	150	5:22	111
23:33–36	96, 96 n. 22, 97, 99, 100, 135	7:5	280 n. 79
		8:24	280 n. 79
23:34	96, 96 n. 24, 98, 98 n. 26, 130, 135 n. 109	10:10	119 n. 82
		11:4–9	214
23:34–36	135	11:16–30	213, 214, 224
23:35	116 n. 77	11:29	213
23:36	96, 98, 116 n. 77, 135, 135 n. 109	13–14	225, 225 n. 131
		13:1–33	211, 216
23:37	116 n. 77	13:1–14:25	224
23:39	96, 98, 130, 135, 135 n. 109	13:20	216
		13:28	216
23:39–40	96	14	211
23:39–42	96, 98	14:4	161, 211, 211 n. 95
23:39–43	96 n. 22, 97, 131, 131 n. 95, 135	14:11	213, 213 n. 100
		14:14	207, 213

14:15	104	28:26–31	100, 281
14:18	211	29:1	101, 116, 116 n. 77, 117, 118, 275
14:18–20	211		
14:19–20	211	29:1–6	99, 281
14:23	213, 213 n. 100	29:1–39	99
14:30	210 n. 93	29:7	116 n. 77, 150, 275
14:39–45	210	29:7–11	99, 281
15:1–16	10 n. 23	29:12	98, 116 n. 77, 275
15:19	284	29:12–32	98
15:20–21	284, 287	29:12–38	96, 96 nn. 22 and 24, 97, 99, 132, 135 n. 109, 281
15:22–29	281		
15:32–36	274, 287	29:12–39	100
15:34	114	29:22	275
18:6	280 n. 79	29:35	135
18:12	284	29:39	281
18:12–13	287	30:3	269 n. 59
18:13	282	30:11	269 n. 59
18:15	132, 283 n. 88	30:14	269 n. 59
18:15–16	283	33:8	206
18:15–18	283 n. 88	35:5	215
18:16	283 n. 88	36:1	129 n. 91
18:17–18	283, 287	36:13	107
18:21	280 n. 79, 284, 287		
18:21–28	284 n. 90	**Deuteronomy**	20, 135
18:23	280 n. 79	1:8	210, 215
18:25–32	284	1:10	215, 215 nn. 108–9
18:26	284, 287	1:16–17	10 n. 23
18:28	284	1:28	216
20:8	209, 225	1:33	207, 207 nn. 82–83
20:1–13	214, 225	1:43	210
20:14	221	1:45	117
20:15	205 n. 76	2:7	214
21:21–35	215	2:24–3:7	215
22:31	111	3:5	216
22:34	163	3:20	219
25:6	117	4:1	210, 215
28:1–29:39	281	4:6	270 n. 61
28:1–30:1	275, 287	4:19	202
28:3–8	281	4:34	205
28:5	281	4:37	202
28:9–10	281	4:47	215
28:11–15	101, 281	5:1	270 n. 61
28:16–25	100, 281	5:12	208, 208 n. 89
28:16–29:38	96 n. 23	5:12–15	274, 287
28:18	116 n. 77, 275	5:14	275
28:25	116 n. 77	5:33	207 n. 83, 208
28:26	116 n. 77, 275	6:10–11	216

6:11	216, 216 n. 112
6:12–13	216
6:13	223
6:18	210, 215
6:20–24	226, 226 n. 132
6:22	205
7:1	272, 272 n. 65
7:1–6	271 n. 64
7:3	271, 271 n. 64, 272, 272 n. 66, 273, 287
7:7	202
7:9	221, 221 n. 121
7:11	270 n. 61
7:19	205
7:24	215
8:1	210, 215
8:2	207 n. 83
8:4	214, 214 n. 106
8:7–10	216
8:10	110, 216
8:11–13	216
8:12	216
9:1	216
9:3	215
9:4	210
9:5	204, 204 n. 73
9:7	217
9:9	209
9:18	209
9:23	217
9:24	217
10:11	210, 215
10:12	223
10:14	200 201
10:15	202
10:16	210
10:17	111 n. 65, 221, 221 n. 121
10:20	223
10:22	215 n. 109
11:8	210, 215
11:10–15	216
11:13	223
11:15	216
11:16–17	216
11:28	210
11:31	210
11:32	270 n. 61
12:1	270 n. 61
12:7	118, 119 n. 82
12:10	219
12:12	119 n. 82
12:18	118, 119, 119 n. 82
12:21	203
13:1	205
13:2	205
13:5	207 n. 83, 208, 223
14:2	202
14:22–26	284 n. 90
14:22–29	284 n. 90
14:23–26	285, 287
14:24	203
14:26	118, 119 n. 82
14:27–29	284 n. 90
14:28	284 n. 90
14:28–29	118, 284 n. 90, 285, 287
15:1–3	287
15:2	276, 276 nn. 70–71, 278, 278 n. 77, 279
15:12–13	278 n. 76
15:19–20	283 n. 89
16:1–13	96 n. 23
16:1–16	283 n. 86
16:1–17	100
16:8	135
16:11	119 n. 82
16:13	96, 98, 98 n. 26, 130
16:13–15	99, 135, 135 n. 109
16:13–17	95, 95 n. 22, 97, 98
16:14	119 n. 82, 150
16:14–15	98, 134
16:15	96, 96 nn. 24–25, 98, 119 n. 82, 132
16:16	98 n. 26, 130
16:18	10 n. 23
17:3	202
17:8–13	10 n. 23, 112
18:4	284, 287
20:20	216
21:5	112
23:4	209
23:23	270 n. 61
24:1	257
24:3	257
24:5	119 n. 82

24:8	112	31:11	96 n. 24, 98, 108, 132
24:10	276, 276 n. 71	31:12	98, 106 n. 49, 223
24:11	276 n. 71	31:20	216
25:19	219	31:23	134
26:1–11	282, 287	32:15	216
26:2	109 n. 61	32:29	130
26:5–9	226, 226 n. 132	32:39	201
26:8	205	32:44–47	135
26:9	109 n. 61	32:46	223
26:10	109 n. 61	33:10	112
26:11	119 n. 82	33:18	119 n. 82
26:12–15	118	34:8	117
26:16	270 n. 61	34:9	134
26:19	116	34:11	205
27:1–8	135		
27:6	132, 132 n. 98	**Joshua**	
27:7	119 n. 82	1:2	104 n. 42
27:15–26	111, 111 n. 67	1:5	212
27:26	223	1:7	223
28:3–8	216	1:7–8	135
28:15–46	216	1:11	210
28:32	277 n. 73	1:13	219
28:46	205	1:15	219
28:47	119 n. 82	2:17	269 n. 59
28:47–48	224	2:20	269 n. 59
28:58	223	3:4	207 n. 83
28:62	215 n. 109	3:13	270
28:69	107, 107 n. 54	5:14–15	201 n. 61
29:3	205	7:6	150
29:4	214, 214 n. 105	8:30–35	97 n. 25, 107, 122, 135, 136
29:6	214	8:31	107, 107 nn. 55–56, 134
29:9–20	269	8:32–35	134
29:11	256, 269	8:34	108, 122, 134
29:13	256, 269	8:34–35	135, 136
29:18	269	8:35	106 n. 49, 134, 136
29:19	269	9:20	269 n. 59
29:20	269	14:12	216
29:25	205 n. 76	15:5	215
29:29	223	18:3	210
31:6	212	18:9	210
31:8	212	18:14–15	215
31:9	98	19:51	129 n. 91
31:9–13	95 n. 22, 96, 96 n. 23, 97, 98, 99, 106 n. 49, 122, 135	21:44	219
		22:4	219
		22:5	209
31:10	98 n. 26, 130	22:17	221
31:10–13	96	22:23	219

Index of Primary Sources

22:33	110	20:11	104
22:34	202	20:23	117
23:1	219	20:26	149
23:1–16	134	21:19	96 n. 25
23:6	107, 107 n. 56, 134	21:21	118
24	21		
24:1–28	97 n. 25, 122, 134, 136	**Ruth**	
24:2	104, 134	2:23	283 n. 86
24:6	205 n. 76		
24:14	205 n. 76	**1 Samuel**	
24:16	21 n. 60	1:4	118
24:17	205 n. 76, 207 n. 83	1:9	118
24:26	113, 134, 135	1:23	204 n. 73
24:27	104, 134	2:6	201
		4:12	150
Judges		7:3	219
2:11–13	217	7:6	149
2:11–18	219	8:19	211
2:11–23	217, 228 n. 134	10:18	219
2:12	205 n. 76	10:25	257
2:14	218, 218 n. 117	11:7	104
2:14–15	217	12:6	205 n. 76
2:16	217	12:8	205 n. 76
2:17	217	12:10	163
2:18	217, 219, 228 n. 134	12:10–11	219
2:19	217	17:47	133 n. 100
2:22	207 n. 83, 208	19:4	152 n. 32
3:9	217, 219	19:14	104
3:15	219	20:3	117
3:19	92 n. 16	22:2	276 n. 71
4:3	217, 218	22:8	256
4:9	207 n. 83	24:9	112 n. 68
4:23	215	25:28	270
6:9	219	25:41	112, 112 n. 68
6:13	205 n. 76	28:12	152 n. 32
6:16	104	28:14	112, 112 n. 68
9:27	96 n. 25, 118	31:13	149
10:6–8	224	31:10	224
11:18–22	215	31:12	224
13:7	101 n. 35		
14:8	224	**2 Samuel**	
14:9	224	1:2	150
15:1	283 n. 86	6:19	118
18:6	207 n. 83	7:1	219
18:9	95 n. 21	7:1–29	29
20:1	104	7:11	219
20:8	104	7:25	204 n. 73

12:15b–23	149	18:4	218
12:21–22	117	18:13	218
13:37	117	18:21	202
14:2	117	18:37	202
15:32	150	19:4	270 n. 61
16:6	110	19:10	218
19:1	117	19:14	218
19:2	117	21:8	260
19:2–3	117	21:21	223 n. 128
19:15	104	21:27	150
21:7	269 n. 59	22:19	110
21:10	101 n. 35	22:19–23	201 n. 61
24:1–17	280		
24:15	101 n. 35	**2 Kings**	
		1:31	112 n. 68
1 Kings		1:40	120 n. 83
1:3	112	2:3	95 n. 21
2:3	270 n. 61	2:5	95 n. 21
2:4	204 n. 73	4:1	276, 276 n. 71, 277
3:1	28	7:9	95 n. 21
3:8	202	8:2	135 n. 109
5:18	219	8:65	135 n. 109
6:12	204 n. 73, 270 n. 61	10:31	269
6:13	212	14:6	107 n. 56
8:15	32 n. 103	15:19–20	222
8:17	32 n. 103	15:29	222
8:20	32 n. 103, 204 n. 73	17:3–6	222
8:21	203, 205 n. 76	17:7–18	219
8:23	32 n. 103, 221, 221 n. 121	17:13	107, 218, 218 n. 116
8:25	32 n. 103	17:14	210
8:26	32 n. 103	17:15	223
8:27	200	17:20	151
8:32	218	17:24	222
8:34	218	17:34	107, 203
8:36	207 n. 83, 208, 218	17:37	208, 270 n. 61
8:43	218	17:39	219
8:49	218	18:9–12	222
8:53	205 n. 76	18:13–19:37	222
9:3	203	18:26	101 n. 34
9:9	205 n. 76, 223 n. 128	19:15	200, 200 n. 60
11:1–8	28	19:19	200, 200 n. 60
11:36	203	21:3	202
12:15	204 n. 73	22:3	95 n. 21
12:28	212	21:12	223 n. 128
13:17	207 n. 83	21:15	205 n. 76
14:9	217, 217 n. 114	22:16	223 n. 128, 269 n. 60
14:10	223 n. 128	22:19	117

Index of Primary Sources

23:1–3	104	23:1–32	28
23:2	108, 122	23:1–25:31	27
23:3	109	23:2	258
23:26–27	228 n. 134	23:9	129 n. 91
24:20	228 n. 134	23:24	129 n. 91
25:8	149 n. 24	23:29	281 n. 82
25:21	228 n. 134	24:1–6	263
25:25	149 n. 24	24:1–27:34	29
		24:6	129 n. 91, 258

1 and 2 Chronicles 23 n. 66, 24, 25, 26, 28, 30, 110, 111, 112, 113, 118 n. 79, 120 n. 83, 129 n. 91, 130, 133, 133 n. 100, 217

		24:7	263 n. 50
		24:7–18	261, 263
		24:9	262
		24:11	262
		24:19	263
		24:31	129 n. 91

1 Chronicles

1:1–9:44	23 n. 66, 29	25:1–31	27
3:19	27 n. 87	25:7	115
7:11	129 n. 91	26:21	129 n. 91
8:13	129 n. 91	26:26	129 n. 91
9:2	37 n. 115	26:32	129 n. 91
9:2–17	37 n. 115, 69 n. 21	27:1	129 n. 91
9:32	281 n. 82	27:23	215 n. 109
9:34	129 n. 91	28:1–21	28
10:1–29:30	23 n. 66	28:9	28
11:1	28	28:21	258
13:4	133 n. 100	29:1	133 n. 100
15:1–2	28	29:9	120, 120 n. 83
15:12	129 n. 91	29:10	111, 133 n. 100, 153, 153 n. 36
15:22	115		
16:1	109	29:10–19	162
16:7–36	162	29:19	270 n. 61
16:12	211	29:20	111, 112, 133 n. 100, 153
16:13	151 n. 30	29:22	118, 120, 120 n. 83
16:16	269	29:28	29 n. 90
16:27	119, 119 n. 80, 146, 147		
16:36	101 n. 35, 111, 111 n. 66, 153, 153 n. 34, 154, 154 n. 38, 239	**2 Chronicles**	24 n. 73, 28 n. 87
		1:1–36:23	23 n. 66
		1:2	129 n. 91
		1:3	133 n. 100
16:40	107, 107 n. 52	2:6	200
17:1–27	27, 29	2:12	114
21:18–22:16	27	2:15–16	27
21:21	112, 112 n. 68	5:3	135 n. 109
22:1	202	5:7	109
22:6	32 n. 103	5:12–13	27
22:12	107 n. 53, 114	6:4	32 n. 103
22:13	107 n. 53	6:5	28
22:19	202		

6:7	32 n. 103	20:19	152
6:10	32 n. 103, 204 n. 73	20:20–30	154
6:13	109	20:22	154
6:14	32 n. 103, 221	20:22–23	28
6:14–42	162	20:26	111, 154
6:16	32 n. 103, 207 n. 83, 208, 269	21:1	29 n. 90
		21:19–20	29 n. 90
6:17	32 n. 103	22:9	29 n. 90
6:18	200	23:2	129 n. 91
6:20	203	23:3	133 n. 100
6:23	218	24:5	280
6:25	218	24:6	280, 280 n. 81
6:27	207 n. 83, 208, 218	24:9	280 n. 81
6:33	218	24:19	218, 218 n. 115, 220, 220 n. 119
6:39	218		
7:3	112, 112 n. 68	24:20–22	218
7:8–9	135 n. 109	24:25–26	29 n. 90
7:13–16	28	25:27–28	29 n. 90
7:18	256	26:12	129 n. 91
7:22	223 n. 128	26:23	29 n. 90
8:11	28	27:9	29 n. 90
8:13	130	28:14	133 n. 100
10:15	204 n. 73	28:27	29 n. 90
11:16	32 n. 103	28:28	133 n. 100
11:31	29 n. 90	29:1–31:21	21 n. 58
12:5	219	29:1–36	28
12:8	224	29:3–31:21	21
12:12–16	29	29:7	32 n. 103
12:16	29 n. 90	29:30	111
13:4–12	29	29:31–32	109 n. 61
13:11	281 n. 82	29:32	10 n. 23
13:19–23	29	29:33	29 n. 90, 281
13:23	29 n. 90	30:1	32 n. 103
14:4	223	30:1–12	28
15:1–7	29	30:2	133 n. 100
15:1–18	21, 21 n. 58	30:4	133 n. 100
15:8–15	269	30:5	32 n. 103, 131
15:9–15	28	30:6–9	29
15:12	269	30:8	210
15:15	269	30:13–27	27
16:14	29 n. 90	30:16	113
17:7–9	112	30:21	114, 120, 120 n. 83
18:18	110	30:22	114
19:8	129 n. 91	30:23	133 n. 100
19:10	10 n. 23, 208, 208 n. 87	30:25	28, 133, 133 n. 100
20:5–15	162	30:26	29, 120, 133, 120 n. 83
20:18	112, 112 n. 68	31:2–19	285

Index of Primary Sources

31:4	285	1:1–2			231
31:5	285	1:1–3a			24
31:5–6	109 n. 61	1:1–4	28, 34 n. 108, 39, 48, 49,		
31:10	109 n. 61		52, 54 n. 169, 55, 60, 61,		
31:12	109 n. 61, 285		63, 64, 67, 231, 257, 289,		
32:1–23	222		298		
32:16	202	1:1–11			6 n. 11
33:3	202	1:1–3:13			23 n. 66
33:8	130	1:1–4:5			23 n. 66
33:16	32 n. 103	1:1–4:23			46
33:20	29 n. 90	1:1–4:24			63 n. 7
33:24	29 n. 90	1:1–6:22	15, 42 n. 132, 54 n. 169,		
34:3–35:18	21		60		
34:12	115	1:1–10:44			6 n. 11
34:14–28	269	1:2			30
34:24	269	1:2–4	15, 29, 33, 36, 61, 62, 63		
34:27	117		n. 6, 77, 104		
34:29–35:19	21 n. 58	1:3	31 n. 99, 32 n. 103, 103,		
34:30	104, 108		103 n. 39		
34:31	109, 113, 270, 270 n. 61	1:3–4			51
35–36	24	1:4		56 n. 172, 281, 289	
35:1–36:23	6 n. 11	1:5	50, 51, 62, 64, 65, 105 n.		
35:3	113, 281		44, 129, 129 n. 91, 184,		
35:6	130		203, 220, 231, 268		
35:8	258	1:5–11		36, 55, 60, 64	
35:10	113	1:5–6:15			54 n. 169
35:10–18	27	1:5–6:22			61
35:18	29, 133	1:5–Neh 7:72		49, 50, 55	
35:22–24	28	1:7			56 n. 172
35:24–25	29 n. 90	1:7–11			62
36:1–13	29 n. 90	1:7–6:22			49, 61
36:13	210	1:8			30, 61
36:20–21	25, 64 n. 8	1:9–11	34 n. 108, 37 n. 118, 40		
36:22	24, 64 n. 8, 131	1:11			62
36:22–23	24, 25	2–6			298
		2:1	49, 69 n. 19, 103, 220,		
Ezra	30 nn. 95–96, 31 n. 99,		232		
	34 n. 109, 26, 33, 34, 35, 36, 37	2:1–67		49, 51, 55	
1–6	31, 31 nn. 99–100, 32 n.	2:1–68			48, 52
	103, 33, 39, 40, 41, 42,	2:1–70	16 n. 39, 29, 33, 34 n.		
	42 n. 132, 44 n. 138, 45,		108, 37 n. 118, 55 n. 170,		
	47, 48 n. 148, 50, 51, 54,		60, 62, 64, 70, 72, 203,		
	59, 60, 61, 61 n. 2, 62,		245, 264, 265, 267, 268,		
	63–65, 67, 298		268 n. 57		
1:1	30, 46, 48, 61, 62, 63 n.	2:1–3:1			33
	7, 64, 64 n. 8, 131, 184,	2:1–4:5			6 n. 11
	257 n. 29	2:1–5:2			36

2:1b	40	3:5	70 n. 23
2:2	41, 47	3:6	37, 72, 100
2:2–64	40	3:6–8	52
2:2–69	40	3:7	30, 61, 109 n. 60, 127 n. 90
2:28	56 n. 172	3:7–10	62
2:36–39	268 n. 57	3:8	27, 41, 56 n. 172, 63 n.
2:38–39	262 n. 47		7, 70 n. 23, 71 n. 23, 105
2:40	140 n. 2, 237, 263, 264, 268 n. 57		n. 44, 129, 232
		3:8–9	62, 64
2:41	268 n. 57	3:8–13	102
2:43	37 n. 115	3:9	56 n. 172, 64, 263, 264
2:43–54	268 n. 57	3:10	27
2:58	37 n. 115	3:10–11	103 n. 41
2:61	250 n. 16	3:10–13	62, 64
2:62	72, 257 n. 29	3:11	103, 103 n. 39, 162
2:63	115	3:12	34 n. 108, 117, 119 n. 81,
2:64	104, 133, 133 n. 100, 136		129 n. 91, 130, 152 n. 33
2:68	48, 56 n. 172, 70 n. 23, 129 n. 91	3:12–13	31 n. 101, 103 n. 41, 119
		3:13	31, 31 n. 97, 119 n. 81
2:68–69	70 n. 23	4:1	31 n. 99, 32 n. 103, 232
2:68–70	55 n. 170	4:1–3	28, 52, 56, 65
2:68–3:13	36	4:1–5	44, 48, 62
2:69	70 n. 23, 71 n. 23	4:1–24	52, 56, 60, 64
2:70	37 n. 115, 40, 71 n. 26, 268, 268 n. 57	4:2	30 n. 96, 47, 129 n. 91, 222
		4:2–3	65
2:70–3:1	72 n. 27	4:3	27, 30, 31 n. 99, 32 n. 103,
3	102 n. 37		41, 47, 48, 61, 129 n. 91
3:1	33, 37, 64, 70, 72, 99, 99 n. 27, 101, 102 n. 37, 103, 104, 128	4:4	215, 272, 297
		4:4–5a	40
		4:4–6:12	65
3:1–6	85, 102	4:5	30, 61, 63 n. 7
3:1–7	102	4:5b	40
3:1–13	27, 60, 64, 67, 70, 70 n. 23	4:6	43, 257 n. 29
		4:6–16	257
3:1–16	55 n. 170	4:6–24a	40
3:1–4:3	40	4:6–6:18	23 n. 66
3:2	27, 31 n. 99, 32 n. 103, 34, 36, 41, 47, 62, 64, 107 n. 57, 131, 132, 132 n. 98, 233 n. 138, 252 n. 21, 257 nn. 29–30, 282	4:7	30, 61, 257 n. 29
		4:7–22	29, 43, 44
		4:7–24	6 n. 11
		4:8	61, 257 n. 29, 261 n. 45
		4:8–16	40
3:2–3	282	4:8–22	45
3:3	70 n. 23, 220, 272, 282, 297	4:8–6:18	65 n. 10
		4:9–22	52
3:4	34 n. 108, 98 n. 26, 130, 131, 132, 257 n. 29	4:10	222
		4:11	61
3:4–6	62, 99, 136	4:11–16	10, 15, 33, 62, 289

Index of Primary Sources

4:11–22	56	6:2–12	33, 36, 61 n. 4, 63, 63 n. 6, 77, 257, 289, 298
4:12	52, 65, 65 n. 10		
4:13	52	6:3	56 n. 172
4:15	65	6:3–5	33, 39
4:16	52	6:3–12	10, 15, 29
4:17	10 n. 21	6:5	56 n. 172
4:17–22	10, 10 n. 21, 15, 33, 61 n. 4, 63 n. 6, 257, 289	6:6–12	33, 39, 52
		6:7	56 n. 172
4:17–23	39	6:7–12	55, 65 n. 10
4:18	113, 113 n. 70	6:8	56 n. 172, 65 n. 10
4:19	10 n. 21	6:9	63 n. 6
4:20	10 n. 21	6:9–10	281, 289
4:21	10 n. 21, 52	6:12	56 n. 172, 63 n. 6
4:22	10 n. 21	6:13–15	64
4:23	61, 65 n. 10	6:13–22	27, 36
4:24	30, 44, 46, 52, 56, 56 n. 172, 63 n. 7	6:14	30, 31 n. 99, 31 n. 100, 32 n. 103, 43, 46 n. 145, 48, 50, 56 n. 173, 61, 62, 63, 64, 65 n. 10, 77 n. 35, 218, 231, 257, 298
4:24–6:15	62		
4:24b	40		
4:42	268 n. 57		
5:1	31 n. 99, 32 n. 103, 65 n. 10, 126	6:14–15	29, 40
		6:15	37, 46, 61, 63 n. 7
5:1–2	29, 218	6:16	31 n. 101, 40 n. 126, 56 n. 172, 62, 64, 103, 119, 119 n. 81, 134, 203
5:1–6:12	40		
5:1–6:15	60, 64		
5:1–6:19	23 n. 66	6:16–18	64, 136
5:1–6:22	46, 63 n. 7	6:16–22	54 n. 169, 60, 62, 64, 67
5:2	27, 41, 56 n. 172	6:17	28, 56 n. 172, 260, 281
5:3–6:12	34 n. 108	6:18	34, 36, 62, 64, 131, 132, 257 n. 29
5:5	65 n. 10		
5:6–17	40, 257, 289	6:19	37, 72, 232
5:7	257 n. 29	6:19–22	27, 40, 64, 268
5:7–17	15, 29, 33	6:20	62, 232
5:7b–17	10	6:21	31 n. 99, 32 n. 103, 41, 103, 133, 232, 268, 268 n. 58
5:8	56 n. 172, 65		
5:8–17	52		
5:10	257 n. 29	6:22	30 n. 96, 31 n. 99, 31 n. 101, 32 n. 103, 56 n. 172, 65
5:12	31 n. 100, 65		
5:13	56 n. 172		
5:13–15	52, 55, 61	6:22b	40 n. 126
5:14	56 n. 172	7–8	6
5:15	56 n. 172	7–10	5, 7, 7 n. 14, 8, 11 n. 26, 24, 31 nn. 99–100, 32 n. 103, 39, 39 n. 122, 40, 41, 42, 42 n. 132, 45, 50, 51, 54, 61 n. 2, 65 n. 11
5:16	56 n. 172, 101 n. 35		
5:17	56 n. 172		
6:2	257 n. 29		
6:2–5	52, 61		
6:2–6	55	7–Neh 12	50

7–Neh 13	23 n. 66, 31, 33, 46, 47, 48 n. 148, 50, 59, 60, 61, 62, **65–67**, 298	7:12–26	8, 9, 10 n. 21, 12, 17, 20, 28, 29, 31, 33, 50, 52, 61, 63, 63 n. 6, 66, 77, 257, 289, 298
7:1	12, 13 n. 33 30, 31 n. 100, 40, 43, 61, 62, 63 n. 7, 87 n. 9	7:12–27	55
		7:12–9:15	13
7:1–5	34, 34 n. 108, 35 n. 110	7:13	10 n. 21
7:1–6	61, 109	7:13–14	8 n. 16
7:1–10	13, 13 n. 33, 14 n. 33, 15, 31, 60, 85, 120, 161	7:13–20	6, 11
		7:14	7, 7 n. 12, 11, 11 n. 26, 32, 61, 67, 77 n. 35
7:1–11	9		
7:1–26	45, 54 n. 169	7:14–24	9
7:1–10:44	1, 6, 23 n. 66, 42 n. 132, 46, 49, 54 n. 169, 60, 63 n. 7, 65, 66 n. 14	7:14–26	12
		7:15	31 n. 99, 32, 32 n. 103
		7:15–20	36, 62 n. 5
7:1–Neh 8:18	61	7:16	56 n. 172
7:6	8 n. 16, 10 n. 23, 13 n. 33, 31 n. 99, 32 n. 103, 34 n. 108, 35 n. 110, 36, 36 n. 114, 37 n. 116, 50, 62, 66, 67, 106, 106 n. 51, 107 n. 57, 108, 231, 233 n. 138, 257 n. 30	7:16–17	11 n. 27
		7:17	10 n. 23, 56 n. 172
		7:19	56 n. 172
		7:20	56 n. 172
		7:21	10, 10 n. 23, 12, 35 n. 110, 36, 66, 107 n. 57, 116
7:6–10	107	7:21–24	6, 11, 12 n. 27, 116, 281, 289
7:7	4, 36, 37 n. 115, 46, 61, 72 n. 27, 103, 103 n. 38	7:23	10 nn. 21 and 23, 56 n. 172
7:7–8	51, 63 n. 7		
7:7–9	2, 5, 14 n. 34, 62	7:24	10 n. 21, 37 n. 115, 56 n. 172
7:8	5, 7, 13 n. 33, 37, 44 n. 136	7:25	10 n. 23, 11, 103 nn. 39–40, 112
7:9	5, 14 n. 33, 37, 37 n. 116, 46, 62, 66	7:25–26	7, 8 n. 16, 10, 11, 11 n. 26, 32, 61, 63 n. 6, 66, 67, 77 n. 35, 116
7:10	8 n. 16, 10 n. 23, 11 n. 26, 35 n. 110, 36, 36 n. 114, 53, 62, 67, 107 n. 57, 208, 223, 233 n. 138, 257 n. 30	7:26	13, 17, 52, 107 n. 57
		7:27–28	13
		7:27–8:36	60
7:11	8 n. 16, 10, 10 n. 2312, , 13 n. 30, 31, 35 n. 110, 36, 36 n. 114, 47, 50, 67 39, 60, 61, 231	7:27–9:15	13, 45, 66 n. 14, 292
		7:27–10:17	54 n. 169
		7:27–10:44	9, 32
7:11–26		7:27–Neh 7:72a	107
7:12	10, 10 n. 21, 10 n. 23, 18 n. 47, 35 n. 110, 36, 47, 50, 66, 107 n. 57, 116	7:28	12, 37 n. 116
		8	5, 32, 44 n. 136
		8–Neh	8, 12
7:12–14	7	8:1	2, 12, 36, 61, 72
7:12–20	11, 13, 63 n. 6, 116	8:1–14	8, 12, 13, 17, 37 n. 118, 40, 66 n. 13
7:12–23	17		

Index of Primary Sources   345

8:1–24	51	8:34	257 n. 29
8:1–9:5	13	8:35	11, 11 n. 27, 31 n. 99, 32
8:2–14	264, 265		n. 103, 62 n. 5, 103, 232,
8:3	72		260, 281
8:6	111	8:35–36	7, 11 n. 27, 13 n. 30
8:12	5	8:36	12 n. 27, 34 n. 108, 56 n.
8:14	5, 257 n. 29		172, 66
8:15	8, 12, 161, 257 n. 29	9	5, 13 n. 32, 44 n. 136
8:15–20	8 n. 16, 28, 34 n. 109, 66	9–10	6, 21, 21 n. 58, 22, 117
	n. 13		n. 78, 150, 150 n. 27
8:15–23	11	9:1	14, 36, 53, 150, 161, 204,
8:15–32	62		204 n. 71, 220, 258, 268,
8:15–34	11, 12 n. 27		272, 297
8:16	106 n. 50	9:1–2	9, 220, 271, 272 n. 65, 273
8:16–17	112	9:1–3	32 n. 103
8:16–20	121	9:1–4	7, 13, 14
8:17	8, 37 n. 115, 56 n. 172,	9:1–5	14
	109 n. 60, 177, 208 n. 86	9:1–15	12 n. 27
8:18	37 n. 116, 62, 66, 109 n.	9:1–10:44	60, 66, 67, 271
	60, 114, 264	9:2	14, 34 n. 108, 41, 56,
8:18–19	263, 264 n. 52		150, 151, 220, 272, 273
8:19	62		n. 67, 297
8:20	37 n. 115	9:4	14, 31 n. 99, 32 n. 103,
8:21	8, 66, 149, 161		104, 104 n. 43, 203, 220
8:21–23	149	9:4–5	14
8:21–30	67	9:5	14, 111, 161, 228
8:22	32 n. 102, 37 n. 116, 62, 66	9:6	31 n. 98, 32 n. 102, 229
8:23	66, 149	9:6–9	221
8:24	260	9:6–15	13, 21 n. 58, 28, 29, 31,
8:24–25	5		31 n. 98, 32, 40, 66, 67,
8:24–28	40		77, 162, 209, 220, 225,
8:24–30	7, 11		228, 229, 298
8:24–34	9, 13, 14	9:7	31 n. 98, 32 n. 102, 206,
8:24–36	36		222, 229
8:25	56 n. 172	9:7–8	229
8:25–26	62 n. 5	9:8	31 n. 98, 32 n. 102, 228,
8:26–27	17, 62		229, 282
8:28	116	9:8–9	229, 231
8:29	258	9:9	30, 31 n. 100, 56 n. 172,
8:30	56 n. 172, 109, 109 n. 60,		126, 212, 221, 224, 229
	112	9:9–10	209
8:31	8, 37, 37 n. 116, 62, 66,	9:10	221, 228
	72, 161	9:10–11	209 n. 91
8:32	66	9:10–12	34 n. 108, 218
8:32–34	7, 11	9:10–15	32 n. 103, 152, 221
8:33	56 n. 172, 62	9:11	220, 272, 297
8:33–34	62–63 n. 5	9:11–14	229

9:12	14, 268, 271, 272, 272 n. 66, 273	10:12	104, 133, 133 n. 100, 136, 152 n. 33
9:13	31 n. 98, 32 n. 102, 223, 223 n. 128	10:12–14	292
		10:13	8
9:14	31 n. 98, 32 n. 102, 219	10:14	12, 69 n. 19, 133, 133 n. 100
9:14–15	229	10:16	5, 7, 9, 14 n. 34, 34, 34 n. 108, 35 n. 110, 36, 37, 108, 109, 129 n. 91, 161, 232
9:15	31 n. 98, 31 n. 99, 32 n. 102, 32 n. 103, 206, 222, 222 n. 126, 223, 229		
10	6	10:17	7, 12, 14 n. 34, 37, 46
10:1	14, 34 n. 108, 36, 56 n. 172, 66, 104, 105, 105 n. 48, 106, 106 n. 49, 117, 151, 152, 161	10:17–18	12
		10:18	12, 47
		10:18–19	66
		10:18–44	12, 13, 37 n. 118, 40, 51, 54 n. 169
10:1–4	53		
10:1–5	8 n. 16, 14	10:19	12, 31 n. 98, 32 n. 102
10:1–15	7	10:20–44	8
10:1–17	13, 67, 104	10:25	87 n. 9
10:1–44	13, 14 n. 33, 15, 45, 292	10:25–43	265
10:2	12, 14, 21 n. 58, 216, 272, 297	10:25–44	87 n. 9
		10:30	87 n. 9
10:2–3	12, 14, 163	10:31	87 n. 9
10:2–4	51	10:33	87 n. 9
10:3	12, 14, 21 n. 58, 34 n. 108, 36, 62, 107, 107 n. 57, 223, 233 n. 138, 241, 256, 257, 257 n. 30	10:44	6

Ezra-Nehemiah 24 n. 73, 25, 25 n. 76, 28 n. 87, 30 n. 93, 30 n. 95, 32 n. 102, 37 n. 115, 37 n. 118, 59, 60, 61, 62, 63, 72, 78, 105 nn. 44 and 47, 110 n. 63, 112, 113, 119 n. 81, 126, 127 n. 90, 129, 129 n. 91, 130, 132, 133, 133 n. 100, 134, 134 n. 108, 136, 152 n. 33

10:5	21 n. 58, 258
10:6	14, 56 n. 172, 66, 117, 149, 161, 209, 220
10:6–8	203
10:7	131, 232
10:8	36, 104, 220, 232
10:9	5, 7, 8, 8 n. 16, 14 n. 34, 28, 44 n. 136, 56 n. 172, 72, 85, 102, 102 n. 37, 103, 103 n. 39, 128, 203
10:9–12	103 n. 41
10:9–15	9
10:9–17	120
10:9–44	14, 21 n. 58, 218
10:10	12, 31 n. 98, 32 n. 102, 34, 34 n. 108, 35 n. 110, 109, 161
10:10–11	163
10:11	36, 150, 216, 268, 272, 273, 297

Nehemiah 30 nn. 95–96, 31 n. 99, 32, 33, 34, 34 n. 109, 35, 37, 120 n. 83, 161, 162, 177, 204, 208, 209, 215, 217, 218, 220, 221, 223, 231, 232

1–6	40, 41
1–7	5, 36, 39, 42, 42 n. 132, 50, 51, 54, 61 n. 2, 65 n. 11
1–9	36
1–13	45, 47
1:1	2, 2 n. 2, 5, 36, 36 n. 113, 37, 61, 63 n. 7, 72, 261
1:1–2:8	54–55 n. 169, 60

Index of Primary Sources

1:1–6:19	16, 17 n. 41	2:17–4:17	66
1:1–7:5	1, 13 n. 32, 15, 26, 26 n. 80, 33, 34 n. 109, 45, 49, 54 n. 169, 55	2:18	37 n. 116, 62, 66, 69 n. 20
		2:19	2 n. 2, 62, 273
		2:19–20	62
1:1–7:5a	16, 70, 292	3:1–2	34 n. 108, 52, 56, 63 n. 5
1:1–7:5	66 n. 14	3:1–32	16 n. 39, 17 n. 41, 34 n. 108, 37 n. 118, 40, 51, 53, 60, 264, 265, 266, 267
1:1–7:72	16 n. 39, 42 n. 132, 60, 65, 66 n. 14, 85, 116, 288, 298		
1:1–13:3	63 n. 7	3:4	266, 266 n. 55
1:2	31 n. 98, 32 n. 102, 65 n. 10, 232	3:5	109 n. 60
		3:6	266
1:3	232	3:7	266
1:4	66, 117, 149, 228	3:8	266
1:5	31 n. 98, 32 n. 102, 111, 221, 221 n. 121, 228, 229	3:11	266
		3:12	266
1:5–11	29, 40, 66, 67, 77, 152, 162, 209, 225, 228, 229, 298	3:13	266
		3:14	266
		3:15	69 n. 19, 152
1:6	103, 151, 152	3:17	34 n. 109, 264, 266
1:6–9	34 n. 108	3:17–18	264
1:7	208, 209, 209 n. 91	3:18	264
1:8	231	3:23	266
1:8–10	229	3:26	37 n. 115, 101 n. 36, 102
1:9	109 n. 60	3:28	87
1:11	229	3:29	266
2:1	2, 2 n. 2, 5, 6, 36, 36 n. 113, 37, 46, 61, 63 n. 7, 72, 99	3:30	266, 266 n. 55
		3:31	35, 37 n. 115, 266, 266 n. 55
2:1–8	62, 231	3:32	35
2:3	69 n. 19	3:33	65 n. 10, 273
2:4–6	62	3:33–34	2 n. 2
2:5	69 n. 19, 249 n. 15	3:33–4:17	62
2:7–8	33, 66	3:33–4:23	60
2:7–10	289	3:37	31 n. 98, 32 n. 102
2:7–11	62	4:1	2 n. 2, 273
2:8	37 n. 116, 62, 66, 69 nn. 19–20, 127 n. 90	4:5	71 n. 23
		4:6	65 n. 10
2:9	33, 66	4:8	69 n. 20, 268
2:9–20	60	4:9	71 n. 23
2:9–6:15	62	4:10	71 n. 23
2:9–6:19	54 n. 169	4:11	71 n. 23
2:10	2 n. 2, 62, 103, 103 n. 38, 273	4:13	69 n. 20, 71 n. 23
		4:14	69 n. 20
2:11	66	4:15	71 n. 23
2:12	69 n. 20	4:16	71 n. 23
2:16	65 n. 10, 69 n. 20, 70 n. 23	4:19	69 n. 20

5:1	65 n. 10, 279	6:7	29 n. 89
5:1–5	276, 296	6:8	33
5:1–13	67, 104, 269, 270, 276, 278	6:9	71 n. 23
		6:10	36, 56, 56 n. 172
5:1–19	60	6:10–14	29 n. 89
5:2	250 n. 16, 277 n. 75	6:12	2 n. 2, 177, 208 n. 86, 273
5:2–4	277	6:14	2 n. 2, 40, 69 n. 20, 218, 273
5:3	250 n. 16, 277 n. 75		
5:3–4	276	6:15	37, 44 n. 136, 46, 72 n. 27, 99
5:4	277 n. 75		
5:5	269, 276, 277, 277 n. 75, 279, 288, 296	6:15–7:5a	73
		6:16	71 n. 23
5:7	53, 69 n. 20, 276, 276 n. 71, 277, 278	6:18	250 n. 16, 269 n. 59, 273
		6:18–19	289
5:7–13	120	6:19–22a	40 n. 126
5:8	65 n. 10, 277	7–9	40
5:8–13	22	7–13	41
5:10	53, 276, 276 n. 71, 277, 278	7:1	34 n. 108, 34 n. 109
		7:1–2	63 n. 5
5:10–11	279	7:1–3	69
5:11	276 n. 71, 277, 277 n. 74, 278	7:1–4	52, 66
		7:1–5	16, 54 n. 169, 70
5:12	260, 278, 292	7:1–10:44	8 n. 16
5:12b–13a	278	7:1–72	55
5:13	104, 111, 111 n. 67, 133, 133 n. 100, 136, 204, 278	7:2	69, 223
		7:3	69
5:14	3, 3 n. 2, 4 n. 5, 41, 47, 61, 63 n. 7, 66, 81 n. 1, 116, 260	7:4	69, 69 n. 19, 70, 71, 72
		7:4–5a	70
		7:4–5	33, 40 n. 126
5:14–19	16 n. 39, 53	7:4–10:40	68 n. 18
5:15	81 n. 1, 116, 250 n. 16, 260	7:5	69, 69 n. 20, 70, 72, 73, 130, 257 n. 29
5:16	71 n. 23		
5:17	65 n. 10	7:5a	69, 69 n. 20, 70
5:18	47, 81 n. 1, 116	7:5b	68, 70, 72 n. 27
5:19	40, 69 n. 20	7:5b–72a	16 n. 39, 36, 60, 69, 72
6:1	2 n. 2, 53	7:5b–10:40	40 n. 126, 68, 68 n. 18
6:1–2	273	7:6	69 n. 19, 103, 232
6:1–19	62, 66	7:6–68	55 n. 170
6:1–7:4	60	7:6–72a	16 n. 39, 34 n. 108, 62, 66 n. 13, 68, 69, 70, 72, 73, 203, 232, 245, 264, 265, 267, 268 n. 57, 292
6:1–7:5a	72		
6:2	2–3 n. 2		
6:2–9	40		
6:2b–12	65		
6:3	71 n. 23	7:6–72	33, 33, 37 n. 118, 49, 51, 55, 55 n. 170
6:5	2 n. 2		
6:6	65 n. 10, 257 n. 29	7:6–12:26	26, 26 n. 80
6:6–7	33, 62	7:6–13:3	45

Index of Primary Sources

7:6b	40		7:72b–8:18	1, 5, 11, 76 n. 32, **79–137**
7:7	260		7:72b–9:5	74, 76, 77, 291, 292
7:7–66	40		7:72b–10:40	1, 5, 6, 21, 29, 57, 59, 59 n. 1, 60, 65, 66, 67, **68–78,** 81, 85, 104, 107, 109, 116, 122, 123, 139, 141, 157, 177, 190, 252, 278, 291
7:7–72	40			
7:15	265 n. 54			
7:25–26	137			
7:39	71			
7:39–42	268 n. 57			
7:41–42	262 n. 47			
7:43	71, 263, 268 n. 57		7:72b–12:43	42 n. 132
7:44	268 n. 57		7:73	40
7:45	71, 268 n. 57		8	5, 6, 7, 7 nn. 13–14, 8, 9, 9 n. 20, 13 n. 32, 36 n. 114, 47
7:46	37 n. 115			
7:46–56	268 n. 57			
7:60	37 n. 115, 71		8–9	39, 68 n. 16
7:63	250 n. 16		8–10	7 n. 14, 9 n. 20, 11 n. 26, 21, 21 n. 58, 22, 39, 39 n. 122, 42, 42 nn. 130 & 132, 43, 49, 57, 61 n. 2, 68 n. 16, 69
7:64	72, 257 n. 29			
7:65	115, 249 n. 15			
7:66	71, 104, 133, 133 n. 100, 136			
7:67	71		8:1	8 n. 16, 20, 34, 35 n. 110, 36, 37, 70, 73, 76, 76 nn. 32–33, 141, 141 n. 6, 142, 145, 161, 189, 194, 248 n. 14, 287, 288, 293, 294, 296
7:69	71 n. 23, 81 n. 1, 115, 129 n. 91			
7:69–71	71 n. 23			
7:69–72	55 n. 170			
7:70	71 n. 23, 129 n. 91			
7:70–9:5	39		8:1–2	293
7:72	37 n. 115, 103		8:1–3	155, 233 n. 138, 297
7:72a	61, 71, 71 nn. 25–26, 72, 255, 267, 267 n. 56, 268		8:1–12	62, 68, 73, 76 nn. 32–33, 243, 245, 246, 293
7:72b	61, 68, 71, 72, 72 n. 27, 73, 75 n. 30, 141, 142, 143, 232, 255, 268 n. 57, 275, 293		8:1–18	5, 7, 8 n. 16, 12 n. 27, 13, 13, 14 n. 33, 15, 34, 40, 41, 42, 51, 55 n. 170, 62, 67
7:72b–8:1	8 n. 16		8:1–10:40	49, 67
7:72b–8:1a	70, 75		8:1–13:31	49
7:72b–8:3	**84–86, 99–109,** 293, 294		8:1b–8	75
7:72b–8:12	23 n. 66, 60, 74, 75, 76, 77, 78, 120, 142, 145, 292, 293, 295, 296		8:2	5, 7, 14 n. 34, 34, 35 n. 110, 36, 37, 52, 74, 76, 76 n. 32, 141, 141 n. 6, 143, 180, 189, 247, 249, 255, 275, 281, 293, 295
7:72–8:13a	6, 6 n. 11, 8 n. 16			
7:72–8:18	41, 70, 72, 76, 291			
7:72b	5, 6, 41, 44, 46		8:2–3	144, 247, 288, 296
7:72b–8:1	33, 235, 242		8:2–6	296
7:72b–8:8	11		8:2–12	288
7:72b–8:12	6, 24, 57, **79–122,** 248, 252, 288		8:3	20, 73, 74, 76, 76 n. 32, 141, 142, 143, 144, 145,

(8:3) 148, 148 n. 22, 149, 155, 156, 189, 194, 247, 249, 252, 288, 293, 294, 295
8:4 34, 35 n. 110, 142, 145, 152, 245, 252, 267, 295, 297
8:4–5 144
8:4–6 **86–89, 109–12,** 155, 293, 294
8:5 34, 35 n. 110, 142, 143, 145, 194, 294
8:5–7 162
8:6 142, 143, 145, 146, 146 n. 12, 154, 162, 172, 194, 239, 294, 297
8:7 76 n. 32, 140 n. 2, 142, 143, 145, 189, 244, 245, 293, 295
8:7–8 8 n. 16, **89–91, 112–15,** 143, 144, 162 n. 5, 242, 288, 293, 294, 296, 297, 297 n. 4
8:7–9 233 n. 138
8:8 20, 74, 76 n. 32, 142, 145, 155, 156, 184, 189, 245, 247, 293, 295
8:9 2, 4, 7, 34, 34 n. 108, 35 n. 110, 36, 47, 66 n. 14, 67, 70, 73, 74, 76, 76 n. 32, 142, 143, 146, 156, 189, 194, 196, 242, 243, 244, 246 n. 11, 250, 253, 293, 294, 295, 296
8:9–11 75, 162, 250, 275
8:9–12 **91–95, 115–20,** 293, 294, 297
8:10 31 n. 101, 74, 74 n. 29, 142, 146, 248, 250
8:11 74, 142, 143, 146, 194, 242, 250, 294, 297 n. 4
8:12 31 n. 101, 74, 74 n. 29, 75, 76, **119–20,** 143, 162, 177, 194, 293, 294, 295, 296
8:13 34, 34 n. 108, 35 n. 110, 37, 52, 53, 72, 73, 74, 75, 76, 76 nn. 32–33, **125,** **129–30,** 141, 142, 143, 144, 145, 155, 156, 297 n. 4, 161, 184, 189, 196, 242, 244, 245, 246, 246 n. 11, 293, 294, 295, 296, 297
8:13–14 233 n. 138
8:13–15 155, 297
8:13–18 20, 57, 60, 62, 68, 73, 74, 75, 76, 76 nn. 32–33, 77, 78, **122–37,** 142, 151, 248, 252, 281, 292, 293, 294, 295, 296
8:14 20, 37, 76 nn. 32–33, 141, 143, 178, 178 n. 31, 189, 242, 248, 248 n. 14, 249 n. 15, 287, 293, 294
8:14–15 75, **126, 130–32,** 162, 293
8:14–16 141, 297
8:14–17 34 n. 108
8:14–18 283
8:15 69, 74, 74 n. 29, 142, 146, 187, 232, 242, 249 n. 15, 252, 253 n. 22, 294, 295, 296
8:16 36, 56 n. 172, 74, 74 n. 29, 76, 76 n. 32, 105 n. 47, 141 n. 6, 252, 294, 295, 296
8:16–17 74, **127–28, 132–34,** 162, 293
8:16–18 75
8:17 29, 31 n. 101, 76, 76 n. 33, 141, 143, 148, 148 n. 22, 194, 194 n. 56, 203, 232, 246, 293, 294, 298
8:18 20, 53, 74, 76, 76 n. 32, **128–29, 134–35,** 141, 142, 143, 144, 145, 148, 148 n. 22, 149, 189, 233 n. 138, 247, 275, 293, 294
9 8, 9, 9 n. 20, 47 n. 147, 222 n. 125
9–10 21, 21 n. 60
9:1 37, 41, 72, 73, 74, 76, 85, 103, 104, 235, 242, 272 n. 65, 293

Index of Primary Sources

9:1–2	9, 75, 76, 275	9:7–8	**172–73**
9:1–3	**143–45, 149–52,** 239, 243, 247, 288, 291, 292, 293, 296, 297	9:8	**203–5,** 241, 242 n. 5, 251, 256, 286, 287, 294, 298
		9:9	**205,** 293, 294
9:1–4	53	9:9–15	**173–79, 205–10**
9:1–5	57, 60, 74, 77, 78, **139–56,** 161, 245, 292, 294, 295, 296	9:9–21	**173–85, 205–14**
		9:9–22	249
		9:10	**205–6,** 251, 294
9:1–37	57, 68, 75, 76	9:11	**206–7,** 273
9:1–10:40	60, 73, 75, 76, 81, 82 n. 3, 85, 125, 129, 139, 140, 141, 142, 151, 155, 248, 249, 252, 256, 288, 296	9:12	**207–8,** 273
		9:13	107 n. 57, **208,** 251, 294
		9:13–14	21, 62, 241, 248, 250, 287, 295, 298, 299
9:2	9, 31 n. 98, 32 n. 102, 33, 36, 41, 199, 232, 246, 249, 293, 295, 296	9:14	95, 107 n. 57, 130, **208–9,** 248 n. 13, 250, 287, 293, 294, 298
9:2–3	52, 53	9:15	**209–10,** 251, 294
9:3	20, 62, 74, 75, 85, 87, 107 n. 57, 108, 189, 233 n. 138, 239, 253, 293, 294, 295, 296	9:16	**210,** 248, 293, 294
		9:16–17b	144, 241, 249, 295
		9:16–21	**179–85, 210–14**
		9:17	31 n. 98, 32 n. 102, **211–12,** 251, 255, 294
9:4	80, 87, 90, 190, 237, 244, 245, 253, 293, 294, 295, 297	9:18	144, **212–13,** 241, 249, 294
		9:19	**213,** 255, 294
9:4–5	75, **145–49, 152–55,** 242, 245, 297 n. 4, 293, 296	9:20	**213–14,** 251, 294
		9:21	**214**
		9:22	**214–15,** 251, 294
9:5	74, 75, 77 n. 34, 87, 88, 90, 101, 101 n. 35, 162, 193, 237, 239, 244, 245, 253, 293, 294, 295, 297	9:22–25	**185–88, 214–16**
		9:22–31	**185–93, 214–20**
		9:23	109 n. 60, **215,** 247, 249, 294
9:5–37	34 n. 108, 40, 51, 77	9:23–25	249
9:5–10:1	239	9:24	**215–16,** 247, 249, 251, 272, 293, 294, 296
9:6	9 n. 17, 115, 141, 145 n. 11, 148 n. 19, **170–72, 200–2,** 293, 294	9:25	118, **216,** 253, 294, 295
		9:26	21, 29, 62, 107 n. 57, 144, **217–18,** 241, 242, 248, 249, 293, 294, 298
9:6–8	**170–73, 200–5**		
9:6–31	**170–93, 200–20**		
9:6–37	1, 9, 21, 21 n. 60, 28, 29, 31, 31 n. 98, 32 n. 102, 42, 60, 67, 68, 74, 75, 76, 77, 78, 104, 139, 141, 149, 152, 153, 155, **157–233,** 238, 241, 242 n. 5, 287, 292, 296, 297 n. 4, 298	9:26–31	**188–93, 217–20,** 298
		9:27	**218–19,** 251, 293, 294
		9:28	34 n. 108, 144, 152, **219,** 241, 249, 293, 294
		9:29	62, 107 n. 57, 144, **219,** 241, 242, 248, 251, 289, 293, 294, 298
9:6–10:40	77, 291, 292	9:29–30	**219–20,** 241, 248, 249, 295
9:7	115, **202–3,** 293, 294		

9:30	29, 144, **220,** 242, 247, 272, 293, 294, 296, 297, 298, 299	10:2–29	37 n. 118
		10:3–9	297
		10:4	87 n. 9
9:31	21, 31 n. 98, 32 n. 102, **220,** 228, 255, 294	10:8	87 n. 9
		10:10	140
9:32	21, 29, 30 n. 96, 31 n. 98, 32 n. 102, 68 n. 17, 103, 103 n. 39, 105 n. 44, 111, **221–22,** 241, 242, 244, 246 n. 11, 287, 293, 294, 297	10:10–11	145
		10:10–14	90, 140 n. 2, **244–45, 263–64,** 297, 297 n. 4
		10:11	90
		10:12	90
		10:13	90
9:32–37	**193–99, 220–25,** 242	10:14	90
9:33	76, 144, **222–23,** 241, 294	10:15–28	87 n. 9, **245, 264–67,** 297
9:33–35	289		
9:34	21 n. 62, 31 n. 98, 62, 68 n. 17, 107 n. 57, **223,** 241, 242, 243, 244, 246 n. 11, 248, 293, 294, 298	10:17	5
		10:19	87 n. 9
		10:21	87 n. 9
		10:23	87 n. 9
9:35	31 n. 98, 144, **223–24,** 251, 294	10:25	87 n. 9
		10:26	87 n. 9
9:36	76, **224,** 241, 293, 294	10:28	87 n. 9, 106 n. 49
9:36–37	298	10:29	36, 37 n. 115, 67 n. 15, 71 n. 25, 105, 105 n. 44, 106, 106 n. 49, 107 n. 57, 129, 130, 144, 144 nn. 9–10, 151, 175, 192, 206, 208, 293, 294, 296, 297 n. 4, 298
9:37	76, 77 n. 34, 141, **224,** 238, 239 n. 3, 241, 254, 289, 293, 294, 297, 297 n. 4		
10	8, 9, 68, 68 n. 16		
10–13	39, 40		
10:1	21, 21 n. 59, 68, 68 nn. 16–17, 76, 77 n. 34, 297 n. 4, 162, 173, **241–42, 255–58,** 293, 294, 298	10:29–30	62, 75, 77, 233 n. 138, **245–48, 267–70,** 292, 293, 295, 298, 299
		10:29–40	1, 9, 20, 61, 67, 77, 78, 230, 232, **245–55, 267–86,** 295, 296
10:1–27	40		
10:1–28	29, 75, 77, 90, **241–45, 255–67,** 292, 296, 299	10:30	21, 107 n. 57, 178, 178 n. 31, 190, 293, 297, 298
10:1–40	34 n. 108, 39, 41, 42, 51, 57, 60, 67 n. 15, 68, 75, 76, 77, 77 n. 34, 78, 139, 141, 154, 155, 162, 232, **235–89,** 292, 294, 296	10:31	9, 67 n. 15, 175, 186, 206, 296, 297, 298
		10:31–32	**271–79**
		10:31–40	21, 21 n. 60, 68, 75, 77, **248–55, 270–86,** 292, 295, 298
10:1–13:29a	40		
10:2	2, 73, 81, 81 n. 1, 115, 116, **243–44, 260–61,** 297	10:32	67 n. 15, 109, 109 n. 60, 116, 175, 178, 186, 206, 293, 296, 297, 298
10:2–9	87 n. 9, **244, 261–63**		
10:2–27	68	10:33	56 n. 172, 193, 294
10:2–28	34 n. 108, 52, **242–45, 258–67,** 295	10:33–40	35, 36, 67, **279–86**

10:34	56 n. 172, 71 n. 23, 178, 193, 294	11:9	69 n. 19
		11:10–18	34 n. 109
10:35	56 n. 172, 62, 67 n. 15, 68 n. 17, 107 n. 57, 109, 109 n. 60, 131, 132, 233 n. 138, 293, 294, 297, 297 n. 4	11:10–24	69 n. 21
		11:11	35, 56 n. 172, 87 n. 9
		11:16	35, 56 n. 172, 62
		11:18	52, 56, 63 n. 5, 66, 69 n. 19, 73
10:36	30 n. 96, 109, 109 n. 60, 193, 294	11:20	129
		11:20–24	69, 70
10:36–40	67 n. 15, 297	11:21	37 n. 115
10:37	56 n. 172, 62, 107 n. 57, 109, 109 n. 60, 131, 132, 193, 233 n. 138, 293, 294	11:21–24	69 n. 21
		11:22	35, 56 n. 172
		11:23	256
10:38	56 n. 172, 67 n. 15, 109, 109 n. 60, 294	11:25–36	37 n. 118, 40, 68, 69 n. 21, 70, 73
10:38–40	67 n. 15, 297, 297 n. 4	12:1	49, 262
10:39	56 n. 172, 193, 294	12:1–7	261, 262, 262 n. 49
10:39–40	68 n. 17	12:1–26	3 n. 2, 34 n. 109, 36, 37 n. 118, 43, 49, 69 n. 21, 73
10:40	21 n. 60, 56 n. 172, 61, 68, 71, 71 n. 25, 72, 75 n. 30, 85, 103, 109, 109 n. 60, 141, 193, 293, 294, 297	12:2	262
		12:3	262
		12:6–7	262 n. 49, 263 n. 50
		12:7	69 n. 21, 87 n. 9
11	68	12:8	152, 263
11–13	42, 42 n. 132	12:8–9	264 n. 52
11:1	33, 40 n. 126, 52, 56, 61, 63 n. 5, 66, 68, 68 n. 17, 69, 69 nn. 19–20, 70, 71, 71 n. 25, 73, 109 n. 60, 267	12:10	261
		12:10–11	2 n. 2, 3 n. 2
		12:10–25	40
		12:12	69 n. 21, 129 n. 91
		12:12–21	261, 262, 262 n. 49
11:1–2	16 n. 39, 68, 68 n. 17, 69, 69 n. 20, 70, 72, 141	12:13	262
		12:14	262
11:1–3	71	12:15	262
11:1–20	69 n. 21, 73	12:19–21	262 n. 49, 263 n. 50
11:1–24	267	12:21	87 n. 9
11:1–36	232	12:22	2 n. 2, 30, 69 n. 21
11:1–12:26	49, 51, 60, 72, 73, 292	12:22–23	3 n. 2, 257 n. 29
11:1–12:43	60, 61, 61 n. 2, 65, 73	12:23	69 n. 21, 129 n. 91, 264 n. 52
11:1–13:31	116		
11:2	148 n. 21	12:24	140 n. 2, 263, 264 n. 52
11:3	37 n. 115, 71, 71 n. 25, 129	12:24–25	263 n. 52
		12:26	2, 4, 34, 35 n. 110, 40, 47, 66 n. 14, 69 n. 21, 73, 81, 81 n. 1, 116, 129, 261, 264 n. 52
11:3–9	37 n. 115		
11:3–19	69, 70		
11:3–24	37 n. 118, 40, 68		
11:3–36	68, 69 n. 21, 73	12:27	31 n. 101, 62, 109 n. 60, 119 n. 81
11:3–12:26	34 n. 108, 45		

12:27–43	16, 16 n. 39, 40, 41, 44 n. 135, 45, 46, 49, 51, 55, 60, 61, 62, 63 n. 7, 66, 67, 72, 73, 136, 292	13:2	102, 103 n. 38, 209
		13:3	55, 62, 107 n. 57, 151, 233 n. 138, 257 n. 30
		13:4	35, 43 n. 135, 56, 56 n. 172
12:27–13:3	49		
12:27–13:31	1, 26, 26 n. 80, 33, 65 n. 10	13:4–5	67 n. 15, 285, 289
		13:4–14	16 n. 39
12:28	104, 104 n. 43	13:4–31	1, 16, 16 n. 39, 45, 47, 49, 60, 63 n. 7, 77, 230, 257, 270, 271 n. 63, 288, 289, 292, 298, 299
12:30	52, 62, 63 n. 5		
12:31	69 n. 20, 116		
12:31–32	16, 69 n. 20		
12:31–36	73	13:5	286
12:31–43	66 n. 14, 73	13:6	2 n. 2, 3 n. 2, 4 n. 5, 31 n. 100, 61, 63 n. 7, 231 n. 137, 298
12:32–42	37 n. 118		
12:33	66 n. 14, 116, 129		
12:36	2, 4, 35 n. 110, 66 n. 14, 109, 116, 129	13:6–7	3, 46, 289
		13:7	4 n. 5, 35, 56, 56 n. 172, 128
12:37	34, 69 n. 19, 101 n. 36, 102, 152		
		13:9	35, 56, 56 n. 172
12:37–40	16, 69 n. 20	13:10–13	270, 286, 297
12:38	2, 4, 116	13:10–14	67 n. 15
12:39	102	13:11	35, 56, 56 n. 172, 113, 270, 286, 286 n. 92, 297
12:40	35, 56, 56 n. 172, 61		
12:43	16, 31, 31 n. 97, 31 n. 101, 119 n. 81, 120, 120 n. 83, 134	13:12	109, 109 n. 60, 286
		13:13	261
		13:14	35, 40, 53, 56, 56 n. 172
12:44	31 n. 101, 43 n. 135, 55, 61, 62, 63 n. 7, 67 n. 15, 107 n. 57, 119 n. 81, 233 n. 138, 257 n. 30, 285	13:15	43 n. 135, 109 n. 60, 275
		13:15–16	275
		13:15–22	16 n. 39, 67 n. 15, 178, 270, 274 n. 68, 275, 297
12:44–46	40	13:15–31	43 n. 135
12:44–47	285	13:16	109 n. 60, 126, 275
12:44–13:3	60, 63 n. 7, 292	13:18	34 n. 108, 69 n. 19, 109 n. 60, 223 n. 128
12:44–13:4	61		
12:44–13:14	43 n. 135	13:19	249 n. 15
12:44–13:31	42 n. 132, 44 n. 135, 60, 61, 61 n. 2, 65, 65 n. 11, 67, 67 n. 15	13:21–24	273
		13:21–27	273
		13:22	40, 52, 249 n. 15
12:45	285	13:23	43 n. 135, 65 n. 10
12:45–46	27	13:23–25	9
12:47	36, 40, 43, 285	13:23–27	33, 67, 270, 271, 297
13	68 n. 16	13:23–29	67 n. 15
13:1	20, 43 n. 135, 63 n. 7, 104, 108, 130, 249 n. 15, 257 n. 29	13:23–31	16 n. 39
		13:24	177, 208 n. 86
		13:25	271, 272, 273, 273 n. 67
13:1–3	34 n. 108, 41, 67 n. 15, 150	13:26	28, 66
		13:28	2 n. 2, 273, 289

Index of Primary Sources

13:29		40	28:8		119
13:29b–31		40	33:6		201
13:30		62, 151	33:19		201
13:30–31		67, 289	34:1		111
13:31	40, 67 n. 15, 282, 282 n. 84, 283, 297		35:2		155 n. 42
			35:13		150
13:44		285	37:28		212
			37:33		212, 219
Esther		118, 118 n. 79	37:39		119
1:8		215	40:3		155 n. 43
2:9		118	41		153
3:12		260	41:2		123
4:1		150	41:3		201
4:3		150, 150 n. 26	41:14	101 n. 35, 146, 147, 153, 153 n. 34, 154, 154 n. 38, 239	
6:2		130			
8:8		260			
8:10		260	44:21		155 n. 43
9:5		215	44:26		155 n. 42
9:19		118	47:4		202
9:22		118	48:2		155 n. 43
9:31		150	48:9		155 n. 43
			48:15		155 n. 43
Job			50:3		155 n. 43
1:22		256	50:17		217 n. 114, 218
2:10		256	66:8		155 n. 43
2:12		150	67:7		155 n. 43
30:31		117	66:17		154
33:4		201	71:20		201
			72:19		153, 154, 154 n. 40
Psalms		111	74:22		155 n. 42
3–41		153	76:11		155 n. 43
3:8		155 n. 42	78	207, 225, 226, 227, 227 n. 132, 228 n. 134	
7:7		155 n. 42			
8:2		270, 270 n. 62	78:5		227
8:10		270, 270 n. 62	78:8		217, 223
9:10		212	78:8–11		227
9:20		155 n. 42	78:11		211
10:12		155 n. 42	78:12		205 n. 76, 227
16:7		111	78:13		206
17:13		155 n. 42	78:14		207
18:32		155 n. 43	78:15		209
19:11		118	78:17		217
20:6		155 n. 43	78:17–18		227
20:8		155 n. 43	78:20		209
22:23		151	78:20–22		227
27:1		119	78:21–22		227
28:2		111	78:24		209

78:30–41	227	106:7	130, 205 n. 76, 211, 217
78:31	227	106:13–15	227
78:32	211, 256	106:17–18	227
78:32–34	227	106:22	211
78:40	217	106:23	227
78:42–51	227	106:33	217
78:43	205	106:40–47	228
78:56	217	106:43	217, 219
78:56–66	227	106:44	217
78:59–64	228	106:46–47	228
78:60–64	227	106:47	155 n. 43
78:67–72	227	106:48	101 n. 35, 111, 111 n. 66, 146, 147, 153, 153 n. 34, 154, 154 n. 38, 239
80:19	201		
82:8	155 n. 42		
85:7	201	107:6	218
86:10	200, 200 n. 60	107:28	218
86:15	211, 211 n. 96	109:11	276 n. 71
89:23	276 n. 71	110:6	224
89:53	111, 111 n. 66, 153	113:1	155 n. 44
90–106	153	113:4	154
90:2	101 n. 35, 153	113:5	155 n. 43
90:17	155 n. 43	115:3	155 n. 43
92:14	155 n. 43	115:18	147
94:14	212	116:5	155 n. 43
94:23	155 n. 43	117:1	155 n. 44
95:7	155 n. 43	119:1	269
96:2	154	119:34	113
96:6	119, 119 n. 80	119:73	113
98:3	155 n. 43	119:125	113
99:5	155 n. 43	119:130	110
99:8	155 n. 43	119:137	208
99:9	155 n. 43	119:142	208
100:4	154	119:156	213
103:1–2	155	122:9	155 n. 43
103:8	211, 211 n. 96	123:2	155 n. 43
103:17	101 n. 35, 153	130:4	211
104:1	155	132:8	155 n. 42
105	207, 225, 226, 227, 227 n. 132	134:1	111
		134:1–2	155
105:5	211	134:2	111
105:7	155 n. 43	135	225, 226, 227, 227 n. 132
105:9	269	135:1	155 n. 44
105:27	205	135:2	155 n. 43
105:39	207	135:4	202
105:40–41	209	135:5	270
106	153, 214 n. 103, 225, 226, 227, 227 n. 132, 228 n. 134	135:9	205
		135:11	215

Index of Primary Sources

135:12	215	**Isaiah**			109
135:19	111	5:2			256
135:20	111	5:25			16 n. 40
136	225, 226, 227, 227 n. 132	6:1–8:18			16 n. 40
		6:1–9:6			
136:1	155 n. 44	6:10			216
136:21	215	6:13			150 n. 29
138:7	201	8:18			205
143:10	214, 214 n. 104	9:12			256
143:11	201	9:17			256
145:1	154	9:21			256
146:1	155 n. 44	10:4			256
146:4	150	12:3			102 n. 37
146:6	201, 201 n. 62	13:4			201 n. 61
147	155 n. 44	14:1			202
147:1	155 n. 43	20:3			205
147:5	270	22:13			118
147:7	155 n. 43	23:18			116
148:4	200	24:2			276 n. 71
		24:13			283 n. 86
Proverbs		25:5			101 n. 35
3:27	277 n. 73	36:1–37:38			222
8:9	105 n. 46	37:16			200, 200 n. 60
10:29	119	37:20			200, 200 n. 60
12:8	114	41:2			64 n. 8
16:20	130 n. 92	41:8			202
16:22	114	41:8–9			202
17:10	105 n. 46	41:17			212
17:24	105 n. 46	41:20			130
19:11	114	41:25			64 n. 8
20:6	203	42:5			205 n. 74
22:26	276 n. 71	42:6			205
28:2	105 n. 46	42:16			212
28:7	105 n. 46, 106	43:16			206
28:9	108	44:1–2			202
28:11	105 n. 46	45:11–12			205 n. 74
29:1	210	45:12			201
		45:13			24, 64 n. 8. 205
Ecclesiastes		45:25			151
2:24	118	48:18			223
3:13	118	49:23			112, 112 n. 68
5:19	118	50:1			276, 276 n. 71, 277
8:15	118	51:1–2			202
9:7	118	56:1–8			274
		58:3			150
Song of Songs		58:5			150, 150 n. 26
5:16	118	58:13–14			274

63:7–64:11	214 n. 103	30:11	220, 225
63:10	217	31:32	205 n. 76
63:11	213, 213 n. 103	31:36–37	151
63:12	206	31:40	116
65:15	269 n. 59	32:10–11	237 n. 1, 258, 260
		32:11	258 n. 33
Jeremiah		32:12	257
1:18	221	32:14	258, 258 n. 33, 260
2:7	224, 224 n. 130	32:17	200
2:26	221	32:17–25	225, 228, 229
2:30	218, 225	32:18	111, 221, 221 n. 121, 228
3:10	256	32:20	206, 228
4:4	224	32:20–21	205
5:1	203	32:24	228
5:18	220, 225	32:25	229
5:19	224	32:44	258, 260
5:28	216	34:8–16	278 n. 76
6:26	150	34:13	205 n. 76
7:7	101 n. 35, 153 n. 37	34:14	278 n. 76
7:22	205 n. 76	36:6	149
7:25	205 n. 76	36:9	149
7:26	210, 225	36:10	108, 122
8:2	202	36:13	108
11:4	205 n. 76	36:21	108
11:7	205 n. 76	40:10	283 n. 86
11:10	211, 225	40:12	283 n. 86
12:1	222	41:1–3	149 n. 24
13:10	211, 225	42:3	207 n. 83
14:11–12	149	44:10	269
15:10	276 n. 71	44:17	221
17:19–27	274 n. 68	44:21	221
17:23	210, 225	44:22	224
18:18	112	44:23	269
19:15	210	46:28	220, 225
21:12	224	51:11	24, 64 n. 8
23:2	224	52:12	149 n. 24
23:22	224		
25:5	153 n. 37, 224	**Lamentations**	
25:11–12	64 n. 8	2:10	150, 150 n. 25
26:3	224	3:5	221
26:4	269		
26:20–23	218	**Ezekiel**	
28:5	110	1:11	224
28:6	204 n. 73	1:23	224
28:11	110	7:26	112
29:10	64 n. 8, 204 n. 73	11:13	152 n. 32
29:10–12	25	11:15	202, 203 n. 65

Index of Primary Sources

11:16–21	202	9:4	111, 152, 221, 221 n. 121, 228
11:20	270 n. 61		
17:16	269	9:4–19	152, 220, 225, 228, 228 n. 135, 229
17:18	269		
17:19	269	9:5	217
18:19	270 n. 61	9:6	222
20:1–31	225	9:7	222, 222 n. 127, 229
20:5	202	9:8	222
20:8	217, 225	9:9	211, 217
20:11	219, 225	9:10	269
20:13	217, 219, 225	9:11	247 n. 12, 269
20:16	274	9:12	204 n. 73, 223 n. 128
20:17	220, 225	9:13	223 n. 128
20:19	270 n. 61	9:14	222, 222 n. 127, 229
20:21	217, 219, 225	9:15	206, 228
20:23	210 n. 93	9:16–19	229
20:24	274	9:18	213
20:25	208	9:20	152
20:28	210, 210 n. 93, 225	10:1	15 n. 36
20:36	205 n. 76	10:4	149
20:42	210, 210 n. 93	10:6	224
22:8	274	11:3	215
22:26	274	11:16	215
23:35	217, 217 n. 114	11:36	215
23:38	274	12:1	130
27:30	150	12:2	150
27:30–31	150 n. 25		
33:24	202, 203 n. 65	**Hosea**	
33:25–29	202	6:2	201
35:12	213	7:10	256
36:7	210 n. 93		
36:27	270 n. 61	**Joel**	
36:35	216 n. 113	2:13	211, 211 n. 96
37:24	270 n. 61		
39:23	218, 218 n. 117	**Amos**	
40:1	100	4:4	285
44:30	283, 284	6:10	92 n. 16
45:25	135 n. 109	8:1–2	283 n. 86
47:12	216, 216 n. 113	8:3	92 n. 16
47:14	210 n. 93	8:5	274
		9:11–15	25
Daniel	15 n. 36		
2:20	101 n. 35	**Jonah**	
5:12	203, 203 n. 67	3:5	150
8:4	215	3:6	150
8:16–17	105 n. 45	4:2	211, 211 n. 96
9:3	150, 150 n. 26, 152, 228	4:6	120 n. 83

Micah		14:18	130
2:1	277 n. 73	14:19	130
Nahum		14:20	116
1:7	119	14:21	116
2:2–3:19	222		
3:3	224	**Malachi**	
		1:13	109 n. 61, 221 n. 123
Habakkuk		2:6	208
2:20	92 n. 16	2:7	112
		3:10	109 n. 61, 285
Zephaniah		3:22	209
1:5	202		
1:7	92 n. 16	**Sirach**	
		5:1	277 n. 73
Haggai	47, 48	14:11	277 n. 73
1:1	41	24:23–29	137
1:2	48	44:20	203, 204
1:12	41		
1:14	41	**1 and 2 Esdras**	35
2:1–9	27 n. 87		
2:2	41	**1 Esdras**	6, 6 nn. 10–11, 7, 7 n. 13,
2:4	41		8, 23, 23 n. 66, 24, 25, 25 n. 76, 80
2:5	256	1–10	36
2:10	149	1:1–58	25
2:11	112	3:1–5:6	6 n. 11, 25
2:20	149	5:7–9:59	25
2:20–23	27 n. 87, 41	5:45	71 n. 26
2:21–22	47	5:46	102 n. 37
2:23	47	8:1–9:55	6, 8 n. 16
		9:16–17	7
Zechariah	47, 48	9:37	7
1:4	224	9:38	102 n. 37
1:7	149	9:44	80
2:13	92 n. 16	9:48	80, 81 n. 1, 102 n. 37
3:1–5	41	9:49	80
3:6–9	41	9:52	81
4:6–10	27 n. 87, 41		
4:12–14	41	**2 Esdras**	
6:9–15	41	1–13	36
6:12–13	27 n. 87, 47	1–23	35
7:3	149	18:9	80
7:5	149	18:10	81
7:8–14	220	19:4	140
7:9	220	19:6	9 n. 17, 148, 161
7:12	220	19:8	161
8:19	149	19:17	161
14:16	130	19:19	161

Index of Primary Sources

19:22	161	20:17–18	260 n. 42
20:1	237	25:18–19	260 n. 42
20:9	237	28:15–16	260 n. 42
20:19	238	30	3 n. 2
		30:18	2 n. 2
Tobit	15 n. 36	30:29	2 n. 2
1:1–2	15 n. 36	30:30	2 n. 2
1:3–2:14	15 n. 36	43:12	260 n. 42
3:1–6	15 n. 36	46:12–15	260 n. 42

1 Maccabees   **Josephus,** *Antiquities*

2:52	203	11.120–158	6 n. 10
		11.154–158	9
CAP (Cowley, *Aramaic Papyri*)		11.297–301	3 n. 2
1:8–11	260 n. 42	11.297–328	3 n. 2
2:19–21	260 n. 42	11.309–311	3 n. 2
5:15–19	260 n. 42		
6:17–21	260 n. 42	**Eusebius,** *Hist. eccl.*	
8:29–34	260 n. 42	4.26.14	35
9:17–22	260 n. 42	6.25.2	35, 36 n. 112
10:22	260 n. 42		
11:10–14	260 n. 42	**Talmud**	
13	259 n. 37	*b. B. Bat.* 15a	35 n. 111
13:17–18	259, 260	*b. Sanh.* 93b	35 n. 111
13:18–20	260 n. 42		
14:12–13	260 n. 42	**Dead Sea Scrolls**	
15:37–39	260 n. 42	1QS	59 n. 1
17	113 n. 71	4QSam^a	25 n. 78
17:3	113, 113 n. 71	4QSam^b	25 n. 78
18:4–5	260 n. 42		

Index of Modern Authors

Abba, R. 112 n. 69
Ackroyd, P. R. 28 n. 88
Ahlemann, F. 8 n. 15
Albright, W. F. 4 n. 6
Alter, R. 82 n. 3
Anderson, C. R. 184 n. 39, 200 n. 59, 206 n. 79, 213 n. 100
Avigad, N. 258 n. 36
Baltzer, K. 21, 21 nn. 57–58, 59 n. 1
Barr, J. 256 nn. 25–26
Batten, L. W. 24 n. 72, 30 n. 93, 68 n. 16, 69 nn. 20, 123 n. 84, 133 n. 101
Begrich, J. 162 n. 7
Bickerman, E. J. 36 n. 113
Blenkinsopp, J. 5 n. 9, 10 n. 23, 11 n. 25, 19 n. 48, 27 n. 86, 30 nn. 92–93, 59 n. 1, 64 nn. 8–9, 68 n. 18, 69, 69 nn. 20–21, 70, 71 n. 26, 76 n. 32, 81 n. 1, 87 n. 8, 131 n. 97, 134 n. 107, 147 nn. 16–17, 150 n. 28, 153 n. 36, 161 n. 2, 201 n. 63, 213 n. 100, 258 n. 35, 261 nn. 45–46, 263 n. 52, 271 n. 63,
Borowski, O. 283 n. 86
Braun, R. 27 n. 86
Brichto, H. C. 247–48 n. 12
Bright, J. 3 n. 3
Brin, G. 283 n. 88
Cazelles, H. 4 n. 27, 20 n. 51, 27 n. 86
Childs, B. S. 38, **41**, 41 n. 129, 212 n. 99
Chrostowski, W. 195 n. 57
Clines, D. J. A. 9 n. 20, 20 n. 56, 30 n. 93, 36 n. 113, 68 n. 16, 69 n. 20, 76 n. 32, 100 n. 29, 101 n. 33, 150 n. 28, 163 n. 9, 215 n. 110, 263–64 n. 52, 271 n. 63, 288 n. 94
Cody, A. 115 n. 75
Couroyer, B. 210 n. 94

Cowley, A. E. 2 n. 2, 113 n. 71
Cross, F. M. 4 n. 4, 23 n. 66, 25, 25 n. 78, 258 n. 35, 259 nn. 36 and 39, 260 n. 40, 261 n. 43
Curtis, E. L. 24 n. 73
da Deliceto, G. 36 n. 113
Dentan, R. C. 212 n. 97
Di Lella, A. A. 228 n. 135, 277 n. 73
Dommershausen, W. 281 n. 82
Driver, G. R. 170 n. 4
Driver, S. R. 7 n. 14, 108 n. 58
Eerdmans, B. D. 20 n. 55
Eichrodt, W. 100 n. 31
Eissfeldt, O. 16 n. 40
Elliger, K. 163 n. 7
Emerton, J. A. 4 n. 5
Eskenazi, T. C. 24 n. 71, 25, 25 nn. 75–76, 38, 45 n. 139, **48–56**, 57, 73 n. 28, 75 n. 31, 162, 162 n. 4, 239 n. 3, 243 n. 7, 257 n. 31, 271 n. 63, 291 n. 1, 292 nn. 2–3
Falk, Z. W. 114 n. 73
Fensham, F. C. 5, 5 n. 8, 30 n. 93, 76 n. 32, 80 n. 1, 133 n. 102, 140 n. 5, 227 n. 133
Finegan, J. 37 n. 117, 100 n. 30
Fishbane, M. 20 n. 56, 114 n. 74, 131 n. 97, 132 n. 99, 288 n. 94
Fitzmyer, J. A. 10 n. 21
Galling, K. 110 n. 62
Gertner, M. 115 n. 75
Gilbert, M. 163 n. 10, 169 nn. 20–21, 186 n. 44, 189 n. 51, 200 n. 59, 208 n. 88, 209 n. 90, 213 n. 102, 214 n. 107, 216 n. 113, 217 n. 114, 222 n. 124, 223 n. 129, 228 n. 135
Giraudo, C. 173 n. 29
Green, A. R. W. 3 n. 2
Grol, H. W. M. van 13–14 n. 33

Index of Modern Authors

Gunneweg, A. H. J. 30 n. 93, 68 n. 18, 110 n. 62, 134 n. 107, 216 n. 111
Guthrie, H. H. 149 n. 23
Haag, H. 257 n. 28
Halpern, B. 44 n. 138, 56 n. 173
Haran, M. 24 n. 73, 280 n. 80
Hartman, L. F. 80, 228 n. 135
Hasel, G. F. 256 n. 26
Hensley, L. V. 10 n. 21
Hoglund, K. 4 n. 4, 20 n. 50
Holladay, W. L. 274 n. 68
Holmgren, F. C. 242 n. 5
Hoonacker, A. van 4 n. 7
Houtman, C. 20 n. 55, 131 n. 96
In der Smitten, W. Th. 110 n. 62, 115 n. 76, 133 n. 103
Irvine, S. A. 16 n. 40
Jagersma, H. 285 n. 91
Japhet, S. 23, 23 nn. 67–68, 24 n. 74, 25, 25 nn. 77–78, 26, 26 n. 84, 27 n. 86, 28 n. 87, 29 n. 91, 37 n. 115, 38, **44–48**, 53 n. 168, 61, 61 n. 3, 119 n. 80, 202 n. 64, 216 n. 111, 220 n. 120, 280 n. 81
Jensen, J. 16 n. 40
Jepsen, A. 262 n. 48
Kaiser, O. 151 n. 30
Kalimi, I. 23 n. 70, 21 n. 59
Kalluveettil, P. 21 n. 59
Kapelrud, A. S. 6 n. 10, 8 n. 14, 10 n. 22, 18, 18 n. 46, 23
Kaufmann, Y. 112 n. 69
Kegel, M. 20 n. 51, 57, 57 n. 174
Kellermann, U. 17, 17 n. 44, 18, 20 nn. 52–53, 21 n. 58, 59 n. 1, 66 n. 12, 69 n. 20, 110 n. 62
Kidner, D. 239 n. 3
Klein, R. W. 2 n. 2, 16 n. 39
Knohl, I. 96 n. 22
Koch, K. 8 n. 15, 134 n. 108
Koehler, L. 114 n. 73
Kooij, A. van der 114 n. 72
Kraeling, E. G. 259 n. 36
Kraemer, D. 30, 30 n. 84, 33, 34, 34 nn. 105–9, 35, 35 n. 110
Kraus, H.-J. 97 n. 25, 153 n. 35
Kugel, J. L. 163 n. 7

Kutsch, E. 116 n. 77, 135 n. 110,
Le Déaut, R. 113 n. 72
Levin, S. 115 n. 75
Levine, B. 225 n. 131
Liver, J. 280 nn. 79 & 81
Macdonald, J. 221 n. 122
MacRae, G. W. 97 n. 25
Madsen, A. A. 24 n. 73
Margalith, O. 20 n. 50
McCarthy, D. J. 21, 21 n. 57, 22, 22 nn. 61 and 64, 59 n. 1, 257 n. 27
McConville, J. G. 134 n. 108
McFall, L. 3 n. 2
McKane, W. 130 n. 92
Meyers, C. L. 149 n. 24
Meyers, E. M. 149 n. 24
Milgrom, J. 96 n. 22, 116 n. 77
Moore, C. A. 118 n. 79
Morgenstern, J. 37 n. 117, 100 n. 28
Moscati, S. 257 n. 32
Mowinckel, S. 4 n. 7, 6 n. 10, 7 n. 13, 8 n. 15, 14, 15 nn. 35–36, 16 n. 38, 17, 17 n. 45, 18, 20 n. 51, 100, 100 n. 28, 102 n. 37, 117 n. 78, 131 n. 96, 258 n. 33
Muddiman, J. 149 n. 23
Mullen, E. T., Jr. 201 n. 61
Myers, J. M. 30 n. 93, 76 n. 32, 87 n. 10, 123 n. 84, 134 n. 106, 140 n. 5, 147 n. 17, 161 n. 2, 200 n. 59
Neufeld, E. 277 n. 74, 279 n. 78
Newsome, J. D. 27 n. 86
North, R. 276 n. 70, 279 n. 78
Noth, M. 8 n. 14, 11 n. 26, 12 n. 28, 17, 17 n. 43, 18, 20 n. 54, 23, 95–96 n. 22, 116 n. 77
Olmstead, A. T. 19–20 n. 49
Otzen, B. 258 n. 34
Pavlovsky, V. 4 n. 5
Pohlmann, K.-F. 6 n. 11, 102 n. 37, 110 n. 62, 117 n. 78
Polzin, R. 25, 25 n. 79, 26, 26 n. 80
Porten, B. 259 n. 36
Rad, G. von 20 n. 54, 97 n. 25, 226 n. 132, 229 n. 136, 233 n.139
Rehm, M. D. 112 n. 69
Reich, N. J. 19 n. 49

Rendtorff, R. 110 n. 62
Rowley, H. H. 2 n. 2, 4 n. 7
Rubenstein, J. L. 96 n. 25, 131 n. 95, 132 n. 99
Rudolph, W. 4 n. 5, 5 n. 9, 8 n. 15, 12 n. 27, 18, 18 n. 47, 30 n. 93, 36 n. 113, 76 n. 32, 101 n. 36, 117 n. 78, 133 n. 104, 140 n. 1, 146 n. 13, 147 n. 18, 150 n. 27, 161 n. 3, 163 nn. 7–8, 178 n. 32, 252 n. 20
Saley, R. J. 2–3 n. 2
Saydon, P. P. 195 n. 58
Schaeder, H. H. 9 n. 20, 10 n. 22, 18, 18 n. 47, 113 n. 70, 162 n. 7
Scharbert, J. 111 n. 64, 212 n. 97
Scott, W. R. 132 n. 99, 134 n. 105
Scullion, J. J. 205 n. 74
Segal, M. H. 203 n. 68
Segert, S. 162 n. 6, 178 n. 32
Skehan, P. W. 277 n. 73
Spiegelberg, W. 19 n. 49
Steuernagel, C. 32 n. 103
Talmon, S. 27 n. 86, 38, **39–41**
Talshir, D. 26, 26 nn. 83–84, 27 n. 85
Throntveit, M. 26, 26 nn. 81–82, 73 n. 28, 75 n. 31, 292 n. 3
Torrey, C. C. 7 n. 14, 9 n. 20, 17, 17 nn. 41–42, 18, 23, **38–39,** 140 nn. 2–3, 146 n. 13, 147, 147 nn. 15 & 18, 148, 161 n. 3, 243 n. 8
VanderKam, J. C. 30, 30 nn. 93 and 95–96, 31, 31 n. 98, 32, 33, 33 n. 104, 35, 37 n. 117, 56 n. 173, 100 n. 30
Vaux, R. de 4 n. 4, 20 n. 49, 97 n. 25, 100 n. 31, 112 n. 69, 278 n. 77

Veltri, G. 114 n. 72
Vogt, H. C. M. 105 n. 44
Watson, W. G. E. 277 n. 73
Weil, H. M. 278 n. 77
Weinberg, W. 114 n. 74
Welch, A. C. 222 n. 125
Wellhausen, J. 97 n. 25
Westermann, C. 155 n. 44
Widengren, G. 3 n. 3
Wiéner, C. 105 n. 45
Wildberger, H. 16 n. 40
Williamson, H. G. M. 3 n. 3, 5 n. 9, 8 n. 15, 9 nn. 18–19, 10 n. 21, 11 n. 24, 12 nn. 27 and 29, 13 n. 32, 14 n. 33, 15 n. 37, 18, 18 n. 47, 23, 23 n. 69, 24 n. 71, 25, 25 n. 75, 26, 27 n. 86, 30, 30 nn. 93 and 95, 38, **42–44,** 45, 46 n. 145, 52 n. 164, 59 n. 1, 64 n. 8, 69 n. 21, 70 n. 22, 71 n. 24, 76 n. 32, 80–81 n. 1, 87 n. 8, 92 n. 14, 101 n. 36, 108 n. 59, 134 nn. 106 and 108, 140 nn. 2–3, 143 n. 7, 146 nn. 13–14, 147 n. 17, 150 n. 27, 161 n. 2, 165 n. 15, 185 n. 41, 201 n. 63, 203 n. 65, 213 n. 103, 239 n. 3, 258 n. 34, 263 n. 51, 264 n. 52, 271 n. 63, 280 n. 80
Wong, G. C. I. 119 n. 81
Yaron, R. 259 nn. 37–38, 260 n. 41
Zadok, R. 261 n. 44
Zevit, Z. 284 n. 90
Zimmerli, W. 100 n. 31
Zunz, L. 22, 22 n. 65

Index of Subjects

Abraham   111, 157, 164, 167, 169, 172–73, 175, 178, 179, 186, 191, 193, 194, 202–5, 215, 224, 225, 226, 229, 230, 231, 232, 233, 241, 242 n. 5, 256, 286, 287, 298, 299
Achaemenid administration   9, 33, 43, 44, 61 n. 2, 113 n. 70, 115 n. 75, 258, 258 n. 34, 281. See also Persia.
Aramaic   2 n. 2, 9–10, 10 n. 21, 19 n. 49, 23 n. 66, 31 nn. 99 and 101, 33, 39, 55, 65, 65 n. 10, 103 nn. 39–40, 107 n. 57, 113, 113 nn. 70 and 72, 114, 115 n. 75, 119, 119 n. 81, 131, 134, 203, 203 n. 67, 257 n. 29, 258 n. 35, 259 nn. 36–37, 260
Artaxerxes I   2, 2 n. 2, 3, 3 n. 2, 4, 5–6, 6 n. 11, 8, 9, 10, 10 n. 21, 11, 11 n. 26, 12, 13 nn. 31 and 33, 17, 19, 20, 31 n. 100, 33 , 36, 36 n. 113, 37, 43, 44, 46, 50, 52, 60, 61, 61 n. 4, 62, 62 n. 5, 63 nn. 6–7, 66, 67, 72 n. 27, 77, 99, 103 n. 40, 112, 116, 137, 231 n. 137, 270, 281, 289, 298
Artaxerxes II   2 n. 2, 4
Artaxerxes III   2 n. 2, 3 n. 2

Babylon   3 n. 2, 5, 11, 12, 13, 14 n. 33, 17, 31 n. 100, 37 n. 117, 39, 41, 46, 62, 64, 64 n. 8, 71, 99, 103 n. 38, 104, 113 n. 70, 133, 134 n. 108, 264, 281
Benjamin   28, 37 n. 118, 44, 51, 52, 64, 69 n. 21, 104, 202, 220
Book of the law   19–20, 21, 55, 76, 79, 81, 82, 83, 84–86, 88, 90, 99, 106–8, 109, 112, 113, 117, 120, 121, 122, 123, 124, 126 n. 86, 127, 128, 134, 135, 136, 139, 142, 144, 155, 189, 239, 245, 269, 292, 293, 295, 296, 297

Booths, festival of   29, 34 n. 108, 35, 57, 62, 68, 70, 75, 76, 76 nn. 32–33, 77, 78, 79, 81, 95–98, 99, 100, 102, 104, 105, 106 n. 49, 107, 108, 120, 122, 123, 124, 125, 127, 128, 129–35, 136, 141, 148, 150, 151, 178, 194, 232, 242, 246, 247, 275, 281, 283, 283 n. 86, 293, 295, 296
Bread   31 n. 101, 64, 96 n. 23, 114, 120, 149, 158, 165, 167, 176, 178, 179, 183, 184, 207, 209, 209 n. 92, 225, 236, 281, 281 n. 82, 284

Calendar   19 n. 48, 37, 37 n. 117, 99–100, 116 n. 77, 150, 275, 281, 283 n. 86
Census   16 n. 39, 29, 33, 35, 37 n. 118, 40, 49, 51, 52, 55, 55 n. 170, 60, 62, 64, 68–71, 72 n. 27, 280, 288
Children of Israel   64, 72, 72 n. 27, 73, 82 n. 3, 85, 102, 122, 128, 130, 134, 136, 143, 149, 242
Chronicler, the   7–8 n. 14, 9 n. 20, 11 n. 25, 16–18, 21 n. 58, 22, 23, 23 n. 66, 25 n. 76, 38–39, 39 nn. 121–22, 68 n. 16, 133, 135 n. 109, 154, 223, 269–70, 280, 285
Commandment   14, 77 n. 34, 93, 95 n. 21, 107 n. 53, 122, 123 n. 84, 124, 126, 127, 136, 137, 142, 143, 146, 147, 147 n. 15, 148, 153, 154, 155, 158, 160, 165, 166, 167, 168, 169, 170, 177, 178, 179, 180, 181, 184, 185, 187, 189, 191, 192, 193, 196, 207, 208, 209, 210, 211, 219, 223, 248, 250, 270, 274, 283, 286, 294
Covenant   21, 22, 22 n. 62, 28, 34 n. 108, 35, 66, 67 n. 15, 81, 104, 107, 108, 109, 111, 118, 118 n. 78,

134, 135, 136, 157, 160, 164, 172, 173, 179, 186, 193, 194, 202, 203, 204, 212, 214, 229, 230, 231, 233, 235, 238, 239, 239 n. 3, 240, 241, 242, 242 n. 5, 243, 245, 256, 264, 267, 268, 269, 270, 271 n. 64, 273, 274, 286, 287, 298, 299

Covenant renewal   1, 2, 6, 21–22, 29, 42, 49, 57, 59, 59 n. 1, 60, 65, 67, 68, 68 n. 17, 70, 71, 71 n. 23, 72, 73, 75–78, 79, 81, 82 n. 3, 83, 84, 85, 88, 90, 97 n. 25, 101, 103, 104, 105 n. 47, 106 n. 49, 107, 110, 111, 113, 116, 122, 123, 125, 126, 129, 130, 134, 139, 141, 142, 145, 157, 172, 173, 177, 178, 180, 184, 186, 190, 192, 193, 196, 208, 230, 232, 233, 235, 242, 244, 245, 246, 246 n. 11, 247, 248, 249, 249 n. 15, 250, 250 n. 16, 251, 252, 253, 255, 256, 263, 267, 268, 269, 275, 278, 279, 282, 286, 291, 292, 293, 294, 295, 296, 297, 297 n. 4, 298, 299

Creation   163, 164, 167, 169, 170–72, 177, 179, 179 n. 33, 200–2, 226, 230, 298

Cyrus   24, 24 n. 73, 31 n. 100, 33, 43, 44, 46, 48, 50, 51, 52, 60, 61, 62, 63, 63 nn. 6–7, 64, 64 n. 8, 65, 72 n. 27, 104, 129, 130, 205, 257 n. 29, 281, 289

Darius I   19, 19 n. 49, 25, 44, 46, 50, 61, 61 n. 4, 62, 63 nn. 6–7, 65, 281, 289

Debt-slavery   22, 251, 260, 268–69, 270, 276, 277, 277 n. 75, 279, 279 n. 78, 288, 296

Dedication   27, 31 n. 101, 32 n. 103, 37 n. 118, 41, 42, 43, 44 n. 135, 46, 46 n. 144, 49, 51, 52, 55, 60, 61, 62, 63 n. 7, 64, 65, 67, 69 n. 20, 72, 73, 101 n. 36, 102, 103, 104, 108, 109, 112, 116, 120, 129, 134, 135 n. 109, 136, 218, 221, 245, 281, 289

Demotic Chronicle   19 n. 49

Deuteronomistic History   21, 104, 135 n. 109, 202, 203, 204, 207, 210, 212, 217, 218, 219, 221, 223, 224, 228 n. 134, 269 n. 60, 270 n. 61

Deuteronomic legislation   10 n.23, 20, 95, 95 n. 22, 96, 96 n. 24, 98, 106 n. 49, 107, 108, 118, 118, 122, 132, 134, 135, 137, 210, 223, 223 n. 128, 226 n. 132, 257, 269, 271 n. 64, 272, 272 n. 66, 273, 276, 278, 278 n. 76, 279, 282, 283 n. 89, 284, 284 n. 90, 285, 287

Divorce   12, 13, 257

Election   164, 167, 172–73, 193, 200, 202–5, 225

Elephantine   2–3 n. 2, 258 nn. 34 and 36, 259, 260, 260 nn. 41–42

Exile   24–25, 39, 41, 42, 47, 48, 50, 51, 60, 62, 63 n. 7, 64, 64 n. 8, 66 n. 13, 68, 69, 70, 72, 72 n. 27, 73, 100, 102, 103, 104, 117, 133, 136, 149, 151, 152, 193, 202, 203, 203 n. 65, 210, 214 n. 103, 215, 218, 220, 228, 228 n. 134, 229, 230, 232, 242 n. 5, 245, 257, 257 n. 31, 261, 263, 264, 265, 267, 268, 268 n. 57, 282, 298

Exodus   97 n. 25, 134, 134 n. 108, 163, 164, 167, 173, 174, 175, 179, 180, 182, 205, 206, 207, 226, 228, 229, 230

Ezra Memoir   5, 15, 16–19, 26, 27 n. 85, 32, 33, 44 n. 136, 61 n. 2

Fasting   14, 66, 143, 144, 149–50, 150 n. 26, 152, 275

Firstfruits 236, 240, 253–54, 282–83, 287

Foreigners   7, 9, 14, 19 n. 48, 21, 28, 32 n. 103, 36, 41, 67 n. 15, 117 n. 78, 130, 139, 142, 143, 144, 144 n. 9, 149, 150, 151, 151 n. 30, 156, 173, 209, 219, 222, 232, 240, 246, 249, 250, 256, 271, 271 n. 64, 273, 274, 275, 295, 296, 299

Gatekeepers   71, 71 n. 25, 236, 240, 246, 255, 268 n. 57, 294

Governor   2–3 n. 2, 20 n. 50, 34 n. 108, 35 n. 110, 47, 66, 80, 81 n. 1,

Index of Subjects

115, 116, 235, 239, 240, 243, 246 n. 11, 260–61, 261 n. 45, 297

Haggai 27 n. 87, 45, 47, 48, 64, 218
Holiness Code 152, 219
House of God. See Temple.

Jeshua 29, 36, 39, 41, 42, 43, 47, 49, 51, 65, 80, 90, 123, 128, 139, 140, 145, 146, 152, 162 n. 5, 235, 244, 245, 252, 262, 262 n. 49, 263, 264
Joshua 21, 102, 103, 104, 104 n. 42, 106 n. 49, 107, 108, 113, 122, 128, 133, 134, 134 n. 108, 135, 136, 209, 262
Joy. See Rejoicing.
Judah 2–3 n. 2, 12, 17, 19, 20, 28, 29, 37 n. 118, 43, 44, 48, 49, 51, 52, 61, 64, 65, 69 n. 21, 70, 71, 72, 72 n. 27, 78, 100, 112, 126, 151 n. 29, 153 n. 37, 154, 202, 203, 203 n. 65, 214 n. 103, 218 n. 116, 220, 222, 231, 231 n. 137, 245, 256, 257, 257 n. 31, 271, 289, 298
Judahites 19, 65, 65 n. 10, 115, 268, 274, 275, 277

Kings, kingship 2 n. 2, 11, 12, 12, n. 27, 13, 19 n. 48, 21, 28, 29, 29 n. 90, 30, 30 n. 96, 31, 31 nn. 98 and 100, 33, 43, 46 n. 145, 47, 48, 50, 61, 62, 63 n. 7, 65, 66, 77, 77 n. 35, 100 n. 28, 112, 113, 159, 160, 164, 170, 183 n. 36, 185, 186, 187, 194, 195, 195 n. 57, 196, 197, 198, 199, 200, 203 n. 67, 215, 218, 222, 223, 229, 231, 231 n. 137, 232, 243, 246, 246 n. 11, 280, 289, 294, 298. See also Artaxerxes I; Cyrus; Darius I.

Land 9, 22, 33, 41, 48, 64, 65, 73, 103, 106 n. 50, 118, 122, 128, 130, 134, 135, 136, 150 n. 29, 153 n. 37, 157, 158, 159, 160, 161, 163, 164, 165, 166, 167, 168, 168 n. 19, 169, 170, 172, 173, 174, 175, 177, 178, 179, 181, 182, 184, 185–93, 195–99, 202,

203, 204, 205, 207, 210, 211, 212, 214–20, 224, 224 n. 130, 225, 226, 227, 228 n. 134, 229, 230, 231, 232, 236, 242, 242 n. 5, 247, 249, 250, 251, 253, 268, 271 n. 64, 272, 272 n. 65, 273, 274, 275, 275 n. 69, 284, 288, 293, 295, 296, 298, 299
Leaders (of the people) 2, 7, 9, 21 n. 58, 29, 31 n. 98, 41, 42, 47, 47 n. 148, 51, 53 n. 168, 60, 68, 68 n. 17, 70, 71, 75, 76, 78, 82, 83, 84, 86, 87, 87 nn. 9–10, 88, 90, 92, 92 n. 16, 93, 104, 110, 116, 117, 119, 121, 122, 123, 124, 125, 126, 127, 128, 129–30, 131, 135, 136, 137, 143, 144, 145, 152, 152 n. 33, 155, 156, 162, 177, 178, 184, 190, 194, 195, 196, 197, 208 n. 87, 213, 221, 223, 225, 229, 235, 237, 239, 240, 241, 242, 243, 244, 245, 246 n. 11, 247, 248, 250, 252, 260, 264–67, 271, 272 n. 65, 273, 273 n. 67, 288, 291, 292, 294, 295, 296, 297–98, 299
Levites 8 n. 16, 11, 28, 33, 34 n. 109, 37 n. 118, 43, 49, 51, 52, 57, 62, 64, 66 n. 13, 67 n. 15, 68, 69 n. 21, 71, 71 nn. 25–26, 75, 77, 77 n. 34, 78, 80, 81 n. 1, 82, 83, 84, 85, 87, 87 n. 10, 88, 89–91, 92, 92 nn. 14 and 16, 94, 95 n. 21, 97, 98, 105, 105 n. 45, 106 n. 50, 110, 111, 112–15, 116, 117, 120, 121, 122, 124, 125, 129, 132, 136, 139, 141, 142, 143, 144, 145–49, 152–55, 156, 157–233, 235, 236, 237, 238, 239, 240, 241, 242, 243, 244–45, 246, 246 n. 11, 247, 248, 250, 252, 253, 254, 255, 258, 263–64, 266, 267, 268 n. 57, 270, 280 n. 79, 284, 284 n. 90, 285, 286, 289, 291, 292, 293, 294, 295, 296, 297, 297 n. 4, 298–99

Manna 158, 183, 184, 209, 214, 225, 226
Marriage 5, 7, 9, 12, 13, 14, 15, 21, 32, 32 n. 103, 33, 34 n. 108, 35, 36, 37 n. 118, 41, 42, 46, 47, 49, 51, 60, 65,

66, 67, 103, 104, 107, 109, 117, 117 n. 78, 131, 133, 136, 149, 150, 151, 152 n. 33, 206, 216, 218, 220, 223, 229, 238, 240, 248, 249, 250 n. 16, 256, 268, 271, 272, 273, 274, 287, 288, 289, 292
Mercy 28, 160, 164, 165, 167, 168, 169, 169 n. 23, 179, 180, 182, 183, 188, 189, 191, 192, 193, 210, 211, 212, 213, 217, 228, 230, 231, 294
Moses 20, 21, 32 n. 103, 64, 67, 79, 84, 85, 102, 103, 106, 107, 107 nn. 52–53, 108, 111, 122, 126 n. 86, 127, 130, 134, 158, 177, 178, 179, 190, 209, 213, 214, 231, 233, 236, 269, 271 n. 64, 274, 280, 280 n. 81, 281 n. 82, 282, 287, 298
Mourning. *See* Weeping.

Nehemiah Memoir 15, 16, 16 nn. 39–40, 17, 18, 26, 27, 27 n. 85, 29 n. 89, 33, 40, 49, 61 n. 2, 65 n. 10, 69, 69 n. 20,
New Year 7, 36 n. 113, 99, 100, 100 nn. 28–29, 101, 102 n. 37, 118 n. 78

Passover 27, 28, 29, 41, 60, 64, 65, 67, 96 n. 23, 103, 131, 133, 136, 268, 275, 281, 283 n. 86
Penitential confessions, prayers, or rites 9, 22, 28, 29, 31, 60, 68, 75, 76, 77, 78, 104, 108, 111, 139–56, 172, 173, 174, 200, 206, 225, 226, 228–29, 243, 245, 269, 292, 293, 294, 295, 296, 298
People of the land 9, 106 n. 50, 249, 268
Persia 2 n. 2, 3 n. 3, 10, 10 n. 21, 11, 11 n. 27, 13 n. 33, 18, 18 n. 47, 19, 19 n. 48, 20, 20 n. 50, 28, 30, 30 n. 96, 31, 31 n. 100, 33, 37 n. 117, 43, 46 n. 145, 47, 48, 50, 55, 61, 62, 63 n. 7, 65, 66, 77, 77 n. 35, 113, 116, 137, 229, 230, 231–32, 254, 257, 257 nn. 29 and 31, 280, 289, 297, 298. *See also* Achaemenid administration.

Pillar of Cloud or Fire 158, 165, 167, 168, 176, 177, 183, 207, 213, 226, 233
Pledges 21 n. 60, 66, 68, 68 n. 16, 75, 77, 77 n. 34, 90, 116, 145, 162, 178, 208, 236, 240, 249, 250, 250 n. 18, 251, 275, 276, 276 n. 70, 277, 277 n. 74, 278, 278 n. 77, 279, 279 n. 78, 281, 288, 289
Priestly legislation 20, 95, 96, 96 nn. 22 and 24, 98, 99, 100, 116, 116 n. 77, 117, 118, 131, 134, 135, 135 n. 109, 137, 207, 210, 210 n. 93, 217, 225, 225 n. 131, 274, 275, 276, 279, 280 n. 79, 281, 282, 283, 284, 287
Priest 2–3 n. 2, 9, 11, 19, 19 nn. 48–49, 31 n. 98, 33, 34, 34 nn. 108–9, 35, 35 n. 110, 37 n. 117, 39, 41, 43, 47, 49, 51, 52, 56, 60, 62, 64, 66, 66 nn. 13–14, 68, 69 n. 21, 71, 71 nn. 23 and 25, 79, 80, 85, 87, 87 n. 9, 107, 109, 110, 112, 113, 116, 121, 122, 125, 129, 132, 136, 144, 156, 160, 194, 195, 195 n. 57, 218, 222, 232, 236, 237, 238, 238 n. 2, 239, 240, 242, 243, 244, 246, 246 n. 11, 248, 252, 254, 255, 258, 260, 261–63, 267, 268 n. 57, 270, 273, 281, 282, 283, 284, 285, 286, 294, 296, 297
Prophet, prophecy 16 n. 40, 22, 25, 29, 29 n. 89, 31 n. 98, 41, 45, 64, 110, 112, 130 n. 92, 149, 151, 159, 160, 184, 189, 190, 192, 194, 196, 201, 202, 209, 216, 216 n. 113, 217, 218, 218 nn. 115–16, 219, 220, 220 n. 119, 224, 225, 231, 246 n. 11, 270, 274, 274 n. 68, 299
Psalms, historical 200, 206, 207, 211, 217, 225, 226–28, 229, 231

Reading 1, 2, 3 n. 2, 4, 5, 6 n. 11, 7, 7 n. 13, 8 n. 16, 11, 13 n. 32, 15, 21 n. 58, 22, 31 n. 101, 34, 34 n. 108, 36, 41, 44, 44 n. 136, 49, 55 n. 170, 57, 60, 61, 66 n. 14, 68, 70, 73, 74, 75, 76, 76 nn. 32–33, 78, 79, 81, 82, 85, 88, 89, 91, 91 n. 11, 92, 93, 94,

Index of Subjects 369

95, 97, 98, 99, 101, 102, 102 n. 37, 103, 104, 105, 106 n. 49, 107, 108, 109, 110, 110 n. 62, 113, 114, 114 nn. 72 and 74, 115, 115 n. 75, 117, 119, 121, 122, 123, 124, 125, 128, 129, 132, 134, 135, 137, 142, 143, 144, 145, 148, 149, 151, 155, 156, 239, 243, 245, 247, 292, 293, 295, 296, 297
Rebellion 62, 65, 164–70, 179–85, 187, 188–93, 195, 196, 210–14, 217–20, 223, 225, 226, 227, 228, 230, 231, 248, 251, 255, 289, 295, 298, 299
Rehum 6 n. 11, 10 n. 21, 63 n. 6, 65, 235, 261 n. 45, 262, 264, 266
Rejoicing 22, 31, 31 n. 101, 62, 64, 76, 80, 82, 93, 93 n. 18, 94 n. 19, 96 n. 24, 97, 98, 103 n. 41, 118, 118 n. 78, 119, 119 nn. 80–82, 120, 121, 122, 123, 128, 134, 136, 143, 269, 293

Sabbath 67 n. 15, 95, 116, 158, 177, 178, 184, 186, 206, 208, 209, 223, 236, 240, 249, 250, 270, 274, 274 n. 68, 275, 276, 281, 287, 288, 289
Sacrifice 11 n. 27, 33, 34, 34 n. 108, 55 n. 170, 63 n. 6, 96 n. 24, 102, 104, 132, 203, 221 n. 123, 252, 283, 283 n. 88,
Scribe 9, 17, 18 n. 48, 19, 19 nn. 48–49, 32 n. 103, 34, 34 n. 108, 35, 35 n. 110, 36, 36 nn. 113–14, 47, 50, 60, 66, 67, 79, 80, 85, 86 n. 6, 107, 109, 110, 113 n. 70, 116, 121, 122, 242, 246 n. 11, 258, 260 n. 41, 261, 261 n. 45
Sea of Reeds 173, 174
Seal 21, 236, 237, 242, 257, 258, 258 nn. 34–36, 259, 260
Seventh month 5, 6, 7, 33, 37, 44, 44 n. 136, 46, 68, 72, 73, 79, 82 n. 3, 84, 97, 98, 98 n. 26, 99, 100, 101, 101 n. 32, 116, 120, 122, 123, 129, 130, 135, 135 n. 109, 141, 149, 149 n. 24, 150, 155, 194, 235, 236, 239, 245, 248, 275, 281, 283, 293

Seventh year 240, 249, 250, 251, 275, 275 n. 69, 278, 278 n. 76, 279, 287, 296
Sinai 21, 108, 158, 169, 176, 177, 178, 179, 183, 184, 189, 190, 192, 208, 209, 212, 226, 233, 233 n. 139, 248, 250, 271 n. 64, 274, 282, 287, 295, 298, 299
Tattenai 65, 257 n. 29
Temple 1, 6, 7, 7 n. 12, 9, 11, 11 n. 27, 13, 14, 17, 19 nn. 48–49, 21 n. 60, 25, 27, 28, 29, 31 n. 101, 32, 32 n. 103, 33, 34, 34 n. 108, 35, 36, 37, 37 n. 118, 38, 41, 42, 43, 44, 45, 46, 46 n. 144, 47, 48, 49, 50, 51, 52, 54, 54 n. 169, 55, 56, 56 nn. 172–73, 60, 61, 62, 62 n. 5, 63, 63 nn. 6–7, 64, 64 n. 8, 65, 67, 67 n. 15, 70, 70–71 n. 23, 71, 73, 85, 100, 101 n. 36, 102, 102 n. 37, 103, 104, 108, 109, 112, 117, 119, 119 n. 80, 122, 127 n. 90, 128, 130, 133, 134, 134 n. 109, 136, 152 n. 33, 193, 218, 221, 231, 232, 236, 239, 240, 241, 244, 245, 246, 248, 249, 251, 252, 253, 254, 255, 256, 257, 257 n. 29, 263, 264, 267, 268 n. 57, 270, 279–86, 287, 288, 289, 294, 298
Temple tax 240, 249, 251, 279–80, 287, 288, 289
Tithe 67 n. 15, 68 n. 17, 118, 236, 238, 240, 245, 253, 254–55, 284–86, 287
Torah 17, 31 n. 101, 32 n. 103, 34, 34 n. 108, 35, 36, 36 n. 114, 41, 44, 44 n. 136, 46, 59, 50, 51, 52, 53, 54, 55, 55 n. 170, 60, 61, 62, 66, 66 n. 14, 67, 68, 70, 72, 73, 74, 75, 76, 76 nn. 32–33, 77, 77 n. 35, 78, 100, 104, 110, 113 n. 72, 137, 143, 154, 155, 156, 177, 178, 189, 192, 196, 217, 230, 232, 233, 239, 240, 241, 242, 243, 244, 245–48, 251, 257, 257 n. 29, 260, 267–70, 281, 287, 292, 295–96, 297, 299

Usury 22, 276 n. 71. See also Debt-slavery.

Walls of Jerusalem   6, 10 n. 21, 16, 16 n. 39, 31 n. 101, 33, 34 n. 108, 37 n. 118, 41, 42, 44, 44 nn. 135–36, 46, 49, 50, 51, 52, 53, 54, 55, 56, 60, 61, 62, 63 nn. 5 and 7, 65, 66, 66 n. 14, 67, 69, 69 n. 20, 71 n. 23, 72, 73, 99, 101, 101–2 n. 36, 102, 104, 108, 109, 116, 120, 134, 136, 264, 265, 267, 268, 289, 298

Water   149, 158, 159, 165, 167, 175, 176, 178, 179, 183, 184, 206, 207, 209, 209 n. 92, 214, 225, 226, 233

Water Gate   2, 11, 21, 67, 70, 76, 79, 81, 83, 84, 87, 101–2, 107, 108, 117, 122, 123, 128, 134, 141 n. 6

Weeping   34 n. 108, 35, 36, 66, 80, 92, 92 nn. 14–15, 93, 94, 94 n. 19, 103 n. 41, 115, 117, 117–18 n. 78, 119, 120, 125 n. 85, 143, 152 n. 33, 156, 296

Wilderness   28, 96, 103 n. 38, 158, 159, 164, 165, 166, 167, 168, 169, 170, 173–85, 189, 190, 191, 192, 193, 194, 196, 205–14, 217, 220, 221, 224, 226, 227, 229, 230, 231, 232, 233, 249, 251, 295

Women   12, 79, 84, 85, 86, 97, 98, 105, 105 n. 44, 106 n. 49, 122, 134, 247, 249, 273, 288, 296

Wood   67 n. 15, 79, 109, 127, 127 n. 90, 132, 152, 236, 240, 245, 249, 252, 252 n. 20, 270, 274, 281, 282, 287, 288

Yehud. *See* Judah.

Zechariah   27 n. 87, 45, 47, 48, 64, 79, 87 n. 9, 218, 219, 262

Zerubbabel   25, 27, 27–28 n. 87, 28, 36, 39, 40, 41, 42, 43, 47, 49, 51, 65

Index of Select Hebrew Words

אבות 73, 74, 124, 129, 129 n. 91, 142, 152 n. 31, 163 n. 11, 164, 165, 165 n. 13, 166, 174, 180 n. 34, 181, 185, 185 n. 42, 187, 194, 195, 196, 197, 198, 199, 205, 205 nn. 75–76, 210 n. 93, 223, 238 n. 2, 245, 252, 293

אמן 86, 88, 89, 111, 111 n. 66, 154n. 38, 173, 203, 233, 241, 286, 287, 298

אמנה 21, 21 n. 59, 173, 233, 241, 246, 247, 251, 256, 257, 260, 286, 287, 298

אמת 177, 178, 195, 208, 223

אסף 73, 74, 76, 76 n. 33, 82, 85, 96 n. 25, 98, 100, 104, 104 n. 43, 123, 124, 126, 141, 142, 151, 293

ארץ 103, 112, 112 n. 68, 115, 144, 161, 168, 168 n. 19, 169, 170, 171, 172, 173, 175, 179, 179 n. 33, 185, 185 n. 41–43, 186, 187, 192, 196, 197, 198, 199, 200, 201 n. 62, 204 n. 72, 205, 206, 210, 210 n. 93, 212 n. 98, 213, 215, 215, 216, 220, 224 n. 130, 232, 246, 268 n. 58, 270 n. 62, 294

בוא 74 n. 29, 84, 85, 86, 109, 124, 127, 132, 185, 185 n. 42, 186, 187, 195, 204, 206 n. 78, 210, 223, 223 n. 128, 224 n. 130, 238, 246, 247, 248, 252, 252 n. 20, 253, 254, 255, 269, 274, 282 n. 85, 285

בית אלהים 35, 52, 56 n. 172, 241, 251, 252, 253, 254, 255, 279, 286 n. 92, 294

בית יהוה 30 n. 96, 241, 252, 253, 282 n. 85, 294

ברית 21, 21 nn. 58–59, 107 n. 54, 108, 164 n. 12, 173, 193, 194, 204, 204 n. 69, 221 n. 121, 231, 233, 241, 242, 256, 256 n. 25, 269, 270, 286

ברך 86, 88, 110, 111 nn. 64 and 66, 112, 140, 141, 143, 146, 146 n. 14,

147, 147 n. 15, 148, 148 nn. 19 and 21, 153, 153 nn. 34 and 36, 154, 154 n. 40, 155, 155 n. 41, 170

חוה 86, 88, 89, 111, 112, 112 n. 68, 142, 144, 145, 145 n. 11, 153, 171, 172, 202, 293

טוב 114, 169, 178, 183, 184, 184 n. 38, 187, 188, 196, 197, 198, 208, 214, 214 n. 104, 216, 216 n. 112, 224 n. 130, 294

ירש 165, 170, 179, 185, 185 nn. 41–42, 186, 187, 210, 215, 294

ישראל 31 n. 99, 32, 32 n. 103, 71, 84, 98, 106 n. 51, 107 nn. 52–55, 111 n. 66, 126, 132 n. 98, 147, 153 n. 36, 248 n. 14, 258, 268 n. 58, 279, 281, 282, 283 n. 87, 284

בני ישראל 61, 64, 72, 74, 75 n. 30, 80, 84, 85, 102, 103, 107 nn. 54–55, 124, 126, 127, 128, 134, 141, 142, 143, 206 n. 78, 255, 285, 293

זרע ישראל 144, 150, 151, 151 n. 30, 172, 246, 249, 295

כל־ישראל 61, 71, 72, 108, 255, 260, 268

מצוה 113, 168 n. 18, 169, 177, 178, 180, 181, 184, 191, 192, 196, 208, 209, 209 n. 91, 210, 239, 248, 252, 270, 270 n. 61, 286, 294

נתן 106 n. 51, 161, 164, 165, 166, 168, 169, 169 n. 20, 172 n. 27, 173, 174, 175, 177, 178, 179, 181, 183, 184, 185, 185 nn. 41 and 43, 187, 188 nn. 46 and 48–49, 189 n. 50, 190, 192, 196, 197, 198, 204 nn. 70 and 72, 205, 210 n. 93, 211 n. 95 218 n. 117, 213, 215, 220, 233, 238, 248 nn. 13–14, 250, 251, 252 n. 20, 255, 283, 272, 284, 294

ספר 83, 83 n. 5, 84, 85, 86, 88, 89, 90, 91, 109, 120, 123, 137, 294
ספר דתא (Aram.) 18 n. 47
ספר הברית 108
ספר היחש 72, 72 n. 27
[ה]ספר [ה]תורה 74, 76, 83, 84, 85, 90, 91 n. 11, 107, 108, 135, 248 n. 14, 293, 295
ספר תורת האלהים 74, 113, 115 n. 75, 124, 129, 134, 135, 142
ספר תורת יהוה 112
ספר תורת יהוה אלהיהם 74, 142, 144
ספר תורת משה 84, 86, 90, 106 n. 51, 107 nn. 52 and 54–56, 126, 134
עוד 166, 170, 188, 191, 196, 197, 220 n. 119, 242, 294
עזב 164, 166, 169 n. 23, 182, 183, 184, 185, 187, 188 nn. 46 and 49, 189 n. 50, 191, 192–93 n. 55, 194, 212, 219, 238, 255, 277, 286 n. 92, 294
עם 71, 71 n. 25, 73, 82, 83, 89, 90, 91, 91 n. 13, 94, 95 n. 21, 98, 106 n. 49, 112, 115, 124, 127, 164, 175, 185 n. 43, 186, 188 n. 49, 192, 194, 204 n. 69, 205, 205 n. 75, 206, 215, 216, 220, 223 n. 129, 243, 245, 246, 252, 267 n. 56, 279, 294
כל־העם 73, 74, 82, 83, 84, 85, 86, 86 n. 7, 87, 88, 89, 90, 91, 91 n. 11, 92, 93, 94, 103, 103 n. 40, 104, 104 n. 42, 108, 110, 111, 117, 121, 124, 128, 129, 132, 134, 154, 154 n. 38, 194, 205, 243, 245, 246, 294, 295
עם הארץ 144, 175, 186, 188 n. 49, 192, 206, 215, 216 n. 111, 220, 247, 249, 250, 268, 268 n. 58, 272, 272 n. 65, 273, 293
שאר העם 71 n. 25, 246, 252, 267, 268
עמד 86, 88, 89, 90, 91, 109, 113, 142, 144, 145, 239, 251
עץ 109, 127, 127 n. 90, 131, 131 n. 94, 152, 216, 216–17 n. 113, 252, 253, 254, 254 n. 23, 282, 282 nn. 83–84
עשה 74 n. 29, 86, 88, 93, 94, 109, 124, 125, 127, 128, 131, 164, 165, 168, 169, 169 n. 21, 171, 171 n. 25, 178,

180, 182, 188, 189, 190, 191 n. 54, 193, 195, 196, 201, 201 n. 62, 211, 212 n. 98, 213, 215, 223, 225, 238, 242, 248, 269, 270, 270 n. 61, 294
קהל 85, 98, 104, 105 n. 48, 111, 124, 125, 127, 128, 132, 133, 134, 232, 280, 280 n. 81
כל־הקהל 71, 133 n. 100, 246
כל־קהל ישראל 106 n. 49
קרא 74, 76, 85, 89, 90, 91, 91 n. 12, 94, 108, 113, 113 n. 70, 115 n. 75, 123, 125, 126, 129, 134, 136, 137, 142, 144, 154, 295
מקרא 89, 91, 91 n. 11, 94, 95, 100, 115, 115 n. 75, 116, 116 n. 77, 117, 118, 136,
רחם 161, 164, 166, 168 n. 17, 169, 182, 188 n. 48, 189, 189 n. 50, 190, 191, 192, 192–93 n. 55, 211 n. 96, 213, 228 n. 134, 231, 294
שמח 31 n. 101, 118, 119, 119 n. 82, 134
שמחה 31, 31 nn. 97 and 101, 64, 76, 93, 94, 118, 119, 119 nn. 81–82, 120, 120 n. 83, 128, 134, 293
שמע 31 n. 97, 84, 85, 86, 91, 92, 94, 105, 105 n. 44, 106 n. 48, 108, 117, 123 n. 84, 125, 126, 128, 130, 168 n. 18, 170, 174, 180, 180 n. 34, 181, 188, 190, 191, 192, 210, 211, 213, 217, 218, 247, 294, 295
תורה 83, 83 n. 5, 85, 86, 89, 90, 94, 106, 106 n. 50, 107, 108, 113, 117, 125, 126, 129, 130, 169, 177, 178, 178 n. 31, 189, 189 n. 51, 190, 190 n. 53, 192, 196, 208, 209, 223, 242, 248, 248 n. 14, 252, 257, 257 n. 30, 269, 282, 287, 293, 294
דברי התורה 74, 76, 92, 94, 98, 110, 117, 123, 124, 125, 126, 136, 223, 245, 293
תורת האלהים 90, 144, 178 n. 31, 190, 245, 246, 247, 248, 248 nn. 13–14, 257, 268 n. 58, 287
תורת יהוה 107 n. 52
תורת יהוה אלהיך 107 n. 53
תורת משה 106 n. 51, 252 n. 21, 282

www.ingramcontent.com/pod-product-compliance
Lightning Source LLC
Chambersburg PA
CBHW021114300426
44113CB00006B/152